cache
nurturing achievement

Early Years Educator

FOR THE CLASSROOM-BASED LEARNER

Carolyn Meggitt

Tina Bruce

Contributor: Julian Grenier

Assessment Guidance: Sheila Riddall-Leech

HODDER
EDUCATION
AN HACHETTE UK COMPANY

Orders: please contact Bookpoint Ltd, 130 Milton Park, Abingdon, Oxon OX14 4SB. Telephone: (44) 01235 827720. Fax: (44) 01235 400454. Lines are open from 9.00 to 5.00, Monday to Saturday, with a 24-hour message answering service. You can also order through our website www.hoddereducation.co.uk

If you have any comments to make about this, or any of our other titles, please send them to educationenquiries@hodder.co.uk

British Library Cataloguing in Publication Data

A catalogue record for this title is available from the British Library

ISBN: 9781471808029

This edition published 2014

Impression number   10 9 8 7 6 5 4 3 2

Year   2018 2017 2016 2015 2014

Copyright © 2014 Carolyn Meggitt and Tina Bruce

Hachette UK's policy is to use papers that are natural, renewable and recyclable products and made from wood grown in sustainable forests. The logging and manufacturing processes are expected to conform to the environmental regulations of the country of origin.

Cover photo © BJI/Blue Jean Images/Getty Images.

Typeset in India.

Printed in Dubai.

Contents

Theme 4 Professional development — 529

Acknowledgements

I would like to thank the following people for their contributions: Laura Meggitt (teacher) for her valuable insights and for providing many of the early years case studies; Kirsty Meggitt (recruitment consultant) for help with the section on SMART targets in Unit 4.1.

I would also like to thank the editorial team at Hodder Education: Stephen Halder, publisher; Sundus Pasha, development editor; and Llinos Edwards, freelance copy editor, for all their hard work.

This book uses intellectual property/material from books previously co-authored with Tina Bruce and Julian Grenier, who willingly agreed to its inclusion in this book in order to share what is important for high-quality early childhood practice.

Picture credits

Every effort has been made to trace the copyright holders of material reproduced here. The authors and publishers would like to thank the following for permission to reproduce copyright illustrations.

The publishers would like to thank all the staff, children and families at Vanessa Nursery School, Ark Alpha Nursery, Bright Horizons Family Solutions, and Kate Greenaway Nursery School and Children's Centre for their help with many of the photographs, taken by Jules Selmes, Andrew Callaghan, and Justin O'Hanlon. A special thanks to Michele Barrett, Julie Breading and Susan Goodbrand for all their assistance with the organisation of the photo-shoots.

Crown copyright material is licensed under the Open Government Licence v1.0.

p.3: © Crown copyright material as reproduced with the permission of the controller of HMSO and the Queen's Printers of Scotland; p.7: © Crown copyright material as reproduced with the permission of the controller of HMSO and the Queen's Printers of Scotland; p.9 © Vadim Ponomarenko – Fotolia; p.21 © eye35.pix / Alamy; p.28 © Crown Copyright. Contains public sector information licensed under the Open Government Licence v2.0; p.29 © Freeze Frame Photography-Fotolia; p.45 l © PHOTOTAKE Inc./Alamy, r © Medical-on-Line/Alamy; p.46 t © Dr P. Marazzi/Science Photo Library, b © Courtesy of Community Hygiene Concern; p.77 © Hodder Education; p.102 l © Ian Hooton/Science Photo Library, m © Carolyn A Mckeone/Science Photo Library, r © Amawasri/iStock/Thinkstock; p.103 © Wong-Baker FACES Foundation 1983, www.WongBakerFACES.org; p.132 © Astier/Science Photo Library; p.145 © Gideon Mendel/Corbis; p.147 © tungfoto- Fotolia; p.183 © Andres Rodriguez – Fotolia; p.187 a KITEMARK and the BSI Kitemark device are reproduced with kind permission of The British Standards Institution. They are registered trademarks in the United Kingdom and in certain other countries, b © The British Toy & Hobby Association; p.197 © Gusto Images/Science Photo Library; p.257 © matka_Wariatka – Fotolia; p.498 © Jaren Wicklund – Fotolia

How to use this book

This book contains all the units you need to master the skills and knowledge for the new CACHE Level 3 Diploma in Early Years Education and Care (Early Years Educator), and is divided into four themes:

1. Health and well-being
2. Legislation, frameworks and professional practice
3. Play, development and learning for school readiness
4. Professional development

This book should be taught in conjunction with the most up-to-date Level 3 Early Years Educator Classroom-based specification document available on www.cache.org.uk. In the LO and AC headings, 'EYP' refers to the role of the Early Years Practitioner. References to parents are intended to include other carers as well.

Key features of the book

LO1 Understand the impact of food and nutrition on children's health and development

Understand all the requirements of the new qualification with clearly stated learning outcomes and assessment criteria fully mapped to the specification

AC 1.1 Explain what is meant by healthy eating

Learning outcomes

By the end of this unit you will:

1 Understand the impact of food and nutrition on children's health and development.

Prepare for what you are going to cover in the unit

Key term

nutrients Nutrients are the essential components of food which provide the individual with the necessary requirements for bodily functions.

Understand important terms

Reflective practice

Think about a situation in which you have found communication unsatisfactory. Why do you

Learn to reflect on your own skills and experiences

In practice activity

Observing transitions
Choose a child who is new to the setting and make detailed observations during the period.

Apply your knowledge in the work setting

In practice

Involving parents and carers
Early years practitioners could do the following:

Checklist of key points to remember to help you in the work setting and develop your professional skills

Case study

A serious case review
The serious case review into Little Stars Nursery in

See how concepts are applied in settings with real-life scenarios

Activity

Observation Arrange to observe a group of children during mealtime.

Short tasks to help enhance your understanding of assessment criteria

Research activity

Different traditions
Find out about the dietary requirements and

Enhance your understanding of topics with research-led activities encouraging you to explore an area in more detail

Discussion point

IEPs set out targets which can be described as SMART (Specific, Measurable,

Activities that encourage debate and discussion in the classroom

Guidelines for weaning

● Try to encourage a liking for savoury foods.

Tips and guidelines to help you develop your professional skills

Progress check

Weaning is the gradual introduction of solid food to the baby's diet.

Summarise key points and underpinning knowledge

Assessment practice

Summary of unit
Whistleblowing is an important aspect of

Test your knowledge with questions linked to assessment criteria to help you generate evidence

Useful resources

Books
Lindon, Jennie (2009) *Safeguarding*

Includes references to books, websites and other various sources for further reading and research

In profile

My name is Susan and I am the Nursery Manager of a 68-place day nursery.

Learn about the experience of real practitioners, their roles and day-to-day duties

Unit 1.1 Support healthy lifestyles for children through the provision of food and nutrition

Unit 1.2 Support healthy lifestyles for children through exercise

Unit 1.3 Support physical care routines for children

Unit 1.4 Promote children's emotional well-being

Unit 1.5 Understand how to support children who are unwell

Unit 1.6 Understand the needs of the mother and baby during pre-conception, pregnancy and the first year of life

Unit 1.1 Support healthy lifestyles for children through the provision of food and nutrition

This unit provides the learner with the knowledge, understanding and skills to support healthy lifestyles for children.

Learning outcomes

By the end of this unit you will:

1 Understand the impact of food and nutrition on children's health and development.
2 Understand how food choices impact on health and development during pre-pregnancy, pregnancy and breastfeeding.
3 Understand the nutritional needs of children.
4 Understand the impact of poor diet on children's health and development.
5 Understand individuals' dietary requirements and preferences.
6 Be able to support healthy eating in your own setting.

LO1 Understand the impact of food and nutrition on children's health and development

AC 1.1 Explain what is meant by healthy eating

The principles of healthy eating

A healthy diet consists of a wide variety of foods to help the body to grow and to provide energy. It must include enough of these **nutrients** (proteins, fats, carbohydrates, vitamins, minerals and fibre) as well as water to fuel and maintain the body's vital functions.

Key term

nutrients Nutrients are the essential components of food which provide the individual with the necessary requirements for bodily functions.

Good nutrition, or healthy eating, is important for children under five to:

- ensure that they get the right amount of energy (calories) and nutrients needed when they are growing rapidly
- ensure that they do not consume too much energy (calories), which may lead to children becoming overweight or obese
- encourage them to eat a wide variety of foods and to develop good dietary habits to take with them into later childhood and adulthood.

What does a healthy diet for very young children look like?

- Plenty of choice and balance
- Lots of fruit and vegetables
- Lots of starchy foods, bread, rice, potatoes, pasta
- Contains calcium and iron-rich foods – milk and dairy, and other sources of protein, such as meat, fish, eggs, beans
- Regular healthy meals and snacks
- Low in salt and in added sugar.

Activity

Check that you know which nutrients are needed for a healthy diet, and explain what is meant by healthy eating.

In a group, discuss what you think is meant by healthy eating. What are the main features of a healthy diet?

AC 1.2 Evaluate national and local initiatives which promote healthy eating

The Eat Better, Start Better programme

This programme is run by The Children's Food Trust and aims to help early years settings meet children's nutritional needs more consistently, and to help families with young children to develop the cooking skills and confidence they need to cook and eat more healthily. Their practical guide includes the government-backed **Voluntary Food and Drink Guidelines for Early Years Settings in England**, as well as advice on encouraging children to eat well, including managing fussy eating and special dietary requirements.

The Schools Fruit and Vegetable Scheme (SFV)

It is recommended that children – like adults – eat at least five portions of fruit and vegetables every day. Children aged between four and six who attend a fully state-funded infant, primary or special school are entitled to receive a free piece of fruit or vegetable each school day.

Figure 1.1.1 'Just eat more' portion poster for the NHS 5 A DAY programme

Feeding Young Imaginations

The Pre-School Learning Alliance's campaign, Feeding Young Imaginations, supports parents and early years groups by providing information to promote a balanced diet for under-fives.

The Children's Food Campaign

Sustain (the alliance for better food and farming) launched the Children's Food Campaign to improve young people's health and well-being through:

- good food and real food education in every school
- protecting children from junk food marketing
- clear food labelling that everyone, including children, can understand.

Cool Milk

Cool Milk works in partnership with local authorities and early years groups to supply free and subsidised school milk to children in pre-schools, nurseries and primary schools. Cool Milk aims to make the provision of milk easier for schools, nurseries, local authorities and parents, while promoting the important health benefits and learning opportunities that school milk offers.

Change4life

The School Food Trust supports the NHS Change4life programme by ensuring that as many children as possible are eating healthy school food. All school lunches must now meet *nutrient-based standards* to ensure that they provide children with the fuel they need to lead a healthy, active lifestyle. Change4life also provides guidance and resources on the following:

- healthier breakfast clubs
- healthier tuck shops
- water provision
- healthier vending machines
- healthier lunchboxes
- dining room environment
- healthier cookery clubs.

The Nursery Milk Scheme

The Nursery Milk Scheme enables:

- children under five to receive free of charge 189 ml (one-third of a pint) of milk for every day they attend approved day care facilities for two hours or more
- babies aged under 12 months may instead receive dried baby milk made up to 189 ml (one-third of a pint).

Day care providers who have been approved to supply milk under the scheme can be reimbursed for the cost of the milk they supply.

Eat Smart, Play Smart

Eat Smart, Play Smart is a Food Standards Agency teaching resource developed for primary school teachers throughout the UK to use with children aged five to seven years. Eat Smart, Play Smart materials have been developed to:

- help children to understand the need for healthy diets and to choose appropriately from different food groups for their meals
- encourage children to be more active in their home and school lives and to understand the benefits of being active in fun, energetic and easy-to-follow ways.

Activity ·

Find out about and evaluate local initiatives to promote healthy eating in your area. See, for example, the information for Change4life in the Useful resources section on p 24.

· ·

AC 1.3 Describe food and drink requirements in relation to current frameworks

The statutory framework for the Early Years Foundation Stage (EYFS) states the following:

- Where early years settings give children meals, snacks and drinks, these must be healthy, balanced and nutritious.
- Before a child is admitted to the setting, the provider must also obtain information about any special dietary requirements, preferences and food allergies that the child has, and any special health requirements.
- Fresh drinking water must be available and accessible at all times.
- Settings must record and act on information from parents and carers about a child's dietary needs.
- There must be an area which is adequately equipped to provide healthy meals, snacks and drinks for children as necessary.
- There must be suitable facilities for the hygienic preparation of food for children, if necessary including suitable sterilisation equipment for babies' food.
- Settings must be confident that those responsible for preparing and handling food are competent to do so. In group provision, all staff involved in preparing and handling food must receive training in food hygiene.

Food requirements vary according to age, gender, size, occupation or lifestyle, and climate. Different foods contain different amounts of energy per unit of weight; foods that contain a lot of fat and sugar have high energy values.

Food energy is traditionally measured in calories (kcal) or kilojoules (kJ).

1 kcal = 4.2 kJ
1000 kJ = 1 MJ (mega joule) = 239 kcal

An excess of calories will result in weight gain, as the surplus 'energy' is stored as fat; an insufficient intake of calories will result in weight loss, as the body has to draw on fat reserves to meet energy requirements. Babies and young children have relatively high energy requirements in relation to their size. The food and drink requirements for young children are discussed in LO3 on pp 7–9.

Activity ·

Read through the statutory framework requirements for food and eating. Does your setting comply with all the requirements? For example, is fresh drinking water available and accessible at all times?

· ·

LO2 Understand how food choices impact on health and development during pre-pregnancy, pregnancy and breastfeeding

AC 2.1 Explain impact on health and development of food choices during pre-pregnancy, pregnancy and breastfeeding

Pre-conceptual diet

Following a healthy balanced diet before a woman becomes pregnant will allow her to build up reserves of the nutrients vital to the unborn baby in the first three months. Guidelines for a healthy pre-conceptual diet include:

- **Eat something from the four main food groups** every day (potato and cereals, fruit and vegetables, milk and milk products and high-protein foods).
- **Cut down on sugary foods** and eat fresh foods where possible.

- **Avoid pre-packed foods** and any foods which carry the risk of **salmonella** or **listeria** – such as soft or blue-veined cheeses, pate, liver and raw meat.
- **Do not go on a slimming diet**: follow your appetite and do not eat more than you need.
- **Vegetarian diets** which include milk, fish, cheese and eggs provide the vital protein the baby needs.
- **Vegans** should eat soya products and nuts and pulses to supply protein, and vitamin B12 may need to be taken as a supplement.
- **Folic acid tablets and a diet rich in folic acid** taken both pre-conceptually and in pregnancy help the development of the brain and spinal cord, and also help to prevent defects such as **spina bifida**. Sources of folic acid include broccoli, nuts and wholegrain cereals.

Diet during pregnancy

Every pregnant woman hears about 'eating for two' but the best information available today suggests that this is not good advice. Research shows that the

> ### Key term
>
> **spina bifida** This occurs when the spinal canal in the vertebral columns is not closed (although it may be covered with skin). Individuals with spina bifida can have a wide range of physical disabilities. In the more severe forms the spinal cord bulges out of the back, the legs and bladder may be paralysed, and obstruction to the fluid surrounding the brain causes hydrocephalus.

quality (not quantity) of a baby's nutrition before birth lays the foundation for good health in later life. Therefore, during pregnancy women should eat a well-balanced diet. See the guidelines in the box below.

Foods to avoid during pregnancy

During pregnancy, women should avoid certain foods. Sometimes this is because they cause problems such as food poisoning. At other times, certain foods contain harmful bacteria and toxins which can cause serious problems for the unborn baby.

Guidelines for a healthy diet in pregnancy

- Lean meat, fish, eggs, cheese, beans and lentils are all good sources of nutrients. Eat some every day.
- Starchy foods like bread, potatoes, rice, pasta and breakfast cereals should – with vegetables – form the main part of any meal.
- Dairy products, like milk, cheese and yoghurt, are important as they contain **calcium** and other nutrients needed for the baby's development.
- Citrus fruit, tomatoes, broccoli, blackcurrants and potatoes are good sources of **vitamin C**, which is needed to help the absorption of iron from non-meat sources.
- Cut down on sugar and sugary foods like sweets, biscuits and cakes, and sugary drinks like cola.
- Eat plenty of fruit and vegetables that provide **vitamins**, **minerals** and **fibre**. Eat them lightly cooked or raw.
- Green, leafy vegetables, lean meat, dried fruit and nuts contain iron, which is important for preventing anaemia.
- Dairy products, fish with edible bones like sardines, bread, nuts and green vegetables are rich in calcium, which is vital for making bones and teeth.

- Margarine or oily fish (e.g. tinned sardines) contain **vitamin D** to keep bones healthy.
- Include plenty of **fibre** in the daily diet; this will prevent constipation, and help to keep the calorie intake down.
- Cut down on fat and fatty foods. Reducing fat has the effect of reducing energy intake; it is important that these calories are replaced in the form of carbohydrate. Fat should not be avoided completely, however, as certain types are essential for body functioning, as well as containing **fat-soluble vitamins**.
- **Folic acid** is a B vitamin, which is very important throughout pregnancy, but especially in the first 12 weeks when the baby's systems are being formed. (Most doctors recommend that pregnant women take a folic acid supplement every day, as more folic acid is required than is available from a normal diet.)
- **Department of Health** advice is to eat according to appetite, with only a small increase in energy intake for the last three months of the pregnancy (an increase of 200 kcal a day).

Foods to avoid	Reasons
• Soft and blue-veined cheese, such as Camembert, Brie, stilton and chèvre, goat's cheese • Paté (any type, including liver paté and vegetable paté) • Prepared salads (such as potato salad and coleslaw) • Ready-prepared meals or reheated food, *unless* they are piping hot all the way through	**Listeria** High levels of the listeria bacteria are occasionally found in prepared foods. Some ready-prepared meals are not always heated at a high enough temperature to destroy the bacteria. Listeriosis (infection with listeria bacteria) can cause problems for the unborn child, such as: • miscarriage • stillbirth • meningitis • pneumonia.
• Raw or partially cooked eggs, such as home-made mayonnaise, and some mousses and sauces • Unpasteurised milk (both goat's and cow's milks)	**Salmonella** Salmonella is found in unpasteurised milk, raw eggs and raw egg products, raw poultry and raw meat. Eggs should only be eaten if they are cooked until both the white and the yolk are solid. Salmonella food poisoning could cause: • miscarriage • premature birth.
• Some types of fish, such as shark, swordfish and marlin, must be avoided altogether	**High levels of mercury** High levels of mercury can harm a baby's developing nervous system. Women should eat no more than two tuna steaks a week (or four cans of tinned tuna). High levels of mercury can cross the placenta and may cause delayed development.
• Unwashed raw fruit and vegetables Raw or undercooked meat • Unpasteurised goat's milk or goat's cheese	**Toxoplasmosis** Toxoplasmosis is an infection caused by a parasite found in cat faeces. It can also be present in raw or undercooked meat, and in soil left on unwashed fruit and vegetables. Although rare, the infection can occasionally be passed to the unborn baby, which can cause serious problems, such as: • miscarriage • stillbirth • eye damage • hydrocephalus.
• Liver and liver products (e.g. liver paté)	**Too much vitamin A** Women should avoid eating liver and liver products such as pate and avoid taking supplements containing vitamin A or fish liver oils (which contain high levels of vitamin A). If high levels of vitamin A build up in the body they can cause serious problems, including birth defects.
• Peanuts and foods that contain peanuts	**Peanut allergy** Avoiding foods like peanuts – and foods that contain peanuts – may reduce the baby's chances of developing a potentially serious peanut allergy. This is especially true if there is a history of allergies, such as hay fever or asthma, in the family.

Table 1.1.1 Foods to avoid during pregnancy

Nutrition for mothers who breastfeed their baby

If the mother is going to breastfeed her baby, she should follow the principles for the healthy diet in pregnancy. Both calcium and energy requirements increase dramatically when the woman is lactating, and most women find that breastfeeding is also one of the most effective ways of regaining their pre-pregnancy weight. The mother should have at least half a litre of milk and a pot of yoghurt or some cheese each day to satisfy her body's need for extra calcium, and should try to drink one-and-a-half to two litres of water a day. The Food Standards Agency recommends that breastfeeding mothers take supplements containing 10 micrograms (mcg) of vitamin D each day.

Activity

1 Why is it important to eat a healthy diet *before* conceiving a baby?
2 Why is folic acid an important part of the diet during pregnancy?
3 List **five** foods that should be avoided during pregnancy – and explain the reasons why.

LO3 Understand the nutritional needs of children

AC 3.1 Explain the nutritional value of the main food groups

A healthy diet for young children combines foods from each and all of the **four food groups** in Table 1.1.2.

The eatwell plate

Use the eatwell plate to help you get the balance right. It shows how much of what you eat should come from each food group.

Fruit and vegetables

Bread, rice, potatoes, pasta and other starchy foods

Meat, fish, eggs, beans and other non-dairy sources of protein

Foods and drinks high in fat and/or sugar

Milk and dairy foods

Figure 1.1.2 The Eatwell Plate

Food groups	Examples of food included	Main nutrients provided	Recommended servings
Starchy foods	Bread, potatoes, sweet potatoes, starchy root vegetables, pasta, noodles, rice and other grains, breakfast cereals	Carbohydrate, fibre, B vitamins and iron	Four portions each day Provide a portion as part of each meal (breakfast, lunch and tea) and provide as part of at least one snack each day
Fruit and vegetables	Fresh, frozen, canned, dried and juiced fruit and vegetables, and pulses	Carotenes (a form of vitamin A), vitamin C, zinc, iron, and fibre	Five portions each day Provide a portion as part of each main meal (breakfast, lunch and tea) with some snacks
Meat, fish, eggs, beans and non-dairy sources of protein	Meat, poultry, fish, shellfish, eggs, meat alternatives, pulses, nuts* * **Nuts:** children under five should not be offered whole nuts as they may cause choking. Nut butters and ground or chopped nuts in recipes are fine. However, it is important to check if a child has a nut allergy before offering nuts. See p 20, allergies.	Protein, iron, zinc, omega 3 fatty acids, vitamins A and D	Two portions each day Provide a portion as part of lunch and tea (Two to three portions for vegetarian children)
Milk and dairy foods	Milk, cheese, yoghurt, fromage frais, custard, puddings made from milk	Protein, calcium, and vitamin A	Three portions each day provided as part of meals, snacks and drinks

Table 1.1.2 Summary of the four food groups and the nutrients they provide

Explain the nutritional value of the main food groups. How does your setting ensure that all snacks and meals are healthy and nutritious? Have a look at your setting's food policy.

AC 3.2 Use current government guidance to identify nutritional needs of babies until they are fully weaned

The nutritional needs of babies

The way in which babies are fed involves more than simply providing enough food to meet nutritional requirements; for the newborn baby, sucking milk is a great source of pleasure and is also rewarding and enjoyable for the mother. The *ideal* food for babies to start life with is breast milk, and **breastfeeding** should always be encouraged as the first choice in infant feeding; however, mothers should not be made to feel guilty or inadequate if they choose not to breastfeed their babies.

Breastfeeding

During pregnancy, the breasts produce **colostrum**, a creamy, yellowish fluid, low in fat and sugar, which is uniquely designed to feed the newborn baby. Colostrum also has higher levels of antibodies than mature milk and plays an important part in protecting the baby from infection. Mature milk is present in the breasts from around the third day after birth. Hormonal changes in the mother's bloodstream cause the milk to be produced, and the sucking of the baby stimulates a steady supply.

The advantages of breastfeeding

- Human breast milk provides food constituents in the correct balance for human growth. There is no trial and error to find the right formula to suit the baby.
- The milk is sterile and at the correct temperature; there is no need for bottles and sterilising equipment.
- Breast milk initially provides the infant with maternal **antibodies** and helps protect the child from infection – e.g. against illnesses such as diarrhoea, vomiting, chest, ear and urine infections, eczema and nappy rash.
- The child is less likely to become overweight, as overfeeding by concentrating the formula is not possible, and the infant has more freedom of choice as to how much milk he or she will suckle.
- Generally, breast milk is considered cheaper, despite the extra calorific requirement of the mother.
- Sometimes it is easier to promote mother–infant bonding by breastfeeding, although this is certainly not always the case.
- Some babies have an intolerance to the protein in cow's milk (which is the basis of formula milk).

Bottle-feeding

Commercially modified baby milks (formula milks) *must* be used for bottle-feeding. Any other type of milk, such as cow's milk or goat's milk, will not satisfy a baby's nutritional needs, and should not be given to babies under one year of age. A young baby's digestive system is unable to cope with the high protein and salt content of cow's milk, and it is likely to cause an adverse reaction. Soya-based milks can be used if the baby develops an intolerance to modified cow's milks (this happens very rarely). For the first four to six months, the baby will be given infant formula milk as a substitute for breast milk; he or she may then progress to follow-on milk, which may be offered until the age of one year.

Government guidelines state that as each baby will have his or her own individual requirements, it is best to let them feed on demand. Newborn babies may take quite small volumes of infant formula milk to start with, but by the end of the first week of life most babies will ask for approximately 150–200 ml per kg per day (although this will vary from baby to baby) until they are six months old.

The health visitor and National Childbirth Trust can support mothers who are breastfeeding but it is important to remember that the decision to breastfeed will depend on the choice of the mother and her individual circumstances.

Figure 1.1.3 Bottle-feeding

AC 3.3 Explain how to plan a weaning programme

The principles of weaning and its importance to the baby's development

Weaning is the gradual introduction of solid food to the baby's diet. The reasons for weaning are to:

- meet the baby's nutritional needs – from about six months of age, milk alone will not satisfy the baby's increased nutritional requirements, especially for iron
- satisfy increasing appetite
- develop new skills – for example, use of feeding beaker, cup and cutlery

- develop the chewing mechanism – the muscular movement of the mouth and jaw also aids the development of speech
- introduce new tastes and textures – this enables the baby to join in family meals, thus promoting cognitive and social development.

When to start weaning

Department of Health guidelines advise parents to wait until their baby is around six months' old before starting him or her on solid food. When the following three key signs are present together, it means that the baby is ready for solid food:

1 The baby can stay in a sitting position while holding his or her head steady.
2 The baby can coordinate his or her eyes, hands and mouth – that is, look at food, grab it and put it in his or her mouth by him or herself.
3 The baby can swallow his or her food – if the baby is not ready, most of it will be pushed back out.

Babies who are born prematurely should not be introduced to solid foods just because they have reached a certain age or weight. They will need individual assessment before weaning.

Giving solids too early – often in the mistaken belief that the baby might sleep through the night – places a strain on the baby's immature digestive system. It may also make the baby fat and increases the likelihood of allergy.

If parents do choose to introduce solid foods before 26 weeks, they should consult their health visitor or GP first. There are also some foods they should avoid giving their baby. These include:

- foods containing gluten, which is in wheat, rye, barley, oats
- eggs
- fish and shellfish
- liver
- citrus fruit juices
- nuts and seeds.

NB Babies under the age of one year should not be given honey because it is not pasteurised and can cause infant botulism – a rare but very serious illness, which occurs when Clostridium botulinum or related bacteria produce toxins in the intestines of babies under one year old.

Stages of weaning

Every baby is different. Some enjoy trying new tastes and textures, moving through weaning quickly and easily, while others need a little more time to get used to new foods.

Stage 1 (around six months)

Give puréed vegetables, puréed fruit, baby rice and, finely, puréed dhal or lentils. Milk continues to be the most important food.

Stage 2 (about six to eight months)

Increase variety; introduce puréed or minced meat, chicken, liver, fish, lentils and beans. Raw eggs should not be used, but cooked egg yolk can be introduced from six months, along with wheat-based foods – for example, mashed Weetabix® and pieces of bread. Milk feeds decrease as more solids rich in protein are offered.

Stage 3 (about nine to twelve months)

Cow's milk can safely be used at about 12 months, along with lumpier foods such as pasta, pieces of cooked meat, soft cooked beans, pieces of cheese and a variety of breads. Additional fluids can be given – for example, water. Three regular meals should be taken, as well as drinks.

Methods of weaning

Some babies take to solid food very quickly; others appear not to be interested at all. The baby's demands are a good guide for weaning – mealtimes should never become a battleground. Even very young children have definite food preferences and should never be forced to eat a particular food, however much thought and effort have gone into the preparation. Table 1.1.3 offers guidelines on introducing new solids to babies.

The best baby food is home-made from simple ingredients, with no sugar, salt or spices. Any leftovers can be frozen in ice cube trays. Puréed, cooked vegetables, fruit and ground cereals such as rice are ideal to start weaning. Chewing usually starts at around the age of six months, whether or not the baby has teeth, and slightly coarser textures can then be offered. The baby should be fed in a bouncing cradle or high chair – not in the usual feeding position in the carer's arms.

Food can be puréed by:

- rubbing it through a sieve using a large spoon
- mashing it with a fork (for soft foods such as banana or cooked potato)
- using a mouli sieve or hand-blender
- using an electric blender (useful for larger amounts).

Guidelines for weaning

- Try to encourage a liking for savoury foods.
- Only introduce one new food at a time.
- Be patient if the baby does not take the food – feed at the baby's pace, not yours.
- Do not add salt or sugar to feeds.
- Make sure that food is at the right temperature.
- Avoid giving sweet foods or drinks between meals.
- Never leave a baby alone when he or she is eating.
- Limit the use of commercially prepared foods – they are of poorer quality and will not allow the baby to become used to home cooking.
- Select foods approved by the baby's parents or primary carers.

Finger foods

Finger foods are any foods that can be given to a baby to manage by him or herself. After weaning, encourage the baby to chew – even if there are no teeth – by giving finger foods or foods that have a few lumps. Examples of finger foods include:

- wholemeal toast
- pitta bread
- banana or peeled apple slices
- cubes of hard cheese – for example, Cheddar
- chapatti
- breadsticks
- cooked carrots or green beans.

Always stay near to the baby during feeding to make sure he or she does not choke, and to offer encouragement.

Baby-led weaning

Some parents use a technique for weaning their babies called baby-led weaning. This involves letting the baby select those items of food that can be held or grasped by the baby and taken to his or her mouth. Starter foods may include pieces of broccoli, carrot or fruit cut into 'chip' shapes and offered to the baby on a tray. The use of bowls and

	4–6 months	6–8 months	9–12 months
You can give or add	<ul><li>Puréed fruit</li><li>Puréed vegetables</li><li>Thin porridge made from oat or rice flakes or cornmeal</li><li>Finely puréed dhal or lentils</li></ul>	<ul><li>A wider range of puréed fruits and vegetables</li><li>Purées which include chicken, fish and liver</li><li>Wheat-based foods, e.g. mashed Weetabix®</li><li>Egg yolk, well cooked</li><li>Small-sized beans such as aduki beans, cooked soft</li><li>Pieces of ripe banana</li><li>Cooked rice</li><li>Citrus fruits</li><li>Soft summer fruits</li><li>Pieces of bread</li></ul>	<ul><li>An increasingly wide range of foods with a variety of textures and flavours</li><li>Cow's milk</li><li>Pieces of cheese</li><li>Fromage frais or yoghurt</li><li>Pieces of fish</li><li>Soft cooked beans</li><li>Pasta</li><li>A variety of breads</li><li>Pieces of meat from a casserole</li><li>Well-cooked egg white</li><li>Almost anything that is wholesome and that the child can swallow</li></ul>
How	Offer the food on the tip of a clean finger or on the tip of a clean (plastic or horn) teaspoon	On a teaspoon	On a spoon or as finger food
When	A very tiny amount at first, during or after a milk feed	At the end of a milk feed	At established mealtimes
Why	The start of transition from milk to solids	To introduce other foods when the child is hungry	To encourage full independence
Not yet	<ul><li>Cow's milk – or any except breast or formula milk</li><li>Citrus fruit</li><li>Soft summer fruits</li><li>Wheat (cereals, flour, bread, etc.)</li><li>Spices</li><li>Spinach, swede, turnip, beetroot</li><li>Eggs</li><li>Nuts</li><li>Salt</li><li>Sugar</li><li>Fatty food</li></ul>	<ul><li>Cow's milk, except in small quantities mixed with other food</li><li>Chillies or chilli powder</li><li>Egg whites</li><li>Nuts</li><li>Salt</li><li>Sugar</li><li>Fatty food</li></ul>	<ul><li>Whole nuts</li><li>Salt</li><li>Sugar</li><li>Fatty food</li></ul>

Table 1.1.3 Introducing new solids to babies

weaning spoons is discouraged. The principles behind this way of feeding babies are that baby-led weaning:

- offers the baby the opportunity to discover what other foods have to offer, as part of finding out about the world around him or her
- utilises the baby's desire to explore and experiment, and to mimic the activities of others
- enables the transition to solid foods to take place as naturally as possible – by allowing the baby to set the pace of each meal, and maintaining an emphasis on play and exploration rather than on eating.

For more information, visit this website: http://babyledweaning.com.

Activity •

Using the information in this section and the guidelines below, plan a weaning programme for a baby at each stage of the process: first stage: around six months; second stage: six to eight months; third stage: nine to twelve months.

• •

AC 3.4 Discuss the nutritional requirements of children aged one to seven years

Children need a varied energy-rich diet for good health and growth. For balance and variety, choose from the **four main food groups** (see Table 1.1.2). A healthy diet should also include foods rich in calcium, iron and vitamin D.

Iron, calcium and vitamin D in children's diets
Iron

Iron is essential for children's health. Lack of iron often leads to **anaemia**, which can hold back both physical and mental development. Children most at risk are those who are poor eaters or on restricted diets. Iron comes in two forms, found either in:

- foods from animal sources (especially meat), which is easily absorbed by the body, or
- plant foods, which are not quite so easy for the body to absorb.

If possible, children should be given a portion of meat or fish every day, and kidney or liver once a week. Even a small portion of meat or fish is useful because it also helps the body to absorb iron from other food sources.

If children do not eat meat or fish, they must be offered plenty of iron-rich alternatives, such as egg yolks, dried fruit, beans and lentils, and green leafy vegetables. It is also a good idea to give foods or drinks that are high in **vitamin C** at mealtimes, as this helps the absorption of iron from non-meat sources.

Calcium and vitamin D

Children need calcium for maintaining and repairing bones and teeth. Calcium is:

- found in milk, cheese, yoghurt and other dairy products
- absorbed by the body only if it is taken with vitamin D.

The skin can make all the vitamin D that a body needs when it is exposed to gentle sunlight. Sources of vitamin D include:

- milk
- oily fish
- fortified margarine
- tahini paste*
- fortified breakfast cereals
- meat
- soya mince, soya drink
- tofu.

(* Tahini is made from sesame seeds; these may cause an allergic reaction in a small number of children.)

The Department of Health recommends that from six months to five years of age, children should be given a vitamin supplement containing vitamins A, C and D unless they are drinking 500 ml of infant formula a day or are eating a varied diet with a wide range of foods to provide an adequate intake of vitamins and minerals.

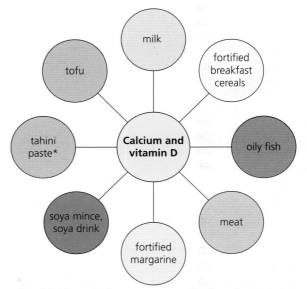

(* Tahini is made from sesame seeds; these may cause an allergic reaction in a small number of children.)

Figure 1.1.4 Sources of calcium and vitamin D

Dietary fibre

Dietary fibre – or roughage – is found in cereals, fruits and vegetables. Fibre is made up of the indigestible parts or compounds of plants, which pass relatively unchanged through our stomach and intestines. Fibre is needed to provide roughage to help to keep the food moving through the gut. A small amount of fibre is important for health in pre-school children but too much can cause problems as their digestive system is still immature. It could also reduce energy intakes by 'bulking up' the diet. Providing a mixture of white bread and refined cereals, white rice and pasta as well as a few wholegrain varieties occasionally helps to maintain a healthy balance between fibre and nutrient intakes.

How much food should children be given?

Children's appetites vary enormously, so common sense is a good guide to how big a portion should be. Always be guided by the individual child:

- do not force them to eat when they no longer wish to, but
- do not refuse to give more if they really are hungry.

Some children always feel hungry at one particular mealtime. Others require food little and often. You should always offer food that is nourishing as well as satisfying their hunger. Table 1.1.4 gives examples of foods to provide for a balanced diet.

Breakfast	• Orange juice • Weetabix® + milk, 1 slice of buttered toast	• Milk • Cereal, e.g. corn or wheat flakes, toast and jam	• Apple juice • 1 slice of toast with butter or jam	• Milk • Cereal with slice of banana, or scrambled egg on toast	• Yoghurt • Porridge, slices of apple
Morning snack	• Diluted apple juice • 1 packet raisins	• Blackcurrant and apple drink • Cheese straws	• 1 glass fruit squash • 1 biscuit	• Peeled apple slices • Wholemeal toast fingers with cheese spread	• Diluted apple juice • Chapatti or pitta bread fingers
Lunch	• Chicken nuggets or macaroni cheese • Broccoli • Fruit yoghurt • Water	• Thick bean soup or chicken salad sandwich • Green beans • Fresh fruit salad • Water	• Vegetable soup or fish fingers/cakes • Sticks of raw carrot • Kiwi fruit • Water	• Sweet potato casserole • Sweet corn • Spinach leaves • Chocolate mousse • Water	• Bean casserole (or chicken drumstick) with noodles • Peas or broad beans • Fruit yoghurt • Water
Afternoon snack	• Diluted fruit juice • Cubes of cheese with savoury biscuit	• Milk shake • Fruit cake or chocolate or biscuit	• Diluted fruit juice • Thin-cut sandwiches cut into small pieces	• Hot or cold chocolate drink • 1 small packet dried fruit mix, e.g. apricots, sultanas	• Lassi (yoghurt drink) • 1 banana • 1 small biscuit
Tea or supper	• Baked beans on toast or ham and cheese pasta • Lemon pancakes • Milk or yoghurt	• Fish stew or fish fingers • Mashed potato • Fruit mousse or fromage frais • Milk or yoghurt	• Baked potatoes with a choice of fillings • Steamed broccoli • Ice cream	• Home-made beef burger or pizza • Green salad • Pancakes • Milk	• Lentil and rice soup • Pitta or whole grain bread • Rice salad • Milk

Table 1.1.4 Providing a balanced diet

Providing drinks for children

An adequate fluid intake will prevent dehydration and reduce the risk of constipation. Milk and water are the best drinks to give between meals and snacks as they do not harm teeth when taken from a cup or beaker. Research into how the brain develops has found that water is beneficial. The best drinks for young children are **water** and **milk.**

Milk is an excellent nourishing drink which provides valuable **nutrients** (see p 2). All toddlers should drink whole (full-fat) milk until they are two years old. Children above this age who are eating well can change to semi-skimmed milk.

Other drinks

All drinks which contain sugar can be harmful to teeth and can also take the edge off children's appetites. Examples are flavoured milks, fruit squashes, flavoured fizzy drinks, and fruit juices (containing natural sugar).

Unsweetened *diluted* fruit juice is a reasonable option for children – although not as good as water or milk – but ideally should only be offered at mealtimes. Low-sugar and diet fruit drinks contain artificial sweeteners and are best avoided. Tea and coffee should not be given to children under five years, as they prevent the absorption of iron from foods. They also tend to fill children up without providing nourishment.

Providing drinks for children aged one to three

The normal fluid requirement for children aged one to three years is 95 ml per kg of body weight per day. The Guidelines for Early Years Settings state that:

- Children must have access to drinking water throughout the day and be encouraged to help themselves to water.
- Children need six to eight drinks (each of 100–150 ml) a day to make sure they get enough fluid.
- Children may need extra drinks in hot weather or after physical activity as they can dehydrate quite quickly.
- Sweetened drinks, including diluted fruit juice, should only be consumed *with*, rather than

between, meals to lessen the risk of dental decay. Consumption of sugar-free fizzy or fruit-based drinks, although not recommended, should also be confined to mealtimes because the high acidity level of these drinks can cause dental decay.

Providing drinks for children aged four to seven years

The normal fluid requirement for children aged four to seven years is 85 ml per kg of body weight per day. The following drinks are recommended: still water, milk, plain or flavoured, diluted pure fruit juice, fruit and milk/yoghurt smoothies, vegetable juices and no-added-sugar (sugar-free) squashes – well diluted.

In between meals and snacks, water and plain milk are still the best drinks as they will not damage teeth as acidic and sugary drinks do.

NB Recent research showed that some parents never offer children water to drink as they do not drink water themselves; some parents even consider it cruel to offer water in place of flavoured drinks.

Providing nutritious snacks

Some children really do *need* to eat between meals. Health guidelines recommend children should not go longer than three hours without refreshment. Children's stomachs are relatively small and so they fill up and empty faster than adult stomachs. Sugary foods should not be given as a snack, because sugar is an appetite depressant and may spoil the child's appetite for the main meal to follow. Healthy snack foods include:

- fruit – banana, orange, pear, kiwi fruit, apple or satsuma
- dairy foods such as cheese or plain yoghurt with added fruit
- fruit bread or wholemeal bread with a slice of cheese
- milk or home-made milk shake
- raw vegetables such as peeled carrots, sweet pepper, tomato, cucumber or celery (all well washed)
- dried fruit – such as raisins or dried apricots
- wholegrain biscuits, breadsticks, cream crackers, matzos, melba toast, crispbread, oatcakes or sesame seed crackers

Guidelines for reducing salt in children's diets

- Cut down gradually on the amount of salt used in cooking so that children become used to less salty foods.
- If preparing baby food at home do not add salt, even if it tastes bland. Manufactured baby food is tightly regulated to limit the salt content to a trace.
- Try using a low-salt substitute, such as LoSalt®, Solo® or a supermarket's own-brand low sodium salt in cooking or at the table. These products substitute up to 70 per cent of the sodium chloride with potassium chloride.

any type of bread including fruit bread, crumpets, teacakes, muffins, fruit buns, malt loaf, bagels, pitta bread or sandwiches. Suitable fillings for sandwiches might be cheese, yeast extract, banana, salad or combinations of these.

The dangers of too much salt

On average children are eating twice the recommended amount of salt. The Recommended Nutrient Intake (RNI) for infants aged between one and three years is not more than 1.25 g of salt each day; four- to six-year-olds should consume no more than 1.75 g. Many manufactured foods are marketed at children, and some of these can exceed their daily salt requirement in a single serving, a bag of crisps for example. A small can (200 g) of pasta shapes in tomato sauce contains twice the daily RNI of salt for a one- to three-year-old and a third more than the daily RNI for a four- to six-year-old.

Foods to avoid giving to children

- **Salt**: there is no need to add salt to children's food. Even when buying processed food made specifically for children, remember to check the information given on the labels to choose those with less salt.
- **Nuts**: do not give whole or chopped nuts to children under five years old because of the risk of choking.
- **Raw eggs**: avoid food that contains raw or partially cooked eggs because of the risk of **salmonella**, which causes food poisoning. Make sure that eggs are always cooked until both the white and yolk are solid.
- **Undiluted fruit juice**: these contain natural sugars which are known to cause tooth decay;

they are best only given at mealtimes and should be diluted when given to young children.
- **High-fibre foods** like brown rice and wholemeal pasta are too bulky for children under five; too much fibre can also make it more difficult for the body to absorb some essential nutrients, like **calcium** and **iron**.
- **Shark**, **swordfish** and **marlin** should not be given because these fish contain relatively high levels of **mercury**, which might affect a child's developing nervous system.
- **Raw shellfish**: to reduce their risk of developing food poisoning.

Activity ·

Make sure you know the current guidelines and nutritional requirements concerning the provision of a healthy diet, including guidelines for providing drinks and avoiding extra salt and sugar. Find out about the food policy in your setting.

· ·

AC 3.5 Explain strategies to encourage healthy eating

The early years setting is an ideal place to provide meal and snack times that make eating an enjoyable social event. When children positively enjoy their food-related experiences, they are less likely to develop food-related problems. Also, children are more likely to try new foods if they see their friends trying them in a relaxed and happy atmosphere. There will be opportunities to talk about food, their likes and dislikes and the texture, colour and smell of different foods. Every child is unique; they gradually develop a whole catalogue of likes, strong dislikes and mild preferences regarding food and mealtimes; for example:

- Some like their food bathed in sauces, while others prefer it dry.
- Some like every food kept separate from the others on the plate.
- Many do not like 'tough' meat or foods that are difficult to chew.

It is important to respect a child's likes and dislikes, and offer alternative foods from the same food group where necessary.

Introducing new foods

When introducing children to new foods, the following points are important:

- They should have the chance to try the same food on more than one occasion. The first time they try a food it can be the fact that it is new or that they do not like the texture that makes them not want to eat it. The second time they try it, it is not so unfamiliar and their preferences may change.

- When trying new foods, children need to know that they do not have to swallow the food. If they know they can spit it into a tissue, they are less likely to be worried about putting a new type of food into their mouth.

LO4 Understand the impact of poor diet on children's health and development

AC 4.1 Explain the impacts of poor diet on children's health and development in the short and long term

Healthy eating – or good nutrition – during childhood makes it easier to maintain a healthy weight, and has been shown to improve children's concentration and behaviour. It can also help to reduce the risk of developing many common

Guidelines: the role of the practitioner in promoting healthy eating

- **Set an example**: children will imitate both what you eat and how you eat it. It will be easier to encourage a child to eat a stick of raw celery if you eat one too! If you show disgust at certain foods, young children will notice and copy you.
- **Offer a wide variety of different foods**: give babies and toddlers an opportunity to try a new food more than once; any refusal on first tasting may be due to dislike of the new rather than of the food itself.
- **Be prepared for messy mealtimes**: present the food in a form that is fairly easy for children to manage by themselves (for example, not difficult to chew).
- **Do not use food as a punishment, reward, bribe or threat**: for example, do not give sweets or chocolates as a reward for finishing savoury foods. To a child this is like saying 'Here's something nice after eating those nasty greens.' Give healthy foods as treats, such as raisins and raw carrots, rather than sweets or cakes.
- **Introduce new foods in stages**: for example, if switching to wholemeal bread, try a soft-grain white bread first. Always involve the children in making choices as far as possible.
- **Teach children to eat mainly at mealtimes** and avoid giving them high-calorie snacks (such as biscuits and sugary drinks) which might take the edge off their appetite for more nutritious food. Most

young children need three small meals and three snacks a day.
- **Ensure that children sit down at a table to eat** their snacks, that they are supervised during these times and are monitored to ensure that they eat an appropriate amount of food safely to reduce the risk of choking.
- **Presentation is important**: food manufacturers use a variety of techniques to make their children's food products exciting – colours, shapes, themes and characters. Using these tactics can make mealtimes more fun.
- **Avoid adding salt to any food**: too much salt can cause dehydration in babies and may predispose certain people to hypertension (high blood pressure) if taken over a lifetime.
- **Allow children to follow their own individual appetites** when deciding how much they want to eat. If a child rejects food, never force-feed them. Simply remove the food without comment. Give smaller portions next time and praise the child for eating even a little.
- **Never give a young child whole nuts to eat** – particularly peanuts. Children can very easily choke on a small piece of the nut or even inhale it, which can cause a severe type of pneumonia. Rarely, a child may have a serious allergic reaction to nuts. Always check whether a child has a known allergy to nuts.

diseases including heart disease, cancer, diabetes, obesity, osteoporosis and dental decay.

Malnutrition and under-nutrition

In recent years there has been increasing public concern about the quality of children's diets, rapidly increasing rates of **child obesity**, diet-related disorders, and low consumption of fruit and vegetables by children. There are various conditions that may occur in childhood that are directly related to a poor or unbalanced diet; these are a result of either **malnutrition** or **under-nutrition** and include:

- **failure to thrive*** (or faltering growth): poor growth and physical development
- **dental caries** or tooth decay: associated with a high consumption of sugar in snacks and fizzy drinks
- **obesity**: children who are overweight are more likely to become obese adults.
- **nutritional anaemia**: due to an insufficient intake of iron, folic acid and vitamin B12
- **increased susceptibility to infections**: particularly upper respiratory infections, such as colds and bronchitis.

(*Failure to thrive can also result from child abuse: physical abuse, emotional abuse, neglect and sexual abuse.) This subject is discussed in Unit 2.1.

> ### Key terms
>
> **under-nutrition** This occurs when people do not get enough to eat.
>
> **malnutrition** A person's diet is lacking the necessary amounts of certain elements that are essential to growth, such as vitamins, salts and proteins.

Food refusal

Many children go through phases of refusing to eat certain foods or not wanting to eat anything much at all. This is particularly common in children up to the age of five, and is a normal part of growing up and asserting their independence. Eating can quickly become a focus for conflict and tension at home, with parents feeling anxious and out of control. Food refusal often starts because it is one of the few ways in which children can exert influence over their parents. Reasons for food refusal in young children include the following:

- **Slower growth and small appetites**: growth slows down in a child's second year. This means that toddlers often have small appetites and need less food. Children eat according to their appetite, and this can vary from day to day. Some children eat in spurts; they may eat much one day and very little the next. It also depends on how active they have been during the day.
- **Distraction**: young children have no concept of time. Their world has become an exciting place to explore and food can seem less important when there are so many other things to do.
- **Grazing and snacking**: toddlers rarely follow a traditional meal pattern. They tend to need small and regular snacks. Parents may offer sweets or crisps throughout the day so that children 'won't go hungry'. Children then become even less inclined to eat their meals when they know that they can fill up on their favourite snacks. Large quantities of milk or other drinks throughout the day also take the edge off a child's appetite.
- **Fussy eating and food fads**: showing independence is part of normal child development, and this often includes refusing to eat foods 'to see what will happen'. It is quite normal for children to have certain times when their food choices become very limited. For example, they will only eat food prepared and presented in a certain way. Some decide they do not like mixed-up food or different foods touching each other on the plate, and they develop strong likes and dislikes that frequently change.
- **New textures and tastes**: children are experimenting with, or being asked to try, new textures and tastes. Rejecting a food does not always mean the child does not like it; they may eat it the very next day.
- **Seeking attention**: children may seek to gain attention in different ways. They may test their parents' reactions and learn the effects of their uncooperative behaviour. They may have learnt to say 'no' and may welcome all the attention they are getting, for example, by refusing to eat (or taking ages to eat) a lovingly prepared meal.

How to cope with food refusal

Research shows that one-third of all parents worry that their child is not eating enough, but unless they are ill, young children will never voluntarily starve themselves. If a child seems to be healthy and energetic, they are almost certainly eating enough. There is plenty of advice for parents and carers from health experts and child dieticians on how to cope with their child's refusal of food, including the following tips:

- Never force-feed a child, either by pushing food into his mouth or by threatening punishment or withdrawal of a treat.
- Keep calm and try not to make a fuss of whether their child is eating or not. Instead, try to make mealtimes pleasant, social occasions, because if children associate mealtimes with an enjoyable event, they will want to repeat it.
- Encourage self-feeding and exploration of food from an early age, without worrying about the mess.
- Offer alternative foods from every food group: if a child dislikes cheese, they may eat yoghurt.
- Provide healthy, nutritious snacks between meals as these play an important part in the energy intake of young children. Ideas include fresh and dried fruits, crackers with cheese or peanut butter, yoghurt.

Activity

Observation Arrange to observe a group of children during mealtime. Note in particular children who seem reluctant or 'fussy' eaters. Note also each child's food preferences.

LO5 Understand individuals' dietary requirements and preferences

Research activity

Different traditions
Find out about the dietary requirements and restrictions in one cultural or religious group different from your own. Choose from:

- Jewish
- Muslim (Islamic)
- Hindu
- Rastafarian.

AC 5.1 Identify reasons for special dietary requirements and keeping and sharing coherent records with regard to special dietary requirements

Apart from the dietary implications of multicultural food provision, there are several other dietary requirements – some based on family preferences, and others required because the child has a disorder or allergy.

Children on vegetarian diets

Children who are on a vegetarian diet need an alternative to meat, fish and chicken as the main sources of protein. Alternatives might include:

- milk
- cheese and eggs
- pulses (lentils and beans).

They also need enough iron. As iron is more difficult to absorb from vegetable sources than from meat, a young child needs to obtain iron from sources such as:

- leafy green vegetables – such as spinach and watercress
- pulses (beans, lentils and chickpeas)
- dried fruit (such as apricots, raisins and sultanas) – although some dentists believe that dried fruit contributes to dental decay, and so it should be given sparingly
- some breakfast cereals.

It is easier to absorb iron from our food if it is eaten with foods containing vitamin C, such as fruit and vegetables, or with diluted fruit juices at mealtimes. Do not give young children tea or coffee, especially at mealtimes, because this reduces the amount of iron they can absorb.

The vegan diet

A vegan diet completely excludes all foods of animal origin; that is, animal flesh, milk and milk products, eggs, honey and all additives which may be of animal origin. A vegan diet is based on cereals and cereal products, pulses, fruits, vegetables, nuts and seeds. Human breast milk is acceptable for vegan babies.

Muslim diets	Hindu diets	Sikh diets
Muslims practise the Islamic religion, and their holy book, The Koran, provides them with their food laws. Unlawful foods (called haram) are: pork, all meat which has not been rendered lawful (halal), alcohol and fish without scales. Wheat, in the form of chapattis, and rice are the staple foods. The Koran dictates that children should be breastfed up to the age of two years. Fasting: during the lunar month of Ramadan Muslims fast between sunrise and sunset; fasting involves abstinence from all food and drink, so many Muslims rise early to eat before dawn in order to maintain their energy levels. Children under 12 years and the elderly are exempt from fasting.	Wheat is the main staple food eaten by Hindus in the UK; it is used to make types of bread called chapattis, puris and parathas. Orthodox Hindus are strict vegetarians as they believe in Ahimsa – non-violence towards all living beings – and a minority practise veganism. Some will eat dairy products and eggs, while others will refuse eggs on the grounds that they are a potential source of life. Even non-vegetarians do not eat beef as the cow is considered a sacred animal, and it is unusual for pork to be eaten as the pig is considered unclean. Ghee (clarified butter) and vegetable oil are used in cooking. Fasting: common for certain festivals, such as Mahshivrati (the birthday of Lord Shiva).	Most Sikhs will not eat pork or beef or any meat that is killed by the halal method. Some Sikhs are vegetarian, but many eat chicken, lamb and fish. Wheat and rice are staple foods Fasting: Devout Sikhs will fast once or twice a week, and most will fast on the first day of the Punjabi month or when there is a full moon.

		Rastafarian diets
		Dietary practices are based on laws laid down by Moses in the Book of Genesis in the Bible. These laws state that certain types of meat should be avoided. The majority of followers will only eat Ital foods, which are foods considered to be in a whole or natural state. Most Rastafarians are vegetarians and will not consume processed or preserved foods. No added salt; no coffee.

Afro-Caribbean diets	Jewish diets	Festivals from different cultures	
The Afro-Caribbean community is the second largest ethnic minority group in the UK. Dietary practices within the community vary widely. Many people include a wide variety of European foods in their diet alongside the traditional foods of cornmeal, coconut, green banana, plantain, okra and yam. Although Afro-Caribbean people are generally Christian, a minority are Rastafarians.	Jewish people observe dietary laws which state that animals and birds must be slaughtered by the Jewish method to render them kosher (acceptable). Milk and meat must never be cooked or eaten together, and pork in any form is forbidden. Shellfish are not allowed as they are thought to harbour disease. Only fish with fins and scales may be eaten. Fasting: The most holy day of the Jewish calendar is Yom Kippur (the Day of Atonement), when Jewish people fast for 25 hours.	Shichi-go-san (Japanese festival for young children)	November 15
		Chinese New Year	Late January/ early February
		Shrove Tuesday (Mardi Gras)	40 days before Easter
		Rosh Hoshanah (Jewish New Year)	Usually September
		Holi (Hindu Spring festival)	February or March
		Id Al Fitir (major Muslim festival)	At end of Ramadan
		Divali (Hindu New Year)	October or November
		Rastafarian New Year	January 7

Table 1.1.5 Multicultural provision and dietary implications

Food intolerances and food allergies
Food intolerance

Food intolerance is an adverse reaction to some sort of food or ingredient that occurs *every time* the food is eaten, but particularly if larger quantities are consumed. Food intolerance is *not* the same as

- a **food allergy** because the **immune system** is not activated, or
- **food poisoning**, in which toxic substances would cause symptoms in anyone who ate the food.

Food intolerance does not include *psychological* reactions to food; it is much more common than food allergy.

Some babies develop an intolerance to cow's milk protein; the most common symptoms are vomiting, diarrhoea and failure to thrive. After weaning, foods most likely to cause an adverse reaction in babies are:

- hen's eggs
- citrus fruits
- pork.
- fish
- wheat and other cereals

Sometimes an adverse reaction will be temporary, perhaps following an illness, but the offending food should always be removed from the baby's diet. Dietetic advice should be sought before any changes to a balanced diet are made.

Food allergies

A food allergy is an abnormal response (an allergic reaction) of the immune system to otherwise harmless foods. Up to 5 per cent of children have food allergies. Most children outgrow their allergy, although an allergy to peanuts and some other tree nuts is considered lifelong.

There are eight foods that cause 90 per cent of all food allergic reactions. These are:

- peanuts
- tree nuts (such as almonds, walnuts, pecans, etc.)
- wheat
- shellfish
- fish.
- soy
- milk
- eggs

Milk is the most common cause of food allergies in children, but peanuts, nuts, fish and shellfish commonly cause the most severe reactions.

What are the symptoms of an allergic reaction?

Symptoms of an allergic response can include:

- vomiting
- hives (or urticaria) – an itchy raised rash usually found on the trunk or limbs
- itching or tightness in the throat
- diarrhoea
- eczema
- difficulty breathing
- cramps
- itching or swelling of the lips, tongue or mouth
- wheezing.

Allergic symptoms can begin within minutes to one hour after ingesting the food.

Anaphylaxis

In rare cases of food allergy, just *one bite* of food can bring on **anaphylaxis**. This is a severe reaction that involves various areas of the body simultaneously. In extreme cases, it can cause death.

Anaphylaxis is a sudden and severe potentially life-threatening allergic reaction. It can be caused by insect stings or medications, as well as by a food allergy. Although potentially *any* food can cause anaphylaxis, **peanuts**, **nuts**, **shellfish**, **fish** and **eggs** are foods that most commonly cause this reaction.

Symptoms of anaphylaxis may include all those listed above for food allergies. In addition, the child's breathing is seriously impaired and the pulse rate becomes rapid. Anaphylaxis is fortunately very rare, but is also very dangerous:

- Symptoms can occur in as little as five to fifteen minutes.
- As little as half a peanut can cause a fatal reaction in severely allergic individuals.
- Some severely allergic children can have a reaction if milk is splashed on their skin.
- Being kissed by somebody who has eaten peanuts, for example, can cause a reaction in severely allergic individuals.

Emergency treatment of anaphylaxis

- **Summon medical help immediately**. The child will need oxygen and a life-saving injection of adrenaline.

- **Place the child in a sitting position** to help relieve any breathing difficulty.
- Be prepared to resuscitate if necessary.

In some settings attended by a child or children known to be at risk from anaphylaxis, the staff may be trained to give the adrenaline injection.

How can food allergies be managed?

The only way to manage food allergies is strictly to avoid the foods to which the child is allergic. It is important to learn how to interpret ingredients on food labels and how to spot high-risk foods. Many children outgrow earlier food-allergic symptoms as they get older, but parents will need professional support and advice to ensure that their child is receiving a safe, balanced diet.

Key terms

allergy Abnormal sensitivity reaction of the body to substances that are usually harmless.

anaphylaxis An immediate and severe allergic response; a shock reaction to a substance.

Recording and sharing information about children's special dietary requirements

Each setting will have its own method for recording and sharing information about special dietary requirements – some have a separate policy for this aspect of care.

Activity

Find out how such information is recorded in your setting. How is the information shared with other practitioners? How often are these records updated?

AC 5.2 Explain the role of the EYP in meeting children's individual dietary requirements and preferences

Meeting children's individual dietary requirements and preferences

All staff in early years settings should be aware of the identities of children who have food allergies, and should have clear instructions on how to

deal with each case. In particular, lunchtime supervisors need to be kept informed. Most settings display a photograph of any child with a special dietary requirement or allergy in the food preparation area to ensure that permanent and supply staff are aware of each individual child's needs.

In practice activity

Special dietary requirements
Find out about the policy in your work setting covering special dietary requirements. In particular, find out about:

- special diets (which have been medically advised)
- preference diets (where there is no degree of risk attached)
- food allergies.

How does your setting ensure that any special dietary requirements are identified, and that every child is offered the appropriate food and drink?

When a child has been diagnosed as having a **severe allergy** to a particular food, staff *may* decide to minimise the risk of exposure by avoiding having the food or ingredient in the setting. In severe cases it is essential that there is regular access to up-to-date advice from a registered dietician because ingredients in processed foods change frequently. Everybody involved in the care of children with known allergies should know:

- how to recognise the symptoms of a food allergy or intolerance
- how to avoid the foods the child is sensitive to
- what to do if they have an allergic reaction
- how to use their adrenaline injector or EpiPen®, if they have one
- when and how to record and report any suspicion of food allergy or intolerance.

Figure 1.1.5 An EpiPen

Progress check

Allergies and intolerances

- All staff should be aware of which children suffer from an allergy and to which food, and of the policy regarding first aid and administering medication.
- All staff involved in the care of that child must be aware of the foods and ingredients being offered to the child.
- Care must be taken in the preparation and serving of food not to cross-contaminate food being served to a child with an allergy.

- If you ever notice swelling of a child's mouth or face or breathing difficulties when eating, seek medical advice immediately. Symptoms such as a rash or vomiting after eating may also suggest that there has been a reaction to a food. Always inform the parent or carer.
- To lessen the risk of peanut allergies, peanut-containing foods should not be given to children under three years of age if the child has a parent or sibling with a diagnosed allergy. Whole nuts should not be given to any child under the age of five years because of the risk of choking.

In practice activity

Food allergies and intolerances

In your setting:

- Find out how many (if any) children have food allergies or intolerances.
- How is information displayed about children's allergies?
- Is there a policy document relating to reporting and recording allergies and intolerances?

AC 5.3 Describe benefits of working in partnership with parents/carers in relation to special dietary requirements

Many early years settings have written procedures for children with special dietary needs. This helps practitioners to work in partnership with parents to find out more about their child's requirements and to reassure them that their child's needs will be met. A procedure may include the following points:

- Before a child begins attending the nursery, the child's parents will be asked by the key person to outline the child's dietary needs.
- If the child has a food allergy or requires a special diet the parents may, for example, be asked to complete a 'Special Dietary Needs Form' which identifies in detail any food allergies or special dietary needs that their child has depending on how the setting records this information.
- The key person will give the form to the Nursery Manager and ensure that all members of staff who may come into contact with the child know about the child's individual needs and any actions required.

- The Nursery Manager will ensure that a suitable individual menu is drawn up for the child (expert advice will be sought if necessary).
- Parents should advise the setting manager which foods can be given as alternatives, ones to be avoided and any triggers. They should also provide confirmation in writing.
- The child's parents will be given a copy of the individual menus and asked to sign an agreement that their child may have all the foods and drinks listed.
- The cook will be given a copy of the child's signed menu and will inform all other staff who may be involved in preparing the child's food about the child's individual needs and any actions required.
- The child's parents will be asked to give permission for their child's individual allergies or individual dietary needs to be displayed discreetly in the nursery to ensure that all staff members are aware of what the child may and may not be given to eat and drink.
- If a child is provided with particular products on prescription, for example gluten-free bread, it may be possible for parents to provide a quantity of these to the setting for cooks to use when preparing a meal.

Activity

Find out about the policy or procedures for children with special dietary requirements in your setting. Why is it beneficial to children when staff work in partnership with parents in relation to special dietary requirements?

LO6 Be able to support healthy eating in own setting

AC 6.1 Plan an activity to support healthy eating in own setting

Raising awareness of healthy eating

Almost all children have some experience of cooking, or at the very least food preparation, in their own homes. This experience can range from watching tins being opened and the contents heated, seeing fruit being peeled and cut, or bread being put in a toaster and then spread, to a full meal being cooked.

Food preparation and cooking activities are also useful in raising children's awareness of healthy and nutritious foods, educating them about diet and choice. For example, by discussing the need for an ingredient to sweeten food, children can be introduced to the variety available and be made aware of healthy options instead of sugar.

Children learn through active involvement so any cooking activity must be chosen carefully to ensure that children can participate. There is very limited value in them watching an adult carry out the instructions and occasionally letting them have a stir!

Other learning outcomes include:

- development of **physical skills** through using the equipment – pouring, beating, whisking, stirring, etc.
- **aspects of counting, sorting, measuring** – size and quantity, sharing, fractions, ordinal number (i.e. first, second), sequencing and memory through following and recalling the recipe instructions
- **independence skills** through preparation, controlling their own food and equipment, tidying up
- **expressing their ideas**, opinions, likes and dislikes
- understanding **how to present food** attractively through arrangement and decoration.

Planning a cooking activity with young children

When selecting a cooking activity, remember:

- that parental wishes must always be respected
- to check that all children can eat the food to be cooked
- to check that there are no problems regarding allergies or religious dietary restrictions
- to follow the basic food safety and hygiene guidelines on p 52.

Ideas for planning and implementing a cooking activity include:

- cutting and preparing fruit, vegetables, salad items or cheese
- spreading breads, crackers or crispbreads with a variety of foods – butter, jam, cream cheese, yeast extract, etc.
- making biscuits or cakes.

AC 6.2 Implement an activity to support healthy eating in own setting

Having planned your activity, make sure you allow plenty of time for preparation, and follow the guidelines below.

Guidelines: implementing a cooking activity with children

- Always prepare surfaces with antibacterial spray and clean cloths.
- Always ensure children have washed their hands and scrubbed their fingernails.
- Always provide protective clothing and, if necessary, roll up long sleeves.
- Always tie back long hair.
- Always check equipment for damage.
- Always follow the safety procedures and policies of the work setting.

- Always ensure adequate supervision.
- Always remind children not to cough over food or put their fingers or utensils in their mouths when handling food.
- Always check the use-by dates of food items and store them correctly.
- Always check for 'E' numbers and artificial ingredients in bought food items.
- Check any allergies/individual dietary requirements.

Evaluation

After the activity, evaluate your activity. How successful were you in achieving your aims? Were all the children involved? What do you think the children learnt about healthy eating?

AC 6.3 and AC 6.4 Reflect on own role when supporting healthy eating and Make recommendations for healthy eating in own setting

Consider your own role when supporting healthy eating in your setting. Try to answer the following questions to help you reflect on your own experiences:

- Am I a good role model for the children?
- Do I always seek to promote healthy eating – through a thorough understanding of what constitutes a healthy diet?
- Are mealtimes and snack times enjoyable for all the children?

- Do I encourage children to help themselves to water throughout the day?
- Do I observe children to ensure they are eating a healthy diet?
- Am I aware of the food preferences of individual children or of their needs for a particular diet?
- Do I consult with parents or carers about their child's dietary needs?
- Do I try to involve both children and their families when planning food-related activities?

Activity

- Create a weekly plan which shows all the meals, drinks and snacks for the children in your setting.
- Identify how your plan meets the children's nutritional needs, using the Guidelines in Table 1.1.4 on p 13.
- Describe the methods you have used to identify each child's needs and preferences.
- Describe the steps you would take to cope with a child who refuses to eat.

Assessment practice

1. What is meant by healthy eating? Describe the nutrients which make up a healthy diet.
2. How far do you think that national and local initiatives have succeeded in promoting healthy eating?
3. Why is it so important that young children have access to drinking water throughout the day? What are the food and drink requirements in early years settings?
4. Why is a healthy diet important in the pre-conceptual period, during pregnancy, and when breastfeeding?
5. What are the main food groups? Why do children require vitamins, iron and calcium?
6. Identify the nutritional needs of babies until they are fully weaned using current government guidance.
7. Why is breast milk best for a baby? When is it safe to give cow's milk to a baby?
8. What is weaning? How could you plan a weaning programme to meet the nutritional needs of babies?

9. Describe the nutritional requirements for children aged between one and seven years. Which foods should be avoided and what sorts of food should be limited as part of a healthy diet?
10. Describe some strategies you could use to promote healthy eating.
11. Explain the short- and long-term impact of poor nutrition on children's health and development.
12. Describe the need for special dietary requirements, and keeping and sharing coherent records with regard to special dietary requirements. What is your role in meeting children's individual dietary needs and preferences?
13. Why is it important to work with parents/carers in relation to special dietary requirements?
14. Plan and implement an activity to support healthy eating in your own setting.
15. Reflect on your own role, and describe ways in which you can promote healthy eating in your setting.

Useful resources

Organisations

Change4Life: www.nhs.uk

Eat better, start better: *Voluntary Food and Drink Guidelines for Early Years*

Settings in England – A Practical Guide: www.childrensfoodtrust.org.uk

Vegetarian Society: www.veg.org/veg/org/vegsocuk

Vegan Society: www.vegansociety.com

Unit 1.2 Support healthy lifestyles for children through exercise

This unit provides the learner with the knowledge, understanding and skills to support healthy lifestyles for children through exercise.

Learning outcomes

By the end of this unit you will:

1 Understand children's need for exercise.
2 Understand inclusive practice in relation to the use of provision for children's exercise.
3 Be able to support children's exercise in an outdoor space.

LO1 Understand children's need for exercise

Physical activity is essential for children's growth and development, because it:

- reduces their risk of developing heart disease in later life
- strengthens muscles
- helps strengthen joints and promotes good posture
- improves balance, coordination and flexibility
- increases bone density, so that bones are less likely to fracture.

Apart from these obvious physical benefits, regular exercise develops a child's self-esteem by creating a strong sense of purpose and self-fulfilment; children learn how to interact and cooperate with other children by taking part in team sports and other activities.

AC 1.1 Outline the benefits of exercise for children

The importance of physical activity for young children's holistic development

Physical activity and the development of movement skills help children to develop holistically in the following areas:

- **Expressing ideas and feelings**: children become aware that they can use their bodies to express themselves by moving in different ways as they respond to their moods and feelings, to music or to imaginative ideas.
- **Developing skills requiring coordination** of different parts of the body: for example, hands and eyes for throwing and catching, legs and arms for skipping with a rope.
- **Exploring what their bodies can do** and become aware of their increasing abilities, agility and skill. Children's awareness of the space around them and what their bodies are capable of can be extended by climbing and balancing on large-scale apparatus, such as a climbing frame, wooden logs and a balancing bar, and by using small tricycles, bicycles and carts.
- **Cooperating with others** in physical play and games. Children become aware of physical play both as individuals and as a social activity: in playing alone or alongside others, in playing throwing and catching with a partner, in using a seesaw or push cart, or in joining a game with a larger group.
- **Developing increasing control of fine movements** of their fingers and hands (fine motor skills). For example, playing musical instruments and making sounds with the body, such as clapping or tapping, help develop fine motor skills in the hands and fingers, while also reinforcing the link between sound and physical movement. Helping with household tasks – washing up, pouring drinks, carrying bags – also develops fine motor skills.
- **Developing balance and coordination**, as well as an appreciation of distance and speed; energetic play that involves running, jumping and skipping helps children to develop these skills.
- **Developing spatial awareness**: for example, dancing and moving around to music develop a spatial awareness while also practising coordination and muscle control.

Effects on short- and long-term health and well-being

Physical activity and exercise are no longer a regular feature in many children's lives. Some children never walk or cycle to school, or play sport. Children need to be physically active in order to prevent harmful effects on their health, in both the long and short term.

Short-term health

Physical activity boosts energy, and helps to alleviate stress and anxiety. Children who are physically active are more likely to fall sleep easily and to sleep for longer. They are also less likely to develop infections, such as colds and flu, because their immune system is made stronger by having regular exercise and sufficient sleep.

Long-term health

Physical activity in young children also helps in the long term with:

- **controlling weight** – and so preventing **obesity**. A recent study found that teenagers who carry a gene for obesity are less likely to become overweight or obese if they are physically active for an hour a day. If an overweight child becomes an overweight or obese adult, they are more likely to suffer from health problems, including diabetes, stroke, heart disease and cancer.
- **increasing bone density** in children and helping to maintain strong bones in adolescents. It also slows down bone degeneration later in life. This can help to prevent osteoporosis, a condition when bones become brittle and more prone to break.
- **reducing blood pressure**: if an individual has high blood pressure, they are more likely to have a stroke or heart attack.
- **reducing the risk of diabetes**: keeping active can help lower the risk of developing type 2 diabetes later on in life.
- **reducing the risks of some kinds of cancer**.

General well-being

Children who are physically active have improved psychological well-being. They gain more self-confidence and have higher self-esteem. Children benefit from playing outdoors in the fresh air and having lots of space in which to move freely. They also benefit socially from playing alongside other children and making friends.

AC 1.2 Identify the requirements of current frameworks for outdoor access and regular exercise for children

The Early Years Foundation Stage (EYFS) states that in order to give all children the best opportunities for effective physical development, early years practitioners should give particular attention to:

- planning activities that offer appropriate **physical challenges**
- providing sufficient space, **indoors and outdoors**, to set up relevant activities
- giving sufficient time for children to use **a range of equipment**
- **providing resources** that can be used in a variety of ways or to support specific skills
- introducing the **language of movement** to children, alongside their actions
- **providing time and opportunities for children with physical disabilities** or motor impairments to develop their physical skills, working as necessary with physiotherapists and occupational therapists
- **using additional adult help**, if necessary, to support individuals and to encourage increased independence in physical activities.

In addition to the EYFS framework guidelines, there are also the following UK Physical Activity guidelines specifically aimed at children under five years old.

UK Physical Activity Guidelines

The introduction of UK early years physical activity guidelines reflects a growing awareness of the importance of physical activity and follows the lead of other major international countries. They are based on evidence from research and the combined input from experts in this field of study. All children aged under five years should minimise the amount of time spent being sedentary (being restrained or sitting, i.e. children in harnesses/prams/highchairs or a child that is in a playpen or bouncer) for extended periods (except time spent sleeping).These guidelines are relevant to all children under the age of five and are aimed at the following groups:

For Early Years (under fives) – infants who cannot yet walk unaided

Physical activity should be encouraged from birth, particularly through floor-based play and water-based activities in safe environments. From birth, babies need to have daily opportunities to move freely on their stomach or back in a variety of safe spaces, without being constrained for long periods by clothing or straps (e.g. in car seats or baby chairs or bouncers). They need opportunities to practise important movements such as:

- 'tummy time'* – this includes any time spent on the stomach including rolling and playing on the floor
- reaching for and grasping objects
- turning the head toward stimuli
- pulling, pushing and playing with other people, objects and toys.

*Remember'tummy time' is only for when babies are awake and supervised. Babies should always be placed on their backs to sleep.

Pre-school children who can walk unaided

Children of pre-school age who are capable of walking unaided should be physically active daily for at least 180 minutes (three hours), spread throughout the day. The 180 minutes can be activity of any intensity. For this age group, the amount of physical activity is more important than the intensity.

Physically active play is the best way for young children to be physically active. Physically active play opportunities should encourage young children to:

- use large muscle groups, e.g. back, shoulders, legs, arms etc.
- engage in more energetic forms of physical activity, e.g. running and chasing games. These need to be encouraged through short bouts of activity, rather than be expected to take place for extended periods of time

- practise a wide range of different movements, e.g. locomotor, stability and object control skills
- experience a variety of play spaces and equipment
- have fun and feel good about themselves and what they can do.

Key term

physically active play Play that involves movements of all the major muscle groups, e.g. legs. It can range from activities with small intermittent movements, such as clapping hands, to large movements involving the whole body, such as climbing and running. It tends to be used to describe young children's physical activity.

Activity

Find out more about the UK Physical Activity Guidelines for children from birth to five years from the British Heart Foundation website (see Useful resources, p 36).

AC 1.3 Evaluate national and local initiatives which promote children's exercise

Play England

Play England campaigns for all children to have the freedom and space to play throughout childhood. As the national organisation for children's play, Play England works with all those who have an impact on children's lives to support and champion play as an essential part of childhood.

Love Outdoor Play

Love Outdoor Play is led by Play England and supported by the Free Time Consortium, a growing collective of local and specialist organisations working together to increase freedom to play.

Play4life

Play4life is a sub-brand of the Change4life programme backed by the Department of Health that aims to help every family in England eat well, move more and live longer.

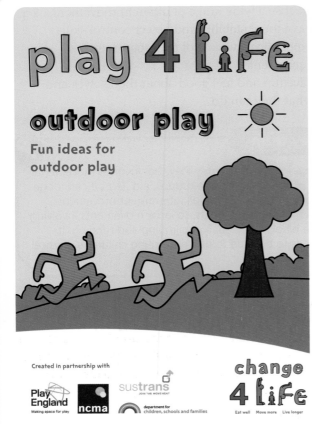

Figure 1.2.1 Play4Life – outdoor play leaflet

AC 1.4 Describe benefits of working in partnership with parents/carers in relation to supporting children's exercise

Early years settings can do a great deal to promote children's exercise. Apart from promoting this aspect of development in their everyday practice, it is important to involve parents as much as possible.

Physical activity begins at home. Research suggests that parental physical activity impacts positively on how much physical activity their children participate in. Children who are physically active usually have parents or carers who:

- encourage them to participate in physical activity
- participate in physical activity with them
- watch them play or compete, and
- transport them to physical activity and sports events.

Early years practitioners should work with parents to promote the importance of physical activity for their child or children and to encourage parents to interact with them in a physically active way as often as possible. This will encourage a child to be more active, to enjoy the experience and stimulate further participation. Parents and carers are important role models for their children, and being physically active themselves has many health benefits too.

LO2 Understand inclusive practice in relation to the use of provision for children's exercise

AC 2.1 Evaluate a local indoor provision in relation to inclusive practice

Both the indoor and the outdoor environments should be carefully planned and prepared to provide opportunities for physical activity and the development of movement skills.

The following factors are important in planning for physical activity that is inclusive (that is, it includes *all* children and uses the indoor provision effectively).

- **Time**: you will need to allow sufficient time for babies and children to become familiar with newly introduced equipment and activities, and also to practise both new and existing skills.

- **Space:** you need to plan for sufficient space to set up appropriate activities for physical play. Movement is important but it does require a lot of room. Additional space may be necessary for children who have physical disabilities or motor impairments, to take into account specialised equipment and also extra professional support such as physiotherapy or occupational therapy.
- **Indoor environments:** opportunities for physical activity should ideally be provided both inside and out. Regular sessions of indoor physical play are particularly important when the weather limits opportunities for outdoor play.

Figure 1.2.2 Playing hopscotch involves many movement skills such as jumping, skipping, hopping, turning and balancing

Providing variety, risk and challenge in play
Play England states that:

All children both need and want to take risks in order to explore limits, venture into new experiences and develop their capacities, from a very young age and from their earliest play experiences.

Physically challenging activities that involve safe risk-taking help children to build and extend their strength and fitness levels. You need to plan activities that are interesting to children, and that offer physical challenges and plenty of opportunities for physical activity. When assessing risk and challenge in physical play, you need to decide whether the activity is developmentally appropriate. Children quickly become frustrated if activities are *too* challenging or difficult, but they also lose interest in activities that are lacking in challenge or that they find too easy.

Problem-solving in physical play
Children need to develop the skills of making assessments and solving problems. Any conscious movement involves making judgements or assessments. Assessment of the situation and of your ability (speed, power, etc.) will help you to make the appropriate movement. For example, a child might make an assessment of:

- how hard to throw
- how fast to run
- how much effort to use to jump so high
- when to begin to stop.

Inclusive practice: meeting the needs of all children
Girls and boys
Boys are routinely offered more opportunities for energetic play – for example, rough-and-tumble games with parents and early introduction to football games. You need to offer the same opportunities for physical play to boys *and* girls.

Children with a disability
Some children may need special equipment for physical play or they may need to have existing equipment adapted; for example, a child with cerebral palsy may have limited control over his or her body movements and need to use a tricycle with differently positioned handles or pedals.

A child with a hearing impairment can be encouraged to dance to music as they can usually feel the vibrations through the floor. Early years practitioners must ensure that hearing aids are looked after carefully as sand and dirt can damage them.

Children of different ages

Babies need physical play just as much as older children. From just a few weeks old, babies can be placed on the floor and encouraged to kick their legs freely. Activities need to be planned that are developmentally appropriate for every child or group of children.

Activity ·

Choose a particular indoor activity in your setting and evaluate it in relation to inclusive practice.

· ·

AC 2.2 Evaluate a local outdoor provision in relation to inclusive practice

The outdoor environment can provide a scale and freedom for a type of play that is difficult to replicate indoors.

Keeping children safe

Children who play in a physically safe environment are more likely to develop confidence, self-esteem and self-reliance. In modern society it is often dangerous for children to play outside in the street. Safety considerations have had a huge impact on what parents and carers allow their children to do, and the freedom to play outdoors out of a carer's sight is now extremely rare.

It is therefore very important that when children attend group settings they can be physically safe. Safety issues should always be borne in mind when working with young children so that accidents are prevented. This is called **risk assessment** because adults are thinking ahead about possible physical danger to children. Children need to be supervised carefully; it is important for adults never to sit with their back to the group, either indoors or outdoors. Without supervision, children might become involved in unacceptable or inappropriate behaviour, such as throwing stones at a window or snatching a tricycle from another child.

The importance of natural outdoor environments

We have seen how important movement is and how it requires a lot of room. The natural outdoor environment – such as woodland,

---

Case study

A child-centred outdoor environment

The design of Cowgate Under 5s Centre in Edinburgh reflects the centre's philosophy inspired by the educationalist Friedrich Froebel, who believed that children learn best through spontaneous child-centred play, and that they should be surrounded by kindness, understanding and beauty.

Good design has enabled a wide range of experiences to be offered within a small space. Nearly all of the resources are made from natural materials, have been chosen to enhance the children's curiosity, and provide both challenge and risk. There are two timber houses at either end of the site (one of which is two storeys high), a pergola with climbing plants; bird boxes, feeders and insect homes; a sandpit; a rabbit run with a rabbit; planted beds with sensory plants such as rosemary and lavender; an adventure playground with a rope climb, wobbly bridge and tyre swing; a greenhouse for growing; large-scale musical instruments; a raised wet area and a seating area with a storytelling seat.

The children are allowed to use all the equipment at all times as a member of staff is always present. First thing in the morning, the doors are opened wide and the children are free to move between the indoors and outdoors.

1 How does the Cowgate Under 5s Centre provide for children's physical activity?
2 Why is it important for children to play outdoors?

fields and beaches – provides young children with a wonderful and constantly varying 'playground'. An exciting outdoor space provides an opportunity for children to explore the environment at their own individual levels of development.

Planning and implementing physical activities

Opportunities for physical activity

When planning physical activities, you need to consider the following factors:

- **Observation**: before planning how to provide physical activity, take some time to observe children's natural and spontaneous movements. You should observe:
    - how they move
    - their object control skills
    - their coordination and balance skills
    - which activities individuals prefer.
- You can observe their movement and object control skills, and plan their physical play by extending an activity: for example, a baby who is sitting but not yet moving (crawling or bottom shuffling) could be supported in trying to move if you provide some exciting objects that are just out of reach.

- **Balance of child-initiated and adult-led activities**: the EYFS in England requires that a balance is struck between activities initiated by the child and those that are adult-led.
- **Range of skills and movements**: you need to consider the wide range of motor skills, movement skills and balance and coordination when planning activities.
- **Time**: children need to be allowed to play at their own pace. Some children are slow to begin and may need support to attempt a new skill.
- **Interests**: children need to have their interests valued and taken into account when planning. This is where your observations of children playing will be useful.

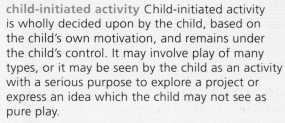
Developmentally appropriate activities

Table 1.2.1 suggests a range of developmentally appropriate activities. For children with disabilities or special needs, you may need to seek advice from other professionals and their parents when planning play for them.

Age and motor skills development	Activities for movement skills	Activities for fine manipulative skills
By 6 months:		
• grasps adult finger • arm and leg movements jerky and uncontrolled • holds a rattle briefly	• gentle bouncing games on the carer's knee to songs • encourage baby to kick, lying on back and front, to build muscles in neck and back • swinging in a baby swing to promote balance	• rattles and soft, squashy toys • books • waterproof books in bath
By 9 months:		
• rolls from front to back • sits up unsupported • may crawl or bottom shuffle • grasp object and passes it from one hand to other	• encourage balance by placing toys around seated baby • encourage mobility by placing objects just out of reach • play 'rolling over' games with them	• picture books • toys to transfer safely to the mouth • simple musical instruments, e.g. xylophone
By 12 months:		
• sitting for longer periods • mobile – crawling or rolling • may be walking, usually with hand/s held • stands, holding on to furniture	• push and pull brick trolleys • roll balls to and from baby • low climbing frames • swimming sessions	• stacking and nesting toys • messy play • painting and drawing
By 18 months:		
• walking independently • bends and squats to pick up objects • climbs up and down stairs with help • uses pincer grasp to pick up small objects	• walker trucks, pull-along animals etc. • low, stable furniture to climb on • space to run and play • trips to parks and woodland • low climbing frames • swimming sessions	• posting toys and shape sorters • threading toys • jigsaw puzzles • hammer and peg and pop-up toys • messy play, sand and water play • play dough
By 2 years:		
• runs and jumps • rides a tricycle propelling with feet • walks up and down stairs	• toys to ride and climb on • space to run and play • ball play: throwing and catching • trips to parks and woodland • swimming sessions	• threading toys • jigsaw puzzles • messy play, sand and water play • play dough • models to build (e.g. Duplo®)
By 3 years:		
• rides a tricycle using pedals • walks and runs • jumps from a low step • stands on one foot and walks on tiptoe	• climbing frames • scooters and tricycles • trips to parks and woodland • swimming sessions • dancing to music	• creative activities: painting, drawing, modelling • jigsaw puzzles • messy play, sand and water play • play dough
By 3 to 4 years:		
• walks with arms swinging • climbs upstairs with one foot on each step and downwards with two feet on each step	• balls and bean bags for throwing and catching • simple running games	• creative activities: painting, drawing, modelling • jigsaw puzzles ➔

Table 1.2.1 Activities which are developmentally appropriate for babies and young children

Age and motor skills development	Activities for movement skills	Activities for fine manipulative skills
<ul><li>catches, throws, kicks and bounces a ball</li><li>can stand, walk and run on tiptoe</li></ul>	<ul><li>rope swings, climbing frames, slides, suitable trees</li><li>party games such as musical statues</li><li>running to music: fast or slow, loudly or quietly according to the music</li><li>trips to parks and woodland</li><li>swimming sessions</li><li>party games such as musical statues</li><li>running to music: fast or slow, loudly or quietly according to the music</li><li>bikes with stabilisers</li></ul>	<ul><li>messy play, sand and water play</li><li>small world play</li></ul>
By 4 to 5 years and beyond:		
<ul><li>good sense of balance</li><li>catches, throws and kicks a ball</li><li>runs up and down stairs, one foot per step</li><li>can run and dodge lightly on the toes</li><li>climbs, skips and hops forwards on each foot separately</li><li>shows good coordination and fine motor skills</li></ul>	<ul><li>climbing frames, rope swings</li><li>skipping ropes and hoops</li><li>hopping and jumping</li><li>action songs and games</li><li>riding tricycles, bikes, with or without stabilisers</li><li>trampoline</li><li>simple running games</li><li>team sports</li><li>trips to parks and woodland</li><li>obstacle courses for bike riders</li></ul>	<ul><li>dressing and undressing practicing.</li><li>creative activities: painting, drawing, modelling</li><li>small world play</li><li>construction toys</li></ul>

Table 1.2.1 Activities which are developmentally appropriate for babies and young children   (*Continued*)

Case study

Taking your cue from children

Rebecca, Shana and Chris work in a pre-school setting with children aged three to five years. On quieter days, they like to take the children to the local park. One day, they plan an outing with ten children. Rebecca, the room leader, ensures that they have drinks, first aid kit and mobile phone with them. She has checked that all the parents and carers have signed up-to-date outing permission slips. As they walk through the park, four-year-old twins Chloe and Oscar run ahead to a fallen tree. The other children are delighted by their find and rush to join them. Rebecca decides that they will stop here to let the children play. The staff help the children to climb and balance, and encourage them to jump off the lower end of the tree trunk onto the soft grass. The children love the activity and it promotes much discussion when they return to the setting.

The next time they plan to go to the park, Rebecca includes Shana and Chris in thinking of ways to promote the children's movement skills as they play. They decide to take quoits, markers and a canvas tunnel, and they set about making an obstacle course that incorporates the fallen tree as a central obstacle. The children are shown the course, and how to complete it and are supported to have a go, one at a time. The children waiting for their turn join in with the staff, shouting encouragement. Chris decides to vary the course after every child has had a turn, and he involves the children in helping him. The children are encouraged to offer their ideas, and are supported in working as a team to put the objects in the right places.

- List the areas of development being promoted.
- How are the children being empowered during this activity?
- This activity can be extended in many ways to promote children's movement and balance skills. Think of other activities that could be used with the children, incorporating the children's interests, such as the fallen tree.

LO3 Be able to support children's exercise in an outdoor space

AC 3.1 Plan an activity which supports children's exercise in an outdoor space

Planning for physical activities

Children need to feel motivated to be physically active. You can support them to develop movement skills through:

- valuing and following their interests (letting them initiate an activity)
- praise
- encouragement
- appropriate guidance.

Your plan should:

- Meet the individual movement skills needs of babies and children.
- Promote the development of movement skills.
- Encourage physical play.

Whenever possible, you should involve children in your planning – by finding out what they would like to do and what equipment they would like to use.

Figure 1.2.3 This girl enjoys playing on the slide

AC 3.2 Implement an activity which supports children's exercise in an outdoor space

Again, careful observation is vital to the successful implementation of a plan. You will need to observe the way in which children are playing, and be ready to adapt the activity if it does not seem to be meeting the children's needs and stimulating their interest. Sometimes your plan might be 'taken over' by the children. They may find a different way of playing with a piece of equipment, or they may introduce other play props into their play.

Building opportunities for physical activity into everyday routines

Children need to have opportunities for physical activity every day. They need opportunities to walk, run, jump, climb and swing. Most of these activities will take place outdoors, but there are other ways in which you can build in opportunities for physical activity in the setting. Everyday routines are those that are usually built in to a setting's provision and include:

- dressing and undressing
- hanging up their own coats
- tidying up and putting away equipment
- wiping and setting tables for meals and snacks
- pouring their own drinks
- washing and drying up.

The importance of physical activity in everyday routines

Helping children to develop physical skills in everyday routines will promote their confidence and self-esteem, as well as providing a positive pattern for later in life. Children also need to have opportunities to go for a walk every day, so that being outside and walking in the fresh air become a regular, enjoyable experience.

How to provide opportunities in practice

It is important to stand back and consider how physical activity is built into your own practice. It is often quicker and easier to do things ourselves, but children can be encouraged to develop self-help and social skills if we build opportunities into our practice. Toddlers can be asked to fetch their own coat or shoes, for example, or you could make a game out of tidy-up time, involving children in sweeping up and putting away the toys they have been playing with.

Reflective practice

Physical activity in everyday routines

Think about a session in your setting:

- How many opportunities are there for children to be engaged in everyday routines that could involve physical activity?
- How much time do children spend outdoors? Are these opportunities limited by rainy or cold weather?
- How could you improve the provision of physical activity opportunities?

AC 3.3 Reflect on an activity which supports children's exercise in an outdoor space

When evaluating the effectiveness of our provision and practice, we need to be able to identify and record ways of continually improving our practice.

Assessing the effectiveness of planned provision

The main way of evaluating our practice is by observing children's participation and assessing whether their needs have been met. The following points should be considered:

Observing and assessing children

Select one child (or a group of children) and carry out a structured observation over a number of sessions or a few weeks. Your aims are to find out:

- how their physical activity has been supported – in particular their progression in movement skills, and
- how their confidence has improved.

Obtaining feedback
From the child or children

You can obtain direct feedback from the child or children by listening to them and noting their comments or by asking them questions. It is usually easy to see whether children have enjoyed a physical activity, as they will often be clamouring to do it again.

From colleagues and parents

Parents know their own child best and they are often able to provide valuable insight into the effectiveness of activities. Colleagues are often well placed to give feedback as they may be able to observe children during an activity. Feedback can also be obtained by filming the children during the activity and observing the children's reactions and comments. You should always have written permission from the parent or carer to photograph or film a child; see Unit 3.14, p 519 for the correct procedure.

AC 3.4 Make recommendations for the outdoor provision for own setting

Identifying and recording areas for improvement

Having obtained feedback, you now need to identify areas for future development. This can be recorded as an action plan. You should draw up a plan that identifies:

- areas for improvement
- reason for action
- detail of action to be taken
- equipment and resources needed
- date for implementation.

Reflecting on your own practice

Reflect on your daily practice and think about how well you provide appropriate physical play experiences for the children you work with. For example:

- How do you consider the balance between child-initiated activity and adult-led activity?
- Do you join in with physical activity?
- How do you enable children and their parents to express opinions and be listened to?
- How confident are you in planning for children's individual needs and in observing and assessing their progress?
- How do you ensure that there is sufficient challenge in the activities you provide?
- How can you improve your practice?

Assessment practice

1 What are the benefits of exercise for children?
2 What are the requirements of current frameworks for outdoor access and regular exercise for children?
3 Evaluate the success of campaigns which seek to promote children's exercise.
4 Describe the benefits of working in partnership with parents/carers in relation to supporting children's exercise.
5 Evaluate a local indoor provision in relation to inclusive practice, using the guidelines for inclusive provision.

6 Evaluate a local outdoor provision in relation to inclusive practice, using the guidelines for inclusive provision.
7 Plan and implement an outdoors activity which promotes children's exercise.
8 Reflect on an outdoors activity which promotes children's exercise.
9 Make recommendations for the outdoor provision in your own setting.

Useful resources

Books

Hughes, B. (1996a), *Play Environments: A question of quality*. PLAYLINK.

Meggitt, C. (2012), *An Illustrated Guide to Child Development* (3rd edn). Oxford: Heinemann.

Organisations for the UK

JABADAO

A national charity which works in partnership with the education, health, arts and social care sectors to bring about a change in the way people work with the body and movement: www.jabadao.org

British Heart Foundation National Centre (BHFNC)

The BHF publishes the UK Physical Activity Guidelines for Early Years: www.bhfactive.org.uk

Organisations for England

Learning, Playing and Interacting: Good practice in the Early Years Foundation Stage

A toolkit to support early years practitioners' work with advice on pedagogy, practice and assessment: www.nationalstrategies.standards.dcsf.gov.uk/earlyyears

Start4Life and Play4Life (Department of Health)

The early years section of the Department of Health's (DH) Change4Life campaign, aimed at health care and childcare professionals. Active play resources are available which can be downloaded from www.dh.gov.uk (search Start4Life).

Play England

www.playengland.org.uk

Unit 1.3 Support physical care routines for children

This unit provides the learner with the knowledge, understanding and skills to support children's physical care as part of a healthy lifestyle.

Learning outcomes

By the end of this unit you will:

1 Understand the physical care needs of children.
2 Understand hygienic practice in preparing formula feeds.
3 Understand hygienic practice in relation to control of infection.
4 Be able to use hygienic practice to minimise the spread of infection.
5 Understand rest and sleep needs of children.
6 Understand childhood immunisation.
7 Be able to support children in personal care routines.

LO1 Understand the physical care needs of children

From the moment they are born, all children depend completely on an adult to meet all their needs, but the way in which these needs are met will vary considerably according to family circumstances, culture and the child and the caring adult.

To achieve and maintain healthy growth and development (that is, physical, intellectual, emotional and social development) certain basic needs must be fulfilled, as shown in Table 1.3.1.

At each developmental stage, children will have different skills and abilities. Although children do not make significant progress in **self-care** until the toddler years, there are signs of growing independence much earlier.

- **At about eight months**, babies begin to understand how objects relate to one another and may begin using them for their intended function: for example, brushing their hair, 'chatting' on the play phone, etc.

Basic needs for healthy growth and development		
food	cleanliness	sleep, rest and activity
protection from infection and injury	intellectual stimulation	relationships and social contacts
shelter, warmth, clothing	fresh air and sunlight	love, and consistent and continuous affection
access to health care	appreciation, praise and recognition of effort or achievements	security and nurture

Table 1.3.1 Children need these basic needs to be fulfilled in order to develop

- **At around ten to eleven months**, babies start learning how to drink out of a cup, and will also begin to hold out their arms or legs to help when getting dressed.
- **By around 12 to 15 months,** babies are able to hold a cup in both hands and drink from it, and will recognise themselves in the mirror.
- **By 18 months** most children go through a period of saying 'NO'; it is their way of asserting their new feelings of self-identity.
- Between **one and four years**, children can:
  - *Use a fork and spoon*: they may start wanting to use utensils as early as 13 months; most children have mastered this skill by 17 or 18 months.
  - *Take off their own clothes*: children usually learn to do it between 13 and 20 months.
  - *Brush their teeth*: they may start wanting to help with this task as early as 16 months, but probably will not be able to do it on their own until sometime between the third and fourth birthday.

- *Wash and dry their hands*: this skill develops between 19 and 30 months and is something children should learn before or at the same time as using the toilet.
- *Get dressed*: they may be able to put on loose clothing as early as 20 months, but will need a few more months before they can manage a T-shirt, and another year or two months after that before they are able to get dressed all by themselves. By 27 months, they will probably be able to pull off their shoes.
- *Use the toilet*: most children are not physically ready to start toilet training until they are at least 18 to 24 months old, and some will not be ready to begin for as much as a year after that. Two key signs of readiness include being able to pull their own pants up and down, and knowing when they have to go before it happens.
- *Prepare their own breakfast*: children as young as three may be able to get themselves a bowl of cereal when they are hungry, and most can do it by the time they are four and a half.
- **Children aged four to eight:** children aged four and five can eat skilfully with a knife and fork and can undress and dress themselves, except for laces, ties and back buttons. By six to seven years old, children are completely independent in washing, dressing and toileting skills.

AC 1.1 Describe routine physical care needs for children in relation to: nappy changing; toilet training; washing and bath time; skin, teeth and hair; mealtimes

The importance of care routines

Routines around mealtimes and bedtimes can be very useful in helping babies and toddlers to adapt both physically and emotionally to a daily pattern, which suits both them *and* those caring for them. This is especially helpful during times of transition and change in their lives, such as starting nursery or moving house. If certain parts of the day remain familiar, they can cope better with new experiences. Having routines for everyday activities also ensures that care is consistent and of a high quality. This does not mean that caring for children is, or should be, in

itself a routine activity. Anyone looking after children should be able to adapt to their individual needs, which will change from day to day. Therefore, you need to be flexible and prepared to adapt or even abandon the activity to enable children to initiate their own play.

How to meet the care needs of children in ways that maintain their security and respect their privacy

It is important that children have their rights to privacy respected when having their care needs met. Intimate, personal care such as nappy changing, toileting, dressing and undressing should be coordinated by a **key person**. When developmentally appropriate, young children should be asked to *consent* to offers of intimate care. You might say, for example, to a toddler in the toilet: 'Would you like me to help pull your pants down?' rather than just going ahead and doing it. Similarly, a child who has had a toileting accident should be encouraged sympathetically to help when changing his or her clothing.

AC 1.2 Explain the role of the EYP during: nappy changing; toilet training; washing and bath time; care of skin, teeth and hair; mealtimes

Children like to feel independent, but sometimes they need an adult's encouragement to feel that they are capable and that adults believe that they can do it. Teaching independence with self-care skills such as hand washing, brushing teeth, and dressing and undressing is an important step in development that can be achieved when children are supported in a positive and encouraging way.

Nappy changing

Nappies must be changed regularly to avoid nappy rash, and should always be changed immediately after they have been soiled. Whenever possible, the baby's key person should change the baby's nappy as this helps to develop a close, trusting relationship and enables the key person to report any concerns to the parents. Young babies will need several changes of nappy each day, whenever the nappy is wet or soiled. As with any regular routine, have everything ready before you begin. This includes:

a plastic-covered padded changing mat	a bowl of warm water (or baby wipes)
baby lotion	barrier cream, such as zinc and castor oil cream
nappy sacks for dirty nappies	cotton wool
baby bath liquid	new, clean nappy.

It is important to pay attention to the differences between boys and girls when cleaning the nappy area – see the guidelines below. If you are using a special changing table or bed, make sure the baby cannot fall off.

Never leave the baby unattended on a high surface. As long as there are no draughts and the room is warm, the changing mat can be placed on the secure baby changing unit.

NB Never leave a baby or toddler unsupervised on the changing mat.

For information on disposing of waste in the early years setting, see your setting's Health and Safety policy on disposal of waste.

Guidelines for cleaning the nappy area

1 Wash your hands and put the baby on the changing mat.
2 Undo the clothing and open out the nappy. It is quite common for baby boys to urinate just as you remove the nappy, so pause for a few seconds with nappy held over the penis.
3 Clean off as much faeces as possible with the soiled nappy.
4 **Boys**: moisten cotton wool with water or lotion and begin by wiping his tummy across, starting at his navel. Using fresh cotton wool or baby wipes, clean the creases at the top of his legs, working down towards his anus and back. Wipe all over the testicles, holding his penis out of the way. Clean under the penis. Never try to pull back the foreskin. Lift his legs using one hand (finger between his ankles) and wipe away from his anus, to buttocks and to back of thighs.
5 **Girls**: use wet cotton wool or baby wipes to clean inside all the skin creases at the top of her legs. Wipe down towards her bottom. Lift her legs using one hand (finger between her ankles) and clean her buttocks and thighs with fresh cotton wool, working inwards towards the anus. Keep clear of her vagina and never clean inside the lips of the vulva.
6 Dry the skin creases and the rest of the nappy area thoroughly. Let the baby kick freely and then apply barrier cream if required.
7 Dispose of soiled nappies and wipes according to your setting's hygiene policy. For information on PPE go to Unit 1.3 and page 50.

In practice

Procedure for changing nappies in a group setting

Nappy changing is an important time and you should ensure that the baby feels secure and happy. Singing and simple playful games should be incorporated into the procedure to make it an enjoyable experience. Every setting will have its own procedure for changing nappies. The following is an example:

- Nappies should be checked and changed at regular periods throughout the day.
- A baby should never knowingly be left in a soiled nappy.
- Collect the nappy and the cream needed. Put on apron and gloves. Ensure that you have warm water and wipes.
- Carefully put the baby on the changing mat, talking to them and reassuring them.
- Afterwards dispose of the nappy and discard the gloves.
- Thoroughly clean the nappy mat and the apron with an antibacterial spray.
- Wash your hands to avoid cross-contamination.

Record the nappy change on the baby's **Nappy Chart**, noting the time, whether it was wet or dry or if there has been a bowel movement. Also note any change you have observed – such as in colour or consistency of the stools, or if the baby had difficulty in passing the stool. Also, note if there is any skin irritation or rash present.

Check nappy mats for any tears or breaks in the fabric and replace if necessary.

Toilet training

Newborn babies pass the waste products of digestion automatically – in other words, although they may appear to be exerting a physical effort when passing a stool or motion, they have no conscious control over the action. Parents used to boast with pride that all their children were potty-trained at nine months, but the reality is that they were lucky in their timing! Up to the age of 18 months, emptying the bladder and bowel is still a totally automatic reaction – the child's central nervous system (CNS) is still not sufficiently mature to make the connection between the action and its results.

Recognising that a child is ready to move out of nappies

There is no point in attempting to start toilet training until the toddler shows that he or she is ready, and this rarely occurs before the age of 18 months. The usual signs are:

- increased interest when passing urine or a motion: the child may pretend play on the potty with their toys
- they may tell the carer when they have passed urine or a bowel motion, or look very uncomfortable when they have done so
- they may start to be more regular with bowel motions, or wet nappies may become rarer; this is a sign that the bladder is developing
- they can stand on their feet and sit on potty seat or a toilet. Some experts assess a child's readiness by their ability to climb stairs using alternate feet, that is, one foot per step.

When to start toilet training

Toilet training should be approached in a relaxed, unhurried manner. If the potty is introduced too early or if a child is forced to sit on it for long periods of time, he or she may rebel and the whole issue of toilet training will become a battleground.

Toilet training can be over in a few days or may take some months. Becoming dry at night takes longer, but most children manage this before the age of five years. Before attempting to toilet train a child, make sure that he has shown that he is ready to be trained. Remember that, as with all developmental milestones, there is a wide variation in the age range at which children achieve bowel and bladder control.

Guidelines for toilet training

- **Be positive and supportive to the child's efforts**: be relaxed about toilet training and be prepared for accidents.
- **Structuring the physical environment to facilitate training**: have the potty close at hand so that the child becomes familiar with it and can include it in his or her play. It helps if the child sees other children using the toilet or potty. It is also helpful if children are dressed in clothes that are easy for them to manage by themselves, such as pull-up trousers rather than dungarees.
- **Working in partnership with parents and carers**: it is important to work closely with parents so that you take a similar approach to toilet training, otherwise the child may become anxious. If a parent starts training their toddler when there is a new baby due, be prepared for some accidents. Many children react to a new arrival by regressing to baby behaviour.
- **Encouraging and praising**: always praise the child when he or she succeeds and do not show anger or disapproval if the opposite occurs; the child may be upset by an accident. It is important not to over-encourage children as this can make them anxious about letting you down.
- **Treating child with respect and avoiding guilt**: do not show any disgust for the child's faeces. He or she will regard using the potty as an achievement and will be proud of them. Children have no natural shame about their bodily functions (unless adults make them ashamed).
- **Establishing a routine**: offer the potty regularly so that the child becomes used to the idea of a routine, and learn to read the signs that a child needs to use it. Cover the potty and flush the contents down the toilet. Always wear disposable gloves. Encourage good hygiene right from the start, by washing the child's hands after every use of the potty.
- **Flexible personalised approach**: some children feel insecure when sitting on a potty with no nappy on – try it first still wearing a nappy or pants if the child shows reluctance. The child may prefer to try the 'big' toilet seat straightaway; a toddler seat fixed onto the normal seat makes this easier. Boys need to learn to stand in front of the toilet and aim at the bowl before passing any urine; you could put a piece of toilet paper in the bowl for him to aim at. Some children are frightened when the toilet is flushed; be tactful

and sympathetic. You could wait until the child has left the room before you flush.
● **Providing plenty of fluids and fibre to prevent hard stools**: children need to drink plenty of water or other drinks in order for them to learn what having a full bladder feels like. They also need to be given foods that contain fibre (such as fruit and vegetables) to prevent constipation.

● It is important to encourage self-care skills when children are using the toilet independently. They should be encouraged to pull their own pants down and shown how to wipe their bottoms – for example, showing girls how to wipe from the front to the back. You also need children to learn that going to the toilet is a private activity and to withdraw by partially closing the door while remaining nearby in case help is needed.

Dealing with accidents

Even once a child has become used to using the potty or toilet, there will be occasions when they have an 'accident' – that is, they wet or soil themselves. This happens more often during the early stages of toilet training, as the child may lack the awareness and control needed to allow enough time to get to the potty. Older children may become so absorbed in their play that they simply forget to go to the toilet.

You can help children when they have an accident by:

● not appearing bothered; let the child know that it is not a big problem, just something that happens from time to time
● reassuring the child in a friendly tone of voice and offering a cuddle if he or she seems distressed
● being discreet – deal with the matter swiftly; wash and change the child out of view of others and with the minimum of fuss
● an older child could be supervised discreetly and encouraged to manage the incident themselves, if they wish to do so
● following safety procedures in the setting – for example, wear disposable gloves and deal appropriately with soiled clothing and waste.

Discussion point
Toilet training

In class, discuss the problems that can arise with toilet training and compare the strategies used by different families.

Washing and bath time
Hand washing

Babies and toddlers need to have their hands washed frequently. This is because they are constantly picking things up and putting their hands in their mouths, and they may also pick up an infection. It is important to build regular hand washing into routine care, for example washing their hands before and after eating.

Hand washing is an important skill that children need to learn. It can be made into a fun activity by singing 'This is the way we wash/dry our hands … on a cold/hot and frosty/sunny morning'. Children soon learn that hand washing is a routine task that must always be done after going to the toilet, before meals and after playing outdoors.

Washing the face

Most young children dislike having their faces washed as they feel they are being suffocated. Always use a clean cloth and wipe each part of the face separately and gently. Dry thoroughly with a soft towel.

Topping and tailing

A young baby does not have to be bathed every day because only their bottom, face and neck, and skin creases get dirty, and her skin may tend to dryness. If a bath is not given daily, the baby should have the important body parts cleansed thoroughly – a process known as 'topping

Research activity

Toilet training
● Arrange to interview a parent or carer who has recently toilet-trained a child.
● Try to find out the methods they used and any problems they encountered.
● Write a report of the methods used.

In small groups, make a colourful, eye-catching wall display that provides tips for parents and carers on toilet training.

Guidelines: a topping and tailing routine

- Wash your hands.
- Remove the baby's outer clothes, leaving on her vest and nappy.
- Wrap the baby in the towel, keeping her arms inside.
- Using two separate pieces of cotton wool (one for each eye; this will prevent any infection passing from one eye to the other), squeezed in the boiled water, gently wipe the baby's eyes in one movement from the inner corner outwards.
- Gently wipe all around the face and behind the ears. Lift the chin and wipe gently under the folds of skin. Dry each area thoroughly by patting with a soft towel or dry cotton wool.

- Unwrap the towel and take the baby's vest off, raise each arm separately and wipe the armpit carefully as the folds of skin rub together here and can become quite sore – again dry thoroughly and dust with baby powder if used.
- Wipe and dry the baby's hands.
- Take the nappy off and place in lidded bucket.
- Clean the baby's bottom with moist swabs, then wash with soap and water; rinse well with flannel or sponge, pat dry and apply protective cream if necessary.
- Put on clean nappy and clothes.

and tailing'. This process limits the amount of undressing and helps to maintain good skin condition. Whatever routine is followed, the newborn baby needs to be handled gently but firmly, and with confidence. Most babies learn to enjoy the sensation of water and are greatly affected by your attitude. The more relaxed and unhurried you are, the more enjoyable the whole experience will be.

Babies do not like having their skin exposed to the air, so should be undressed for the shortest possible time. Always ensure the room is warm, no less than 20°C (68°F) and that there are no draughts. Warm a large, soft towel on a not-too-hot radiator and have it ready to wrap the baby afterwards.

Collect all the equipment you will need before you start:

- changing mat
- water that has been boiled and allowed to cool
- cotton-wool swabs
- lidded buckets for soiled nappies and used swabs, and clothes
- bowl of warm water
- protective cream such as Vaseline®
- clean clothes and a nappy.

Bathing the baby

When the bath is given will depend on family routines, but it is best not to bath the baby immediately after a feed, as she may be sick. Some babies love being bathed; others dislike even being undressed. Bath time has several benefits for babies, as it provides:

- the opportunity to kick and exercise
- the opportunity to clean and refresh the skin and hair
- the opportunity for the carer to observe any skin problems, such as rashes, bruises, etc.
- a valuable time for communication between the baby and the carer
- a time for relaxation and enjoyment.

Before you start ensure the room is warm and draught-free, and collect all necessary equipment:

• small bowl of boiled water and cotton swabs (as for 'topping and tailing' procedure)	• baby bath filled with warm water – test temperature with your elbow, not with hands as these are insensitive to high temperatures; the water should feel warm but not hot
• changing mat	• lidded buckets
• two warmed towels	• clean nappy and clothes
• brush and comb	• toiletries and nail scissors.

Caring for children's skin

Apart from ensuring that babies and children's skin is kept clean, it is also important that they are protected from the sun.

Guidelines for a bathing routine

- Undress the baby except for her nappy and wrap her in a towel while you clean her face, as for 'topping and tailing'.
- Wash her hair before putting her in the bath: support her head and neck with one hand, hold her over the bath and wash her head with baby shampoo or soap; rinse her head thoroughly and dry with second towel.
- Unwrap the towel around her body, remove her nappy and place it in bucket.
- Remove any soiling from the baby's bottom with cotton wool; remember to clean baby girls from front to back to avoid germs from faeces entering the urethra or vagina.
- Lay the baby in the crook of one arm and gently soap her body front and back with baby soap. (If preferred, use baby bath liquid added to the bath beforehand.)
- Lift the baby off the towel and gently lower her into the water, holding her with one arm around the back of her neck and shoulders and holding the far arm to stop her slipping.
- Talk to the baby and gently swish the water to rinse off the soap, paying particular attention to all skin creases – under arms, between legs and behind knees. Allow time for the baby to splash and kick, but avoid chilling.
- Lift the baby out and wrap in a warm towel; dry her thoroughly by patting, not rubbing.
- Baby oil or moisturiser may now be applied to the skin; do not use talcum powder with oils as it will form lumps and cause irritation.
- Check if fingernails and toenails need cutting. Always use blunt-ended nail scissors and avoid cutting nails too short.
- Dress the baby in clean nappy and clothes.

Additional guidelines on keeping babies clean

- Cultural preferences in skin care should be observed; cocoa butter or special moisturisers are usually applied to babies with black skin and their bodies may be massaged with oil after bathing.
- Always put cold water in the bath before adding hot water – many babies have been severely scalded by contact with the hot surface of the bath.
- Do not wear dangling earrings or sharp brooches and keep your own nails short and clean.
- Never leave a baby or child under ten years alone in the bath, even for a few seconds.
- Do not top up with hot water while the baby is in the bath; make sure that taps are turned off tightly as even small drops of hot water can cause scalds.
- From a few months old, babies may be bathed in the big bath, keeping the water shallow and following the same guidelines regarding temperature and safety. A non-slip mat placed in the bottom of the bath will prevent slipping.
- Avoid talcum powder because of the risk of inhalation or allergy; if it is used, place on your hands first and then gently smooth it on to completely dry skin.
- Do not use cotton-wool buds – they are not necessary and can be dangerous when poked inside a baby's ears or nose, which are self-cleansing anyway.
- Nail care should be included in the bathing routine. A young baby's nails should be cut when necessary. Do this after a bath when they are soft.
- Hair should be washed daily in the first few months, but shampoo is not necessary every day. A little bath lotion added to the bath water could be gradually worked into the baby's scalp until a lather forms and may then be rinsed off using a wrung out flannel.
- If the baby dislikes having her hair washed, try to keep hair washing separate from bath time so that the two are not associated as unpleasant events.

Protection from sun

Babies benefit from being outside in the fresh air for a while every day. When air is trapped in a building it becomes stale, the level of humidity rises and there is an increased risk of infections spreading. When working in nurseries, early years practitioners should ensure that rooms are well ventilated and that there are opportunities for babies to go outside. Sunlight is beneficial too, but care should be taken with babies and young children:

- Keep all children out of the sun when it is at its most dangerous, between 11 am and 3 pm; those caring for young children should plan outdoor activities to avoid this time unless children are well protected by hats and sun protection cream. Permission must be obtained from the child's parent or carer before applying sunscreen creams.

- Specialists advise keeping babies up to nine months of age out of direct sunlight altogether to prevent the risk of developing skin cancer in later life. Permission must be obtained from the child's parent or carer before applying sunscreen creams.
- Use sun hats with a wide brim that will protect face, neck and shoulders on older babies.
- Use sun protection cream on all sun-exposed areas.
- Use sunshades or canopies on buggies and prams.

Caring for a child with eczema

Eczema (from the Greek 'to boil over') is an itchy and often unsightly skin condition that affects millions of people to some degree. The most common type which affects children is **atopic eczema**. About one in eight of all children will show symptoms at some time, ranging from a mild rash lasting a few months, to severe symptoms that persist over years.

- Eczema is *not* infectious.
- It often starts as an irritating red patch in the creases of the elbows or knees, or on the face.
- It can spread quickly to surrounding skin that becomes cracked, moist and red.

- In severe cases it can blister and weep clear fluid if scratched.
- Later, the skin becomes thickened and scaly.
- Skin damaged by eczema is more likely to become infected, particularly by a bacterium called staphylococcus aureus that produces yellow crusts or pus-filled spots.

Causes

There is no single known cause, but certain factors predispose a child to suffer from eczema:

- an allergy to certain foods, such as cow's milk
- an allergy to airborne substances like pollen, house dust, scales from animal hair or feathers, or fungus spores
- environmental factors, such as humidity or cold weather
- a family history of allergy
- emotional or physical stress.

In severe cases, the GP will refer the child to a skin specialist (dermatologist).

Caring for a child with eczema in the early years setting

- **Food allergies** can create problems with school lunches; the cook must monitor carefully what the child eats.

Guidelines for managing eczema

In mild cases where the child's life is not disrupted, the following measures are usually advised:

- **Do not let the child's skin become dry**: apply a moisturising cream or emollient to the skin several times a day. Aqueous cream is a good moisturiser and can also be used for washing instead of soap. Apply the cream with downward strokes – do not rub it up and down. (Try to put some cream on when you feed the baby or change a nappy.)
- **Identify triggers**: identify and avoid anything that irritates the skin or makes the problem worse; for example, soap powder, pets and other animals, chemical sprays, cigarette smoke or some clothing.
- **Avoid irritants**: avoid substances that dry or irritate the baby's skin, such as soap, baby bath, bubble bath or detergents; bathe the child in lukewarm water with a suitable skin oil added. Avoid wool and synthetics – cotton clothing is best.

- **Prevent scratching**: use cotton mittens for small children at night; keep the child's nails short.
- **Foods to avoid**: do not cut out important foods, such as milk, dairy products, wheat or eggs, without consulting the GP or health visitor. However, citrus fruits, tomatoes and juice can be avoided if they cause a reaction.
- **House dust mite**: the faeces of the house dust mite can sometimes make eczema worse. If the child has fluffy or furry toys in the bedroom, the house dust mite collects on them. Limit these toys to one or two favourites, and either wash them weekly at 60°C or put them in a plastic bag in the freezer for 24 hours to kill the house dust mite.
- **Apply steroid creams** as prescribed by the GP: these must be used sparingly as overuse can harm the skin.

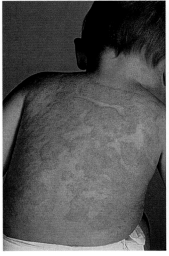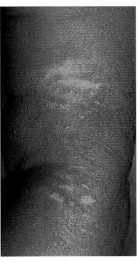

Figure 1.3.1 Eczema appears as a dry, scaly rash which becomes red and may start to 'weep'

- **Clothing**: wearing woolly jumpers, school uniforms (especially if not cotton) and football kits can all make the eczema worse.
- **A special cleaner** may be needed rather than the school soap; they may also need to use cotton towels as paper towels can cause a problem.
- **Extra time and privacy** may be needed for applying creams at school; children may need to wear bandages or cotton gloves to protect their skin.
- **Changes in temperature** can exacerbate the condition: getting too hot (sitting by a sunny window) or too cold (during PE in the playground).
- **Difficulty holding a pen**: if the eczema cracks, they may not be able to hold a pen.
- **Pain and tiredness**: eczema may become so bad that the child is in pain or needs to miss school, due to lack of sleep, pain or hospital visits.
- **Irritability and lack of concentration** can result due to tiredness: sleep problems are very common as a warm, cosy bed can lead to itching and therefore lack of sleep.
- **Using play dough, clay and sand**: some children with eczema may have flare-ups when handling these materials.
- Early years practitioners should find out from the child's parents or specialist nurse which activities are suitable and which should be avoided; you should also provide alternatives so that the child is not excluded from the normal daily activities in the setting.

Caring for children's teeth

Although not yet visible, the teeth of a newborn baby are already developing inside the gums. A baby's first teeth are called milk teeth and these begin to appear at around six months. Dental care should begin as soon as the first tooth appears, with visits to the dentist starting in the child's second year. Teeth need cleaning *as soon as they appear*, because plaque sticks to the teeth and will cause decay if not removed. Caring for the first teeth, even though they are temporary, is important for the following reasons:

- This develops a good hygiene habit which will continue throughout life.
- Babies need their first teeth so that they can chew food properly.
- First teeth guide the permanent teeth into position. If first teeth are missing, the permanent teeth may become crooked.
- Painful teeth may prevent chewing and cause eating problems.
- Clean, white shining teeth look good.

It is essential to establish **a tooth-brushing routine**. Children should brush after meals, after snacks, and before bedtime, so that it becomes a lifelong habit. Offering children a choice during routines increases the likelihood that they will do the activity and gives them a sense of control. So for example, when brushing teeth, you could say, 'Do you want to use the minty toothpaste or the strawberry toothpaste?'

In practice

Caring for teeth

1 Use a small amount (a smear) of baby toothpaste on a soft baby toothbrush or on a piece of fine cloth (such as muslin) to clean the plaque from the teeth. Gently smooth the paste onto the baby's teeth and rub lightly. Rinse the brush in clear water and clean her mouth.
2 Brush twice a day – after breakfast and before bed.
3 After their first birthday, children can be taught to brush their own teeth – but will need careful supervision.
4 They should be shown when and how to brush, that is, up and down away from the gum. They may need help to clean the back molars.
5 Avoid sweets and snacks between feeds or mealtimes.

Caring for children's hair

Most parents will style their own children's hair. If you need to care for their hair while they are in the setting, it is important to follow the parents' preferences; for example, using a wide-toothed comb, or using hair oil rather than shampoo.

Head lice

Head lice are a common affliction. Anybody can 'catch' head lice, but they are particularly prevalent among young children, probably because they tend to put their heads together when playing.

See Table 1.3.2 for detailed information on head lice.

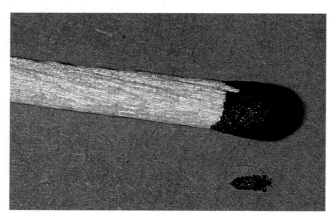

Figure 1.3.2 A head louse

Many people only realise that they have head lice when the itching starts, usually after two to three months. The

They are tiny grey-brown insects with six legs, ending in claws.	Head lice only live in human scalp hair: they cannot be caught from animals.
They have mouths like small needles which they stick into the scalp and use to drink the blood.	They are unable to fly, hop or jump. They cling to hair shafts and climb swiftly between them.
Head lice are not the same as **nits**, which are the cases or shells of eggs laid by female lice, 'glued' on to hair shafts. Nits remain glued in place after the lice hatch; they are pinhead sized and pearly white.	
Head lice are between 1 and 3 mm in size – from pinhead to match head length (see Figure 1.3.2).	Head lice generally remain close to the scalp, for warmth, food and cover, and do not wander down the hair shafts. They move away in response to disturbance.
Head lice do not discriminate between clean and dirty hair, but cease to move around in really wet hair.	They are caught just by head-to-head contact with someone who is infested. When heads touch, the lice simply get across by climbing through the dry hair.

Table 1.3.2 Features of head lice

itching is due to an allergic reaction to the louse bites which takes time to develop. Sometimes a rash may be seen on the back of the neck where lice droppings (a black powder, like fine pepper) irritate the skin.

Treatment

The Community Hygiene Concern charity (www.chc.org) has developed the '**bug buster**' kit; this contains specially designed combs, which are used in wet hair to detect and cure head lice methodically without having to subject children to chemical treatments. This method has been approved by the Department of Health.

Figure 1.3.3 How the Bug Buster kit works

Prevention

The best way to prevent lice is for families to learn how to check their own heads reliably. National Bug Busting Days are educational days that many schools in the UK take part in. The aim is to inform children and their parents about the behaviour of head lice and how to detect and remove them. Co-ordinating Bug Busting Days across the country can help to prevent head lice circulating. See www.chc.org for more information about Bug Busting for schools.

Mealtimes

Meal and snack times should be enjoyable occasions for both staff and children. The following safety guidelines should be followed to ensure health and safety at these times:

- **Hygiene**: wipe all surfaces where food will be served, before and after meals and snacks. Refer to your setting's policy and clean the surfaces in the recommended way – often this is done using an antibacterial spray and disposable cloth. Make sure that children have washed and dried their hands before eating.
- **Serving food**: check that the food you are giving children is appropriate for them; check they have no allergies, for example to milk or wheat. Never give peanuts to children under four years old as they can easily choke or inhale them into their lungs, causing infection and lung damage. Food should be cut up into manageable pieces and should be served at the correct temperature – not too hot or too cold.
- **Seating**: babies should be securely strapped into high chairs, using a five-point harness.
- **Supervision**: supervise children carefully: never leave children unattended with drinks or food in case they choke. Never leave a baby alone, eating finger foods. Babies can choke silently when eating soft foods such as pieces of banana, so you should make sure that you know what to do if choking occurs. Never leave babies propped up with a bottle or feeding beaker.

Routines for mealtimes for toddlers should include allowing time for them to feed themselves and planning to make the experience as enjoyable as possible. Special dietary needs and parental preferences must always be taken into account.

Feeding babies

The advantage of family groups in early years settings is that babies can easily be part of mealtimes. When a whole row of babies all need feeding together, there are often tears and staff become anxious and frustrated, because it seems impossible to get each baby fed quickly enough. Meals become times of stress instead of times of pleasure.

Babies learn more if they are given finger foods as soon as this is appropriate. A carrot stick is a wonderful learning experience, and makes a good contrast with a metal teaspoon. Observing a baby's learning at mealtimes is fascinating – for example, does the baby pass the spoon from one hand to the other? Is the spoon held with a palmar grip? Does the baby try to pick up the carrot stick with a pincer grip?

Case study

Using everyday events for learning

At lunchtime, a group of sitting babies and toddlers were encouraged to choose their pudding. A plate of freshly prepared fruit was placed on the table. A tiny portion was given to the babies to try out. Several showed they wanted more through their movements. The key person passed the plate to the babies, who were allowed to take more for themselves. This encouraged:

- learning that one portion of fruit is the same as the next
- physical coordination
- a feeling of control over what happens
- decision-making.

Activity

Explain your role when attending to the physical care needs of babies and children.

AC 1.3 Identify situations in which non-routine physical care is required

There are various occasions when you will need to give physical care to a child that is not part of the normal routine. These include the following:

- when a child has had a toileting accident
- when a child has been sick

- when a child develops a sudden illness – possibly along with a fever that needs to be reduced by tepid sponging
- when a child comes into the setting in a state of physical neglect.

In these circumstances, you will need to provide respectful and personalised personal care – always being aware of the child's individual needs and preferences.

Activity ·

Think about how you would give physical care in a non-routine situation.

· ·

AC 1.4 Describe benefits of working in partnership with parents/carers in relation to individual physical care routines

Parents develop their own way of caring for their child which reflects their culture and personal preferences. It is important to consult parents and carers about these ideas and preferences. This involves respecting their decisions and acknowledging them as being the people who know their child best. Early years practitioners can then use this knowledge to plan individualised and culturally sensitive care.

While each setting must adopt physical care routines which benefit every child, there may be instances when parental wishes and preferences could be taken into account. For example, parents may:

- request that their child has a rest or sleep at a set time each day, or
- use towelling nappies for their baby, or
- be using baby-led weaning techniques.

Each parent's preferences should be considered, and accommodated where possible.

Reflective practice

Think about the way physical care routines are carried out in your setting. Are parental wishes listened to and acted upon? What do you consider are the benefits of working in partnership with parents in this context?

LO2 Understand hygienic practice in preparing formula feeds

AC 2.1 Outline hygienic practice when preparing formula feeds and sterilising equipment

Preparation of formula feeds

How to prepare a formula feed:

1 Fill the kettle with at least 1 litre of *fresh* tap water (do not use water that has been boiled before).
2 Boil the water. Then leave the water to cool for no more than 30 minutes so that it remains at a temperature of at least 70°C.
3 Clean and disinfect the surface you are going to use.
4 **Wash your hands**: this is very important.
5 If you are using a cold-water steriliser, shake off any excess solution from the bottle and the teat, or rinse the bottle with cooled boiled water from the kettle (not the tap).
6 Stand the bottle on a clean surface.
7 Keep the teat and cap on the upturned lid of the steriliser. Avoid putting them on the work surface.
8 Follow the manufacturer's instructions and pour the correct amount of water that you need into the bottle. Double-check that the water level is correct. Always put the water in the bottle first, while it is still hot, before adding the powdered infant formula.
9 Loosely fill the scoop with formula, according to the manufacturer's instructions, and level it off using either the flat edge of a clean, dry knife or the leveller provided. Different tins of formula come with different scoops. Make sure you use only the scoop that is enclosed with the powdered infant formula that you are using.
10 Holding the edge of the teat, put it on the bottle. Then screw the retaining ring onto the bottle.
11 Cover the teat with the cap and shake the bottle until the powder is dissolved.
12 It is important to cool the formula so it is not too hot to drink. Do this by holding the bottom half of the bottle under cold running

water. Make sure that the water does not touch the cap covering the teat.

13 Test the temperature of the infant formula on the inside of your wrist before giving it to your baby. It should be body-temperature, which means it should feel warm or cool, but not hot.

14 If there is any made-up infant formula left after a feed, throw it away.

Guidelines for bottle-feeding

- Always wash hands thoroughly before preparing feeds for babies.
- As manufacturers' instructions vary as to how much water and powder to use, it is important to follow the instructions on the product very carefully.
- Do not add extra powdered infant formula when making up a feed. This can make the baby constipated and may cause dehydration. Too little powdered infant formula may not provide the baby with enough nourishment.
- Never add sugar or salt to the milk, and never make the feed stronger than the instructions state – this could result in too high a salt intake which can lead to severe illness.
- Never warm up infant formula in a microwave as it can heat the feed unevenly and may burn the baby's mouth.
- Always check the temperature of the milk before giving it to a baby.
- Always check that the teat has a hole of the right size and that it is not blocked.
- Never prop up a baby with a bottle – choking is a real danger.

Sterilising equipment

There are several ways of sterilising the feeding equipment. For example, by:

- using a cold water sterilising solution
- steam sterilising or
- sterilising by boiling.

Remember, before sterilising, **always**:

- Clean the feeding bottles, teats, caps and covers in hot, soapy water as soon as possible after a feed, using a clean bottle brush. Teats may be cleaned using a special teat cleaner; turn teat inside out

to ensure all milk deposits are removed and wash as the bottles.
- Rinse **all** the equipment in clean, cold running water before sterilising.

Cold water sterilising solution

- Follow the manufacturer's instructions.
- Change the sterilising solution every 24 hours.
- Leave feeding equipment in the sterilising solution for at least 30 minutes.
- Make sure that there are no air bubbles trapped in the bottles or teats when putting them in the sterilising solution.
- Keep all the equipment under the solution with a floating cover.

Steam sterilising (electric steriliser or microwave)

- It is important to follow the manufacturer's instructions as there are several different types of sterilisers.
- Make sure the openings of the bottles and teats are facing down in the steriliser.
- Manufacturers will give guidelines on how long you can leave equipment that you are not using immediately (straight after sterilising) before it needs to be resterilised.

Sterilising by boiling

- When using this method, care must be taken to ensure safety and prevent scalds or burns. Hot pans and liquids should not be left unattended, especially if children are present.
- Make sure that whatever you sterilise in this way is safe to boil.
- Boil the feeding equipment in water for at least ten minutes, making sure that all items stay under the surface of the water.
- Remember that teats tend to get damaged faster with this method. Regularly check that teats and bottles are not torn, cracked or damaged.
- Wash your hands thoroughly. Clean and disinfect the surface where you will put together the bottle and teat.
- It is best to remove the bottles just before they are used.

NB Once sterilised, if the bottles are not being used immediately, they should be put together fully with the teat and lid in place. This is to prevent the inside of the sterilised bottle from being contaminated, along with the inside and outside of the teat.

Activity ●

Describe the procedures for preparing formula feeds and for sterilising equipment. What makes good hygienic practice for preparing formula feeds and for sterilising equipment?

● ●

AC 2.2 Explain how poor hygiene may affect the health of babies in relation to preparing formula feeds and sterilisation

The importance of hygienic practice when preparing formula feeds and sterilising equipment

A baby's immune system is not as strong or as well developed as an adult's. This means that babies are much more susceptible to illness and infection. Therefore, **good hygiene** is essential when making up a feed:

● All equipment used to feed the baby must be sterilised
● Bottles, teats and any other feeding equipment need to be cleaned and sterilised before each feed to reduce the chances of the baby falling sick or getting diarrhoea.
● Use boiled drinking water from the tap to make up a feed.
● Do not use bottled water: bottled water is not recommended to make up a feed as it is not sterile and may contain too much salt (sodium) or sulphate. If you *have* to use bottled water to make up a feed, check the label to make sure the sodium (also written as Na) level is less than 200 milligrams (mg) per litre, and the sulphate (also written as SO or SO4) content is not higher than 250mg per litre. It is not usually sterile, so it will still need to be boiled, like tap water, before you prepare the feed.

Bacteria in infant formula

Even when tins and packets of powdered infant formula are sealed, they can sometimes contain bacteria such as *Cronobacter sakazakii* and, more rarely, *Salmonella*. Although these bacteria are very rare, the infections they cause can be life-threatening. Bacteria multiply very fast at room temperature. Even when the feed is kept in a fridge, bacteria can still survive and multiply, although they do this more slowly.

To reduce the risk of infection:

● Always make up each feed as the baby needs it
● Always use boiled water at a temperature of at least 70°C, but remember to let the feed cool before you give it to the baby. (Water at this temperature will kill any harmful bacteria that may be present.)

Activity ●

What are the risks to the health of babies if formula feed preparation and sterilisation of equipment are not carried out with strict adherence to hygienic practice?

● ●

LO3 Understand hygienic practice in relation to control of infection

AC 3.1 Describe the role of the EYP in relation to hand washing, food hygiene, dealing with spillages safely, safe disposal of waste, using correct personal protective equipment

Cross infection is the spread of infection from one person to another. Infections are very common in childhood and are responsible for the majority of illnesses that occur in babies and children under the age of five years. A particular concern for early years settings is that young children often lack basic hygiene skills and must rely on others for their care. Shared toilets and washing facilities, toys, equipment and utensils further increase cross-infection risks. Repeated close physical contact with other children, adults and at-risk areas of the environment (such as toilet facilities) increases the risk of acquiring infections.

What is cross-infection?

Infections are caused by bacteria, fungi and viruses. These pathogenic (disease-causing) organisms or germs can spread in various ways, the main methods being:

- **airborne**: the germs are carried by the air, such as the chicken pox virus
- **droplet spread**: infectious droplets of moisture are coughed or breathed out during infection. They settle on surfaces and may be transferred to another person's eyes or mouth, usually by their hands
- **direct contact**: the germs are spread by touching someone who has the infection, such as scabies or impetigo
- **indirect contact**: the germs are spread by coming into contact with dirty equipment or other materials.

The importance of hand washing

Effective hand washing is an essential way of preventing cross-infection in early years settings. Some simple facts illustrate the importance of regular hand washing in preventing the spread of infection:

- The number of bacteria on fingertips doubles after using the toilet.
- Bacteria can stay alive on our hands for up to three hours.
- 1,000 times as many bacteria spread from damp hands than from dry hands.
- Even after thorough washing, certain bugs can remain under long fingernails.
- Right-handed people tend to wash their left hand more thoroughly than their right hand, and vice versa.
- Millions of bacteria can hide under rings, watches and bracelets.

How you should wash your hands

We all think we know how to wash our hands, but many of us do not do it properly. Figure 1.3.4 shows how we often miss certain parts of our hands when washing them.

Figure 1.3.4 Parts commonly missed when hand washing (red); sometimes missed (orange); and rarely missed (cream)

A step-by-step guide to effective hand washing

- Wet your hands thoroughly under warm running water and squirt liquid soap onto the palm of one hand.
- Rub your hands together to make a lather.
- Rub the palm of one hand along the back of the other and along the fingers. Then do the same with the other hand.
- Rub in between each of your fingers on both hands and around your thumbs.
- Rinse off the soap with clean running water.
- Dry hands thoroughly on a clean dry towel, paper towel or air dryer.

When you should wash your hands

You should wash your hands **before**:

- starting work – this is particularly important when working in any caring environment
- preparing food
- eating
- putting a plaster on a child or giving medicines, etc. Note that plasters will be found in a first aid box, but should only be used where permission has been given
- looking after babies and young children;

between handling raw foods (meat, fish, poultry and eggs) and touching any other food or kitchen utensils; and **after**:

- handling raw foods, particularly meat, fish and poultry and raw eggs in their shells
- going to the toilet
- coughing or sneezing (into your hands or a tissue)
- touching your hair or face
- playing outside
- touching rubbish/waste bins; cleaning cat litter boxes or using chemical cleansers
- changing nappies
- caring for someone who is ill, especially with tummy upsets
- handling and stroking pets or farm animals; gardening, even if you wear gloves
- smoking.

Food hygiene

The term 'food hygiene' refers to the practices which should be followed to ensure that food is safe and wholesome throughout all the stages of production to the point of sale or consumption.

Food hygiene is important to everyone. The food we eat is one of the key factors in good health. If you are working with children you will almost always be involved in handling food in some way. Examples include:

- preparing and serving snacks or meals for children in a nursery or other setting
- preparing and serving snacks or meals in the child's own home
- supervising mealtimes in a school.

The causes of food poisoning

Any infectious disease which results from consuming food or drink is known as food poisoning. The term is most often used to describe the illness, usually diarrhoea and/or vomiting, caused by bacteria, viruses or parasites.

Most cases of food poisoning result from eating large numbers of pathogenic (or harmful) bacteria which are living on the food. Most food poisoning is preventable, although it is not possible to eliminate the risk completely.

Good working practices

If you handle food as part of your job, you are responsible for ensuring that food does not become **contaminated**. You need to understand how current legislation affects your work and to follow good working practices.

These include the following:

- Keep yourself clean by following rules of personal hygiene.
- Know how to store and prepare food safely and hygienically.
- Ensure that areas for serving food are clean and safe.
- Protect food from anything which could cause harm.
- Be alert to food safety hazards.
- Ensure that children are given the opportunity to wash their hands before a meal.

Dealing with spillages

When dealing with **water spillages**:

- ensure when clearing them up that the surface is left completely dry
- no water is to be left on the surface.

When dealing with **body fluids**:

- *before* clearing them away, ensure that you are wearing gloves and the correct protective apron
- use a dilute bleach (hypochlorite) solution to mop up any spillages or product specified by your setting's policy.
- clean the surface until it is completely dry.

Safe disposal of waste

All types of waste (nappies, used tissues and food scraps) can contain germs and must be disposed of promptly and correctly. Children should not be able to gain access to any waste bins. See also Unit 2.3, p 189.

Using correct personal protective equipment (PPE)

The term 'PPE' includes single-use disposable gloves and single-use disposable plastic aprons. Whether you need to use PPE will depend on you coming into contact with blood and body fluids.

- Always wash your hands before putting on and after taking off PPE.

- Disposable gloves and disposable plastic aprons must be worn where there is a risk of splashing or contamination with blood or body fluids – for example, dealing with a nosebleed or nappy changing.
- Some larger settings supply disposable aprons in different colours – for example, red for dealing with blood.

Activity ·

Check your setting's policy for the following procedures: hand washing, food hygiene, dealing with spillages safely, safe disposal of waste, using correct personal protective equipment.

· ·

LO4 Use hygienic practice to minimise the spread of infection

AC 4.1 Use hygienic practice in relation to hand washing, food hygiene, dealing with spillages safely, safe disposal of waste, using correct personal protective equipment

Having read and understood the information for AC 3.1, you will be expected to use hygienic practice at all times to minimise the spread of infection.

LO5 Understand rest and sleep needs of children

AC 5.1 Explain the rest and sleep needs of babies and children from six weeks to seven years

Sleep and rest

Everyone needs sleep, but the amount that babies sleep varies enormously, and will depend on the maturity of the brain (the pre-term baby may sleep for long periods) and on the need for food. Sleep is divided into two distinct states:

- **Rapid eye movement (REM)**, which is termed active sleep.
- **Non-rapid eye movement (NREM)**, which is termed quiet sleep.

In REM sleep the mind is active and is processing daytime emotional experiences. In NREM sleep the body rests and restoration occurs. In babies under one year, more of the sleep is active (REM). It is important not to wake babies during deep sleep, as it plays a vital part in restoring energy levels.

The importance of rest and sleep

Rest and sleep are important for our health and well-being. By the end of the first year, most babies are having two short sleeps during the day – before or after lunch and in the afternoon – and sleeping through the night, although there is much variation between individual children. It is important to have 'quiet periods', even if the baby does not want to sleep.

When we sleep, we rest and gain energy for a new day. But sleep does more than that. When we dream, we process all the events of our daily life. After a night without enough sleep we often feel exhausted and irritable, but after a good night's sleep we feel rested, refreshed and full of energy. It is important to parents that their child sleeps through the night, as it influences the entire family's life and well-being. Children need more sleep than adults because the brain is developing and maturing, and they are physically growing as well. Sleep is important to child health because:

- it rests and restores our bodies
- it enables the brain and the body's metabolic processes to recover (these processes are responsible for producing energy and growth)
- during sleep, growth hormone is released; this renews tissues and produces new bone and red blood cells
- dreaming is believed to help the brain sort out information stored in the memory during waking hours.

Children vary enormously in their need for sleep and rest. Some children seem able to rush around all day with very little rest; others will need to 'recharge their batteries' by having frequent periods of rest. You need to be able to recognise the signs that a child is tired; these may include:

- looking tired – dark rings under the eyes and yawning
- asking for their comfort object

- constant rubbing of the eyes
- twiddling their hair and fidgeting with objects
- showing no interest in activities and in their surroundings
- being particularly emotional – crying or being stubborn
- withdrawing into themselves – sucking thumb and appearing listless.

The sleep and rest needs of children from six weeks to seven years

Getting the right rest is crucial for the learning of babies and young children. Not all babies will need to sleep at the same time, and it is very worrying to find a practice where all babies are expected to have their nappies changed at the same time and to sleep at the same time. These are very individual things. It is important for babies to feel that they are near someone when they sleep. Some babies sleep best on a mat, with a cover to keep them warm, on the floor of a quiet area that is gated. Others sleep better in a darkened room in a cot kept for them. This area should not be too full of stimulation. It is important to relax and let go when falling asleep. Neutral colouring is best, and the room should not be cluttered.

It is also important to keep to the sleep-time rituals and patterns that are familiar to the baby at home. Some babies need to have a cuddle, being lowered into their cot as they fall asleep. Others might never go to sleep on a lap, but need to be in a cot, in a quiet room, with their teddy, in order to fall asleep.

Sleep and rest needs of a baby aged six weeks

Newborn babies tend to sleep a great deal. At around six weeks old, a baby will probably sleep for shorter spells during the day and longer periods at night. The baby will have more deep, non-REM sleep and less light sleep, but will probably still wake for a feed or more than one feed at night. Sleep and rest periods are spread throughout the 24 hour period, usually comprising four to five periods of rest and sleep lasting two-and-a-half to three hours.

A baby aged six weeks needs to sleep and rest for approximately 15 hours in a 24-hour period.

Sleep and rest needs of a baby aged seven months

From four-and-a-half months onwards, most babies are capable of sleeping for eight hours at night without needing a feed. By seven months, babies usually have two to three daytime sleeps, each between one-and-a-half and two hours.

A baby aged seven months needs between 13 to 14 hours' sleep and rest in a 24-hour period.

Sleep and rest needs of a baby aged 15 months

From 12 months up until the age of two, babies tend to sleep for approximately 11 hours at night. The rest of their sleep will be in daytime naps. At around 15 to 18 months, many babies have just one longer daytime sleep, rather than two shorter naps.

A baby aged 15 months needs 14 hours' sleep and rest in a 24-hour period.

Sleep and rest needs of a child aged two-and-a-half years

Most children between the ages of two and three years still need one nap a day, which may range from one to three-and-a-half hours long. At this age children usually go to bed between 7 and 9 pm and wake up between 6 and 8 am.

A child aged two-and-a-half years needs a total of 13 hours' sleep and rest in a 24-hour period.

Sleep and rest needs of a child aged four to five years

By the age of four years, most children meet all their sleep and rest needs at night, although a few may still need a short daytime rest or sleep.

A child aged four to five years needs a total of eleven to eleven-and-a-half hours' sleep and rest in a 24-hour period.

Sleep and rest needs of a child aged six to seven years

By this age, the need for daytime sleeps has disappeared, and all the sleep needs are met at night-time.

A child aged six to seven years needs a total of between ten-and-a-half and eleven hours' sleep and rest in a 24-hour period.

Different views about sleep and rest

There are cultural differences in how parents view bedtime and sleep routines. In some cultures it is normal for children to sleep with parents and to have a much later bedtime in consequence. Some families who originate from hot countries where having a sleep in the afternoon is normal tend to let

their children stay up in the evening. Such children are more likely to need a sleep while in your care; as long as the overall amount of sleep is sufficient for the child, it does not matter. It is always worth discussing bedtime routines with parents when toddlers are struggling to behave well. Some areas have sleep clinics managed by the health visiting service to help parents whose children have difficulty sleeping.

Even after they have established a good sleep routine, children's sleep patterns can become disrupted between the ages of one and three years. There are thought to be a number of factors for this, including developmental changes and behavioural issues.

Guidelines: Establishing a routine for rest and sleep

Children will only sleep if they are actually tired, so it is important that enough activity and exercise is provided. Some children do not have a nap during the day but should be encouraged to rest in a quiet area.

When preparing children for a daytime nap, rest or bedtime sleep, you need to:

- Treat each child uniquely; every child will have his or her own needs for sleep and rest.
- Find out all you can about the individual child's sleep habits; for example, some children like to be patted to sleep, while others need to have their favourite comfort object.

- Be guided by the wishes of the child's parents or carers; some parents, for example, prefer their child to have a morning nap but not an afternoon nap, as this routine fits in better with the family's routine.
- Reassure children that they will not be left alone and that you or someone else will be there when they wake up.
- Keep noise to a minimum and darken the room; make sure that children have been to the toilet – children need to understand the signals which mean that it is time for everyone to have a rest or sleep.
- Provide quiet, relaxing activities for children who are unable or who do not want to sleep; for example, jigsaw puzzles, a story tape or reading a book.

Guidelines: Establishing a bedtime routine for babies

- Between three and five months, most babies are ready to settle into a bedtime routine:
- Give the baby a bath or wash and put on a clean nappy and nightwear.
- Take her to say goodnight to other members of the household.
- Carry her into her room, telling her in a gentle voice that it is time for bed.
- Give the last breast- or bottle-feed in the room where the baby sleeps.
- Sing a song or lullaby to help settle her, while gently rocking her in your arms.

- Wrap her securely and settle her into the cot or cradle, saying goodnight.
- If she likes it, gently 'pat' her to sleep.
- The routine can be adapted as the baby grows. Advice from **The Lullaby Trust** (formerly The Foundation for the Study of Infant Deaths) is that the safest place for a baby to sleep is in a cot in the parents' room for the first six months. After six months, the baby can be safely left in her own room.

AC 5.2 Explain safety precautions which minimise the risk of sudden infant death syndrome

Sudden infant death syndrome (SIDS)

Sudden infant death syndrome is often called 'cot death'. It is the term applied to the sudden unexplained and unexpected death of an infant.

The reasons for cot deaths are complicated and the cause is still unknown. Although cot death is the commonest cause of death in babies up to one year old, it is still very rare, occurring in approximately two out of every 1,000 babies. Recent research has identified various risk factors, and the Lullaby Trust has written the following guidelines.

Guidelines for parents from the Lullaby Trust

- Cut smoking in pregnancy – fathers too!
- Do not let anyone smoke in the same room as your baby.
- Place your baby on the back to sleep.
- Do not let your baby get too hot.
- Keep baby's head uncovered: place your baby with their feet to the foot of the cot, to prevent wriggling down under the covers.
- If your baby is unwell, seek medical advice promptly.
- The safest place for your baby to sleep is in a cot in your room for the first six months.

- It is dangerous to share a bed with your baby if you or your partner:
  - are smokers (no matter where or when you smoke)
  - have been drinking alcohol
  - take drugs or medication that makes you drowsy
  - feel very tired.
- It is very dangerous to sleep together on a sofa, armchair or settee.

Guidelines for reducing the risk of sudden infant death syndrome

- The room where an infant sleeps should be at a temperature that is comfortable for lightly clothed adults (16–20°C).
- If the baby is a natural tummy-sleeper, keep turning him over and tuck in securely with blankets (as long as the weather is not too hot); a musical mobile may help to keep him happy while lying on his back.
- Always invest in a brand new mattress if the baby's cot is second-hand.
- A pillow should never be used for sleeping; if the baby is snuffly or has a blocked nose, place a small pillow under the mattress, but make sure he does not slide down to the end of his cot.
- Never allow the baby to come into contact with smoky rooms; ask visitors not to smoke in the house.

The risk factor increases with the number of cigarettes smoked.
- Learn to recognise the signs and symptoms of illness and know how to respond.
- Use a room thermometer if necessary and check the baby's temperature by feeling his tummy, making sure your hands are warm beforehand.
- Babies over one month of age should never wear hats indoors, as small babies gain and lose heat very quickly through their heads.
- Learn and practise on a special baby resuscitation mannequin how to perform artificial ventilation and cardiac massage. This should always be practised under the supervision of a qualified first aider.

Research activity

Sudden infant death syndrome (SIDS)
In groups, prepare a display that details the risk factors implicated in sudden infant death syndrome. Using the information provided, make a poster for each risk factor and state clearly the precautions that should be taken to prevent cot death. Access the website: www.lullabytrust.org.uk for up-to-date recommendations.

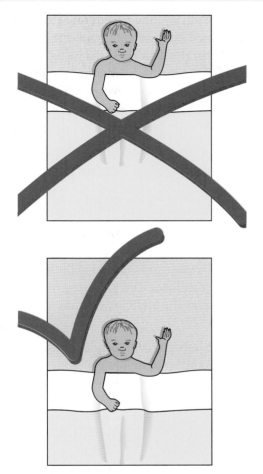

Figure 1.3.5 Preventing SIDS: the feet-to-foot position

LO6 Understand childhood immunisation

Immunisation is a way of protecting children against serious disease. Once children have been immunised, their bodies can fight those diseases if they come into contact with them. If a child is not immunised they will be at risk from catching the disease and will rely on other people immunising their children to avoid becoming infected.

An immunisation programme protects people against specific diseases by reducing the number of people getting the disease and preventing it being passed on. With some diseases – like **smallpox** or **polio** – it is possible to eliminate them completely.

AC 6.1 Outline the reasons for immunisation

Reasons for immunisation against disease

How immunity to disease and infection can be acquired

Babies are born with some **natural immunity.** They are:

- able to make their own infection-fighting cells
- further protected by antibodies and other substances found in breast milk.

A child's own experiences of infection boost his or her immunity. For some infections – e.g. measles – immunity is lifelong, while for others it is short-lived. Certain illnesses, such as the common cold, are caused by one of several strains of virus, which is why having one cold does not automatically prevent another one later. Sometimes the immune system does not work properly, as in the case of **HIV/AIDS** infection and some other rare conditions. Sometimes it *over*-works and causes **allergy**. It can also be affected by emotional distress and physical exhaustion.

There are two types of immunity: **active immunity** and **passive immunity**. As discussed above, immunity can be induced by contact with an infection. It can also be induced by **immunisation** against certain infective agents.

Active immunity

Active immunity is when a vaccine triggers the **immune system** to produce **antibodies** against the disease as though the body had been infected with it. This also teaches the body's immune system how to produce the appropriate antibodies quickly. If the immunised person then comes into contact with the disease itself, their immune system will recognise it and immediately produce the antibodies needed to fight it.

Passive immunity

Passive immunity is provided when the body is given **antibodies** rather than producing them itself. A newborn baby has passive immunity to several diseases, such as measles, mumps and rubella, from antibodies passed from its mother via the placenta.

Passive immunity only lasts for a few weeks or months. In the case of measles, mumps and rubella (MMR) it may last up to one year in infants – this is why the MMR immunisation is given just after a child's first birthday.

Herd immunity

If enough people in a community are immunised against certain diseases, then it is more difficult for that disease to get passed between those who are not; this is known as herd immunity. Herd immunity does not apply to all diseases because they are not all passed on from person to person. For example, tetanus can only be caught from spores in the ground.

> ### Key terms
>
> **antibodies** Antibodies are proteins made by the body's immune system.
>
> **immunisation** Immunisation protects children (and adults) against harmful infections before they come into contact with them in the community.
>
> **immunity** A condition of being able to resist a particular infectious disease.
>
> **vaccine** A substance that stimulates the body's immune response in order to prevent or control an infection.

The **advantages of immunisation** include the following:

- Children who are not immunised run a risk of catching diseases and having complications.
- Immunisation is the safest way to protect children from particular diseases which may have long-lasting effects.
- Having children immunised at an early age means they are well protected by the time they start playgroup or school, where they are in contact with lots of children.
- Immunisation also protects those children who are unable to receive immunisation, by providing herd immunity.

The **disadvantages of immunisation** include the possibility of **side effects**. The possible risks that follow certain childhood immunisations must be weighed up against the possible risks of complications of the childhood illness. For example, with the MMR vaccine there is a risk of 1 in a 1,000 of febrile convulsions (fits). However, if a child catches the measles disease, the risk of convulsions is 1 in 200 people with the disease.

AC 6.2 Identify the immunisation schedule.

Not every disease that affects children can be immunised against. There is no routine vaccination for chicken pox or scarlet fever in the UK although the chicken pox vaccine is offered with the MMR in some other countries. The following diseases are all included in the NHS programme of routine immunisation (2013).

- **Diphtheria:** a bacterial infection which starts with a sore throat but can rapidly get worse, leading to severe breathing difficulties. It can also damage the heart and nervous system.
- **Tetanus**: a bacterial infection caused when germs found in soil and manure get into the body through open cuts and burns. Tetanus is a painful disease which affects the muscles and can cause breathing problems.
- **Pertussis** (or whooping cough): a bacterial infection that can cause long bouts of coughing and choking, making it hard to breathe. It is not usually serious in older children, but it can be very serious and can kill babies under one year old. It can last for up to ten weeks.
- **Polio**: a highly infectious viral disease spread mainly through close contact with an infected person. The polio virus attacks the nervous system and can paralyse muscles permanently. If it attacks the muscles in the chest, or those that control swallowing, it can be fatal.
- **Hib:** Hib (*Haemophilus influenzae type* b) is an infection that can cause a number of major illnesses like blood poisoning, pneumonia and meningitis. All of these illnesses can kill if not treated quickly. The Hib vaccine protects the child against only *one* type of **meningitis** (Hib). It does not protect against any other type of meningitis.

When to immunise	Diseases protected against	Vaccine given	Immunisation site
Two months old	Diphtheria, tetanus, pertussis (whooping cough), polio and Haemophilus influenzae type b (Hib)	DTaP/IPV/Hib (Pediacel)	Thigh
	Pneumococcal disease	PCV (Prevenar 13)	Thigh
	Rotavirus	Rotavirus (Rotarix)	By mouth
Three months old	Diphtheria, tetanus, pertussis, polio and Hib	DTaP/IPV/Hib (Pediacel)	Thigh
	Meningococcal group C disease (MenC)	Men C (NeisVac-C or Menjugate)	Thigh
	Rotavirus	Rotavirus (Rotarix)	By mouth
Four months old	Diphtheria, tetanus, pertussis, polio and Hib	DTaP/IPV/Hib (Pediacel)	Thigh
	Pneumococcal disease	PCV (Prevenar 13)	Thigh
Between 12 and 13 months old – within a month of the first birthday	Hib/MenC	Hib/MenC (Menitorix)	Upper arm/thigh
	Pneumococcal disease	PCV (Prevenar 13)	Upper arm/thigh
	Measles, mumps and rubella (German measles)	MMR (Priorix or MMR VaxPRO)	Upper arm/thigh
Two and three years old[3]	Influenza[4] (from September)	Flu nasal spray (Fluenz) (annual) (if Fluenz unsuitable, use inactivated flu vaccine)	Nostrils Upper arm
Three years four months old or soon after	Diphtheria, tetanus, pertussis and polio	dTaP/IPV (Repevax) or DTaP/IPV (Infanrix-IPV)	Upper arm
	Measles, mumps and rubella	MMR (Priorix or MMR VaxPRO) (check first dose has been given)	Upper arm

[3] This is defined as children aged two or three years (but not four years) on 1 September 2013.

[4] The vaccine is given prior to the flu season – usually in September and October.

Table 1.3.3 Routine immunisations for children from birth to five years old, 2014 (taken from the NHS complete routine immunisation schedule 2013/14)

- **Meningococcal disease:** this is one of the serious causes of **meningitis** – an inflammation of the lining of the brain – and serious blood infections in children. Although fairly rare now, before the introduction of the vaccine it was the most common killer in the one to five years age group. The Men C vaccine protects the child against only *one* type of meningitis (meningococcal).

- **Measles**: the measles virus is highly contagious and causes a high fever and rash. Around 1 in 15 of all children who get measles are at risk of complications including chest infections, fits and brain damage. In very serious cases, measles kills. In the year before the MMR vaccine was introduced in the UK (1988), 16 children died from measles.

- **Mumps:** mumps is caused by a virus which can lead to fever, headache and painful, swollen glands in the face, neck and jaw. It can result in permanent deafness, viral meningitis (swelling of the lining of the brain) and encephalitis. Rarely, it causes painful swelling of the testicles in males and the ovaries in females.
- **Pneumococcal disease:** this is the term used to describe infections caused by the bacterium *Streptococcus pneumoniae*. It can cause pneumonia, septicaemia (blood poisoning) and meningitis, and is also one of the most common bacterial causes of ear infections. The bacterium is becoming increasingly resistant to antibiotics in the UK and worldwide.
- **Rotavirus:** rotavirus is a highly infectious stomach bug that typically strikes babies and young children, causing an unpleasant bout of diarrhoea, sometimes with vomiting, tummy ache and fever. Most children recover at home within a few days, but nearly one in five will need to see their doctor, and one in ten of these end up in hospital as a result of complications such as extreme dehydration. A very small number of children die from rotavirus infection each year.
- **Rubella:** (German measles) is caused by a virus. In children it is usually mild and can go unnoticed. Rubella infection in the first three months of pregnancy causes damage to the unborn baby in nine out of ten cases; it can seriously damage their sight, hearing, heart and brain. In the five years before the MMR vaccine was introduced, about 43 babies a year were born in the UK with congenital rubella syndrome.

Immunisations are usually carried out in child health clinics. The doctor will discuss any fears the parents may have about particular vaccines. No vaccine is completely risk-free, and parents are asked to sign a consent form prior to immunisations being given. Immunisations are only given if the child is well, and may be postponed if the child has had a reaction to any previous immunisation or if the child is taking any medication that might interfere with their ability to fight infection. The effects of the disease are usually far worse than any side effects of a vaccine.

Activity •

Recap the diseases included in the NHS programme of routine immunisation (2013). The latest Immunisation Schedule was issued in 2013. Make sure you check with the NHS website for any updates of the schedule.

• •

AC 6.3 Explain the reasons why some children are not immunised

In the UK, the childhood immunisation programme is not compulsory, and therefore parental consent has to be obtained before the child is immunised. Although primary immunisation uptake in the UK is relatively high (95 per cent of children are immunised by the age of two years, not including MMR), a small percentage of children are not immunised. Reasons why children may not be immunised include:

- parental preferences – e.g. for homeopathy
- religious reasons
- an unwell child when first immunisations were due
- general lack of belief in the validity of immunisation
- fear of being responsible for any possible side effects to the immunisation
- previous diagnosis with the disease.

Fear of side effects

In the past, children with epilepsy or a family history of epilepsy were not given the pertussis (whooping cough) vaccine. There were concerns that the vaccine could directly cause febrile convulsions and epilepsy. Studies since then have shown there is no link. The whooping cough vaccine is now routinely given to children with epilepsy

A study in 1998 by Dr Andrew Wakefield suggested that the MMR immunisation could cause **autism**. This is not the case. The study was flawed and has since been discredited. Extensive research since then has shown that there is no link between MMR and autism. The recent epidemic of measles – mostly in Swansea, Wales – was thought to have been caused by a severe drop in the number of children receiving the MMR jab, possibly because of the now discredited research into links with autism.

LO7 Support children in personal care routines

AC 7.1 Support children in personal care routines

See ACs 1.2 and 5.1 for further information on personal care routines in relation to toileting, washing and/or bath time, skin, teeth and hair, meal times, resting and/or sleeping

Good routines can provide valuable opportunities for promoting health and development, whether in a home or group setting. Everyday care routines for babies and young children provide opportunities for the promotion of:

- **intellectual and language skills**: talking to babies and children when carrying out routine care promotes communication skills and understanding.
- **emotional development**: babies and children feel secure when handled and treated in an affectionate and competent manner.
- **social skills**: young children see and understand that they are treated equally when routines are carried out, and will learn the concepts of sharing and taking turns. They will also experience a feeling of belonging, which is very important.
- **development of independence**: good routines allow time and space for toddlers to try to do things for themselves, rather than being rushed by the adult.

Engaging with children during care routines to support their learning and development

Encourage

It is very important that you encourage *all* attempts when the child is first learning how to do a routine. If you discourage children because it was not done *quite* right, their attempts at trying might stop.

Practice makes perfect

Remember that young children need a lot of practice (and support) before they are able to carry out new tasks independently. As children gain the skills required for the task, we need to slow down the routine and expect that it might take extra time to complete.

Step by step

Break down routine activities and tasks into easy, manageable steps; for example:

- Use a footstool to reach the bathroom basin.
- Use small steps and a toilet seat to make the child feel more secure when going to the 'big' toilet.

Support

It is important to let children know that you understand their feelings when they are becoming frustrated, and that you will support them so that they feel successful. For example: 'I know it's hard to get your hands really dry; let me help.'

Praise

Praise every little attempt to do any step. Attention to a child's use of a new skill will strengthen that skill. Effective praise is **descriptive praise**; for example, 'Thank you for putting your cup on the side there – it stopped it from being knocked over,' or 'Putting your shoes on all by yourself so quickly was great as now we have more time to play outside.' Children will learn that when you offer descriptive praise (rather than just saying 'Clever boy'), you are teaching them what you like and why you liked it. They are more likely to do it again.

Modelling

First, model how to do the first step and then say, 'Now you show me.' Show one step at a time, allowing time for the child to process the information and imitate what you did before moving to the next step.

Daily and weekly routines

Routines should be planned and organised around the needs of individual babies and children. The routines should ensure that each baby or child has all his or her personal care needs met in a positive environment. Factors to take into consideration when planning and implementing routines include:

- sleep, rest and stimulation
- feeding
- nappy changes
- play preferences
- consultation with each child's parents or carers
- stage of development.

Make sure you know about the policies and procedures in your setting relating to care routines. Think of ways in which you can support individual children during routine care activities.

· ·

Assessment practice

1 What are physical care needs? Describe routine physical care needs for children in relation to nappy changing, toilet training, washing and bath time, skin teeth and hair, mealtimes, and the roles of the EYP during these.

2 Explain the importance of routines when promoting the physical care of babies and young children.

3 Under what circumstances might non-routine physical care be required?

4 What are the benefits of working in partnership with parents/carers in relation to individual physical care routines?

5 Find out about your setting's policy and procedures for the safe, hygienic preparation of formula feeds and sterilising equipment.

6 How can poor hygiene affect the health of babies in relation to the preparation of formula feeds and sterilisation of equipment?

7 Describe your role in relation to hand washing, food hygiene, dealing with spillages safely, safe disposal of waste, using correct personal protective equipment.

8 Describe how you have used hygienic practice in relation to hand washing, food hygiene, dealing with spillages safely, safe disposal of waste and using correct PPE.

9 Why are sleep and rest so important for babies and young children?

10 How can you ensure that a child's needs for sleep and rest are provided for within the setting?

11 What is sudden infant death syndrome (SIDS)? Explain how you can minimise the risk of sudden infant death syndrome.

12 Which childhood illnesses can be prevented by immunisation?

13 What is the current immunisation schedule for babies and young children in the UK?

14 Give four reasons why some children are not immunised.

15 Describe how you have been able to support children in personal care routines in your setting.

Useful resources

Organisations

Birth to five is a guide to parenting in the early years and has 150 pages of NHS-accredited information, videos and interactive tools: www.nhs.uk/Planners/birthtofive

The Lullaby Trust offers confidential support to family, friends and carers affected by the sudden and unexpected death of a baby or toddler: www.lullabytrust.org.uk

Unit 1.4 Promote children's emotional well-being

This unit provides the learner with the knowledge, skills and understanding to promote children's emotional well-being.

Learning outcomes

By the end of this unit you will:

1 Understand children's needs in relation to emotional well-being.
2 Understand the requirements for promoting emotional well-being in relation to current frameworks.
3 Understand the needs of children during transition and significant events.
4 Be able to promote the emotional well-being of children in own setting.
5 Be able to critically evaluate provision in own setting in relation to promoting emotional well-being in line with current frameworks and theoretical perspectives.

LO1 Understand children's needs in relation to emotional well-being

A child's emotional well-being is the result of healthy development within a nurturing environment. In the early years, babies and young children make emotional attachments and form relationships which lay the foundation for future mental health and well-being. Attachment relationships are particularly important and have far-reaching effects on the development of personal, emotions, social and cognitive skills.

Children need to be in a safe, secure, loving and stimulating environment in order to develop healthily in all areas. Within their home and wider environment, every child needs the following conditions:

● love and security
● to have friends and feel as if they belong
● new experiences and opportunities for play
● praise and recognition
● responsibility.

AC 1.1 Explain theoretical perspectives on emotional well-being

From the 1920s onwards, an interest in the work of Sigmund Freud and the other early psychoanalysts began to influence English nursery childcare, with specific attention paid to children's emotional development.

John Bowlby and attachment theory

John Bowlby's work was important because it led to the introduction of key person systems in institutions. Children no longer had a series of different nurses looking after them as each work shift changed. They were placed in smaller 'family' groups and were consistently looked after by the same team of staff. Also, increasing numbers of children began to be fostered in family homes rather than placed in large institutions. This helped children to form good attachments with a limited number of people who cared for them. Children could develop warm, physical, loving relationships, and found it easier to communicate with their carers. Theories of attachment and bonding are also discussed in Unit 3.13.

Harry and Margaret Harlow

The adverse effects of long-term maternal separation were confirmed by research carried out with rhesus monkeys in the USA. Harry and Margaret Harlow conducted a series of experiments in the 1950s to determine the source of attachment and the effects of maternal separation. Such experiments would be considered very cruel and shocking today. In their most famous study, they separated infant monkeys from their natural mothers at a very early age and placed them in individual cages with two inanimate surrogate (substitute) mothers. These surrogates were dummies made to look something like real monkeys:

● one surrogate was made from wire mesh – and contained the food bottle

- one surrogate was padded with foam and covered with towelling cloth – no food was provided.

The monkeys showed a clear preference for the soft padded 'mother' even if they were always fed from a bottle attached to the wire mesh mother. They would only go to the wire mesh mother to feed, and would then go back and cling to the soft, padded mother.

In other experiments, the monkeys had access to the wire mesh dummy only. These monkeys showed more signs of emotional disturbance – rocking, clutching and failing to explore – than the monkeys reared with the padded mother. The Harlows' research refuted the behaviourist (conditioning) theory that attachment develops because the parent feeds the child and that affectionate behaviour is reinforced by food. Results from the many Harlow experiments consistently showed that a warm, comfortable area to which to cling was more likely to promote attachment than a mere source of food.

Mary Ainsworth: The Strange Situation

Mary Ainsworth, formerly a student of Bowlby, studied the development and pattern of attachments in a psychological laboratory using a device called The Strange Situation. The purpose of the procedure is to observe how different babies (aged between 12 and 24 months) *respond to a stranger* when they are:

- with their mothers
- left alone, and
- reunited with their mothers.

The procedure consists of a series of episodes involving collaboration between an observer and a mother. The baby's behaviour is recorded by strategically placed video cameras.

Each episode lasts approximately three minutes – being concluded if the child is distressed, and prolonged if more time is needed for the child to become re-involved in play. Trained observers, using a detailed coding scheme, then code the video recording of the whole session. In particular they will look for instances of the infant seeking

1st episode	The child and the mother are brought into a comfortable, well-equipped playroom and the child is given the opportunity to play with the toys and to explore the room while the mother is watching. After the mother and her child have settled, the mother sits reading a magazine and after a few minutes, a stranger enters and sits quietly on the free chair.
2nd episode	After an interval, the stranger starts talking in a friendly way with the mother, and after a while, moves to the floor and starts to play with the child.
3rd episode	The stranger moves closer to the child and after a few minutes the mother leaves as unobtrusively as possible.
4th episode	The child is left in the room with the stranger, who joins in with the child's activities – e.g. accepting a toy when proffered, etc. (If the child becomes very distressed, the session is concluded.)
5th episode	After a few minutes, the mother returns to comfort her child and to settle her down to play.
6th episode	When she leaves the room again, she waves goodbye, drawing attention to her departure.
7th episode	The stranger returns and remains in the room with the child.
8th episode	The mother returns once more.

Table 1.4.1 The Strange Situation

proximity to the mother, maintaining contact and showing signs of avoidance or resistant behaviour.

After careful consideration of the coding, a security classification is arrived at, defining the quality of the attachment. The typical reaction of the child on entering the room with the mother is to stay close to her, at first physically touching her. Later, the child moves away to explore, but looks back from time to time – as if to check that the mother is still there. When a stranger enters the room, the child tends to rush back to the mother and will only play with the stranger after some time. If the mother leaves the room, most children tend to cry and to stop playing.

Ainsworth and her colleagues identified three types of attachment relationship:

Type A: anxious-avoidant

A child with an anxious-avoidant attachment style will avoid or ignore the mother and show little emotion when she departs or returns. The child will not explore very much, regardless of who is there. Strangers will not be treated very differently from the mother. There is not much emotional range displayed regardless of who is in the room or if it is empty.

Type B: securely attached

A child who is securely attached to the mother will explore freely while she is present, will engage with strangers, will be visibly upset when the mother departs, and happy to see her return. The child will not engage with the stranger if the mother is not in the room.

Type C: anxious-ambivalent

A child with an anxious-ambivalent attachment style is wary of exploration and of strangers, even when the mother is present. When the mother departs, the child is extremely distressed. The child will be ambivalent when she returns and will seek to remain close to the mother, but will be resentful and angry, and also resistant when the mother initiates attention.

The most common attachment pattern observed in The Strange Situation was Type B: securely attached (70 per cent of the sample). Further studies using this technique found that there were wide cultural differences in the ways in which attachment patterns are expressed. For example, when reproduced in Japan, babies became very distressed in the Strange Situation because, in their culture, they are never normally left alone at 12 months. Ainsworth also linked her research to her observations of mothers at home with their babies – this was a more common situation in the 1970s –

and concluded that the development of attachment was greatly influenced by the responses of the primary carer to the child.

A fourth pattern of attachment, **disorganised attachment**, was later added to the three above, to include those children who did not demonstrate a consistent coping mechanism, and who showed fear and confusion about the parental relationship. This pattern is seen most frequently in families where there is high social risk or child abuse.

Attachment theory reassessed

Bowlby's work has been criticised by other researchers in the field – most notably Michael Rutter. Michael Rutter (1981) conducted a major review of maternal deprivation research and – unlike Bowlby – did *not* find a direct causal link between early experiences of separation from parents and later emotional distress. Rutter believed that:

- **Separation from the parent does not in itself cause harmful effects**. The quality of sensitive support given to the child during the experience of separation is highly significant. The adverse effects on children in care, especially institutionalised children, which Bowlby and others attributed to separation from the mother, have been shown by subsequent researchers to be due to a variety of different causes.
- **The quality of family relationships affects the child more than the actual fact of separation or divorce**. For example, children separated because of discord between their parents are more likely to show the sort of 'deprivation reaction' described by Bowlby than children separated by the death of a parent.
- **Children can form multiple attachments with various people without harm** – as long as there is not an *extreme* form of shared care, for example, with tens of adults involved.
- **Children often appear to be extremely resilient to situations of deprivation.** Other factors – such as under-stimulation and minimal social contact – play an unquantifiable part in the overall picture of deprivation.

It is now widely accepted that emotional and social development is affected by attachment, and that how children interact with their parents or primary carers has a significant effect upon how their parents or carers behave towards them.

James and Joyce Robertson: attachment and substitute care

James and Joyce Robertson made a series of films in the 1950s that showed Bowlby's theory about maternal deprivation in action. The films were of young children who were separated from their parents and showed that they went through various stages in their loss and grief:

- They *protested*: they cried out but were able to be comforted.
- They *despaired* about what was happening – and were inconsolable.
- They showed *denial* – and became detached in the way that they related to others. Superficially, they seemed unconcerned about the separation, but denied any affection or response to the mother when eventually reunited.

Robertson's research shows that maternal deprivation does seem to cause emotional difficulties for children. However, further research showed that long-term effects on development could be prevented by providing high-quality **substitute emotional care** with a single substitute caregiver.

D.W. Winnicott and transitional objects

Writing in 1964, Donald Winnicott emphasised the importance of the teddy bears and other comforters that children seem to need to carry about with them. He called these transitional objects. Parents often describe them as 'comfort objects'.

Winnicott believed that children need such objects to help them through the times when they begin to realise that they are a separate person. The teddy might stand for the mother, when she leaves the baby in the cot; it is a symbol of the mother who will return. It helps children through being alone or feeling sad.

Anna Freud

Freud's daughter, Anna, was a nursery teacher and set up a residential nursery school during the Second World War in Hampstead to help care for children whose parents were working or otherwise absent. She arranged for each child in the Hampstead Nursery to have a constant 'maternal figure', later writing that:

repeated experience proves the importance of the introduction of this substitute mother relationship into the life of the residential nursery. A child who forms this kind of relationship to a grown up not only becomes amenable to educational influence in a very welcome manner, but shows more vivid and varied facial expressions, develops individual qualities and unfolds his whole personality in a surprising way.

(Anna Freud, 1973)

Key term

transitional object Often a soft toy or blanket to which a child becomes attached, a transitional object is used by a child to provide comfort and security while he or she is away from a secure base, such as parents or home.

In practice activity

Do you think it is important for children to have unlimited access to their transitional object in early years settings?

Find out if your setting includes information on transitional objects – either in information given to parents and carers or as part of a policy document.

AC 1.2 Explain the process of bonding, attachment and developing secure relationships

The needs of children in relation to emotional well-being

The process of bonding, attachment and developing secure relationships can be explored by looking at young children's needs. These include:

- The need for love and security.
- The need to have friends and to feel as if they belong.
- The need for new experiences and opportunities for play.

- The need for praise and recognition.
- The need for responsibility, independence and self-reliance.

The need for love and security

This is probably the most important need as it provides the basis for all later relationships. Research shows that children who do not get enough love and attention in early childhood are less likely to become well-adjusted adults. Every child needs to experience **unconditional love** from their parents or carers – this means that they are totally accepted with no restrictions or conditions imposed on them.

Security

Babies learn about love from the words and actions of those who care for them. In their first year, their need for security may be met by having a comforter or **comfort object**: this is often a blanket or a favourite soft toy. Some children use their thumb or a dummy as a comfort object, while some children do not have a comfort object at all. Comforters provide security for children, particularly at night; they represent something familiar for the child and help them to adjust when their parents are separated from them.

Routine

Another aspect of the child's need for love and security is the need for routine and predictability. This is why having daily routines is so important when caring for children. By meeting children's need for routine, parents and carers are helping the child to feel acknowledged and independent, and this increases their self-esteem.

Bonding and attachment

Bonding is a term used to describe the feelings of love and responsibility that parents have for their babies. It is a very close, two-way relationship which develops between a baby and an adult. Attachment means a warm, affectionate and supportive bond between a child and his or her carer, which enables the child to develop secure relationships.

The need to have friends and to feel as if they belong

Children need friends in order to develop emotionally and socially. Through interacting with friends, children learn how:

- to share and to take turns
- to set up rules, and
- to weigh alternatives and make decisions when faced with dilemmas.

Children and their families need an environment that is welcoming and reassuring; children need to feel that they belong. This sense of belonging can be promoted by:

- making all children feel valued for who they are – for example, celebrating their own cultures, achievements or significant events in their lives
- encouraging a strong sense of identity both individually and within a group
- giving children the chance to explore and talk about physical characteristics, things they like to do or to eat. These are important aspects of **self-identity** and also help children to learn about each other
- understanding and respecting the importance of each child's race, culture, ability and gender.

The need for new experiences and opportunities for play

Children learn best through first-hand experiences. These experiences help children to develop the skills of communication and concentration. They also provide opportunities for children to develop positive attitudes and to consolidate their learning. Children find stimulation, well-being and happiness through play, which is also the means by which they grow physically, intellectually and emotionally.

The need for praise and recognition

Growing up requires an enormous amount of learning – emotional, social and intellectual. Consequently, children need strong incentives to help them cope with any difficulties that they will inevitably encounter. The most effective incentives are praise and recognition sustained over time. Praise for new achievements helps to build the child's self-esteem and children love to be able to do things for themselves.

Good role models

Children need adults as good role models. Children learn to imitate our behaviour. They learn more from how they *see us act* than they do from anything we tell them.

Self-fulfilling prophecy

Children feel like failures when they cannot live up to the unrealistic hopes of their parents and are less likely to repeat their efforts. The lower the expectation of the adult, the lower the level of effort and achievement of the child – sometimes called the **self-fulfilling prophecy**.

Example: If an early years practitioner expects a child to underachieve, he or she may provide less encouragement, fewer challenging tasks and take less responsibility for that child's learning. Conversely, if the practitioner expects a child to achieve, he or she may provide more encouragement, more challenging tasks and take more responsibility for that child's learning. Each situation can create the environment for the expectation (or prophecy) to come true – a self-fulfilling prophecy.

Intrinsic motivation

If you make children feel anxious when they have not succeeded they will avoid activities likely to lead to failure. It is important to praise children appropriately when they try hard or have achieved something new, however small it might seem. This will motivate children to greater effort and lead to the desire to achieve something for its own sake; this is called intrinsic motivation, and promotes children's feelings of self-worth and self-esteem.

Example: Most people's hobbies are intrinsically motivated. People collect things or build complicated models just for the pleasure gained from doing so.

The need for responsibility, independence and self-reliance

Being responsible involves knowing what is to be done and how to do it. Children have different levels of understanding at different ages. The need for responsibility is met by allowing children to gain personal independence:

- firstly, through learning to look after themselves in matters of everyday care;
- then through a gradual extension of responsibility over other areas until they have the freedom and ability to decide on their own actions – for example, choosing for themselves what to wear or what game to play.

Encouraging children's self-reliance is an important part of helping them to develop the independence and resilience which will enable them to face life's demands and challenges in preparation for their adult lives. Encouraging self-reliance involves helping children to develop:

- independence (or autonomy) – the ability to think and act for themselves
- dependence on their own capabilities and personal resources
- competence in looking after themselves
- trust in their own judgement and actions
- confidence in their own abilities and actions.

Bonding

Donald Winnicott called the effect of the hormonal changes in late pregnancy 'primary maternal preoccupation'. He described it as a 'state of heightened sensitivity, almost an illness' which made the mother ready to fall in love with her baby, thus creating a mother–infant 'bond'. It used to be thought that this bonding happens rapidly in the first few days (or even hours) after the baby's birth, and a lack of early bonding meant problems in the future. It is now recognised that bonding is a process which is established over a period of time, and that it is the **quality** of the time the child spends with people which determines whether or not the child becomes attached to them.

Attachment

Attachment means a warm, affectionate and supportive bond between a child and his or her carer, which enables the child to develop **secure relationships**. When children receive warm, responsive care, they feel safe and secure.

The importance of attachment between infant and parent/carer

- **Secure attachments** are the basis of all the child's future relationships. Because babies experience relationships through their senses, it is the expression of love that affects how they develop and that helps to shape later learning and behaviour.
- **Children who are securely attached** tend to be more inquiring, to get along better with other children and to perform better in school than children who are less securely attached.
- With children who have a strong attachment to their parent or primary carer, the process of becoming attached to the practitioner is *easier*, not harder, than it is for children with a weaker attachment. Remember, though, that all parents or carers find separation difficult, whether or not they have formed a strong attachment with their child.

> **Key term**
>
> **attachment** A warm, affectionate and supportive bond between child and carer that enables the child to develop secure relationships.

The importance of loving, secure relationships

Babies learn and begin to make sense of the world through responsive care and loving, secure relationships. These relationships are equally important with their primary carer(s) and with their key person in the setting.

Babies and children who do not have loving, secure relationships with the important people in their lives are likely to find it difficult to settle and to enjoy being in the setting. This in turn may lead to difficulties with concentration, with engaging with others and with their general ability to learn.

> **Activity**
>
> - What happens during the process of bonding?
> - Why is it so important for children to develop secure attachments?
> - How do children develop secure, loving relationships?

AC 1.3 Evaluate the impact of secure relationships on a child's emotional well-being

The importance of secure attachments

When babies learn that they can rely completely on at least one person for their physical and emotional needs, they form what is known as a **secure attachment**. A baby or child who has internalised a strong attachment figure is then able to separate from that attachment figure and make relationships with other important adults in their lives.

Emotional security

Babies and children need to be able to trust others in order to feel emotionally secure. When there has been insecure or poor attachment – whether it is with their primary carer or parent, with adults in a setting, or both – they may begin to show antisocial behaviour and aggression towards others.

Effects on mental health

Babies and young children with poor-quality attachments may show less interest in exploring their environment than those with secure attachments. They may also display anxiety and even depression later on in life, although it is difficult to predict the cause-and-effect relationship as there are many other factors at work.

Effects on relationships with parents and professional carers

A baby's primary attachment is at its most intense between the ages of six months and one year, and it is then that the baby is likely to be acutely distressed when being left with a new carer. Babies who have experienced poor attachments at home may not feel able to trust the new carer enough to be able to form an attachment relationship. This is an unconscious self-defence mechanism – the baby does not want to experience emotional distress again.

Case study

Attachments

Maya is 11 months old and has recently started attending a local Children's Centre. Jennie, her key person, has observed that she appears uninterested in the adults in the centre, and also does not seem to notice a difference between regular staff and strangers who visit. Maya shows no anxiety or distress when her mother leaves her every day and Jennie is worried that there does not seem to be a close relationship between Maya and her mother. She has also observed that Maya does not seem to engage properly with play activities – she appears listless and apathetic, but rarely cries.

● What should Jennie do in this situation to ensure that Maya's needs are being met?

Temperament

Temperament is the term used to describe the different styles of behaviour in infancy; it interacts with experience to produce **personality**. The individual baby's temperament may have an influence on the quality of **attachment** to the main carer:

● A mother who is unresponsive and shows little sensitivity to her baby is likely to affect her baby's behaviour.
● A baby who likes to be cuddled and obviously wants plenty of contact with their primary carer tends to be more placid and easier to look after.
● A baby who actively resists being hugged or held tight even when ill or tired tends to be much more active and restless generally.

Treating each child as a unique individual

Although it is important to understand about differences in temperament and about how personality and temperament 'clashes' occur, we should always be wary of applying labels to children (and adults) as this leads to stereotyping and loss of self-esteem. It is very important that adults working with young children establish and maintain positive relationships with all children, and that they do not discriminate against any children.

LO2 Understand the requirements for promoting emotional well-being in relation to current frameworks

The **EYFS** in **England** states that: every child in a group setting must be assigned a key person. Providers must ensure support for children's emotional well-being to help them to know themselves and what they can do.

All frameworks in the UK emphasise the need for a key person system in every early years setting.

AC 2.1 Analyse the role of the key person in promoting emotional well-being

The importance of the key person

The way in which babies and young children are cared for may have a huge impact on how they will respond to difficulties and relationships later in life. Babies are totally dependent on our ability to be responsive to their needs. If they learn to feel and enjoy their parents' love, care, comfort and protection, they will start to feel secure and understood. Being in warm, loving surroundings, with plenty of physical contact, is the single most important factor for improving a baby's physical and emotional well-being. Babies and toddlers are more likely to feel safe and loved when the same familiar people are looking after them each day. As early years practitioners, you need, above all, to have 'empathy': to be able to appreciate the world from a baby's point of view.

Key term

key person The EYFS glossary defines a key person as: 'The named member of staff with whom a child has more contact than other adults. This adult shows a special interest in the child through close personal interaction day to day. The key person can help the young child to deal with separation anxiety.'

The role of the key person

A key person is sometimes thought of as the person who collects observations and updates records for a specific child. Although it is important for settings to have systems and procedures like these, they do not constitute a key person system.

A key person is:

- a named member of staff who has more contact than others with the child
- someone to build relationship with the child and parents
- someone who helps the child become familiar with the provision
- someone who meets children's individual needs and care needs (e.g. dressing, toileting, etc.)
- someone who responds sensitively to children's feelings, ideas and behaviour
- the person who acts as a point of contact with parents.

(from Dearnley, Elfer, Grenier, Manning-Morton and Wilson, 2008)

The **key person role** benefits the baby or child, the parents or carers and the key person. The benefits for **babies** are that:

- within the day-to-day demands of a nursery, each child feels special and individual, cherished and thought about by someone in particular while they are away from home
- the baby will experience a close relationship that is affectionate and reliable in the nursery as well as at home.

The benefits for **parents** are that:

- there is an opportunity to build a personal relationship with 'just one person' rather than 'all of them' in the nursery

- there is the possibility of building a partnership with professional staff who may share with them the pleasures and stresses of child rearing. It is liaising with someone else who loves your baby or child too.

The benefits for the **key person** are that:

- you feel that you really matter to a child and to their family
- you will probably have a profound influence on the baby's well-being, their mental health and their opportunities to learn.

The key person approach is very demanding physically and emotionally on the individual, as the relationship formed is intense. However, it also has benefits for the setting as an organisation, with more satisfied staff and fewer absences; better care and learning for the babies and children; and a parent clientele who are likely to develop a more trusting confidence in the abilities, qualities and dedication of professional staff.

Providing consistent, individual care

In nursery and crèche settings, each baby should be allocated to a key person who, ideally, is responsible for:

- the routine daily hands-on care, such as feeding, washing, changing
- observing the baby's development
- encouraging a wide range of play activities tailored to the baby's individual needs
- recording and reporting any areas of concern
- liaising with the baby's primary carers or parents and establishing a relationship that promotes mutual understanding.

Any setting that uses the key person system should have a strategy for dealing with staff absence or holidays.

Guidelines for supporting parents

It takes time for staff to get to know a parent but you can help to alleviate some of their concerns, and to provide quality care and education for children by doing the following:

- Show empathy – try to put yourself in the parent's shoes and follow the guidelines on p 142 for settling in new children.

- Welcome parents and make time for them – make friendly contact with the child's parents. You need to be approachable. Try not to appear rushed even when you have a really busy nursery.
- Help parents to separate from their baby – when a baby is handed from the parent to a new carer, it is best if:

→

- you approach slowly
- you talk gently before picking up and taking the baby from the parent
- the baby is held looking at the parent during the handover.
- Explain how you will be caring for the baby – for example, describe the daily routines and the layout of the setting.
- Be aware of your particular situation and your responsibilities – you need to maintain a professional relationship with parents (even if they also happen to be your friends) and work as a team member in an early years setting.

- Show that you enjoy being with the baby – physical contact is important; encourage 'conversations' with babies; smile and talk to them.
- Always act in the interests of the child – use your knowledge of holistic development and your powers of observation to enable you to tailor the care you give to the individual baby's needs.
- Keep parents and other staff members informed – you need to know how and when to pass on information to parents about their baby's care; and to observe the rules of confidentiality (see pp 166–67).

Activity ·

What is the role of the key person in promoting children's emotional well-being? Analyse the different responsibilities involved in the role.

· ·

LO3 Understand the needs of children during transition and significant events

AC 3.1 Identify transitions and significant events that a child may experience

What are transitions?

A transition is a period of change from one stage or state to another. Children and young people naturally pass through a number of stages as they grow and develop. Often, they will also be expected to cope with changes such as movement from nursery education to primary school, and from primary to secondary school.

You may have just made the transition from secondary school to a tertiary college or sixth form. Along with the excitement of a new course and possibly making new friends, you are likely to have felt some apprehension about the change to your life. This is likely to affect you more if you have experienced many changes in your life. These changes are commonly referred to as transitions.

Types of transitions

Transitions can affect all areas of the development of children and young people:

- **Emotional**: personal experiences, such as parents separating, bereavement, entering or leaving care
- **Physical**: moving to a new educational setting, a new home or care setting
- **Intellectual**: moving from nursery to primary school, or primary to secondary school
- **Physiological**: puberty or a long-term medical condition.

Expected transitions

Many transitions are universal; they are experienced by almost everyone, and can usually be anticipated, or expected. **Babies** experience transitions when they:

- are weaned onto solid food
- are able to be cared for by others, such as at nursery or a childminder's home
- progress from crawling to walking
- move from needing nappies to being toilet trained.

Children experience transitions when they:

- start and move through day care
- start nursery and then primary school
- move up to secondary school.

Unexpected transitions

Not every transition is experienced by every child, and not all transitions can be anticipated. These unexpected transitions include:

- the birth of a new baby in the family (although this is a very common transition, it is not always expected)
- an unexpected change of school or childcare provider
- moving house
- living outside of the home
- violence or abuse within the family
- parents divorcing; having a new step-parent and perhaps new stepfamily
- serious illness, accident or death in the family.

Supporting the child and family through transitions

Children and young people need practitioners who are able to recognise the importance of attachment and emotional well-being during periods of transition, and who are able to identify the needs of an individual child and his or her family. The **key person** approach is vital to supporting young children through transitions, and is also frequently used in health care and social care settings when transitions are necessary. The key person system supports children through transitions by providing opportunities for:

- respecting the child as unique, with individual emotional needs
- warm, affectionate relationships between practitioners and babies and young children
- practitioners to listen to children and tune in to them.

Some families will have a lead professional working with them to ensure that there is more joined-up thinking and that different professionals link with each other.

AC 3.2 Describe potential effects of transitions and significant events on a child's life

Understanding the potential effects of transitions

You need to be able to identify transitions and understand what you can do to support children through them. Before we can fully understand the importance of transitions in children's lives, we need to learn about the concepts of attachment and separation, and the effects of multiple transitions in a child's life.

Separation

Many of the times that prove to be difficult for children are connected with separation. Going to bed is separation from the main carer and is often a source of anxiety in children. Some young children can be terrified as a parent walks out of the room. How children react to separation is as varied as children's characteristics. For some children every new situation will bring questions and new feelings of anxiety; other children love the challenge of meeting new friends and seeing new things.

The effects of multiple transitions

Children who have had to make many moves or changes may feel a sense of loss and grief. These changes may have a profound effect on their emotional and social development. Reasons for transitions include:

● Divorce or separation: children whose parents have separated or divorced may have to live and get along with several 'new' people, such as stepfathers, stepmothers, half-brothers and half-sisters, etc.

● **Changes in childcare arrangements**: children who experience many different childcare arrangements; for example, frequent changes from one nanny or childminder to another.

● Children who are in local authority care – either in residential children's homes or in foster care.

● Children whose families have moved house several times, perhaps for employment reasons, or as Travellers.

How children feel when they transfer to a new setting

You need to be able to identify transitions and understand what you can do to support children through them. Many of the problems relating to transitions in childhood are associated with **separation**. As children become older, they start to cope better with being separated from their parents or main carers, but the way in which they cope will still depend on their early experiences of separation and how earlier transitions were managed. Children who have had multiple transitions (perhaps changing schools or homes many times, possibly caused by changes to a parent's job) often find it harder to settle in and make new friends and relationships.

Transitions can affect the development of children and young people in different ways. There can be positive as well as negative effects; they can also be short-term or long-term, depending on the individual child or young person and on how effectively they are supported. Possible effects of transitions are given in Table 1.4.2.

How a child may react	Effect of this experience on the child
Emotional withdrawal	Children may withdraw from new relationships with other children and with carers, because they do not trust the separation not to happen again.
Disorientated	No sooner have children settled in one place and got to know a carer, they may be uprooted and have to face the same process again.
A sense of loss	Every time children make a move, they lose the friends they have made and also the attachments they have formed with their carers.
Regressive	Reverting to behaviour usually shown by younger children; for example, a child who was previously dry at night may start to wet the bed, or an older child might start to talk in a more 'babyish' way.
Depression	This may show in a number of ways: sadness, problems in sleeping, crying and lack of appetite.
Separation anxiety	Children become clingy and need to be near their parent or primary carer to feel reassured.
Changes in behaviour	Young children may have frequent tantrums; older children may show challenging behaviour.
Lack of motivation	Children may have difficulty in concentrating on schoolwork and become easily distracted.

Table 1.4.2 Effect of transitions on children

AC 3.3 Explain the role of the EYP in preparing a child for a planned transition

Strategies to support and prepare children for transfers and transitions

Being separated from our loved ones is difficult at any age, and a feeling of bereavement can be experienced. In situations where children are repeatedly separated from their families, through home circumstances or war and conflict, it helps when the adults with whom the child is left understand the elements discussed in this chapter, so that vulnerable children feel a sense of belonging and well-being, and feelings of being valued, loved and respected.

Guidelines for preparing children for transfers and transitions

- Remember that if the parent is anxious about leaving their child, the child will be anxious about being separated from the parent. Make sure that every adult and child is welcomed. Put notices in the languages of the community as well as in English.
- A noticeboard with photographs of staff and descriptions of their role helps people to feel familiar with the environment.
- An attractive display of some of the recent experiences gained by the children helps people to tune in to the setting's way of working.

- A notice with the menu for the week gives valuable information to parents and carers.
- Something for children to do is vital; watching fish in a fish tank or having a turn on a rocking horse are popular examples.

It is also important to remember that Anna Freud, working with children who had experienced the Holocaust, found that their friendships with each other were very important, and so was having a normal childhood with opportunities for sensitively supported play. Play seemed to have a self-healing power.

AC 3.4 Explain the role of the EYP in supporting children's needs during transition and significant life events

It is important that times of transition are as positive as possible, both for the individual child and the family as a whole. Transitions can be painful, and some of the separations in the list of examples could never be happy experiences for children or those who love them and whom they love. However, it is always possible to ease the impact of difficult separations through thoughtful, organised and sensitive support.

From the home environment to the early years setting

This might be when the family visits the early years setting or it might be through a home visit. It is important that parents do not feel forced into accepting a home visit from staff. Often families welcome home visits as an opportunity to get to know the early years practitioner. A home visit, or a visit to the setting before the child starts there, gives staff the chance to find out what the parents are expecting from the setting. All this helps parents and children to make the transition from being at home to starting in a group setting. Childminders and nannies often make photograph albums with short captions in the same spirit.

Parents and children often appreciate having a booklet of their own to keep, and this can build into a record of the child's time with the setting, childminder or nanny. This often helps a child to make future transitions.

When settling a child and family, transitions are made easier if there is sensitivity about the way you use gesture and body language, such as eye contact.

The photographs in the brochure can be invaluable when staff and family do not share the same language.

Settling children into the setting

Probably the most important thing an early years practitioner does is to settle a child into an early years group, in partnership with the parents or carers. This is usually called the settling-in period.

This is a very important time for everyone. Parents will not necessarily know what sort of approaches will help their child, and what will hinder the process of settling in. Equally, practitioners will not know the child well and what the child finds soothing or upsetting. So it is important to maintain good communication with parent throughout the process. The parent knows the child best, the practitioner has the most experience of helping children to settle in: it is by combining their knowledge that they can best help the child.

Every child, and every family, is unique. Children's responses to starting nursery will vary from full-on enthusiasm, to wariness, to a great deal of crying and clinging. None of these responses is, in itself, a cause for concern and it is helpful to reassure parents about this. No child's needs can fully be met by a key person: there is bound to be some unhappiness, or uncertainty.

The first few days at a nursery or playgroup can be very daunting for some children. They may not have been left by their parents or primary carers ever before and some children will show real distress. You need to be able to recognise their distress and to find ways of dealing with it. Children show their distress at being separated from their carer by crying and refusing to join in with activities. Parents too can feel distressed when leaving their children in the care of others; they may feel guilty because they have to return to work, or they may be upset because they have never before been separated from their child.

How to support the needs of children during transition

You can help a child to settle in by following the suggestions given below.

- **Trying to plan for the separation**: nursery staff can help by visiting the child and their parents at home. This gives both parents and children the opportunity to talk about their fears and helps them to cope with them. When children know in advance what is going to happen, they can think about and get used to their feelings about it. Parents can be encouraged to prepare their child for the change by:
  - visiting the nursery with their child so that they can meet the staff
  - reading books about starting at a nursery or going to hospital, and
  - involving their child in any preparation, such as buying clothing or packing a 'nursery bag'.
- **Encouraging parents to stay with their child until the child seems settled**: this does not mean that the parents should cling to their child. Children can always sense a parent's uncertainty. Although young children do not have a very good sense of time, parents and carers should make it very clear when they will be back (e.g. saying 'I'll be back in one hour').
- **Allowing the child to bring a comforter** – for example, a blanket or a teddy bear – to the nursery. If it is a blanket, sometimes the parent can cut a little piece and put it in the child's pocket if they think there will be any embarrassment. Then the child can handle the blanket and feel comforted when feeling lonely.
- **Having just one person to settle the child**: hold and cuddle the child and try to involve him or her in a quiet activity with you (e.g. reading a story). Most settings now employ a key person who will be responsible for one or two children during the settling-in period.
- **Contacting the parent or primary carer** if the child does not settle within 20 minutes or so. Sometimes it is not possible to do this, and you will need to devise strategies for comforting and reassuring the child. Always be honest with parents regarding the time it took to settle their child.

Figure 1.4.1 This child uses his teddy as a comfort object

Research activity

Settling-in period at nursery
Watch **Life at Two: Attachments, Key People and Development** from www.sirenfilms.co.uk which shows Eva as she first visits and then settles into her nursery. What did the nursery staff do to help Eva and her mother?

Early years settings usually have a policy and procedure for settling-in periods. The leaflet on settling-in produced for parents of children at Kate Greenaway Nursery School helps parents to understand the ways in which the nursery supports children during this transition.

Other transitions and significant events

Where children are facing other transitions or significant events in their lives – such as bereavement or loss, or the arrival of a new sibling – their key person will need to be especially sensitive to their feelings and always take time to talk with them about how they are feeling. Opportunities should be provided for children to express their feelings in a safe and unthreatening environment. For example, some children may be encouraged to use play dough to release pent-up feelings of frustration; others may choose to use role play.

The importance of providing continuity of experiences for children

Whenever there is a transitional point for a child and family, it is important to look at *what went before*. This is so that we can learn about and tune in to the child, and support them and make as seamless a transition as possible. There should

---

The settling-in period

The settling-in period is this time when you are here with your child in the Nursery School. It is a time for your child to get to know his or her key person – with the reassurance of having you here too. As the relationship develops, your child will be able to trust that:

- the key person and the other staff in the nursery are able to meet her or his needs
- they can be helpful, comforting and deal positively with any problems
- they can provide interesting experiences which make it worthwhile to come to Nursery.

The settling-in process gives you a chance to check out:

- what type of nursery this is
- how the staff work
- what kinds of experiences we offer to the children.

Our aim is to settle children in at their own pace – when children are ready to move away from their parents, we will encourage and support this. We have found that in the long run, this means more settled and happier children – and parents!

The settling-in process

1. The home visit (if you chose to have one). This can be very special for a child – often children remember it for a long time. The home visit helps your child to begin an attachment with the key person on 'home territory'.

2. Your child spending time in the Nursery room with you. During this time, you are available to support your child and to help staff get to know your child. It is best to be available to your child but not too interesting! We are aware that both you and your child may be feeling stress, and your child may not be on 'best behaviour'. Please don't worry about this.

3. Your child spending time in the Nursery room whilst you are in another part of the building. It will be up to you and your key person to decide when your child is ready. This might be for quite a short period of time at first, and then for longer stretches of time. Please note that is always very important that you say clearly to your child that you will be leaving the nursery room. It's tempting to nip out when your child is busy, but if your child turns round a few minutes later to find you have unexpectedly gone, she or he may be really upset.

4. Finally, it is for you to judge – with the support of the key person – when your child is ready to be left in the nursery with the staff. Your child might be very sad or angry at the moment of parting, but if the settling-in process has gone well, she or he will be able to manage this with the support of the key person and other members of staff. If your child continues to be upset after you have gone, please be reassured that we would contact you and would not put your child through an ordeal. When saying goodbye, some parents find it easiest to set a limit on how long they will stay (e.g. 'I'll read two books with you and then it will be time for me to go.') Other parents like to have a special ritual like:

- going to the sofa and reading a book
- waving goodbye through the glass doors
- kiss-cuddle-high five.

It is up to you how you manage this, but please do ask for support or advice if it will be helpful. Please make sure that you always bring your child right into the nursery room and make your key person or another member of staff aware before you leave.

It is not uncommon for a child to settle very well into the nursery, and then unexpectedly a few weeks later to find it difficult to come in. This might be for any one of a variety of reasons, and again we will offer our support or help if you would like it. You are always welcome to phone and ask how your child is getting on at any time of the day.

Figure 1.4.2 Leaflet on settling-in for parents from Kate Greenaway Nursery School and Children's Centre

In practice activity

An activity to support children in settling in

This activity will help a child who is new to the setting to realise that he or she is not alone, and that other children also feel shy and alone at times.

- **Introduction**: choose a teddy and introduce him to the group, saying something like: 'Teddy is rather shy and a little bit lonely. How can we help him to feel better?'
- **Discussion and display**: take photos of Teddy – using a digital camera if possible – with different groups of children, and in different places in the nursery (for example, playing in the sand, reading a book, doing a puzzle) and use later for discussion and display.
- **Circle time**: in circle time, pass Teddy round, and encourage each child to say something to him:

'Hello Teddy, my name is Lara' or 'Hello Teddy, I like chocolate …', etc.

- **Taking Teddy home**: every child takes it in turns to take Teddy home. Include a notebook and encourage parents to write a few sentences about what Teddy did at their house that evening. The children can draw a picture.
- **Story time**: read and act out the story of Goldilocks and the Three Bears, with the different-sized bowls, beds and chairs.
- **Cooking**: use a shaped cutter to make teddy-shaped biscuits or dough teddies.
- **Teddy bears' picnic**: Arrange a teddy bears' picnic where each child brings in a favourite bear. What does your teddy like to eat? Are there enough plates, biscuits and cups for all the bears?

---

be **continuity**, not discontinuity of experience for the child and family. This means that every practitioner working with young children in the birth-to-five-years age range should know what comes before and what comes after the time the child will spend with them. For example, a practitioner working in England will need to know about:

- Early Years Foundation Stage
- Curriculum Guidance for the Foundation Stage
- Key Stage 1.

The DfES has developed a mainstream training package for the transition between the Foundation Stage and Key Stage 1, called *Continuing the Learning Journey*.

LO4 Promote the emotional well-being of children in own setting

AC 4.1 Identify children's needs in own setting in relation to emotional well-being

Your role in identifying children's needs

If you become concerned about a possible emotional, behavioural or mental health problem in a child, you should work to find out how you can promote their emotional well-being.

Careful observations are the key to this process of identification of needs.

Observations

Observation is the key to finding solutions for children who are struggling to manage their feelings. By observing closely, practitioners can find out what happens before the child behaves in an antisocial way, exactly how they react and what happens next.

- Observe the child over a period of time. Many problems are transient, so it is important to build up a picture over a set period.
- Write down your observations about the behaviour or situation.
- Consider the potential impact on development, well-being or learning.

Action

- Decide what action should be taken. Talk with the child and/or with their parents or caregivers, depending on their age and stage of development.
- Discuss your observations sensitively and explain your concerns in regard to the child's development, well-being or learning.
- Ask about any factors at home that may be affecting the child.

Involving colleagues

- Talk with your line manager or teacher to develop a plan for assisting the child within your setting.

- Referral for specialist intervention and support may be needed – for example, the family's GP or Inclusion Support Agency.

Activity •

Observe a child whom you have noticed may be having problems with any aspect of emotional well-being. For example, you may have noticed a child who appears withdrawn or miserable, or a child who is experiencing problems with a transition. Discuss your observations with a colleague, and decide what action, if any, may be required to promote the child's well-being.

• •

AC 4.2 Work with children in a way that promotes their emotional well-being

Working with children in a way that supports independence

Children need the freedom to develop their independence in ways that are appropriate to their overall development. Some children may need more encouragement than others to become increasingly independent and less reliant on other people.

Most children start wanting to do things for themselves from about 18 months to two years onwards. While young children want to do things for themselves (for example, getting dressed, making things), they may become frustrated if they cannot do things for themselves. Many conflicts arise between young children and other people as children increase their independence and expand the boundaries of their world.

Adults caring for children should avoid inhibiting the child's need for independence as this can lead to either emotional dependence, excessive shyness and an overcautious nature or emotional detachment, antisocial behaviour and a rebellious nature. Adults should also avoid unrestricted independence as the child may be exposed to danger and physical harm (for example, from fire, boiling water, traffic) and/or the child may become selfish and unable to recognise the needs and rights of others. Adults should strike a balance between these two extremes. You should provide a balance between allowing for the individual child's need for independence, and

providing supervision with guidelines for socially appropriate behaviour which takes into account the needs of everyone in the early years setting.

Working with children in a way that builds resilience and perseverance

Children who are resilient have high self-esteem. Children need inner strength to deal competently with the many challenges and demands they encounter. This ability to face the ups and downs of life and to cope with the its demands is called resilience. They have learnt to set realistic goals and expectations, and have developed the ability to solve problems and make decisions. Being resilient also involves having good relationships with their peers and with adults.

You can help children to build resilience by:

- **Being empathetic**: showing that, even if you disagree with their point of view, you can put yourself in their shoes and that you always try to value their ways of thinking.
- **Communicating effectively – by tuning in to children and listening actively**: effective communication involves actively listening to children; loving our children in ways that help them feel special and appreciated.
- **Accepting children for who they are** and helping them set realistic expectations and goals. When children feel accepted, it is easier for them to respond to requests and limits because they experience these in an atmosphere of love and support.
- **Helping children to experience success**: it is important to identify and promote each child's strengths rather than focusing on their weaknesses.
- **Setting realistic expectations**: children need to know that they are accepted and loved even when they make mistakes. Resilient children tend to view mistakes as opportunities for learning, whereas children who have not developed resilience often feel they are failures.
- **Supporting children to solve problems and make decisions**: try to engage them in thinking about possible solutions to a problem, so that they feel they are in control of the situation.

Guidelines: How to show a child that you are actively listening

1 **STOP**: pay attention. When a child or young person approaches you with something to share, stop what you are doing and pay attention. This lets her know that you are listening and that you value what she is saying.
2 **LOOK**: make eye contact. Get down to her level, face her directly and make eye contact. Also show that you are listening through body language, such as by smiling and nodding.

3 **LISTEN**: listen attentively. Focus your attention on what she is saying by listening to her words and tone of voice. Listen carefully to what she actually says as well as what she might be trying to say.
4 **RESPOND**: respond appropriately. Having listened carefully to what has been said, you could paraphrase what she has just said, ask open-ended questions, or prompt her to say more, by saying 'That's interesting' or 'Oh, I see.'

● **Showing fairness and consistency**: children need to know what is and what is not allowed. Positive feedback and encouragement are important. Each child's needs must be considered; for example, a confident, talkative child or a child with behavioural difficulties may take up a lot of your time, but it is important to watch out for the quiet child who seems not to need you when playing alone.

Key term

active listening The process of actively seeking to understand the meaning of another person's communication, whether the communication is spoken or conveyed in a different way. Active listening includes the use of verbal and non-verbal skills.

Working with children in a way that builds confidence and supports self-reliance

The self-confidence and self-esteem of young children can be greatly boosted by a strong key person approach in the setting. Many aspects of this approach support the safeguarding of children.

● **Listening and tuning in to a child** – this will include noticing changes in a child's behaviour and emotional well-being, and developing a trusting relationship so that the child can tell you if things are upsetting him or her. Taking a child's concerns seriously is important. Often, when a child has been bullied or abused in some way, he or she will try to communicate what has happened. The child needs to know that

you are there to listen and, most importantly, that you will believe what he or she tells you.
● **Allowing a child to express his or her feelings** – if a child is allowed to express sadness and anger, as well as happiness and enjoyment, he or she may feel more confident that it is all right to have a range of emotions. The child will be more likely to tell other people how he or she is feeling.
● **Increasing a child's confidence** – this involves making a child feel a sense of belonging, and that he or she is special for his or her unique qualities. It is important to show a genuine interest in what a child has to say, and to praise him or her for any achievements. A quick 'That's lovely, Suhail' is really not enough to show a child that you value him.
● **Observing a child** and keeping **regular records** of his or her behaviour – the key person is in a strong position to note any changes of behaviour or signs of insecurity that could result from child abuse.

Working with children in a way that equips children to protect themselves

Child protection not only involves the detection of abuse and neglect but also the prevention of abuse by helping children to protect themselves. As part of this preventative role you should help children to do the following:

● understand what is and is not acceptable behaviour towards them
● stay safe from harm
● speak up if they have worries and concerns
● develop awareness and resilience.

Being actively involved in prevention helps children to keep safe both now and in the future. Children need to know how to take responsibility for themselves and to understand the consequences of their actions. Children should know and understand:

- that they all deserve care and respect
- their rights and how to assert them
- how to do things safely and how to minimise risk
- how to deal with abusive or potentially abusive situations
- when and how to ask for help and support.

Critical thinking and decision-making are also essential for helping children to keep themselves safe. You can help them to develop these skills by encouraging them to participate in decision-making within the setting and providing opportunities for cooperation.

Working with children in a way that builds relationships between children

Socialisation involves how children relate socially (and emotionally) to other people. Children need to learn how to deal appropriately with a whole range of emotions, including anger and frustration, within a supportive environment. Socialisation occurs through the observation, identification, imitation and assimilation of the behaviour of other people. Children model their attitudes and actions on the behaviour of others. You need to be aware of the significant impact you make on children's social (and emotional) development, and ensure that you provide a **positive role model**. An essential aspect of socialisation involves getting young children to behave in socially acceptable ways without damaging their self-esteem: that is, rejecting the children's unacceptable behaviour, not the children themselves. Socialisation begins from birth, as babies interact with the people around them and respond to their environment.

Activity ·······································

Describe ways in which you can work with children to support their emotional well-being.

·······························

AC 4.3 Plan an activity to promote emotional well-being in own setting

Unit 3.2 provides information to assist with the planning and implementing of play activities. When choosing an activity to promote emotional well-being in your setting, consider the following questions:

What sort of activities in the setting help children to think about:

- the things that make them feel good about themselves?
- the people who help them?
- how to keep themselves safe?
- how to recognise and avoid possible danger?
- reasons for making particular choices?
- the reason they are allowed to do or to have some things and not other things?

Suggested activities may focus on:

- role-play opportunities
- imaginative play which takes into account different cultures and lifestyles through a variety of utensils, costumes and small world props
- play with malleable materials, e.g. sand and water, dough
- musical activities that provide opportunities for releasing pent-up emotions
- dolls and puppets which reflect a mix of both gender and cultural diversity
- stories, songs and poetry that explore different emotions
- toys and games which require cooperative play
- games which encourage turn-taking
- activities to promote self-reliance skills: e.g. hand-washing routines, skills in dressing self and managing buttons and shoelaces.

AC 4.4 Implement an activity to promote emotional well-being in own setting

Carry out the activity you have planned, noting what works particularly well in order to evaluate the activity.

Activity

Implement an activity for a group of children in your setting which promotes emotional well-being. Afterwards, reflect on what worked particularly well in the activity. For example:

- Were all children able to join in?
- How could you improve the activity next time?

AC 4.5 Reflect on own role when promoting emotional well-being in own setting

In line with the CACHE values, you need to ensure that the child is at the *centre* of your practice; their needs are paramount. This means that every child is valued for his or her individuality. As a practitioner, your role is:

- to listen to children
- not to impose your own agenda on them
- not to single out any one child for special attention
- to ensure that children maintain control over their own play
- to be friendly, courteous and sensitive to their needs
- to praise and motivate them; display their work
- to speak to the child – not at the child; with young children, this means getting down to their level and maintaining eye contact
- to respect their individuality

- to develop a sense of trust and caring with each child.

Reflecting on your own practice

Being able to reflect on your practice in planning and providing opportunities for play will help you to understand which things have worked well – and which have not worked so well. This will help you to think of ways to improve your practice. There are various ways to reflect on your practice. These include:

- observing the children's responses during play – their enjoyment and skill development
- reviewing what worked well and what did not work so well – in terms of equipment provided, numbers of children involved and an assessment of how involved children were in their play
- asking children for feedback
- asking colleagues for feedback
- recording your reflections in a Reflective Diary.

Identifying your strengths and weaknesses and how to improve your practice

Practitioners need to reflect on their own contributions to good practice. This involves identifying their strengths and weaknesses.

Activity

Identify your own strengths and weaknesses when promoting emotional well-being in your own setting. How could you improve your practice in this area?

In practice

How to praise and encourage children

- Give praise and positive feedback for all achievements, however small.
- Be prompt in giving praise and encouragement, as the effect is much greater when delivered immediately after the effort or achievement.
- Encourage children to make choices and to try new things; sometimes they need to learn by their mistakes.
- Avoid making comparisons with another child.
- Always remember the child is an individual.

- Encourage them to feel included in decision-making and respond to their questions in a considerate way.
- Be specific about why you are praising them: Avoid general praise, such as: 'You've done well today.' Instead say: 'Well done, Jack, for helping to clear away all the blocks.'

Guidelines for promoting a positive self-image and sense of well-being in children

- Value children for who they are, not what they do or how they look.
- A child needs love, security and a feeling of trust. There is no single way to give these feelings to children: it will depend on where children live, their family and culture. There is no standard family or institution, or a single best way to love children and give them self-esteem.
- People who give children positive images about themselves (in terms of skin colour, language, gender, disability, features, culture and economic background) help children to develop good self-esteem. Look at the book area and the displays on the walls in your setting. Are you giving positive messages?
- Visitors to the nursery can provide positive images. The people children meet occasionally or on a daily basis will all have a strong influence on them. If children almost never see men working in early years settings or women mending pieces of equipment, they form very narrow ideas about who they might become. Books, pictures, outings and visitors can all offer positive images which extend children's ideas of who they might be.
- Adults who are positive role models help a child's self-esteem.
- Children need to feel some success in what they set out to do. This means that adults must avoid having unrealistic expectations of what children can manage, such as dressing, eating or going to the toilet. It is important to appreciate the efforts that children make.
- They do not have to produce perfect results: the effort is more important than the result.

- Adults help children's self-esteem if they are encouraging. When children make mistakes, do not tell them they are silly or stupid. Instead say something like, 'Never mind, let's pick up the pieces and sweep them into the bin. Next time, if you hold it with two hands it will be easier to work with.'
- Children need to feel they have some choices in their lives. Obviously, safety and consideration for others are important, but it is usually possible to allow children to make some decisions.
- Children need clear, consistent boundaries or they become confused. When they are confused they begin to test out the boundaries to see what is consistent about them.
- Children need consistent care from people they know. Many early years settings have now introduced a key person or family person system, which provides continuity.
- Children need to have a feeling of trust that their basic needs for food, rest and shelter will be met. Rigid rituals are not helpful, but days do need a shape or routine. This will give children a predictable environment. They will have the know-how to help in setting the table, for example, or washing their hands after going to the toilet.
- Children and their families need to be given respect so that they can then develop self-respect. Children, parents and staff need to speak politely and respectfully to each other.
- Children have strong and deep feelings. They need help, support and care from adults.

LO5 AC 5.1 Critically evaluate provision in own setting in relation to promoting emotional well-being in line with current frameworks and theoretical perspectives

In order to critically evaluate provision in relation to the promotion of emotional well-being, you need to use your critical abilities to:

- examine the strengths and weaknesses, and
- evaluate the ways in which the provision promotes emotional well-being with reference to current frameworks and the theoretical perspective discussed above.

Activity

Using the information provided in this unit, particularly LO1 and LO2, write a report which critically evaluates the provision in your own setting in relation to promoting well-being.

1 Evaluate how your setting provides for children's needs for:
- love and security
- having friends and for feeling that they belong
- new experiences and opportunities for play
- praise and recognition
- responsibility.
2 Evaluate how the key person system provides children with support during times of transition – both planned and unplanned.

Assessment practice

1 What do you understand by the term emotional well-being? Explain the theoretical perspectives on emotional well-being.

2 Explain what is meant by the processes of bonding, attachment and developing secure relationships.

3 Evaluate the impact of secure relationships on a child's emotional well-being.

4 Describe and analyse the role of the key person in promoting emotional well-being.

5 What is meant by a transition? Describe the different transitions a child might experience.

6 Describe the potential effects of transition and significant events on a child's life.

7 Describe your role in preparing a child for a planned transition.

8 Describe your role in supporting the needs of children during transition and significant life events.

9 Identify the needs of children in your own setting in relation to emotional well-being.

10 Describe the way in which you should work to support children's emotional well-being.

11 Plan and implement an activity in your own setting to promote emotional well-being.

12 Reflect on your own role when promoting emotional well-being in the setting.

13 Using the current frameworks and theoretical perspectives, critically evaluate provision in your own setting in relation to promoting emotional well-being.

Useful resources

Films

Siren Films: High-quality DVDs showing the importance of attachments and key people in the EYFS: www.sirenfilms.co.uk

Books and articles

Bowlby, J. (1969), *Attachment and Loss. Vol. I: Attachment.* London: Hogarth Press.

Bruce, T. (2005), *Early Childhood Education and Care* (3rd edn). London: Hodder Arnold.

Elfer, P. and Dearnley, K. (2007), 'Nurseries and emotional well-being: Evaluating an emotionally containing model of continuing professional development', *Early Years: An International Journal of Research and Development* 27(3): 267–79.

Dearnley, K., Elfer, P., Grenier, J., Manning-Morton, J. and Wilson, D. (2008) 'Appendix 1: The key person in reception classes and small nursery settings', in *Social and Emotional Aspects of Development: Guidance for Practitioners Working in the Early Years Foundation Stage*. Nottingham: DCSF Publications, available at http://nationalstrategies.standards.dcsf.gov.uk/node/132720.

Freud, A., in collaboration with Dorothy Burlingham (1973) *The Writings of Anna Freud. Vol. III: Infants Without Families [and] Reports on the Hampstead Nurseries, 1939–1945*. New York: International Universities Press.

Isaacs, S. (1945), *Childhood and After: Some Essays and Clinical Studies*. London: Agathon Press.

Winnicott, D.W. (1964), *The Child, the Family and the Outside World*. London: Penguin Books.

Unit 1.5 Understand how to support children who are unwell

This unit provides the learner with the knowledge and understanding of how to support children who are unwell.

Learning outcomes

By the end of this unit you will:

1 Know common childhood illnesses.
2 Know the signs of ill health in children.
3 Understand legal requirements for reporting notifiable diseases.
4 Understand the role of the early years practitioner in minimising ill health in children.
5 Understand care routines when a child is ill.
6 Understand how to support children for planned hospital admission.
7 Understand the therapeutic role of play in hospitals.
8 Understand the role of the early years practitioner when supporting children who are chronically ill.

LO1 Know common childhood illnesses

Infections are a major cause of illness in children, and they range from a mild attack of the common cold to a life-threatening illness such as meningitis. Children are particularly susceptible to infection because their immune systems have not yet built up resistance. Most common childhood infections are not serious and clear up quickly. Some serious viral infections, such as measles and rubella, are less common now because of routine immunisation. Bacterial infections can usually be cured rapidly by antibiotics.

How infection is spread

Infectious diseases are caused by both bacteria and viruses. Infection enters the body in several ways:

- **droplet infection**: this occurs by breathing in air containing tiny droplets of infected mucus from an infected person's sneeze or cough. For example, colds, flu, pneumonia and whooping cough are spread by coughs and sneezes.

- **touching infected people:** germs can be spread by touching (or kissing) someone who is infected or by using the things they have used, e.g. towels, combs and cups. (This may also be called a contagious disease.) For example, chickenpox and measles can be caught by touching infected people, and athlete's foot can be caught by walking on wet floors or mats used by infected people.

- **infected food or drink**: food and drink can be infected with germs by coughs and sneezes, dirty hands, flies, mice and pet animals. For example, infected food and drink cause food poisoning and dysentery.

AC 1.1 and AC 1.2 Identify common childhood illnesses and Describe signs and symptoms

Illness in babies

Common illnesses in babies include colds, coughs, fevers and vomiting. Babies also often have skin disorders, like nappy rash or cradle cap. Many of these problems are not serious, but some may require medical help. Table 1.5.1 shows the more common illnesses in babies.

Key terms

colic Colic is persistent, unexplained crying in a healthy baby between two weeks and five months of age.

cyanosis A bluish discoloration of the skin and mucous membranes resulting from inadequate oxygenation of the blood.

hypothermia Hypothermia, a potentially fatal condition, occurs when body temperature falls below 35°C (95°F).

meningitis Infection or inflammation of the membranes (meninges) that cover the brain and spinal cord.

possetting When a baby regularly vomits small amounts of her feeds but has no sign of illness. Usually caused by a weakness of the muscle at the opening of the stomach.

Illness in babies		
Condition	**Signs and symptoms**	**Role of the carer**
Colic	This occurs in the first 12 weeks. It causes sharp, spasmodic pain in the stomach, and is often at its worst in the late evening. Symptoms include inconsolable high-pitched crying, drawing her legs up to her chest, and growing red in the face.	Try to stay calm and seek medical intervention. Gently massage her abdomen in a clockwise direction, using the tips of your middle fingers.
Diarrhoea	Frequent loose or watery stools. Can be very serious in young babies, especially when combined with vomiting, as it can lead to severe dehydration.	Give frequent small drinks of cooled, boiled water containing glucose and salt or a made-up sachet of rehydration fluid. If the baby is unable to take the fluid orally, they must be taken to hospital urgently and fed intravenously, by a 'drip'. If anal area becomes sore, treat with a barrier cream.
Gastro-enteritis	The baby may vomit and usually has diarrhoea as well; often has a raised temperature and loss of appetite. May show signs of abdominal pain, i.e. drawing up of legs to chest and crying.	Reassure baby. Observe strict hygiene rules. Watch out for signs of dehydration. Offer frequent small amounts of fluid, and possibly rehydration salts.
Neonatal cold injury – or hypothermia	The baby is cold to the touch. Face may be pale or flushed. Lethargic, runny nose, swollen hands and feet. Pre-term infants and babies under 4 months are at particular risk.	Warm *slowly* by covering with several light layers of blankets and by cuddling. Do not use direct heat. Offer feeds high in sugar and seek medical help urgently.
Reflux	Also known as gastro-intestinal reflux (GIR) or gastro-oesophageal reflux (GOR). The opening to the stomach is not yet efficient enough to allow a large liquid feed through. Symptoms include 'grizzly' crying and excessive possetting after feeds.	Try feeding the baby in a more upright position and bring up wind by gently rubbing her back. After feeding leave the baby in a semi-sitting position. Some doctors prescribe a paediatric reflux suppressant or antacid mixture to be given before the feed.
Tonsillitis	Very sore throat, which looks bright red. There is usually fever and the baby will show signs of distress from pain on swallowing and general aches and pains. May vomit.	Encourage plenty of fluids – older babies may have ice-lollies to suck. Give pain relief, e.g. paracetamol. Seek medical aid if no improvement and if fever persists.
Cough	Often follows on from a cold; may be a symptom of other illness, e.g. measles.	Keep air moist. Check the baby has not inhaled an object. Give medicine if prescribed. ➜

Table 1.5.1 Illness in babies

Illness in babies		
Condition	Signs and symptoms	Role of the carer
Croup	Croup is an infection of the voice box or larynx, which becomes narrowed and inflamed. Barking cough (like a sea lion), noisy breathing, distressed; usually occurs at night.	If severe, seek medical help. Reassure the baby and sit them up. Keep calm and reassure the baby. Increasing the humidity using a room humidifier will help to create an appropriate atmosphere. While there is little scientific evidence to support it, some people have found that allowing their child to breathe in steam from a hot bath or shower in a closed room has eased symptoms. Steam treatment should only be used under careful supervision as there is a risk of scalding your child. [Source: NHS website]
Bronchiolitis	A harsh dry cough which later becomes wet and chesty; runny nose, raised temperature, wheeze, breathing problems, poor feeding or vomiting. May develop a blue tinge around the lips and on the fingernails (known as cyanosis).	Observe closely. Seek medical help if condition worsens. Increase fluids. Give small regular feeds. Give prescribed medicine. Comfort and reassure.
Febrile convulsions (high temperature)	Convulsions caused by a high temperature (over 39°C, 102°F) or fever are called febrile convulsions. Baby will become rigid, then the body may twitch and jerk for one or two minutes.	Try not to panic. Move potentially harmful objects out of the way and place the baby in the recovery position. Loosen clothing. Call doctor. Give tepid sponging. Comfort and reassure.
Otitis media	Will appear unwell; may have raised temperature. May vomit, may cry with pain. May have discharge from ear.	Take to doctor, give antibiotics and analgesics (or painkillers). Increase fluids; comfort and reassure.
Conjunctivitis	Inflammation of the thin, delicate membrane that covers the eyeball and forms the lining of the eyelids. Symptoms include a painful red eye, with watering and sometimes sticky pus.	Take to doctor who may prescribe antibiotic eye drops or ointment. Bathe a sticky eye gently with cool boiled water and clean cotton wool swabs. Always bathe the eye from the inside corner to the outside to avoid spreading infection.
Common cold	Runny nose, sneeze; tiny babies may have breathing problem.	Keep nose clear. Give small frequent feeds. Nasal drops if prescribed.
Meningitis	Raised temperature, may have a blotchy rash; may refuse feeds; may have a stiff neck; may have a seizure; bulging fontanelle, may have a shrill, high-pitched cry.	Seek medical help urgently. Reduce temperature. Reassure.

Table 1.5.1 Illness in babies   (*Continued*)

AC 1.3 and AC 1.4 Explain treatments for common childhood illnesses and Identify exclusion periods

Common childhood illnesses

Table 1.5.2 shows the common illnesses in childhood and their incubation periods. As with babies, most of them are not serious and clear up quickly. Others will need medical intervention. Table 1.5.7 on page 97 shows exclusion periods.

Disorders of the digestive tract

One of the most common signs that something is wrong with the digestive system is diarrhoea, when the bowel movements are abnormally runny and frequent. Other symptoms of infection or illness are vomiting and abdominal pain. Although these symptoms are often distressing – to both the child and his carer – they are rarely a serious threat to health.

Disease and cause	How it spreads	Incubation	Signs and symptoms	Rash or specific sign	Treatment	Possible complications
Common cold (coryza) Virus	Airborne/ droplet, hand-to-hand contact	1–3 days	Sneeze, sore throat, running nose, headache, slight fever, irritable, partial deafness		Treat symptoms. Apply a product such as Vaseline® to nostrils	Bronchitis, sinusitis, laryngitis
Chickenpox (varicella) Virus	Airborne/ droplet, direct contact	10–14 days	Slight fever, itchy rash, mild onset, child feels ill, often with severe headache	Red spots with white centre on trunk and limbs at first; blisters and pustules	Rest, fluids, calamine to rash, cut child's nails to prevent secondary infection	Impetigo, scarring, secondary infection from scratching
Dysentery Bacillus or amoeba	Indirect: flies, infected food, poor hygiene	1–7 days	Vomiting, diarrhoea, blood and mucus in stool, abdominal pain, fever, headache		Replace fluids, rest, medical aid, strict hygiene measures	Dehydration from loss of body salts. Shock, can be fatal
Food poisoning Bacteria or virus	Indirect: infected food or drink	1½ to 36 hours	Vomiting, diarrhoea, abdominal pain		Fluids only for 24 hours; medical aid if no better	Dehydration, can be fatal
Gastro-enteritis Bacteria or virus	Direct contact. Indirect: infected food/drink	Bacterial: 7–14 days Viral: 1½ to 36 hours	Vomiting, diarrhoea, signs of dehydration		Replace fluids – water or Dioralyte®; medical aid urgently	Dehydration, weight loss, death
Measles (morbilli) Virus	Airborne/ droplet	7–15 days	High fever, fretful, heavy cold – running nose and discharge from eyes; later cough	Day 1: Koplik's spots, white inside mouth. Day 4: blotchy rash starts on face and spreads down to body	Rest, fluids, tepid sponging. Shade room if photophobic (dislikes bright light)	Otitis media, eye infection, pneumonia, encephalitis (rare)

➜

Table 1.5.2 Common childhood infections

Disease and cause	How it spreads	Incubation	Signs and symptoms	Rash or specific sign	Treatment	Possible complications
Meningitis (Inflammation of the meninges which cover the brain) Bacteria or virus	Airborne/droplet	Variable Usually 2–10 days	Fever, headache, drowsiness, confusion, photophobia (dislike of bright light), arching of neck	Can have small red spots or bruises	Take to hospital, antibiotics and observation	Deafness, brain damage, death
Mumps (epidemic parotitis) Virus	Airborne/droplet	14–21days	Pain, swelling of jaw in front of ears, fever, pain when eating and drinking	Swollen face	Fluids: give via straw, hot compresses, oral hygiene	Meningitis (1 in 400) Orchitis (infection of the testes) in young men
Pertussis (whooping cough) Bacteria	Airborne/droplet, direct contact	7–21 days	Starts with a snuffly cold, slight cough, mild fever	Spasmodic cough with whoop sound, vomiting	Rest and assurance; feed after coughing attack; support during attack; inhalations	Convulsions, pneumonia, brain damage, hernia, debility
Rubella (German measles) Virus	Airborne/droplet, direct contact	14–21 days	Slight cold, sore throat, mild fever, swollen glands behind ears, pain in small joints	Slight pink rash starts behind ears and on forehead. Not itchy	Rest if necessary. Treat symptoms.	Only if contracted by woman in first 3 months of pregnancy: can cause serious defects in unborn baby
Scarlet fever (or scarlatina) Bacteria	Droplet	2–4 days	Sudden fever, loss of appetite, sore throat, pallor around mouth, 'strawberry' tongue	Bright red pinpoint rash over face and body – may peel	Rest, fluids, observe for complications, antibiotics	Kidney infection, otitis media, rheumatic fever (rare)
Tonsillitis Bacteria or virus	Direct infection, droplet	2–4 days	Very sore throat, fever, headache, pain on swallowing, aches and pains in back and limbs	Throat reddened, tonsils swollen and may be coated or have white spots on them	Rest, fluids, medical aid antibiotics, iced drinks to relieve pain	Quinsy (abscess on tonsils), otitis media, kidney infection, temporary deafness

Table 1.5.2 Common childhood infections (*Continued*)

Vomiting

Vomiting is the violent expulsion of the contents of the stomach through the mouth. A single episode of vomiting without other symptoms happens frequently in childhood. It could be a result of over-eating or too much excitement. Vomiting has many causes, but in most cases there is little warning and after a single bout the child recovers and quickly gets back to normal. Table 1.5.3 details possible causes of vomiting in children over one year old and what to do about it.

Helping a child who is vomiting

- Reassure the child, who may be very frightened.
- Stay with the child and support their head by putting your hand on their forehead.
- Keep the child cool by wiping the face with a cool, damp cloth.
- Offer mouthwash or sips of water after vomiting.
- Give the baby sips of oral rehydration solution (ORS) a few times an hour.
- Encourage the child to rest lying down with a bowl by their side. Do not leave them until they have fallen asleep – and stay within call in case they vomit again.

Possible causes of vomiting with accompanying symptoms	What to do
Gastro-enteritis The child also has diarrhoea	See the doctor within 24 hours Prevent dehydration (see p 91)
Intestinal obstruction The child's vomit is greenish-yellow	Call an ambulance; do not give the child anything to eat or drink
Meningitis The child has a fever, a stiff neck or flat, purplish spots that do not disappear when pressed	Call an ambulance
Head injury The child has recently suffered a blow to the head	Call an ambulance; do not give the child anything to eat or drink
Appendicitis The child has continuous abdominal pain around the navel and to the right side of the abdomen	Call an ambulance; do not give the child anything to eat or drink
Infection The child seems unwell, looks flushed and feels hot	Reduce the fever; see the doctor within 24 hours
Hepatitis The child has pale faeces and dark urine	See the doctor within 24 hours
Travel sickness When travelling, the child seems pale and quiet and complains of nausea	Give the child a travel sickness remedy before starting journey; take plenty of drinks to prevent dehydration
Migraine The child complains of a severe headache on one side of the forehead	See the doctor if accompanied by severe abdominal pain – it could be appendicitis
Whooping cough (pertussis) The child vomits after a bout of coughing	See the doctor within 24 hours

Table 1.5.3 Possible causes of vomiting

Diarrhoea

Most children have diarrhoea at some time, usually after an infection involving the digestive tract – for example, **gastro-enteritis**. If the fluid lost through passing frequent, loose, watery stools is not replaced, there is a danger the child will become **dehydrated**. Babies become dehydrated very quickly and can become seriously ill as the result of diarrhoea. Diarrhoea can also be caused by:

- emotional factors – overtiredness, excitement and anxiety
- allergy
- reaction to certain drugs and medicines.

Toddler's diarrhoea

Toddler's diarrhoea occurs when an otherwise healthy child (between the ages of one and three) passes loose, watery faeces. The cause is uncertain, but it is thought to be the result of poor chewing of food.

Signs and symptoms

- loose, watery faeces often containing recognisable pieces of food – e.g. raisins, corn, carrots and peas
- nappy rash if the child is in nappies.

What to do

- Consult a doctor to exclude other causes of diarrhoea, such as an infection.
- Encourage the child to chew foods thoroughly.
- Mash or liquidise foods which are difficult to chew and digest.
- Children generally grow out of toddler's diarrhoea by three years of age. As it is not an infectious condition, there is no need for the child to be kept away from friends or from nursery.

Care of a child with diarrhoea

- Reassure the child – who may be very distressed.
- Prevent dehydration by giving regular drinks of water.
- Keep a potty nearby.
- Be sympathetic when changing soiled underwear; soak any soiled clothing in a nappy sterilising solution before washing.

- Maintain a high standard of hygiene; hand washing by both you and the child is vital in preventing the spread of infection.
- Unless it is toddler diarrhoea, keep child away from other children; early years settings will have an exclusion policy in the case of infectious illness, such as gastro-enteritis.

Dehydration

Children can lose large amounts of body water through fever, diarrhoea, vomiting or exercise; this is called **dehydration**. In severe cases, they may not be able to replace this water simply by drinking and eating as usual. This is especially true if an illness stops them taking fluids by mouth or if they have a high fever.

Signs of dehydration in babies

- **Sunken fontanelles**: these are the areas where the bones of the skull have not yet fused together; they are covered by a tough membrane and a pulse may usually be seen beating under the **anterior fontanelle** in a baby without much hair.
- **Fretfulness**
- **Refusing feeds**
- **Dry nappies**: because the amount of urine being produced is very small.

Mild to moderate dehydration	Severe dehydration
Dry mouth	Very dry mouth
No tears when crying	Sunken eyes and dry, wrinkled skin
Refusing drinks	No urination for several hours
At first thirsty, then irritable – then becomes still and quiet	Sleepy and disorientated
Inactive and lethargic	Deep, rapid breathing
Increased heart rate	Fast, weak pulse
Restlessness	Cool and blotchy hands and feet

Table 1.5.4 Signs of dehydration in children

What to do

If you think a baby or child might have dehydration, do not try to treat them at home or in the setting. Call the doctor immediately, or take the child to the nearest Accident and Emergency Department. The doctor will prescribe oral rehydrating fluid to restore the body salts lost.

LO2 Know the signs of ill health in children

AC 2.1 Describe the signs and symptoms of ill health in children

Recognising general signs of illness in babies and children

Small children are not always able to explain their symptoms, and may display non-specific complaints such as headache, sleeplessness, vomiting or an inability to stand up. Babies have even less certain means of communication, and may simply cry in a different way, refuse feeds or become listless and lethargic. Many, but not all infectious diseases are accompanied by fever.

Detection of symptoms relies on the child being able to describe how they are feeling.

> **Key terms**
>
> **signs of illness** Those that can be observed directly, for example, a change in skin colour, a rash or a swelling.
>
> **symptoms of illness** Those experienced by the child, for example, pain, discomfort or generally feeling unwell.

Identifying signs of illness in children with different skin tones

Both within and between different ethnic groups there is a wide variety of skin tones and colours affecting the way skin looks during illness. When dark-skinned children are ill, they may show the following signs:

- **Skin appearance**: normal skin tone and sheen may be lost; the skin may appear dull and paler or greyer than usual. You must pay attention to those parts of the body with less pigmentation – the palms, the tongue, the nailbeds and the **conjunctiva** (the insides of the bottom eyelids), all of which will be paler than usual.
- **Rashes**: in children with very dark skin, raised rashes are more obvious than flat rashes.
- **Bruising**: the discolouration that is obvious in pale skin may not be easily observed in darker-skinned children. When bruised, the skin may appear darker or more purple when compared with surrounding skin.
- **Jaundice**: in a fair-skinned child, gently press your finger to his forehead, nose, or chest, and look for a yellow tinge to the skin as the pressure is released. In a darker-skinned child, check for yellowness in his gums or the whites of his eyes.

Recognising illness in babies

The responsibility of caring for a baby who becomes ill is enormous; it is vital that carers should know the signs and symptoms of illness and when to seek medical aid. You should:

- **Observe the baby carefully** and note any changes; record his or her temperature and take steps to reduce a high temperature (see p 102).
- **Give extra fluids** if possible and carry out routine skin care. The baby may want extra physical attention or prefer to rest in his cot.

Meningitis in babies

Meningitis is an inflammation of the lining of the brain. It is a very serious illness, but if it is detected and treated early, most children make a full recovery. The early symptoms of meningitis – such as fever, irritability, restlessness, vomiting and refusing feeds – are also common with colds and 'flu. However, a baby with meningitis can become seriously ill within hours, so it is important to act quickly if meningitis is suspected.

General signs and symptoms of illness in children

When children feel generally unwell, you should ask them if they have any pain or discomfort and treat it appropriately. Take their temperature and look for other signs of illness, such as a rash or swollen glands. Often, feeling generally unwell is the first sign that the child is developing an **infectious disease**. Some children can also show general signs of illness if they are anxious or worried about something, either at home or at school.

Children react in certain characteristic ways when they are unwell. Some of the more common **emotional and behavioural changes** include:

- being quieter than usual
- becoming more clingy to their parents or primary carer
- attention-seeking behaviour
- changed sleeping patterns; some children sleep more than usual, others less
- lack of energy
- crying: babies cry for a variety of reasons. Older children who cry more than usual may be physically unwell or you may need to explore the reasons for their unhappiness.
- regression: children who are unwell often regress in their development and behaviour. They may:
  - want to be carried everywhere instead of walking independently
  - go back to nappies after being toilet-trained
  - start to wet the bed
  - play with familiar, previously outgrown toys.

The following are common signs and symptoms of illness in children:

- **Loss of appetite** – the child may not want to eat or drink; this could be because of a sore, painful throat or a sign of a developing infection.
- **Lacking interest in play** – he may not want to join in play, without being able to explain why.
- **Abdominal pain** – the child may rub his or her tummy and say that it hurts; this could be a sign of gastro-enteritis.
- **Raised temperature (fever)** – a fever (a temperature above 38°C) is usually an indication of viral or bacterial infection, but can also result from overheating.
- **Diarrhoea and vomiting** – attacks of diarrhoea and/or vomiting are usually a sign of gastro-enteritis.
- **Lethargy or listlessness** – the child may be drowsy and prefer to sit quietly with a favourite toy or comfort blanket.
- **Irritability and fretfulness** – the child may have a change in behaviour, being easily upset and tearful.

- **Pallor** – the child will look paler than usual and may have dark shadows under the eyes; a black child may have a paler area around the lips and the conjunctiva may be pale pink instead of the normal dark pink.
- **Rash** – any rash appearing on the child's body should be investigated; it is usually a sign of an infectious disease.

High temperature (fever)

The normal body temperature is between 36°C and 37°C. A temperature of above 37.5°C means that the child has a fever.

A child with a fever may:

- look hot and flushed; the child may complain of feeling cold and might shiver. This is a natural reflex due to the increased heat loss and a temporary disabling of the usual internal temperature control of the brain
- be either irritable or subdued
- be unusually sleepy
- go off their food
- complain of thirst.

Children can develop high temperatures very quickly. You need to know how to bring their temperature down (see page 102) to avoid complications, such as dehydration and febrile convulsions.

Activity ·

Describe the signs and symptoms that would lead you to believe that a child is unwell.

· ·

AC 2.2 Give examples of when medical intervention is necessary

When to call a doctor or call for an ambulance

If you think the child's life is in danger, **dial 999** if you are in the UK, **ask for an ambulance** urgently and explain the situation. Contact the **family doctor** (GP) if the child has any of the symptoms shown in Table 1.5.5. If the doctor cannot reach you quickly, take the child to the accident and emergency department of the nearest hospital.

Contact the GP if a child shows these symptoms	
Has a temperature of 38.6°C (101.4°F) that is not lowered by measures to reduce **fever**, or a temperature over 37.8°C (100°F) for more than one day	Has **convulsions**, or is limp and floppy
Has severe or persistent **vomiting** and/or **diarrhoea,** seems **dehydrated** or has projectile vomiting	**Cannot be woken**, is unusually drowsy or may be losing consciousness
Has symptoms of **meningitis**	Has symptoms of **croup**
Is pale, listless, and **does not respond** to usual stimulation	**Cries or screams** inconsolably and may have severe pain
Has bulging **fontanelle** (soft spot on top of head of a baby) when not crying	Appears to have severe abdominal pain, with symptoms of **shock**
Refuses two successive feeds (babies)	Develops **purple-red** rash anywhere on body
Passes bowel motions (stools) containing **blood**	Has jaundice
Has a suspected **ear infection**	Has been injured, e.g. **by a burn which blisters and covers** more than 10% of the body surface
Has inhaled something, such as a peanut, into the air passages and may be **choking**	Has swallowed a **poisonous** substance, or an object, e.g. a safety pin or button
Has bright pink cheeks and swollen hands and feet (could be due to **hypothermia**)	Has difficulty in **breathing**

Table 1.5.5 When to contact the GP

LO3 Understand legal requirements for reporting notifiable diseases

AC 3.1 Identify notifiable diseases

The HPA list of notifiable diseases

Table 1.5.6 lists infectious diseases which are notifiable (to Local Authority Proper Officers) under the Health Protection (Notification) Regulations 2010. (HPA is now part of Public Health England.)

Policies and procedures for infection control

There are some general rules about excluding children from childcare settings:

- Children who are ill should *not* attend the childcare setting. If a child becomes ill while in childcare, a parent or carer should be asked to take the child home as soon as possible.
- Children with diarrhoea or vomiting illnesses should not be in early years settings. Parents

should contact their GP for advice regarding the child's illness and possible need for collection of samples. The exclusion period should last until at least 48 hours after the last episode of diarrhoea or vomiting.

- Parents should be advised if there are known cases of infection within the early years setting. It is particularly important that the parents of children whose immunity may be impaired due to illness or treatment (such as leukaemia, HIV) are given this information. It is also important that mothers who are pregnant are made aware of the following infections: chicken pox/shingles, rubella, slapped cheek syndrome and measles.
- It is good practice that a child requiring antibiotics does not come into the early years setting for 48 hours after they have begun treatment. This is so that the child's condition has an opportunity to improve, and that in the unlikely event of a reaction to antibiotics, the parent or carer can be with the child and is able to seek further help

Notifiable diseases		
Acute encephalitis	Acute infectious hepatitis	Acute meningitis
Acute poliomyelitis	Anthrax	Botulism
Brucellosis	Cholera	Diphtheria
Enteric fever (typhoid or paratyphoid fever)	Food poisoning	Haemolytic uraemic syndrome (HUS)
Infectious bloody diarrhoea	Invasive group A streptococcal disease	Legionnaires' disease
Leprosy	Malaria	Measles
Meningococcal septicaemia	Mumps	Plague
Rabies	Rubella	SARS
Scarlet fever	Smallpox	Tetanus
Tuberculosis	Typhus	Viral haemorrhagic fever (VHF)
Whooping cough	Yellow fever	

Table 1.5.6 Notifiable diseases

or advice from the GP. It is possible that some infections may take the child much longer to recover from and feel well enough to attend childcare. Other infections are subject to specific exclusions advice.

Exclusion policies

The **2010 Health Protection Agency (HPA, now part of Public Health England)** orange poster 'Guidance on Infection Control in Schools and other Child Care Settings' details the current guidelines for whether – and when – to exclude a child with an infectious disease from the setting. Every early years setting must have an **exclusion policy** for infectious diseases, and parents should be informed of their responsibilities. The exclusion criteria for some of the more common infections are given in Table 1.5.7.

Note: the diseases marked* in Table 1.5.7 are **notifiable**. This means that under the Public Health (Infectious Diseases) Regulations 1988, these infections and *all cases of food poisoning* must be reported to the local authority proper offices.

AC 3.2 Describe the process for reporting notifiable diseases

If the manager or teacher has reason to believe that any child or staff member is suffering from a notifiable disease the following steps must be taken:

- Contact the Local Health Protection Agency and follow any advice given.
- Record the incident detailing the child's or staff member's details and the type of infection.
- Ensure any advice received is also noted and ensure that the incident is recorded.
- Ensure that staff are made aware of procedures or of any symptoms that are likely to occur.
- Ensure confidentiality.

Activity

Find out about your setting's policy relating to notifiable diseases and their policy relating to excluding children when they have an infectious illness.

Infectious illness	Recommended period for exclusion from the setting
Chicken pox	For 5 days from onset of rash (see also section on female staff and pregnancy below)
Diarrhoea and/or vomiting	For 48 hours from last episode of diarrhoea or vomiting. Exclusion from swimming should be for 2 weeks following last episode of diarrhoea
Hand, foot and mouth	None. Exclusion is ineffective as transmission takes place before the child becomes unwell
Impetigo	Until lesions are crusted or healed, or 48 hours after commencing antibiotic treatment
Measles*	For 4 days from onset of rash
Meningococcal meningitis*	The local Health Protection Unit (HPU) will give advice on any action needed. There is no reason to exclude from school siblings and other close contacts of a case
Non-meningococcal meningitis*	None. Once the child is well, infection risk is minimal. Meningitis C is preventable by vaccination
Meningitis due to other bacteria*	Exclude until recovered. There is no reason to exclude from school siblings and other close contacts of a case. Hib meningitis and pneumococcal meningitis are preventable by vaccination
Mumps*	For 5 days from onset of swelling
Rubella* German measles	For 6 days from onset of rash (see section on female staff and pregnancy below)
Shingles	Exclude only if rash is weeping and cannot be covered (see section on female staff and pregnancy below)
Scabies	Child can return after first treatment has commenced
Slapped cheek disease (Fifth disease /Parvovirus)	None. Exclusion is ineffective as nearly all transmission takes place before the child becomes unwell (but see section on female staff and pregnancy below)
Whooping cough*	For 5 days from commencing antibiotic treatment

Table 1.5.7 Exclusion criteria for infectious diseases

LO4 Understand the role of the EYP in minimising ill health in children

AC 4.1 Explain how the EYP can minimise ill health in children

Minimising ill health in children: infection control procedures

The EYFS 2012 states: Children learn best when they are healthy, safe and secure, when their individual needs are met, and when they have positive relationships with the adults caring for them. The Safeguarding and Welfare Requirements are designed to help providers create high-quality settings which are welcoming, safe and stimulating, and where children are able to enjoy learning and grow in confidence.

Your responsibility for promoting a healthy hygienic environment

Staff with infections can place children and others at risk, therefore staff suffering from particular conditions must be **excluded** from their work in accordance with Health Protection Agency guidelines:

- Any member of staff who handles food and becomes sick with diarrhoea, vomiting or infected skin problems must report this to his or her supervisor.
- Any member of staff with diarrhoea or vomiting should be excluded from work until at least 48 hours after symptoms have stopped. Staff with infected wounds or skin infections on exposed parts of their bodies should be similarly excluded until the lesions are healed or they have been advised that it is safe to return to work by the GP.

- Any member of staff with other conditions that could spread infections, such as the common cold, should take sensible precautions. Staff should inform their supervisor.

Basic hygiene routines for minimising ill health in children

Children who play closely together for long periods of time are more likely than others to develop an infection – and any infection can spread very quickly from one child to another. All settings should have set routines for tidying up and for cleaning the floors, walls and furniture. Good hygiene routines will help to prevent infection. Children will take their cue from you, so you need to ensure that you are a good role model by setting a good example of a high standard of personal hygiene. Guidelines for keeping the setting clean and hygienic are discussed in Unit 2.3.

When to wear protective clothing

It is recommended that a new disposable plastic apron and gloves be worn:

- during nappy changing (see Unit 1.3 for guidelines on nappy changing)
- when cleaning up blood or body fluid (faeces, urine and vomit) spills.

Procedure for cleaning up blood or body fluid spillages

1 Put on disposable gloves and plastic apron.
2 Use paper towels to mop up any excess and dispose of them in a plastic bag.
3 Do not use a mop to clean up spillages.
4 Wash area with hot water and detergent using a disposable cloth, and dry using paper towels.
5 Discard apron and gloves into disposable bag and dispose of appropriately in a bin.
6 Always wash your hands thoroughly after removing gloves and aprons.
7 If staff clothing is contaminated by body fluid spillages, clothes should be changed as soon as possible and placed in a plastic bag and sealed. These clothes should be washed at the highest temperature possible for the item. Correct hand washing and drying are essential after touching the clothes.

In practice

Disposal of waste

You should always:

- Protect yourself from infection by wearing a protective apron and disposable gloves.
- Protect children by keeping them away from spillages at all times.
- Dispose of waste safely and hygienically – in special bins.
- Clean up spillages that could cause infection – using special solutions. If children are likely to come near the affected area, ask another member of staff to keep them away while you deal with the incident.
- Wrap children's soiled clothes in a polythene bag and give them to the parents when they arrive.
- When a child uses a potty, make sure that it is emptied straightaway after use and cleaned appropriately. Refer to Unit 1.3 for more information on disposal of body fluids.

In practice activity

Infection control policy

Find out about the infection control policy in your own setting.

1 When should you wear protective clothing?
2 When should you wear gloves?
3 How should you dispose of waste?
4 Which conditions should you report to your supervisor and not attend for work?

Activity

Minimising ill health in children

1 Why is good hygiene so important in early years settings? Give three reasons.
2 When should children wash their hands?
3 Why should children's toys and playthings be checked for hygiene and regularly cleaned?
4 How should you dispose of a soiled nappy in an early years setting?
5 When preparing and serving food and drinks for children, you must follow the rules of food hygiene. State three important ways in which you can prevent infection from food or drink.

LO5 Understand care routines when a child is ill

AC 5.1 Describe the needs of a child who is ill

Children who are ill have:

- **physical needs** – food and drink, rest and sleep, temperature control, exercise and fresh air, safety, hygiene and medical care
- **intellectual and language needs** – stimulation, appropriate activities
- **emotional and social needs** – love, security, play and contact with others.

The most important part of caring for children who are ill is to show that you care for them and to respond to all their needs. If a child is going to be nursed for some weeks, it is often useful to draw up a **plan of care**, just as nurses do in hospital. This has the following benefits:

- It helps you to keep a record of any changes in the child's condition and to ask for outside help if necessary.
- It reassures you that you are providing for all the child's needs.
- It enables you to plan a simple programme of activities to keep the child entertained and occupied.
- It enables another family member or colleague to assist in the general care, allowing you a break.

Meeting physical needs
Food and drink

Children who are ill often have poor appetites – a few days without food will not harm the child but fluid intake should be increased as a general rule.

Drinks should be offered at frequent intervals to prevent dehydration – the child will not necessarily request drinks.

Guidelines for encouraging sick children to drink

- Provide a covered jug of fruit juice or water; any fluid is acceptable according to the child's tastes, for example, milk, meaty drinks or soups.
- If the child has mumps, do not give fruit drinks because the acid causes pain to the tender parotid glands.
- A sick toddler who has recently given up his bottle may regress. Allow him to drink from a bottle until he is feeling better.
- Try using an interesting curly straw.
- Give the child an 'adult' glass to make them feel special.
- Try offering drinks in a tiny glass or eggcup, which makes the quantities look smaller.
- Offer fresh fruit juices, such as pear, apple or mango; dilute them with fizzy water to make them more interesting, but avoid giving more than one fizzy drink a day; vary the drinks as much as possible.
- If the child does not like milk, add a milkshake mix or ice cream.

Guidelines for encouraging a sick child to eat

- Most children with a fever do not want to eat, so while you should offer food, you should never force a child to eat.
- Allow the child to choose their favourite foods.
- Give the child smaller meals but more often than you would normally.
- If the child has a sore throat, give ice cream or an iced lolly made with fruit juice or yoghurt.
- If the child is feeling slightly sick, offer plain foods such as mashed potato.
- Offer snacks regularly and always keep the child company while they eat.
- Most children who are sick do not find ordinary food very appetising, but may be tempted to eat with 'soldiers' of fresh bread and butter, slices of fruit or their favourite yoghurt.
- Try to make food as attractive as possible; do not put too much on the plate at once and remember that sick children often cope better with foods that do not require too much chewing, such as egg custard, milk pudding, thick soups, chicken and ice cream.

Guidelines for caring for a child in bed (caring for a child in their own home)

- Use cotton sheets – they are more comfortable for a child with a temperature.
- Change the sheets daily if possible – clean sheets feel better.
- Leave a box of tissues on a table next to the bed.
- If the child has bouts of vomiting, pillows should be protected and a container should be kept close to the bed. This should be emptied and rinsed with an antiseptic or disinfectant, such as Savlon®, after use.
- Wet or soiled bed linen should be changed to prevent discomfort. Paper tissues that can be disposed of either by burning or by sealing in disposal bags are useful for minor accidents.
- A plastic mattress cover is useful as a sick child's behaviour may change and cause him or her to wet the bed.

Guidelines for a hygiene routine for a sick child at home

- The child's room should be well ventilated and uncluttered. Open a window to prevent stuffiness but protect the child from draughts.
- Provide a potty to avoid trips to the lavatory.
- Protect the mattress with a rubber or plastic sheet.
- A daily bath or shower is important. During an acute phase of illness, this can be done in the form of a bed bath – an all-over wash in bed.
- Brush hair daily.
- Clean teeth after meals and apply a product such as Vaseline® to sore, cracked lips.
- Keep the child's nails short and clean, and prevent scratching of any spots.
- Dress the child in cool, cotton clothing; put a jumper and socks or slippers over pyjamas if the child does not want to stay in bed the whole time.

Personal care

All children benefit from having a routine to meet their hygiene needs, and this need not be altered drastically during illness.

Rest and sleep

Children usually dislike being confined to bed and will only stay there if feeling very unwell. There is no need to keep a child with a fever in bed; take your lead from the child. Making a bed on a sofa in the main living room will save carers the expense of extra heating and of tiring trips up and down stairs. The child will also feel more included in family life and less isolated. The room does not have to be particularly hot – just a comfortable temperature for you. If the child *does* stay in bed in his own room, remember to visit him often so that he does not feel neglected.

Emotional well-being

Play is an important part of recovery for a sick or convalescent child. Children who are ill often regress and may want to play with toys that they have long since outgrown. While they are ill, children have a short attention span and tire quickly, so toys and materials should be changed frequently. You will need to be understanding and tolerant of these changes in behaviour. Never put pressure on a child to take part in an activity they do not want to. If a child is ill for some time, you can achieve variation in toys and games by borrowing them from a local toy library. If the child wishes to draw or paint, or do some other messy activity, use protective sheets to protect the bed covers. Many activities are easier to manage if you supply a steady surface such as a tray with legs or a special beanbag tray.

Activities which sick children might enjoy

- Jigsaw puzzles: the child could start with simple puzzles and progress to more challenging ones, perhaps with family help
- Board games, such as Lotto, Ludo and Halma
- Card games, such as Uno, Snap and Happy Families

- Making a scrapbook: provide magazines, photos, flowers, scissors and glue to make a personal record
- Drawing and painting: provide poster paints, lining paper and a protective plastic apron; children also love to paint with water in 'magic' painting books
- Play dough: either bought or home-made; playing with dough is creative and provides an outlet for feelings of frustration
- Making models with Duplo® or Lego®
- Playing with small world objects, such as toy farms, zoos and Playmobil®
- French knitting or sewing cards can be used with older children
- Crayons, felt tip pens and a pad of paper
- Books to be read alone or with an adult
- Audiotapes of songs, rhymes and favourite stories
- Videos, cartoons, and computer games in moderation
- Encourage other children and adults to visit once the child is over the infectious stage.

Dignity and respect

When caring for young children, it is important to preserve their dignity and to show respect. This can be achieved by:

- recognising each child as a unique individual whose best interests must be paramount, while considering their physical, psychological, social, cultural and spiritual needs, as well as those of their families
- listening to the child and providing a means for them to express their opinions and feelings – and using these to guide decisions about the way they are cared for
- promoting and protecting the individual rights of children in all settings where they receive care
- ensuring privacy and confidentiality at all times
- respecting the right of children, according to their age and understanding, to appropriate information about their care.

Observation and monitoring

Careful observations of the child's behaviour, and regular monitoring of the child's symptoms – body temperature, evidence of pain and drowsiness – should be carried out and recorded on a timed chart. If the child's condition deteriorates, be prepared to call a doctor or an ambulance.

Temperature control

If the child has a fever, you will need to take their temperature regularly and use tepid sponging to reduce it (see page 102).

How to take a temperature

All family first aid kits should contain a thermometer. There are many types, but the most widely used in the home are digital thermometers and temperature strips.

Digital thermometers: these are battery-operated and consist of a safe narrow probe with a tip sensitive to temperature. They are easy to read via a display panel and are available as in-ear thermometers under the armpit or in the mouth thermometers:

1 Place the narrow tip of the thermometer in the ear or under the child's armpit – or for older children, place under their tongue.
2 Read the temperature when it stops rising; some models beep when this point is reached.

Forehead temperature strip: this is a rectangular strip of thin plastic which contains temperature-sensitive crystals that change colour according to the temperature measured. It is placed on the child's forehead. It is not as accurate as other thermometers but is a useful check.

1 Hold the plastic strip firmly against the child's forehead for about 30 seconds.
2 Record the temperature revealed by the colour change.

Whatever the cause of a high temperature, it is important to try to reduce it. There is always the risk a fever could lead to convulsions or fits.

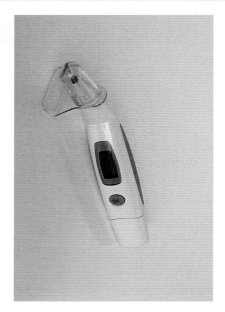

Figure 1.5.1 Forehead temperature strip and digital thermometers

Guidelines for bringing down a high temperature

- Offer cool drinks: encourage the child to take small, frequent sips of anything he will drink (though preferably clear fluids like water or squash, rather than milky drinks). Do this even if the child is vomiting because, even then, some water will be absorbed.
- Remove clothes: keep the child as undressed as possible to allow heat to be lost.
- Reduce bedclothes: use a cotton sheet if the child is in bed.
- Sponge the child down: use tepid water (see tepid sponging below).
- Give the correct dose of children's paracetamol: make sure you have written consent from the parents to use it in case of emergency. If not, contact the parents and try to obtain consent.

- Cool the air in the child's room: use an electric fan or open the window.
- Reassure the child: they may be very frightened. Remain calm yourself and try to stop a baby from crying as this will tend to push the temperature higher still.
- If the temperature will not come down, **call the doctor**. Always consult a doctor if a high fever is accompanied by symptoms such as severe headache with stiff neck, abdominal pain or pain when passing urine.

NB Medicines should not be given unless the written permission of the parent or next of kin is obtained.

Guidelines for tepid sponging to reduce a temperature

- Make sure the air in the room is comfortably warm – not hot, cold or draughty.
- Lay the child on a towel on your knee or on the bed and gently remove their clothes; reassure them by talking gently.
- Sponge the child's body, limbs and face with tepid or lukewarm water – not cold; as the water evaporates from the skin, it absorbs heat from the blood and so cools the system.

- As the child cools down, pat the skin dry with a soft towel and dress only in a nappy or pants; cover them with a light cotton sheet.
- Keep checking the child's condition to make sure that he does not become cold or shivery; put more light covers over the child if he is shivering or obviously chilled.
- If the temperature rises again, repeat sponging every ten minutes.

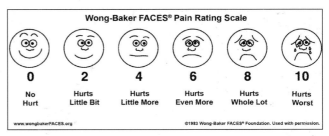

Figure 1.5.2 The Wong – Baker FACES® Pain Rating Scale

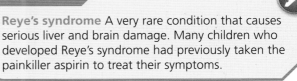

Key term

Reye's syndrome A very rare condition that causes serious liver and brain damage. Many children who developed Reye's syndrome had previously taken the painkiller aspirin to treat their symptoms.

Helping children who are in pain

Very young children or children who are very sick are not always able to express how they are feeling. Parents know their child's usual reactions and behaviour and so may be able to tell if their child is in pain, but it is often difficult for adults to know how much pain a young child is in. Signs that a young child is in pain include:

- crying or screaming
- facial changes or pulling a face
- changes in their sleeping or eating patterns
- becoming quiet and withdrawn
- refusing to move.

Often a child with acute earache will not be able to describe where they are hurting, but may pull or rub at their earlobes. Hospitals and clinics use a scale such as the Wong-Baker FACES® Pain Rating Scale: see Figure 1.5.2. This involves asking the child to point to the face that shows how much hurt they are feeling from 'no pain' on the left through to 'hurts worst' on the right.

Pain can cause acute distress to the affected child. Distraction techniques can help with minor pain – for example, blowing bubbles, playing with puppets etc. Children's ibuprofen or paracetamol can be administered with parental permission.

NB Aspirin must never be given to any child under the age of 16 years, because of the risk of Reye's syndrome.

Activity

How would you draw up a plan of care that provides for all the needs of a sick child? Include their physical needs, intellectual and language needs, and emotional and social needs.

AC 5.2 Outline the procedures for storage of medication, administration of medication, and record-keeping with regard to medication

Procedures for storage of medication

All medicines must be stored in their original containers, be clearly labelled and be kept in a locked cupboard inaccessible to the children.

Make sure that each medicine is labelled for a particular child; always check the label for the child's name before giving it. The only exception to this is **inhalers for asthma**, which should be kept nearby for the child. This should still be in a cupboard, out of reach but one that is accessible by staff at all times.

Keep a written record of medicines given, including the child's name, date, time, the medicine and dose, any problems with giving it.

Procedures to follow for the storage and administration of any medicines must comply with the regulations for England.

Procedures for administering medication

Most early years settings have a policy on the giving of medicines. This usually states that *no drugs* will be given to the child while at the setting. However, there are certain exceptions to this rule. For example, if a child has a condition (such as asthma) that requires an immediate response or has a condition (such as eczema or glue ear) that requires long-term medication, parents should discuss this with the manager or supervisor.

Medicines prescribed by a doctor and paracetamol may be given to these children only after the parent's or carer's written consent is obtained.

In England, the EYFS issued a guidance document: *Managing Medicines in Schools and Early Years Setting*. This requires settings to do the following:

- **Policy**: have a policy about the management and administration of medicines.
- **Written record**: every medicine given to children must be written down, and this record is shared with the child's parents or carers.
- **Parent consent forms**: ensure that parent consent forms have been completed, giving permission for each and every medicine prior to it being administered. The consent form must be very precise and contain the following information:
  - full name of child and date of birth
  - name of medication and strength
  - who prescribed it
  - dosage to be given in the setting
  - how the medication should be stored (such as in the fridge) and the expiry date
  - any possible side effects that may be expected
  - signature, printed name of parent and date.

If the administration of the medicine requires any technical or medical knowledge, individual training should be provided for the staff team from a suitably qualified health professional. The manager will decide who administers the medication in your setting.

Procedures for record-keeping with regard to medication

It is good practice for two members of staff to be present when administering medication, and for each of them to sign the record sheet, which should include date, time, dosage, and space for the parent's or carer's signature when he or she collects the child.

The parents will then sign the record book to acknowledge that the medicine has been given. If there is any problem with giving the medicine – for example, if the child refuses it or is sick shortly after – this should also be recorded and the parents should be informed. Always make sure that you understand how and when to give a child's medicine – if in doubt, ask your manager or supervisor.

Activity

Find out about the policy for management of medicines in your setting.

AC 5.3 Explain procedures which are followed when a child is taken ill in a setting

Reporting and recording when a child becomes ill

Reporting illness

Children who are sick should not be at school or nursery; early years settings are not appropriate places in which to care for sick children. However, it is often at an early years setting that the child first shows signs and symptoms of an illness. Childminders and nannies working in the family home also need to know how to act to safeguard children's health.

Nannies and childminders should always contact the child's parents directly in case of accident or illness.

In schools or nurseries, you should notify a senior member of staff if you notice that a child is unwell; that person will then decide whether and when to contact the child's parents.

Keeping records

Every child's record should contain the following information:

- child's full name
- address and telephone number of child's home
- address and telephone number of child's GP and health visitor

- date of birth
- address and telephone number of parent or carer's place(s) of work
- names and addresses of child's primary carers
- additional emergency contact telephone number, possibly a relative.

Recording illness

Records of a child's illness should be kept so that the child's parents and doctor can be informed; as with the accident report book (see p 198), these records should include:

- when the child first showed signs of illness
- the signs and symptoms
- any action taken – for example, taking the child's temperature
- progress of the illness since first noticing it – for example, are there any further symptoms?

Helping a child who becomes unwell

- Staff in early years settings should offer support and reassurance to a child who may have to wait a while to be taken home.
- Any incident of vomiting or diarrhoea should be dealt with swiftly and sympathetically to minimise the child's distress and to preserve their dignity.
- A member of staff – preferably the child's key person – should remain with the child at all times and keep them as comfortable as possible.
- All early years settings should have a written policy on when to exclude children for childhood infections.

Activity ·······································

What should you do when you notice a child is unwell at the setting? Check the relevant policy at your setting.

··

LO6 Understand how to support children for planned hospital admission

Preparing for hospitalisation

Every year one in four children under five years old goes into hospital, and over two million children are seen in accident and emergency units. How a child reacts to a hospital visit depends on:

- their age
- the reason for hospitalisation
- the tests and treatment needed
- the ambience of the ward
- their personality
- their previous experience of hospitals
- the attitude and manner of the doctors, nurses and other staff
- the carer's own anxieties and perceived ability to cope with what is often a very stressful situation.

When a child has to be admitted to hospital, either for medical treatment or for a surgical operation, it is best, if possible, to prepare them in advance. Often, the experience is stressful for parents, particularly if they have their own negative childhood memories of hospitalisation. In the event, the majority of children do enjoy their hospital stay, but adverse reactions can be avoided in younger children by careful preparation and complete honesty in all information given.

AC 6.1 Describe how the EYP supports a child to prepare for a stay in hospital

Preparing a child for a stay in hospital

For many children the idea of going to hospital for the first time can be very frightening. They are likely to be worried about having to stay away from home, and may be very afraid of what will happen to them in hospital. Parents and carers can help children to avoid much of this distress. They can help in the following ways:

- to help the child cope with the change in routine
- to help the child feels less frightened
- to help the child understand why they are going to hospital
- to correct any wrong ideas the child may have about hospital.

Many hospitals now have pre-admission units where children can go a few days before admission to be examined and to become familiar with the hospital environment. Common questions children in hospital ask are:

Guidelines for preparing children for hospitalisation

The best way to prepare a child is by giving them information – but not to overload them.

- If possible, arrange to visit the ward a few days before admission – most wards welcome such visits and are happy to talk with carers. (This helps to overcome fear of the unknown.)
- Encourage children to talk about their feelings so that you know how to help them.
- Always be honest – never say that something will not hurt if it might, and only tell them that you will be there all the time if that is your plan.
- Keep explanations simple – reading a book about a child going to hospital may help allay fears.
- If the child is going to have an operation, explain that they will have a special hospital 'sleep' which will stop them from feeling any pain. Following the operation, explain that they may feel a little sore but the nurses will give them something to take the pain away.

- Do not let the child see your own worry, as this will make him or her feel frightened.
- Always tell the child the truth. Do not lie by saying, for example, that something will not hurt when it might. This will destroy their trust in adults.
- Play hospital games using toys to help the child act out any fears.
- Try to be involved in the child's care as fully as possible.
- Take the child's favourite toy or 'comforter' as a link with home – the child could even help to pack their case.
- Tell the ward staff about the child's eating and sleeping patterns, and about particular preferences or special words that may be used for the toilet, etc.
- If the child is of school age, the hospital school will provide educational activities. Play specialists, nursery nurses or teachers will provide play activities for younger children.

- Will I get better?
- What will the doctors and nurses do to me?
- Will I be blamed – or laughed at?
- Can I go home?

Activities that may help a child

There are many ways in which you can help a child prepare for a hospital stay: see Figure 1.5.3.

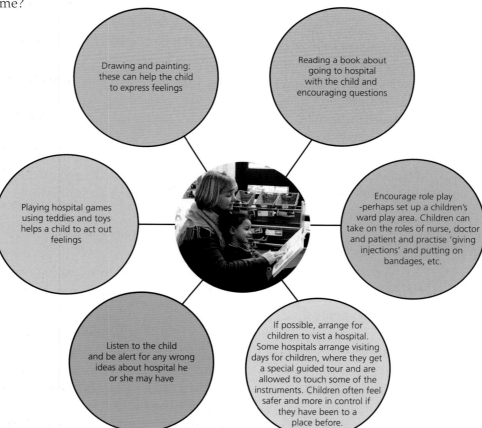

Drawing and painting: these can help the child to express feelings

Reading a book about going to hospital with the child and encouraging questions

Playing hospital games using teddies and toys helps a child to act out feelings

Encourage role play -perhaps set up a children's ward play area. Children can take on the roles of nurse, doctor and patient and practise 'giving injections' and putting on bandages, etc.

Listen to the child and be alert for any wrong ideas about hospital he or she may have

If possible, arrange for children to vist a hospital. Some hospitals arrange visiting days for children, where they get a special guided tour and are allowed to touch some of the instruments. Children often feel safer and more in control if they have been to a place before.

Figure 1.5.3 Helping a child prepare for a hospital stay

The day before admission

Depending on the age of the child, you can involve them in packing the things they need to take with them:

- comfort blanket or special cuddly toy, if used – plus a spare if possible
- some toys and books. Children usually regress when they are feeling ill, so choose books and toys that are on the young side
- pyjamas or nightie; dressing gown and slippers; wash bag with their own toiletries
- photo of family
- favourite fruit drink.

What the hospital needs to know

Apart from general information such as name, age and date of birth, on admission the nurse will also find out about any allergies and medication the child is taking. They also need to know about the child's normal routine and preferences:

- **Communication**: What is the child's level of understanding and language development? Does the child need a hearing aid or glasses?
- **Hygiene**: What is the child's usual routine for bathing, washing and cleaning teeth?
- **Rest and sleep**: What is the usual pattern of naps and bedtime sleep?
- **Food and drink**: If a baby, is the baby bottle-fed, breastfed or weaned? Are there any dietary restrictions? Can an older child feed himself?
- **Play**: Does the child have any favourite toys or games? What sort of play does the child enjoy?
- **Comfort**: Does the child have any comfort habits, e.g. thumb-sucking or holding a comfort object or teddy?
- **Toilet habits**: Does the child wear nappies? How independent is the child in going to the toilet? What are the normal bowel movements?

The care plan

The nurse will work with the parents to write an individual care plan for their child, which will cover all the categories of need mentioned above. The role of the parents will be discussed and arrangements made for them to stay with their child, if possible. If the child is going to have an operation, a hospital play specialist will prepare them for the event and parents are encouraged to accompany them to the anaesthetic room and stay until they are asleep. When the operation is over, the parent is invited to collect their child from theatre with the ward nurse.

Activity
How could you support the child and his or her family to prepare for a planned hospital stay?

LO7 Understand the therapeutic role of play in hospitals

AC 7.1 Describe the therapeutic role of play in hospital in supporting children's recovery

The therapeutic role of play in hospital

For children, play is at the very centre of their lives. From the earliest age, playing helps children to learn, to relate to others and to have fun. Play can make a real difference to children in hospital, as they are at their most vulnerable – ill, separated from their friends and familiar surroundings. Play is important in hospital because it:

- creates an environment where stress and anxiety are lessened
- helps the child to regain confidence and self-esteem
- provides an outlet for frustration and anger
- helps the child understand what is going to happen to them
- helps in assessment and diagnosis
- speeds recovery and rehabilitation.

The role of the health play specialist

Formerly called hospital play specialists, health play specialists work as part of a multidisciplinary team in hospital wards and departments. Their role is to:

- organise daily play and art activities in the playroom or at the bedside
- provide play to reach developmental goals
- help children to cope with anxieties and difficult feelings
- use play to prepare children for hospital procedures

- support families and siblings
- contribute to clinical judgements and diagnoses through their play-based observations
- act as the child's advocate
- teach the value of play for the sick child
- encourage peer group friendships to develop
- organise parties and special events.

Types of therapeutic hospital play
Play as preparation for a medical or nursing procedure

During a medical assessment, a child may have a series of nursing procedures, such as having their temperatures taken, blood tests, oxygen levels measured, blood pressure taken or being given medicine for pain relief. Using play as preparation helps by:

- distracting the very young child, as their level of understanding is limited and they may be frightened of unfamiliar investigations
- showing children what will happen to them so that they know what to expect and what is expected of them
- assessing their level of understanding and likes and dislikes, and providing appropriate toys and play activities
- listening to children and encouraging them to ask questions about procedures.

A variety of techniques may be used – always geared to the individual child and their specific needs:

- Bubbles are a very good way of amusing and distracting a young child. They are also a useful assessment tool, for example, if medical staff are querying an arm injury, a child will only use the healthy arm to catch the bubbles, leaving the injured arm limp.
- Dolls with injection sites and intravenous infusions which can be used with coloured water.
- Puppets and small world figures can be used to act out certain hospital procedures, such as being wheeled on a trolley to the operating theatre.
- Books, DVDs, audiotapes and photographs can all help to make the planned procedure less threatening.

Play as therapy after a medical or nursing procedure

After an uncomfortable medical or nursing procedure or after surgery, many children will have no choice but to lie in bed until they are physically recovered. Using play after a procedure helps by:

- reassuring children that life goes on as normal
- assessing their understanding of the treatment and their reaction to it
- encouraging children to play out their experiences and so feel more accepting
- giving children control over what they are doing – the child is in control of the play process.

A variety of techniques may be used – always geared to the individual child and their specific needs:

- dolls specially adapted to show the specific treatment the child has had – for example, the doll may have an intravenous infusion (a drip) attached to one arm or may have a large bandage covering its head
- medical equipment such as stethoscopes and syringes (without needles)
- books and photos showing children at various stages of recovery
- musical activities: many hospitals will have musical equipment for family use through music therapy, physiotherapy or occupational therapy departments. Passive music activities can be performed with little or no active participation on the part of a child who is required to stay quiet – or a child who is unable to move actively after surgery or procedures
- for children unable to leave their hospital rooms, small hand instruments – such as castanets, bells, tambourines, etc. – can be played to music or on their own
- basic art supplies can be used by children to draw while listening to music
- active musical activities, such as songs that require hand or body movements can be adapted to various activity levels of children. For all ages, moving to music can provide gentle exercise.

Case study

Using play in an accident and emergency unit

Georgia is a two-year-old child who was brought into A&E by her mother. She had suffered a burn to her shoulder from boiling hot water. The skin was very red and had several large blisters. Georgia was assessed by the nursing and medical team and given pain relief, then taken to a cubicle. The cubicle is used to provide a private area for the child and parent to relax and play while waiting for the pain relief to take effect.

Armed with lots of noisy toys and a bubble-making machine, the health play specialist, Lauren, went to see Georgia. Sitting on the floor at the child's level, blowing bubbles with laughs and squeaks from Georgia, Lauren started to get to know Georgia and her mother better. Georgia's mother felt guilty about the accident and found it very useful to talk to Lauren during the play session. As the three of them established a good relationship, Lauren learnt a lot about Georgia's likes and dislikes – information that would be needed during the cleaning and dressing of the burn.

The time came for the dressing of the burn. Georgia sat on her mother's lap for comfort and support. Lauren used toys to distract Georgia and encouraged the mother to be a part of her daughter's treatment. Georgia occasionally protested by crying: this seemed to be partly due to discomfort and partly because no two-year-old likes to sit still for long. But the dressing was completed without any delays and a calm, relaxed atmosphere was maintained throughout.

1 List the feelings that both Georgia and her mother might be experiencing when they arrived at the A&E unit.
2 What specific skills did Lauren use to help Georgia and her mother?

Activity

How would you provide play for a four-year-old child who has just had an operation to remove his tonsils and adenoids? Think about play before the operation and also in the child's recovery period.

LO8 Understand the role of the EYP when supporting children who are chronically ill

What is a chronic illness?

A chronic illness tends to last a long time – in contrast with acute illnesses, i.e. those of sudden onset and of short duration. A child with a chronic illness shows little change in symptoms from day to day and may still be able – though possibly with some difficulty – to carry out normal daily activities. The disease process is continuous with progressive deterioration, sometimes in spite of treatment. The child may experience an acute exacerbation (flare-up) of symptoms from time to time.

Some examples of chronic illness in young children are:

- juvenile rheumatoid arthritis
- diabetes mellitus (type 1)
- thalassaemia major – an inherited blood disorder
- chronic renal failure
- atopic eczema
- sickle cell disorders (sickle cell anaemia).

Long-term illness may mean that the child's ability to exercise freedom of choice in daily activities is curtailed. Frequent periods of hospitalisation disrupt family and social life, and impose strain on all members of the family; siblings often resent the extra attention given to the sick child, and the parents themselves may also need financial support. Social workers based at hospitals will give advice on any benefits and can provide a counselling service. They may also be able to put parents in touch with a voluntary organisation for the parents of children with similar conditions. Most children's units in hospitals have a separate playroom with trained staff who provide the sick child with an opportunity for a choice of play activities.

AC 8.1 Describe the responsibilities of the EYP when supporting a child who has a chronic health condition

The impact on parents and other family members when children are ill

Having a child with a serious or chronic illness is bound to have an effect on the whole family. Family members will be worried and under considerable stress. While a child is being treated in hospital it is best for everyone if life continues as normally as possible. Parents may be tempted to spoil their child , but as this could cause problems in the long run, the advised approach would be to maintain the same level of discipline. The child will feel more secure if discipline is as usual. Each family is unique in the way that it will react initially and adjust in the long term. Parents whose baby or child develops a chronic or life-threatening illness may react in the following ways, which are part of what is known as the grieving process:

- **Disbelief, shock, numbness, pain and withdrawal**: even when parents suspect that there is something seriously wrong with their child, having their suspicions confirmed may still produce feelings of shock and panic. Explanations from health professionals may be impossible to fully comprehend, and they may feel numb and withdraw initially from others while they try to take in what has happened.
- **Despair and anger**: there may be powerful feelings of resentment and anger – 'Why is this happening to us?' Some of this anger may be directed towards professionals who are responsible both for breaking the bad news and for providing treatment and care.
- **Guilt**: parents may feel that they could have prevented the illness or disability. 'If only we had noticed sooner that something was wrong …' is a common reaction as parents make a great effort to come to terms with a child's serious or life-threatening illness.
- **Confusion**: parents may be unable to understand what is happening, begin to question their ability to be good parents and worry about how they will cope in the future.
- **Isolation and feeling a loss of control**: parents may feel an increasing sense of isolation and feel that they have no control over events. They may feel that nobody else can fully appreciate what they are feeling and nothing can take away their pain.
- **Missing social life**: parents may have less time for each other and for social activities outside the home. Plans for evenings out or holidays may have to be cancelled.

The reactions of brothers and sisters

Just as there are variations in the way parents react to a child's illness, the ways in which the sick child's brothers and sisters react will differ greatly. Their reaction will depend upon their age and stage of development – and particularly on their level of understanding. Common reactions include:

- **Jealousy**: children may feel jealous of all the attention the sick child is getting. Parents and other relatives appear to be focusing all their attention on the ill child, with disruption of previous routines. Some children regress and develop attention-seeking behaviour in an effort to claim more of their parents' time.
- **Guilt and fear**: siblings may feel guilty that they are well and able to play and do things that their sick brother or sister cannot. They may be frightened at the strength and power of their parents' feelings of sadness and may even be afraid that they too could develop the same illness.
- **Neglect**: siblings can feel unloved and neglected by parents and others, whose loving attention may seem exclusively reserved for the sick child. They feel somehow very different from their friends, for whom life seems to go on as normal.
- **Grief**: children may go through a similar grieving process to adults. They may feel overpowering feelings of sadness and loss; these feelings can result in:
  - loss of appetite and lack of energy
  - mood swings – one minute seeming full of energy and optimism, and the next seeming withdrawn and uncommunicative
  - sleeping problems.

The impact of ill health on the development of the child
Physical development

Physical development will almost always be affected when a child has a chronic illness. Depending on the nature and course of the condition, children may experience:

- **Delay in gross motor and fine motor skills development**: this could be because their treatment takes place mostly in a bed or chair, or because the illness itself prevents full mobility. The child may feel constantly tired and lacking in energy.

- **Faltering growth**: this may occur when a child's condition causes an inability to take in the nutrients necessary for growth and development.

Communication and language development
Although children who are away from their peers for long periods of time lack the normal conditions for communication, many children develop very good communication skills because of the increased attention from adults communicating with them.

Intellectual development
Children of school age will be able to have school lessons in hospital, but these have to be fitted in around treatments and care procedures. Also the child may lack the ability or energy to concentrate, and so may fall behind in all aspects of learning.

Emotional and social development
Chronic illnesses can interfere with children's happiness and how they feel about themselves. This can make treatment difficult, as when children are distressed or unhappy their illness may be harder to control.

Increased physical symptoms caused by the illness can also have an effect on a child's emotional development. Other effects include:

- **Poor self-esteem**: feeling unable to do the normal things his or her peers can do because of missing school may cause the child to have poor self-esteem.
- **Feelings of frustration**: children may develop attention-seeking behaviour or become aggressive when they see others doing things they want to do.
- **Regression**: babies and younger children particularly may revert to behaviour typical of a younger age group by becoming clingy, lethargic, tearful or withdrawn.

Family-centred support
It is important that support given to the child and family is **family-centred**. This means that the child's parents have a key role in making decisions about the sort of care their child receives, where the care takes place and how they can establish networks of support.

Professional carers, such as doctors, nurses, social workers and early years practitioners should recognise the needs of the child and the whole family, and aim to meet those needs in an honest, caring and supportive manner.

Parents should be involved in every aspect of their child's illness and encouraged to make decisions about the care their child will receive, for example how much they will be involved in practical care. Parents should never feel pressurised to undertake nursing tasks, such as changing dressings, unless they feel comfortable about them.

Information about the child's illness and the care and treatment involved must be given in a way that is easy to understand, and professionals should operate an 'open door' policy which encourages parents to ask about any aspect of care they are unsure about.

Care plans should be drawn up with the parents' involvement, and should take account of the physical, emotional and social needs of the whole family. Parents and carers who are caring for a sick child at home may experience feelings of isolation and stress. Support groups can help enormously, by putting parents in touch with others who are going through the same difficulties.

Financial help should be available for all parents caring for a chronically ill child at home or in hospital. Extra costs incurred as a direct result of their circumstances include:

- transport costs to get to the hospital or assessment centre
- increased household bills for heating, lighting and laundry
- one parent having to give up work to look after the sick child
- increased telephone bills as parents have to keep in touch with hospital staff, family and friends.

The Benefits Agency can advise parents about the different allowances payable in individual circumstances.

Providing support in the child's early years setting
Whether you are working in the family home as a nanny, in a nursery or in a school, you will need to keep well informed about the family's situation and

to offer appropriate support. You will need to be aware of:

- the child's needs and their stage of development
- how they may be feeling
- any behaviour changes.

Guidelines for how you can help

- You need to offer practical and emotional support to the child and to his or her family.
- Key persons can develop a strong emotional bond with the child and provide a safe, trusting relationship which will help the child and the parents; there should always be a back-up person to help when the child's key person is away.
- Always find time to listen to the child.
- Observe the child closely and try to see if the child is experiencing any areas of difficulty.
- Allow the child to express his or her feelings; encourage children to use play as a form of therapy to release feelings of tension, frustration and sadness; you could offer activities such as playing with dough, bubble-blowing, water play, small world play and home corner play.
- Reassure them that they are very much loved by their family and their carers.

Training and development needs

Those working with children who are chronically ill should consider how to improve their understanding and skills in relation to the individual child's needs. Most settings arrange training opportunities for staff, and some also offer them to parents. You should always be willing to increase your understanding of children's developmental and learning needs. Each member of staff should have a Personal Development Plan or Continuing Professional Development Plan that includes training and personal development goals and how these relate to the aims of the setting. It may be helpful to see a trained counsellor to enable you to talk things over. Ask your tutor or supervisor for support: they should be able to recommend a counsellor.

Partnership working

In hospital, the child and family are helped and supported by a multidisciplinary team of professionals, which includes:

- paediatric nurses
- doctors
- social workers
- play leaders and nursery nurses
- play therapists and health play specialists: they may hold a Level 3 qualification in childcare and education, a Health Play Specialist Certificate, a psychotherapy qualification or other childcare qualification
- teachers: hospital-based teachers provide lessons for children of school age who are in hospital for longer than a week
- counsellors
- representatives of different religious faiths.

Other professionals who may help the child in hospital include physiotherapists, occupational therapists, speech and language therapists, medical social workers and dieticians.

In the community, support is offered by:

- the primary health care team: the GP, district nurse, health visitor and practice nurse
- paediatric specialist nurses: some health authorities operate a 'hospital at home' service
- Macmillan nurses: trained district nurses who specialise in caring for people with life-threatening conditions.

Inclusive practice: multi-agency working and the sharing of information

Inclusive practice in the setting aims to encourage the participation of all children within a mainstream setting. This means that each child is valued as a unique individual and is given appropriate support to enable them to participate fully in the play and learning activities. As with all multi-agency working, the child is the central focus. Members of the primary health care team (the PHCT) will work together in the best interests of the sick child and his or her family. The GP will be responsible for arranging the services and professional help necessary in each individual case. Hospital staff will keep the GP informed of treatment and progress. If a child is of school age, the school nurse will liaise with both the hospital and the GP so that the relevant educational support is put in place.

The support for parents and families who are looking after children who are ill

There are a number of local support groups for the families of children who are ill. Parents can find out about the general and specialist support groups in their area from:

- the reference section in the local public library
- health visitors and GP centres.

There are also a number of useful organisations at national level, most of which have local branches to support families in their own neighbourhood. These include Action for Sick Children and Contact a Family (see Useful resources section below).

Support for self

There may be occasions when you feel overwhelmed by events, or feel inadequate to cope with the demands of your work role. Caring for young children is hard work, and when a child you are caring for has a chronic illness, you will need to be able to talk over your concerns with colleagues. Simply expressing any anxieties will help, but you may also need to find strategies to help you to continue to be effective in your role. One way of doing this is to use your skills of reflective practice. Ask yourself what has worked particularly well – and what has not worked well. Draw up an action plan that will help you to improve your practice.

Activity

Choose one particular chronic illness – for example, type 1 diabetes, epilepsy or cystic fibrosis – and find out how to obtain further information and training. How can you ensure that your practice is inclusive? How can you look after yourself by accessing the appropriate support?

Assessment practice

1. Identify the most common childhood illnesses.
2. Describe the signs and symptoms of common childhood infectious illnesses.
3. Explain the treatments for common childhood illnesses.
4. Identify exclusion periods for common childhood illnesses.
5. What are the signs and symptoms of general ill health in children?
6. When should you call for a doctor or an ambulance?
7. What are notifiable diseases? Describe the process for reporting notifiable diseases.
8. How can the early years practitioner minimise ill health in children?
9. Describe the holistic care needs of a child who is ill.
10. What are the procedures for the storage and administration of medication? What is the procedure for record-keeping in relation to medication in the early years setting?
11. What are the procedures to follow when a child is taken ill in the setting?
12. Explain how you would support a child to prepare for a hospital stay.
13. How does play help to support children's recovery?
14. What is your role when supporting children who are chronically ill?
15. How can you ensure inclusive practice?

Useful resources

Organisations

Action for Sick Children

The UK's leading health charity, specially formed to ensure that sick children always receive the highest standard of care possible. Provides useful information for parents and professionals on all aspects of health care for children: www.actionforsickchildren.org

Contact a Family

This website is for families who have a disabled child and those who work with disabled children or who are interested to find out more about their needs: www.cafamily.org.uk

Health Play Staff

Aims to promote the physical and emotional well-being of children and young people who are patients in hospital, hospice or receiving medical care at home: www.nahps.org.uk.

Unit 1.6 Understand the needs of the mother and baby during pre-conception, pregnancy and the first year of life

This unit provides the learner with the knowledge and understanding of pre-conceptual care, pregnancy, and health and developmental checks during the first year of life.

Learning outcomes

By the end of this unit you will:

1 Understand development from conception to end of gestation.
2 Understand the potential effects on development of pre-conception, pre-birth and birth experiences.
3 Understand post-natal care.
4 Understand developmental checks from birth to 12 months.

LO1 Understand development from conception to end of gestation

AC 1.1 Describe stages of development from fertilisation to end of gestation

Conception

The human reproductive system contains all the organs needed for reproduction or producing babies. Conception occurs in the fallopian tube when a male sperm meets the female egg (the ovum) and fertilises it. The fertilised ovum now contains genetic material from both mother and father, and conception has taken place: a new life begins.

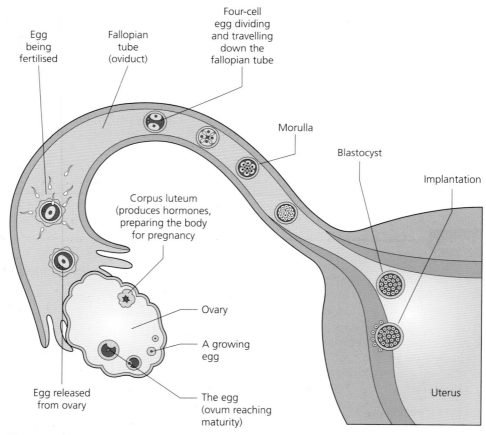

Figure 1.6.1 Ovulation, conception and implantation

Fertilisation

Fertilisation happens when an egg cell meets with a sperm cell and joins with it. This happens after sexual intercourse. Sperm cells travel in semen from the penis and into the top of the vagina. They enter the uterus through the cervix and travel to the egg tubes. If a sperm cell meets with an egg cell there, fertilisation can happen. The fertilised egg divides to form a ball of cells called an **embryo**. This attaches to the lining of the uterus and begins to develop into a **foetus** and finally a baby.

Genes and inheritance

Each cell in the human body contains 23 pairs of **chromosomes** – i.e. 46 chromosomes in total (except the sex cells (sperm and ova), which have 23 chromosomes). When fertilisation takes place, the male and female chromosomes from these sex cells join together to form a new cell, called a **zygote**, which has its full 23 pairs.

Girl or boy?

In humans, sex is determined by the male. Sperm cells contain an X or a Y chromosome, but egg cells contain only X chromosomes. If a sperm cell carrying an X chromosome fertilises the egg, the resulting baby will be female; if the sperm cell is carrying a Y chromosome then the baby will be male.

Each chromosome contains thousands of **genes**. Each gene is responsible for certain individual characteristics inherited from the parents, including eye colour, hair colour and height.

The early days of life

Within about 30 hours of fertilisation, the egg divides into two cells, then four, and so on (see Figure 1.6.3); after five days it has reached the 16-cell stage and has arrived in the uterus (womb).

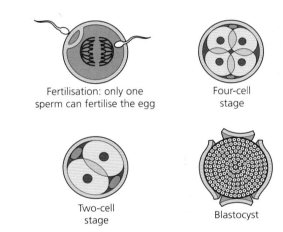

Fertilisation: only one sperm can fertilise the egg

Four-cell stage

Two-cell stage

Blastocyst

Figure 1.6.3 The early days of life

Sometimes a mistake happens and the ovum implants in the wrong place, such as in the fallopian tube; this is called an **ectopic pregnancy** and it is not sustainable. By about the tenth day, the cell mass forms a tiny ball of new tissue called a **blastocyst** and has embedded itself entirely in **endometrium**, and the complex process of development and growth begins. The outer cells of the blastocyst go on to form:

● **the placenta** (called chorionic villi during early development). The placenta (afterbirth) provides the foetus with oxygen and nourishment from the mother via the **umbilical cord** and removes the foetal waste products. The placenta also acts as a

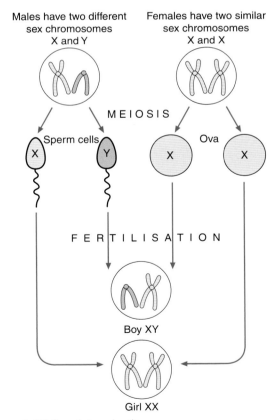

Males have two different sex chromosomes X and Y

Females have two similar sex chromosomes X and X

MEIOSIS

Sperm cells X Y

Ova X X

FERTILISATION

Boy XY

Girl XX

Figure 1.6.2 Sex determination

barrier to certain micro-organisms, but some may cross this barrier and cause damage to the embryo or foetus.

- **amniotic sac** (or membranes). This sac is filled with amniotic fluid (mostly composed of water) and provides a protective cushion for the foetus as it develops and becomes more mobile.

The inner cell mass goes on to form the embryo proper. Until eight weeks after conception, the developing baby is called an **embryo**; from eight weeks until birth, the developing baby is called a **foetus**. The embryonic cells are divided into three layers:

1. The **ectoderm** – forms the outer layer of the baby, the skin, nails and hair; it also folds inwards to form the nervous system (brain, spinal cord and nerves).
2. The **endoderm** – forms all the organs inside the baby.
3. The **mesoderm** – develops into the heart, muscles, blood and bones.

Development of the embryo and foetus

At four to five weeks the embryo is the size of a pea (5 mm), and yet the rudimentary heart has begun to beat, and the arms and legs appear as buds growing out of the sides of the body (Figure 1.6.4).

Embryo 4–5 weeks   Embryo 6–7 weeks

Figure 1.6.4–1.6.5

At six to seven weeks the embryo is 8 mm long and the limb buds are beginning to look like real arms and legs; the heart can be seen beating on an ultrasound scan (Figure 1.6.5).

At eight to nine weeks the unborn baby is called a **foetus** and measures about 2 cm. Toes and fingers are starting to form and the major internal organs (brain, lungs, kidneys,

liver and intestines) are all developing rapidly (Figure 1.6.6).

Foetus 8–9 weeks   Foetus 10–14 weeks

Figure 1.6.6–1.6.7

At 10–14 weeks the foetus measures about 7 cm and all the organs are complete. By 12 weeks the unborn baby is fully formed and just needs to grow and develop. The top of the mother's uterus (the fundus) can usually be felt above the pelvic bones (Figure 1.6.7).

At 15–22 weeks the foetus is large enough for the mother to feel its movements. A mother who has had a child before may feel fluttering sensations earlier as she is able to identify them. At 22 weeks the greasy, white protective film called **vernix caseosa** has begun to form and the foetus is covered with a fine, downy hair called **lanugo** (Figure 1.6.8).

Foetus 15–22 weeks   Foetus 23–30 weeks

Figure 1.6.8–1.6.9

At 23–30 weeks, the foetus is covered in vernix and the lanugo has usually disappeared. From 28 weeks the foetus is said to be **viable** – that is, if born now, he has a good chance of surviving, although babies have survived from as early as 23 weeks. The mother may be aware of his response to sudden or loud noises, and he will be used to the pitch and rhythm of his mother's voice. At 30 weeks the foetus measures 42 cm (Figure 1.6.9).

At 31–40 weeks, the foetus begins to fill out and become plumper; the vernix and lanugo

amniotic sac Often called 'membranes' or the 'bag of waters', the amniotic sac is the bag of amniotic fluid that surrounds and cushions the foetus.

blastocyst The rapidly dividing fertilised egg when it enters the woman's uterus.

embryo The unborn child during the first eight weeks after conception.

endometrium The lining of the womb which grows and sheds during a normal menstrual cycle and which supports a foetus if a pregnancy occurs.

fertilisation The moment when sperm and egg meet, join and form a single cell. It usually takes place in the Fallopian tubes. The fertilised egg then travels into the uterus, where it implants in the lining before developing into an embryo and then a foetus.

foetus the unborn child from the end of the eighth week after conception until birth.

lanugo Downy, fine hair on a foetus. Lanugo can appear as early as 15 weeks of gestation, and typically begins to disappear sometime before birth.

umbilical cord The cord connecting the foetus to the maternal placenta. It contains blood vessels that carry nutrients to the placenta and remove waste substances from the placenta.

vernix A protective white greasy substance that often covers the skin of the newborn baby.

viable Able to maintain an independent existence – to live after birth.

---

disappear and the foetus usually settles into the head-down position ready to be born. If his head moves down into the pelvis it is said to be 'engaged', but this may not happen until the onset of labour (Figure 1.6.10).

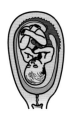

Foetus 31–40 weeks

Figure 1.6.10

Activity

- Where does fertilisation take place?
- When does the embryo become a foetus?
- At what stage is the foetus considered to be viable – i.e. capable of independent life outside the womb?

AC 1.2 Describe antenatal developmental checks

Pregnancy

The signs and symptoms of pregnancy occur after the fertilised ovum has implanted in the lining of the uterus. All women then start to produce a hormone (HCG – human chorionic gonadotropin), which can be detected in the blood or the urine.

Testing for pregnancy

The pregnancy is usually confirmed by a simple urine test which detects the presence of HCG in the urine.

Home pregnancy testing kits are widely available in large supermarkets and chemist shops; they almost always give an accurate result.

Signs and symptoms of pregnancy

- **Missed period (amenorrhoea)**: missing a period is a very reliable symptom of pregnancy if the woman has no other reason to experience a change to her menstrual cycle; occasionally periods may be missed because of illness, severe weight loss or emotional upset.
- **Breast changes**: sometimes the breasts will tingle and feel heavier or fuller immediately; surface veins become visible and the primary **areola**, the ring around the nipple, will become darker. This is more noticeable on fair-skinned women. As pregnancy continues (at about 16 weeks) colostrum can be expressed from the nipple.

- **Passing urine frequently**: the effect of hormones and the enlarging uterus result in women having to pass urine more often than usual.
- **Tiredness:** this can be noticeable in the first three months of pregnancy but usually lifts as the pregnancy progresses.
- **Sickness**: nausea (feeling sick) or vomiting can occur at any time of the day or night, but is usually referred to as 'morning sickness'. Some unlucky women experience nausea throughout pregnancy.

Antenatal care

The main aim of antenatal care is to help the mother deliver a healthy baby. Women are encouraged to see their family doctor (GP) as soon as they think they may be pregnant. The team of professionals – midwife, doctor, health visitor and obstetrician – will discuss the options for antenatal care, delivery and post-natal care with the mother. The women most at risk of developing complications during pregnancy are those in poor housing, on a poor diet or whose attendance at antenatal clinics is infrequent or non-existent. The midwife and health visitor will be aware of the risks such factors pose for both mother and baby, and will target such individuals to ensure that preventive health care, such as surveillance and immunisation, reaches them.

The following is a general guide. Each Area Health Authority will have their own protocol for antenatal care.

Early antenatal care (the first 12 weeks, or first trimester)

The booking appointment

Wherever the woman decides to give birth, early in her pregnancy she will attend a lengthy interview with the midwife, and the medical team will perform various tests. If necessary, a bed is booked for a hospital delivery for around the time the baby is due. Recognition of cultural differences and personal preferences, such as a woman's wish to be seen by a female doctor, is important and most antenatal clinics try to meet such needs. Relatives are encouraged to act as interpreters for women who do not understand or speak little English, and leaflets explaining common antenatal procedures are usually available in different languages.

Taking a medical and obstetric history

This is usually carried out by the midwife and covers the following areas:

- details of the **menstrual cycle** and the date of the last period; the expected delivery date (EDD) is then calculated
- details of any previous **pregnancies**, miscarriages or births
- **medical history** – diabetes, high blood pressure or heart disease can all influence the pregnancy
- **family history** – any serious illness, inherited disorders or history of twins
- **social history** – the need for support at home and the quality of housing will be assessed, especially if the woman has requested a home delivery.

Medical examination

A doctor will need to carry out the following physical examinations:

- listening to the heart and lungs
- **examining breasts** for any lumps or for inverted nipples which might cause difficulties with breastfeeding
- noting the presence of **varicose veins** in the legs and any swelling of legs or fingers.

Clinical tests

- **Height**: this can give a guide to the ideal weight; small women (under 1.5 m or 5ft) will be more carefully monitored in case the pelvis is too narrow for the baby to be delivered vaginally.
- **Weight**: this will be recorded at every antenatal appointment: weight gain should be steady (the average gain during pregnancy is 12–15 kg).
- **Blood pressure**: readings are recorded at every antenatal appointment, as **hypertension** or high blood pressure in pregnancy can interfere with the blood supply to the placenta and may mean a risk of pre-eclampsia.

- **Urine tests**: urine is tested at every antenatal appointment for:
  - **sugar (glucose)**: occasionally present in the urine during pregnancy, but if it persists may be an early sign of diabetes
  - **protein (albumen)**: traces may indicate an infection or be an early sign of **pre-eclampsia** – a special condition only associated with pregnancy where one of the main signs is high blood pressure
  - **ketones**: these are produced when fats are broken down; the cause may be constant vomiting or dieting, or there may be some kidney damage.
- **Blood tests:** a blood sample will be taken and screened for:
  - **blood group**: in case transfusion is necessary; everyone belongs to one of four groups: A, AB, B or O
  - **Rhesus factor**: positive or negative (see p 000)
  - **syphilis**: can damage the baby if left untreated
  - **rubella immunity**: if not immune, the mother should avoid contact with the virus and be offered the vaccination after birth to safeguard future pregnancies
  - **sickle cell disease**: a form of inherited anaemia which affects people of African, West Indian and Asian descent
  - **thalassaemia**: a similar condition which mostly affects people from Mediterranean countries
  - **haemoglobin levels**: the iron content of the blood is checked regularly to exclude **anaemia**.

Dating scan
Women are offered an ultrasound scan called the **dating scan** between 10 and 13 weeks to estimate when the baby is due (the EDD). The scan also determines whether she is expecting more than one baby.

Antenatal notes
A record of antenatal care and appointments will be made, and these are known as the antenatal notes (or Cooperation Card). It will usually be the woman's responsibility to look after these notes, and she should bring them with her to each appointment. They should also be carried on her person throughout the pregnancy, so that, should she fall ill while away from home, all the up-to-date medical information is available to other medical personnel. The hospital or midwife keeps duplicate copies of scans and routine tests.

Antenatal care from 13 to 28 weeks (second trimester)
Visits to the antenatal clinic, GP or community midwife will be monthly during this stage of pregnancy, or more often if problems are detected. However, if the pregnancy is uncomplicated and the woman is in good health, she may not be seen as often as someone who needs to be more closely monitored. On each occasion the following checks are made and recorded on the Antenatal notes:

weight: the average weight gain at this stage is 12 oz or 0.5kg per week	**blood pressure**: a rise in blood pressure could mean there is risk of pre-eclampsia
foetal heart: heard through a portable ear trumpet or using electronic equipment (a **sonic aid**); the normal foetal heart rate is 100–115 beats per minute	**urine test**: a sample of urine is tested routinely for glucose (sugar), albumen (protein) and **ketones**
fundal height (the size of the uterus): this is done by feeling the 'bump' and checking whether the size corresponds to the EDD	**checking for signs of oedema** (or swelling) of ankles and fingers – an early warning sign of pre-eclampsia
an **ultrasound** screening test is usually offered at around 18 to 20 weeks	

By 28 weeks, the hospital will expect to have the mother booked in for a hospital delivery.

Antenatal care from 29 weeks to the birth (the third trimester)
Although this is the shortest trimester, it can often seem to go slowly, as the woman feels heavier and less mobile.

- The unborn baby or foetus is now **viable** – which means that should he or she be born early, there is a very good chance of survival.

- Visits to the antenatal clinic, GP or midwife are fortnightly from 28 weeks and once a week in the final month of pregnancy.
- The same tests are carried out as in the second trimester. By **palpating** (or lightly pressing) the surface of the woman's abdomen to feel the uterus underneath, the doctor or midwife can now predict the baby's weight and its position in the uterus.

Screening tests in pregnancy

Screening tests estimate the risk of the baby being born with certain conditions, such as **Down's syndrome** or **spina bifida**. They aim to detect a disease or condition in the early stages before it causes significant problems, and where treatment can be offered. They are very safe, painless and do not affect the unborn baby in any way.

Ultrasound scan

How does it work?

The operator slowly scans across the abdomen with a hand-held transducer that detects sound waves bounced off the uterus and the baby's body. These are transmitted to a computerised monitor for a visual interpretation. Parents are often offered the first photo of their baby while in the womb.

When and why is it used?

An ultrasound scan may be used at any stage of pregnancy:

- **At eight weeks**: in this early stage of pregnancy, as well as checking the size of the foetus and looking for more than one baby, ultrasound is used to diagnose early complications such as miscarriage
- **At 11 to 13 weeks**: it is now often possible to determine the sex of the baby. The same checks are carried out as at eight weeks and may also be used with the **nuchal fold translucency test** – see below
- **At 18 to 22 weeks**: most women have a more detailed ultrasound scan. Checks are made to ensure that the right amount of fluid surrounds the baby, and the baby's head, heart, spine, limbs and internal organs are examined in detail. The

position, size and function of the **placenta** are also checked. (The placenta joins the mother and foetus and allows exchange of nutrients and waste products between them.) This scan can also identify some physical abnormalities, such as cleft lip or skeletal abnormalities, and can confirm spina bifida if blood tests have shown the baby is at high risk.

Nuchal fold translucency test

This is a screening test for Down's syndrome which is usually offered at 11–14 weeks. It involves an ultrasound scan to measure the thickness of the layer of fluid at the back of the baby's neck. Babies with Down's syndrome have a thicker layer. If it is thicker than average, women are usually offered a further test such as **amniocentesis** (see below) or **CVS** for diagnosis.

AFP (alpha-fetoprotein) test

This is a blood test offered at around 15 to 18 weeks which measures the amount of alpha-fetoprotein (AFP) in the woman's blood. (AFP is a protein made by all unborn babies.) Low levels of AFP can mean that the developing baby has an increased chance of having Down's syndrome, while high levels may indicate an that there is more than one baby or, rarely, an increased chance of neural tube defects such as spina bifida.

Maternal serum screening (MSS)

This simple blood test is offered to women at about 15–16 weeks into pregnancy. It is also sometimes called the Bart's, double or triple test. The sample is tested for certain hormones and proteins, including AFP and HCG with or without oestriol. The measurements are analysed in combination with the mother's age, weight and exact **gestation** (or length of pregnancy), to assess the chance, or risk, of the baby having Down's syndrome. The results of the test are expressed as either a risk value, e.g. 1 in 300, or as a positive or negative screening. Having a positive screening (increased risk) does not mean that the baby will definitely have Down's syndrome. Having a negative screening (low risk) is not a guarantee that the baby will not have Down's syndrome.

Women with a positive result will be offered amniocentesis.

Activity •

- Describe the main antenatal development checks.
- What is an ultrasound scan? What is it used for?
- What is the function of screening tests in pregnancy?

• •

AC 1.3 Identify actions to take in response to outcomes of antenatal developmental checks

Diagnostic tests in pregnancy

Diagnostic tests confirm whether a baby has a certain condition, and are offered if the screening tests predict an increased risk of a problem. Unlike the screening tests, these tests do carry a slight risk of miscarriage.

Amniocentesis

Amniocentesis is a diagnostic test which is usually used between 15 and 19 weeks of pregnancy. It is offered to any woman who has a higher risk of carrying a baby with Down's syndrome – either because she is in the higher age group (over 35) or because prior tests (such as the MSS) have detected a higher risk of abnormality. A fine needle is inserted into the amniotic fluid surrounding the baby. Ultrasound is used to guide the positioning of the needle. The amniotic fluid contains some cells from the baby that are cultured in the laboratory and then analysed in detail. Full results can take up to four weeks.

This is an accurate way of finding out whether the baby has a number of genetic or inherited disorders, such as Down's syndrome or cystic fibrosis. Amniocentesis carries a slight risk of harming the baby or causing a miscarriage.

Chorionic villus sampling (CVS)

For CVS, a fine instrument is inserted through the woman's cervix into the uterus and a sample of the **chorionic villi** (tiny finger-like projections found in the placenta) is removed. These have the same genetic material as the baby. This test looks for similar problems as amniocentesis, although it does not test for neural tube defects. CVS is performed earlier – usually between 10 and 12 weeks of pregnancy – and the results are usually available within a few days. The results are not quite as accurate as amniocentesis, the procedure is technically quite difficult and it is not always successful. There is a slightly higher risk of miscarriage with CVS than with amniocentesis.

Key terms

alpha-fetoprotein A protein produced by the foetus's liver which can be detected in the mother's blood most accurately between the 16th and 18th weeks of pregnancy. High levels of AFP may be associated with spina bifida; low levels may be associated with Down's syndrome.

cystic fibrosis A condition which affects certain organs in the body, especially the lungs and pancreas, by clogging them with thick sticky mucus. New treatments mean people with cystic fibrosis can live relatively healthy lives.

Down's syndrome A genetic disorder resulting from the presence of an extra chromosome; children usually, but not always, have learning difficulties.

neural tube defects This term includes anencephaly, encephalocoele and spina bifida. These conditions occur if the brain and/or spinal cord, together with its protecting skull and spinal column, fail to develop properly during the first month of embryonic life.

spina bifida This occurs when the spinal canal in the vertebral columns is not closed (although it may be covered with skin). Individuals with spina bifida can have a wide range of physical disabilities. In the more severe forms the spinal cord bulges out of the back, the legs and bladder may be paralysed, and obstruction to the fluid surrounding the brain causes hydrocephalus.

LO2 Understand the potential effects on development of pre-conception, pre-birth and birth experiences

AC 2.1 Explain the potential effects on development of pre-conception experiences; pre-birth experiences; birth experiences

The potential effects on development of pre-conception experiences

Pre-conceptual care means both partners work to reduce known risks before trying to conceive in order to create the best conditions for an embryo to grow and develop into a healthy baby – in other words, actively planning for a healthy baby. Caring for the *woman's* health is particularly important because in the very early weeks of pregnancy she may not even know she is pregnant – but the first twelve weeks of life in the womb (or uterus) are the most crucial as this is when all the essential organs are being formed. A balanced diet is important in allowing the woman to build up reserves of the nutrients vital to the unborn baby in the first three months. The known risks to the baby's development are similar to those during pregnancy – for example, if the mother-to-be smokes or drinks alcohol or takes recreational drugs, the unborn baby's development can be impaired.

The potential effects on development of pre-birth experiences

Different factors may affect the growth and development of the foetus while in the womb.

Diet during pregnancy

Every pregnant woman hears about 'eating for two', but the best information available today suggests that this is not good advice. Research shows that it is the quality (not quantity) of a baby's nutrition

before birth that lays the foundation for good health in later life. Therefore, during pregnancy, women should eat a well-balanced diet, and also should do the following:

- **Avoid pre-packed foods** and any foods which carry the risk of salmonella or listeria (such as soft or blue-veined cheeses, pate, liver and raw meat). Listeria can cause miscarriage, premature labour or severe illness in a newborn baby.
- **Take folic acid tablets and have a diet rich in folic acid**: when taken both pre-conceptually and in pregnancy, folic acid helps the development of the brain and spinal cord, and also helps to prevent defects such as spina bifida. Sources of folic acid include broccoli, nuts and wholegrain cereals.

The mother's age

The best age to have a baby from a purely *physical* point of view is probably between 18 and 30 years.

- **Younger mothers**: under the age of 16 years there is a higher risk of having a small or premature baby, of becoming anaemic and suffering from high blood pressure
- **Older first-time mothers**: first-time mothers over the age of 35 run an increased risk of having a baby with a chromosomal abnormality. The most common abnormality associated with age is Down's syndrome. A woman in her twenties has a chance of only one in several thousand of having an affected baby, but by 40 years the risk is about 1 in every 110 births, and at 45 the risk is about 1 in every 30. Amniocentesis can detect the extra chromosome which results in Down's syndrome; it is usually offered routinely to women who are 37 or over.

> **Key terms**
>
> **chromosomal abnormality** An abnormality in the number or structure of chromosomes. Chromosomes are the structures that hold our genes.
>
> **genes** The individual instructions that tell our bodies how to develop and function. They govern our physical and medical characteristics, such as hair colour, blood type and susceptibility to disease.

Number of pregnancies

Some problems occur more frequently in the first pregnancy than in later ones, e.g. breech presentation, pre-eclampsia (see p 000), low birth weight and neural tube defects. First babies represent a slightly higher risk than second and third babies do. The risks begin to rise again with fourth and successive pregnancies; this is partly because the uterine muscles are less efficient, but it also depends to a certain extent on age and on the social factors associated with larger families.

Maternal health

Pre-eclampsia is a complication of later pregnancy that can have serious implications for the well-being of both mother and baby. The oxygen supply to the baby may be reduced and early delivery may be necessary. It is characterised by:

- a rise in blood pressure
- **oedema** (swelling) of hands, feet, body or face, due to fluid accumulating in the tissues
- protein in the urine.

In severe cases, pre-eclampsia may lead to **eclampsia**, in which convulsions (seizures) can occur. This can occasionally threaten the life of both mother and baby. If pre-eclampsia is diagnosed, the woman is admitted to hospital for rest and further tests.

Smoking

Smoking during pregnancy cuts the amount of oxygen supplied to the baby through the placenta. Babies born to mothers who smoke are more likely to be born prematurely or to have a low birth weight. (It is also important to continue not to smoke after the baby is born, as babies born into a household where there is a smoker are more at risk of cot death, chest infections and asthma.)

Alcohol can harm the foetus if taken in excess. Babies born to mothers who drank large amounts of alcohol throughout the pregnancy may be born with foetal alcohol syndrome. These babies have characteristic facial deformities, stunted growth and learning difficulties. Even moderate drinking may increase the risk of miscarriage. It is best to avoid alcohol when trying to conceive, during pregnancy and whilst breastfeeding.

Substance misuse

Most drugs taken by the mother during pregnancy will cross the placenta and enter the foetal circulation. Some of these may cause harm, particularly during the first three months after conception:

- **Prescription drugs**: drugs are sometimes prescribed by the woman's doctor to safeguard her health during pregnancy, such as antibiotics or anti-epilepsy treatment. These have to be very carefully monitored to minimise any possible effects on the unborn child.
- **Non-prescription drugs**: drugs such as aspirin and other painkillers should be checked for safety during pregnancy.
- **Illegal drugs**: recreational drugs such as cocaine, crack and heroin may cause the foetus to grow more slowly. Babies born to heroin addicts are also addicted, and suffer painful withdrawal symptoms. They are likely to be underweight and may even die.

Infection

Viruses and small bacteria can cross the placenta from the mother to the foetus, and may interfere with normal growth and development. During the first three months of a pregnancy, the foetus is particularly vulnerable. The most common problematic infections are:

- **Rubella (German measles)** – a viral infection which is especially harmful to the developing foetus as it can cause congenital defects such as blindness, deafness and learning difficulties. All girls in the UK are now immunised against rubella before they reach childbearing age, and this measure has drastically reduced the incidence of rubella-damaged babies.
- **Cytomegalovirus (CMV)** – this virus causes vague aches and pains, and sometimes a fever. It poses similar risks to the rubella virus such as blindness, deafness and learning difficulties, but – as yet – there is no preventative vaccine. It is thought to infect as many as one per cent of unborn babies, of whom about 10 per cent may suffer permanent damage.

- **Toxoplasmosis** – an infection caused by a tiny parasite. In about one-third of cases, toxoplasmosis is transmitted to the foetus and may cause blindness, hydrocephalus or learning difficulties. Infection in late pregnancy usually has no ill effects. Toxoplasmosis may be caught from eating anything infected with the parasite, including:
  - raw or undercooked meat, including raw cured meat such as Parma ham or salami
  - unwashed, uncooked fruit and vegetables
  - cat faeces and soil contaminated with cat faeces
  - unpasteurised goat's milk and dairy products made from it.
- **Syphilis**: a bacterial sexually transmitted disease (STD). It can only be transmitted across the placenta after the 20th week of pregnancy, and causes the baby to develop congenital syphilis or can even lead to the death of the foetus. If the woman is diagnosed as having the disease at the beginning of pregnancy, it can be treated satisfactorily before the 20th week.

Activity

1 What effects can smoking during pregnancy have on the unborn baby?
2 What effects can drinking alcohol during pregnancy have on the unborn baby?

Research activity

'Foetal Alcohol Syndrome is the biggest cause of non-genetic mental handicap in the western world and the only one that is 100% preventable.' (Foetal Alcohol Syndrome Aware UK)

Visit www.fasaware.co.uk to find out about foetal alcohol syndrome. In groups, prepare a poster that highlights the problems associated with heavy drinking during pregnancy.

The potential effects on development of birth experiences

Birth

The majority of babies are born safely, usually in hospital, but sometimes in a special midwife-led unit or at home.

Most women give birth vaginally, but sometimes the delivery is **assisted** medically, using forceps, vacuum delivery or a Caesarean section.

Key terms

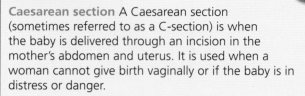

Caesarean section A Caesarean section (sometimes referred to as a C-section) is when the baby is delivered through an incision in the mother's abdomen and uterus. It is used when a woman cannot give birth vaginally or if the baby is in distress or danger.

pre-eclampsia A condition that a mother may develop late in pregnancy, marked by sudden oedema, high blood pressure and protein in the urine. It can lead to eclampsia where the mother has convulsions; antenatal care staff monitor women carefully for the warning signs.

premature (or preterm) baby A premature baby is one who is born before 37 weeks of gestation.

Forceps delivery

Forceps are like tongs that fit around the baby's head to form a protective 'cage'. They are used during the second stage of labour to help deliver the head under the following circumstances:

- to protect the head during a breech delivery (when the baby presents bottom first)
- if the mother has a condition, such as heart disease or high blood pressure, and must not overexert herself
- if the labour is very prolonged and there are signs of foetal distress
- if the baby is very small or pre-term (premature).

Vacuum delivery (ventouse)

This is an alternative to forceps, but can be used before the cervix is fully dilated; gentle suction is applied via a rubber cup placed on the baby's head.

Caesarean section

A Caesarean section is a surgical operation performed under either a general or an epidural anaesthetic; the baby is delivered through a cut in the abdominal wall. The need for a Caesarean section may be identified during pregnancy and is called an **elective** (planned) operation; for example, when the woman is expecting twins or triplets. A Caesarean section may be performed as an emergency in the following circumstances:

- when induction of labour has failed
- when there is severe bleeding
- when the baby is too large or in a position (such as breech) which makes vaginal delivery difficult
- in *placenta praevia* – when the placenta is covering the cervix
- in cases of severe foetal distress
- if the mother is too ill to withstand labour.

Birth trauma

Occasionally, a baby may suffer from foetal distress during the birth process. This is usually caused by a lack of oxygen to the baby's brain (anoxia). During labour, midwives and doctors look out for signs of foetal distress and will often accelerate the delivery by using forceps.

Premature birth

Babies who are born before the 37th week of pregnancy are premature babies. Around 10 per cent of babies are born before 38 weeks of pregnancy, and most of them weigh less than 2,500 g. The main problems for premature babies are as follows:

- **Temperature control** – heat production is low and heat loss is high, because the surface area is large in proportion to the baby's weight, and there is little insulation from subcutaneous fat.
- **Breathing** – the respiratory system is immature and the baby may have difficulty breathing by him or herself; this condition is called respiratory distress syndrome (RDS). This is caused by a deficiency in surfactant, a fatty substance that coats the baby's lungs and is only produced from about 22 weeks of pregnancy.
- **Infection** – resistance to infection is poor because the baby has not had enough time in the uterus to acquire antibodies from the mother to protect against infection.

- **Jaundice** – caused by immaturity of the liver function.

Premature and multiple births: potential effects on development

The extent to which prematurity and multiple births affect the healthy development of the foetus and baby varies a great deal and is linked to how *early* a baby or babies are born. Babies born earlier than 34 weeks may need extra help breathing, feeding and keeping warm. The earlier they are born, the more help they are likely to need in these areas.

Advances in the medical and nursing care of babies born prematurely have meant that many babies born after 35 weeks are able to breathe and feed independently, and their healthy development is not usually affected. However, babies who are born very early – such as around 25 weeks – require intensive neonatal care, which means being nursed in incubators (to maintain their body temperature) and receiving medical assistance with breathing and feeding. These vulnerable babies have a higher risk of developing hearing and sight problems and learning difficulties than those who are born at full term.

Post-term birth

Babies born after the expected date of delivery (after 40 weeks of pregnancy) may also experience problems with breathing, feeding and keeping warm. This is because the placenta stops functioning after about 42 weeks, and so fails to provide the larger baby with enough oxygenated blood.

Activity

- Which foods should be avoided by a pregnant woman, and why?
- What are the potential effects on the unborn child if a woman misuses alcohol and other drugs?
- If contracted by a woman in pregnancy, which infections may have an adverse effect on the foetus?
- Describe three medical interventions used to assist a woman in labour. What are the possible problems for the baby associated with each intervention?

LO3 Understand post-natal care

AC 3.1 Describe post-natal care for the mother and the baby

The post-natal needs of the mother and baby

The pattern of post-natal care is determined by the needs of the woman and her family and – by law – a midwife **must** be in attendance on a woman for at least ten days following delivery. If the mother has had a complicated birth, the midwife can visit for 28 days after the birth. In these first weeks, families need:

- support from their own family and friends
- information, advice and support from the community health service – their GP, midwife and health visitor
- to register the birth of the baby up to six weeks after the birth (or up to three weeks in Scotland).

Post-natal care during the first six weeks after birth

The period from birth to six weeks is called the **puerperium**. For the first ten days the mother will receive help and advice from a midwife, either in hospital or at home. The midwife will:

- feel if the uterus is getting back to its pre-pregnancy size
- check any stitches have dissolved and that healing is complete
- take the mother's blood pressure
- give advice on minor problems, such as constipation
- help to establish feeding
- watch for signs of post-natal depression.

From ten days onwards the health visitor visits mother and baby at home. The purpose of these visits is to:

- offer advice on health and safety issues, including advice on special exercises to strengthen the pelvic floor muscles, which will have been stretched after a vaginal delivery
- check that the baby is making expected progress
- offer support and advice on any emotional problems, including referral to a specialist if necessary

- advise the parents to attend a baby clinic
- discuss a timetable for immunisations
- put the parents in touch with other parents locally.

Giving birth is a momentous event; everyone reacts differently and while many mothers feel an immediate rush of love and excitement, others can feel quite detached, needing time to adjust. Early contact with their newborn baby is as important for fathers as for mothers, and learning how to care for a newborn baby can make couples feel closer.

The 'baby blues'

About half of new mothers will feel a bit weepy, flat and unsure of themselves on the third or fourth day after having a baby; this is called the 'baby blues'. It is a feeling of mild depression caused by hormonal changes, tiredness and reaction to the excitement of the birth, and it passes after a few days. It is more common in first-time mothers and in those who have experienced problems with pre-menstrual syndrome (PMS or PMT). If these feelings persist for longer than a few days, the mother may develop a more serious condition, post-natal depression, and she will need medical help.

Post-natal depression

Post-natal depression (PND) usually develops within the first month following childbirth. Around one in ten mothers experience PND. It may or may not develop out of the 'baby blues', and the mother will show similar symptoms to those seen in 'ordinary' depression:

- **Feeling low, miserable and tearful** for no apparent reason: these feelings persist for most of the time, though they may be worse at certain times of day, particularly the morning.
- **Feeling resentful and angry**: this may be particularly noticeable in first-time mothers who feel that they are not enjoying having a new baby in the way they anticipated.
- **Feeling constantly tired**: disturbed sleep patterns are a natural part of looking after a new baby. But mothers with post-natal depression find it hard to go to sleep even though they are tired, or they wake early in the morning.
- **Feeling tense and anxious**: the normal worries and anxieties which any mother feels for a new

baby may become overwhelming. Also some mothers experience 'panic attacks', which are episodes lasting several minutes when they feel as if something disastrous is about to happen – such as collapsing or having a heart attack.

- **Feeling unable to cope**: when people are depressed, they sometimes feel that there is no way out of their problems and even the simplest of tasks seems too much.
- **Loss of appetite**: mothers may not feel hungry and forget to eat at a time when they need to have a good healthy diet.

Nobody knows why some mothers become depressed after childbirth, although it may occur partly because of the hormonal changes following childbirth.

Treatment for post-natal depression

It is treated in much the same way as ordinary depression. The following measures are helpful:

- talking about the problem with somebody, such as the health visitor or general practitioner
- getting extra support and help with looking after the baby from partner and close family members
- medication in the form of antidepressants may be necessary.

In severe cases of post-natal depression the mother and her baby will be admitted to a psychiatric hospital for more intensive therapy. (Post-natal depression should not be confused with the much more serious condition puerperal psychosis: this is a very rare mental illness – affecting fewer than 1 in 500 women – which always requires treatment in a psychiatric unit.)

Post-natal care for the mother and baby
The post-natal check: six weeks after the birth

At the end of the puerperium, a post-natal check is carried out by a GP or hospital doctor. The mother has the following checks:

- **Weight**: breastfeeding mothers tend to lose weight more quickly than those who are bottle-feeding, but most mothers are almost back to their pre-pregnancy weight.

- **Urine test**: to make sure the kidneys are working properly and that there is no infection.
- **Blood pressure** may be checked.
- **Perineal check**: the mother will be asked if she has any concerns about the healing of any tear, cut or stitches in her perineum (the area between the vagina and the rectum). If she is concerned, the midwife or doctor will offer to examine her.
- **Rubella immunity check**: if she is not immune to rubella (German measles) and was not given an immunisation before leaving hospital, the mother will be offered one now.
- **Discussion points**: the doctor will ask about the following:
  - whether the mother has had a period yet or if there is any discharge
  - any concerns about contraception or any aspect of sex
  - how the mother is feeling – e.g. if very tired, low or depressed.

The baby's six-week check

The baby's six-week check is usually carried out at the same time as the mother's. This is a thorough examination of the baby's health and development; for example, the baby's heart is listened to, his or her weight and length measured and general behaviour noted. The mother is asked about any problems and the information is recorded on the **Personal Child Health Record** (PCHR). See Figure 1.6.11 for an example.

Key terms

perineum The skin between the vagina and the rectum.

post-natal The first days and weeks after the birth of the baby (post = after, natal = birth).

puerperium The period of about six weeks which follows immediately after the birth of a child.

Activity

- What is the role of the health visitor during the post-natal period?
- What is the difference between the 'baby blues' and post-natal depression?
- List four checks carried out on the mother at the post-natal check at six weeks after the birth.

Do you feel well yourself?	yes ☐	no ☐	not sure ☐
Do you have any worries about feeding your baby?	yes ☐	no ☐	not sure ☐
Do you have any concerns about your baby's weight gain?	yes ☐	no ☐	not sure ☐
Does your baby watch your face and follow with his/her eyes?	yes ☐	no ☐	not sure ☐
Does your baby turn towards the light?	yes ☐	no ☐	not sure ☐
Does your baby smile at you?	yes ☐	no ☐	not sure ☐
Do you think your baby can hear you?	yes ☐	no ☐	not sure ☐
Is your baby startled by loud noises?	yes ☐	no ☐	not sure ☐
Are there any problems in looking after your baby?	yes ☐	no ☐	not sure ☐
Do you have any worries about your baby?	yes ☐	no ☐	not sure ☐

Any other issues you would like to discuss? ....
....
....

Results of newborn bloodspot screening

Condition	Results received? yes / no / not done	Follow-up required? no / yes & reason	If follow-up, outcome of follow-up
PKU			
Hypothyroidism			
Sickle Cell			
Cystic Fibrosis			
Other			

Figure 1.6.11 Personal Child Health Record

AC 3.2 Describe concerns parents may have following the birth of a baby

Having a baby and becoming a parent are one of the greatest changes in anyone's life, and a variety of emotions may be experienced. The arrival of a new person in the family usually brings great happiness, but it also signals a loss of freedom and many conflicting demands.

Feeding in the early days

Newborn babies tend to feed at least 8 to 12 times in a 24-hour period. At first, babies may feed more at night than during the day. Although breast milk is the perfect food for a baby, and is recommended by the NHS, not all mothers choose to breastfeed. They should not be persuaded into breastfeeding against their real feelings or forced into it out of a sense of guilt. The most important thing is that the mother feels relaxed and is able to enjoy her new baby in a way that suits her best.

Whether breastfeeding or using formula feeds, common concerns include the following:

- how often to feed
- how to know that the baby is getting enough.

With a new baby it helps to be aware of 'early feeding cues', which are signals that the baby is ready to feed. The baby might put her hands to her mouth or turn her head from side to side, for instance – or start crying.

Babies feed for many reasons – mainly to get the food and drink they need to grow and stay healthy, but they also feed in order to establish a relationship with the mother, for reassurance, and for closeness.

In the early days, parents can be reassured that their baby is feeding enough if she is gaining weight as expected, producing at least six wet nappies a day and appears to be contented and healthy.

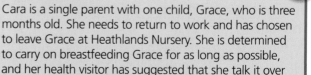

Case study

Cara is a single parent with one child, Grace, who is three months old. She needs to return to work and has chosen to leave Grace at Heathlands Nursery. She is determined to carry on breastfeeding Grace for as long as possible, and her health visitor has suggested that she talk it over with the baby room supervisor before returning to work.

1. What are the main points Cara needs to consider when leaving Grace in full-time nursery care?
2. As Grace's key person, how can you help to smooth the way for Cara to continue breastfeeding?

Crying in young babies

Crying is a baby's way of expressing his or her needs. Finding out why a baby is crying is often a matter of elimination, so it is important that all carers should understand the physical and emotional needs of a baby at each stage of development (see Table 1.6.1).

Persistent crying

Periods of inconsolable crying are not unusual in newborn babies. Some babies do cry a great deal more than others, and are difficult to soothe and comfort. Parents and carers can feel quite desperate through lack of sleep and may develop personal problems; they may suffer guilt at not being able to

Hunger

This is the most common cause of crying. It is quite likely unless the baby has just been fed. Breastfed and bottle-fed babies should be fed on demand in the early weeks. By the age of six months, the baby will probably need solid foods.

Being undressed

Most new babies hate being undressed and bathed, because they miss the contact between fabric and bare skin. One solution is to place a towel or shawl across the baby's chest and tummy when she is naked.

Discomfort

Until they can turn themselves over, babies rely on an adult to change their position. Babies show marked preferences for sleeping positions.

Nappy needs changing

Some babies dislike being in a wet or dirty nappy and there may be nappy rash.

Twitches and jerks

Most new babies make small twitching and jerking movements as they are dropping off to sleep. Some babies are startled awake and find it difficult to settle to sleep because of these twitches. Wrapping a baby up firmly – or swaddling – usually solves the problem.

Overtired or overstimulated

Some babies can refuse to settle if there is too much bustle going on around them, e.g. loud noises, too much bouncing or bright lights in a shopping centre; take her somewhere quiet and try rhythmical rocking, patting and generally soothing her.

Pain or illness

A baby might have a cold or snuffles and be generally fretful or may have an itchy rash, such as eczema. (For signs and symptoms of illness in babies, see Unit 1.3.)

Allergy

An Intolerance of cow's milk could cause crying; seek medical advice.

Thirst

In particularly hot weather, babies may be thirsty and can be given cool boiled water. Breastfed babies may be offered an extra feed as breast milk is a good thirst-quencher.

Feeling too hot or too cold

Temperature control is not well developed in the young baby. If too hot, he or she will look red in the face, feel very warm and may be sweaty around the neck folds; loosen clothes and wrappings and remove some layers of bedding, but watch for signs of chilling. If too cold, he or she may also have a red face or may be pale. To check, feel the hands, feet, tummy and the back of the neck. Cuddle the baby, wrap a blanket around him or her and try a warm feed.

➜

Table 1.6.1 Causes of crying

Boredom/need for physical contact
Babies find being cuddled or carried reassuring; talk to her and provide interesting objects for her to look at and a mobile; put pram under a tree or near a washing line so that he or she can see movements (NB: remember to fix a cat net to prevent insects and other unwanted visitors).

Colic
If the baby cries after being fed or has long bouts of crying, especially in the evening, he or she may be suffering from colic.

Child abuse
A baby who has been abused in any way may cry and the carer should seek help from appropriate professionals (see Unit 2.2).

Table 1.6.1 Causes of crying   (*Continued*)

Guidelines for helping a crying baby

- Make sure the baby is not hungry or thirsty.
- Check that the baby is not too hot or cold.
- Check that the baby is not physically ill (see Unit 1.5 for signs of illness in babies).
- Check if the baby's nappy needs changing.
- Treat colic or teething problems.
- Cuddle the baby and try rocking gently in your arms (the most effective rate of rocking is at least 60 rocks a minute; the easiest way to achieve this rapid and soothing rocking without getting exhausted is to walk while rocking her from side to side).
- Rock the baby in a cradle or pram.
- Talk and sing to the baby.
- Take the baby for a walk or a car ride.
- Leave the baby with someone else and take a break.
- Play soothing music or a womb-sounds recording.
- Talk to a health visitor, GP or a parent's helpline.

- Accept that some babies will cry whatever you do.
- Remember that this phase will soon pass.

If the crying ever feels too much to bear:

- Take a deep breath and let it out slowly. Put the baby down in a safe place, like a cot or a pram. Go into another room and sit quietly for a few minutes, perhaps with a cup of tea and the television or radio on to help take your mind off the crying. When you feel calmer, go back to the baby.
- Ask a friend or relative to take over for a while.
- Try not to get angry with the baby. She will instinctively recognise your displeasure and will probably cry even more.
- Never let things get so bad that you feel desperate. There are lots of organisations at the end of a telephone line that can help.

make their baby happy or lack confidence in caring for her. Such feelings of desperation and exhaustion can unfortunately result in physical violence to the baby – throwing her into the cot, shaking her or even hitting her. Parents experiencing such stress need a great deal of support.

Colic

Some babies keep on crying even when you have tried everything and there are no obvious signs of illness. Colic is excessive crying or extended and repeated periods of crying or fussing in babies who are otherwise healthy and thriving. Common

symptoms in babies usually begin within the first few weeks of life and generally end by around three months.

Reflux

Excessive crying might also be caused by reflux, which occurs when the stomach contents – food (milk) and acid – come back up into the throat or into the mouth. Most babies have reflux to a certain degree because the muscular valve at the end of their food pipe, which acts to keep food in the stomach, has not developed properly yet. This is painful for only a small proportion of babies.

The effects on the family when a baby is in a special care baby unit

Parents whose baby has been transferred to a special care baby unit (SCBU) or neonatal intensive care unit often feel very anxious and helpless. Such an environment can be very frightening for the parents, and staff will do everything they can to keep any separation to the minimum.

- **Feeling of helplessness**: the baby they had so eagerly anticipated now seems totally at the mercy of strangers and is surrounded by highly technical and often very noisy machinery. Often parents feel that there is nothing that they can do to protect and care for their own child. Sometimes they feel guilty – that they did or did not do something which has caused their child to be ill.
- **Worry about the baby**: low birth-weight babies usually sleep more and may seem less alert than full-term babies, and parents will welcome reassurance from the staff that this is normal behaviour. Premature babies also look very thin and frail, and may have red wrinkled skin. Parents will naturally worry whether their baby will survive and be healthy.
- **Bonding**: some mothers may be too ill to visit their baby straightaway. Staff caring for neonates value the importance of early mother–baby bonding and encourage parents and close family to talk to and touch the baby, after observing the required hygiene precautions. If the baby is too ill or frail to leave the incubator, the hospital will take a photograph of the baby that the parents can have immediately.
- **Family members under strain**: other children in the family will need caring for while the mother is with the new baby. Fathers may have to fit their visits around their normal working day.

AC 3.3 Identify sources of support for parents following the birth of a baby

After the baby has arrived, it is the role of midwives and health visitors to help parents look after their baby as well as themselves. All families receive a visit from a health visitor around two weeks after their baby is born, to check that the baby is healthy and developing well and to support parents with the challenges of early parenthood.

The role of the health visitor

The health visitor is a qualified registered nurse, midwife, sick children's nurse or psychiatric nurse with specialist qualifications in community health, which includes child health, health promotion and education. The health visitor's role is to offer support and encouragement to families through the early years from pregnancy and birth to primary school and beyond. They work closely with GPs and cover the geographical area of the GP practice.

Every family with children under five has a named health visitor. Health visitors offer help and advice to parents on the following:

- their child's growth and development
- common infections in childhood
- common skin problems
- behaviour difficulties
- sleeping, eating, potty training, temper tantrums and teething
- breastfeeding, weaning, healthy eating, hygiene, safety and exercise
- post-natal depression, bereavement and violence in the family.

Health visitors are also involved in:

- working in partnership with families to tailor health plans to their needs
- coordinating child immunisation programmes
- organising and running baby clinics
- breastfeeding support groups
- parent support groups, and parenting courses.

The general practitioner (GP)

This is a doctor who has taken further training in general practice. Every family should be registered with a GP, and he or she is the first port of call in cases of illness in the family.

The paediatrician

This is a doctor who has specialised in the care of children up to the age of 16 years. Paediatricians attend all difficult births in case the baby needs resuscitation. The GP may refer a baby or child to a paediatrician for specialist support.

Self-help groups

Often just talking to others helps the carer to feel less isolated. Self-help groups such as Cry-sis or the

National Childbirth Trust Post-natal Support System can help by offering support from someone who has been through the same problem.

LO4 Understand developmental checks from birth to 12 months

AC 4.1 Explain routine checks carried out for the newborn and the baby during the first year of life

Routine checks carried out for the newborn

The first question usually asked by parents is: 'Is the baby okay?' The doctor and midwife will observe the newborn baby closely and perform several routine tests and checks that will show whether the baby has any obvious physical problem (see Figure 1.6.12).

The Apgar score

This is a standard method of evaluating the condition of a newborn baby by checking five vital signs (See chart below). The **Apgar score** is assessed at one minute and five minutes after birth; it may be repeated at five-minute intervals if there is cause for concern.

Most healthy babies have an Apgar score of nine, only losing one point for having blue extremities; this often persists for a few hours after birth. A low score at five minutes is more serious than a low score at one minute. In hospital, the paediatrician will be notified if the score is six or under at five minutes. Dark-skinned babies are assessed for oxygenation by checking for redness of the conjunctiva and inside the mouth.

Interpreting the Apgar score

- 10: the baby is in the best possible condition
- 8–9: the baby is in good condition
- 5–7: the baby has mild asphyxia (lack of oxygen in the blood) and may need treatment
- 3–4: the baby has moderate asphyxia and will need treatment
- 0–2: the baby has severe asphyxia and needs urgent resuscitation.

The face is examined for cleft palate – a gap in the roof of the mouth, and facial paralysis – temporary paralysis after compression of the facial nerve, usually after forceps delivery

Eyes are checked for cataract (a cloudiness of the lens)

Hands are checked for webbing (fingers are joined together at the base) and creases – a single unbroken crease from one side of the palm to the other is a feature of Down's syndrome

The head is checked for size and shape: any marks from forceps delivery are noted

The heart and lungs are checked using a stethoscope; any abnormal findings will be investigated

The neck is examined for any obvious injury to the neck muscles after a difficult delivery

Feet are checked for webbing and talipes (club foot), which needs early treatment

Genitalia and anus are checked for any malformation

Skin – vernix and lanugo may still be present, milia may show on the baby's nose; black babies appear lighter in the first week of life as the pigment, melanin, is not yet at full concentration

The spine is checked for any evidence of spina bifida

Hips are tested for cogenital dislocation using Barlow's test

The abdomen is checked for any abnormality, e.g. pyloric stenosis, where there may be obstruction of the passage of food from the stomach; the umbilical cord is checked for infection

Figure 1.6.12 Examination of the newborn baby

Signs	0	1	2
Heartbeat	absent	slow – below 100	fast – over 100
Breathing	absent	slow – irregular	good; crying
Muscle tone	limp	some limb movement	active movement
Reflex response (to stimulation of foot or nostril)	absent	grimace	cry, cough, sneeze
Colour		body oxygenated, hands and feet blue	well oxygenated

Table 1.6.2 The Apgar score

Neonatal screening tests

Three screening tests are carried out on the newborn baby to check for specific disorders that can be treated successfully if detected early enough.

Barlow's test: this is a test for congenital dislocation of the hip and is carried out soon after birth, at six weeks and at all routine developmental testing opportunities until the baby is walking. There are varying degrees of severity of this disorder; treatment involves the use of splints to keep the baby's legs in a frog-like position.

The newborn bloodspot test: all babies are screened for **phenylketonuria** and **congenital hypothyroidism**; in some areas babies are also screened for **cystic fibrosis**, **sickle cell disorders** and some other conditions. A small blood sample is taken from the baby's heel and sent for analysis.

- **phenylketonuria** is very rare, affecting 1 in 10,000 babies; it is a metabolic disorder which leads to brain damage and learning delay. Early diagnosis is vital since treatment is very effective. This involves a special formula protein diet which has to be followed throughout the person's life.
- **congenital hypothyroidism** (CHT) affects 1 in 4,000 babies in UK. Babies born with this condition do not have enough thyroxin; untreated babies develop serious, permanent, physical and mental disability. Early treatment with thyroxin tablets prevents disability and should start by 21 days of age.

Screening for hearing impairment
The otoacoustic emissions (OAE) test
Newborn babies are usually screened using the otoacoustic emissions (OAE) test. A tiny earpiece is placed in the baby's outer ear and quiet clicking sounds are played through it. This should produce reaction sounds in a part of the ear called the cochlea, and the computer can record and analyse these. It is painless and can be done while the baby is asleep. Sometimes clear results are not obtained from the OAE test. Then a different method can be used, called the automated auditory brainstem response (AABR): small sensors are placed on the baby's head and neck, and soft headphones are placed over the ears. Quiet clicking sounds are played through the earphones and a computer analyses the response in the brain, using information from the sensors.

Screening for visual disorders
Screening tests for visual problems are carried out on all children at: the newborn examination, the six-week check and the pre-school (or school-entry) vision check.

The newborn examination and six-week check
The eyes of newborn babies are examined for any obvious physical defects, including cross eyes, cloudiness (a sign of cataracts) and redness. This examination includes:

- **The red reflex**: this test uses an **ophthalmoscope**. Light is directed into the baby's eyes and a red reflection should be seen as the light is reflected back. If the reflection is white instead, the child will be referred to a specialist immediately, as it can be a sign of a cataract or other eye condition.

- The **pupil reflex** is checked by shining a light into each eye from a distance of 10 cm. The pupils should automatically shrink in response to brightness.
- **General inspection of the eyes** may suggest other conditions. For example, one eye larger than the other may indicate glaucoma.

A **specialist examination** is indicated in babies who have:

- an abnormality detected in the above routine examinations, or
- a known higher risk of visual disorders; for example, low birth-weight babies at risk of retinopathy of prematurity; babies who have a close relative with an inheritable eye disorder; and babies with known hearing impairment.

Key terms

orthoptist A professional who investigates, diagnoses and treats defects of vision and abnormalities of eye movement.

retinopathy of prematurity An abnormal growth of blood vessels in the retina at the back of a premature baby's eye; when severe it can cause loss of vision.

Developmental reviews during the baby's first year
Personal Child Health Record

All parents are issued with a PCHR (or Red Book) that enables them to keep a record of their child's development. This form is completed by doctors, health visitors and parents, and is a useful source of information if the child is admitted to hospital or is taken ill when the family are away from home.

Centile growth charts

Each child's growth is recorded on a centile chart in the child's PCHR. This allows parents and health professionals to see how their height and weight compare to other children of the same age. Boys and girls have different charts because boys are on average heavier and taller, and their growth pattern is slightly different.

Since May 2009, the centile charts in the PCHR or red book have been based on measurements taken by the World Health Organization from healthy, breastfed children with non-smoking parents from a range of countries.

The charts are used to plot height (or, in young babies, length), weight and head circumference. See Figure 1.6.13.

- The 50th centile (or percentile) is the **median**. It represents the middle of the range of growth patterns.
- The 15th centile is close to the bottom of the range. If the height of a child is on the 15th centile, it means that in any typical group of 100 children, 85 would measure more and 15 would measure less.

The 85th centile is close to the top of the range. If the weight of a child is on the 85th centile, then in any typical group of 100 children, 85 would weigh less and 15 would weigh more.

Developmental reviews

Parents will want to know as soon as possible if their child has problems: it is easier to come to terms with a serious problem in a young baby than in an older child. Early years practitioners are usually very astute in recognising abnormalities in development because of their experience with a wide variety of children.

Developmental reviews give parents an opportunity to say what they have noticed about their child. They can also discuss anything that concerns them about their child's health and behaviour. Child development is reviewed by doctors and health visitors, either in the child's home or in health clinics. The areas that are looked at are:

- **gross motor skills** – sitting, standing, walking, running
- **fine motor skills** – handling toys, stacking bricks, doing up buttons and tying shoelaces (gross and fine manipulative skills)
- **speech and language** – including hearing
- **vision** – including squint
- **social behaviour** – how the child interacts with others, such as family and friends.

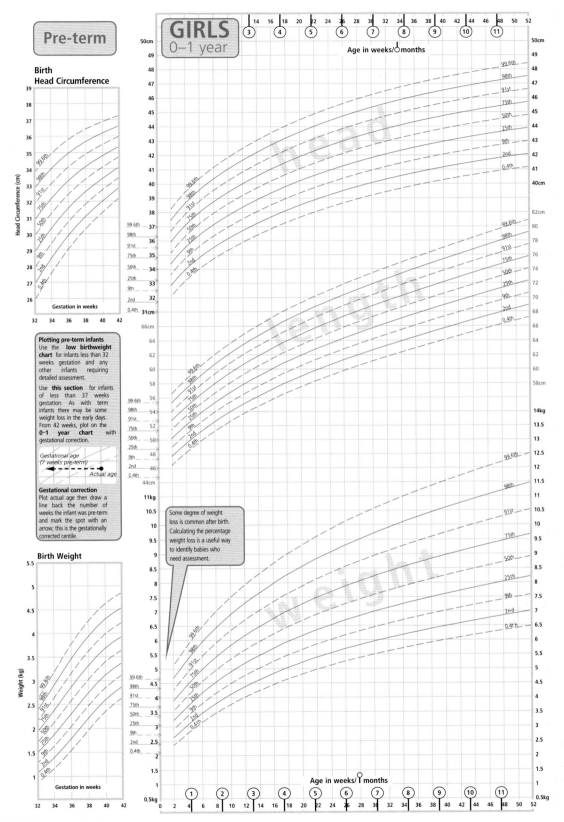

Figure 1.6.13 Growth chart

Early detection is important as:

- early treatment may reduce or even avoid permanent damage in some conditions
- an early diagnosis (of an inherited condition) may allow genetic counselling and so avoid the birth of another child with a disabling condition.

6- to 8-week check			
Parental concerns	**Observation**	**Measurement**	**Examination**
The doctor will ask the parent about: - feeding - bowel actions - sleeping - micturition (passing urine).	While the parent is undressing the baby for examination, the doctor will look out for: - the responsiveness of the baby – smiles, eye contact, attentiveness to parent's voice, etc. - any difficulties the parent has holding the baby – which may indicate maternal depression - jaundice and anaemia. The general appearance of the baby will give an indication of whether he or she is well nourished.	- The baby is weighed naked and the weight is plotted on the growth chart (see page 133). - The head circumference is measured and plotted on the growth chart.	- The eyes are inspected using a light – the baby will turn his or her head and follow a small light beam. An ophthalmoscope is used to check for a cataract. - The heart is auscultated (i.e. listened to with a stethoscope) to exclude any congenital defect. - The hips are manipulated, again to exclude the presence of congenital dislocation of the hips. - The baby is placed prone and will turn his or her head to one side; hands are held with the thumbs inwards and the fingers wrapped around them. - The posterior fontaneile is usually closed by now; the anterior fontaneile does not close until around 18 months.
Hearing			
Most babies will have been screened soon after birth. There is no specific test at this age. The parent is asked if or she thinks the baby can hear. A baby may startle to a sudden noise or freeze for some sounds.			
Health education points			
The doctor will discuss the following health topics, give the first immunisation and complete the personal child health record. - Nutrition: breastfeeding, preparation of formula feeds, specific feeding difficulties. - Immunisation: discuss any concerns and initiate a programme of vaccinations. - Passive smoking: babies are at risk of respiratory infections and middle ear disease. - Illness in babies: how to recognise symptoms. - Crying: coping with frustration and tiredness. - Reducing the risk of cot death (SIDS: sudden infant death syndrome).			

Table 1.6.3 Developmental checks in the first six to eight weeks

6- to 9-month check			
Parental concerns	**Observation**	**Measurement**	**Examination**
The doctor or health visitor will enquire again about any parental concerns.	The doctor will look out for: ● socialisation and attachment behaviour ● visual behaviour ● communication – sounds, expressions and gestures ● motor development – sitting, balance, use of hands, any abnormal movement patterns.	Head circumference and weight are plotted on the growth chart.	Manipulation of the hips is carried out. ● The heart is listened to with a stethoscope. ● The testes are checked in boys. ● The eyes are checked for a squint – if this is present, the child is referred to an ophthalmologist (eye specialist); visual behaviour is checked. ● Hearing is sometimes tested by the distraction test.

Health education points

● Nutrition: weaning; control of sugar intake.
● Immunisations: check they are up to date.
● Teeth: regular brushing once teeth appear; information on fluoride; visit the dentist.
● The need for play and language stimulation.
● Accident prevention.

2-year check

This check is similar to the previous tests. It is often easier for the health visitor to carry out the check during a home visit. The parent is asked about any general concerns. A physical examination is not normally carried out at this age.

● The height is measured if the child is cooperative.
● Weight is only checked if there is reason for concern.
● The parent is asked if there are any concerns about vision and hearing, and the child is referred to a specialist if necessary.
● A check is made that the child is walking and that the gait (manner of walking) is normal.
● Behaviour and any associated problems are discussed (e.g. tantrums, sleep disturbance, poor appetite or food fads).
● The possibility of iron deficiency is considered. It is common at this age and may be a cause of irritability and developmental and behavioural problems, as well as anaemia.

Health education points

● Nutrition and dental care: the child will be referred to the dentist if teeth are obviously decayed.
● Immunisations: check they are up to date.
● Common behavioural difficulties, such as temper tantrums, sleep disturbance, toilet training.
● Social behaviour: learning to play with other children and to share possessions.
● Accident prevention.

→

Table 1.6.4 Developmental checks at six to nine months

Parental concerns	Observation	Measurement	Examination
This check is usually carried out by the GP and the health visitor. The parent is asked if there are any general concerns about the child's progress and development, or any behavioural or emotional problems.	• Motor skills – can the child walk, run and climb stairs? Does the child tire more quickly compared with other children? • Fine manipulative skills – can the child control pencils and paintbrushes? • Behaviour – parents are asked about the child's ability to concentrate, to play with others and to separate from his or her parents without distress. • Vision, language and hearing – observation and discussion with the parent will determine any problems that may need specialist assessment.	Height and weight are measured and plotted on the growth chart.	• The heart is listened to for any abnormal sounds. • The lungs are listened to for wheezing. • In a boy, the testes will be checked again; if still not descended, he will be referred to a surgeon. • The spine is inspected for signs of curvature or spina bifida occulta. • Blood pressure is usually measured only if the child has a history of renal disease or growth problems.

Health education points

• Immunisation: pre-school booster.
• Dental care: diet – danger of sweets and snacks; brushing teeth; dental decay; visits to the dentist.
• The child's needs for play, conversation and social learning.
• The recognition and management of minor ailments.
• Accident prevention.

8-year check

This is carried out by the school nurse, and parents are encouraged to attend the sessions at school. It involves the following:

• a general review of progress and development; the parent may voice concerns such as bedwetting (enuresis) or food fads
• height and weight are measured
• vision is tested and, if a problem is found, the child is referred to an ophthalmologist or optician.

Health education points

• Accident prevention: particularly safety on the roads and awareness of 'stranger danger'
• Diet
• Exercise
• Dental health.

Hearing

Parents who are concerned that their child is not hearing properly should have access to hearing testing. This is particularly important if the child has had:

• meningitis
• measles
• mumps
• recurrent ear infections or glue ear.

Table 1.6.4 Developmental checks at six to nine months (*Continued*)

Activity

Visit your local baby clinic or child development clinic and find out about the developmental checks carried out on babies during their first year.

Assessment practice

1 Describe the stages of development from fertilisation to the end of gestation.
2 Describe the developmental checks carried out during the antenatal period. What is the purpose of the ultrasound scans?
3 If routine screening shows any deviation from the expected, what other tests may be offered to the pregnant woman?
4 Why is it important for a couple to eat a balanced healthy diet before conceiving a child?
5 What are the potential risks to the foetus if the mother smokes or drinks throughout pregnancy?
6 Describe the potential effects on development of birth experiences.
7 What is meant by post-natal care? When do both mother and baby receive a medical health check after the birth of the baby?
8 What are the main concerns for parents following the birth of a baby?
9 Identify sources of support for parents following the birth of a baby.
10 Describe the routine checks carried out for (a) the newborn, and (b) the baby until one year old.

Useful resources

Organisations

Cry-sis has advice on coping with a crying or sleepless baby. The Cry-sis helpline – 08451 228 669 (08451 ACT NOW) – is open seven days a week from 9am to 10pm, and can give parents the number of a volunteer contact who has experienced similar problems in the past and can understand what they are going through.

Home-Start has a parent-helper visiting scheme and a helpline 08000 68 63 68 (Monday–Friday 8am–8pm and Saturday 9am–12pm).

National Childbirth Trust (NCT) is a support group for parents. It aims to give accurate, impartial information so that parents can decide what is best for their family, and introduces them to a network of local parents to gain practical and emotional support. The NCT is the UK's largest charity for parents, and campaigns as the voice for parents on the issues they care about.

In profile

My name is Sian and I have been working in the baby room in a large nursery for three years. During this time, I have met many different families with very different backgrounds and upbringings. Working with babies can be challenging especially when there are three hungry mouths to feed and only one of me!

I have six key children for whom I take the key role of care and track their development, providing activities that will help them achieve their next steps. The thing I enjoy most about working with babies is the bond that is formed between us and the partnership formed with the family as we are usually the first people they are entrusting their children with. It is a very special relationship and we do all we can to include parents within the setting, from sending messages and pictures home via email, digital photo frames, and regular stay and plays where parents and carers can come into the nursery setting and spend time with their child. During this time they can meet other parents and share information with each other and us.

The nursery in which I work has large premises and we are lucky to have so much outdoor space in which the children can grow and develop. I am particularly proud of our garden area which we have just redeveloped, making it more child-friendly and now includes more natural features.

Unit 2.1 An introduction to the role of the early years practitioner

This unit provides the learner with an introduction to the role of the early years practitioner.

Learning outcomes

By the end of this unit you will:

1 Understand the role of the early years practitioner.
2 Be able to communicate to meet individuals' needs and preferences.
3 Understand working relationships in early years.
4 Understand why Continuing Professional Development is integral to the role of the early years practitioner.

LO1 Understand the role of the early years practitioner

All those working with children and young people are bound by legislation to respect the rights of children, young people and their families. In addition to the legal aspects, being a professional means that you must ensure that all children feel included, secure and valued; this is the cornerstone of a positive, integrated environment. As a professional, your practice should adhere to the CACHE values and also to any policies and codes of practice in your work setting. Professional practice should include:

- developing **positive relationships with parents** in order to work effectively with them and their children
- understanding the extent of your **responsibilities** and being accountable to others for your work
- working effectively as part of **a team**
- knowing **the lines of reporting** and how to get clarification about your role and duties
- understanding what is meant by **confidentiality** and your role in the preserving of confidential or privileged information that parents or others share with you about their children or themselves.

AC 1.1 Identify the skills, knowledge and attributes required for the role of the early years practitioner

Above all else, an early years practitioner needs to like children and to enjoy being with them. Caring as a quality is largely invisible, difficult to quantify and more noticeable when absent than when present. The main individual characteristics required are shown in the guidelines box below.

Guidelines for the skills, knowledge and attributes required by an early years practitioner

- **Knowledge**: a secure knowledge of early childhood development and how that leads to successful learning and development at school is essential. This CACHE EYE course provides all the underpinning knowledge necessary for those working with young children.
- **Listening**: active listening is a vital part of the caring relationship. Sometimes a child's real needs are communicated more by what is left unsaid than by what is actually said. Facial expressions, posture and other forms of body language all give clues to a child's feelings. A good early years practitioner will be aware of these forms of non-verbal communication (EYFS Positive Relationships – Listening to Children).

- **Comforting**: this has a physical and an emotional aspect. Physical comfort may be provided in the form of a cuddle at a time of anxiety, or by providing a reassuring safe environment to a distressed child. Touching, listening and talking can all provide emotional comfort as well (EYFS Positive Relationships – Key Person).
- **Empathy**: this should not be confused with sympathy. Empathy means being able to 'project' yourself into the other person's situation and experience, in order to understand them as fully as possible. Some people find it easy to appreciate how someone else is feeling by imagining themselves in that person's position. A good way of imagining how a strange environment

appears to a young child is to kneel on the floor and try to view it from the child's perspective.

- **Sensitivity**: this is the ability to be aware of and responsive to the feelings and needs of another person. Being sensitive to other people's needs requires the carer to anticipate their feelings; for example, those of a child whose mother has been admitted to hospital, or whose pet dog has just died.
- **Patience**: this involves being patient with children and tolerant of other people's methods of dealing with problems, even when you feel that your own way is better.
- **Respect**: an early years practitioner should have an awareness of a child's personal rights, dignity and privacy, and must show this at all times. Every child is unique, and so your approach will need to be tailored to each individual's needs.
- **Interpersonal skills**: a caring relationship is a two-way process. Warmth and friendliness help to create

a positive atmosphere and to break down barriers. Acceptance is important: you should always look beyond the disability or disruptive behaviour to recognise and accept the person.
- **Self-awareness**: an early years practitioner is more effective if he or she is able to perceive what effect their behaviour has on other people. Being part of a team enables us to discover how others perceive us and to modify our behaviour in the caring relationship accordingly.
- **Coping with stress**: caring for others effectively in a full-time capacity requires energy, and it is important to be aware of the possibility of professional emotional stress. In order to help others, we must first help ourselves: the early years practitioner who never relaxes or develops any outside interests is more likely to suffer emotional stress than one who finds his or her own time and space.

The skills required by the professional early years practitioner need to be practised with regard to certain responsibilities.

Activity

Reading through this section on what is required in your role as an early years practitioner may seem a little daunting. However, by putting the child at the centre of your practice, you can build on all the other skills and attributes. List six personal qualities that you believe to be most important in your role of early years practitioner.

Guidelines: your responsibilities as a professional early years practitioner

- **Respect the principles of confidentiality**: confidentiality is the preservation of confidential (or privileged) information concerning children and their families which is disclosed in the professional relationship. It is a complex issue which has at its core the principle of trust. The giving or receiving of sensitive information should be subject to a careful consideration of the needs of the children and their families; for example, a child who is in need of protection has overriding needs which require that all relevant information be given to all the appropriate agencies, such as social workers, doctors, etc. Within the childcare and education setting, it might be appropriate to discuss sensitive issues, but such information must never be disclosed to anyone outside the setting unless there are concerns regarding safeguarding.

- **Commitment to meeting the needs of the children**: the needs and rights of all children should be paramount, and the early years practitioner must seek to meet these needs within the boundaries of the work role. Any personal preferences and prejudices must be put aside; all children should be treated with respect and dignity, irrespective of their ethnic origin, socio-economic group, religion or disability.
- **Responsibility and accountability in the workplace**: the supervisor, line manager, teacher or parent will have certain expectations about your role, and your responsibilities should be detailed in the job description. As a professional, you need to carry out all your duties willingly and to be accountable to others for your work. It is vital that all workers know the lines of reporting and how to obtain clarification →

of their own role and responsibility. If you do not feel confident in carrying out a particular task, either because you do not fully understand it or because you have not been adequately trained, then you have a responsibility to state your concerns and ask for guidance.

- **Respect for parents and other adults**: the training you have received will have emphasised the richness and variety of child-rearing practices in the UK. It is an important part of your professional role that you respect the wishes and views of parents and other carers. You should also recognise that parents are usually the people who know their children best; and

in all your dealings with parents and other adults, you must show that you respect their cultural values and religious beliefs (EYFS Positive Relationships – Parents as Partners).

- **Communicate effectively with team members and other professionals**: the training you are receiving emphasises the importance of effective communication in the workplace. You will also be aware of the need to plan in advance for your work with young children: knowledge of children's needs in all developmental areas will enable you to fulfil these within your own structured role.

AC 1.2 Identify settings which provide early years education and care

The main types of provision for children

Provision for children means the whole range of services that are specifically provided for children. Provision includes health services, social services, education and care services and leisure and recreation services.

Services for children may be divided into four categories:

1. **Statutory services**: these are provided by the government (or state). The services that are provided are set by legislation passed in Parliament.
2. **Voluntary services**: these are provided by organisations such as charities. Volunteers and paid staff provide services in the same way as in the statutory sector. Some or all of their funding comes from donations, and some are subsidised by the state.
3. **Private services**: these are profit-making services offered by private providers, and include private nurseries and independent preparatory schools; and childminders. They are inspected for the EYFS and to ensure that the health and safety of the children are maintained.
4. **Independent services**: these are provided independently of the state and do not receive government funding; they include childminders, and also independent schools. The EYFS framework is mandatory for all early years

providers: this includes maintained schools, non-maintained schools, independent schools, childminders and all providers on the Early Years Register.

Health services for children and their families

Most health services for children are statutory and free. The government's Department of Health is responsible for providing health care through the National Health Service (NHS), which was set up in 1948 to provide free health care to the entire population. Children are entitled to receive free health services provided by:

- GPs – or family doctors
- health visitors
- clinics
- hospitals
- other medical professionals including dentists and opticians.

Social services for children

Most social care services for children are statutory and free. Statutory social services were brought together under a director of children's services in each local authority following the Children Act 2004.

Social services provide a range of care and support for children and families, including:

- social workers
- residential childcare
- foster care
- outreach service through Children's Centres.

Education services for children: integrated care and education

Statutory services

Most education services are statutory and free. Statutory education services include the following:

- The **Sure Start programme** (introduced in 1999) which brought together services for pre-school children and their families including early education, childcare, health and family support.
- The **Early Years Foundation Stage** (EYFS): a comprehensive statutory framework (introduced in 2008) that sets the standards for the care, learning, and development of young children from birth to five.
- **Children's Centres**: the majority of these were developed from Sure Start local programmes, Neighbourhood Nurseries and Early Excellence Centres. Sure Start Children's Centres are places where children under five years old and their families can receive seamless holistic integrated services and information, and where they can access help from multidisciplinary teams of professionals.
- **Maintained nursery schools**: these offer either fulltime or part-time places for children of three years to the equivalent of the end of the Reception year. Some children may start at two years, but only if there is a recommendation and joint decision by the education, health and social services departments.

Figure 2.1.1 Children's Centres provide a wide range of services for children and their families

- **Nursery classes and nursery units**: nursery classes are attached to primary schools. The head teacher of the primary school may or may not be an expert in early years education. Nursery units are usually in a separate building with a separate coordinator.
- **Primary schools**: children start at primary school between the ages of four and five in a Reception class. Reception is the final part of the EYFS . Pupils then transfer to Year 1 in the September following their fifth birthday, and to Year 2 the following year. At the end of this time, pupils will move to a linked primary school.

Voluntary services

These services include:

- **Community nurseries**: these are often funded by voluntary organisations, such as Barnardo's, the Royal National Institute for the Blind (RNIB), SENSE and SCOPE.
- **Pre-schools and playgroups**: many (but not all) are affiliated to the Pre-school Learning Alliance, which was set up in 1961 at a time when there was concern from parents at the lack of nursery education available. They usually offer part-time services, and offer perhaps two or three half-day sessions a week, often in a church hall. This type of provision is often the only one available in rural areas.
- **Day schools**, residential special schools, or specialist voluntary groups which support children in mainstream education.

Private services

These services include:

- **Private nurseries**, **nursery schools** and **day nurseries**: these are legally required to be registered and inspected, and to follow the current EYFS statutory framework.
- **Private primary schools**: these are usually called preparatory schools. These schools are also required to follow the EYFS in Reception year.
- **Childminders, nannies and grandparents**: children are looked after in the childminder's home (home-based childcare or childcare on

domestic premises), or in their own homes by grandparents or nannies. Childminders are required to attend programmes for training before registration is granted. They are offered training through PACEY (Professional Association for Child Care and Early Years), CACHE and childminding networks in local authorities. Nannies sometimes live with a family, but not always. Sometimes they look after children from several different families.

Key terms

Sense Sense is a national charity that supports and campaigns for children and adults who are deaf blind. Sense provides tailored support, advice and information as well as specialist services to all deaf blind people, their families, carers and the professionals who work with them. It also supports people who have a single sensory impairment with additional needs.

Scope Scope is a charity that works with disabled people of all ages and their families, across England and Wales.

Leisure and recreation services

Some of these services are statutory and are provided by the local authority, while others are privately owned and managed:

- sports centres, children's gyms
- music groups
- parks
- adventure playgrounds and soft play areas
- holiday schemes and activities
- lessons, such as dance and drama
- clubs, for example, Beavers, Cubs and Scouts; Rainbows, Brownies and Guides; Woodcraft Folk
- libraries.

The implications of funding for the statutory and independent sectors
Statutory services

These services are provided free of charge. Some statutory services are provided by central government and are funded from central taxation – for example, the National Health Service (NHS). Others are provided by local government and funded by a combination of local and central taxation – for example, education and social service departments.

Voluntary services

These organisations (mostly charities) rely on donations for most or all of their funding. They may also provide some of the statutory services, and will be paid by the local authority or government for these services. They are often staffed by volunteers and do not make any profit; any spare income is used to improve the quality of their service.

Private and independent services

These services include private day nurseries, private nursery schools, preparatory schools and kindergartens. They are available for those parents who can afford them, although some financial support is available through government schemes.

Government financial schemes
Childcare Tax Credit

Those parents who are eligible for Tax Credits may be eligible for Childcare Tax Credit, which can help with up to 70 per cent of their childcare costs. This help is based on the parents' income.

Free Entitlement

The government has recently introduced a scheme under which all three- and four-year-olds will get a free place at a nursery for at least 15 hours per week: three days per week for five hours per day, or five days per week for three hours per day. Childminders graded good or outstanding can offer free entitlement with effect from September 2013 and they do not have to be a member of a network. Free entitlement can be spread across a year – it does not have to be taken in term time but funding is only provided for 15 hours a week for 28 weeks. The local authority pays the grant directly to the early education provider up to a certain maximum for three terms. If parents use a nursery for full day care, the grant will pay for part of the day and parents will continue to pay for the rest. From September 2014 in England, approximately 40 per cent of all two-year-olds are also entitled to access to nursery education.

Figure 2.1.2 Many local authorities provide play facilities for children

Research activity

Choose one of the following services for young children and their families:

- children's gyms or dance lessons
- parent and toddler groups
- adventure playgrounds
- children's clubs.

Find out what services are available in your local area. Your local library will have information to help you.

How are the services run, and how much do they cost?

AC 1.3 Describe the relationship between legislation, policies and procedures

Every aspect of early years care and education is subject to legislation in the relevant area of the UK. These laws are reinforced by the use of policies and procedures. Policies describe the requirements for each early years setting, and procedures outline the ways in which policies can be carried out. For example, every setting must conform to the current legislation on health and safety. Each setting has its own policy with regard to meeting those requirements. This aspect of early years practice is discussed fully in Units 2.2, 2.3 and 2.4.

Activity

Find out how and when to access the policies and procedures documents in your setting. How are they produced and how do managers ensure they are kept up to date with current legislation? Make a list of the policies and procedures in your setting.

AC 1.4 Describe the role of the EYP in relation to current frameworks

All early years practitioners should work within a framework that embodies sound values and principles. The CACHE Statement of Values is a useful tool for checking that you are upholding important childcare values.

CACHE Statement of Values

You must ensure that you:

1 Put the child first by:
   - ensuring the child's welfare and safety
   - showing compassion and sensitivity
   - respecting the child as an individual
   - upholding the child's rights and dignity
   - enabling the child to achieve his or her full learning potential.
2 Never use physical punishment.
3 Respect the parent as the primary carer and educator of the child.
4 Respect the contribution and expertise of staff in the childcare and education field, and other professionals with whom they may be involved.
5 Respect the customs, values and spiritual beliefs of the child and his or her family.
6 Uphold the Council's Equality of Opportunity Policy.
7 Honour the confidentiality of information relating to the child and his or her family, unless its disclosure is required by law or is in the best interests of the child.

All children deserve the best possible start in life and support that enables them to fulfil their potential. Children develop quickly in the early years and a child's experiences between birth and age five years have a major impact on their future life chances.

A secure, safe and happy childhood is important in its own right. Together with good parenting, high-quality early learning provides the foundation which children need to make the most of their abilities and talents as they grow up.

The Early Years Foundation Stage (EYFS) 2012
The EYFS:

- **ensures quality and consistency** across early years settings, so that every child makes good progress and no child gets left behind
- **provides a secure foundation** through learning and development opportunities which are planned around the needs and interests of each individual child, assessed and reviewed regularly
- **supports partnership working** between professionals and parents, and between different early years settings
- **provides equality of opportunity** and **anti-discriminatory practice**, ensuring that every child is included and supported.

The four overarching principles of the EYFS are:

1 A unique child
2 Positive relationships
3 A positive environment
4 Children develop and learn in different ways and at different rates.

Each principle is supported by four commitments which emphasise inclusive practice (children's entitlements, early support, equality and diversity).

A curriculum which includes all children
Most children learn in a rather uneven way. They have bursts of learning and then they have plateaux when their learning does not seem to move forward (but they are actually consolidating their learning during this time). This is why careful observation and assessment for learning of individual children plus a general knowledge of child development are all very important. In the EYFS, observation, inclusion, assessment and record-keeping will be supported by DfES guidance (Enabling Environments, EYFS). Catching the right point for a particular bit of learning during development is a skill. So is recognising the child's pace of learning. Children have their own personalities and moods. They are affected by the weather, the time of day, whether they need food, sleep or the toilet, the experiences they have, their sense of well-being and their social relationships with children and adults.

Gifted and talented children
People who are talented in music, dance and mathematics, for example, tend to show promise early in their lives. The most important thing is that adults provide a rich and stimulating learning environment, indoors and outdoors, which encourages children to develop and extend their thinking, understand and talk about their feelings, and understand themselves and others. It is frustrating for gifted children when they are constrained and held back in their learning.

It is also important to remember that however gifted or talented a child may be in a particular respect, he or she is still a child. They need all the things that any child needs, and should not be put under pressure to behave and learn in advance of their general development.

Children with Special Educational Needs (SEN) and disabilities
Some children will be challenged in their learning, and those working with children with SEN and disabilities will need to be particularly resourceful and imaginative to support their development.

Many children with SEN and disabilities are underestimated by the adults working with them. For example, most six-year-old children can run confidently across a field. However, in general, children with visual impairments in mainstream settings are not expected to try to do this, and so they do not attempt it. No one suggests it to them or offers them help to do it. With the right help, the child might manage it, becoming physically more confident and mobile as a result. The experience of running across a field depends on the child's development, personality and mood. Walking hand-in-hand first might be important. Talking as you go helps. The child may need tips about picking up their feet, and eventually perhaps running towards your voice. If the child tumbles he will need reassurance, and not an anxious adult. Saying 'Can I help you up?' is more helpful than rushing over and asking 'Are you hurt?'

Activity ·······························

Describe your role in relation to the current learning, development and care requirements frameworks in your area of the UK. In particular, take any opportunities presented to you to attend training sessions relating to frameworks for learning.

·····································

AC 1.5 Identify everyday routine tasks which ensure a safe and stimulating setting

How routine tasks help to ensure a safe and stimulating setting

Routines are an important part of the day for babies and young children, and can be used not only as valuable learning opportunities, but also as ways to develop young children's independence and imagination. Doing things in the same order helps children to know what to expect when they are in the setting. For example, toddlers may know that when the early years practitioner says it is lunchtime, they need to put away their toys, go and wash their hands, sit down at their place at the table and wait for the practitioner to sit down. Most children who have been in the setting for a while remember the basic routines and are more comfortable when the routine is consistent.

Routine tasks include:

- **personal physical care routines** for babies and children not yet able to take care of themselves – such as changing, cleaning, dressing and feeding
- **familiar daily routines** – such as hanging up coats, self-registration, hand washing, snack and mealtimes, tidy-up time, etc. Physical care routines are discussed in Unit 1.3.

Although young children have the same *basic* needs, it is important to understand that babies and children are unique individuals – and that, within the routine, you should aim to meet children's needs in an individual way that supports the individual's development and learning. Even though the routines are part of a group setting's framework, routines should not adopt a 'one approach for all'; rather, each routine should allow for flexibility to take account of individual preferences.

For example: babies and children have the same basic needs for food, warmth, affection and stimulation. However, there will be many differences in the way that an individual baby likes to be fed and also variations in what they like to eat. Every baby will also have a unique preference for how an adult can comfort them and show them affection.

Case study

Planning and implementing a self-service snack system

Background
The Nursery Manager has decided to introduce a different system for children's snack time. Having a rigidly defined group snack time inevitably interrupts many children's play at an inappropriate time. A self-service snack system – sometimes called a 'rolling' snack bar – would allow children to sit together in pairs or in small groups and also allow others to continue in their play.

Aim
To plan a flexible routine for snack time in a pre-school setting that will help young children to learn healthy eating habits and to develop positive attitudes toward food.

Rationale
Young children have small stomachs and high energy levels so they need nutritious snacks and meals frequently. A flexible self-service snack system will enable children to access snacks at a natural break in their play, or when they feel hungry.

Brainstorming
At a staff meeting, everyone was encouraged to put forward their ideas and concerns about the new system. These included concerns about:

- the supervision of hand washing and of eating
- ensuring that every child participated
- responsibility for preparation and washing up
- children with food intolerances
- disruption to the nursery's normal routine. ➜

The plan

The snack bar was created from two small tables covered in colourful washable fabric in a corner of the room. This limited the number of children who could visit at any one time, and the four chairs around the table also served as a reminder to keep numbers low. The snack area would be available from 10 am to 10.50 am every day.

On the tabletop was a basket of name cards, a tray of milk cartons, plates with today's snack and plates or napkins for the children. Next to the table was a bucket for waste cartons. Each day, a photo of 'Today's snack' was displayed on the wall above the tables (these photos were taken by staff and printed via the computer). There were also photographs and captions showing the sequence to follow when the children arrived for their snack:

1 Find your name card.
2 Put your name card in the basket.
3 Choose your drink.
4 Sit at the table.
5 Put your milk carton in the bucket.

Children would be encouraged to be independent from the introduction of the scheme. Early years practitioners would be responsible for their 'key' children – supervising their hand washing and use of the snack area. Any problems encountered when implementing the scheme should be reported on the same day to a designated staff member. It was agreed that the new system would run for at least three months and then staff would evaluate its success.

Discussion point

In a group, discuss:

- the advantages and disadvantages of a self-service snack system
- how snack time is managed in your setting
- whether it can be improved in any way.

Activity

Choose two routines used in your setting. Write a paragraph stating how each routine promotes development in *each* of the following areas: physical, cognitive, language and communication, emotional and social development.

Figure 2.1.3 Showing independence during snack time

AC 1.6 Describe reasons for adhering to the agreed scope of the job role

You need to understand the expectations about the agreed scope of your job role as expressed in relevant standards, including codes of practice, regulations, minimum standards or national occupational standards. For example, the government document published in 2005 by the DfES, Key Elements of Effective Practice (KEEP), provides a framework for early years practitioners to do the following:

- reflect on their work
- understand what effective practice looks like
- record their qualifications
- formulate their self-development plan
- allow managers to understand staff experience/qualifications and training needs to support the development of the setting.

KEEP sets out the six areas of expertise that everyone working with children, young people and families should be able to demonstrate:

- effective communication and engagement with children, young people and families
- child and young person development
- safeguarding and promoting the welfare of the child or young person
- supporting transitions
- multi-agency and integrated working
- information-sharing.

If the agreed scope of the job role is not adhered to:

- children may not be looked after appropriately – in accordance with current frameworks
- children's needs may not be met
- accidents could happen.

In addition, you may be uncertain of your own role, and could undertake tasks for which you are ill-prepared or even unqualified.

Activity

Working as a team, show your commitment to the CACHE statement of values in your daily practice.

Outline the standards of professional practice expected from you and your colleagues. (This information may be included in a code of practice for staff in the staff handbook and/or set out in best practice benchmarks, such as KEEP.)

LO2 Communicate to meet individuals' needs and preferences

AC 2.1 Identify reasons why people communicate

When working in early years settings, you need to be able to communicate effectively with a wide range of other people, such as:

- children
- their parents, families and carers
- colleagues and managers
- different professionals, such as teachers, doctors, nurses and social workers.

Communication may take the form of one-to-one interactions with a child or a parent, or group interactions, such as activities with children, case conferences and staff meetings.

Reasons why people communicate

The main reasons why people communicate in early years settings are given below, with examples:

- **To promote relationships and to offer support**: a social worker arranges regular contact with a family 'in need' and builds up a mutual system of support.
- **To maintain relationships**: a child's key person will ensure that he or she gets to know the child and his or her family, so that a trusting relationship is built and maintained.
- **To exchange information**: a father gives information to the nursery manager about his daughter's dietary requirements. The nursery manager gives the father information about the ways in which the setting will support his child and ensure that she receives the correct diet.
- **To negotiate and liaise with others**: a nursery manager will liaise with other professionals, parent groups and committees to discuss policies and procedures.
- **To express needs and feelings**: children should be given opportunities to express themselves freely, confident that adults will acknowledge them and meet their needs. Communicating with children is discussed in Unit 3.11.

AC 2.2 Explain how communication affects all aspects of own practice

Although your main job is to care for and educate young children, you will also need to develop positive relationships with adults. These adults will (for the most part) be your colleagues and parents of the children. However, you may also need to interact or communicate with other family members and other professionals involved with the children.

Establishing good relationships in the work setting enables you to support other people and also to expect support from them in times of stress or difficulty. If you work alongside practitioners whom you like and respect – and who you know will be there to support you – then you will help to create a positive working environment in which:

- both you and your colleagues experience job satisfaction
- children's holistic development is supported
- practitioners work together in a team – with the common aim of providing the best possible service for children
- transitions (such as settling in to a new setting) are managed sensitively
- parents and carers know that they can trust practitioners, because information is regularly shared and any concerns addressed within an environment that encourages open communication.

Research activity

Different ways of communicating with children
Find out about different methods of communicating with children such as Makaton, Signalong and PECS. (See the list of useful websites on p 159.)

Activity

1 Identify the main reasons why people communicate in your work setting. For each reason identified, provide an example of the methods in which communication is carried out. (For example, in a nursery, one reason people communicate may be: 'To share information with parents or carers about the key person approach'. One method of communication could be a leaflet or brochure produced by the setting and given directly to the parents.)
2 Explain how communication affects relationships in your work setting. For example, you could look at:
- the ways in which colleagues communicate with each other
- how information is shared with other practitioners
- the nature of the relationship between children and their key person.

AC 2.3 Use communication methods that meet individuals' communication needs and preferences

The way in which we communicate with other people should always take account of each individual's needs, wishes and preferences. For example, parents and carers may express a preference to be addressed by their full title, or they may ask to be addressed by their first name.

Empathetic listening

Empathy means being able to 'project' yourself into the other person's situation and experience, in order to understand them as fully as possible. Early years practitioners need to be able to listen with sympathy and understanding, and give support at the appropriate time. They also need to be able to encourage people who lack confidence that other people will value what they say. For more information on how to communicate well with children, see Unit 3.11.

Communicating with parents

You will find that there are many occasions when you are responsible for passing information clearly to parents. However, parents will also want to talk to you, as well as listen. You will therefore need to develop good listening skills. Try to set a particular time for parents so that they do not take your attention when you are involved with the children. For some parents this can be very difficult to arrange, especially if they are working. See also Unit 2.5.

Factors to consider when promoting effective communication

The key to effective communication is the consideration of **individual needs**. Early years practitioners need to be flexible in their choice of communication method and to be aware of the need to ask for help if they perceive any barriers to communication. There are many factors to consider when promoting effective face-to-face communication.

Environment

Various environmental factors influence communication, such as:

- the design or layout of the space
- decoration
- lighting
- colour
- furniture
- smells
- noise.

A busy, noisy environment will inhibit effective communication, and early years practitioners often need to find a quiet place in order for children and young people to feel relaxed and for the practitioner to convey genuine warmth when responding to their needs.

Personal space

The concept of personal space concerns the distance you are from another person. It is sometimes called **proxemics** or physical proximity. Psychologists now believe that air rage and other violent outbursts are often caused by 'invasions' of personal body space. In care relationships, those giving care should be conscious of the power they may have over the physical and personal space of the person receiving care.

Reflective practice

Being aware of personal space

Think about an occasion when you have felt uncomfortable, or have felt that your personal space has been invaded.

How do you protect your own personal space in the library, in a queue or on a crowded train?

How could care settings such as hospitals or residential homes take account of people's need for personal space?

Communication methods and styles

Good communication involves **listening**, **questioning**, **understanding** and **responding**. It is important to remember that communication does not only happen through the spoken word, but also involves:

- facial expressions and eye contact
- body language: posture and actions or gestures which help to convey meaning
- tone of voice: this can alter the meaning of what has been said. For example, the tone used by other people to say our name instantly tells us whether we are in trouble, being appealed to or just having our attention drawn (particularly if it is our parent!)
- pauses
- turn-taking.

It is thought that approximately 80 per cent of messages are conveyed through **non-verbal** ways.

When communicating with other people, it is also important to:

- take account of culture and context, such as where English is an additional language
- build a rapport by showing understanding, respect and honesty.

In order to meet individual needs, you will need to know how to choose the most effective method of face-to-face communication. This will include both non-verbal and verbal communication methods.

Non-verbal aspects of communication

Non-verbal communication is widely used by everyone, often without any words being spoken. Waving hello or goodbye, beckoning someone, a smile or 'thumbs up' sign convey messages. Used in conjunction with speech they aid understanding.

- **Eye contact**: perhaps the most important aspect of non-verbal communication is eye contact. It is extremely difficult to hold a conversation or communicate in any way without it. An early years practitioner who is listening to a child, parent or carer will therefore use eye contact to express sincerity and empathy – and to show that he or she is attending carefully.
- **Body language**: this refers to the way we stand or sit (upright, slouched, tense, relaxed), the way we hold ourselves, or our posture.
- **Gestures**: most of us use gestures when we speak: shrugging, shaking the head or perhaps to

 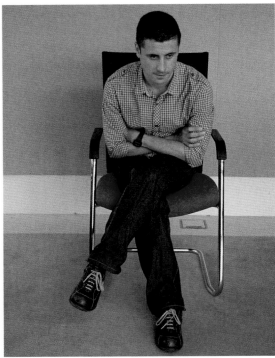

Figure 2.1.4 (a) An open posture encourages communication (b) A closed posture inhibits communication

point to something. Indeed, some people cannot communicate without using their hands and arms!

- **Touch**: sometimes it may be appropriate to use touch as a gesture of sympathy, reassurance or guidance, or particularly when communicating with a person who is visually impaired.
- **Facial expressions**: our facial expressions are important in conveying what we mean and how we feel. We judge whether another person has understood what we are saying and how they feel about it by watching facial expressions.

Failure to make eye contact and a 'closed' body stance (arms folded or held across body, hunched body) can make effective communication very difficult. Similarly, an adult with a tense, possibly aggressive, body stance also poses difficulties in communicating effectively. When faced with either of these examples, it is important to interact and respond in a way that reassures him/her.

Barriers to communication

There can be many barriers to communication:

- a visual or hearing impairment
- a different first or 'preferred' language
- strong accent or dialect
- technical or specialist language not being understood
- too much background noise or poor acoustics
- poor lighting so that facial expressions cannot be seen clearly.

Activity

Active listening

Working in threes, with one observer, one sender (parent, in this case) and one receiver (practitioner), carry out a conversation in which the parent talks about his/her difficulty sleeping and his/her tiredness.

- In the first instance, the receiver should not give any eye contact or indication that he or she is listening – no nodding, grunting or murmuring.
- How long can the sender try to make conversation? Discuss how the sender feels.
- Then change to active listening: the receiver should try to adopt an 'open' posture, maintain eye contact (without staring), indicate that he or she is listening and, at an appropriate point in the conversation, reflect back what he or she has been told.
- Change roles so that everyone tries each one.

Active listening

Developing good listening skills is very important. Most importantly, active listening involves eye contact (or, for visually impaired people, a light touch on the hand or arm to show your presence), an open body position, an interested facial expression and some murmurs of encouragement or nodding to reassure the speaker or sender that attention is being paid. To be an effective listener, you need to concentrate on the sender and understand the message that is being sent. This is different from an ordinary conversation in which you may exchange information about similar experiences and compare them. To ensure that you have understood the message, you should 'reflect back' the main points or concerns, using some of the same words and checking before the sender continues.

In the following example, the early years practitioner immediately recalls her own experiences rather than focusing on and responding to the parent.

Parent: I slept very badly last night, I just couldn't get comfortable.

Practitioner: I'm really tired too. My little boy kept crying and I couldn't get him off to sleep till 3 o'clock this morning.

Key term

active listening Active listening is about focusing not only on what is being said, but the accompanying emotions and feelings that are also being expressed. It provides a safe structure for a child to voice his or her concerns, and to receive feedback from the adult.

Reflective practice

Communicating with children

As practitioners we need to think carefully about what we say and how we say it, and we should also be fully aware of what our **body language** is communicating.

- Do we look interested when a child is talking to us?
- How do we make sure that the child knows we are listening?
- How do we convey the feeling that what the child is saying and feeling is important to us?
- How could you improve the ways in which you communicate with children?

Activity

Describe communication methods you have used in your setting or in your learner group that meet individual needs and preferences.

LO3 Understand working relationships in early years

AC 3.1 Explain how a working relationship is different from a personal relationship

A **working relationship** describes a relationship with a work colleague. You do not necessarily have to like the people you work with and you may need to keep personal opinions and feelings to yourself. Features of a working relationship usually involve each individual working:

- in a business or professional relationship
- as a member of a team
- within agreed guidelines
- within professional codes of conduct, towards the achievement of shared aims and objectives.

A **personal relationship** is a relationship formed through choice – except for family relationships – with someone whom you like, and with whom you may share interests and feelings. In a personal relationship there are no sets of rules and procedures to follow and you are able to voice your personal opinions, thoughts and feelings. Features of a personal relationship usually involve each individual forming a bond:

- with a friend
- with a family member
- within a social group.

AC 3.2 Identify different working relationships in early years settings

Working relationships in a team

Effective practice as a team member will depend on liaising with others, and reporting on and reviewing your activities. Conflicts between team members often arise from poor communication – for example, an early years practitioner who fails to report, verbally or in writing, that a parent will be late collecting his or her child on a particular day may cause conflict if a colleague then challenges the parent's conduct.

Most early years practitioners work with colleagues within a team. There are certain benefits for each individual from working in a team. These include:

- the sharing of responsibility – as well as knowledge
- a sense of belonging and a sharing of problems, difficulties and successes
- staff weaknesses being balanced by other people's strengths
- children benefit from seeing people working well together.

There will always be areas in your work where you experience conflict or stress – these are discussed on p 158.

Developing appropriate relationships with children

In line with the CACHE values, you need to ensure that the child or young person is at the centre of your practice – that their needs are paramount.

Treat children with respect

This means you:

- give only essential directions and allow children to make choices
- set appropriate directions which are realistic and consistent
- ask open-ended questions to encourage language development
- avoid labelling children
- are warm and positive in a way which affirms children.

Keep children safe

This means you ensure children are:

- supervised at all times
- safe at all times: make sure that all potentially dangerous materials and objects are kept out of their reach and that consideration is made of a child's stage and individual ability in the use of scissors, knives, etc.

Value and respect children

This means you:

- listen to them
- do not impose your own agendas on them
- do not single out any one child for special attention
- ensure that children maintain control over their own play
- are friendly, courteous and sensitive to their needs
- praise and motivate them; display their work
- speak *to* the child not *at* the child; with young children, this means getting down to their level
- respect their individuality
- develop a sense of trust and caring with each child and young person.

Emotional attachment to children

Early years practitioners are often concerned, or feel that parents are anxious, about young children becoming too attached to staff. However, babies and young children need to form close attachments with significant adults in their lives, and they cannot become too closely attached. Some young children spend many hours in group settings outside the home – they need and ought to develop attachments to their key person. Parents who work long hours may experience a conflict of emotions. They want their child to be happy and secure in nursery care, but they do not want to feel forgotten or pushed out; parents often feel a real anxiety when their child shows affection for their key person.

Physical contact with babies and young children

Babies and very young children need physical contact – they need to be held and cuddled in order to develop emotionally. Hugging a baby, comforting a child when they are upset, putting a plaster on them, changing their wet pants – all these are everyday ways in which adults care for young children. However, there is a growing concern among childcare professionals about touching children in their care. Researchers say that there is anxiety and uncertainty about what is acceptable and what is not when it comes to innocent physical contact with children. If teachers and other childcare professionals are no longer allowed to offer comforting hugs – or sometimes even to put on a plaster or sun cream – their relationship with the children they look after will certainly suffer.

Your setting should have a code of conduct which will give clear guidelines on appropriate physical contact with the children or young people in your care. What is appropriate physical contact with a baby or toddler – such as hugging them when upset or sitting them on your lap to explain something – will not be seen as appropriate with an older child (the EYFS also gives guidance on this).

Maintaining a professional attitude

It is important to remember that your relationship with the children in your care is a professional one. You should always be friendly and approachable but not try to take the place of the child's parents. Similarly, you should communicate with each child at a level which is appropriate to their stage of development and their holistic needs – you should not yourself behave as a child when interacting with them.

Establishing and maintaining relationships with parents

The parent or carer is a deeply important person to the child, and the relationship between parent and child is always very emotional. Emotional relationships can be a source of great strength but they can also be demanding. It is important to recognise that parents and staff have different kinds of relationships with the children in their care.

Practitioners need to develop consistent, warm and affectionate relationships with children, especially babies, but they do not seek to replace the parents. Babies need to be with the same people each day to develop social relationships. This is why the EYFS requires all early years settings that each child must be assigned a key person in all early years settings.

Parents and practitioners have one thing in common which is very important: they all want the best for the child. The roles involved are not the same, but they are complementary:

- Staff have knowledge of general child development.
- Parents know their own child the best.

If the partnership between parents, staff and child is going to develop well, each needs to be able to trust and respect the other. The self-esteem and well-being of the people in the partnership – the parents, the staff members and the child – are important when they are working together. How we feel about ourselves influences how we relate to other people.

Parents may have had bad experiences at school, and when their child joins a group setting, all those past feelings may come rushing back to the surface. Parents may be anxious and suffer low self-esteem. They might expect your setting to be like the one they went to, and this will make them fear for their child. This is often so when parents are required to bring their child to the early years setting under a child protection order. Staff will need to be sensitive to the feelings of parents in this sort of situation. The relationship – or partnership – with parents is discussed in more depth in Unit 2.5.

Activity

Think about the different working relationships within your setting. Consider also relationships formed with other professionals, such as health visitors, special needs coordinators, etc.

AC 3.3 Explain reasons for working in partnership with others

Partnership working enables different services and professionals to join forces in order to prevent problems occurring in the first place. It is an effective way of supporting children and families with additional needs, and helps to secure improved outcomes. Partnership working involves everyone who works with children, whether part-time or full-time. Early years practitioners need to understand the importance of working together in an integrated way and to build it into their everyday practice. Partnership working is also referred to as integrated and multi-agency working.

Key term

partnership working When everyone supporting children works together effectively to put the child at the centre, meet their needs and improve their lives.

The importance of partnership working

Before partnership working became the accepted way of working, the parents of a child with special or additional needs would probably face many different appointments with several different people, none of whom would have spoken to each other and all of whom would expect the parents to give a detailed breakdown of their child's disability. Partnership working is designed to cut across this by bringing together professionals with a range of skills to work across their traditional service boundaries.

AC 3.4 Identify skills and approaches needed for resolving conflict

Children and conflict

Children need to be able to deal with conflict effectively. This is an important life skill and will help children and young people to resolve conflicts in an assertive, but not aggressive, manner. They will be more confident in situations if they feel they can stand up for themselves, without needing others to look out for them. If you see children arguing, try not to step in straightaway. Most conflicts in early childhood relate to sharing and taking turns. For example, if two children are arguing over whose turn it is to use the computer, stay nearby and observe, and allow the children time to sort the dispute out for themselves. Only step in immediately if a child is being hurt, or is at risk of being hurt.

If you *do* decide to intervene, follow these guidelines:

- Give both children the opportunity to be heard without interruption.
- Invite the children to come up with their own solutions to the problem.
- Acknowledge the feelings and emotions from *both* sides.
- Suggest one or two solutions if necessary.
- Acknowledge the attempts made to resolve conflict: 'That seems like a good idea, Tom. What do you think, Ivan?'

Stress and conflict in the workplace

Working with young children and their families is demanding. It is work which draws on your personal qualities and skills and demands emotional engagement – unlike, for example, most office work.

This means that the work can be very satisfying, and can lead to feelings of great personal achievement and pleasure in helping others. Teamwork can offer support, but tensions can quickly build and disputes can flare up between staff members. There may be:

- low morale – individuals may feel unsupported and undervalued in their role
- confusions over individual roles in the hierarchy of the organisation
- stresses associated with the responsibility and accountability for providing care for children who are ill or disadvantaged
- a lack of communication with superiors and colleagues
- ambiguity over which tasks should take priority during the working day
- an excessive workload in both quantitative (i.e. having too much to do) and qualitative (i.e. finding work too difficult) terms
- feelings of personal inadequacy and insecurity, often following destructive criticism of one's work.

Resolving conflict in the workplace

If conflict is not dealt with immediately and effectively, it could flare up into open hostility and then it becomes destructive. However, if managed appropriately, conflict can add to the strength of the team, leading to improved shared understanding. Wherever possible, it is better for practitioners to find their own solutions with the senior practitioner or manager acting as a facilitator or mediator.

Staff members need time and space to express their feelings and to raise concerns. This alone can often resolve the conflict, therefore all practitioners need to know:

- who (and when) to approach if they have a problem at work
- that their concerns will be taken seriously.

A senior practitioner or manager needs to:

- encourage open expression of opinions and be trained to handle difficult conversations with staff
- have clear grievance and disciplinary procedures to deal with conflict
- focus on what the individual is saying, rather than on personalities.

Think about a situation when you have felt stressed at work, because of conflict within the staff team. Try to analyse the reasons for the conflict and identify the skills and approaches needed for resolving it.

LO4 Understand why Continuing Professional Development is integral to the role of the EYP

AC 4.1 Explain why CPD is integral to the role of the EYP

Working in the field of early years care and education can be physically and emotionally exhausting, and professionals will need to consolidate their skills and develop the ability to be reflective in their practice. It is important to keep abreast of all the changes in childcare practices by reading the relevant magazines, such as *Nursery World* and *Early Years Educator,* and by being willing to attend training courses when available. There are greater opportunities than ever before for practitioners to enhance their qualifications up to and beyond degree level. It is clear that the future in early years education and care will favour those who are the best qualified.

Continuing Professional Development

Continuing Professional Development (CPD) should be considered essential in all settings. Having trained practitioners in the early years setting will help to develop and maintain high standards of care and education for the benefit of the children and families while also creating a positive culture of continuous improvement.

As a practitioner you can ensure that your skills are maintained and your practice is up to date by attending regular training. This will include both core training and CPD.

According to the Early Years Quality Improvement Support Programme, attendance at training should be on average more than one session in three

months and have a sustained and continuous impact. Ofsted also has an expectation that staff should access training to keep up to date, reflect upon the effectiveness of their practice and strive to improve.

CPD is an ongoing and planned learning and development process. It focuses on what you learn and how you develop but may include a formal process of recording it (through supervision, submission of assignments, etc.). It does not always involve attending a course or completing assignments; for example, CPD could involve doing some work-shadowing, reading some information in a book or on a website, or talking to colleagues about how they handled a difficult situation. The key feature of CPD is to reflect on your learning and think about how it will influence your job or role in the future.

CPD includes:

- all training and development which goes beyond the basic 'core' training
- any type of learning that you undertake which increases your knowledge, understanding and experiences of a subject area or role
- any training which improves the quality of the setting and its staff.

CPD is integral to your role of early years practitioner because it:

- gives you new information that may help you to deal with new or complex situations
- can help you achieve your career goals by focusing on learning and development
- will give you confidence in your role
- demonstrates your commitment to developing your skills and expertise in a subject area.

How do you share information and develop practice within your own setting? What are the benefits of staff coming together to share CPD opportunities and experiences? Explain why CPD is integral to the role of the early years practitioner.

Assessment practice

1 What do you consider to be the main skills and attributes required for the role of the early years practitioner?

2 Identify six different early years settings in your area, and describe their role in providing care and education.

3 Describe the relationship between legislation, policies and procedures.

4 Describe the role of the early years practitioner in relation to current frameworks.

5 Why is it important to have routines for young children within the setting? Identify everyday routine tasks which ensure a safe and stimulating setting.

6 Find out about the work role of a qualified early years practitioner. List the main roles and responsibilities described in the job specification. Describe reasons for adhering to the agreed scope of the job role.

7 Give five reasons why people communicate with each other.

8 Explain how communication affects all aspects of own practice.

9 What is body language and why is it so important?

10 How can you select appropriate communication methods to meet individuals' communication needs and preferences?

11 Describe the working relationships within your own setting. How is a working relationship different to a personal relationship? How often do you meet your mentor or senior practitioner?

12 Why is it important to work in partnership with others? Identify skills and approaches needed for resolving conflict.

13 Why is it important to incorporate Continuing Professional Development into your practice?

Useful resources

Organisations

Makaton was developed to help people with learning disability to communicate. It is now widely used with a variety of children with communication difficulties: www.makaton.org

Picture Exchange Communication (**PECS**) uses functional and practical interventions to teach individuals how to communicate, function

independently and be successful in their schools, homes, places of employment and the community: www.pecs.org.uk

Signalong empowers children and adults with impaired communication to understand and express their needs, choices and desires by providing vocabulary for life and learning: www.signalong.org.uk

Unit 2.2 Understand legislation relating to the safeguarding, protection and welfare of children

Safeguarding children's welfare means protecting them from physical, emotional or sexual abuse, or neglect. It also means helping children to grow up into confident, healthy and happy adults.

Learning outcomes

By the end of this unit you will:

1 Understand legislation and guidelines for the safeguarding, protection and welfare of children.
2 Understand policies and procedures for the safeguarding, protection and welfare of children.
3 Understand how to respond to evidence or concerns that a child has been abused or harmed.
4 Understand the purpose of serious case reviews.

LO1 Understand current legislation and guidelines for the safeguarding, protection and welfare of children

Keeping children safe – everyone's responsibility

There is one aspect of work with babies, toddlers and young children that must always come first: the requirement to keep them safe, and to protect them from significant harm. All this work with children and families falls under the umbrella term of safeguarding.

AC 1.1 Summarise current legislation and guidelines for the safeguarding, protection and welfare of children

'Working together to safeguard children' (2013)

This document applies to those working in education, health and social services as well as the police and the probation service. It is relevant to those working with children and their families in the statutory, independent and voluntary sectors. The document covers the following areas:

- A summary of the nature and impact of child abuse and neglect.
- How to operate best practice in child protection procedures.
- The roles and responsibilities of different agencies and practitioners.
- The role of Local Safeguarding Children Boards (LSCBs).
- The processes to be followed when there are concerns about a child.
- The action to be taken to safeguard and promote the welfare of children experiencing, or at risk of, significant harm.
- The important principles to be followed when working with children and families.
- Training requirements for effective child protection.

All early years practitioners should read 'working together to safeguard children' in order to understand the principles and to perform their roles effectively. However, those who work regularly with children and young people and who may be asked to contribute to assessments of children and young people in need should read the relevant sections.

The new 'Working together to safeguard children (2013)' streamlines previous guidance documents to clarify the responsibilities of professionals towards safeguarding children and strengthen the focus away from processes and onto the needs of the child. It replaces

- Working together to safeguard children (2010)
- Framework for the assessment of children in need and their families (2000), and
- Statutory guidance on making arrangements to safeguard and promote the welfare of children under section 11 of the Children Act 2004 (2007).

What to do if you're worried a child is being abused (2006)

This is a guide for professionals working with children which explains the processes and systems contained in 'Working together to safeguard children' and 'Framework for assessment of children in need and their families'.

Protection of Children Act 1999

As a further safeguard to children's welfare, this Act requires childcare organisations (including any organisation concerned with the supervision of children) not to offer employment involving regular contact with children, either paid or unpaid, to any person listed as unsuitable to work with children on the Department of Health list.

The Disclosure and Barring Service (DBS)

The Disclosure and Barring Service helps employers make safer recruitment decisions and prevent unsuitable people from working with vulnerable groups, including children. (It replaces the Criminal Records Bureau (CRB) and Independent Safeguarding Authority (ISA)). The DBS acts as a central access point for criminal records checks for all those applying to work with children and young people.

The Children Act 2004

This Act placed a duty on local authorities and their partners (including the police, health service providers and the youth justice system) to cooperate in promoting the well-being of children and young people and to make arrangements to safeguard and promote the welfare of children.

The Act put the new Local Safeguarding Children Boards on a statutory footing (replacing the non-statutory Area Child Protection Committees), and gave them powers of investigation and review procedures which they use to review all child deaths in their area, as required by the 'Working together to safeguard children' statutory guidance. The Act also revised the legislation on physical punishment by making it an offence to hit a child if it causes mental harm or leaves a lasting mark on the skin. This repealed the section of the Children and Young Persons Act 1933 which provided parents with the defence of 'reasonable chastisement'. See Useful resources on page 177 for other reference documents that are useful to read on safeguarding, protection and welfare.

See Useful resources on page 177 for other reference documents that are useful to read on safeguarding, protection and welfare.

Activity

Make sure you are familiar with the current safeguarding requirements in your area. Do they meet the legislation and advised guidelines? Could they be improved in any way?

AC 1.2 Identify policies and procedures relating to the safeguarding, protection and welfare of children

All early years settings in the UK must be registered by the appropriate organisation and are also regularly inspected. Each of the home countries of the UK has its own system for registering and inspecting settings. All settings must demonstrate (through policies and codes of practice) how they intend to ensure that they meet the legal, regulatory requirements. All workplace policies and codes of practice must be drawn up within the framework of current legislation.

Key term

policy A safeguarding policy is a statement that makes it clear to staff, parents and children what the organisation or group thinks about safeguarding, and what it will do to keep children safe.

In addition to the policy, each early years settings will need clear **procedures** about what to do when there is a concern about a child. These should include:

- keeping a clear, written record of any concern identified
- reporting any concerns to a line manager, or the designated member of staff who is responsible for safeguarding, who will then decide what (if any) further action is required
- guidelines about how and whether to discuss the concern with the child and/or family.

Policies and codes of practice are usually kept in the staff room or manager's office. It is the employer's duty to ensure that each member of staff knows about the policies and procedures within the setting.

However, it is your responsibility to ensure that you have read and understood the documents. If you come across any policy matter that you are unsure about, you should know where to find the relevant document in order to find out what is expected of you in practice.

Legal requirements for all settings

All early years settings and schools must nominate a member of staff to oversee safeguarding and child protection. This person must be specifically trained to undertake this role. The whole team (including volunteers and students) must work together to promote children's welfare and keep them safe. The whole team will need regular training and updating, and it is best practice that such training provides staff with time to explore different experiences, attitudes and opinions as steps towards agreeing policy and practice.

Every adult working in the setting must be a *suitable person* to work with young children, and must have a full **DBS clearance** – see p. 162 above. This includes students on placements and regular volunteers.

Activity ·

Find out what is meant by the legal term 'suitable person' in relation to the care of young children.

Familiarise yourself with the safeguarding policy in your placement.

· ·

AC 1.3 Analyse how current legislation and guidelines for safeguarding inform policy and procedure

There is one aspect of work with babies, toddlers and young children that must always come first: the requirement to keep them safe, and to protect them from significant harm. All early years settings are bound by the laws described above – and by the many laws relating to health and safety. See Unit 1.2.

Schools and early years settings are places where children spend a considerable amount of their lives. Early years practitioners are some of the most important adults that young children will come into contact with. As a staff team, they can create an atmosphere and ethos which profoundly affects the child's experience of being cared for, listened to, valued, guided and stimulated. Early years settings and schools therefore play a considerable part in promoting children's best interests.

Safeguarding children in early years settings and schools

An early years setting or school keeps children safe by:

- having effective procedures around safe recruitment, management and its general operating policy; for example, if children are encouraged to speak out when they feel unhappy or uncomfortable, they will be much less vulnerable to abuse.
- ensuring that children's intimate care – nappy changing, toileting, dressing and undressing – is coordinated by a key person. This reinforces the child's right to privacy, and the child would not then expect that just anyone could take them aside and undress them.

LO2 Understand policies and procedures for the safeguarding, protection and welfare of children

AC 2.1 Explain the roles and responsibilities of the EYP in relation to the safeguarding, protection and welfare of children

Safeguarding systems
Common Assessment Framework (CAF)
The Children Act 2004 requires different agencies – for example, across education, health, children's social care and housing – to cooperate in the best interests of children and young people. The CAF provides a structure to facilitate this cooperation. (Although the CAF is specific to England, the same approach of working together is recommended in all the countries of the United Kingdom.)

Shared assessment
One of the many difficult issues when working with vulnerable children and families is making an

assessment of what the needs of the child and the family are. In the example we will consider here, a health visitor may notice that a three-year-old girl presents as slightly more prone to infections than is usual, and appears a little low in energy. Her development may seem satisfactory in terms of number of words spoken and understood, walking and running, and building with blocks in the clinic.

However, the early years practitioners working with the child may have noticed that she appears sociable at first, but is not able to play with or alongside other children. It may have been observed that while the child remains playing in areas of the nursery for some time, this involvement is only superficial and she is merely repeating the same actions over and over again.

As a result of these concerns, the child's **key person** could arrange to meet with the parents and the health visitor to discuss the extent to which the child is:

- healthy
- safe from harm
- learning and developing well
- socialising and making positive relationships with others
- not significantly impaired by the effects of poverty.

Team Around the Child (TAC)

This type of meeting is called **Team Around the Child.** There is a pre-assessment checklist for the CAF which early years practitioners can consult before calling such a meeting. It is important to remember that meetings like this, and the process of drawing up a CAF, are voluntary. Early years ractitioners should only proceed with the informed consent of parents.

Key term

Informed consent When anyone, child or adult, is given sufficient information to be able to make a genuine decision to say 'yes' or 'no' to a request.

Using our example of the three-year-old girl, in such a meeting the mother might explain that her child sometimes gets very little sleep at night because her older brother, with whom the girl shares a room, has disabilities and needs care through the night. The mother might explain that the family is feeling overwhelmed and very stressed, and that there is little time for positive attention for her daughter.

By bringing together the information from the health visitor, the early years practitioner and the parent, an assessment of needs can be made in the following areas:

- development of the child
- parents and carers
- family environment.

This assessment, and the action plan based on the assessment, will be recorded on a standard CAF form, or electronically (the eCAF). In this case, the possible benefits of the CAF could be:

- a referral to the Children's Centre family support service, in order to investigate whether the family could be entitled to disability carers' allowance with respect to the older sibling
- a local voluntary group might be contacted, to provide respite care for several hours a week so that the older brother can be cared for while the rest of the family have some time together
- an application for more suitable housing could be made, supported by the different agencies.

The parent will be asked to nominate a lead professional to coordinate this plan. With the CAF, the parents will not constantly need to fill out different forms and repeat the same information to different agencies.

It is possible that without this support, the child's development and play could have fallen further behind those of her peers in nursery, leading to her becoming more isolated and unhappy. The stress of the family's situation could have led to the child's needs being neglected at home. In a small number of cases, stress of this kind can lead to mistreatment of one or both children.

Research activity

To read the guidance on the CAF, including the pre-assessment checklist, search online for 'CAF' or go to www.dcsf.gov.uk/everychildmatters/strategy/deliveringservices1/caf

---

There are no specific mandatory laws in the UK that require professionals to report any suspicions they may have of child abuse to the authorities. In Northern Ireland, however, it is an offence not to report an arrestable crime to the police, which by definition, includes crimes against children. In England, government guidance 'Working together to safeguard children' (DCSF, 2013) states that:

Everybody who works or has contact with children, parents and other adults in contact with children should be able to recognise, and know how to act upon, evidence that a child's health or development is or may be being impaired – especially when they are suffering, or likely to suffer, significant harm.

The guidelines also state that all staff members who have or become aware of concerns about the safety or welfare of a child or children should know:

- *who* to contact in what circumstances, and *how*; and
- *when* and *how* to make a referral to local authority children's social care services or the police.

If there are any child welfare concerns, 'relevant information about the child and family should be discussed with a manager, or a named or designated health professional or a designated member of staff depending on the organisational setting'.

Following the procedures for safeguarding children

All the legislation and guidance in recent decades, including the Children Act 2004, make it clear that the child's interests must come first. All professionals must work together to promote the child's welfare before all else. For example, imagine that you found out that a father has slapped his child on the face, leaving a mark. You may have developed a very close relationship with this parent and you may be very sympathetic to the difficulties he is experiencing. You may feel that this incident is a 'one-off', that he genuinely loves and cares for the child, and that he would be devastated if you did not keep this to yourself. All the same, you are required to put the child's interests before your feelings about the family. The actions you might take are discussed later in this chapter.

Activity •

Explain your role and responsibilities in relation to the safeguarding, protection and welfare of children within your setting. Would you know whom to contact and how to report any concerns you have?

• •

AC 2.2 Describe the lines of reporting and responsibility to meet the safeguarding, protection and welfare requirements of children

Duty of care

All adults, whether paid or unpaid, who work with or on behalf of children have a **duty of care** in that they are accountable for the way they exercise their authority, manage risk, use resources and otherwise act to safeguard children. In carrying out their work the child's welfare must be paramount.

This means that they have a duty to:

- keep children safe, and protect them from sexual, physical and emotional harm and neglect
- treat children with dignity and respect at all times
- take reasonable steps to ensure children's safety and well-being; failure to do so may be regarded as neglect
- ensure that confidential information about children is only shared when it is in the child's interests to do so.

These duties are fulfilled by:

- developing respectful and caring relationships between adults and children
- consistently behaving as a professional adult in ways that demonstrate integrity, maturity and good judgement.

Progress check

Safeguarding children

- All adults working with children have a statutory **duty of care** to safeguard children, and children's welfare is paramount.
- Everybody involved in an early years and childcare setting needs to be clear about their **roles and responsibilities** around safeguarding.
- **All adults should receive safeguarding information** as part of their induction, appraisal and supervision.

- Everybody involved in the early years and childcare setting must attend appropriate **safeguarding training** and ensure learning is embedded in practice.
- All settings must have **safeguarding policies and procedures** in place that are reviewed in line with local and national guidance and legislation.

Activity

- What are your responsibilities for reporting information on possible abuse to a senior colleague or external agency?
- How and to whom should you pass on information from a child's personal disclosure of abuse? For example, your responsibilities for providing information on the disclosure to a senior colleague or external agency.

AC 2.3 Explain the boundaries of confidentiality in relation to the safeguarding, protection and welfare of children

Confidentiality and 'need to know'

In general, you must keep sensitive information confidential. If information circulates too freely, parents can feel very exposed and vulnerable. They may stop sharing information with staff.

Allegations made against staff

Schools and early years settings are usually some of the safest places for children to be. However, sadly there have been incidents when children have been harmed or abused by the adults who work with them and care for them. Cases include the discovery in 2009 that a nursery nurse, Vanessa George, had sexually assaulted and made and distributed indecent pictures of some of the children in her care.

Generally, an early years setting or school keeps children safe by having good procedures around safer recruitment, management and its general operating policy; for example, if children are encouraged to speak out when they feel unhappy or uncomfortable, they will be much less vulnerable to abuse. Children's intimate care – nappy changing, toileting, dressing and undressing – should be coordinated by a **key person**. This means that children do not have the

Guidelines for confidentiality

- **Where appropriate, seek consent before you share information** – you might find out on a home visit that a child's mother has a serious mental health difficulty, which is well managed by medication and therapy. However, the medication can make her feel rather tired first thing in the morning, and she tells you that she can struggle to take in information or hold a conversation then. So you might say, 'I'll need to tell my manager this, but shall we also let the staff team know, so they can talk with you at the end of the day and not in the morning?' The parent can then give or withhold consent freely.
- **Never disclose any information about a child's welfare in an inappropriate way** to people outside the setting or school – for example, you would not tell

friends or family about a child protection conference you had attended.
- **Put the child's interests first** – if sharing information will help to ensure a child's safety, you must do this. In nearly all cases, you would start by explaining to the parent why you wish to share the information and how this would help the child. If a parent refuses, ask for advice and guidance from the named person for safeguarding or the manager/head of the setting. If a parent says something like 'I did smack her round the head, but you won't tell anyone will you? They'll take her into care,' you will need to explain clearly that you are legally required to pass on information like this.

experience that anyone can take them aside and undress them, and their right to privacy is upheld. It is good practice, where developmentally appropriate, to ask children to consent to offers of intimate care and to give them as much control as possible. So you might say to a toddler in the toilet, 'Would you like me to help pull your pants down?' rather than just going ahead and doing it.

However, no system alone can protect children: what matters, beyond good policies and procedures, is that adults are confident to raise concerns, and that children are encouraged to say if they are unhappy or uncomfortable with anything that happens to them.

All early years settings and schools are required to have a policy to deal with allegations made against staff. This will cover cases where a child makes a disclosure, or an adult is seen or overheard behaving in an inappropriate way. But there are other examples that might give rise to a concern, without a specific allegation being made:

- a child who seems fearful of a particular member of staff
- a member of staff seeming to try to develop a very close relationship with a child – for example, offering small presents and special treats, or arranging to meet the child outside the setting or school
- a parent expressing a general concern about how a member of staff relates to their child, without being able exactly to say what is wrong.

In cases like these, you will need to discuss your concerns with the named person for safeguarding. Discussions like these are awkward, but it is important to share any concerns you have – the child's welfare is paramount.

AC 2.4 Analyse the benefits of partnership working in the context of safeguarding, protection and welfare of children

Partnership working is important to ensure that children's and young people's welfare is safeguarded regardless of where they are and who is looking after them. For example, where children receive education and care in more than one setting, early years practitioners must ensure continuity and coherence by sharing relevant information with each other and with parents or carers.

Different professionals and agencies should work together to help the child and family early on when there are difficulties. They should not wait until something serious happens before taking action. For example, a health visitor might notice that a mother is getting very stressed by the behaviour of her toddler and is struggling to cope. Early intervention might involve talking to the mother, showing sympathy, and perhaps finding some support for her at the local Children's Centre or setting up a programme of home visits. This would be much better than waiting to see if the situation becomes worse before doing anything. Although there is still a common view that social workers swoop in to take children away from their families, in reality the vast majority of social work is about helping different agencies work together to support the family, so that the child's safety and well-being are assured.

Initial assessment

An initial assessment is undertaken by specialist children's social workers in response to referrals made by, for example, schools, doctors, nurses and early years settings. The initial assessment informs the decision of what to do next. Possible decisions include:

- **Offering services to support the child and family**, if it is judged that the child is not at immediate risk of harm but is at risk of poor developmental outcomes.
- **Urgent action to protect the child from harm** (e.g. apply for a court order to take the child into care). Social workers cannot take children away from their parents: only the courts can direct this. However, a police officer can take a child into police protection in an emergency.
- **Holding a strategy discussion**. This would happen where the assessment indicates that the child may be suffering significant harm. Other professionals, like GPs, health visitors, teachers and early years practitioners who know the child and family, may be invited to this discussion. Specialist police officers must always be represented in strategy discussions. Where appropriate, a **child protection conference** will be arranged.

It is important to remember that staff in early years settings and schools should *not* investigate possible abuse or neglect. The role of the early years practitioner is to refer concerns to children's social care, contribute to the initial assessment and attend meetings as requested.

The initial assessment can lead to:

- further work and assessment being undertaken by specialist children's social workers (called the **Core Assessment**);
- help being offered to the child and family on a voluntary basis, usually coordinated under the **CAF**.
- a **Child Protection Conference** being convened. Key staff working with the family, and the child's parents, will be invited to this conference. The meeting will be organised by an independent chair who has not previously been involved in the

case in any way, and who reports to the Director of Children's Services.

Child Protection Conference

The Child Protection Conference seeks to establish, on the basis of evidence from the referral and the initial assessment, whether the child has suffered ill treatment, or whether his health or development has been significantly impaired as a result of physical, emotional or sexual abuse or neglect. A professional judgement must be made about whether further ill treatment or impairment is likely to occur. It is possible to hold a Child Protection Conference pre-birth if there are significant concerns that the newborn baby will be at risk of immediate harm (for example, in a family where there has been significant previous child abuse, or where a mother has abused drugs or alcohol during pregnancy).

If this is established, then the child will be made the subject of an inter-agency **child protection plan**. The child's early years setting or school should be involved in the preparation of the plan. The role of the school or early years setting to safeguard the child, and promote his welfare, should be clearly identified. Examples of this role might include:

- carefully monitoring the child's heath or well-being in the setting on a daily basis
- making referrals to specialist agencies, e.g. educational psychology
- offering support and services to the parents, e.g. a parenting class run at the setting
- monitoring the child's progress against the planned outcomes in the agreed plan.

Discussion point

One of your key children is subject to an inter-agency child protection plan, under the category of neglect. During the day, you notice that the child looks rather grubby. Other children are avoiding him because he smells.

How would you talk to the parent at the end of the day? What information would you pass on to the child's social worker?

The Core Group

The Core Group of professionals and the child's parents must meet within ten working days of a child being made subject to a child protection plan. The group will be called together by the child's social worker in the role of the **lead professional** (sometimes called the key person), and will then meet regularly as required. This group should include a member of staff from the child's early years setting or school. The Core Group develops the child protection plan into a more detailed working tool, outlining who will do what and by when. Both this working plan and the overall child protection plan should be based on the assessments undertaken by the specialist social worker and others, and should address the issues arising in relation to:

- the child's developmental needs
- parenting capacity
- family and environmental factors.

There should be a review child protection conference within three months of the initial conference. Further reviews should be held at least every six months while the child remains subject to a child protection plan.

The plan may be ended if it is judged that there have been significant improvements to the well-being and safety of the child. These improvements might have taken place as a result of:

- a change in circumstances (for example, the abusing parent has moved out of the family home and no longer has unsupervised contact with the child)
- the family responding positively to the requirements set out in the plan, and following advice given
- the child being given the medical or other treatment she needs.

At this stage, there might be no further involvement from Children's Services, or the family may continue to be offered further help and support by the different agencies, usually coordinated under the CAF. This only happens once Children's Services are satisfied that their involvement is not required because the child is no longer considered to be 'in need'.

Activity

1 What is the Common Assessment Framework (CAF) and how can it help children and their families?
2 Who can take children into protective care if they are in immediate danger?
3 Why might a child be made subject to an inter-agency child protection plan?
4 If early years practitioners suspect a child is being abused, should they investigate their concerns?

LO3 Understand how to respond to evidence or concerns that a child has been abused or harmed

AC 3.1 Explain child protection in relation to safeguarding

What is safeguarding?

For some children, universal services such as early years education and health visiting are not enough to ensure their healthy, safe and happy development. These children might, for periods of time, be vulnerable. They may experience emotional difficulties, fall behind in their development or learning, or suffer the adverse effects of poverty, poor housing or ill health. The CAF exists to support children and families with appropriate help and advice for a brief period.

Child protection is a part of safeguarding and promoting welfare.

- It refers to the activity that is undertaken to protect specific children who are suffering, or are likely to suffer, significant harm.
- There are also *children in need*, who are judged to be unlikely to reach or maintain a satisfactory level of health or development unless they are offered additional services. This group includes children with disabilities.
- Finally, there are children who are subject to an inter-agency child protection plan. These children are judged to be at risk of significant harm without the provision of additional services, as well as close and careful monitoring by specialist children's social workers.

All this work with children and families falls under the umbrella term of **safeguarding**.

In the Department for Education (DfE) document 'Working together to safeguard children' (2013), safeguarding and promoting the welfare of children are defined as:

- protecting children from maltreatment
- preventing impairment of a child's health or development
- ensuring that children grow up in circumstances consistent with the provision of safe and effective care, and
- taking action to enable all children to have the best outcomes.

Key terms

Inter-agency protection plan If a child's health or development has been significantly impaired as a result of physical, emotional or sexual abuse or neglect, an inter-agency protection plan may be drawn up. The plan will identify the steps that the family needs to take to safeguard the child, with the support of Children's Services and other agencies. The child's safety, health, development and well-being will be regularly monitored throughout the plan.

Safeguarding This term includes: all the steps you would take in an early years setting or school to help children to feel safe and secure; protecting children from neglect or abuse; ensuring that children stay safe, healthy and continue to develop well.

This unit offers concise, useful and accurate information about safeguarding. If you have any doubts or concerns about a child, however trivial you might think they are, we strongly advise you to speak to the manager or head teacher of the early years setting or school where you are working. Always ask for information and guidance.

Definitions of abuse and neglect

Abuse and neglect are forms of maltreatment of a child. Somebody may abuse or neglect a child by inflicting harm, or by failing to act to prevent harm. Children may be abused in a family or in an institutional or community setting, by those known to them or, more rarely, by a stranger, for example, via the internet. They may be abused by an adult or adults, or another child or children.

Working Together to Safeguard Children: A Guide to Inter-agency Working to Safeguard and Promote the Welfare of Children, DCSF, 2010

There are four categories of abuse: physical, emotional and sexual abuse, and neglect. These are outlined below.

Physical abuse

Physical abuse is the most apparent form of child abuse. It includes any kind of physical harm to a child, which can include hitting, shaking, throwing, poisoning, burning or scalding, drowning and suffocating.

Physical harm may also be caused when a parent or carer fabricates the symptoms of illness in a child, or deliberately induces illness – for example, giving a child so much salt that he or she becomes very ill, so that medical staff think the child has a gastric illness or a brain condition.

Emotional abuse

Emotional abuse is difficult to define and can be difficult to detect. It involves continual emotional mistreatment which results in significant damage to the child's emotional development. The child may come to feel worthless, unloved, inadequate or valued only if they meet the expectations or needs of another person. Emotional abuse includes the following:

- The parent having expectations that are well outside what is suitable for the child's age and development. This includes unreasonable expectations, like continuously trying to force a child to achieve more, and then constantly criticising the child for his or her failures. At the other end of the spectrum, some parents may fail to stimulate their child adequately – for example, keeping a two-year-old in a playpen with only a couple of baby toys.
- Preventing a child from participating in normal social interaction with other children, either by keeping the child at home, or by taking the child out but being so overprotective, fearful or controlling that the child cannot join in.
- Failing to protect the child from witnessing the mistreatment of others – for example, cases of domestic violence.

All children will experience some emotional difficulties as part of the ordinary processes of growing up. It becomes abusive if the result is significant damage to the child's emotional development. All cases of child abuse will include some degree of emotional abuse.

Sexual abuse

Sexual abuse involves forcing or encouraging a child to take part in sexual activities. The child may or may not be aware of what is happening. Activities may involve physical contact – for example, rape, including forced anal sex or oral sex – or non-penetrative acts like touching or masturbation.

The abuse may include non-contact activities, such as involving children in looking at or in the production of sexual images online or on mobile phones, watching sexual activities or encouraging children to behave in sexually inappropriate ways.

Neglect

Neglect means that the parent persistently fails to meet the child's basic physical needs, psychological needs or both. The result is that the child's health or development is significantly impaired.

Neglect can occur during pregnancy if the mother abuses drugs or alcohol, which can have serious effects. Neglect of babies and young children includes the failure to:

- provide adequate food, clothing and shelter
- keep the child safe from physical and emotional harm or danger
- supervise the child adequately, including leaving the child with inadequate carers
- make sure the child is seen promptly by medical staff when ill
- respond to the child's basic emotional needs.

AC 3.2 Describe signs, symptoms, indicators and behaviours that may cause concern

Early years practitioners are good at recognising when all is not well with a child. Historically, the biggest difficulty has *not* been in recognising problems, but in communicating concerns to others

(including the child's parents) and acting on them. Often practitioners worry about the consequences of passing on information, and worry that it might lead to the family being split up. It is important to remember that in the vast majority of cases, the different services will work *with* the family to ensure the child's safety. But the decision about what is best for the child should be made by a trained social worker, acting on the best possible information. When practitioners feel worried but do not communicate their concerns to others, a child can be put in danger.

The National Society for the Prevention of Cruelty to Children (NSPCC) states:

Children and young people often find it very difficult to talk about the abuse they are experiencing. So adults have a vital role to play in looking out for the possible signs.

The following section draws on the NSPCC's guide, *Learn How to Recognise the Signs of Child Abuse*. It is not always possible to be completely certain that a child is being abused, but there are signs and indicators that all early years practitioners should look out for:

- A baby or toddler who is always crying.
- A child who often has injuries or bruises.
- A child who is often very withdrawn. Withdrawn children are not simply quiet or shy – they shrink from adult attention, lack interest in their surroundings and try to occupy themselves without being noticed.
- A child who is often in very dirty clothes, looks unwashed for a period of time or is very smelly.
- A child who is frequently very hungry.
- A child who is often inappropriately dressed for the weather or time of year. This would include children who often come to the setting in thin T-shirts, shorts or dresses through the winter. It would also include children who come into the setting on a hot day in very warm clothes.
- Any indication that a child is being left home alone, or left unsupervised in risky circumstances at home.

- A child who does not receive the medical treatment he or she needs.
- A child who is mocked, sworn at, constantly joked about and made to feel foolish or useless.
- A child who expresses fear about particular adults, or seems reluctant to be picked up by a particular adult or afraid to be left alone with that person.
- A child with very strong mood swings – anxiety, depression, uncontained anger or severe aggression.
- A child whose sexual knowledge, use of sexual words or sexual behaviour is not appropriate for their age or development.
- A child who is witnessing domestic violence.
- A child who is witnessing significant drug or alcohol abuse.

There may be valid explanations for some of these signs. Equally, there are many other indications of possible abuse, and other circumstances that could be unsafe for a child. The NSPCC advises:

*The most important thing to remember is that if you have a gut feeling that something is not right, **trust your judgement** and take action.*

Research activity

You can read the full NSPCC guide *Learn How to Recognise the Signs of Child Abuse* at www.nspcc.org.uk

Progress check

Remember that when practitioners feel worried but do not communicate their concerns to others, a child can be put in danger. Make sure to:

- use your observational skills to learn how to recognise the indicators that may cause concern.
- understand what is expected behaviour for children, and
- be aware of any unusual signs and symptoms that could indicate abuse.

If possible, arrange to attend a course to further your understanding of this complex subject.

AC 3.3 Describe actions to take if harm or abuse is suspected and/or disclosed

Allegations

Sometimes a child may allege information that leads you to think that he or she is being abused. With young children, this may happen in a number of ways. A child might tell you something directly: 'Mummy and daddy went out yesterday, and me and Scarlet were scared because we were all alone.' Or a child might use play to communicate – for example, you might observe a child in the home corner shouting at and slapping one of the dolls.

In all cases, your role when a child alleges is to listen very carefully and show concern. Reaffirm that it is good for the child to tell you things that are worrying or upsetting him or her. Say that you believe the child. If you are not sure about something the child has said, then ask for clarification: 'I'm not sure I quite understood – did you say it was your arm that hurts?'

However, there are also some things that you must not do. You must not question or cross-examine a child or seem to put words into a child's mouth. So you would not ask a question like 'Does this happen every day?' because the child might just agree with you, or repeat your words. You are there to listen and observe – you are not an investigator.

A child may make an allegation to anyone – his or her key person, the caretaker, the dinner supervisor, a student on placement. For that reason, it is very important that everyone who comes into contact with children has training on safeguarding and knows what to do if they have any reason to be worried about a particular child.

Key term

disclosure A safeguarding allegation means the giving out of information that might commonly be kept secret, usually voluntarily or to be in compliance with legal regulations or workplace rules. (Allegation used to be known as disclosure.) For example, a child tells an adult something that causes him or her to be concerned about the child's safety and well-being.

Procedure for when abuse is suspected

If a child alleges (makes an allegation) to you, or if you are worried for one or more of the reasons listed by the NSPCC (see p 171):

- Make a note that is as exact as you can make it, recording exactly what the child said, and anything you noticed (signs of an injury, child seeming upset, stressed, angry or ashamed while talking to you). If you have had ongoing concerns, summarise what these are; again, be as accurate as you can.
- Discuss your concerns as a matter of urgency with the named member of staff for safeguarding, however busy that person seems to be.

In most cases, the named member of staff will discuss the concerns with the parent and then make a judgement about what to do next. You should be told what action (if any) is being taken, and why. Responses might include:

- No action – for example, in a case where a parent gives a reasonable explanation for their child's injury or behaviour.
- Advice given – for example, a parent is advised on what sort of clothes will keep their child warm enough in winter. Staff can then check that the child is appropriately dressed on subsequent days.
- Support offered – for example, a parent might agree that she is finding it difficult to manage the child's behaviour, and might welcome the offer of support from a parenting group or an appointment with a clinical psychologist.
- Referral to family support at the local Children's Centre – this will provide structured support and help for the family on a voluntary basis. A similar type of referral might be made to a specialist social work team (Disabled Children's Team, Domestic Violence Project).
- Referral to children's social care (social services) – if the named person judges that the child is at risk of significant harm, a written referral will be made to children's social care.

If you have raised a concern and you think that the action being taken is inadequate, meet the named person again. Explain your opinion, referring to what you have observed or heard. Although such conversations are very difficult, they are essential if we are to uphold the principle that the child's welfare and safety come first.

If you are a student, discuss your concerns in confidence with your tutor. Any worried adult is also entitled to contact children's social care or the NSPCC directly. If you have reason to believe your concern is not being acted on, you should do this.

Activity

Revise the main points of the last pages by answering the following questions:

1 What are the four categories of child abuse?
2 What should you remember to do if a child alleges to you? What should you avoid doing?
3 Why would early years staff share concerns about a child's welfare or well-being with the child's parents, rather than just keeping a record or making a referral?

AC 3.4 Explain the rights of children and parents/carers in situations where harm or abuse is suspected or alleged

When a child is suspected of being abused then the primary concern will be to ensure that the child is protected from further abuse and the child's welfare is paramount.

The rights of children

In cases of alleged abuse or harm, a child has the following rights:

- to be protected against significant harm
- not to be subjected to repeated medical examinations or questions following suspected abuse
- to be involved in decisions that are being made about them
- to be kept fully informed of processes involving them, while also being allowed to express their own views and opinions.

Wherever possible the child may be allowed to remain in their family home, and protection will be achieved by working with the child's parents or carers without the need to remove the child. However, if they are suffering from physical or sexual abuse then they will be removed from their home to protect them from any further harm.

The rights of parents

The rights of parents are modified by their responsibilities towards their children. In cases of alleged abuse or harm to a child, parents or carers have a right to be informed about what is being said and to contribute their own views and opinions. However, if the child is suffering significant harm then the parents or carers have no immediate rights.

AC 3.5 Explain the responsibilities of the EYP in relation to whistleblowing

Whistleblowing

Whistleblowing is an important aspect of safeguarding where staff, volunteers and students are encouraged to share genuine concerns about a colleague's behaviour. The behaviour may not be child abuse but the colleague may not be following the code of conduct or could be pushing the boundaries beyond normal limits.

Whistleblowing is very different from a complaint or a grievance. The term 'whistleblowing' generally applies when you are acting as a witness to misconduct that you have seen and that threatens other people or children.

The Public Interest Disclosure Act 1998, known as the Whistleblowing Act, is intended to protect the public interest by providing a remedy for individuals who suffer workplace reprisal for raising a genuine concern, whether it is a concern about child safeguarding and welfare systems, financial malpractice, danger, illegality or other wrongdoing.

The statutory guidance from the DfE, 'Working together to safeguard children', makes it clear that all organisations that provide services for, or work with, children must have appropriate whistleblowing procedures. They must also have a culture that enables concerns about safeguarding and promoting

the welfare of children to be addressed by the organisation. The concern may relate to something that is happening now, has happened in the past or that you think could happen in the future.

All staff, volunteers and students should be aware of, and follow, their setting's whistleblowing policy and procedures.

Examples of whistleblowing in early years settings

Sometimes a person inside an organisation knows that something is going wrong and is being covered up. This could affect the safety and well-being of children. Examples of this in early years settings and schools include the following:

- A member of staff has reported a number of concerns about a child's welfare. The child's parents are on the management committee of the nursery, and the manager says, 'They are not the sort of people who would harm their child.'
- There are consistently too few staff on duty in the nursery. When the local authority come to visit, supply staff are hired, and during an Ofsted inspection, management and office staff are brought into the room so that legal ratios are met.

In cases like these, it is very important that action is taken before there is a serious incident. If a member of staff has spoken to the manager, head teacher or other appropriate person and made clear that a situation is dangerous and illegal, and no action is taken, it is necessary to 'blow the whistle' and report the concerns directly to an outside body, such as the local Children's Services, Ofsted or the NSPCC.

If you act to protect children or to keep them safe, you are clearly protected by the law. In general, employees who blow the whistle are legally protected against being bullied, sacked or disciplined, if they have acted in good faith.

Research activity

Search online for 'protection of whistleblowers' or find out more at www.direct.gov.uk.

Figure 2.2.1 Children need to be cared for by suitably qualified staff who enjoy their company

LO4 Understand the purpose of serious case reviews

AC 4.1 The need for serious case reviews

In England, the LSCB must undertake a serious case review (SCR) after a child dies and abuse or neglect is believed to be a factor. In addition, serious case reviews are considered in all cases where:

- a child has sustained a potentially life-threatening injury through abuse or neglect, or
- a child has sustained serious and permanent impairment of health or development through abuse or neglect, or
- important lessons for inter-agency working could be learnt.

The government requires that every agency which had a role and responsibility for the child should contribute to the SCR by having an individual management report. The reports are then collated by an overview report author, who must be independent of any of the agencies that had involvement with the child and family. This is all overseen by a review panel of senior staff from the agencies which had no prior involvement with the child or family or decisions taken. The SCR overview report is presented to the local safeguarding children board, which decides what recommendations are to be acted upon and tracked.

Their purpose is to:

- establish whether there are lessons to be learnt from the case about the way in which professionals and statutory and/or voluntary agencies work together to safeguard children
- improve inter-agency working and thus provide better safeguards for children.

Activity ·

Research the incidence of serious case reviews in your part of the UK. Explain why and when serious case reviews are required.

· ·

AC 4.2 Analyse how serious case reviews inform practice

The key purpose of undertaking SCRs is to enable lessons to be learnt from cases where a child dies or is seriously harmed and abuse or neglect is known, or suspected, to be a factor. In order for these lessons to be learnt as widely and thoroughly as possible, professionals need to be able to understand fully what happened in each case, and most importantly, what needs to change in order to reduce the risk of such tragedies happening in the future.

Activity ·

Using the information in this section, give three examples of how serious care reviews inform early years practice.

· ·

Case study

A serious case review

The serious case review into Little Stars Nursery in Birmingham highlighted the failings that allowed Paul Wilson to abuse a child in his care. Paul Wilson was found guilty of raping a child in Little Stars nursery in 2010 and he also admitted 47 counts of 'grooming' teenage girls over the internet. Wilson, whose mother had previously been a manager at the nursery, though not at the time of the attacks, had abused the toddler on at least two occasions. Ofsted had received an anonymous complaint from a staff member about Wilson's behaviour towards the girl, who the review said was from a vulnerable background. It included him cuddling the child, rocking her for hours at a time, wrapping her in a blanket and refusing to leave her. He also spent time with her to the exclusion of others.

The review found that weak safeguarding practices within the nursery had created an environment where factors that might have deterred Wilson from abusing the child were missing.

In the above case, the SCR made eight recommendations based on its findings:

1. Colleges providing early years qualifications should ensure students' application and understanding of child protection procedures have been properly evaluated.
2. Ofsted should ensure the review's findings on safeguarding practices are used in the training of inspectors.
3. Ofsted and Birmingham Children's Services should work together on child protection concerns in early years settings to coordinate intervention.
4. Early years development workers should receive safeguarding training, which includes how to raise concerns about a colleague's conduct.
5. Birmingham Safeguarding Children Board should review local internet safety education campaigns to ensure people are aware of the dangers of internet chat rooms.
6. Information from the setting where a child is the subject of an assessment by children's social care must be incorporated into assessments.
7. Early years settings should adhere to safer recruitment best practice, to prevent unsuitable people working with children and young people.
8. Organisations that complete individual management reviews must provide evidence that action has been taken to address individual and management practice below expected standards.

The lessons to be learnt from the review are that:

- those in charge of settings caring for children must ensure there are strong, clear practices and systems to minimise the risk of abuse
- staff should listen to and ask about children's experiences rather than just speak to adults
- safeguarding children is a job for everyone, and every single person who looks after or cares for children needs to know how to recognise when something is not right and what to do about it, and have confidence they will get the right response when they do act.

Assessment practice

1 Briefly describe the laws and guidelines in your area of the UK which relate to the safeguarding, protection and welfare of children.
2 Select two policy documents relating to the safeguarding of children from your setting. For each document, explain:
   ● how the policy fulfils the setting's legal obligations
   ● the course of action outlined in certain situations.
3 Give two examples of and analyse how current legislation and guidelines for safeguarding influence policy-making and procedure in early years settings.
4 Explain your role and responsibilities in relation to the safeguarding of children.
5 Describe the lines of reporting and responsibility to meet the safeguarding, protection and welfare of children.
6 Describe the boundaries of confidentiality in relation to the safeguarding of children. What is a 'need to know'?

7 What is meant by partnership working, and how does it help in safeguarding children? Analyse the benefits of partnership working in the context of safeguarding, protection and welfare of children.
8 Explain child protection in relation to safeguarding.
9 Describe the different categories of child abuse, and the main signs, symptoms and behavioural indicators that may cause concern.
10 Describe the actions to take if a child alleges or discloses harm or abuse, or if there is reason to suspect any harm or abuse.
11 What are the rights of children and of parents or carers in situations where harm or abuse is suspected or alleged?
12 Outline the responsibilities of the early years practitioner in relation to whistleblowing.
13 Explain the circumstances which give rise to a serious case review being required.
14 How do serious case reviews influence the development of policy and safe childcare practices?

Useful resources

Books

Lindon, J. (2009), *Safeguarding Children and Young People*. London: Hodder Education.

Munro, E. (2011), *The Munro Review of Child Protection: Final Report A child-centred system*. London: Department for Education.

Organisations

National Society for the Prevention of Cruelty to Children (NSPCC)

The NSPCC campaigns against cruelty to children, and runs ChildLine, the free, confidential helpline for children and young people. The NSPCC also offers services to support children and families, and can investigate cases where child abuse is suspected: www.nspcc.org.uk

Working Together to Safeguard Children

This is the government's guide to inter-agency working to safeguard and promote the welfare of children: www.education.gov.uk/aboutdfe/statutory/g00213160/working-together-to-safeguard-children

For LO1, it would be useful to read current versions of Early Years Foundation Stage Statutory Framework, Section 3, 3.1–3.3 inclusive, and The Early Years Foundations for Life, Health and Learning: An Independent Report on the Early Years Foundation Stage to Her Majesty's Government.

Unit 2.3 Use legislation relating to the health and safety of children

Safety is a basic human need. When working with children and young people you need to know how to provide a safe, healthy environment. This involves knowing how to assess risks to children's safety and to ensure that any such risks are minimised. A fine balance must be achieved which allows children to explore their environment and to learn for themselves, but also ensures that the environment in which children are playing and learning is as safe and healthy as possible.

Learning outcomes

By the end of this unit you will:

1 Understand legislation and guidelines for health and safety.
2 Understand policies and procedures for health and safety.
3 Understand how to plan environments that support children's health and safety.
4 Be able to manage risk within an environment which provides challenge for children.
5 Understand how to identify, record and report accidents, incidents and emergencies.

LO1 Understand legislation and guidelines for health and safety

AC 1.1 Summarise current legislation and guidelines relating to the health and safety of children

Every child deserves the best possible start in life with the opportunity to learn and develop in an environment that is both safe and secure. Parents who use early years services should be able to do so confident in the knowledge that their children will be getting the best possible experiences. There are many regulations, laws and guidelines dealing with health and safety. You do not need to know the fine detail, but you do need to know where your responsibilities begin and end. The most relevant laws relating to health and safety in the early years setting are listed in Table 2.3.1.

Relevant laws relating to health and safety	
Health and Safety at Work Act 1974	Health and Safety (First Aid) Regulations 1981
Personal Protective Equipment at Work Regulations 1992	Control of Substances Hazardous to Health Regulations 2002 (COSHH)
Manual Handling Operations Regulations 1992	Food Hygiene Regulations 2006
Reporting of Injuries, Diseases and Dangerous Occurrences Regulations 1995 (RIDDOR)	Care Standards Act 2000
Fire Precautions (Workplace) Regulations 1997 (amended 1999), The Regulatory Reform (Fire Safety) Order 2005	Children Act 1989
Data Protection Act 2000	Childcare Act 2006
Children Act 2004	

Table 2.3.1 Current laws relating to health and safety in the early years setting

Health and Safety at Work Act 1974

Employers have a duty to:

- make their workplace as safe as they are able and ensure that they are also responsible for health and safety of visitors and keeping the building safe
- display a Health and Safety Law poster or supply employees with a leaflet with the same information (available from the Health and Safety Executive)
- decide how to manage health and safety: if the business has five or more employees, this must appear on a written health and safety policy.

As an employee, you have a duty to:

- work safely. If you are given guidance about how to use equipment, you should follow that guidance. You should not work in a way that puts other people in danger.

Fire Precautions (Workplace) Regulations 1997

Fire Safety Officers must check all childcare premises while they are in the first registration process. They will advise on what is needed to make the workplace as safe as possible.

- Evacuation procedures should be in place, known to all the adults, and practised regularly using all available exits at different times, so that everyone can leave the building quickly and safely if an emergency occurs.
- Some exits may be locked to prevent children wandering away or intruders entering, but adults must be able to quickly open them in case of an emergency.
- Designated fire exits must always be unlocked and kept unobstructed. Fire extinguishers should be in place and checked regularly. A fire blanket is needed in the kitchen.
- In accordance with the Regulatory Reform (Fire Safety) Order 2005, the responsible person in the setting is required to carry out a fire risk assessment for all those who are on or around the premises.

Control of Substances Hazardous to Health Regulations 2002 (as amended 2004)

These regulations, known as **COSSH**, require employers to keep a record of substances that could be hazardous to health, where they will be kept, how they will be used and for what purpose, as well as what to do if they contact skin, eyes or are ingested. In a nursery setting, this mainly applies to cleaning chemicals and those used for general maintenance.

Solutions such as bleach or dishwasher powders, some solvent glues and other materials in your setting can be hazardous. You should have a risk assessment that tells you what these things are, and what to do to minimise the risks involved. Any new person coming to the team must be made aware of what to do.

Every workplace must have a COSHH file which lists all the hazardous substances used in the setting. The file should detail:

- where they are kept
- how they are labelled

- their effects
- the maximum amount of time it is safe to be exposed to them
- how to deal with an emergency involving one of them.

Never mix products together as they could produce toxic fumes. Some bleaches and cleaning products, for instance, have this effect.

Manual Handling Operations Regulations 1992

This covers jobs that involve lifting and preventing injuries or accidents while doing this. In early years settings this will apply to lifting and carrying babies and young children, as well as furniture and large play equipment. It requires that risk assessments are carried out, for equipment to be provided when needed and for employers to ensure that staff are trained to lift correctly, in order to reduce back strain and injury caused through work tasks.

Reporting of Injuries, Diseases and Dangerous Occurrences Regulations 1995

These regulations, known as **RIDDOR**, require that serious accidents which result in injuries needing treatment from a doctor are reported to the Health and Safety Executive (HSE). In addition, outbreaks of a serious disease, the death of a child or adult, or a dangerous occurrence, such as an explosion, are also notifiable.

An **accident report book** must be kept in which incidents that happen to staff are recorded. If an incident occurs at work that is serious enough to keep an employee off work for three or more days, employers will need to fill in the relevant paperwork and send the report to the HSE. They may investigate serious incidents and give advice on how to improve practice if needed. It is important to note there are two accident books. One is for accidents within the provision to children and is kept with the first aid box. The other is for accidents to employees, paid or voluntary.

Health and Safety (First Aid) Regulations 1981

Employers should make sure that at least one person at each session has an up-to-date first aid qualification and is the 'appointed' first aider. Each setting should have a suitably stocked first aid box. In early years settings regulated by Ofsted, there is also a requirement for a staff member to be trained in 'Paediatric First Aid'. Methods of dealing with incidents to adults and children are not the same, particularly where resuscitation is involved. Recommendations change, and for this reason, first aid qualifications must be renewed every three years.

Food Hygiene Regulations 2006

The food hygiene requirements in the statutory framework for the Early Years Foundation Stage (EYFS) state that managers/leaders must be confident that those responsible for preparing and handling food are competent to do so. In group provision, all staff involved in preparing and handling food must be supervised or receive training in food hygiene.

Everyone involved in preparing food for young children, or helping them to eat, needs to understand the importance of food safety and hygiene, and be aware of the requirements of the Food Handling regulations. These cover what might be seen as common-sense things:

- washing your hands before preparing food
- making sure that the surfaces and utensils you use are clean and hygienic
- making sure that food is stored safely at the correct temperature
- disposing of waste hygienically.

These regulations also include knowledge of safe practices in the use of chopping boards, having separate sinks for hand washing and preparing foods, how to lay out a kitchen and so on. There should always be people who have completed a Basic Food Hygiene certificate available to ensure that guidance is properly carried out.

Personal Protective Equipment at Work Regulations 1992

Under these regulations, employers must make sure that suitable protective equipment is provided for employees who are exposed to a risk to their health and safety while at work. This is considered a last resort, for the risk should be prevented wherever possible. In childcare the most important piece of personal protective equipment that is provided will be gloves, to be used when dealing with body fluids.

Employees and students should be made aware of the need to use these when changing nappies or dealing with blood spillage or vomit. Good hygiene protects both adults and children.

Data Protection Act 1998

Anyone who keeps records, whether on computers or on paper, should comply with this Act. It should be clear to service users for what purpose the data is being kept. Information about a child should also be accessible to the parent/carer and shared with them (refer to Unit 2.2 for more information on safeguarding). It is not necessary to do this 'on demand'. A convenient time to be able to discuss the information can be arranged. Information should not be kept for longer than necessary, though accident and incident records will need to be kept in case they are needed for reference at some time in the future. Records must also be stored securely.

Children Act 1989

The Children Act 1989 brought together several sets of guidance and provided the basis for many of the standards we maintain with children. It first outlined the amount of space that should be available as well as the adult:child ratio for work with children aged under eight. This is based on the age of the children being cared for. The minimum ratio is set out in Table 2.3.2.

Age of children	Number of adults: children (ratio)
0–1	1:3
2–3	1:4
3–5	1:8

Table 2.3.2 The adult:child ratio in early years settings

Some places have slightly different ratios depending on local conditions, such as the number of rooms used, or the location of the toilets if not directly off the main room. Local authority nursery classes and schools may also work on a ratio of one adult to 13 children where a trained teacher is in charge. Children in Year 1 and above do not have specified ratios, though 1:6 is recommended for outings.

The Children Act also outlined some of the principles that we now take for granted:

- The welfare of the child is paramount.
- Practitioners should work in partnership with parents.
- Parents should care for their children whenever possible.
- Children's opinions should be taken into account when matters concern them.

Childcare Act 2006
This sets out the statutory assessment of settings, including health and safety in the EYFS.

LO2 Understand policies and procedures for health and safety

Each early years setting will have policies and procedures which reflect the philosophy of the setting.

Policies and procedures convey clear messages to staff members about their roles and responsibilities and set the boundaries within which they are expected to work. Standard sets of policies and procedures may be adopted, but it is important that such 'universal' policies are carefully adapted to reflect precisely what happens in each particular setting. For example, the procedure for evacuation

will be very different between settings, according to the layout of the building and the surrounding physical environment. In order to maintain consistency, policies and procedures must be shared with everyone and each person must be given the opportunity to contribute to them. They should never be compiled by just one person, and they should also be regularly reviewed. Each setting will develop its own policies and procedures and these may be covered under different headings from those outlined below.

AC 2.1 Identify policies and procedures relating to the health and safety of children

In practice activity

Infection control policy
Find out about the infection control policy in your own setting.

1 When should you wear protective clothing?
2 When should you wear gloves?
3 How should you dispose of waste?
4 Which infectious illnesses should you report to your supervisor and not attend work?

Safety during outings

Any outing away from the children's usual setting (such as trips to farms, parks and theatres) must be planned with safety and security issues as a top priority. When participating in off-site visits, all early years practitioners (including volunteers) have a duty to take reasonable care to avoid injury to themselves and others, and to cooperate to ensure that statutory duties and obligations are fulfilled. Adults in charge of children during an off-site visit have a duty of care to make sure that the children are safe and healthy. Practitioners have a common law duty to act as would a reasonably prudent parent, and should not hesitate to act in an emergency and to take life-saving action in an extreme situation. As a safeguard to children, volunteer helpers on off-site visits must not be left unsupervised and:

- be appropriate people to supervise children
- be trained in their duties

Unqualified staff or volunteers must not be left in sole charge of children except where it has been previously agreed as part of the risk assessment. Practitioners and volunteers should not be in a situation where they are alone with one child away from the rest of the group.

Risk assessments for outings

There is a legal requirement for settings to carry out risk assessments for outings. (See p 191 for information on risk assessments.) The **EYFS** makes it clear that this should include an assessment of the ratios of adults to children needed for outings, and it must include an assessment of the risks and

hazards that might arise for the children. It is not necessary to carry out a risk assessment before *every* outing, providing there is one in place for that *type* of outing. Each type of outing will carry its own particular risks and practitioners must assess the risks and hazards that may arise and the steps to be taken to remove or minimise and manage them.

Planning the outing

Visit or find out about the place beforehand and discuss any particular requirements, such as what to do if it rains, or specific lunch arrangements. A risk assessment should be carried out to include consideration of potential risks in the environment, such as traffic, dogs, ponds or rivers, etc.

Main policies and procedures relating to health and safety of children	
Health and safety - risk assessment - food safety - health and hygiene - infection control and prevention of illness - fire safety	- first aid - accidents and emergencies - safety at arrival and departure times, and on outings - evacuation procedures - administration of medicine
Safeguarding children - child protection - missing child - critical incidents - non-collection of child - death of a child - complaints against the registered provider or a member of staff	**Record-keeping** - sharing information - confidentiality - children's records
Staffing - staffing ratios - recruitment and deployment - volunteers and parent helpers - disciplinary and grievance procedures - students and induction - whistleblowing	**Partnership with parents and carers** - working in partnership with other agencies - key person system
Equality and inclusion - valuing diversity - special educational needs (SEN)	**Childcare practices** - behaviour management - identification and assessment of children with special educational needs - settling in - daily routines - play and learning

Table 2.3.3 Main policies and procedures relating to health and safety of children

Figure 2.3.1 Children enjoying an outing

Contact numbers
A copy of the children's contact information should be taken on the outing, and the person in charge should regularly check the names of the children against the day's attendance list.

Parental permission
Parents should be informed of what is involved on the outing, such as what the child needs to bring (such as packed meal, waterproof coat), spending money if necessary (state the advised maximum amount). Parents must sign a consent form that gives the setting permission to take their child off the premises.

Supervision and staff ratios
There should always be trained staff on any outing, however local and low key. Usually help is requested from parents so that adequate supervision is ensured. The minimum staff to child ratios are set out in the safeguarding and welfare requirements for every home nation, and must be complied with:

- The adult to child ratio should never exceed one to four.
- If the children are under two years old or have special needs, then you would expect to have fewer children per adult.
- Swimming trips should be attempted only if the ratio is one adult to one child for children under five years old.
- The younger the children, the more adults are required, particularly if the trip involves crossing roads, when an adult must be available to hold the children's hands.

Head counts
Make sure that you all count the children regularly. Always accompany children to public toilets, telling a colleague how many children you are taking with you.

Transport
If a coach is being hired, check whether it has seat belts for children. By law, all new minibuses and

coaches must have seat belts fitted, and minibus drivers must pass a special driving test.

Activity ·

Find out where the health and safety policies are kept in your setting. How often are they reviewed? Who is responsible for keeping them up to date?

· ·

AC 2.2 Analyse how legislation and guidelines for health and safety inform day-to-day work with children

Health and safety legislation is constantly being updated, in response to new research into accident prevention and increased knowledge about health and safety issues. For example, it is hard to imagine a time – some 40 years ago – when children were allowed to sit unrestrained in the backs of family cars, but the laws regarding seat belts and restraints have saved countless lives. All early years settings are bound by the laws described above, and by the EYFS statutory framework. These laws and guidelines provide a framework within which practitioners can work as a team to provide an environment that is as safe and healthy as possible, while still allowing children the freedom to explore their environment in an active way.

The EYFS statutory framework

The EYFS places an obligation on settings to conduct a risk assessment and review it regularly. The guidance on play includes the advice that:

Through play, in a secure but challenging environment with effective adult support, children can take risks and make mistakes.

The duty to balance keeping children safe with encouraging them to learn actively is further developed in the Development Matters section of the EYFS :

- *A Unique Child – Keeping Safe* says: 'being over-protected can prevent children from learning about possible dangers and about how to protect themselves from harm'.
- *A Unique Child – Health and Well-being* identifies one of the key challenges and dilemmas for

practitioners as 'ensuring safety without stopping reasonable risk-taking'.
- *Learning and Development – Play and Exploration* says: 'practitioners always intervene in play if it is racist, sexist or in any way offensive, unsafe, violent or bullying'.
- *Learning and Development – Physical Development* says practitioners should give particular attention to building 'children's confidence to take manageable risks in their play'.

When children undertake a challenging physical activity successfully, they grow in confidence and capability; their skills develop well for their future when they will have to make risk assessments for themselves.

Progress check

Health and safety in early years settings
An early years setting or school keeps children healthy and safe by:

- having effective procedures around safety of equipment, hygiene guidelines and accident prevention
- ensuring that all practitioners have an understanding of the legislation that informs good practice, and
- developing risk assessments that protect children from incurring accidents in the setting.

AC 2.3 Describe procedures for registration of children and collection of children

Supporting children's safety when they move in and out of the setting

Every setting should have clear systems – policies and procedures – in place to ensure the safety of children:

- when being received into the setting
- when departing from the setting, and
- during outings (off-site visits).

During these times, there is often a lot of movement and activity. When children are received into the setting, several children may arrive at once, parents may be in a rush to get to work, and children are keen to rejoin their friends. When leaving the setting, again many children will be leaving at the same time, parents chatting with others and children eager to say goodbye to their friends. During outings, there is usually a great deal of excitement about being in a new place with lots to see and do. Every practitioner should be aware of the policy and procedures that relate to these times in their setting, and should be clear about his or her own role and responsibility.

Receiving children into the setting

All settings must register children on arrival. A daily register of the names of all the children in the setting at any given time is essential not only in case of an emergency evacuation of the setting, but also so that adequate staff supervision (or staffing ratios) is provided. Many early years settings have door entry phones and a password system for parents and staff to enter the premises. The entrance should be secure so that the door cannot be left open for people to wander in and out. In some settings, one member of staff is stationed at the door, greeting and sharing information with each family as they arrive. Some settings have a designated dropping-off area where a calm atmosphere can be created as parents and carers 'hand over' their child to their key person.

In practice activity

Receiving children into the setting

Find out about the system for receiving children in your setting:

1 Who is responsible for registering the children?
2 How does the setting ensure that the entrance door is kept shut between arrivals?
3 How smooth is the transition from reception into the setting to each child being with his or her key person?

Ensuring safety on departure

Every setting will have a policy about correct procedure for when parents and carers come to collect their child. Again, the register must be kept so that it is clear which children are in the setting in case of an emergency. At home time:

- A member of staff must ensure that every child is collected by the appropriate person: the person registered as the child's own parent or carer, or a person who has written authorisation from the parent or carer.
- If parents know that they will not be able to collect their child on a particular occasion, they should notify the setting, giving permission for another named person to collect their child.
- The child's key person should, where possible, be responsible for handover at home times.

Within the setting's safeguarding children policy, there should be a written statement of the procedures in place for an uncollected child.

Reflective practice

Safety at arrival and departure

- Do you know the procedures for arrival and departure in your setting?
- How do you ensure that the person who arrives is authorised to collect the child?
- Do you know what to do if an unknown adult arrives to collect a child?
- Think about the most welcoming and safe way to greet families when they arrive.

AC 2.4 The roles and responsibilities of the EYP in relation to policies and procedure for health and safety

Your setting's health and safety policy will contain the names of staff members responsible for health and safety. All early years practitioners are responsible for health and safety in any setting.

Your responsibilities include:

- taking reasonable care for **your own safety** and that of others
- working with your employer in respect of **health and safety** matters
- knowing about the **policies and procedures** in your particular place of work – these can all be found in the setting's **health and safety** policy documents
- not intentionally damaging any health and safety equipment or materials provided by the employer

- **reporting all accidents**, incidents and even 'near misses' to your manager. As you may be handling food, you should also report any **incidences of sickness** or **diarrhoea**. If you are unable to contact the sick child's parents or carer (or other emergency contact person), then you will need to seek medical advice. Always ask your supervisor or manager if in doubt.
- **reporting any hazards** immediately you come across them.

Apart from your legal responsibilities, knowing how to act and being alert and vigilant at all times can prevent accidents, injury, infections and even death – this could be in relation to you, your fellow workers or the children in your care.

Being a good role model

You need to set a good example by always taking care with your appearance and your own personal hygiene. Often your early years setting will provide you with a uniform – usually sweatshirt and trousers – but if not, choose your clothing carefully, bearing in mind the sort of activity you are likely to be involved in.

Activity •

Think about your role as a positive role model and the responsibilities you have regarding:

- hygienic practice when feeding babies and young children
- promoting hand washing with young children.

How could you improve your practice with regard to the above?

• •

LO3 Understand how to plan environments that support children's health and safety

One of the cornerstones of early years care and education is to offer an exciting range of experiences to children, which will stimulate them and extend their skills in all areas of development. As they grow you need to be responsive to their changing **safety needs** at each stage of development.

Guidelines on being a good role model for personal hygiene

- Personal hygiene involves regular and thorough cleaning of your skin, hair, teeth and clothes.
- The most important defence against the spread of infection is hand washing; wash your hands frequently – especially before eating, and before and after touching your mouth or nose. You should not use the kitchen sink to wash your hands.
- Parents and carers must wash their hands after they blow the nose or wipe the mouth of a sick child.
- Use paper towels to dry your hands if possible; if cloth towels are used, make sure that they are washed daily in hot water.
- Keep your nails clean and short as long fingernails harbour dirt. Do not wear nail varnish because flakes of varnish could chip off into the snack you are preparing.
- Avoid jewellery other than a simple wedding ring and a watch.
- Avoid contact with the secretions (especially on stray facial tissues) of somebody with a runny nose, sore throat or cough.
- Cover any cuts or sores on the hands with a clean, waterproof plaster. Use a new plaster each day.
- Do not share utensils or cups with somebody who has a cold, sore throat or upper respiratory tract infection.
- Wear disposable gloves when changing nappies or when dealing with blood, urine, faeces or vomit.
- Hair should be kept clean, be brushed regularly and be tied back, if long.

NB Close supervision is the most effective way of ensuring children's safety.

Children also need a clean, warm and hygienic environment in order to stay healthy. Although most large early years settings employ a cleaner, there will be many occasions when you have to take responsibility for ensuring that the environment is kept clean and safe; for example if a child has been sick or has had a toileting accident.

All early years settings should have set **routines** for tidying up and for cleaning the floors, walls, furniture and play equipment; details may be found in the setting's written policy for health and hygiene issues.

AC 3.1 Describe factors to consider when planning healthy and safe environments

Guidelines for providing a safe and hygienic indoor environment

- Adequate **ventilation** is important to disperse bacteria or viruses transmitted through sneezing or coughing. Make sure that windows are opened to let in fresh air to the nursery – but also make sure there are no draughts.
- Cleaning routines:
  - All surfaces should be damp dusted daily. Floors, surfaces and the toilet area must be checked on a regular basis for cleanliness.
  - All toys and play equipment should be cleaned regularly – *at least* once a week. This includes dressing-up clothes and soft toys. Use antiseptic solutions such as Savlon® to disinfect toys and play equipment regularly; toys used by babies under one year should be disinfected daily.
  - Check that sandpits or trays are clean and that toys are removed and cleaned at the end of a play session; if the sandpit is kept outside make sure it is kept covered when not in use. Keep sand trays clean by sieving and washing the sand regularly.
  - Water trays should be emptied daily as germs can multiply quickly in pools of water.

- The home area often contains dolls, saucepans and plastic food; these need to be included in the checking and in the regular wash.
- Apart from routine cleaning, you should always clean up any spills straightaway; both young children and adults often slip on wet surfaces.
- Use paper towels and tissues, and dispose of them in covered bins.
- Remove from the nursery any toy that has been in contact with a child who has an infectious illness.
- Throw out any plastic toys that have cracks or splits in them as these cracks can harbour germs. Particular care should be taken to keep hats, head coverings and hairbrushes clean in order to help prevent the spread of head lice.
- Animals visiting the nursery or nursery pets must be free from disease, safe to be with children and must not pose a health risk. Children should *always* be supervised when handling animals and you should make sure they always wash their hands after touching any pet.
- A no-smoking policy must be observed by staff and visitors.

Safety of toys

More than 30,000 children go to hospital every year in the UK following an accident involving a toy. Most of these accidents happen to toddlers between one and three years old. As well as accidents associated with the toys themselves, injuries also happen when children – and adults – trip on toys. The most serious of these accidents occur when toys are left on stairs or steps.

A warning symbol telling you that a toy is not suitable for children under 36 months is important because it means that the toy may contain parts that could

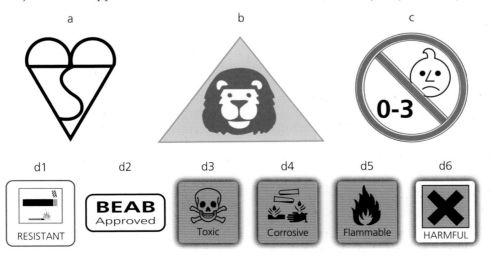

Figure 2.3.2 (a) The Kite Mark (b) The Lion Mark (c) The age advice safety symbol (d) Other safety symbols

choke a very young child. All toys and children's clothes sold in the UK must bear a label to show that the product meets specific safety standards. Toys and playthings display the following labels:

- The **Kite Mark** (see Figure 2.3.2 (a)) confirms that the British Standards Institution (BSI) has tested a product and found it meets a particular standard.
- The **Lion Mark** (see Figure 2.3.2(b)): this symbol is only found on British-made toys and means that they have met the safety standards required.
- The **age advice safety symbol** (see Figure 2.3.2(c)): this means that the toy is unsuitable for children under three years old because it might, for instance, contain small parts. It is very important to choose the right toy for the age of child. (Most toys also have a suggested age range on the packaging. These are mostly for guidance only and reflect what age groups the manufacturer believes will find the toy most appealing.)

NB: Toys and games bought from market stalls, and cheap foreign imports may be copies of well-known brand-name toys but may not meet the UK safety standards.

Providing a safe and hygienic outdoor environment

Children benefit from playing in the fresh air, as long as they are dressed for the weather. All early years settings should be checked regularly to make sure a safe and hygienic environment is being provided.

Policies relating to health and hygiene issues

All early years settings must have a written policy for dealing with health and hygiene issues. The guidelines below include points which are often part of the policy document.

Supervising children's safety

The most important thing to remember when caring for children is to treat each child as an individual – with individual needs. Babies and young children's abilities will differ over time; it may be surprising when they do things for the first time but you should

Guidelines for ensuring a safe outdoor environment

- Check the outdoor play area daily for litter, dog excrement and hazards such as broken glass, syringes or rusty cans.
- Follow the **sun safety code**; provide floppy hats and use sun cream (SPF15) to prevent sunburn (if parents give their permission).
- Check all play equipment for splinters, jagged edges, protruding nails and other hazards.
- Supervise children at all times.
- Keep sand covered and check regularly for insects, litter and other contamination.
- Keep gates locked and check that hinges are secure.

Guidelines for addressing health and hygiene issues

- Always wear disposable gloves when dealing with blood, urine, faeces or vomit.
- Always wash your hands after dealing with spillages – even if gloves have been worn.
- Use a dilute bleach (hypochlorite) solution (or product specified by your setting's policy) to mop up any spillages.
- Make sure paper tissues are available for children to use.
- Always cover cuts and open sores with adhesive plasters.
- Food must be stored and prepared hygienically.
- Ask parents to keep their children at home if they are feeling unwell or if they have an infection.
- Children who are sent home with vomiting or diarrhoea must remain at home until at least 48 hours have elapsed since the last attack.
- Parents must provide written authorisation for early years workers to administer medications to children.

Guidelines for disposing of waste

- Staff should *always* wear disposable gloves when handling any bodily waste, i.e. blood, urine, vomit and faeces. Always dispose of the gloves and wash your hands after dealing with such waste, even though gloves have been worn.
- A dilute bleach (hypochlorite) solution should be used to mop up any spillages.
- Different types of waste should be kept in separate covered bins in designated areas; food waste should be kept well away from toilet waste.
- Soiled nappies, dressings, disposable towels and gloves should be placed in a sealed bag before being put in a plastic-lined, covered bin for incineration.
- Always cover any cuts and open sores with waterproof adhesive plasters.

be able to anticipate, adapt and avoid dangerous situations in order to maintain their safety and security. In particular, babies have no awareness of danger and are therefore totally dependent on their carers for protection and survival. Appropriate levels of **supervision**, provided by you, are therefore essential.

Example: Babies under one year old are able to wriggle, grasp, suck and roll over and are naturally curious. Toddlers, too, can move very quickly, so accidents often happen in seconds. As children get older and their physical skills increase they are better able to explore their environment, which means they are more likely to have knocks and bruises and you need to ensure that they can play in safety.

It is not just broken or damaged equipment and toys that can be a risk to children's safety. You need to make sure that the activity or plaything a child uses is suitable for them; this means that the child is at the right stage of development to be able to play safely with the toy.

Figure 2.3.3 Baby reaching for a toy

Special needs: Children with special needs may need specialised equipment and playthings in order to participate safely in the daily activities in any childcare setting; more often they just need to have very slight changes made to the environment; for example, a child with physical difficulties might benefit from having Velcro® straps attached to the pedals of a bike.

Providing a safe and secure environment for children also involves:

- ensuring that the environment and equipment are checked for safety
- knowing how to maintain the environment to ensure safety for children
- knowing why accidents happen and how to prevent them
- encouraging children to be aware of their own safety and the safety of others
- knowing about safety issues when taking children out of the setting.

Checking the environment and equipment for safety
Doors, gates and windows
These should be appropriately fastened to ensure the safety of the children. Any setting must be secure so that children cannot just wander off without anyone realising; there should also be a policy which guards against strangers being able to wander in without reason.

Many early years settings now have door entry phones, and staff wear name badges or identifiable uniform. Be sure to challenge anyone politely who is unfamiliar to you in the setting or gives you cause for suspicion as to why they are there, and keep a record of any visitors.

Access points and **fire exits** must be unobstructed at all times.

Play equipment

All equipment used for children's play should be checked routinely and any damaged items should be removed from the scene and reported to your supervisor. You will be expected to check for objects which stick out on equipment and could cut a child or cause clothing to become entangled, e.g. screws or bolts on trucks or playground equipment. Plastic toys and equipment can be checked for splits and cracks when you clean them. Check wooden equipment such as wooden blocks or wheeled carts for splinters and rough edges.

Sandpits

Check that sandpits are covered overnight or brought indoors to prevent contamination from animals, such as cats. You should also check that no hazardous litter is in the sand – such as sharp sticks, broken glass or insects.

Safe storage

Sharp objects such as scissors and knives must be stored out of children's reach – scissors used for craftwork should be children's safety scissors – and remember to remove knives from tables where children might grab them.

Water

Check that buckets or bowls of water are never left where children could trip into them as children can drown in water that is only a few inches deep. If there is open water such as a pond, drains or a pool at or near to the setting, make sure they are made safe and inaccessible to children, and that children are closely supervised at all times when playing with or near water.

Electrical equipment

Most early years settings have a variety of electrical equipment – including TV, DVD, CD, MP3 player and a computer. You need to check that the electric sockets are covered with socket covers when not in use and that there are no trailing wires on the floor or where children could grab them.

Outdoor safety

Before outdoor play sessions, you must check that surfaces are safe to play on – for example, not icy or slippery and that objects which could cause children harm have been removed. Also ensure that children are properly equipped for outdoor play. They should always be dressed according to the weather, with waterproof coats and wellington boots in wet weather, and warm hats and gloves in cold weather. You also need to ensure that children are protected against strong sun – by following the sun safety code. Children playing outside should be supervised at all times.

Maintaining a safe environment

On a day-to-day basis you need to be alert to the changing abilities and safety needs of children and also to identify and address hazards in the childcare setting. Your employer will do this on a formal basis, carrying out a Health and Safety risk assessment (see p 190). To ensure children's safety, you need to be able to:

- **identify a hazard** – at every stage of a child's life, you must think again about the hazards that are present and what you can do to eliminate them. This could be play equipment left on the floor and obstructing an exit, or small items which have been left within reach of a baby
- **be aware of the child's interaction with the environment** – this means understanding the different stages of child development – for example, babies explore objects with their mouths and run the risk of choking, and young children tend to run everywhere and could trip over toys on the floor
- **provide adequate supervision** – according to each child's age, needs and abilities
- **be a good role model** – ensuring that the child's environment is kept safe and that you follow the setting's health and safety guidelines
- **know how to use the safety equipment provided** – e.g. safety gates, window locks, baby harnesses and security intercom systems
- **teach children about safety** – encourage children to be aware of their own personal safety and the safety of others.

Activity

What are the main factors to consider when planning a safe and healthy environment in relation to the following?

- indoor hygiene and safety
- safety and hygiene of toys and dressing-up props
- safety outdoors
- play equipment.

AC 3.2 Identify hazards to the health and safety of children, colleagues and visitors

Early years practitioners need to be conscious of any risks in the working environment and the potential impact of these risks. They can then plan ahead to avoid hazards and incidents.

Key terms

hazard A source of potential harm or damage, or a situation with potential for harm or damage.

risk The possibility of suffering harm or loss; danger.

risk assessment The assessment that must be carried out in order to identify hazards and find out the safest way to carry out certain tasks and procedures.

How to identify hazards in the setting

In the early years setting a hazard may be a substance, a piece of equipment, a work procedure or a child's condition. Examples of hazards in settings include:

toys and play equipment	chemical hazards, such as cleaning materials and disinfectants
biological hazards, such as airborne and blood-borne infections, food hygiene infections	the handling and moving of equipment and of children
unsupervised children	security of entry points and exits
administration of medicines	visual or hearing impairment of children

Risk is defined as the chance or likelihood that harm will occur from the hazard. The likelihood is described as 'the expectancy of harm occurring'. It can range from 'never' to 'certain', and depends on a number of factors.

Example 1: A door

The main entrance to a nursery or primary school may present a hazard. The risks are that:

- a child might escape and run into the road, or go missing, or
- a stranger might enter the building.

The likelihood of the hazard of the entrance/door posing a risk will depend on a number of factors:

- the security of the entrance – for example, can it only be opened by using a key pad or entry phone system, and is the door handle placed high up, out of a child's reach?
- policies and procedures being known to parents and other visitors, such as at collection times.

Example 2: A damaged or uneven floor surface

This may present a hazard. The risk is:

- that someone may trip over and become injured.

The likelihood of the hazard of the damaged floor posing a risk will depend on a number of factors:

- the extent of the unevenness or damage
- the number of people walking over it
- the number of times they walk over it
- whether they are wearing sensible shoes
- the level of lighting.

Babies and young children are at particular risk of harm because they:

- lack any appreciation of danger
- are naturally inquisitive
- love to explore and test the boundaries of their world.

You need to help young children to explore within safe boundaries, but to adjust those boundaries according to their capabilities and increasing skill. Useful skills to employ when dealing with inquisitive toddlers include recognising the value of **distraction** – guiding attention away from something dangerous and towards something potentially more interesting, physically removing the child: 'Harry, come with me – I want to show you something.'

Even so, no environment, however carefully planned and designed, can ever be totally without risk to children.

Older children face different risks. For example, they are more likely to travel to school independently and need to be aware of the principles of road safety. They also need to be aware of the risks involved in using the internet.

Safe working practices: protecting children from common hazards

All areas where children play and learn should be checked for hygiene and safety at the start of every session and again at the end of each session – this is often called the **safety sweep** – but do be alert at all times. Look at your setting's written policy for health and hygiene issues. Find out from your manager how to clean toys and other equipment, and remember that many objects (plastic toys and soft toys) end up in children's mouths, which is a good way of passing on and picking up an infection.

Remember that *you* could also be a risk to children's health. For example, if you have a heavy cold or have suffered from diarrhoea or vomiting within the previous 48 hours, you must not attend for work as you could pass on a serious infection to the children.

Safety sweeps

Most practitioners carry out a safety sweep, both indoors and outdoors, on a daily or twice-daily basis – often at the start and end of a session. This is a very useful way to assess risk. The checks are often done informally and not always recorded unless the safety sweep has identified a risk that then requires formal assessment. For example, a safety sweep at the beginning of the day may involve checking the outdoor area for the following hazards:

- Is the 'safer' surfacing in the play area in good condition – e.g. no loose or uneven tiles? Rubberised surfaces can get an almost invisible build-up of algae which can make them very slippery when wet, so always check surfaces for slipperiness.

- Are pathways undamaged and free from obstructions?
- Is the area free from litter, glass or any other dangerous objects?
- Is the area free from animal fouling?

A risk assessment would be required if a safety sweep revealed problems regarding any of the above checks. Any faults should be recorded and reported to the relevant person.

Activity

Find out how safety is promoted in your setting. Do staff perform regular safety sweeps? Are risk assessments routinely carried out for new activities or scenarios?

LO4 Manage risk within an environment which provides challenge for children

Health and safety legislation does not expect *all* risk to be eliminated – but that 'reasonable precautions' are taken and that staff are trained and aware of their responsibilities. This is particularly important in an early years setting, as children should be able to grow and develop being able to take appropriate risks through physically challenging play. Children must also have the opportunity and be encouraged to work out what is not safe and what they should do when they are faced with a risk.

AC 4.1 Explain why it is important to take a balanced approach to risk management

Children need a safe but challenging environment. Almost every human activity involves a certain degree of risk, and children need to learn how to cope with this. They need to understand that the world can be a dangerous place, and that care needs to be taken when they are negotiating their way round it. For example, when a child first learns to walk, he or she will inevitably fall over or knock into things. This is a valuable part of their learning and a natural part of their development.

Children who are sheltered or overprotected from risk and challenge when young will not be able to make judgements about their own strengths and skills, and will not be well equipped to resist peer pressure in their later years. Also, a totally risk-free environment lacks challenges and stimulation; this leads inevitably to children becoming bored and to deteriorating behaviour. Simply being *told* about possible dangers is not enough: children need to see or experience the consequences of not taking care.

The challenge for early years practitioners is balancing the need for safety against the need for children to explore risks. Many adults engage in risky activities such as bungee jumping, skydiving, motor racing, snowboarding. Similarly, children need to explore their own levels of risk-taking, but in safe environments with qualified first aid personnel at hand should accidents arise. If we do not enable children to take risks, then they will seek them out when adults are not around, which may mean more deaths on roads, rivers, railway lines and electric pylons.

Reflective practice

Do you agree that it is important for children to take risks? How can you balance this with the need to promote their safety? Can you remember being allowed to take risks when you were a young child?

(If you would like to learn more about children's need for risk and challenge, read Tim Gill's blog: Rethinking Childhood, at www.rethinkingchildhood.com.)

AC 4.2 Carry out risk assessments within own setting

Risk assessment is a method of preventing accidents and ill health by helping people to think about what could go wrong and devising ways to prevent problems. Risk assessments on aspects such as security of the building, fire safety, food safety, toilet hygiene and nappy changing, outings, and personal safety of staff should already exist. Other examples of activities where risk assessments are required include:

- cooking activities
- supervising children's use of climbing equipment

- a visit from somebody outside the setting who may be bringing equipment – or a pet animal – to show the children as part of a topic
- making reasonable adjustments for disabled children or children with additional needs, and for staff or visitors.

Whatever the reason for the risk assessment, the process remains the same: the **Risk Assessment Processes** identifies five steps that you need to take:

- **Step 1: Identification of risk or hazard** – where is it and what is it?
- **Step 2: Decide who is at risk and how** – for example childcare staff, children, parents, cooks, cleaners.
- **Step 3: Evaluate the risks and decide on precautions** – can you get rid of the risk altogether? If not, how can you control it?
- **Step 4: Record your findings and implement them** – prioritise, make a plan of action if necessary.
- **Step 5: Monitoring and review** – how do you know if what has been decided is working, or is thorough enough? If it is not working, it will need to be amended, or maybe there is a better solution.

It is usually the responsibility of the manager or person in charge to devise the format of the risk assessment using the above points; they must then ensure that they are carried out and that the completed forms are kept to inform procedures that guide your work on a day-to-day basis.

In practice activity

A risk assessment

Carry out a risk assessment for a visit by a parent who is bringing in her pet rabbit to show the children and talk to them about pets in general. Remember to include possible hazards – e.g. allergies, overexcited children, hygiene issues, etc.

AC 4.3 Describe how health and safety risk assessments are monitored and reviewed

It is important to monitor and review risk assessments as there may have been changes – for example, new equipment introduced or new procedures. After completing an initial risk assessment, a date should be set for the next one. This could be once a term, twice a year or annually, depending on the size of the setting, the number of staff changes, changes to the physical environment, additional equipment or resources. When new equipment arrives, a new risk assessment should be completed and the findings added to the original document.

The process of review includes answering the following questions:

- Have there been any changes?
- Are there improvements you still need to make?
- Have you or your colleagues identified a problem?
- Have you learnt anything from accidents or near misses?

Activity ·

In your setting, examine some recent risk assessments and find out if there are any improvements to be made. Find out who is responsible for reviewing risk assessments and for implementing any recommendations.

AC 4.4 Support children in own setting to manage risk

An important aspect of teaching children about risk is to encourage them to make their own risk assessments and think about the possible consequences of their actions. Rather than removing objects and equipment from the environment in case children hurt themselves, adults should teach children how to use them safely. It is important to strike the right balance: protecting children from harm while allowing them the freedom to develop independence and risk awareness.

If a child seems at risk of harming herself in some way, the early years practitioner *must* intervene. Then, using language appropriate to the age and understanding of the child, the adult

could ask open-ended questions for the child to identify why she could come to harm. In this way, the adult and the child work together to reach a solution and children gain a better understanding of why they were stopped from playing and how to identify dangers. (They can then carry on, if appropriate.)

As children become older, talk to them about keeping safe and about how to avoid accidents and injury. Children may also be encouraged to assess risks by being given reasons why they may be asked to do something. For example, when asking children to put the cars and trucks back on to the mat, the adult asks why it should be done and the child learns that if they are not collected, someone may trip over them and could hurt themselves.

Case study

Supporting children to assess and manage risk

Four children are playing in a den they have made in the outdoor play area, using a frame and some cloth. The den looks rather crowded and the children are finding it difficult to carry out their play. Angela, an early years practitioner, asks them: 'How many children do you think should be in the den? How many of you are in the den? How is it making you feel? What could we do to make it less of a squash?' The children all join in with answers, and after a lively debate, two of the children decide to set up a den for themselves. Angela helps them fetch the equipment and the play resumes.

1 What are the hazards when too many children are playing in a confined space?
2 How did Angela support the children in making their own risk assessments?
3 Think of ways in which you could support children in your care to assess and manage risk for themselves.

Activity ·

Think about risk management. In which situations **must** you intervene during children's play?

Figure 2.3.4 Children playing in a den

AC 4.5 Reflect on own role in the setting when managing risk

Step 5 of the risk assessment process is monitoring and review. This part of the risk assessment process allows early years practitioners to reflect upon:

- actions taken against the risks that are identified
- the effectiveness of those actions, and
- any further amendments required.

By building the skills of reflective practice into your everyday work, you will develop the skills of identifying any adjustments that are required in order to minimise risks during an event or experience.

LO5 Understand how to identify, record and report accidents, incidents and emergencies

AC 5.1 Identify accidents and incidents which may occur in a setting

Recognising signs of illness

The responsibility of caring for a child who becomes ill is enormous; it is very important that early years practitioners should know the **signs and symptoms** of illness and when to seek medical aid. When a child is taken ill or is injured, it is vital that the parents or carers are notified as soon as possible.

Case study

A breach of health and safety regulations

A child aged 16 months, who had been left unattended for 20 minutes at a nursery, died after getting her neck trapped in the drawstring of a bag. The toddler had been placed in a cot to sleep with a looped drawstring of a bag placed over the side and became entangled in the loops. She was at the time in the care of a 17-year-old student member of staff while senior managers met upstairs. Following an inquest verdict of unlawful killing, the nursery owner was prosecuted in the Crown Court, where the judge said staff showed 'gross incompetence' by not acting on warnings from the child's parents that she did often wrap things around her neck, adding: 'This was such an obvious risk that virtually no parent in their own home would have considered it, let alone professionals who should have been responsible.'

It emerged that a proper risk assessment had not been carried out, which would have prohibited the leaving of bags and other potentially dangerous objects within reach of children. Safety rules were poorly understood and inconsistently applied; toddlers were supposed to have been checked every 10 minutes. Imposing a £35,000 fine, the judge noted that this was not a case of manslaughter but a breach of health and safety regulations, referring to the tragedy as 'an accident which should have been foreseen'.

(Adapted from a report in the *Guardian*, 30 October 2008)

Study the case history above and discuss the following questions:

1 What factors led to the toddler being unsafe while in nursery care?
2 What sort of risk assessment could have helped to prevent the toddler's death?
3 On a wider subject - do you think that *all* accidents are preventable?

Small children are not always able to explain their symptoms, and may display non-specific complaints such as headache, sleeplessness, vomiting or an inability to stand up. Babies have even less certain means of communication, and may simply cry in a different way, refuse feeds or become listless and lethargic. Most, but not all, infectious diseases will be accompanied by fever.

> ### Key terms
>
> **signs of illness** Those that can be observed directly, for example, a change in skin colour, a rash or a swelling.
>
> **symptoms of illness** Those experienced by the child, for example, pain, discomfort or generally feeling unwell. Detection of symptoms relies on the child being able to describe how they are feeling.

Provide comfort and reassurance

If a child becomes ill while at nursery, he or she may have to wait a while to be taken home. In the meantime you should:

- offer support and reassurance to the child, who may feel frightened or anxious
- always notify a senior member of staff if you notice that a child is unwell; that person will then decide if and when to contact the child's parents or carers
- A member of staff (preferably the child's key person) should remain with the child all the time and keep them as comfortable as possible.

You must deal with any incident of vomiting or diarrhoea swiftly and sympathetically to minimise the child's distress and to preserve their dignity. All settings have an exclusion policy that lets parents know when it is safe for their sick child to return to the group.

Serious conditions

A child who has sustained a serious injury or illness will need to be seen urgently by a doctor. For example:

- a head injury or any loss of consciousness
- a wound that continues to bleed after first aid treatment is given
- suspected meningitis (see below)
- an asthma attack not relieved by child's inhaler
- fracture or suspected fracture, burns and scalds, foreign bodies

- life-threatening incidents such as seizures, poisoning, choking, anaphylaxis, loss of consciousness, respiratory and cardiac arrest.

> ### Key terms
>
> **anaphylaxis** A severe allergic reaction that affects the whole body. It can lead to **anaphylactic shock**.
>
> **anaphylactic shock** A potentially fatal immune response when the body system literally shuts down. The most common causes are a severe allergic reaction to peanuts, insect stings and certain drugs.

Meningitis

Meningitis is an inflammation of the lining of the brain. It is a very serious illness, but if it is detected and treated early, most children make a full recovery. The early symptoms of meningitis, such as fever, irritability, restlessness, vomiting and refusing feeds, are also common with colds and 'flu. However, a baby with meningitis can become seriously ill *within hours*, so it is important to *act quickly* if meningitis is suspected. Table 2.3.4 shows the signs and symptoms of meningitis.

In babies under 12 months
• Tense or bulging fontanelles.
• A stiffening body with involuntary movements, or a floppy body.
• Blotchy or pale skin.
• A high-pitched, moaning cry.
• High temperature.
• The baby may be difficult to wake.
• The baby may refuse to feed.
• Red or purple spots (anywhere on the body) that do not fade under pressure – do the glass test (see below).
In older children
• Headache.
• Inability to tolerate light.
• Neck stiffness and joint pains - the child may arch the neck backwards because of the rigidity of the neck muscles.
• Fever.

Table 2.3.4 Signs and symptoms of meningitis

The 'glass test'

Press the side or bottom of a glass firmly against the rash; you will be able to see if the rash fades and loses colour under the pressure. If it *does not* change colour, summon medical aid *immediately*. If spots are appearing on the child's body, this could be septicaemia – a very serious bacterial infection described as the 'meningitis rash'.

Figure 2.3.5 The 'glass test' for meningitis

Emergency procedures: what to do in the event of a non-medical incident or emergency

There are many different types of emergency (apart from a medical emergency when a person is seriously injured or ill) and it is important to know what procedures to follow, for example:

- if a child goes missing
- in case of fire
- if there is a security incident.

Missing children

Strict procedures must be followed to prevent a child from going missing from the setting. However, if a child *does* go missing, an established procedure must be followed, for example:

- The person in charge will carry out a thorough search of the building and garden.
- The register is checked to make sure that no other child has also gone astray.
- Doors and gates are checked to see if there has been a breach of security whereby a child could wander out.
- The person in charge talks to staff to establish what happened.

If the child is not found, the parent or carer is contacted and the missing child is reported to the police.

Case study

Missing from a nursery

A two-year-old girl walked out of her pre-school nursery one winter morning, leaving her coat behind, and crossed a busy road as she wandered half a mile to her home. The first that the nursery knew of her disappearance was when her furious father turned up demanding to know why he had found his tearful daughter struggling to open their garden gate.

Fortunately, potentially dangerous events like this are very rare, but they should be preventable.

1. How do you think that this could have happened?
2. Consider your own setting and assess whether it could happen there.
3. How could such incidents be prevented?

In case of fire

In the case of fire or other emergency, you need to know what to do to safely evacuate the children and yourselves. Follow the following rules for fire safety:

- No smoking is allowed in any early years setting.
- Handbags containing matches or lighters must be locked securely away out of children's reach.
- The nursery cooker should not be left unattended when turned on.
- Fire exits must be clearly signed.
- Fire drills should be carried out regularly; registers must be kept up to date throughout the day.

- Fire exits and other doors should be free of obstructions on both sides.
- Instructions about what to do in the event of a fire must be clearly displayed.
- You should know where the fire extinguishers are kept and how to use them.
- Electrical equipment should be regularly checked for any faults.

Evacuation procedures

A plan for an escape route and the attendance register must be up to date so that everyone – children and staff – can safely be accounted for at the meeting point of safety. The attendance record must be taken by the person in charge when the building is evacuated. Clearly written instructions for fire drills and how to summon the fire brigade must be posted in a conspicuous place in the setting.

Security issues and violence

Early years settings and schools should be secure environments where children cannot wander off without anyone realising. But they also need to be secure so that strangers cannot enter without a good reason for being there. Occasionally you might encounter a problem with violence – or threats of violence – from a child's parents or carers. Your setting will have a policy that deals with this issue.

AC 5.2 Identify forms for completion in the event of accidents, incidents and emergencies

All early years settings must follow the guidelines of RIDDOR for the reporting of accidents and incidents. (Child protection matters or behavioural incidents between children are *not* regarded as incidents and there are separate procedures for this.)

The accident report book

Every workplace is, by law, required to have an accident report book and to maintain a record of accidents. The accident report book must be:

- kept safely and accessibly
- accessible to all staff and volunteers, who know how to complete it, and

- be reviewed at least half-termly to identify any potential or actual hazards.

Information recorded includes:

- name of person injured
- date and time of injury
- where the accident happened (for example, in the garden)
- what exactly happened (Kara fell on the path and grazed her left knee)
- what injuries occurred (a graze)
- what treatment was given (graze was bathed and an adhesive dressing applied)
- name and signature of person dealing with the accident
- signature of witness to the report
- signature of parent or carer.

One copy of the duplicated report form is given to the child's parent or carer; the other copy is kept in the accident report book at the early years setting.

Reporting accidents and incidents

Under the **EYFS Safeguarding and Welfare Requirements**, *Safeguarding and Promoting Children's Welfare*, Ofsted must be notified of:

- any food poisoning affecting two or more children looked after on the premises, and
- any injury requiring treatment by a general practitioner or hospital doctor, or
- the death of a child or adult as soon as possible or at least within 14 days of the incident occurring.

Local child protection agencies are informed of any serious accident or injury to, or the death of, any child while in the setting's care and the setting must act on any advice given by those agencies.

When there is any injury requiring general practitioner or hospital treatment to a child, parent, volunteer or visitor or where there is a death of a child or adult on the premises, a report is made to the HSE using the format for the RIDDOR.

Reporting to the HSE

In compliance with RIDDOR, a report must be made to the HSE in the following circumstances:

- any accident to a member of staff requiring treatment by a general practitioner or hospital; and

- any dangerous occurrence. This may be an event that causes injury or fatalities or an event that does not cause an accident but could have done, such as a gas leak.

Any dangerous occurrence is recorded in the setting's incident book.

Reportable incident record

Incidents to be recorded include:

- break in, burglary, theft of personal or the setting's property
- an intruder gaining unauthorised access to the premises
- fire, flood, gas leak or electrical failure
- attack on member of staff or parent on the premises or nearby
- any racist incident involving staff or family on the centre's premises
- death of a child, and
- a terrorist attack, or threat of one.

In the incident book the following data is recorded:

- the date and time of the incident
- nature of the event
- who was affected
- what was done about it or if it was reported to the police, and if so a crime number.

Any follow up, or insurance claim made, is also recorded.

Forms relating to health and safety in early years settings

The following forms are required to be kept for each child in all early years settings. They are to be completed when necessary and kept in the child's confidential file. It is your responsibility to find out where the forms are kept and to record relevant information.

- **Accident form**: a form to record any accident or injury to a child while in the care of the setting – whether on the premises on an outing. When completed, a copy is given to parents and the original stored in the child's confidential file.
- **Treatment record form**: a short form to record details of any long-term treatment a child needs, e.g. asthma inhaler. Once completed,

a copy is given to parents and the original stored in the first aid box for reference. When no longer required, this is stored in the child's confidential file.

- **Medication record form**: a short form to record details of any short-term medicine a child needs, e.g. prescription or over-the-counter cough medicines. Once completed, this is stored with the medicine. When treatment has been completed this is stored in the child's confidential file.
- **Parent-administered medication form**: a short form to record details of medicine administered prior to the child's arrival and whether they have had this medicine before (i.e. to ascertain the risk of allergic reaction).
- **Existing injury form**: a short form in which parents can record a recent injury sustained by their child for the setting's information and to record similar information provided by school/ pre-school with a copy being given to parents, e.g. a graze or bruise.
- **Register of attendance**: a file should be used to record arrival and departure times to the nearest five minutes (rather than the time the parents arrive and depart) and to be completed by a parent or the setting.

Reporting to parents

All accidents, injuries or illnesses that occur to children in a group setting must be reported to the child's parents or primary carers. If the injury is minor (such as a bruise or a small graze to the knee), the nursery or school staff will inform parents when the child is collected at the end of the session; or they may send a notification slip home if someone else collects the child. The parents are notified about:

- the nature of the injury or illness
- any treatment or action taken
- the name of the person who carried out the treatment.

In the case of a major accident, illness or injury, the child's parents or primary carers must be notified as soon as possible. Parents need to know that staff members are dealing with the incident in a caring and professional manner, and they will need to be involved in any decisions regarding treatment.

AC 5.3 Describe the lines of reporting and responsibility in the event of accidents, incidents and emergencies

Reporting and recording when a child becomes ill

If a child becomes ill while in a group setting, you should *first* report it to your manager or supervisor and then record the following details in the child's daily record:

- when the child first showed signs of illness
- the signs and symptoms: for example, behaviour changes, a high temperature or a rash
- any action taken: for example, taking the temperature or giving paracetamol (with parental permission agreed beforehand)
- progress of the illness since first noticing it: for example, are there any further symptoms?

What to do in case of serious illness or injury

1 Call for help: stay calm and do not panic! Your line manager (or designated first aider) will make an assessment and decide whether the injury or illness requires medical help, either a GP or an ambulance. He or she will also contact the parents or carers to let them know about the nature of the illness or injury.
2 Stay with the child; comfort and reassure him or her.
3 Treat the injury or assess the severity of the illness and treat appropriately. You are not expected to be able to *diagnose* a sudden illness, but should know what signs and symptoms require medical treatment.
4 Record exactly what happens and what treatment is carried out.

What to do when an accident happens

If a child has had an accident, they are likely to be shocked and may not cry immediately. They will need calm reassurance as first aid is administered, together with an explanation of what is being done to them and why. Parents or carers must be informed and the correct procedures for the setting carried out. If the child needs emergency hospital treatment, parental permission will be needed.

If you work in a setting with others such as a day care facility or school, there is likely to be a designated person who is a qualified in first aid; they should be called to deal with the situation.

Remember! It is essential that you do not make the situation worse, and it is better to do the minimum to ensure the child's safety such as putting them into the **recovery position**. The only exception to this is if the child is not breathing or there is no heartbeat.

Activity

Make sure you know what to do if a child becomes ill or has an accident. Find out where the records are kept and how they should be completed.

Assessment practice

1 Describe the main laws relating to the health and safety of children in your area of the UK.

2 What do the following acronyms stand for: RIDDOR, COSHH and HSE?

3 Identify policies and procedures relating to the health and safety of children.

4 Analyse how legislation and guidelines for health and safety inform day-to-day work with children.

5 Why is it important to work within the EYFS framework and to have a good knowledge of the policies and procedures in your setting?

6 Describe procedures for the registration and collection of children.

7 Outline your role and responsibilities when keeping children safe.

8 What factors should be considered when planning healthy and safe environments?

9 Identify hazards to the health and safety of children, colleagues and visitors.

10 Explain why it is important to manage risk and challenge in the setting but also to take a balanced approach.

11 Choose an activity and carry out your own health and safety risk assessment.

12 Describe how health and safety risk assessments are monitored and reviewed.

13 Describe ways to support children in your own setting to manage risk.

14 Reflect on your own role in the setting when managing risk.

15 Describe the signs and symptoms of illness in babies and young children.

16 What signs and symptoms would lead you to suspect meningitis, and what should you do?

17 Identify accidents and incidents which may occur in a setting, and the forms for completion in the event of accidents, incidents, and emergencies.

18 Why is it important to record accidents and incidents? Describe your role and responsibilities when dealing with and reporting accidents, incidents and emergencies.

Useful resources

Organisations

Health and Safety Executive (HSE)

HSE is the national independent watchdog for work-related health, safety and illness: www.hse.gov.uk

RIDDOR

RIDDOR puts duties on employers, the self-employed and people in control of work premises (the Responsible Person) to report certain serious workplace accidents, occupational diseases and specified dangerous occurrences (near misses): www.hse.gov.uk/riddor

Ofsted

Ofsted is the Office for Standards in Education, Children's Services and Skills. Ofsted inspects and regulates services which care for children and young people, and those providing education and skills for learners of all ages: www.ofsted.gov.uk

Unit 2.4 Use legislation relating to equality, diversity and inclusive practice

Equality, inclusion and anti-discriminatory practice refer to moral and legal obligations and rights for people working in and using public services. As an early years practitioner, you have a role to play in ensuring that in all aspects of your work every person is given real opportunities to thrive, and that any barriers that would prevent them from reaching their full potential are removed. The principles of equality and inclusion are at the heart of work with children and young people in every kind of setting.

Learning outcomes

By the end of this unit you will:

1 Understand how legislation and codes of practice inform equality, diversity and inclusive practice.
2 Understand how policies and procedures inform equality, diversity and inclusive practice.
3 Be able to use information, advice and support to promote equality, diversity and inclusion.
4 Be able to work in ways which support equality, diversity and inclusive practice.

LO1 Understand how legislation and codes of practice inform equality, diversity and inclusive practice

AC 1.1 Describe what is meant by equality, diversity, inclusion and discrimination

Equality

Equality does not mean that everyone has to be treated the same. People have different needs, situations and ambitions. Early years practitioners have a part to play in supporting children and young people to live in the way that they value and choose, to be 'themselves' and to be different if they wish. Every person should have equality of opportunity. This means opening up access for every child and

family to the full participation in all services for children and young people. Lack of access causes:

- poor self-esteem
- misunderstandings
- stereotyping and discrimination
- lack of inclusion
- lack of respect
- lack of confidence.

Diversity

Diversity refers to the differences in values, attitudes, cultures, beliefs, skills and life experience of each individual in any group of people. In the UK, early years curriculum frameworks emphasise the importance of developing each child's sense of identity and promoting a positive sense of pride in each child's family origins. Starting with themselves, young children can develop a sense of belonging to the local community, and begin to understand and respect less familiar cultures.

Inclusion

Inclusion is a term used within education to describe the process of ensuring the equality of learning opportunities for all children and young people, whatever their disabilities or disadvantages. This means that all children have the right to have their needs met in the best way for them. They are seen as being part of the community, even if they need particular help to live a full life within the community.

Discrimination

Discrimination is the denial of equality based on personal characteristics, such as race and colour. Discrimination is usually based on prejudice and stereotypes.

- **Prejudice** means to prejudge people based on assumptions. For example, racial prejudice is the belief that physical or cultural differences (for example in skin colour, religious beliefs or dress) are directly linked to differences in the development of intelligence, ability, personality or goodness.

- The word **stereotype** comes from the process of making metal plates for printing. When applied to people, stereotyping refers to forming an instant or fixed picture of a group of people, usually based on false or incomplete information. Stereotypes are often negative.

We need to be aware of different forms of discrimination so that we can act to promote equality.

The restricting effect of stereotypes

To avoid stereotypes it is important to look beyond the 'fixed picture' or perceptions. For example, the most important thing about working with 'the child with glasses' might be the fact that he loves music. The most important thing about 'the Afro-Caribbean child' might be that she loves mathematics, and can remember all the sequences and measurements of cooking even at three years of age. The most important thing about the girl 'in the pretty dress' might be that she is worried about getting it dirty and so never plays with clay. Gender stereotypes are also restricting because behaviour is seen as 'what boys do' and 'what girls do'. By encouraging boys and girls alike to be active and to explore, to be gentle and nurturing, all children are enabled to lead fuller lives with broader roles. It equips them much better for their future lives.

Adults working with children need to empower them rather than to narrowly stereotype them. To focus on one feature of the child is much too narrow. It is important not to stereotype children through labels. Children are people, and they have names, not labels!

Racial, cultural and religious discrimination

Racism is the belief that some races are superior, based on the false idea that things like skin colour make some people better than others. An example of racial discrimination is refusing a child a nursery place because they are black; an example of cultural discrimination is failing to address the needs of children from a minority religious or cultural group, such as children from Traveller families; and an example of religious discrimination is only acknowledging festivals from the mainstream Christian culture, such as Christmas and Easter.

Disability discrimination

Children with disabilities or impairments may be denied equality of opportunity with their non-disabled peers. Examples are failing to provide children with special needs with appropriate facilities and services; or organising activities in a nursery setting in a way that ignores the special physical, intellectual and emotional needs of certain children.

Sex discrimination

This occurs when people of one gender reinforce the stereotype that they are superior to the other. Examples are routinely offering boys more opportunities for rough-and-tumble play than girls, or encouraging girls to perform traditional 'female' tasks such as cooking and washing.

No law can prevent prejudiced attitudes. However, the law can prohibit discriminatory practices and behaviours that flow from prejudice.

Direct and indirect discrimination

Children can experience the effects of discrimination in a number of ways. Discrimination can be direct or indirect.

Direct discrimination

This occurs when a child is treated less favourably than another child in the same or similar circumstances; for example, when a child or young person is bullied by being ignored, verbally or physically abused, or teased. See also p 302 on bullying.

Indirect discrimination

This occurs when a condition is applied that will unfairly affect a particular group of children when compared to others. This may be either deliberate or unintended; for example, when children from a minority ethnic or religious group (such as Sikh, Muslim or Plymouth Brethren) are required to wear a specific school uniform that causes difficulties within their culture.

The potential effects of discrimination

Discrimination of any kind prevents children and young people from developing a feeling of self-worth or self-esteem. The effects of being discriminated against can last the whole of a child's life. In particular, they may:

Key terms

anti-discrimination An approach which challenges unfair or unlawful treatment of individuals or groups based on a specific characteristic of that group (such as colour, age, disability, sexual orientation, etc.).

diversity The differences in values, attitudes, cultures, beliefs, skills, knowledge and life experience of each individual in any group of people.

discrimination Treating a person less favourably than others in the same or similar circumstances.

equality Ensuring that everyone has a chance to take part in society on an equal basis and to be treated appropriately, regardless of their gender, race, disability, age, sexual orientation, language, social origin, religious beliefs, marital status and other personal attributes.

inclusion Ensuring that every child, young person, adult or learner is given equality of opportunity to access education and care, by meeting their specific needs.

inclusive practice Inclusion in education and care is one aspect of inclusion in society, and means taking necessary steps to ensure that every child, young person, adult or learner is given an equal chance of taking advantage of the opportunities offered to them.

In practice activity

Exploring stereotypes

You could arrange to carry out this activity with a group of children in Reception class. The aim is to develop children's understanding of stereotyping.

1 Present children with a choice of two DVDs: one is in its own bright colourful cover; the other is a very popular film inside a plain box.

2 Ask children which video they wish to watch. After viewing the selected video for five minutes, show the children some of the other video.
3 Repeat with two books, one of which is covered in plain brown paper. Talk to the children about what these examples tell us (you should not judge a book by its cover).

- **be unable to fulfil their potential**, because they are made to feel that their efforts are not valued or recognised by others
- **find it hard to form relationships** with others because of low self-worth or self-esteem
- be so **affected by the stereotypes or labels** applied to them that they start to believe in them and so behave in accordance with others' expectations. This then becomes a self-fulfilling prophecy: for example, if a child is repeatedly told that he is clumsy, he may act in a clumsy way even when quite capable of acting otherwise
- **feel shame** about their own cultural background
- **feel that they are in some way to blame** for their unfair treatment, and so withdraw into themselves
- **lack confidence in trying new activities** if their attempts are always ridiculed or put down
- **be aggressive towards others**: distress or anger can prevent children from playing cooperatively with other children.

AC 1.2 Explain current legislation and codes of practice relating to equality, diversity and inclusive practice

Legislation and codes of practice

The laws and codes of practice relating to equality, diversity and discrimination are listed in Table 2.4.1.

The Special Needs and Disability Act (SENDA) 2001

It is anticipated that a new Special Educational Needs Code of Practice will be ready for implementation in September 2014. (It should, however, be mentioned that SENDA 2001 is due to be replaced by the Children and Families Act.) Until that time the current statutory framework will still apply to provision.

The legislation should have an influence on the way in which organisations provide and organise services, and how practitioners approach their work. You need to be aware of the law as it stands in relation to promoting equality of opportunity.

Legislation and codes of practice	Main points of information
The Equality Act (2010)	The Equality Act 2010 replaces all previous equalities legislation, bans unlawful discrimination and helps achieve equal opportunities in and outside the workplace. All early years settings, whether in the statutory, voluntary, independent or private sectors, including childminders, must comply with the Act. The Equality Act 2010 makes sure that people with particular characteristics are protected from discrimination. These are the protected characteristics: • age • disability • gender reassignment • marriage and civil partnerships • pregnancy or maternity • race • religion or belief • sex • sexual orientation (gay, lesbian or bisexual). The Equality Act sets out the different ways in which it is unlawful to treat someone, such as direct and indirect discrimination, harassment, victimisation and failing to make a reasonable adjustment for a disabled person.
The Special Educational Needs and Disability Act 2001	The Special Needs and Disability Act 2001 is supported by the SEN code of practice and strengthened the right of children with disabilities to attend mainstream educational facilities. It was supported by the Code of Practice 2002.
The Special Educational Needs Code of Practice 2002	The SEN Code has the following general principles: • A child with special needs should have his or her needs met. • The special needs of children will be met in mainstream schools – wherever possible. • The views of children should be sought and taken into account. • Parents have a vital role to play in supporting their child's education – and must be seen as partners with local education authorities (LEAs) and other agencies. • Children with special educational needs should be offered full access to a broad, balanced and relevant education, including an appropriate curriculum for the foundation stage and the national curriculum. • All early years settings have a special educational needs policy and follow the integrated team approach of the EYFS profile. • Early identification, Early Years Action, Early Years Action Plus and for some children, statutory assessment. According to the Code, every school must appoint a member of staff who takes responsibility for special education needs: the Special Educational Needs Coordinator or SENCO.
The United Nations Convention on the Rights of the Child (1989)	As an early years practitioner you must know and understand the basic requirements of the United Nations Convention on the Rights of the Child. These rights are for children and young people (up to the age of 18 years). (The only two countries in the world that have not signed the Convention are the USA and Somalia.) The rights embodied by the UN Convention which particularly relate to childcare and education are these: • Children have the right to be with their family or with those who will care best for them. • Children have the right to enough food and clean water for their needs. • Children have the right to an adequate standard of living. • Children have the right to health care. • Children have the right to play. • Children have the right to be kept safe and not hurt or neglected. • Disabled children have the right to special care and training. • Children must not be used as cheap workers or as soldiers. • Children have the right to free education. • All children should be listened to and their views taken seriously. (Article 12 is Respect for the views of the child. Children have the right to be heard.)

Table 2.4.1 Legislation and codes of practice relating to equality, diversity and discrimination

Figure 2.4.1 Children have special rights, including the right to play

Research activity

Exploring children's rights

In the UK it is still both legal and arguably socially acceptable for parents to smack their children.

After considering the case of a boy who had been beaten regularly by his stepfather with a three-foot garden cane between the ages of five and eight, the European Court of Human Rights ruled that the British law on corporal punishment in the home failed to protect children's rights. The stepfather had been acquitted (found innocent) by a British court of causing actual bodily harm. The stepfather had argued that the beating was 'reasonable chastisement'; this means that parents could use a degree of force in order to discipline their children. Recent changes to the law have removed this defence of 'reasonable chastisement', which dates back to 1860. In an amendment to the Children Bill agreed by peers in 2005, smacking is now outlawed in England and Wales 'if it causes harm such as bruising or mental harm'.

1 Individually, find out all you can about:
   - the arguments against smacking children – in particular, investigate the work of the Children are Unbeatable! Alliance whose aims are (a) to seek legal reform to give children the same protection under the law on assault as adults and (b) to promote positive, non-violent discipline. (www.childrenareunbeatable.org.uk)
   - the arguments for parents' right to smack their own children; for example, look into the Parents Have Rights campaign which is against any legislation that interferes with a parent's right to punish their children as they see fit. (www.families-first.org.uk)
2 Prepare a fact file on the debate on smacking for the use of future students. Include a list of useful addresses and websites. Ensure you find out about any recent changes to these laws in Scotland and elsewhere in the UK.

Discussion point

Smacking children

In two groups, organise a debate on the issue of smacking children.

- Group A will argue that: 'The law should be changed so that physical punishment of children is never permitted.'
- Group B will argue that: 'Parents have the right to use whatever method of discipline works best for their children.'

As an early years practitioner you must know and understand the basic requirements of national legislation relating to children's rights. You also need to know and understand how to carry out research on children's rights and identify the implications for your setting.

Activity ·

Find out about the legislation covering equality and inclusion and how it relates to your setting; for example, the setting's equal opportunities policy and/or inclusion policy.

· ·

LO2 Understand how policies and procedures inform equality, diversity and inclusive practice

All early years settings in the UK must be registered by the appropriate organisation and are also regularly inspected. Each of the home countries of the UK has its own system for registering and inspecting settings. All settings must demonstrate (through policies and codes of practice) how they intend to ensure that they meet the legal, regulatory requirements. All workplace policies and codes of practice must be drawn up within the framework of current legislation. A code of practice is not a legal document, but it does give direction and cohesion to the organisation for which it has been designed. Policy documents cover areas of ethical concern and good practice.

AC 2.1 Identify policies and procedures relating to equality, diversity and inclusive practice

Equal opportunities policy

An equal opportunities policy represents a commitment by an organisation to ensure that its activities do not lead to any individual receiving less favourable treatment on the grounds of:

- gender
- race or skin colour
- ethnic or national origin
- age
- disability
- marital status
- religious belief
- skin colour.

Having such a policy does not mean reverse discrimination, but equality for all. An effective policy will establish a fair system in relation to recruitment, training and promotion opportunities, as well as to the staff's treatment of children, parents and one another.

The policy statement

Every employing organisation should set out a clear policy statement that can be made available to employees and service users. The statement should include:

- a recognition of past discrimination
- a commitment to redressing inequalities
- a commitment to positive action.

Training should be provided to explain to all staff the implications and practical consequences of the policy. The organisation must also provide information about the law on direct and indirect discrimination.

Any policy which attempts to promote equality is only effective if the individuals working in the organisation incorporate its principles into their individual practice.

Special educational needs policy

All schools must have a special educational needs policy. This should include information about:

- how they identify and make provision for children with special educational needs

- the facilities they have, including those that increase access for pupils who are disabled, including access to the curriculum
- how resources are allocated to and among pupils with special educational needs
- how they enable pupils with special educational needs to engage in activities of the school together with pupils who do not have additional needs
- how the governing body evaluates the success of the schools' work with pupils with special educational needs
- their arrangements for dealing with complaints from parents.

Working as a team

It is important to pause at regular intervals and examine what happens in every work setting. Does what the team members say they believe in match what they actually do? Identifying problems in the way adults work with children and in the way children and adults relate to each other is essential before positive action can be taken by the whole team. It helps to work as a team when doing this because it is hard for individual team members to inspect their own thinking in isolation from other people. It helps to share and discuss things with colleagues. The team should devise a **policy of equality of opportunity** and a **code of practice** and then, as a team, review them regularly:

- The policy states the values of the team and the aims of its work.
- The code of practice sets out how the team will put the policy into practice.
- The review process covers all aspects of the team's work in relation to its policy and code of practice.

Activity

Identify the policies and procedures in your setting relating to equality, diversity and inclusive practice. How effective do you think these policies are?

AC 2.2 Explain the roles and responsibilities of the EYP in supporting equality, diversity and inclusive practice

Principles for supporting equality, diversity and inclusive practice

Equality of opportunity is about giving every child full access to the group. You cannot be trained to know everything. You cannot be an expert in every area, but you can be a good networker. This means linking people together who might be useful to each other. Get in touch with people who know about:

- welfare rights and social services
- health services
- voluntary organisations and self-help groups.

Use the experience of your team

It is important to remember that you are part of a multi-professional team and that each member has something different to bring to early childhood work.

Have high expectations for every child

When you meet children, whether they are in a mainstream school, a special school or an early years setting, make sure that your expectations of what each child can do are high enough.

Encourage children to make decisions and exercise choice

Set children tasks that help them to make decisions and to exercise choice. It is important to let all children make choices and decisions so that they feel a sense of control in their lives. When people feel they have some control over what they do, they learn better. It gives them greater equality of opportunity.

Respect yourself and others alike

Try to think why people have different views and customs from your own. Keep thinking about (or reflecting upon) what you do. Think about issues of race, gender, sexual orientation, age, economics, background, disability, assertiveness, culture and special educational needs. Keep changing what you do not like about what you do. Do this without feeling guilt or shame.

Value your knowledge

Value the things you keep learning about equality of opportunity so that you can look forward with positive images about yourself and other people.

Progress check ✓

Understanding and promoting equality of opportunity

Early years practitioners should:

1 know their Equalities Lead Officer or Equalities Coordinator
2 receive support and training in this area
3 work to improve his or her own practice
4 report all incidents of discrimination (an incident is discriminatory if it is felt to be so by anyone involved, even an onlooker)
5 take active steps to make sure that everyone knows about the available services and is able to access them.

Identifying and challenging discrimination in the work setting

The first step in being able to challenge discrimination is to identify when it is taking place. The most obvious and common form of indirect discrimination is when labels are applied to children. You may believe in private, for example, that Mark is a 'spoilt' child who is allowed to behave in a way which you personally think is unacceptable. It would be unnatural not to have an opinion on such matters. However, you should not initiate or join in any discussions which result in Mark being labelled as a 'difficult' or 'spoilt' child. Equally, you will find some children more likeable than others; again this is quite natural. What is important is that you are fair in your treatment of all the children in your care. You should treat them all equally and with respect.

Challenging discriminatory behaviour: the role of the individual member of staff

Each individual worker needs to be committed and empowered to carry out the team's anti-discriminatory policy using the code of practice. You can have a great impact on the lives of the children and families you work with, and you can have an influence on combating discriminatory behaviour.

It is important to be **assertive** but not aggressive. Being assertive means talking clearly and politely about how you feel, which is very different from being rude and angry. For example, you might say, 'I felt very uncomfortable when you asked me to give a drink to the girl with a hearing aid. I felt I needed to know her name, because I am worried that I might stop seeing her as a person if I just think of her as "the girl with a hearing aid".'

Challenging situations

If you see a child hurt or insult someone, explain that such behaviour is not acceptable. Never ignore or make excuses for a child's discriminatory behaviour towards another person. Explain to the child why such behaviour is unacceptable, and encourage them to see how hurtful their comments or actions appear to the other child. Criticise the behaviour rather than the child.

Being aware of discrimination in children's resources

Books which are discriminatory can be discussed with other practitioners, removed and replaced with others (chosen as a team) which contain positive images of people with disabilities, from different cultures and of different genders.

Learn from experience

From time to time you will make mistakes, and regret things which you have said or done. For example, someone who had lived in Dorset all her life came to London and laughed at the idea of people eating goat meat. She quickly realised how insulting this was to her new friends, and apologised, explaining that it was simply a new idea to her.

Learning about other cultures and respecting the differences

It is very important to try to pronounce and spell names correctly, and to understand the systems which different cultures use when choosing names for people. It is also very important to learn about the types of clothes which people wear in different cultures, and to try to learn what these garments are called.

Teaching children to be assertive

We have seen that being assertive is important for staff, but it is also vital for children. Children need to feel protected from aggression and to be able to assert themselves sufficiently to take a full part in the activities provided. Children often pick on weaker children or children who are different; they may tease them or make racial, gender or disability insults. Both the bully *and* the victim need help to be assertive: one needs help with aggression, and the other with timidity. Visualisation techniques can help children and young people to use positive images (seeing themselves as assertive) rather than negative images (being the bully or victim).

> ### In practice
>
> **Practical ways of supporting equality, diversity and inclusive practice**
> - Provide a range of activities which celebrate cultural differences (for example, make children aware of what is involved in celebrations of religious festivals such as Diwali and Chinese New Year, as well as Christmas and Easter, whether or not there are children in the setting who celebrate these occasions).
> - Promote a multicultural approach to food provision; for example, parents could be invited into the setting to cook authentic national and regional dishes – Caribbean food, Yorkshire pudding as a dessert, Welsh bara brith, Irish stew, or Asian sweets.
> - Encourage self-expression in solo and in group activities; for example, by providing 'tools' for cooking and eating from other cultures such as woks, chopsticks, griddles.
> - Celebrate the diversity of language; use body language, gesture, pictures and actions to convey messages to children and young people whose home language is not English.

LO3 Use information, advice and support to promote equality, diversity and inclusion

Firstly, you will need to understand the laws and codes of practice relating to equality, diversity and discrimination and how they apply to you and your work role. In each early years setting, you will meet people of many different backgrounds, cultures and beliefs – your colleagues as well as the children and their families. Make the most of this opportunity. Be open with people, and listen and learn from others about their experiences.

AC 3.1 Access information, advice and support about equality, diversity and inclusion

Sources of information and support

As part of your ongoing personal and professional development, you should always be willing to improve your practice by seeking further information and support from a variety of sources. No one will expect you to know and understand everything, and you may come across situations that you find difficult or challenging. It is your responsibility to seek advice and support from your tutor or line manager, and to use your experience as a valuable learning opportunity.

Colleagues

In most settings, there is a Special Needs Co-ordinator (SENCO), whom you can approach for information or support when working with a child with additional needs. It is important to get to know the strengths and personal expertise of individual members in your staff team; you will often find that they can offer useful support, having encountered a similar situation before.

Parents and families

Remember that parents, carers and family members can be a valuable resource if you need further information about an individual child's:

- disability or condition
- home language
- special dietary needs or allergies, and preferences
- cultural preferences.

Organisations specialising in equality issues

There are various useful sources of information relating to equality, diversity and discrimination:

- the relevant Acts of Parliament: www.direct.gov.uk/en/governmentcitizensandrights

- the Equality and Human Rights Commission (EHRC): EHRC has a statutory remit to promote and monitor human rights; and to protect, enforce and promote equality across the seven 'protected' grounds – age, disability, gender, race, religion and belief, sexual orientation and gender reassignment: www.equalityhumanrights.com
- Early Education: the leading national voluntary organisation for early years practitioners and parents, Early Education promotes the right of all children to education of the highest quality: www.early-education.org.uk
- National Children's Bureau (NCB): NCB is a charitable organisation dedicated to advancing the health and well-being of all children and young people across every aspect of their lives, and providing them with a powerful and authoritative voice: www.ncb.org.uk
- Organisation Mondiale Education Pre-Scholaire (OMEP): OMEP is an international, non-governmental organisation founded in 1948 to benefit children under the age of eight years throughout the world. OMEP's aim is to promote the optimum conditions for all children, in order to ensure their well-being, development and happiness, both within their family unit and the wider communities in which they live: www.omep-international.org

Activity

Journals and magazines can be valuable in keeping you up to date with what is happening in your sector. Early years practitioners can refer to magazines such as *Nursery World*, *EYE* and *Infant Educator*. You can find out which books will be useful from your tutor, and then order them from your local library.

AC 3.2 Reflect on ways information, advice and support about equality, diversity and inclusion can be used to inform practice

Using reflective practice will help you to review and evaluate your own practice. Having accessed information about equality, diversity and inclusion,

practitioners should reflect on the ways in which the information could improve their own practice.

Reflective practice

Welcoming all families equally
- Do you believe your environment is welcoming to all children and their families?
- Do you know how to challenge prejudice?
- Do you record prejudice-related incidents?
- Do you ensure that children's names are spelt and pronounced correctly?
- Do you offer children a secure environment in which to explore their own culture and that of their peers?

Activity

Look at the relevant policy and code of practice on equal opportunities in your own setting and then answer the following questions, making brief notes on current practice:

- How do you show that you value differences between children, and ensure good communication and liaison with parents to ensure that the records for children and young people contain relevant information?
- How do you develop children's sense of identity and raise their self-esteem?
- How does the curriculum planning reflect equal opportunities within every activity and area of learning?
- What do you do to acknowledge the diversity of backgrounds and cater for the individual needs of the children and young people in your setting? (This should include dietary, medical and cultural needs.)
- To what extent do your resources reflect a full range of the diversity within society, avoid stereotypes and promote positive images?
- Who is responsible for planning resources, and how often are the resources reviewed?
- How do you value different spoken and written languages and other forms of communication encountered in your setting?
- To what extent do you take into account the requirements of those with special educational needs and disabilities?

For each question, identify any areas that could be improved, and suggest ways in which this could be achieved.

LO4 Work in ways which support equality, diversity and inclusive practice

Early years practitioners should work in a fair, just and inclusive way, taking into account both the statutory legal framework in the UK and the policies and procedures in their setting. You need to value, and show respect to, all those you encounter in your setting as individuals. Examples of ways of working inclusively are given below.

Definitions of inclusion have developed from being primarily focused on integrating children with special educational needs into a much broader concept concerning social justice and equality for all. Inclusion is the process by which early years settings develop their ethos, policies and practices to include all learners with the aim of meeting their individual needs.

AC 4.1 Interact with children in a way that values them and meets their individual needs

As early years practitioners, we are responsible for ensuring inclusive practice and equal opportunities within our settings. There are many ways in which we can promote such practice. We can do this using the following guidelines shown in Figure 2.4.2.

Promote a sense of belonging

As children grow up, they need to feel that they belong to the group, whether that group is their family, their culture, the community they live in and experience, or their early years setting. Belonging to a group is the result of either:

- being allocated to a group defined by someone else – for example, being British-born; or
- deciding to join a group – for example, choosing to be a vegetarian or joining a football club.

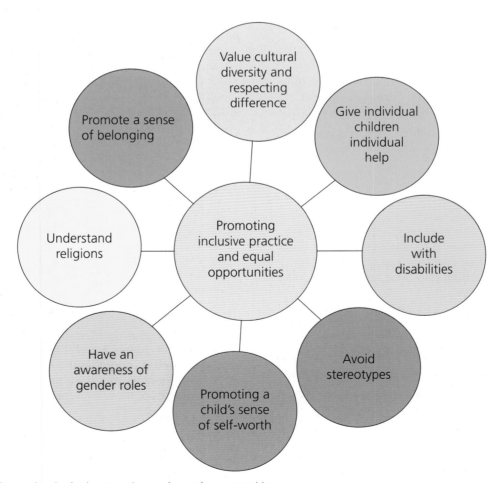

Figure 2.4.2 Promoting inclusive practice and equal opportunities

Until recently, people tended to be seen as belonging to a particular ethnic group if they shared a culture, language, physical feature (such as skin colour) or religion. This way of grouping people is no longer thought to be useful. Increasingly, people *choose* the groups they want to be identified with. The early years setting is often the first group outside the family and its friendship network that the child joins. It is important when welcoming families to a setting that they feel a sense of belonging.

Guidelines: ideas for promoting a sense of belonging through equality of opportunity

1 Be willing to find out about different religions and to respect them. Every religion has variety within it. For example, there are Orthodox and Reformed Jews; Roman Catholic Christians Church of England Christians, Methodist Christians, Quaker Christians, Jehovah's Witness Christians and Mormon Christians. Ask religious leaders and parents for information.

2 Find out about different disabilities. Ask parents and voluntary organisations (e.g. Scope, RNIB, RNID) to help you.

3 Do not be afraid to say that you do not know and that you want to find out and learn. Remember that minority groups of all kinds are as important as the majority groups and are included as part of the whole group.

4 Respect and value the child's home language. Think how you can make yourself understood using body language, gestures and facial expression; by pointing; by using pictures; by using actions with your words. Try asking children if they would like a drink using one of these strategies. You could use objects as props. It is important to be warm towards children. Remember to smile and to show that you enjoy interacting with them. Make sure that you are giving comprehensible language input.

5 Create opportunities for children to talk with other children and adults who are already fluent in English. Try to accompany a child's actions with language by describing what is happening. For example, talk with the child and describe what they are doing when they cook, or use clay.

6 When telling stories you could:
- use puppets and props, flannel boards, magnet boards, etc.
- invite children to act out pictures as you go through the story
- use facial expressions, eye contact and body language to 'tell' a story and make it meaningful for the children.

7 Use books in different languages and tell stories in different languages. Remember that there can be problems with dual-language textbooks because, although a language like English reads from left to right, a language like Urdu reads from right to left.

8 Invite someone who speaks the child's language to come and tell stories. For example, ask a Hindi speaker to tell a story such as *Where's Spot?* in Hindi, using the book in that language but in a session that is for all the children in a story group. Then tell the story and use the book in English at the next session, again with all the children in the story group. Remember that grandparents are often particularly concerned that children are losing their home language as they become more fluent in English (transitional bilingualism). They may enjoy coming into the group and helping in this way.

Figure 2.4.3 It is important to be warm towards children

Standard English is the usual way of communicating in English in public, educational, professional and commercial aspects of life. However, young children need to be confident in talking, reading and writing in their home language and to be supported in this early years setting. This actually helps children to develop fluency and literacy in English. So, it is very important that the child's own language is valued and that efforts are made to develop balanced bilingualism. See p 427 for further information on this.

Value cultural diversity and respecting difference

In the UK we live in a diverse and multicultural society. This means that it is important to appreciate, understand and respect different cultural and religious ideas. The whole environment of the early years setting needs to reflect a multicultural and multilingual approach. For example, the home area, like every other area of the environment, should include objects that are familiar to children and link with their homes and culture. These are often called **cultural artefacts**.

Figure 2.4.4 Reading a picture book in Portuguese

Using everyday activities to explore different cultures

It is particularly important to introduce children to different cultures through the activities of daily life, such as preparing food and cooking. This is because they can most easily relate to these events.

For example, for those children who have not met Chinese people or who have not experienced Chinese food, it might be possible to invite someone to the nursery to demonstrate and introduce the children to another culture. Remember that it is important not to stereotype your visitor. For instance, not all people of Chinese background will use chopsticks at home: some families may be using knives and forks. Sets of cultural artefacts should not be mixed up in one home area, as this confuses everyone. It also makes it difficult for the children to value the area and take pride in keeping it looking attractive.

There are opportunities for mathematical learning in sorting out chopsticks from spoons, knives and forks, and Chinese soup spoons, or in knowing which sets of utensils relate to Chinese life, which to African, Indian or Asian cooking, and which to European culture.

Encouraging children to use what they know

Children gain by using their own cultural experience and knowledge in an open way. For example, the advantage of playdough, rather than pre-structured plastic food, is that children can bring their own experiences to it. They can make it into roti, pancakes, pasties or pies, depending on their own past experiences. All experiences can be valued, not just those that a toy manufacturer has set in plastic.

Figure 2.4.5 Playing with dough

Introducing cultural artefacts

A home area needs to reflect familiar aspects of each child's home. It needs to build on all the children's prior experiences. This means that it should have crockery, cutlery and cooking utensils in the West European style. If, for example, there are children from Chinese backgrounds in the group, it would be particularly important also to have chopsticks, bowls, woks, etc. to reflect their home culture. These would need to be available all the time.

But many children will not know about Chinese woks because they do not meet anyone who cooks with one. These children will need extra help in understanding about cultures other than their own. It is very important to include activities which introduce them to the purpose and function of, for example, Chinese ways of cooking. So, it is important not only that Chinese children see their own culture reflected, but also that other children have the opportunity to learn about different cultures in ways which hold meaning for them and, therefore, are not tokenist (see below).

A child who has never seen a wok before will need to do *real* cookery with it, and be introduced to this by an adult. **Remember, children learn through real first-hand experiences**. It is no good simply putting a wok in the home area and hoping the children will then know about Chinese cooking. That would be tokenist.

Reflective practice

- How do you reflect and acknowledge an understanding of your local community in your setting? Are there cultural references that will mean something to all the children and their families?
- Do you include local cultural events and traditions as well as a range of world festivals and national celebrations?
- How would you support and challenge colleagues who make comments that reflect a limited cultural view such as, for example, 'it's not polite to eat with your fingers'?

Give individual children individual help

There may be children with special educational needs using the home area, for example, and

they might need special arrangements to allow them access: a child in a wheelchair will need a lower table so that a mixing bowl can be stirred; it might be necessary to make a toy cooker of an appropriate height. Children love to construct their own play props; allowing them to do so makes for a much more culturally diverse selection, because they can create what they need in order to make a play setting like their own homes.

Understand religions

In order that every child feels accepted beyond their home, those working with children and young people and their families need to learn about belief structures other than their own. It is also important to remember not to judge people or make assumptions about their values or behaviour based on whether or not they believe in a god or gods. Some children are brought up in families that follow more than one religion. For example, there might be a Roman Catholic Christian father and a Muslim mother, or a Hindu father and a Quaker Christian mother.

Reflective practice

- How do you show respect for beliefs and religious practices that differ from your own – among your colleagues and among children and families within your setting?
- How do you demonstrate that you value all faiths and belief systems equally?

Include children with disabilities

Inclusion is about being able to support, encourage and provide for all with individual needs, whether they are temporary or permanent. Excluding children with disabilities from everyday experiences can lead to a lifetime of segregation. In addition, lack of contact with disabled people can lead to fear and ignorance of those who seem 'different'.

Have an awareness of gender roles

Creating an environment where girls and boys are respected and cared for equally in early

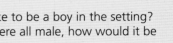

Reflective practice

- What expectations do you have of girls that might be different from those you have of boys? How does this affect your treatment of both?
- Do you find it easier to deal with girls playing with boys' toys than boys playing with dolls or dressing up in frocks?

- What must it be like to be a boy in the setting? If the workforce were all male, how would it be for the girls?

childhood is the first step towards breaking cycles of discrimination and disadvantage, and promoting a child's sense of self-worth as it relates to their gender. It is important to remember that some children will have learnt narrow gender roles. Children need to see adults taking on broader gender roles, and to learn about alternative ways for men and women to behave as themselves.

Avoid stereotypes and labelling

When adults fill in forms, they decide whether to be described as Mr, Ms, Mrs or Miss, and whether or not they wish to describe themselves according to different ethnic categories. An adult with a hearing loss can also choose whether to be described as deaf, hearing impaired or aurally challenged. Children need to be given as much choice as possible about these aspects of their lives.

Reflective practice

Promoting equality of opportunity

Think about different ways in which you have encouraged equality of opportunity in your work with children and young people.

- How can you ensure that your practice is not discriminatory?

- How can you promote equality of opportunity?

Write a short account of ways in which you can ensure that no child, young person or adult is treated unfavourably compared with others.

Guidelines for helping children to have a sense of their own worth

- Provide familiar objects for every child in the different areas of the room. These artefacts of their culture might be cooking utensils, clothes or fabrics.
- Positive images of different children in different cultures are important. Remember that the important thing about a child is not how they look or the extent of their learning difficulty, but that they are a person. The way you behave and talk will give messages about your mental image of each child.
- Make sure you tell stories, and make displays and interest tables with positive images of children with disabilities and children from different cultures. These stories should also be in the book area.
- Make sure that children meet adults with broad gender roles, to show them that men and women are not restricted respectively to a narrow range of activities.

- Encourage children to speak to other children and adults within the early years setting. Remember that children might feel powerless if they cannot speak to other people.
- Use stories from different cultures to introduce children to myths, legends and folk tales. The same themes crop up over and over again in different stories across the world. Find some of these universal themes in the stories you look at from different cultures, e.g. the wicked stepmother, the greedy rich person, good deeds being rewarded after suffering.
- Make sure the indoor and outdoor areas offer full access to activities for children with disabilities.
- Do not forget that you need to have a sense of your own worth too. What did you do today that made you feel that you had a worthwhile day?

Promoting a child's sense of self-worth

Children need to feel a sense of their own worth. This comes from:

- feeling that they matter to other people
- feeling able to take an active part in things
- feeling competent and skilled enough to do so.

Discussion point

Making assumptions

Read the following three scenarios and then discuss the questions below in a group:

1 Harry's mother arrives at the school open day. She is in a wheelchair, being pushed by Paul's father. The teacher welcomes the parents and then asks Paul's father if his wife would like a drink and a biscuit.
2 Patrick and Jo, both early years practitioners, are having a tea break and discussing a new child who has just started at their school. Patrick says, 'I can't stand the way these Travellers think they can just turn up at school whenever they feel like it – they don't pay taxes, you know, and they live practically on top of rubbish dumps … I feel sorry for the kids – they don't know any different.'
3 Rory, Jason, Lucy and Fatima are playing in the role play areas. The practitioner asks Rory and Jason to tidy away the train set and trucks, and asks Lucy and Fatima to put the dolls and cooking pots away, as it is nearly story time.

In both instances, certain assumptions have been made about other people.

- Why do you think these assumptions have been made?
- How would you explain to someone new to early years work why labelling and stereotyping people are wrong?
- Discuss ways in which you can interact with children in a way that values them and meets their needs.

AC 4.2 Analyse the benefits of supporting equality, diversity and inclusive practice

Under the EYFS, all settings must provide and implement an effective equality of opportunity policy. Good practice highlights how children, from a very young age, can learn to place a value on different races, cultures and disabilities. We have already considered the potential effects of discrimination on children and on adults.

The benefits of supporting equality, diversity and inclusive practice include the following:

- **Recognition of our own prejudices**: an awareness of our own bias and prejudices will help us to act to ensure they do not result in discrimination or bias towards others.
- **Welcoming diversity and working with it**: by presenting children with an environment which positively encourages diversity, we are helping children to develop a strong self-identity.
- **Helping young children to develop a sense of belonging**: the EYFS emphasises the importance of developing young children's own sense of identity and a positive sense of pride in their own family origins. By supporting diversity and inclusive practice in the setting, young children can develop a sense of belonging to the local community and begin to understand and respect less familiar cultures.

Reflective practice

Giving everyone a voice

It is everyone's responsibility to promote inclusion, but early years practitioners should actively seek to break down the barriers that prevent those from minority groups having their own voice in the way services are planned and delivered. Think about the following issues within your setting:

- Do you have opportunities within your setting to share ideas about equality issues?
- Do practitioners have a safe space where they can debate and discuss issues of equality, including gender, membership of a minority ethnic group, and disability?

AC 4.3 Evaluate the impact of own attitudes, values and behaviour when supporting equality, diversity and inclusive practice

Inspecting our own attitudes and values

In the UK there is now legislation on race, gender and disability discrimination, which helps teams of people working together to have an impact on

Guidelines for helping children to form positive images of people

- **Storytelling:** ask storytellers (for example, parents) from different ethnic groups to tell stories in their own languages, as well as in English. This helps children to hear different languages, so that the idea becomes familiar that there are many languages in the world.
- **Using arts, crafts and artefacts from different cultures** (fabrics, interest tables, books, posters, jigsaws, etc.). This helps children to realise, for example, that not everyone uses a knife, fork or spoon when eating: they might use fingers or chopsticks instead. Children are helped to learn that there are different ways of eating, something which might seem strange to them at first.
- **Including music and dances from different cultures**: listening to them, watching them, and perhaps joining in a bit. In every culture children love to stand at the edge while people perform. Children often 'echo dance'. Watch out the next time you go to a fête. If there are Morris dancers or folk dancers you are likely to see children watching them and echo dancing at the sides. Being introduced to different cultures in this way helps children not to reject unfamiliar music. For example, Chinese music has a pentatonic scale; African music sometimes has five beats in a bar; European music has two, three or four beats but not usually five. A child who has never seen ballet before or a child who has never seen an Indian dance before might find these strange at first.
- **Doing cookery from different cultures**: you might have multi-language, picture-based cookery books that families can borrow (you might need to make these). For example, there could be a copy of a recipe for roti in English, Urdu and French, or for bread in English, Greek and Swahili; the choice of languages would depend on which were used in the early childhood setting.
- **Planning the menu carefully**: make sure that the menu includes food that children will enjoy and which is in some way familiar. One of the things young children worry about when they are away from home is whether they will like the food. Food and eating with others are a very emotional experience.

racism, sexism, and disablist attitudes and work practices, however unconscious these may be. In addition, it is important that each of us inspects what we do so that we become aware of our attitudes and values. Only then can we act on the unwittingly discriminatory behaviour that we will almost inevitably find. Discriminatory behaviour occurs when, usually without meaning it, we are sexist, racist or disablist. For example, an early childhood worker might ask for a strong boy to lift the chair. We need to look to see whether what we say we believe matches what we actually do. Sometimes it does not! So then we have to do something about it.

Each of us has to work at this all the time, right through our lives. It is not useful to feel guilty and dislike yourself if you find you are discriminating against someone. It is useful to do something about it.

The process of inspecting our basic thinking needs to be done on three levels:

1 within the legal framework
2 in the work setting as part of a team
3 as individuals.

Valuing cultural diversity and respecting difference

Much can be gained from respecting different ways of bringing up children. For example, the Indian tradition of massaging babies is now widely used in British clinics and family centres; so is the way that African mothers traditionally carry their babies in a sling on their backs. It is important to understand and respect what the child has been taught to do at home. For example, in some cultures it is seen as disrespectful for a child to look an adult directly in the eye, whereas in others children are considered rude if they do not look at an adult directly.

Helping children to feel that they belong

Ensure that children who look different, because they are from different cultures or because they have a disability, feel at ease and part of the group. In the early years setting it is important not to have expensive outings or activities, and to be sure to invite all parents to take part in the life of the group. No parent or child should be left out because of their economic background. This is an important equality of opportunity issue.

Activity ···

Working together to promote equality of opportunity and inclusivity

The following ten activities can often be done as a group exercise. Each provides good opportunities for you to develop these important skills:

- **observing** children
- **planning** to meet every child's needs
- **implementing** and **evaluating** the activities.

1 **Plan a multicultural cooking library**: make six cookery books with simple recipes from a variety of cultures. Find or draw pictures to illustrate the books. Write the text in English, and another language if possible. If you write in Urdu or Chinese, remember that you will need to make two separate books, as Urdu and Chinese text runs from right to left. Use the books with groups of children and run a series of cookery sessions. **Observe** the way the children use and respond to the cookery books. **Evaluate** the aim of your plan, the reason for the activity, how the activities were carried out and what you observed in the children's cooking activities.

2 **Storytelling**: plan a story that you can tell (rather than read from a book). Choose a story you enjoy and make or find suitable props. You could make puppets out of stuffed socks, finger puppets out of gloves, stick puppets or shadow puppets; or use dolls and dressing-up clothes and various other artefacts. **Observe** the children listening as you tell the story. Focus on their understanding and their language, especially children whose first language is not English. **Evaluate** your activity.

3 **Religious festivals**: plan how you can make the children you work with more aware of religious festivals in a variety of cultures – for example, how could you introduce the children to Diwali (a Hindu festival with lights, held in October and November) in a way that is not tokenist? Remember to offer children meaningful first-hand experiences. **Observe** the children and assess how much they understand. Look particularly at the reactions of children who are

familiar with the festival you choose, and compare their behaviour to that of children for whom this is a new experience. **Evaluate** your plans and observations.

4 **Inclusion**: plan how you would include a child with disabilities in your early years setting. Remember that your plans will be different according to each child's needs. A child with a hearing impairment will need different help from a child who is a wheelchair user, for example. Carry out and **observe** your plan in action. Focus on how you meet the child's individual needs through your plan. **Evaluate** your plan.

5 **Equality of opportunity**: read your setting's policy on equality of opportunity, and look at actual practices in the daily routine – for example, mealtimes and books. Does what happens match the policy? **Evaluate** your observations.

6 **Musical development**: plan a series of activities which introduce children to the music of a variety of cultures. You will need to help children to listen to music and make music. Make musical instruments out of cardboard boxes, elastic bands, yoghurt pots, masking tape and other materials.

7 **Booklet**: plan a booklet that introduces different religious festivals and helps parents to understand different religious perspectives in your setting. Make the booklet and use it in your early years setting. **Evaluate** it.

8 **Display**: plan and make a display using a multicultural theme. **Evaluate** it. How did the adults use it? How did the children react?

9 **International book**: choose one picture, book, story or poem from each of the seven continents: Africa, North America, South America, Asia, Australia, Antarctica and Europe. Make the collection into a book that you can use with children of three to seven years of age. **Evaluate** the activity.

10 **Multicultural provision**: plan an area of provision that is multicultural in approach – for example, the home area. Perhaps you can add more ideas to those suggested in this section. Implement and **evaluate** your plan.

Assessment practice

Understanding equality, diversity and inclusion

1 What is meant by the following terms: equality, diversity, inclusion, discrimination, prejudice and stereotype?
2 Describe the legal framework relating to equality, diversity and inclusive practice.
3 List the policies and procedures in your setting relating to equality, diversity and inclusive practice.
4 Describe your role and responsibilities in supporting equality, diversity and inclusive practice.
5 How can you access information, advice and support about how to promote equality of opportunity in your setting?
6 Plan and evaluate three different activities with a group of children which will actively promote cultural diversity.

7 How can reflecting on your practice help you to develop the values which support inclusion?
8 Reflect on ways in which information, advice and support about equality, diversity and inclusion can be used to inform practice.
9 How would you challenge discrimination in the setting?
10 Describe ways you would interact with children in a way that values them and meets their individual needs.
11 Describe and analyse the benefits of supporting equality, diversity and inclusive practice within early years settings?
12 Evaluate the impact of your own attitudes, belief systems and behaviour on the ways in which you support inclusive practice and principles of equality of opportunity.

Useful resources

Book

Lindon, J. (2006), *Equality in Early Childhood: Linking theory and practice*. London: Hodder Arnold.

Organisations

The Alliance for Inclusive Education is a national campaigning organisation led by disabled people: www.allfie.org.uk

Early Support provides materials for families and professionals, including a service audit tool, a family pack, and information for parents on certain disabilities and impairments: www.earlysupport.org.uk

KIDS works for disabled children, young people and their families: www.kids.org.uk

Unit 2.5 Work in partnership

This unit provides the learner with the knowledge, understanding and skills required to work in partnership.

Learning outcomes

By the end of this unit you will:

1 Understand the principles of partnership working in relation to current frameworks when working with children.
2 Understand how to work in partnership.
3 Understand challenges to partnership working.
4 Understand recording, storing and sharing information in relation to partnership working.
5 Be able to work with parents/carers in a way which encourages them to take an active role in their child's play, learning and development.
6 Be able to complete records.

LO1 Understand the principles of partnership working in relation to current frameworks when working with children

Partnership working refers to formal ways of working together. It is often also referred to as **integrated** or **multi-agency** working and involves identifying organisations which need and are required to work together for a common purpose, and in setting up a structure for them to come together regularly. A partnership can be formed between a number of individuals, agencies or organisations with a shared interest. There is usually an overarching purpose for partners to work together and a range of specific objectives. These partnerships may be formed to address specific issues, and they may exist for the short or long term.

Key term

working in partnership Different services and professionals working together with other teams of people in order to meet the needs of children, young people and their parents or carers. Also called multi-agency working or integrated working.

AC 1.1 Identify reasons for working in partnership

The key principles of working in partnership are openness, trust and honesty, agreed shared goals and values, and regular communication between the different services, agencies and teams of professionals. When performed well, working in partnership enables agencies and professionals to do the following:

- Maintain a focus on the child by putting them at the centre of everything they do and by involving them. This ensures that everyone communicates about the 'whole' child.
- Improve communication and information-sharing: this involves developing strong partnership links with relevant agencies and within the community.
- Support the early intervention process: early intervention may alleviate existing concerns or prevent further issues from developing.
- Work in an inclusive way: the needs of every child are valued and supported to ensure active participation in all areas of the setting or curriculum. It also means embedding processes of consultation and engagement with children and families in practice.
- Reduce inappropriate referrals: this involves being knowledgeable and well informed about the roles and functions of other professionals, and understanding when and to whom a referral can be made.
- Reduce duplication: this is a key aspect of working in partnership – 'ensuring a child only tells their story once'.
- Maintain confidentiality: this means understanding that confidentiality is paramount in helping to build trust and confidence.

AC 1.2 Describe partnership working in relation to current frameworks

The EYFS

The EYFS (2012) places a specific duty on early years settings to build relationships with parents. In addition to providing safe, stimulating childcare that promotes early learning and development, childcare settings 'must engage, interact and connect with a child and their family'.

The Common Assessment Framework (CAF)

The Common Assessment Framework (CAF) is usually used by practitioners to assess the additional needs of a child and their family, and to help to identify the services required to meet their needs. The lead professional will usually work with the parents and other agencies to draw up a CAF. It is not always necessary to undertake a CAF for a child – for example if a child is making good progress and the agencies are communicating well together. The CAF begins with information-sharing and assessment of:

- the child's development: this is the area in which early years practitioners can usually make the biggest contribution, looking at the child's progress within the framework of the EYFS, including personal, social and emotional development
- parents and carers: this section looks at the care and support offered to the child or young person, including relationships, stimulation and responding to the child's or young person's needs
- family and environment: this takes a wider look at the overall family and environment, and the overall capacity of the parents to support the child's development now and over time.

Drawing on these assessments, the lead professional works with the parents and the **Team Around the Child (TAC)** to put together an integrated plan to protect the child's welfare.

The CAF recognises that a range of factors may affect children's development and vulnerability. A child with complex needs who has supportive parents and a supportive family environment, with good housing and family income, will be much less vulnerable than a child with a lower level of need, but who lives in an overcrowded and potentially dangerous flat with a parent suffering from depression. Where a child does not make the expected progress, or where a child is at risk of significant harm, a referral may be made for safeguarding.

The CAF has three elements:

1 **A simple pre-assessment checklist**: to help practitioners identify children or young people who would benefit from a common assessment.
2 **A three-step process** (prepare, discuss, deliver) for undertaking a common assessment: this helps practitioners to collect and understand information about the needs and strengths of the child or young person, based on discussions with the child or young person, their family and other practitioners as appropriate.
3 **A standard form**: to help practitioners record and, where appropriate, share with others the findings from the assessment, in terms that are helpful in working with the family to find a response to unmet needs.

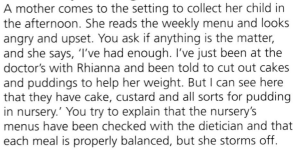

Discussion point

Partnership working

A mother comes to the setting to collect her child in the afternoon. She reads the weekly menu and looks angry and upset. You ask if anything is the matter, and she says, 'I've had enough. I've just been at the doctor's with Rhianna and been told to cut out cakes and puddings to help her weight. But I can see here that they have cake, custard and all sorts for pudding in nursery.' You try to explain that the nursery's menus have been checked with the dietician and that each meal is properly balanced, but she storms off.

Why did the parent/carer storm off? How could this have been handled differently? How could you work with health care professionals to ensure Rhianna's dietary needs are met? Think about why early years practitioners should work closely with health care professionals in order to help in a situation like this. Discuss your ideas with another learner or in a group.

Early Support

Early Support is a Government programme for coordinated, family-focused services for young children with disabilities and their families in local authorities, hospitals and community-based health services across England. Families receive coordinated support through key person/worker systems, effective sharing of information between agencies, family support plans and family-held records.

AC 1.3 Summarise policy and procedural requirements in relation to partnership working

All policies and procedures in the setting should be available to those who have an interest, and may be shared with colleagues, parents and carers and other settings as well as with other agencies and services.

Every setting should have policies and procedures relating to working in partnership, which should include:

- recording, storing and sharing information
- confidentiality
- inclusion and diversity.

The following list is not exhaustive, but includes the policies and procedures used in most early years settings:

Care, Learning and Development Policy	Parents as Partners Policy	Inclusion and Diversity Policy
Behaviour Management Policy and Procedures	Food, Nutrition and Healthy Eating Policy	Procedure for Children with Special Dietary Needs
Rest and Sleep Policy and Procedures	Safeguarding Children Policy and Procedures	Special Educational Needs Policy and Procedures
Complaints Procedures	Health and Safety Policy	Late Collection Policy and Procedures
Health and Safety Procedures	Missing or Lost Child Procedure	Photograph and Filming Policy and Procedures
Confidentiality Policy	Data Protection Policy and Procedures	Internet and Email Usage

Activity

Find out about the policies and procedures in your setting. Who has a right to access them? How often are they checked and updated, and by whom? How often are practitioners required to check their knowledge of them? Then create a general summary of policy and procedural requirements in relation to working in partnership.

LO2 Understand how to work in partnership

AC 2.1 Explain the roles of others involved in partnership working when supporting children

Professionals who may work together to support children

Early years practitioners need to understand the importance of working with others in an integrated way and to build it into their everyday practice. There are many different services and professionals providing integrated support for children: see Figure 2.5.1.

Every setting is unique, and the nature of the partnership working will vary accordingly. For example, childminders are primarily home-based and will work with a varying number of professionals and agencies according to the needs of the children who are placed with them. In order to meet the needs of families accessing support from a range of professionals, the following systems of partnership working have been developed:

Multi-agency panels or the Team Around the Child (TAC)

Practitioners remain employed by their home agencies but meet on a regular basis to discuss children and young people with additional needs who would benefit from multi-agency input.

Multi-agency teams

These are made up of practitioners seconded or recruited into the team, making it a more formal arrangement than a multi-agency panel. The team works with universal services (those available to

Figure 2.5.1 Professionals who may work together to support children

every child) to support families and schools, as well as individual children.

> **Key term**
>
> **agency** In this context, this term covers the range of organisations, services and professional groups who provide services to children and their families.

Integrated working practices

> **Key term**
>
> **extended school** A school which provides a range of services and activities, often beyond the school day, to help meet the needs of its pupils, their families and the wider community.

Examples of integrated working include Children's Centres and extended schools, which offer access to a range of integrated, multi-agency services.

In Children's Centres, for example, practitioners work in a coordinated way to address the needs of children, young people and families, providing services such as:

- integrated early learning and full day care
- family support
- health services
- outreach services to children and families not attending the centre
- access to training and employment advice.

How multi-agency teams work

Within multi-agency teams, practitioners share a sense of team identity and are generally line-managed by the team leader; they may, however, maintain links with their home agencies through supervision and training.

Features of multi-agency teams include the following:

- There is a dedicated team leader – also called the **lead professional**.

- There is a good mix of educational, health care and social care staff.
- The people who work in the team think of themselves as team members. They are recruited or seconded into the team, either on a full- or part-time basis.
- The team works at a range of levels – not just with individual children and young people, but also small group, family and whole-school work.
- The team is likely to share a base, though some staff may continue to work from their home agencies.
- There are regular team meetings to discuss case working as well as administrative issues.

The Behaviour and Education Support Team is one example of multi-agency working.

Behaviour and Education Support Teams (BESTs)

These are multi-agency teams bringing together a complementary mix of professionals from the fields of health, social care and education. The aim of a BEST is to promote emotional well-being, positive behaviour and school attendance, by identifying and supporting those with, or at risk of developing, emotional and behavioural problems.

BESTs work with children and young people aged five to eighteen years, their families and schools. A BEST will aim to intervene early and prevent problems from developing further, and works in targeted primary and secondary schools and in the community, alongside a range of other support structures and services.

A BEST has a number of staff members, who between them have a complementary mix of education, social care and health skills in order to meet the multifaceted needs of children, young people and their parents.

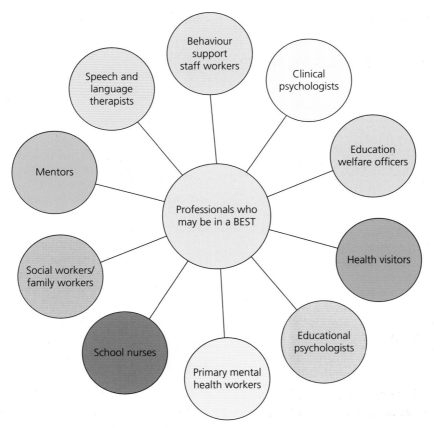

Figure 2.5.2 Professionals who form a BEST

Schools with BESTs include those with high proportions of pupils with (or at risk of developing) behavioural problems, usually demonstrated in levels of exclusions and attendance.

Activity

Find out about other professionals who are involved in partnership working with your setting and explore how your setting uses their expertise to support individual children.

AC 2.2 Evaluate partnership working in relation to meeting children's additional needs, safeguarding children and children's transitions

Meeting children's additional needs

As mentioned above, Early Support is an integral part of the delivery of the EYFS for babies and young children under five with disabilities or emerging special educational needs. It helps staff in early years settings to identify impairments early and to work in partnership with families and other services to provide the best possible care and support for young children with disabilities. An important part of the Early Support programme is the Family File, which the family holds. The Family File:

- is used by the family and professionals together, to plan appropriate support to be provided for the child
- informs the family of the different professionals they meet and their role. It may also include photos to help with recognition for the child
- explains how the different health, education and social services can provide support
- allows parents and carers to share information about their child with the professionals they meet, without having to say the same things to every new person
- provides information about sources of financial support and childcare.

The benefits of early recognition and intervention

Sometimes parents are unaware that their child's development is delayed compared with other children of the same age, especially in the case of their first or oldest child. On other occasions, parents may have felt that 'something is not quite right', but have either been anxious about sharing their worries, or have talked to other professionals but not been fully understood. Sometimes a child can appear to be developing well during a check-up, but have difficulties in less structured environments or in the company of other children. Early identification means that the child can be helped while still very young. In many cases, prompt intervention and support early on can prevent or minimise later difficulties.

Case study

Max

Max is a three-year-old boy who has learning difficulties and has recently been diagnosed as having an autistic spectrum disorder. Max has a baby sister, Zoe, who is four months old. Six months ago, Max's mother, Carol, was contacted by the local Early Support Team, who helped to find him a place in the nursery at her local Children's Centre. Max quickly settled in, and although he does not interact with other children he enjoys his time there and has built relationships with two key people. His favourite activity is playing in the sensory room with his mother or a staff member, and he particularly likes the bubble tubes.

Max's key person, Tom, describes Max as a lovely little boy who has difficulties with social and communication skills, and needs supervision at all times to keep him safe as he has very little understanding of danger. As a member of the Early Support Team, Tom coordinates services for Max and his family, and ensures that the appropriate services are in place to support the family. He works closely with Max's parents and immediately makes sure that they have access to information about autistic spectrum disorder in order to understand Max's needs. Tom also helps to coordinate appointments for Max, organises transport to appointments and makes referrals to other services. For example, he arranged a referral to an occupational therapist to support the family in looking at safety, particularly in the home, and also arranged a referral to the Disability Nursing Team, which supports the family in understanding Max's behaviour. Max also has a Portage worker who helps him to interact socially through play.

1 List the ways in which Early Support is helping to improve outcomes for Max.
2 Find out how Early Support supports children and families in your own area.

Safeguarding children

Safeguarding and promoting the welfare of children depend on effective partnership working between agencies and professionals. Every professional involved in the welfare of children has a duty to safeguard them.

Children's transitions

Moving on to different surroundings, a change in caregiver, or making friends in a new setting are all transitions for young children. Practitioners in early years settings can support children during transitions by working in partnership with parents. Parents can support staff in getting to know children well, while staff support parents as they adjust to change. Transitions and partnership working are discussed in Unit 1.4.

Activity . . . .

- Evaluate how your setting uses partnership working in relation to meeting children's additional needs.
- Make sure you know your responsibilities with regard to safeguarding children.
- Through consultation with parents and children, think of ways in which you could develop and improve transition experiences for children and families.

. . . .

AC 2.3 Identify different family structures

Family structures in the UK

The nature of the family has changed in the UK. It has become more complex, mainly due to changes in society – such as moral attitudes towards marriage and changes to the laws concerning divorce. The word 'family' means different things to different people; this depends upon who you are – your own beliefs and attitudes – and your own experiences of family life.

Even social scientists disagree on what defines a family, but a useful definition for the twenty-first century in the UK is:

A family is a small social group, consisting of at least one adult and child, usually living together, related by blood, marriage or adoption.

The family can include all or some of the following individuals:

- grandparents, uncles and aunts and other relations
- foster parents, step-parents, stepchildren, or only one parent
- two parents living separately
- parents who have chosen to marry or those who have not and are **cohabiting**
- parents of the same sex bringing up children.

Different family structures

In today's society there are many different types of family structure, and children are likely to come from a wide range of home backgrounds. Many children will live with parents who cohabit (or live together) but are not legally married. They may have been given either (sometimes both) of the parents' surnames as their own.

The nuclear family

The nuclear family is the most common family type in the UK today. It is made up of no more than two generations (parents and children): a father, a mother and their 'joint' biological children all live together. They may be married or cohabiting. Often the nuclear family live away from the rest of the family and need to make more effort to maintain links with other family members.

The extended family

The extended family is a nuclear family 'extended' by other relations. It is usually a large group, which may include grandparents, parents, aunts and uncles, brothers, sisters and cousins living in the main family home. Pakistani and Bangladeshi households are the largest – often containing three generations, with grandparents living with a married couple and their children.

The reconstituted family

The reconstituted family (or stepfamily) is one that has two parents, each of whom may have children from previous relationships, but has re-formed into a single unit. In a reconstituted family, children live with one natural parent and a step-parent. Families may also include stepsisters and stepbrothers and/or half-sisters and half-brothers.

The lone-parent family

The lone-parent family is one in which there is only one parent living with the children. It is often assumed that this is the mother but in many instances it is the father. It is sometimes referred to as a 'broken nuclear' family because it often – but not always – arises out of the break-up of a nuclear family. In a lone-parent family, a single parent takes care of children, either through choice or for other reasons. This may be, for instance, because of divorce or separation, or the death of a partner.

The adoptive family

The adoptive family is one in which a child has been adopted, resulting in the parents assuming legal responsibility for the child.

The foster family

The foster family is one which is temporarily caring for a child or children who may or may not have their own families. Foster parents may or may not have 'parental responsibility'.

Residential care home

Children without parents (or whose parents are unable to look after them) are looked after in residential homes by people who are not their parents. Residential care homes are usually run by Social Services.

Key terms

sibling A brother or sister.

stepfamily Stepfamilies consist of married or cohabiting (living together) couples who, between them, have at least one child from a previous relationship who either visits or lives with them.

step-parent (stepmother or stepfather) The individual who is not the biological parent of the child or children is referred to as the step-parent.

stepbrother or **stepsister** A child who has brothers or sisters through the remarriage of a parent to somebody who has children.

half-brother or **half-sister** A sibling with one shared biological or adoptive parent.

The types of family discussed above represent patterns of family life that are commonly found in the UK, but within any of them there will be variations. For example:

- A **reconstituted family** may have not only step-parents and stepchildren but also children from the new adult partnership who become half-siblings (half-brothers or half-sisters) to the existing children. This is also known as the **blended family**.
- In **lone-parent families** the absent parent may remain in contact with, and have access to, the children but may have formed new relationships and had more children. This means that the original children are part of both a lone-parent family and a stepfamily.

Other family types that are less common include:

- **The nomadic family** – one that has no permanent town or village. A nomadic family may live in a 'mobile' home and travel to different sites, settling in any one place for only a short period of time – for example, Traveller families.
- **The communal family** – one in which children live in a commune where, in addition to their parent or parents, they are cared for by other people who share the home.

There is no 'correct' model for a family structure, just as there is no 'best' way of bringing up children. However, certain things do seem to be important for all families. Always remember that every family is different.

Progress check

Early years practitioners need to bear in mind the following facts:

- Every family is different, with different needs and traditions.
- The great majority of parents want to do best for their child, even if they are not always sure what this might be.
- Each one of us only really knows what it is like to grow up in our own family. Parents almost always like some of the things about their own family and the way they were brought up, but they will just as certainly wish that other aspects of their upbringing had been different.
- Parents usually welcome help when trying out some alternative ways of doing things. They will not want to change too much, though, and they will not want rapid changes forced on them by other people. Early years practitioners need to respect parents' wishes.

AC 2.4 Analyse benefits of working in partnership with parents/carers

Working with parents and carers is an essential aspect of work with children. Parents are the first and primary educators of their children. You can strengthen and build on this responsibility so that parents experience an increase in enjoyment of their children and an understanding of child development. Remember that it takes time and regular communication to build good relationships with parents that are founded on mutual trust and respect.

The benefits of working in partnership with parents/carers

Developing a real partnership with parents allows practitioners to learn about the child as an individual and enables the parents to understand and value their own role as their child's primary educator. This equal exchange and understanding brings with it continuity of care for each child as young children experience a consistent approach at home and across all the settings in which they are cared for and educated.

There are many reasons why it is valuable to involve parents or carers in the work setting:

- Parents know their children better than anyone else.
- Children benefit from the extra attention, particularly one-to-one help.
- A range of different skills can be brought to the work setting, e.g. music, sewing, drawing, cooking, etc.

- Parents and carers who do not share the same language or culture as the work setting can extend the awareness and knowledge of both staff and children about the way other people live, cook and communicate.
- Parents and carers can help by sharing lots of books with children from an early age, and by hearing and helping their child read when they start school.
- Involving parents in the play and learning experiences of their children can help to counteract any negative feelings parents may have about education systems, arising perhaps from memories of their own school days.

In many instances you will be working under the supervision of others, and it is likely that parents will pass confidential information directly to another staff member. However, there may be occasions on which you are given information and asked to pass it on, or when you may hear or be told confidential information in the course of the daily routine. This issue is dealt with in the section on **confidentiality** (see p 000), and as long as you follow guidelines, procedures and practices that apply to the work setting you will not go far wrong. Remember that lines of management are in place in most work settings and you should follow them if you need to check your understanding or to ask advice. Try to be aware of the ways in which staff members relate to and communicate with parents, and try to identify which methods seem to be most effective.

Guidelines for working with parents

- Support parents: begin by seeing yourself as a resource and support that can be used by parents to further their child's best interests.
- Respect all parents: the vast majority of parents – including those who abuse their children – love them. It is important not to judge parents, and to respect their good intentions. Almost every parent wants to do the job well, even if on the surface they do not seem to be interested or loving.
- Recognise the good intentions of parents: work positively, with this aim as a central focus. Concentrating on the good intentions of parents helps to give them a positive self-image. Just as children need positive images reflected about

themselves, so do parents. The attitude of the staff must therefore be to show parents respect; bringing up a child is hard.
- Reinforce the parents' sense of dignity and self-esteem: showing parents respect and reinforcing their dignity demonstrates to them that their child also needs respect and a sense of dignity.
- Using your experience: if you are not a parent, you will not have experienced some of the things that parents have. If you are a parent, you will only know about being a parent of your own child; you will not know what it is like to be a parent of other people's children.

Research activity

Parent partnership services
Every local authority (LA) is required to provide Parent Partnership Services. Find out:

1 what type of service is provided in your area by PPS
2 how practitioners and families can access the support provided by these services in your area.

AC 2.5 Identify when parents/carers need support

If the partnership between parents, staff and child is going to develop well, each needs to be able to trust and respect the other. The self-esteem and well-being of the people in the partnership are important when they are working together. How we feel about ourselves influences how we relate to other people. As we discussed in Unit 2.1, parents may have had negative experiences at school, and when their child joins a group setting, all those past feelings may come rushing back to the surface. Parents may be anxious, and this may make them fear for their child. This is often the case when parents are required to bring their child to the early years setting under a Child Protection Order. Staff will need to be sensitive to the feelings of parents in this sort of situation.

Parents start off in an unequal relationship with child care staff. Some parents may feel very anxious, as they are not familiar with the building, the staff or the rules and relationships within the setting. Other factors may increase their uncertainty and feelings of helplessness, for example:

- they may speak a different language from that spoken in the setting
- they may be under emotional pressure about leaving their child
- they may have other worries – e.g. about getting to work, financial problems, etc.

Sharing information and raising concerns

As an early years practitioner, your first duty is to promote the welfare, development and learning of each child. Sometimes this means raising difficult or sensitive issues with a parent. A key person might need to share a concern with parents that their child:

- has special educational needs (discussed in more detail in Unit 3.14)
- is not getting sufficient support and help at home, or that his or her needs are being neglected (discussed in more detail in Unit 2.2)
- is overweight, or otherwise not in good health.

All of these are sensitive issues. It is important that they are raised in a way that shows concern for a child, not criticism of a parent. However, parents feel highly responsible for their children and their initial reactions may well be defensive ('I don't know why you would think that') or hostile ('It is my business what my child has for breakfast and dinner'). In general, if a discussion is sensitively arranged in a confidential space and with a clear focus on the child's best interests, the vast majority of parents will be supportive, even if their first reaction is negative. It is always important to ensure senior practitioners are aware of such discussions – for example, the head teacher, setting manager or SENCO.

Parents becoming angry or upset

Occasionally, parents might become upset and might shout at you. Many early years settings have a policy on how a member of staff can get help from a senior colleague if there is an emergency of any kind. Make sure that you know about this in advance:

- **Call on the head teacher or manager** if you are not sure how to handle a situation. When parents become upset, it is almost always because they are under emotional stress of some kind. The paint spilt on the child's clothing may not seem serious to you, but it might be the last straw for a parent after a stressful day.
- **Try to remain calm and polite**: pointing, shouting or moving angrily towards a parent in a situation like this will almost always make things worse. Your line manager will encourage the parent to move away from the public area, and will help by offering a quiet place to talk.

Parents with different priorities

Sometimes it may appear that a parent prioritises other parts of his or her life at the expense of his or her child's welfare. A parent may work long hours and seem to swoop in at the end of the day, at the last minute (or even late), and expect to pick up the child, all ready for home. Meanwhile, the child might be tired out after a long day at nursery and need a few minutes of unrushed care before being ready to go home. A key person can help by offering advice in a friendly and non-critical manner, perhaps pointing out how every evening there is a scene at picking-up time and suggesting some ways of avoiding this. However, it will always be the case that staff may not see eye to eye with parents at times; as long as the child is adequately cared for and is developing, staff need to accept that in a free society parents may not always act the way we might like them to.

Problems with parental attitudes

When working with issues of equality, it is best to put the main emphasis on positive actions, rather than responding to problems. For example, the parent handbook should make it clear that the setting is positive about diversity, celebrates the different languages children speak and actively opposes discrimination. This should be reinforced through displays and other methods, to establish an atmosphere that is welcoming to all and opposed to racism and prejudice. Occasionally, a child in nursery will show discriminatory behaviour that has come from the home environment – for example, a child may make a racist comment, and when this is discussed with the parent, he or she may display the same prejudice.

In these cases, the manager or head teacher will need to be clear about the legal and moral requirement to oppose discrimination, and to help children learn to be tolerant of others. The parent needs to be told clearly that such views are not acceptable in an early years setting or school.

Differences in rules and expectations

Families have a range of approaches to the problems they face. These approaches may contradict what is expected in an early years setting or school – for example children may be made to stay at the table until they have finished their dinner at home, but an early years setting may allow children to choose what they eat, and how much.

The best approach to difficulties like these is to try to build bridges between home and the setting, while accepting that there are differences. Staff and

parents can explain to a child that there is a different expectation or rule in nursery, for example.

A key person, in response to a parent who does not want the child to play outside on a cold day, might first show sympathy and understanding, then explain the policy on free flow, and finally meet the parent's needs halfway by undertaking to ensure that the child is really well wrapped up, and by arranging a further discussion, if necessary, to explain the nursery's approach.

Activity

Discuss with a fellow learner three occasions when a parent/carer may need help in supporting their child.

AC 2.6 Give examples of support which may be offered to parents/carers

Every situation and family must be treated individually and their needs met through a flexible approach; for example, parents who are dealing with a large family or with family members with disabilities will have different priorities from a lone-parent family with one child. When children have been placed in a setting on the advice of a social worker, there may be some resentment from parents. They may feel that their rights and responsibilities have been overridden. It is important that a positive relationship between parents and the setting is established as soon as possible, with a clear understanding that the interest of the child is everyone's main concern. In these situations there will usually be regular meetings involving parents, staff and other professionals to discuss the child's progress.

Making parents welcome in the setting

You need to be able to see things from a parent's point of view and to do everything possible to make them welcome in the setting. Some useful ideas include the following:

● Names accurately recorded: ensure that you have the parents'/carers' names accurately recorded. Find out how they want to be addressed – do not assume that their family name will be the same as each other, or the same as the child's.

Guidelines for sharing information with parents before the child starts

Parents need to know about:

- settling-in procedures
- how the key person system works, and how their child will be helped if he or she becomes upset, angry, tired or needs a change of clothes
- what type of educational opportunities are offered
- how they can keep up to date with their child's development and progress, and share any concerns that may arise
- meals, snacks and how allergies and other dietary requirements – for example, religious ones – are managed

- policy for collection and non-collection of children
- arrangements for outings and parental permissions
- the policy on the use of photographs and video to record children's progress, and for use in displays and publicity.

Some of this information can be shared with parents by going through a photo album or watching a DVD about the setting together. This could show, in a very practical way, the philosophy, activities and timetabling of the day. Seeing the approach 'in action' can help to make sense of questions about how children learn through play, or the approach taken to meals and snacks.

- Greeting: make a point of greeting parents and smiling at them.
- Name badges: these are useful so that parents know to whom they are talking and whom their children are talking about.
- Photos: a board with staff names and regularly updated photos could be put in the reception area and in newsletters.
- Key person: parents need to know which staff member will be working most closely with their child. Key people are a requirement under the Childcare Act 2006. A key person should be allocated to each child at the setting, as the primary point of contact for the family and child. The key person is responsible for keeping notes and records of progress for a small number of children.

In many nursery settings the children are cared for in groups according to age and/or development and there may be one supervisor for each group. The manager or supervisor of a nursery or the head

teacher in an infant school would still retain overall responsibility.

Children's Centres

Children's Centres generally offer a combination of early years education and childcare, and services, information and advice for parents. Children's Centre services may also be coordinated with or linked to local extended schools services. Extended schools offer services in addition to the standard school day. These can include before- and after-school care, holiday care, sports clubs, cultural activities and clubs – for example, dance, music, art – and outreach services to support children and families who are experiencing difficulties.

Key term

Children's Centre These centres bring together early education, childcare, health services, family support and help for parents wanting to return to work.

Research activity

Children's Centres

You may be working in a Children's Centre, or in a school or setting that is formally linked to a Children's Centre. If your setting or school is not formally linked to a local Children's Centre, there should still be links to enable families to find out about and use the Children's Centre's services.

If you are not sure which is your local Children's Centre, phone the local Family Information Service and they will tell you. You can also find this information by going to http://childrenscentresfinder.direct.gov.uk or searching online for 'Sure Start Children's Centre finder'.

Find out which of the following services is offered by your local centre:

- integrated early education and childcare, led by a specialist early years teacher
- support for parents – parenting advice, help finding local childcare, and access to specialist services for families
- child and family health services – health screening, health visitor services and support with breastfeeding and healthy eating, for example
- helping parents into work – links to Jobcentre Plus and training.

Services that may be offered from a Children's Centre

Parent-and-baby and parent-and-toddler group (or Stay and Play group)

These groups introduce parents and children to being in a group setting in an informal way. Parents might bring their toddler to the group once a week. There will be drinks and healthy snacks for parents and children, together with activities appropriate for toddlers. Adults can talk, exchanging ideas and feelings. Babies can also be brought to the group.

The group may have a regular programme of visits from a range of professionals – for example, a speech and language therapist and a clinical psychologist. Planning for the group may draw on best practice in early years education, offering high-quality treasure baskets for babies, a range of play and first-hand experiences, and outdoor play.

Toy libraries

These can be very beneficial to families, especially those on a low income. Instead of needing to spend a great deal of money on an expensive toy, families can see if the interest in a particular toy is short-lived.

Children can get a broader play experience through regular borrowing, and can enjoy a range of high-quality toys and materials. A good toy library can show how open-ended equipment – for example, a toy set with bricks, animals and people – provides long-lasting and rich play opportunities. On the other hand, many 'educational toys' that are advertised on TV and in catalogues – for example, an electronic toy that speaks the names of letters when you push the buttons – will not usually hold a child's interest for more than a few hours at best. Toy libraries can have a particular role in supporting families with a child with a disability, by offering specialist play equipment.

Book packs and activity packs

The BookStart programme, which began in Birmingham in 1992, initially aimed to provide a pack of free books to every family with a baby. The programme has now expanded to provide a free pack to every baby, toddler and children aged between three and four years, with bilingual packs, packs for children with hearing impairments, and packs for children who are visually impaired.

In addition, some Children's Centres have developed packs to help parents to provide opportunities for early language and literacy, and maths and science experiences in the family home, at no or low cost. They encourage parents to enjoy books and educational activities with their children. Children can begin to learn mathematics and science in a very natural way.

Consolidating and extending the partnership with parents

There is no single way to have a partnership with parents. There needs to be a whole range of ways for parents to access partnership, so that they can find the one that is most suitable for them. Some parents like to have regular home visits and to collect their child quickly at the end of the day, without waiting about for a long chat with the key person. Some parents prefer to use a diary to communicate. In an ideal situation, diaries are updated daily, but more usually they are updated weekly or even monthly. The diary is sent home with the child; parents can add to it and send it back. This is particularly helpful in monitoring the child's progress. Some parents like to come in to the nursery setting to talk to the key person. Staff may be very tired, however, if they have worked a long shift, and it may be difficult to speak to the parent and to care for the other children who have not yet been picked up. So negotiation and understanding of each other's points of view are needed.

Some parents prefer to come to morning or afternoon sessions in the parents' or staff room. Many early years settings now make provision for this. Parents come in to sit with one another and their babies, or to attend a session led by the local health visitor. Subjects covered may include children's feeding routines, sleep patterns and other areas of concern. Many early years settings and schools store each child's Learning journey/journal in a place where it can be easily picked up and read by the child's parents. This can enable parents to keep up to date with the latest observations, assessments and planning for their child. Sometimes parents are encouraged to take the Learning journey/journal home, share it with their child, and add to it themselves. Together with regular reviews when the parent and key person sit down formally together, this type of system can help parents feel that they are up to date and are active participants in planning for their child's development and learning.

Workshops

Parents appreciate workshops run by the setting. These usually take place in the evening; parents come to experience some of the things their children do and staff explain what the children get out of the activities – for example, parents may be surprised to find out about the mathematics that their children are learning when involved in a cooking activity.

Open days and evenings

These are often popular with parents. They can be purely social or may be a mixture of a social occasion and a workshop or talk. Many early years settings combine these.

LO3 Understand challenges to partnership working

AC 3.1 Identify barriers to partnership working

There are many potential barriers to effective partnership working. These will vary from one setting – and one particular circumstance – to another. Some are organisational, while others relate to problems with communication.

Information-sharing

Problems mostly occur around *when* and *how* to share information. Practitioners may be unclear

Figure 2.5.3 Parents need to be made welcome in the setting

about their individual roles and responsibilities, and worry that they might misjudge the situation and be disciplined for sharing information inappropriately. Team meetings need to be arranged at a convenient time and place for everyone, otherwise non-attendance of various professionals can present a barrier to effective working.

Key term

information-sharing The term used to describe the situation whereby practitioners use their professional judgement and experience on a case-by-case basis to decide whether personal information should be shared with other practitioners in order to meet the needs of a child or young person.

Developing a common language

Often there are differences in the cultures of different agencies, and this can lead to difficulties in understanding the specialist terminology and language used by other professionals. Already you will have noticed that there is a whole set of acronyms commonly used in settings with children and young people, such as BEST, CAF, EYFS, etc. You do not need to know what they all mean, only the acronyms used in your area of work. You will find a list of acronyms commonly used in settings with children at the end of this book, on p 555.

The fear of the 'new'

Some practitioners may feel threatened by new approaches which require them to work differently, across service boundaries. Some may resent being managed by a professional with different skills experiences from their own, and may generally feel out of their 'comfort zone'.

Lack of understanding of different agency roles

If practitioners do not fully understand the roles and responsibilities of other services and practitioners, they may lack confidence in them and worry that a different agency may not treat the matter confidentially; they may even fear that other practitioners may make things worse for the child,

young person or family. Not knowing whom to contact for advice and support with information-sharing can also create barriers to effective multi-agency working. This often leads to anxiety and a lack of confidence.

Different professional priorities

Team members need to be clear about their goals and their individual roles and responsibilities. Every team member needs to work together to make use of the other professionals' expertise in the best interest of the child and family. It may take time to establish this understanding and to find a way of working together.

Parents and carers who may not want to become involved

Many parents will want to become involved in their child's setting, especially if there is an open, welcoming atmosphere and a place to meet other parents. However, there will always be some parents who do not want to participate. There could be a number of reasons for this reluctance. These include:

- working full-time or having other daytime commitments
- feeling that they have nothing of value to contribute
- not being interested in spending time with other people's children
- lacking confidence or feeling shy.

It is important that parents do not feel pressured into becoming involved. You should always respect parents' decisions and not assume that this shows a lack of interest in their children.

Some early years settings have a drop-in facility for parents that helps support those feeling isolated and experiencing problems, while a family support group, with a skilled family worker on hand, can help people with parenting skills and other issues.

Barriers to communication

- **Time constraints**: there may be several children arriving at the same time, which puts pressure on staff at a busy time. Parents may be in a rush to get away when bringing their children. It is

Case study

Communicating with parents

1 The parents of three-year-old Thomas have been anxious about their son's appetite since he was ill with a virus. Staff at the day nursery have been observing Thomas, keeping written records and taking photographs, at snack and mealtimes over a period of a week. They have made sure the food is attractively presented, includes some of Thomas' favourite items and offered small portions. They have noticed a great improvement and want to share their findings with his parents and discuss how he is at home.

2 Five-year-old Charlotte has recently become withdrawn from both adults and other children.

For the past week or so she has needed encouragement to complete work tasks which are within her capability and when she has had free-choice activity she has tended to sit alone in the home corner with a soft toy. This represents a change in Charlotte's behaviour and the teacher wants to discuss her concerns with the parents.

- In each case, what method would you use to contact the parents?
- Explain what you would say/write and what you would arrange in order to deal with each situation.

important that you do not interpret this as a lack of interest. Greet them with a friendly nod and pass on any information as briefly as possible.

- **Not seeing parents regularly**: when someone other than the parents brings and fetches the child, staff will need to find other ways to maintain regular communication.
- **Body language and non-verbal communication**: be aware of how parents may be feeling at a particular time, even when they do not mention anything specific.
- **Written communication**: unless sent in the post, there is a chance that some letters and other written notes may not reach the parent. Also some parents might have difficulty reading and writing and not want to seek help. The noticeboard can also be used to display a general letter sent to all parents.
- **Making messages clear**: remember that we understand messages not only from what is said but also from *how* it is said – our tone of voice, gestures and facial expressions can change the meaning of a message. The person on the receiving end of a written message has no such clues. It is important to give careful consideration to the wording of any letter and try to make sure that it cannot be misinterpreted.
- **When English is not the parent's first language**: you can help by signing or – where possible – by involving bilingual staff or translators. Noticeboards can display signs in picture form – for example, showing the activities

their child will be doing during the session. Having written information in a number of different languages is also helpful.

AC 3.2 Explain strategies to overcome barriers when working in partnership

Working effectively as a team

To meet the needs of all the children, the staff members must work effectively together as a team. The roles and responsibilities of individual team members will depend on the organisation of the work setting. In your role as a learner you will be supporting the work of others. You will usually work under the direction (or sometimes supervision) of a nursery manager or teacher, depending on the setting. There may also be professionals from other disciplines (medicine, social services, dentistry, etc.) who are involved with the families and children you work with. A special school or nursery that cares for children with physical disabilities will have a multi-disciplinary team. This team may include teachers, nursery nurses and assistants, trained special care assistants, physiotherapists, paediatricians and, possibly, social workers.

Effective teamwork is vital in such settings to ensure that:

- everyone knows their individual roles and responsibilities
- parents and primary carers know which team member can deal with any specific concerns.

Effective communication in partnership working

Sharing information through communicating with others is vital for early intervention to ensure that children receive the services they require. It is also essential for safeguarding and protecting the welfare of individuals, and for providing effective and efficient services which are coordinated around the needs of an individual or family. The need for every practitioner to have effective communication and teamwork skills is therefore important.

Effective communication between professionals and agencies is important to make sure that everyone:

- shares information in a clear way that focuses on the individual child or young person
- works towards the same aim: to achieve the best positive outcomes for the child or young person and his or family.

The EYFS Guidance states:

It is vital to ensure that everyone is working together to meet the emotional, health and educational needs of children in all settings that they attend and across all services provided.

Being able to communicate effectively with team members, other professionals and with parents is a very important part of your role as a practitioner. You should always:

- be considerate of others and polite towards them
- recognise the contributions made by other team members; we all like to feel we are valued for the work they do. You can help others to feel valued by being aware of their role and how it has helped you fulfil your own role
- explain clearly to the relevant person any changes in routine or any actions you have taken; for example, as a nanny, always informing a parent when a child you are caring for has refused a meal or been distressed in any way, or reporting any behavioural problem or incident to your line manager in a nursery setting.

Progress check

Communication in a multi-agency approach

Each profession has its own jargon and set of rules. You do not need to know about these in depth, but should always be willing to learn from other professionals and to respect the contribution of others working with children and families. You need to be:

- clear about your own role
- aware of the roles of other professionals
- confident about your own standards and targets, and
- respectful of those that apply to other services.

Reflective practice

The need for clear and effective communication

Think about the examples below and reflect on why clear and effective communication between different professionals is important in providing for the needs of every child and young person:

- A six-year-old child has sickle cell anaemia and attends school but is often in hospital for weeks at a time. Health play specialists, hospital teachers and the child's class teacher are all involved in the child's care and education.
- A child with a severe visual impairment attends a mainstream school and has daily support from a dedicated learning support assistant.
- A young child with special educational needs attends a Children's Centre and is also visited at home by a Portage worker.

Appropriate communication methods for different circumstances

Informal communication

Ongoing communication with parents and carers is essential to meet the needs of children and young people. For many parents there can be regular and informal communication when children are brought to, or collected from, the setting. However, it is unusual for both parents to perform this task and, therefore, it is often the same parent who has contact. The methods below can usually work for both parents and practitioners. Finding ways to communicate with parents can sometimes be difficult, especially when staff may not feel confident themselves.

- **Regular contact with the same person**: always meet and greet parents when they arrive. At the start, it is very important that parents meet the same practitioner – preferably their child's teacher or key person – on a daily basis.
- **A meeting place for parents**: ideally, there should be a room that parents can use to have a drink and a chat together.

Information that applies in the longer term should ideally be given in writing; for example, information concerning food allergies or medical conditions, such as asthma or eczema. As well as informing staff members, notices may also need to be attached to a child's own equipment, lunchbox or displayed in particular areas such as food preparation, nappy changing. In a school setting the class teacher should ensure that any other adults involved in the child's care receive information as appropriate.

Copies of all letters received and sent and a record of all communication should be kept for future reference.

Verbal information

Routine information can be – and often is – exchanged verbally. This usually happens at the start and end of the session, when parents and their child's key person chat informally.

- **Talking with parents**: always let parents know about their child's positive behaviour and take the opportunity to praise the child in front of their parents. Then if you need to share a concern with them, they will already understand that you are interested in their child's welfare and are not being judgemental. (Many adults associate being called in to see the person in charge with their own experiences of a 'telling-off'.)

Written information	How and when it is used
Formal letter	Welcome letter prior to admission to the setting
	To give information about parent's evenings or meetings
	To alert parents to the presence of an infectious disease within the setting
	To advise parents about any change of policy or staff changes
Email	To give information about an event; to respond to a request from parent or colleague
Newsletters	To give information about future events – fundraising fairs, open forums and visiting speakers, etc.
Noticeboards	To give general information about the setting, local events for parents, support group contact numbers, health and safety information, daily menus, etc.
Activity slips	To inform parents about what their child has been doing
Admission form	All parents fill in an admission form when registering their child (see sample below). This is confidential information and must be kept in a safe place where only staff have access to it
Home books	To record information from both staff and parents. Home books travel between the setting and the home and record details of the child's progress, any medication given, how well they have eaten and slept, etc.
Accident slips	To record information when a child has been ill or is injured when at the setting
Suggestions box	Some settings have a suggestions box where parents can contribute their own ideas for improving the service
Policy and procedure documents	These official documents should be openly available, and parents should be able to discuss them with staff if they have any concerns

Table 2.5.1 Exchanging routine written information

- **Recording information and passing on messages**: you will need to record some information the parent has talked to you about – especially if you are likely to forget it! You should always write down a verbal message which affects the child's welfare, so that it can be passed on to other members of staff; for example, if someone else is collecting the child, if a favourite comfort object has been left at home, or if the child has experienced a restless night. The person delivering the message also needs confirmation that it will be acted upon. Where there are shift systems in operation a strict procedure for passing on messages needs to be established.
- **Telephone calls**: information received or delivered by telephone should be noted in a diary so that action can be taken.

Activity ·

How does partnership working operate in your area? Find out who would be the relevant 'partners' or agencies in your own work setting.

Try to visit one setting such as a Children's Centre or a special school: find out how referrals are made and how often the multi-agency team meets.

· ·

AC 3.3 Evaluate the complexity of partnership working

There are many ways in which the early years practitioner – in particular, the key person – can work in partnership with parents.

Involving parents in the partnership

- Provide opportunities for parents to contribute to practitioners' developing understanding of the child as a unique individual – through shared observations of their children, in the setting and at home with the parent.
- Encourage parents to help out during sessions, to share their interests or cultures with children and to take part in discussions about the provision.

Sharing information

- Ensure that information about the process of learning is visible for all parents and children.

- Ensure that policies on important areas such as key person, inclusion, behaviour, learning and teaching are made known to parents; parents could also be involved in the drawing up of early years policies.

Supporting parents in developing their own skills

- Many parents find workshops run by the setting a useful way to experience some of the activities their children do, and are able to develop their own skills.

Supporting parents to contribute to planning the learning environment

- Inviting the opinions of parents about the general running of the setting and encouraging them to evaluate the environment with their child's needs and interests in mind.

Obtaining feedback from parents

An important part of evaluating the complexity of partnership working is making sure that parents are given opportunities to feedback on and to shape services for children and families. Different early years settings will have a range of management systems, including:

- Maintained nursery schools, and primary schools, will have a legally constituted governing body that includes parent representatives. The governing body will have formal systems for reporting back to all parents and for acting on suggestions and complaints. There will also be systems to survey parents' views on a regular basis.
- Other settings may have a management committee made up of parents and other volunteers. Voluntary and community settings – for example, a pre-school or a community nursery – will often be led by parents of children currently or previously on roll, and be linked to other community and local groups.
- Children's Centres will usually have a parents' forum, a gathering of parents who give feedback on the services offered and shape the future direction of the centre.

Planning a workshop

1 In conjunction with your setting, plan a workshop for parents that will help them to understand how children learn through activities such as cooking, sand play and painting. Plan the materials you would use for a demonstration, and make instruction cards with diagrams to help parents experiment with the materials.
2 Rehearse what you might say in a presentation to parents about one of the activities.
3 Advertise your workshop to parents and carry out your plan. Do not worry if not many people attend – even one parent taking part will give you valuable experience, and it is common to find that it takes several months of working with parents to encourage high levels of participation.
4 Evaluate how successful your workshop is. Include your own impressions, and information from parental feedback that you have obtained either by talking to the participants or by asking them to fill in an evaluation form.

Activity

Evaluate the partnership with parents. Find ways to obtain feedback from parents about (a) information-sharing, and (b) the framework of development and learning.

LO4 Understand recording, storing and sharing information in relation to partnership working

AC 4.1 Identify records to be completed in relation to partnership working

Record-keeping
The EYFS requires that:

- settings maintain and regularly update records of children's development and progress
- records must be securely stored
- records must be accessible to parents on demand.

It is good practice for observations and records to be shared between practitioners in the setting – for example, at planning meetings. This helps to ensure that staff work together to build up a rounded picture of each child's development, well-being and needs.

Involving parents and upholding their rights
The best approach to working with parents is to develop a culture of mutual trust, respect and sharing of information. This will mean making it easy for parents to access their children's records, however they are kept. Parents will expect to be offered regular meetings to discuss their children's progress, when achievements can be celebrated and concerns can be raised and discussed.

If you want to encourage parents to look regularly at their children's records, you will need to think about how to make them accessible. A folder full of long written observations is unlikely to engage most parents, especially if the observations are handwritten and hard to read. On the other hand, profile books that are carefully illustrated with photos, as well as including written observations, are much more inviting. Video and slide shows of photos are another way to engage parents. The danger here is that the focus on the child's development, learning and well-being can get lost if parents are presented with something that looks like a scrapbook, family album or holiday slide show, full of posed images of smiling children.

The EYFS says:

Parents must be given free access to developmental records about their child (for example, the EYFS Profile). However, a written request must be made for personal files on the children and providers must take into account data protection rules when disclosing records that refer to third parties.

Preparing reports
As part of your role, you may need to prepare reports. A report is a formal document which presents facts and findings, and can be used as a basis for recommendations. Certain reports that you may write will be a statutory requirement within the EYFS framework, and must be made available to any Ofsted inspection. These include accident reports, reporting of illnesses or injuries and any report of concerns about a child.

Reports you may be required to write include:

- **An accident or incident report**: this is quite straightforward, and will involve completing a standardised form.
- **A CAF Pre-Assessment checklist or CAF form**: an official form which is focused and easy to complete.
- **A formal report about a project or plan**: for example, a plan to change the use of a room within the setting.

A formal report has a fairly rigid structure, and is usually divided into sections, probably with subheadings performing a very specific task. The language used should be straightforward and to the point, and the report's structure should make it easy to identify the various parts, and to find specific items of information quite quickly. The three general principles of a report are: Why was it done? How was it done? What does it mean?

A formal report usually has the following features:

- **Title page**: include author's name, date and for whom the report is written.
- **Contents list**: list the main sections, sub-sections and any appendices.
- **Introduction**: the background or context to the report and the aims and objectives.
- **Main body or text**: this describes how the study was conducted and gives the facts, findings and results.
- **Conclusions**: this describes what the study has shown, summarising the main points.
- **Any recommendations** for the implementation of a report's findings.
- **Appendices**: include any supporting information here, such as tables, or information that applies only to certain readers.
- **References**: a list of books or articles used or suggestions for further reading.

Information-sharing

The Government produced a *Guide to information sharing* (2008) for all practitioners working with children and young people. This outlined the important Acts that can be used to develop an information-sharing policy in children's services:

- The Data Protection Act 1998 provides a framework to ensure that information is shared appropriately.
- The Children Act 2004 on the duty to safeguard and promote the welfare of children.
- 'Working together to safeguard children' (2013): the statutory guidance that sets out how organisations and individuals should work together to safeguard and promote the welfare of children (see Unit 2.2 for more detail on safeguarding information).
- *What to do if you are worried a child is being abused* (HMG, 2006).
- The Education and Inspections Act 2006, which sets out the duty to promote the well-being of pupils to governing bodies of maintained schools.
- The Child Health Promotion Programme (DH, 2008).
- Local Safeguarding Children Board (LSCB) policies, procedures, protocols and guidance.

Recording and storing information

Every setting must provide clear policies and procedures about the recording and storing of information. These are governed by the Data Protection Act 1998. Anyone who keeps records, whether on computers or on paper, should comply with the Data Protection Act. It should be clear to service users (in this case, parents or carers) for what purpose the data is being kept. Information about a child should also be accessible to his or her parent or carer and shared with them. It is not necessary to do this 'on demand'. A convenient time to be able to discuss the information can be arranged. Information should not be kept for longer than necessary, although accident and incident records will need to be kept in case they are needed for reference at some time in the future. Records of incidents and accidents must be kept for at least three years after the occurrence. Records must also be stored securely.

Electronic recording and storing of information

If information is kept on computers or sent by email, steps must be taken to ensure that it could not fall into the hands of unauthorised people (for example, by the use of encryption software).

The national electronic CAF (eCAF) enables authorised, trained practitioners from across the children's workforce to electronically store and share CAF information quickly and securely, and to work together to build a holistic picture of a child's or young person's needs. The system reduces the need for children, young people and families to repeat their story for different services.

Information should not be kept for longer than necessary, although accident and incident records will need to be kept in case they are needed for reference at some time in the future. Records must also be stored securely.

Activity . . . .

Find out about the methods used to record and store information about the children and their families in your setting. What information is held? How are such records kept secure? Are computer records password-protected? Who has a right to see the documents held in your setting? Summarise the records to be completed in relation to partnership working.

. . . .

AC 4.2 Explain reasons for accurate and coherent record-keeping

Good practice in the area of record-keeping is based on the following principles. Records and reports should:

- **Be legible and grammatically correct**: handwriting must be neat and care should be taken to ensure that records are free from spelling and grammar errors. It is important that only factual information is included in records – opinions and assumptions must not be recorded.
- **Help to ensure that children's needs are met**: for example, observation records help to identify children's needs and can inform future practice.
- **Help to safeguard the health and well-being of the child**: any concern about the child's health or well-being should be recorded and reported to the line manager.
- **Help to provide continuity of service**: so that another member of staff can take over in the event of the practitioner being ill or unavailable.

- **Provide evidence of the practitioner's work**: this will go towards compiling a record of evidence.
- **Contain information that practitioners can use** to monitor and evaluate their work in order to improve their practice.
- **Help managers to monitor and evaluate** the quality and performance of the service to children and young people.

Activity . . . .

Think about the last time you wrote a report or record in your work setting.

- Were you clear about its purpose?
- Did you have to obtain consent from the child's parents?
- Evaluate the usefulness of the document.

Summarise the reasons for accurate and coherent record-keeping.

. . . .

AC 4.3 Evaluate the reasons for confidentiality when maintaining records

It is essential to maintain confidentiality when working with children and their families, as it imposes a boundary on the amount of personal information and data that can be disclosed without consent. Confidentiality arises where a person disclosing personal information reasonably expects his or her privacy to be protected, such as in a relationship of trust. It is useful to understand fully the meanings of the terms 'consent', 'disclosure' ('allegation') and 'privacy'.

Consent

Consent means agreement to an action based on knowledge of what the action involves and its likely consequences. For example, information on a child should only be collected and stored with the consent of the child's parents or carers – and they should have free access to this information on request. The only exceptions to the rule of consent are the very small number of cases where the child might otherwise be at risk of immediate and significant harm if you shared a piece of information with the parent.

Case study

Confidential information

During a coffee break, practitioners are openly chatting about Harry, a child that you know. Apparently, the people he lives with are not his parents, but his grandparents – although they look young enough to be his parents. They are bringing Harry up because their daughter (his mother) was judged to be unable to look after her child. This happened a few years ago when

Harry was very young, and he had spent some time in social care before his grandparents gained custody. One practitioner noted that Harry always calls them Mummy and Daddy.

1 Is this information confidential? If so, why?
2 Should you inform your line manager of the situation?

Disclosure (allegation)

A safeguarding allegation means the giving out of information that might commonly be kept confidential, usually voluntarily or to be in compliance with legal regulations or workplace rules (allegation used to be known as 'disclosure'); for example, a child tells an adult something that causes him or her to be concerned about the child's safety and well-being.

Privacy

Privacy refers to the right of an individual or group to stop information about themselves from becoming known to people other than those to whom they choose to give the information. For example, when former prime minister Tony Blair's ex-nanny wrote a book about life at Number 10, Downing Street, the Blairs took swift legal action to prevent details being leaked to the press. Tony Blair stated, 'We will do whatever it takes to protect … our children's privacy.'

Activity

Explain and evaluate the reasons why confidentiality is important when maintaining records.

AC 4.4 Analyse the potential tension between maintaining confidentiality and the need to disclose information

The right to confidentiality is not absolute

When working within a multi-agency team, private information about the child may often be shared with other professional persons within the team. The obligation to preserve the child's confidentiality then binds *all* professionals equally. Records should only show information which is essential to provide the service, and in many instances should be available to the scrutiny of the child and his or her family (for example, patients have the right to see their medical records).

The Guidance document *Guide to information sharing* outlined Seven Golden Rules for information-sharing.

When poor practice is identified

All early years settings and schools are required to have a policy to deal with allegations made against staff. This will cover cases where a child makes a

Guidelines for information-sharing: The Seven Golden Rules

1 **Remember that the Data Protection Act is not a barrier to sharing information** but provides a framework to ensure that personal information about living persons is shared appropriately.
2 **Be open and honest with the person** (and/or their family where appropriate) from the outset about why, what, how and with whom information will, or could be shared, and seek their agreement, unless it is unsafe or inappropriate to do so.

3 **Seek advice if you are in any doubt**, without disclosing the identity of the person where possible.
4 **Share with consent where appropriate** and, where possible, respect the wishes of those who do not consent to share confidential information. You may still share information without consent if, in your judgement, that lack of consent can be overridden in the public interest. You will need to base your judgement on the facts of the case. →

5 **Consider safety and well-being**: base your information-sharing decisions on considerations of the safety and well-being of the person and others who may be affected by their actions.

6 **Necessary, proportionate, relevant, accurate, timely and secure**: ensure that the information you share is necessary for the purpose for which you are sharing it, is shared only with those people who need

to have it, is accurate and up to date, is shared in a timely fashion, and is shared securely.

7 **Keep a record of your decision and the reasons for it** – whether it is to share information or not. If you decide to share, then record what you have shared, with whom and for what purpose.

disclosure, or where an adult is seen or overheard behaving in an inappropriate way. For more information, see Unit 2.2.

Where a child is at risk

If you have concerns about the welfare and safety of a child, this concern overrides all other consideration and you may disclose information whether you have consent or not. For more information, see Unit 2.2.

When it is suspected that a crime has been/may be committed

An early years practitioner may have to break confidentiality if he or she suspects that an individual is going to harm themselves or others or if they are going to commit a criminal offence. Such information should be passed on to the person responsible for the care setting.

Activity ·

Make sure you understand your responsibilities regarding the need to disclose information and the duty to maintain confidentiality.

· ·

LO5 AC 5.1 Work with parents/carers in a way which encourages them to take an active role in their child's play, learning and development

Considerable research shows that children's development and learning can be greatly enhanced with the support of parents and the availability of play opportunities at home. This research can lead practitioners in two possible directions:

- **A social control model** of teaching parents to bring up their children. This means the staff

show parents examples of what to do, hoping the parents will copy 'good models'. The parents and the home environment they provide are considered to be deficient; there will often be a list of resources and activities that parents are told they should provide.

- **A developmental partnership** in which professionals do not try to tell parents how to bring up their children. Instead, they seek to find out what the parents think and feel. They respect parents' views and help them to build on what they already know about and want for their children, offering knowledge, information and discussion.

Case study

A developmental partnership

Pen Green Centre for Children and their Families has led practice in involving parents in understanding and supporting their children's development. This programme includes:

- action for the parent – helping parents to reclaim their own education and build up their self-esteem
- action for the child – encouraging parents to child-watch, to be involved in and be respectful of their children's learning process and development.

In a system of Parents Involved in their Children's Learning (PICL), professionals and staff work closely together, sharing and shaping joint understandings. A parent's unique knowledge of the child is respected, and professional knowledge about child development is shared with the parent, including:

- understanding children's well-being and involvement as they play
- noticing and working with children's schemas.

Video of the child, taken by parents in the family home and by staff in the nursery, provides a way of observing and reflecting on children's play.

Find out more about PICL by going to www.pengreen. org, or search online for 'Parents involved in their children's learning'.

● ●

LO6 Complete records comprehensively and accurately

AC 6.1 Complete records that are accurate, legible, concise and meet organisational and legal requirements

As an early years practitioner, you will be expected to maintain records such as observations and planning, tracking and current framework aspirations.

From time to time, these records may need to be summarised to include reports.

Completing records

Make sure you know what is required when completing the following records:

● an accident or incident report
● a CAF Pre-Assessment checklist or CAF form
● a formal report about a project or plan
● observation and planning forms
● developmental records for individual children.

● ●

Assessment practice

1 What do you consider to be the main reasons for working in partnership?
2 Describe partnership working in relation to current frameworks.
3 Which policies and procedures are particularly required for partnership working?
4 Explain the roles of others involved in partnership working with reference to your own setting.
5 Evaluate partnership working in relation to (a) meeting children's additional needs, (b) safeguarding children, and (c) children's transitions.
6 Identify and list different family structures.
7 Describe and analyse the benefits of working in partnership with parents/carers.
8 Describe situations when parents/carers may need support.
9 Give four examples of support which may be offered to parents/carers.
10 Describe some common barriers to partnership working and explain what could be done to overcome them.

11 Evaluate the complexity of partnership working.
12 Identify records to be completed in relation to partnership working.
13 Explain reasons for accurate and coherent record-keeping.
14 Evaluate the reasons for confidentiality when maintaining records.
15 Analyse the potential tension between maintaining confidentiality and the need to disclose information.
16 Describe ways to work with parents/carers in a way that encourages them to take an active role in their child's play, learning and development.
17 Understand your role in recording, storing and sharing information in relation to partnership working.
18 Describe how to complete records that are accurate, legible, concise and meet organisational and legal requirements.

Useful resources

Organisation

National Parent Partnership Network and **Parent Partnership Services** (PPS) are statutory services offering information advice and support to parents and carers of children and young people with special educational needs (SEN): www.parentpartnership.org.uk

In profile

My name is Susan and I am the Nursery Manager of a 68-place day nursery. I have been a manager for nearly two years and every day I learn something new. My biggest achievement to date has been to get my nursery to 'Outstanding' with Ofsted last year.

My nursery is part of a large group which I have been with for seven years now. I have worked in childcare for twelve years and have seen so many changes to the industry and practice in that time. I have wanted to work in childcare ever since I completed my GCSE in child development – I was so fascinated by how children learn and develop and I wanted to be a part of that. I enrolled in college and gained my CACHE DCE Level 3, got my first job in a small 35-place nursery and I haven't looked back!

My role as a manager is very varied and no day is ever the same. I meet new families looking for nursery care and I support my staff team with training, appraisals, supervision meetings and up skilling their knowledge. I deal with the business side of the nursery too which includes managing budgets, completing invoices for families and ensuring that we are always fully compliant in the nursery and keep everyone safe. I also spend time in the rooms as much as I can as I will always be a nursery nurse at heart. I am happy that I can combine my passion for childcare with my ambitions to learn and to take up increased responsibilities, as the company I work for allow me to have the freedom to grow.

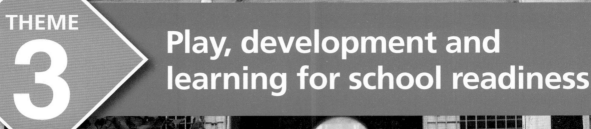

THEME 3

Play, development and learning for school readiness

Unit 3.1 Understand the value of play in early years

Unit 3.2 Plan, lead and review play opportunities which support children's learning and development in relation to current frameworks

Unit 3.3 Apply theoretical perspectives and philosophical approaches to play

Unit 3.4 Contribute to enabling play environments

Unit 3.5 Develop emergent literacy skills of children

Unit 3.6 Develop emergent mathematical skills of children

Unit 3.7 Understand the needs of the child in preparing for school

Unit 3.8 Understand how to plan to meet the needs of the developing child

Unit 3.9 Facilitate the cognitive development of children

Unit 3.10 Develop the speech, language and communication of children

Unit 3.11 Promote the physical development of children

Unit 3.12 Promote the personal, social and emotional development of children

Unit 3.13 Support children with additional needs

Unit 3.14 Use observation, assessment and planning to promote the development of children

Unit 3.15 Use longitudinal studies to observe, assess and plan for children's needs

Unit 3.1 Understand the value of play in early years

Play is an essential part of every child's life, and is vital for the enjoyment of childhood as well as for promoting social, emotional, intellectual, physical and holistic development. This unit provides the knowledge and understanding of the value of play in early years in preparation for practical experience.

Learning outcomes

By the end of this unit you will:

1 Understand the role of play.
2 Understand children's rights in relation to play.
3 Understand play at different stages of children's development.
4 Understand different types of play for all children.
5 Understand inclusive play practice.

LO1 Understand the role of play

What is play?

Play is a word that is widely used in the field of early years, but it is very difficult to define. It is probably one of the least understood aspects of an early years practitioner's work, yet play is probably one of the most important elements of childhood.

A traditional way of talking about play has been to break it up into types of play. The problem with this is that people seem to add more and more types to the list.

Looking at play as a whole concept

Breaking play up into types can help to make play more tangible – that is, less abstract to understand. However, there is much to be said for looking at play as a whole, because it is so central to childhood. Play is one of the most important ways in which children develop and learn. The huge variety of types of play shows that play creeps into most areas of a child's life. A happy childhood will involve children in play, wherever they live in the world. Play takes different forms in different families and in different cultures. Children who are sick or have complex needs might

have difficulty or face challenges in playing, but with support they can be helped to play.

AC 1.1 Explain the innate drive for children to play

All children need to play. The impulse to play is innate – that is to say, children are born with a natural drive to play. Play is a physiological, psychological and social necessity, and is fundamental to the healthy development and well-being of individuals and communities. Research has shown that even when children are living in harsh conditions, or are unwell, they still possess a natural drive to play.

AC 1.2 Analyse how play is necessary for the development of children

It would be inaccurate to say that play is the only way in which children learn. However, play is a major part of learning, opening up possibilities to reflect on and apply ideas and imagination, relationships and feelings, to be physically coordinated, to be capable of flexible thinking, to be ethically thoughtful and to develop a sense of awe and wonder. A life without play can inhibit the holistic development of children.

Children learn through play. Children need opportunities to learn through:

- **Learning to predict**: children learn to predict that something is about to happen. For example, a baby learns to predict that food will soon appear if a bib is tied around his or her neck.
- **Learning the consequences of their actions**: children understand that they can bring about a result by their own actions. For example, a baby learns that if he or she cries, he or she will be picked up and comforted.
- **Asking questions**: as soon as they can talk, children ask questions to try to make sense

of their world and gain information. For example, four-year-old children constantly ask the question 'Why?' whereas a child who is two-and-a-half years old constantly asks 'Who?' and 'What?'

- **Understanding concepts**: experiences with real objects help young children to understand concepts and to develop problem-solving skills. For example, mathematical concepts involve understanding number, sequencing, volume and capacity as well as weighing and measuring.
- **Repetition**: children learn by repeating activities over and over again. For example, they can learn a song or nursery rhyme by hearing it sung to them many times.
- **Imitation**: children learn by copying what others do. For example, they learn how to write by copying letters, and in role play children are copying the way they have observed others behave in certain situations.

Discussion point

Discuss the following in a group:

- What are your memories of your childhood play? Did you play?
- Did you make dens in the garden, under a table or with your bedclothes?
- Did you pretend you were in outer space, on a boat, on a desert island, going shopping, keeping house?
- Did you feel you had hours and hours to play?
- Did you enjoy using inexpensive play props or were your favourite toys expensive, commercially produced toys?

Activity

Why is play essential to the holistic development of children?

LO2 Understand children's rights in relation to play

Play England's *Charter for Children's Play* sets out the basic principles of what play means for children, and what we should do to support their right to enjoy it.

There are eight charter statements that describe children's right to play in detail:

1 Children have the right to play.
2 Every child needs time and space to play.
3 Adults should let children play.
4 Children should be able to play freely in their local areas.
5 Children value and benefit from staffed play provision.
6 Children's play is enriched by skilled playworkers.
7 Children need time and space to play at school.
8 Children sometimes need extra support to enjoy their right to play.

AC 2.1 Identify the rights of children in relation to play as detailed in the UNCRC

The United Nations Convention on the Rights of the Child, adopted by the United Nations in 1989, spells out the basic human rights to which every child, everywhere, is entitled.

The Convention sets out in a number of statements (called articles) the rights of all children and young people up to the age of 18. This includes Article 31, **the right to engage in play and recreational activities**:

- **Article 31.1** Recognise the right of the child to rest and leisure, to engage in play and recreational activities appropriate to the age of the child and to participate freely in cultural life and the arts.
- **Article 31.2** Respect and promote the right of the child to participate fully in cultural and artistic life and shall encourage the provision of appropriate and equal opportunities for cultural, artistic, recreational and leisure activity.
- **Article 23, Rights of disabled children** A mentally or physically disabled child should enjoy a full and decent life, in conditions which ensure dignity, promote self-reliance and facilitate the child's active participation in the community. This includes additional care and assistance where appropriate, free of charge whenever possible.
- **Article 30, Children of minorities or of indigenous people** The right for children from minority communities to enjoy their own culture, and to practise their own religion and language.

AC 2.2 Explain how settings meet the right for children to play

Supporting children's right to play

Early years settings must work within the frameworks for learning in the UK, which for England is the EYFS. Well-planned play, both indoors and outdoors, is an important part of the EYFS, as well as the other frameworks. Children learn by playing and exploring, being active, and through creative and critical thinking which takes place both indoors and outside.

The EYFS framework (2012) applies to children from birth to five years of age. During this Foundation Stage, children might be attending a playgroup, pre-school, nursery school, nursery class, day care setting, reception class or private nursery, or be with a childminder or nanny. The EYFS explains how and what children will be learning to support their healthy development. Children will be learning skills, acquiring new knowledge and demonstrating their understanding through **seven areas of learning and development**.

Children should mostly develop the **three prime areas** first. These are:

- communication and language
- physical development
- personal, social and emotional development.

These prime areas are those most essential for children's healthy development and future learning.

As children grow, they will be able to develop skills in the prime areas complemented by specific areas. These are:

- literacy
- mathematics
- understanding the world
- expressive arts and design.

Activity

Choose the early years curriculum framework for your own home country. Look at the areas of development and learning as set out in the Guidance and think about how each area can be planned for in play.

LO3 Understand play at different stages of children's development

The stages of play

It used to be thought that there were four stages of social play:

- solitary play
- parallel play
- associative play
- cooperative play.

Recent research shows that children do not develop as if they are climbing up a ladder. Instead, brain studies show that their play develops like a network. Sometimes they will play alone (solitary play). Sometimes they will play with others (parallel, associatively or cooperatively). These aspects of play are discussed on p 253.

It will partly depend on their age, but it will also depend on their mood, others around them, where they are, and whether they are tired, hungry or comfortable.

It is certainly easier for toddlers and young children to play together in parallel, associatively or cooperatively if they are in a pair (two children). Larger groups are more of a challenge for young children. Gradually, three or four children might play cooperatively together. This tends to develop from three or four years of age.

Play and the development of physical coordination

See table 3.1.1 for how play opportunities support physical development.

Playing alone
Solitary play: a child plays alone

Solitary play is play that is undertaken alone, sometimes through choice and at other times because the child finds it hard to join in, or because of his or her developmental stage.

In the first stage of play, beginning at about six months, babies play alone. Babies and toddlers need time and space to play alone, but often appreciate having others around them as they do so.

Stage of physical skill development		Supporting physical development through play opportunities
Sit (usually 6–9 months)	• Play with feet (put them in mouth) • Cruise around furniture	• Play with objects using a pincer movement (i.e. finger and thumb) • Transfer toys from one hand to the other • Enjoy dropping objects over the side of the high chair and look to see where they have gone • Play with objects by putting them into the mouth • Enjoy 'treasure baskets' (natural objects and household objects) Provide: • Cups, boxes, pots of different sizes
Crawl (usually 9–12 months)	• When sitting, the baby leans forward and picks up objects • Enjoy playing by crawling upstairs or onto low furniture • Love to bounce in time to music	• Pick things up with a pincer movement • Pull objects towards themselves • Can point at toys • Clasp hands and love to copy adults' actions in play • Love to play by throwing toys on purpose • Hold toys easily in hands • Put objects in and out of pots and boxes Provide: • Push and pull toys
Walk (but with sudden falling into a sitting position) (12–15 months)	• Can manage stairs with adult supervision • Can stand and kneel without support	• Begin to build towers with wooden blocks • Make lines of objects on the floor • Begin using books and turn several pages at a time • Use both hands but often prefer one • Lot of pointing • Pull toys along and push buttons Provide: • Board books and picture books with lines • Big empty cardboard boxes • Messy play with water paints and sand (be alert for physical safety)
Walk confidently (usually 18 months)	• Can kneel, squat, climb and carry things, can climb on chairs • Can twist around to sit • Can creep downstairs on tummy going backwards	• Pick up small objects and threads • Build towers • Scribble on paper • Push and pull toys • Enjoy banging toys (e.g. hammer and peg drums) Provide: • Large crayons and paper for drawing
Jump (usually 2 years)	• Can jump on the spot and run, and climb stairs two feet at a time • Kick but not good at catching ball • Enjoy space to run and play (trips to the park) • Enjoy climbing frames (supervised)	• Draw circles • Build tall towers • Pick up tiny objects • Turn the pages of books one at a time • Enjoy toys to ride and climb on • Enjoy messy play with water paints and sandpits Provide: • Duplo, jigsaws, crayons and paper, picture books, puppets, simple dressing-up clothes, hats, belts and shoes →

Table 3.1.1 How play opportunities support physical development

Stage of physical skill development		Supporting physical development through play opportunities
Hop (usually 3 years)	• Jump from low steps • Walk forwards, backwards and sideways • Stand and walk on tiptoe • Stand on one foot • Try to hop • Use pedals on tricycle • Climb stairs one foot at a time	• Build taller and taller towers with blocks • Begin to use pencil grip • Paint and make lines and circles in drawings • Use play dough, sand for modelling, paint • Hold objects to explore Provide: • Enjoy trip to the park, walks, library, swimming • Enjoy cooking, small world, gluing, pouring, cutting
Skip (usually 4 years)	• Balance (walking on a line) • Catch a ball, kick, throw and bounce • Bend at the waist to pick up objects from the floor • Climbing trees and frames • Can run up and down stairs one foot at a time	• Build tower with blocks that are taller and taller • Draw people, houses, etc. • Thread beads • Enjoy exercise, swimming, climbing (climbing frames and bikes) Provide: • Jigsaws, construction toys, wooden blocks, small world, glue and stick, paint, sand, water, clay, play dough, dressing-up clothes and home area play • Cooking (measuring, pouring and cutting)
Jump, hop, skip and run with coordination (usually 5 years)	• Use a variety of play equipment (slides, swings, climbing frames) • Enjoy ball games • Hop and run lightly on toes, and can move rhythmically to music • Well-developed sense of balance	• Sew large stitches • Draw with people, animals and places, etc. • Coordinate paint brushes and pencils, and a variety of tools • Enjoy outdoor activities (skipping ropes, football – both boys and girls enjoy these) • Make models, do jigsaws
Move with increased coordination and balance (usually 6–7 years)	• Can ride two-wheel bicycle • Hops easily with good balance • Can jump off apparatus at school	• Build play scenarios with wooden blocks • Draw play scenarios in drawings and paintings • Hold pencil as adults do • Enjoy ball games • Enjoy vigorous activity (riding a bike, swimming) (NB children should never be forced to take part, unless they want to) • Enjoy board games and computer games • Often (but not always) enjoys work being displayed on interest tables and walls (NB Children should never be forced to display their work)

Table 3.1.1 How play opportunities support physical development (*Continued*)

- Playing alone gives personal space and time to think, get to know and like yourself.
- When toddlers play alone, they seek interesting experiences, but need support when frustrated.
- Children of all ages engage in solitary play sometimes; playing alone enables older children to concentrate and practise their skills (e.g. when constructing a model).
- It is important to protect the child's play space and toys from interference by other children.

Figure 3.1.1 Baby playing alone

- Children should be allowed to experience 'ownership' of toys and not be pushed to share before they are ready.

Example

A child might play alone – for example, with a dolls' house – because they want to play out a story that they have in their head. Having other children join the play would stop them being able to do this.

Onlooker behaviour

Onlooker 'play' is the passive observation of the play of others without actual participation. Before children begin to play with each other, they go through a brief stage of looking-on behaviour:

- Children will stop what they are doing to watch and listen to what other children are doing.
- Older children may also watch others play if they are new to the group and do not yet feel ready to enter into the play.

- Even a child who is already secure in a group may engage in onlooker behaviour – taking a passive interest in what their friends are doing, but not joining in.

Stages of social play: children play together

Parallel play

Parallel play is when children play alongside each other but quite separately and without communicating with each other. Onlooker behaviour evolves into parallel (or side-by-side) play, which includes a lot of imitation and conversation back and forth between the players:

- During this stage, children like to have exactly the same toys as their peers do, but their own play space.
- They are no longer content to play alone, but they are also not ready for the demands of sharing toys or taking turns.
- Older children also enjoy parallel play with their friends.

Figure 3.1.2 Parallel play

Example

Two children might both put dolls to bed in the home area. They do not take much notice of each other.

Associative play

Associative play is when two or more children actively interact with one another by sharing or borrowing toys, while not doing the same things. Children playing at the **parallel stage** will begin to become aware of other children. They will often begin to communicate through talking to each other or by becoming aware of each other's games and by explaining to each other what they are doing:

* Gradually one child will become involved in the other child's play; this is known as **associative** (or partnership) play.
* Language becomes much more important, imagination increases and dramatic themes begin to come into the play; this category of play may seem to be cooperative, but this is not the case – at this age, children are still too egocentric to have true cooperation.

Figure 3.1.3 Associative play

Example

Two children might play so that one is the cook in the cafe and the other is the waitress. They do not seem to care that they have no customers.

Cooperative play

Cooperative play is when children begin to 'play' together – to share their play. They become more sociable and take on roles in the play. Children begin to be aware of the needs and the roles of their peers and gradually the play can become complex:

- Rules are sometimes devised and some cooperative play will be revisited over several days.
- Cooperative play continues throughout middle childhood, where it evolves into more stylised games with rules.
- In the early stages of cooperative play, the rules are not as important as the sense of belonging to a group and working towards a common goal.

Example of early (or simple) cooperative play

One child might be the baby and the other might be the parent, as they play going to the shops. They talk about their play ideas: 'You say "Mum" and I say "Yes, darling".'

Example of later (or complex) cooperative play

A group of children between three and five years old have been on an outing in the local market. When they return, the adult sets up a market stall. Some children become customers and buy things, while others sell things. John has a hearing impairment and uses sign language. Jack understands his sign to give him three oranges. Other children talk as they play: 'You come and bag these apples.'

Figure 3.1.4 Cooperative play

Activity

Matching stages of play

Read through the section in the book on 'Stages of play' and match the following descriptions to the stage of play and the approximate age when children tend to play in this way.

Stages of play:

- solitary play
- parallel play
- cooperative play.
- onlooker or spectator play
- associative play

1 Four children are making biscuits. They decide how to measure out the ingredients and how to mix them together, sharing the tasks between them. They take turns and there is plenty of discussion.

Stage of play:

Approximate age:

2 Two children are sitting next to each other on the floor. Each is playing with wooden blocks and is totally absorbed, but not taking any notice of each other.

Stage of play:

Approximate age:

3 A baby is sitting on the floor, selecting items from a treasure basket containing natural and everyday objects – an example of heuristic play. (See page 262 for more information on heuristic play.)

Stage of play:

Approximate age:

4 Two children are playing with a farm set. A third child stops what he is doing and watches them intently for a while.

Stage of play:

Approximate age:

5 A group of children are playing at the sand tray. They are starting to talk to each other – explaining to each other what they are doing.

Stage of play:

Approximate age:

AC 3.1 Explain the characteristics of child-initiated play and adult-led play

Child-initiated play

Child-initiated play occurs when children make their own decisions, without suggestion or guidance from adults, about the way in which they use the equipment and resources provided for them. For example, although an adult may have chosen which construction materials to set out (e.g. wooden blocks), two children may decide to work together to build a castle for 'small world' figures or play people. This, then, is a child-initiated activity.

Adult-led play

These activities are planned, prepared and, often, initiated by adults. For example, a water activity might be planned that focuses particularly on 'force' or 'pressure'. The adult may have selected the equipment that lends itself to using water under pressure – squeezy bottles, thin plastic tubing, a water pump – and allowed children to use it in their own way, or played alongside the children, talking about what was happening and questioning them so that they express their ideas.

Even when an activity is adult-led it should always involve *active participation* by the children. Activities that have an 'end product' (e.g. a model or a special occasion card) must allow for children's experimentation and creativity so that each one is different and original. You should not aim to have all the children's work looking the same or 'perfect' (i.e. your idea of what the finished article should look like). Ownership is very important: children need to feel that their work is their own. What children learn from doing the activity – practical skills, understanding of materials, textures, sounds, and so on – is far more important than the finished article.

Structured activities

These should be carefully planned to develop a particular aspect of understanding or skill. They are structured in that there are resources, carefully chosen, and usually a sequence of tasks, or steps, that may lead to a desired learning outcome or objective. An adult usually leads, supervises and monitors children's responses.

In practice activity

A simple sorting activity

Aim: to find out if children can identify and sort all the blue objects from a selection of objects of different colours.

Ask the children individually to find something blue and put it in the sorting 'ring' with other blue things – this ensures that all children participate, and enables the adult to find out if the child has understood the task and can carry it out.

- For this task the child has to know what 'blue' means and be able to distinguish objects of that colour from others.
- Some children may not realise that there are different shades of blue that are still 'blue'.
- Adults working with children on an activity such as this need to talk to them. Asking questions and enjoying a chat together help adults check each child's understanding.

AC 3.2 Identify how children's play needs and preferences change in relation to their stage of development

What are play needs?

Play needs are individual to each child and are directly related to the age, stage of development and interests or preferences of the child.

Progress check

Play needs

Play needs include opportunities to:

- play in safe places
- use a variety of objects and materials
- learn about the physical environment
- develop empathy (being able to imagine what someone else feels or thinks)
- take control of their own learning – at their own pace
- develop relationships with others – both other children and adults
- explore their own feelings – and learn how to control them.

Adults often make assumptions about the play needs of children, but these are not always an accurate reflection of what children both want (play preferences) and need (play needs).

Observing children during their play and discussing their play preferences with them will help to ensure that each child's play needs are met.

Having respect for children and valuing their play preferences

Giving attention to children's play activities can range from being a passive observer through to being fully involved in their play. Our own experience of playing as children and our ideas about play are certain to have an influence on the way we think about how children play. Children quickly pick up on the way in which adults react when they are playing. For example, if you hover over a child who is using the climbing frame for the first time, the child will probably be less adventurous and turn to you for reassurance. Or, if you stereotype children's play by always encouraging boys to play as superheroes and girls to play with the pram and dolls, the children may alter their course of play to fit in with your ideas. One of the most important skills to develop is being able to know when to get involved and when to allow children to carry on playing. The principle behind this is having respect for children and valuing their play preferences. Although you may be involved in planning the play environment, you are not planning the way children play in it. Children need to be able to initiate their own ideas and to be spontaneous.

The play preferences of children from birth to eight years

Babies (from birth to 18 months) are totally dependent on caring adults to provide them with new play experiences. They show a preference for:

- watching movement and listening to rhythmic sounds
- holding rattles, chiming balls and musical toys
- exploring textures – for example, on an activity mat
- playing with stacking beakers and bricks
- exploring objects with their hands and their mouth
- active play with a caring adult
- making noises by banging toys
- playing with empty cardboard boxes
- looking at picture books.

Children aged 18 months to three years have an increasing desire for independence. They show a preference for:

Figure 3.1.5 Babies enjoy looking at picture books

- playing with things that screw and unscrew
- paints and crayons
- sand and water play
- playing with balls – rolling, kicking and throwing.

Towards the end of this period, they show a preference for:

- toys to ride and climb on
- matching and sorting games
- simple jigsaw puzzles
- puppet play and action rhymes
- musical games
- jumping, running and physical games
- role play.

Children aged three to five play with other children. They show a preference for:

- playing outdoors
- active pretend play with other children
- jigsaw puzzles and making models
- simple craft activities and playing with dough
- playing on the floor with bricks, trains, dolls and boxes, alone and with others
- acting out puppet shows
- imaginative play.

Children aged five to eight are learning self-control and enjoy showing what they can do. They show a preference for:

- team games and games with rules
- complicated games on the floor with small world objects
- more elaborate pretend play with others
- playing cooperatively with other children
- fantasy play
- activities that involve precise movements – such as hopscotch or skipping games.

LO4 Understand different types of play for all children

AC 4.1 Describe benefits of: physical, creative, imaginative, and sensory play

Physical play

Physical play promotes a child's health. It links with all other areas of a child's development. The brain works better if children have plenty of fresh air and exercise. It also benefits the general health and well-being of children, it aids rest/sleep and even digestion. That is why both indoor and outdoor play are very important.

Through physical play children learn to challenge gender stereotypes. Boys and girls can enjoy playing ball games (e.g. football play scenarios, running and climbing). Children need to be encouraged in these activities. It helps if they wear clothes and shoes that allow freedom of movement.

The benefits of physical play

Physical play helps children to:

- **Express ideas and feelings**. Children become aware that they can use their bodies to express themselves by moving in different ways as they respond to their moods and feelings, to music or to imaginative ideas.
- **Explore what their bodies can do** and become aware of their increasing abilities, agility and skill. Children's awareness of the space around them and what their bodies are capable of can be extended by climbing and balancing on large-scale apparatus, such as a climbing frame, wooden logs and a balancing bar and by using small tricycles, bicycles and carts.
- **Cooperate with others** in physical play and games. Children become aware of physical play both as an individual and a social activity: in playing alone or alongside others, in playing throwing and catching with a partner, in using a seesaw or push cart, or in joining a game with a larger group.
- **Develop increasing control of fine movements** of their fingers and hands (fine motor skills). For example, playing musical instruments and making sounds with the body, such as clapping or tapping, helps develop fine motor skills in the hands and fingers, while also reinforcing the link between sound and physical movement. Helping with household tasks – washing up, pouring drinks, carrying bags – also develops fine motor skills.

Figure 3.1.6 Children enjoying physical play

- **Develop balance and coordination**, as well as an appreciation of distance and speed; energetic play which involves running, jumping and skipping helps children to develop these skills.
- **Develop spatial awareness**. For example, dancing and moving around to music develop a spatial awareness while also practising coordination and muscle control.

Manipulative play

Manipulative play is an important aspect of physical play. Children need plenty of opportunities to play using manipulative skills. This particularly encourages children to use their hands, which are very important in human development.

Boys and girls can enjoy manipulative play.

EYFS 2012

Manipulative play links with the EYFS Framework, with the area of learning called Physical Development.

Creative play

Children must not be expected to 'make something'. Creative play is about experimenting with materials and music. It is not about producing things to go on display, or to be taken home; for example, when children are involved with messy finger play with paint, nothing is left at the end of the session once it has been cleared away.

Adults can encourage creative play by offering children a range of materials and play opportunities in dance, music, drawing, collage, painting, model-making and woodwork, sand (small world scenarios), water (small world scenarios) and miniature garden scenarios.

The benefits of creative play

Creative play helps children to express their feelings and ideas about people, objects and events. It helps children to:

- be physically coordinated
- develop language

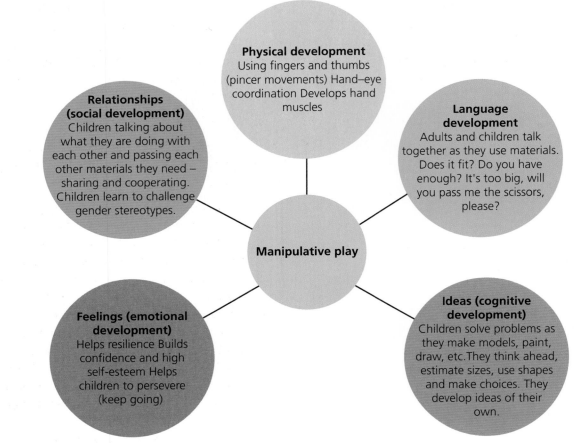

Physical development
Using fingers and thumbs (pincer movements) Hand–eye coordination Develops hand muscles

Relationships (social development)
Children talking about what they are doing with each other and passing each other materials they need – sharing and cooperating. Children learn to challenge gender stereotypes.

Language development
Adults and children talk together as they use materials. Does it fit? Do you have enough? It's too big, will you pass me the scissors, please?

Manipulative play

Feelings (emotional development)
Helps resilience Builds confidence and high self-esteem Helps children to persevere (keep going)

Ideas (cognitive development)
Children solve problems as they make models, paint, draw, etc. They think ahead, estimate sizes, use shapes and make choices. They develop ideas of their own.

Figure 3.1.7 Aspects of manipulative play

- develop ideas (concepts)
- develop relationships with people
- be more confident, and it boosts their self-esteem
- helps promote positive thinking.

Imaginative play

Sometimes called drama or pretend play, imaginative play is where children make play scenarios – for example, about a shop or a boat, a garage, an office or a swimming pool.

The important thing to remember about imaginative play is that there will be nothing left to show anyone when the play finishes. Pretend play scenarios do not last, and it can be difficult to explain to parents the importance of pretend play.

Some adults take video or photographs of children during their play, to try to capture it on film. They want to value imaginative play as they do all the other learning that children do.

What to look out for in imaginative play

- Children use play props – for example, they pretend a box is a fridge, or a stick is a spoon, or a daisy is a fried egg.
- They role play and pretend that they are someone else (e.g. the shopkeeper).
- When they pretend play together, cooperatively, this is called socio-dramatic play.
- Young children pretend play everyday situations: getting up, going to sleep, eating (just as Peppa Pig and George Pig do on television and in books).
- Gradually children develop their pretend play scenarios to include situations that are not everyday events, and that they may only have heard about but not experienced. This is called **fantasy play**. They might pretend to go to the moon or go on an aeroplane. It is not impossible that these things will happen to them.

- Superhero play develops when they use unreal situations, like Superman, Power Rangers or cartoon characters.
- Children use imaginative play to act out situations that they have definitely experienced, like going to the supermarket.

For example, a group of children made a swimming pool out of wooden blocks. One of them pretended to be the lifeguard and rescued someone drowning. All the children had visited a swimming pool so this pretend play was based on a real experience.

The benefits of imaginative play

Imaginative play also links with all areas of a child's development:

- emotional development
- social development
- language development
- cognitive (thinking) development
- physical development.

Sensory play

Sensory play includes any activity that stimulates a young child's senses. It is important to remember that children learn best when they can actually touch, see, smell, taste, hear, and manipulate the materials in their world. Stimulating the senses sends signals to children's brains that help to strengthen neural pathways important for all types of learning. For example, as children explore sensory materials, they develop their sense of touch, which lays the foundation for learning other skills, such as identifying objects by touch and using fine motor skills.

Sensory activities and sensory tables promote exploration and encourage children to use scientific processes while they play, create, investigate and explore.

Examples of sensory play

- Sand and water play: provide interesting objects – pipes, funnels, ladles, scoops, sieves, etc.
- Play dough: provide rolling pins, cutters.
- Play with a variety of malleable materials: shaving cream, cornflour, dried or cooked pasta, dried beans or lentils.

- Natural objects: collect sticks, feathers, fir cones, etc. during a walk in the park or garden.
- Fruits and vegetables: encourage children to touch, smell, taste and play with all the different produce.
- Music activities: singing, dancing, playing musical instruments, etc.

The benefits of sensory play

Spending time stimulating their senses helps children develop cognitively, linguistically, socially and emotionally, physically and creatively:

- **Cognitive development**: sensory play promotes spatial awareness, mathematical thinking, and scientific exploration and discovery. Sensory play provides opportunities for learning colours, counting, sequencing, sorting, and constructing.
- **Language development**: sensory play encourages children to use descriptive and expressive language, and to find meaning behind essentially meaningless words – such as 'slimy' or 'lumpy' – when taken out of context. Children also develop pre-writing skills as they focus on hand–eye coordination tasks while using various materials.
- **Emotional development**: sensory play provides an opportunity way for children to relieve their stress and to express their feelings. Pummelling clay or playing with water, for example, can be very soothing and relaxing to a young child. The open-ended nature of sensory play gives children the opportunity to create or recreate pictures, shapes and designs as many times as they like. Sensory play also eliminates the fear and experience of failure, which can negatively impact a child's self-esteem.
- **Social skills**: when engaged in group sensory play, children often form emotional bonds with other children as they share a common experience. Working closely together at a sand and water table, for example, provides young children with opportunities to observe how their peers handle materials, to share their own ideas and discoveries, and to build relationships. Because playing with play dough or sand does not require the use of language, even very young children can build early social ability through sensory play.

- **The development of fine motor skills**: in the process of rolling and cutting up play dough or scooping and pouring water and beans, children will develop hand–eye coordination and fine motor control. Children are also developing the skills and muscles they will need for handwriting and other fine manipulative skills.
- **Creative development**: sensory play allows children to experiment with a large variety of materials in new and creative ways. Play that is open-ended and uninterrupted by adults allows creativity to flourish. The children are able to use the materials in any way they like, and are able to enjoy the process and have no concern for the end product.

AC 4.2 Explain the principles of heuristic play

Heuristic play is the term used to describe children playing and exploring natural materials using all of their senses. The word 'heuristic' means 'helping to find out or discover'. The concept was developed by Elinor Goldshmied, a child psychologist, from her work watching children and the way they gained knowledge of the world around them. Heuristic play is rooted in young children's natural curiosity. As babies grow, they move beyond being content to simply feel and ponder objects, to wanting to find out what can be *done* with them. Toddlers have an urge to handle things: to gather, fill, dump, stack, knock down, select and manipulate in other ways. Kitchen utensils offer this kind of activity and can occupy a child for surprising stretches of time. When toddlers make an enjoyable discovery – for instance when one item fits into another, or an interesting sound is produced – they often repeat the action several times to test the result. This strengthens cognitive development as well as fine muscle control and hand–eye coordination. Treasure basket play was also developed by Elinor Goldshmied to promote heuristic play.

The benefits of heuristic play

Heuristic play:

- supports inclusion
- is often considered to be therapeutic
- supports children's cognitive development, as they learn through discovery and exploration

- offers children the opportunity to test out their own theories and solve problems.

Activity

Understanding key terms in play

1 Match the category of play in column 1 with the example in column 2.

1 Physical play	A Child using a brush and paint on paper
2 Fantasy play	B Three children are playing in the home area; one is the shopkeeper and the other two are customers
3 Exploratory play	C Child pretending to be a fire-fighter
4 Manipulative play	D Child playing outdoors on a climbing frame and slide
5 Creative play	E Baby playing with treasure basket which contains natural and everyday objects
6 Imaginative play	F Children playing with beakers and wheels at the water tray
7 Heuristic play	G Child threading beads onto a lace
8 Socio-dramatic play	H Child pretending he is flying to the moon on a broomstick

2 Using the headings from column 1, think of two more examples of activities which correspond to each type of play (except for heuristic play).

AC 4.3 Evaluate resources for: physical, creative , imaginative, sensory and heuristic play

All early years settings provide a wide variety of equipment and resources to support young children in their play.

Activity

For **each** of the following categories of play – physical, creative, imaginative, sensory and heuristic play:

- Describe the resources provided in your setting – e.g. wooden blocks for physical play, paints and musical instruments for creative play – and so on.
- Evaluate each resource in terms of the benefits to the children using them.
- Think of ways in which each resource might be improved – or suggest further resources.

In practice activity

Observing a baby with a natural treasure basket

Babies learn about their environment using all their senses – touch, smell, taste, sight, hearing and movement. A treasure basket is a collection of everyday objects chosen to stimulate the different senses. Babies have the chance to decide for themselves what they want to play with, choosing in turn whichever object they want to explore.

1 Choose a sturdy basket or box – one that does not tip over easily.
2 Fill the basket with lots of natural objects or objects made from natural materials so that the baby has plenty to choose from.
  For example:

● fir cones	● large seashells	● large walnuts
● fruit (e.g. apple, lemon)	● brushes	● woollen ball
● wooden pegs	● small baskets	● feathers
● large pebbles	● gourds	● pumice stone

3 Make sure that everything you choose for the basket is clean and safe. Remember that babies often want to put everything into their mouths, so you need to check that all objects are clean and safe.
4 Make sure the baby is seated comfortably and safely, with cushions for support if necessary. Sit nearby and watch to give the baby confidence. Only talk or intervene if the baby clearly needs attention.
5 You should check the contents of the basket regularly, cleaning objects and removing any damaged items.
6 Write an observation of the activity, noting the following:
   ● the length of time the baby plays with each item
   ● what he or she does with it
   ● any facial expressions or sounds made by the baby.

LO5 Understand inclusive play practice

Inclusive play is primarily about all children having equal access to – and equal participation in – local play, childcare and leisure opportunities. Inclusive play is not just the inclusion of children with disabilities. Equally important is the provision of high-quality play opportunities to children regardless of their needs and abilities.

AC 5.1 Summarise inclusive play practice in relation to current frameworks

The EYFS framework and guidance requires that every child can join in play and learning activities at a level appropriate to them. The best way for early years settings to develop inclusive provision is to consider the needs and entitlements of each child in their setting and to build up resources to meet those needs. The legislation relating to inclusive practice is described in Unit 1.3.

AC 5.2 Analyse how play supports the interests and abilities of children

An inclusive approach to play means that the general play environment is planned to be suitable for a variety of play needs, ages and stages.

Providing inclusive play opportunities

Children aged two to three years:

● are easily frustrated, but they can concentrate well if they are allowed to make choices and decide what they do; otherwise, their concentration will last for only a few minutes
● enjoy using wheeled trucks to sit in and be pulled along, and to sit on and scoot with feet on the ground
● will not share easily with other children, so there need to be enough boxes, hats, toy cars, tea set pieces, wooden blocks, and so on, or there will be conflicts.

Children aged three to five years:

● will use the area without so much adult support; even so, adults will need to make sure that children feel confident as they move about indoors and outdoors

- enjoy using tricycles with pedals; a few children may manage to use two-wheeled bicycles
- who are wheelchair users can join in wheeled play in the zone where children have space to go fast and feel freedom of movement together
- need you to think about progression in play, so that you challenge children to learn through their play
- need to play in zones where they have enough space to use wheeled toys safely

- need to have available other areas where they can play without wheeled toys, so that they do not have to worry about being knocked over; this means dividing the outdoor area into wheeled truck zones and other areas where children are not allowed to take wheeled trucks or bikes.

Assessment practice

1 What is meant by the innate drive for children to play?
2 How is play essential to the holistic development of children?
3 What are children's rights in relation to play?
4 How do settings meet the right for children to play?
5 What are the characteristics of child-initiated play, and adult-led play?
6 How do children's play needs and preferences change in relation to their stage of development?

7 What are the benefits of physical play, creative play, imaginative play and sensory play?
8 What is heuristic play?
9 In your setting, evaluate resources for physical, creative, imaginative, sensory and heuristic play.
10 Explain what is meant by inclusive play practice.
11 How does play support the interests and abilities of children?

Useful resources

Organisation

Play England

Promotes free play opportunities for all children and young people, and works to ensure that the importance of play for children's development is recognised: www.playengland.org.uk

Unit 3.2 Plan, lead and review play opportunities which support children's learning and development in relation to current frameworks

This unit provides the knowledge, understanding and skills which a learner needs to be able to plan, lead and review purposeful play opportunities which support children's learning and development.

Learning outcomes

By the end of this unit you will:

1 Be able to plan play opportunities.
2 Be able to lead and support play opportunities.
3 Be able to review how planned play opportunities contribute to your own practice.

LO1 Be able to plan play opportunities

AC 1.1 Create a plan which includes a balance of child-initiated and adult-led play opportunities for physical, creative, imaginative and sensory play

Planning play opportunities

There are no **strict** rules about what planning should look like in the revised EYFS, nor about what types of planning should be in place. The only requirement is that planning should be fit for the purposes described in the revised document and meet the requirements set out by individual schools, settings or groups of settings.

Underpinning all planning should be evaluative questions about its usefulness and whether it makes a difference to teaching and learning in the setting, regardless of whether a child is five months old or five years old.

Planning needs to balance different areas of development and learning, and **play should be central**. Sometimes adults will lead directly (teaching children to cook a recipe, or plant vegetables in the garden). Sometimes adults will lead indirectly, in the way they set up the environment and materials, or engage with children in their play and during their experiences. There needs to be a balance of the adult being involved in direct and indirect teaching, and child-initiated learning.

Working as a team

Planning work also involves working with other people (for example, parents, carers, colleagues and other professionals) to deliver the appropriate curriculum for the children in your setting. You should regularly check and discuss the progress of children with parents, carers and colleagues. Seek additional support especially if children are not progressing as expected, for example by consulting other professionals as appropriate.

The value of observing and involving the children

Remember to observe the children while they are involved in the learning activities and assess whether you need to change or extend these activities to meet their early learning and developmental needs more fully. Children's responses should also be considered when providing support for learning activities. Be sensitive to children's needs and preferences. You should take notice of non-verbal responses and preferences demonstrated by the children; these are just as important as what they say.

Remember to give the children positive encouragement and feedback to reinforce and sustain their interest and efforts in the learning process. You can use children's positive or negative responses to modify or extend activities to meet each child's needs more effectively. For example, if the learning intentions prove too easy or too difficult, you may have to set new goals. By breaking down learning activities into smaller tasks, you may help individual children to achieve success more quickly.

Guidelines: planning play opportunities

- **Discuss your plan with your supervisor or line manager**. Make sure that your setting has the materials and resources required and that your plan takes into account the children's age and stage of development.
- **Decide which areas of development your activity will promote**. How does your activity link to the EYFS or other curriculum framework where you are working?
- **Plan to involve the children** in the planning, setting up and clearing away of the activity. Decide on the group size with regard to their routines for sleep, rest and refreshment.
- **Consider health and safety issues relevant to your activity**: for example, how much supervision will be necessary; health and hygiene factors during a cooking activity, etc.

- Make sure that you are providing **equality of opportunity** for the children: you may need to adapt the activity for a child with a visual or hearing impairment, and make sure that you are promoting positive images and avoiding gender or cultural stereotyping.
- **Plan the timing for the activity**: allow some flexibility within your timescale to allow for spontaneity.
- **Prepare the area beforehand**: for example, protecting tables, organising water tables and appropriate clothing (such as aprons or warm outerwear) for the children.
- **Evaluation**: after the activity, discuss how well it went with the children and with colleagues. Evaluate it in terms of the benefits to the children and to the setting. How could you improve it next time?

In modifying plans, you are continuing a cycle of planning and implementing activities. After the learning activities, you should use all the available relevant information to evaluate the effectiveness of your planning and implementation of the activity; this might include responses from parents, carers, colleagues and other professionals.

Planning for physical play

Children need to move as much as they need to eat and sleep. They learn through action and through language that gives it meaning. They need to be skilled in a range of movements, using both fine and gross motor skills. They need repetition to consolidate. Movement needs to be appropriate – stroke a dog gently, but throw hard to make a splash with a pebble in a puddle.

Large apparatus

Large apparatus includes climbing frame, ropes to swing on, planks to walk on with ladders and things to jump off. Children need to be encouraged to become generally skilled in movement.

Small apparatus

Small apparatus includes bats, balls, hoops, beanbags, ropes and pushcarts. It is very important to encourage turn-taking and cooperation.

Floor work

Floor work enables children to explore:

- weight transfer from one part of the body to another
- travel from one spot to another
- flight: the five basic jumps are on two legs, from one leg to the other, on the left leg, on the right leg, from two legs to one leg.

Guidelines for floor work

- Give children (aged between four and seven years) a general theme to investigate through floor work – for example, starting low and getting higher.
- Do not make children do just one thing, such as a handstand. There are lots of different ways of changing your balance.

- To help children enjoy creating and solving problems about weight transfer, you can say, 'Can you start on your feet and stop with another bit of you touching the floor?' In this way, you are helping children with reasoning and problem-solving as they think about their own movements.

> **In practice activity**
>
> **Physical play**
>
> Plan a group activity to promote physical development in your setting. It could be something as straightforward as playing 'What's the time Mr Wolf?', creating an obstacle course for children riding trikes or a simple game with beanbags.

Planning for creative play

The requirements of the EYFS state that

Children's creativity must be extended by the provision of support for their curiosity, exploration and play. They must be provided with opportunities to explore and share their thoughts, ideas and feelings, for example, through a variety of art, music, movement, dance, imaginative and role-play activities, mathematics, and design and technology.

When talking about what creative development means for all children, the EYFS states that

Creativity is about taking risks and making connections and is strongly linked to play … [It] emerges as children become absorbed in action and explorations of their own ideas, expressing them through movement, making and transforming things using media and materials such as crayons, paints, scissors, words, sounds, movement, props and make-believe.

Children need experiences such as using clay and paint and woodwork. Representing a dog is quite different when using clay, wood at the woodwork bench, paint, or pretending to be a dog in the home corner. Teach children skills when the need arises. Adults need to be effective observers and tune in to these situations.

Children can make models with clay, wet sand, wax, soap-carving, wood, dough, junk and recycled materials. This will involve them in using sticky tape, scissors, rolling pins, string, wire and other materials. Most of the time, these materials can be offered as general areas of provision, available all the time. Clearly, the woodwork can only be used when an adult joins the children, in order to maintain a safe environment.

Drawing and painting

For drawing, it is best to use plain white paper of varied sizes, plus pencils, wax crayons, felt-tip pens, chalks and slates, and charcoal.

For painting, there should be powder paints and different thicknesses of brushes. Materials should be stored carefully so that children can take and access what they need when they need it. Children should be offered pots of basic coloured paints, but they should also be able to mix paints, provided they are taught to do so. They simply need the basic colours – red, yellow, blue – and white and black for light and dark shades of colour.

Book-making

Children love to make books, but need help to do so initially. If they see that you have made recipe books, books of stories and poems, and books for display with information, they will want to do the same. They need to learn how to fold and cut the paper. An early years practitioner may need to be with them so that they do not give up.

Collage and workshop area

This requires glue, found materials, junk and recycled materials, and scissors. Materials can be set out in attractive baskets or boxes covered in wallpaper. Glue should always be non-toxic.

Music

Recent studies in neuroscience show that music is important in helping language and memory to develop. Adults naturally sing 'Up we go,' when they lift a baby or toddler out of a pram. Music helps children to remember words, but music is important in its own right. Everyday sounds have rhythm, such as the tick-tock of an alarm clock, tearing paper, shaking a salt cellar, jangling a bunch of keys, fire engines, and so on. Children love to go on listening walks, and to make the sounds they have heard using home-made musical instruments you can help them to make. The importance of singing and listening to a wide range of music from different cultures cannot be overemphasised.

Planning for imaginative play

Several types of play can be grouped under the umbrella of imaginative play: symbolic play, role play, socio-dramatic play, small world play and fantasy play. Dressing-up clothes and small world play equipment are all useful props in promoting imaginative play.

The home area is one of the most important areas for promoting imaginative play in early years settings. The home area should ideally have:

- some things in it that are like those in the child's home (e.g. cups, cooking pots)
- resources that are familiar to the child
- some things that are from other cultures (e.g. a wok)
- a proper place for everything, and children should be encouraged to tidy up carefully
- a large dresser – with hooks for cups, and cupboards to store dishes and saucepans
- big, middle-sized and small dolls, representing children of different cultures

Progress check

Helping children to make dances

- Use an action phrase – for example, 'shiver and freeze'. Ask the children to move like the words in the phrase.
- Show different objects, perhaps something spiky. Ask the children to move in a spiky way and make a dance.
- Take an idea from nature or everyday life: rush and roar like the wind; be a machine or a clock; dance like shadows moving or fish in an aquarium.
- For inspiration only, use experiences that the children have had very recently.

In practice activity

Promoting children's creativity in the arts

Drawing, painting, weaving, collage, sewing, woodwork, sculpture and model-making, and pottery are examples of arts and crafts. Organise art materials for the children to select and use in their own way.

Case study

Creativity in dance, music and drama

You can use what children do naturally – spinning, running, jumping, stamping – to make up a dance. A 'Singing in the Rain' dance was made up by a group of five-year-old children in Year 1, helped by their teacher, Dee De Wet. The children watched a video extract from the film, *Singing in the Rain*, then they experimented with moving about:

- with fancy feet
- by jumping in puddles
- by swishing through puddles
- by dashing about under an umbrella.

They made a dance sequence. Every child had an umbrella and a raincoat, and used the above sequences in line with the traditional music from the film. Every child made up his or her own dance, yet they all danced at the same time, and were sensitive to each other's movement and ideas.

Guidelines for promoting children's creativity in the arts

Adults often use children's art lessons as a chance to do art for themselves! Therefore:

Do not:

- draw for children
- use templates
- ask children to trace
- ask children to colour in
- ask children to copy your model step by step.

Do:

- give children real, first-hand experiences, such as looking at plants or mini-beasts in the pond
- give children opportunities to represent things, and to keep hold of their experiences (for example, by making a model of the plant out of clay)
- encourage lots of different ideas: it is best when every child in a group has made a different model. This means that children are doing their own thinking and are not dependent on adults for ideas
- remember that children are creative in lots of different ways: arts and crafts are only one area in which children are creative. Children can be creative scientists, creative mathematicians, creative writers, and so on.

- a cooker (this can be home-made – e.g. from a cardboard box)
- wooden boxes, which can be used as beds, tables, chairs
- food can be pre-structured (plastic fruit), transformable (dough), real food (a salad) or pretend
- clothes can be kept in a chest of drawers, labelled with pictures and words
- magazines, notepads and writing implements can be put by the telephone, and perhaps a bookcase with books
- adaptations for children with disabilities (e.g. a child who is a wheelchair user will need a low table so that they can use the bowls and plates).

Providing for imaginative play outdoors

The home area outside is a den. Children at home enjoy playing in outside dens.

- Old furniture can be used outside to make a home area. An old airer (clothes horse) with a sheet or blanket over it makes good walls.
- Children can make pretend food using sand, water and messy materials.
- A rug can be put in the den and furniture can be made by collecting spare cardboard boxes (e.g. they can become tables or beds for dolls).
- Cushions can make seats or beds.
- A box on its side can become a cupboard with flaps as the cupboard doors.
- Cups and saucers can be made out of old yoghurt pots and margarine containers.

Safety

- Wooden equipment should be checked regularly for rough edges and splinters.
- Cutlery must be carefully introduced. Ask your supervisor for advice.
- Glass and china break easily and should not be used in the home area.

Figure 3.2.1 Playing in the home area

Plan an imaginative play activity

Most imaginative play is *child-initiated* and your role will be mostly as an observer and facilitator. Often children gravitate towards the home area and begin to act out roles in their play. Make sure there is a wide variety of play props, such as the dressing-up clothes, small world props and home area resources described above, and encourage children to develop their own play scenarios. Observe the play and evaluate it.

Planning for sensory play

All settings should provide a variety of sensory play activities, to include sand and water play – both indoors and outdoors, play dough, and play with a variety of malleable materials.

AC 1.2 Differentiate planned play opportunities to meet children's individual needs in own setting in relation to current frameworks

Principles influencing early years curriculum frameworks in the UK

1 The best way to prepare children for their adult life is to give them a happy childhood which meets their needs and builds on their interests.
2 Children are whole people who have feelings, ideas, relationships involving a sense of self and others, a sense of awe and wonder; they need to be emotionally, physically and morally healthy.
3 Children do not learn in neat and tidy compartments. Everything new that they learn links with everything they have already learnt.
4 Children learn best when they are respected and helped to be autonomous, active learners.
5 Self-discipline is emphasised as the only kind of discipline worth having. Children need their efforts to be valued in their own right.
6 There are times when children are especially able to learn particular things.
7 What children can do (rather than what children cannot do) is the starting point for a child's learning.
8 There are many different kinds of symbolic behaviour. These show the inner thoughts, feelings and ideas of the child, through the way they draw paint, make things, dance, sing, talk/sign, enjoy making stories, mark-make or pretend play. The Italian educator Malaguzzi called this the 'hundred languages' of children.
9 Relationships with other people are central to a child's emotional and social well-being, and in opening up their possibilities for an intellectual life and a sense of a fulfilled life.
10 A good education is about the child, the context in which development and learning take place, and the knowledge and understanding which evolve as part of the child's learning journey.

(Bruce, 2010)

Differentiating planned play opportunities

When planning activities for children you should remember to include all children. See Unit 2.3 for legislation relating to equality, diversity and inclusive practice.

Rigid plans hold back learning: they do not meet the learning needs or develop the interests of individual children, and lead to an activity-based curriculum which does not help the group or individual children to develop and learn.

Planning begins with the observation of the child as a unique, valued and respected individual, with their own interests and needs. We could say this is all about getting to know the child, but further general planning is also necessary, because there is only so much that children can learn on their own. They need an environment that has been carefully thought through, plus the right help from adults in using that environment. This aspect of planning ensures that the learning environment indoors and outdoors is balanced in what it offers, so that it helps all children in general, but also caters for individual children.

In this way, the curriculum:

- differentiates for individual children
- is inclusive and embraces diversity
- offers experiences and activities which are appropriate for most children of the age range (the group), because it considers the social and cultural context and the biological aspects of children developing in a community of learning

- links with the requirements of legally framed curriculum documents (which include the first three points).

Many early years settings now focus on particular children on particular days. This means that every child is observed regularly, and the curriculum is planned in a **differentiated** way to cater for the interests and needs of individual children.

Key term

differentiation Altering and adapting the way in which activities are presented to children to enable them to access them and to make progress.

The importance of differentiation

As not all children learn in the same way, there will be differences in their progress. For instance, some children understand and remember well if they *see* something. Others need to be more actively involved to make good progress. If a child is making slow progress when being taught in the same way as the rest of the group, staff should try other ways through differentiation to help them succeed. This can mean any or all of the following:

- providing activities at a more basic and simple level
- changing ways of teaching that match the child's way of learning
- moving the child into a small group
- giving different support through a key person
- breaking down complicated information into small steps.

Most children learn in a rather uneven way: they have bursts of learning, and then they have plateaux when their learning does not seem to move forward but they are actually consolidating their learning during this time. This is why careful **observation** and **assessment for learning** of individual children, plus a general knowledge of child development, are very important.

Activity

How does your setting differentiate planned play opportunities to meet the needs of each child?

AC 1.3 Identify features of an environment which support children's play, learning and development

The things that matter most for supporting children's play, learning and development in the early years setting are:

- your relationship and communication with children, their families and the team of staff (that is, people)
- how you support the children in using core experiences and open-ended, continuous material provision, equipment and resources, both indoors and outdoors.

Children need:

- people who give them interesting and engaging experiences
- carefully considered and organised materials for indoors and outdoors
- to be greeted and made to feel welcome with their parent/carer as they arrive
- to be connected with their key person when they part from their parent/carer
- to feel physically, socially and emotionally safe, so that their intellectual lives open up as they relax and enjoy learning.

LO2 Be able to lead and support play opportunities

AC 2.1 Lead a planned play opportunity in own setting

Catching the right time for a particular part of learning during development is a skill, as is recognising the child's pace of learning. Children have their own personalities and moods. They are affected by the weather, the time of day, whether they need food, sleep or the toilet, the experiences they have, their sense of well-being, and their social relationships with children and adults.

Some of the richest learning comes from experiences of everyday living. Examples would be getting dressed, choosing what to do, going shopping, using what you have bought for cooking, using a recipe book, washing up, sharing a story or photographs

Guidelines: Encouraging children's active participation

- Even when an activity is adult-directed, it should always involve active participation by the children.
- Activities that have an 'end product' (e.g. a model or a special occasion card) must allow for children's experimentation and creativity so that each one is different and original.
- There is absolutely no value in directing every aspect of a task. You should not aim to have all the children's

work looking the same or 'perfect' (i.e. your idea of what the finished article should look like).
- Ownership is very important: children need to feel that their work is their own.
- What children learn from doing the activity – practical skills, understanding of materials, textures, sounds, and so on – is far more important than the finished article.
- Young children should also be able to choose whether or not to make a card or a model.

of shared events (visiting the park), laying the table, eating together, sorting the washing and washing clothes. It is a challenge to find ways of making this manageable for children to take part in with independence, but careful planning makes this both possible and enjoyable, and makes for a deep learning experience.

AC 2.2 Support children's participation in a planned play opportunity

Giving attention to children's play activities can range from being a passive observer through to being fully involved in their play. In a planned play opportunity, you need to ensure that each child is actively participating – and that each child is able to make his or own choices within the sphere of activity.

AC 2.3 Demonstrate how play opportunities provide a balance between child- and adult-led play

Adult-led activities are based on our own professional understanding of what we should teach young children and what experiences they should have.

Through **adult-led activities**, practitioners ensure that children are:

- introduced to new ideas
- provided with opportunities to develop their skills so that they experience all seven areas of learning and development in the EYFS.

Although this means that practitioners are in control of the teaching they are providing, what they cannot

have any control over is what young children are learning from these experiences.

Through **child-initiated activities**, children are able to:

- explore their own ideas
- play with resources, and
- use their imagination and creativity.

This is why it is so important to balance adult-led learning with child-initiated activities.

To provide high-quality experiences for young children, practitioners should aim for a balance of one-third adult-directed activities and one-third child-initiated activities. The other third of the time should ideally be taken up by child-initiated activities that are then picked up on and supported by an adult – these are opportunities for **sustained shared thinking** to take place.

Remember, you are planning the play environment. You are not planning the way in which children play in it. Children need to be able to initiate their own ideas in their play and to be spontaneous. This is only possible if the environment is set up to encourage play.

Case study

Planning the play environment

Some of the children visited the market and found it fascinating. Back at the setting, the staff set up a market in the garden, with stalls made of upturned cardboard boxes, and play props that were mainly boxes of stones, leaves, conkers, and so on. The children developed their own play, but the important thing was that they had materials such as paper bags to put stones and leaves into, when they pretended to be customers or stallholders.

Activity

Analyse your planned play activity and describe how it achieves a balance between adult-led learning with child-initiated activities.

AC 2.4 Encourage parents/carers to take an active role in children's play

Parents develop their own way of playing with their child which reflects their culture and personal preferences. It is important to consult parents and carers about these ideas and preferences. This involves respecting their decisions and acknowledging them as being the people who know their child best. Practitioners can then use this knowledge to plan play for children in the setting. Some ways of involving parents in the planning process include:

- **organising information sessions** to explain the ethos underpinning the provision of a rich play environment
- **talking with parents** about their own preferences relating to children's play
- **providing a forum for parents**: this allows parents to give feedback on the play opportunities offered and to help shape the planning process

- **planning a workshop for parents**: this could be related to a specific play activity, such as woodworking or cooking.

LO3 Review how planned play opportunities contribute to own practice

AC 3.1 Evaluate how a planned play opportunity meets children's play, learning and developmental needs

Quality learning takes place when you are able to match what is offered in the curriculum to the interests and needs of individual children. Effective teaching means helping children to learn, so that they make connections with what they already know, and at times are helped to extend this.

Bear these factors in mind when you plan – quality is more likely to result. If you can help children to enjoy learning, you will have given them a good start, which they will take with them through their lives. Both the adult and the child contribute actively when the curriculum is of high quality.

When children feel their efforts are appreciated and celebrated, they learn more effectively. If adults only praise and recognise results (**products of learning**), children are more likely to lose heart and become less motivated to learn. See Unit 3.8 for more advice on planning.

In practice activity

Devise a short questionnaire to give to all parents new to the setting. Keep it simple and try to include the following ideas:

- What sort of games and activities does your child enjoy?
- What sort of things do you enjoy doing with your child?

- Are there any activities you would like to be offered to your child?
- Would you be willing to participate in any play activities, such as reading, cooking, or painting?
- Collate the answers and provide feedback, either individually or using the Parents' noticeboard to keep everyone informed.

Activity

Planning for play and learning

Look at the following list of activities:

sand play	dressing up	outdoor game
board game	poetry	making music
painting	clay	role play
home play	ring (or circle) game	songs
story telling	modelling	dough
natural materials play	water play	drama activity/ mime
cooking	listening game	finger rhymes
drawing	adventure playground	table-top game with rules

1 Choose **one** of the following age ranges:
   - one to two years
   - two to four years
   - four to seven years.
2 Select **three** of the listed activities that you have identified as particularly appropriate for that age range.
3 For **each** of the **three** activities describe:
   - what equipment and resources you would provide
   - the health and safety aspects you would need to consider
   - how you would set up the activity and the immediate environment
   - what the children will actually be doing and what experiences you want them to have
   - what language you would want to encourage or introduce; for example, new vocabulary – names of objects and/or descriptive terms, such as hot/cold, wet/dry, etc.)
   - how your activity will support and stimulate the play
   - how the activity meets the individual needs of the children
   - how you will provide for different cultural backgrounds
   - how you will provide for children who have particular needs.

AC 3.2 Reflect on how a planned play opportunity relates to current frameworks

The EYFS stipulates that the learning environment should provide opportunities for both indoor and outdoor play which will enable young children to:

- select and use activities and resources with help as per own request
- take turns and share resources with appropriate support as required
- talk to other children when playing together, including initiate conversations
- play cooperatively in a group, for example, demonstrate friendly behaviour
- form positive relationships with peers and familiar adults
- move confidently in a range of ways, for example, safely negotiating space when playing racing and chasing games, adjusting speed or changing direction to avoid obstacles
- handle tools effectively for the purpose, including mark-making.

Reflective practice

How a planned play opportunity relates to current frameworks

Reflect on an activity that you have planned and implemented, and describe how your activity relates to each of the requirements of the EYFS framework, described above.

AC 3.3 Analyse own role in relation to planned play opportunities

It is very difficult for children when adults do not stay in one place for long enough for children to engage with them in focused ways. It does not encourage children to focus either. Children usually like to feel that an adult is nearby; it makes them feel safe and secure, especially when they are trying something new and unfamiliar. The first time glue is used or paint is mixed are good examples of this. It is important not to crowd, overwhelm or invade a child's thinking space, but it is vital to support a child's learning by being there for them, smiling and looking interested, and commenting on what they do from time to time; for example, 'You like red best, I think, because I've noticed that you have used it three times in your painting so far.'

It is a good idea, as part of planning the curriculum framework in the learning environments indoors and outdoors, to see where there might need to be *anchored adults* working in depth with children. The following points are important:

- The anchored adult needs to sit at the child's height or on the floor, so as to give full attention to a child or children in one area, while retaining an overview of the rest of the room.
- The practitioner must be free to focus on what the children in a particular area are doing

(such as playing with wooden blocks or in the movement corner) and be able to have engaging conversations: listening to what children say and being sensitive to what they do, allowing them plenty of time (such as when cooking together or planting bulbs in the garden).

- Another adult must be free to help children generally – for example, to deal with children's toilet needs, to hang up a painting or comfort a tearful child, or simply to respond to children who ask for help.
- If every adult has a clear understanding of their role in the team, it helps each practitioner to focus on the children and reduces the temptation to chat with other adults instead of engaging with the children.

Case study

Tuning in to children

Nadia (two years old) is exploring glue and its properties for the first time in her life. She is interested in the way in which the glue falls off the glue stick, and in the soggy mound of glue on the paper. She does not seem to be interested in the function of glue – to join things together. So, does she need to be using this expensive glue? She might gain just as much satisfaction from flour and water glue, which is cheaper. Does she need expensive paper to drip the glue onto? She might learn just as much if the glue is dripped onto newspaper.

It is important to respond sensitively once you have tuned in to a child. Evaluate your practice in relation to this case study. Discuss this in a small group, then take action and try out (implement) the ideas in your practice. In the example explored in the case study, you could consider the following points:

- Always have different kinds of glue available in the workshop. You could offer Nadia flour and water

glue in an attractive pot, showing her how she can use it by demonstrating. Chat about the flour glue.
- When the paper is very soggy, and Nadia wants to continue but it is beginning to flow off the table, replace the paper with newspaper. Chat as you do so, saying you think this might help Nadia to carry out her idea of dripping the glue on the paper.
- Chatting is important in developing communication – not too much, not too little. Give Nadia key words but in sentences, such as, 'This newspaper will be better, I think, for you to drip your flour glue onto. Let's try it out, shall we?' Nadia might well echo, 'Try it out, shall we.'
- Chatting is especially important for children with English as an additional language (EAL) and for children with special educational needs (SEN).
- By tuning in to what Nadia finds interesting about this activity, you can engage further with her and help develop your practice.

Case study

Developing expertise in the block play area

Some children spend a great deal of time in a particular area, every day. Monty has a favourite – block play. It is important to encourage this, so that he will be able to become a specialist in this area. Help him to develop his skill, making bridges, roofs, walls, and so on. Monty likes to focus on his play for a long time.

Unless practitioners observe and tune in to children, they often find their actions and behaviour a worry, when

all the child needs is the right kind of support to get the most out of the learning environment, indoors and outdoors.

- In a small group, discuss how you are helping children.
- What more can you do to support and extend their learning? Children do not know how to use glue, wooden blocks and so on, unless they feel supported and are given the right sort of help, in the right way, at the right time.

Case study

Flitting from one thing to the next?

Hayley comes into the garden. She goes to the two-wheeler bikes with no pedals and rides one to the end of the garden. Then she runs to the watering can and picks it up. She walks around with it, drops it on the path and runs to the practitioner who is putting up the sun umbrella. She looks up at its spokes, standing underneath it. Then she goes to the outdoor sandpit, and chooses to play with the wheel, tipping dry sand in and flicking it with her hand as the sand spins round in it. She takes the sand wheel to the water pump and puts it under the spout, pumping water into it and watching it turn.

Hayley seems to be flitting from one thing to the next, yet everything she has chosen to do has the same pattern in it: everything has a core and radials coming out of it – the spokes on the bicycle wheels, the spout on the watering can, the spokes on the umbrella, the sand wheel, which becomes the waterwheel. The researcher Chris Athey would say that she is 'fitting', not 'flitting'. (For more information on Athey and sustained shared thinking, go to page 333.)

- How should the practitioner respond? Discuss this in a small group, then implement one of your ideas in your practice and evaluate your own practice. What do you need to remember next time?
- Perhaps Hayley would like to be offered similar objects with a core and radials, to broaden her experience.
- The practitioner could have a chat with her as she moves from one thing to another, helping her to build her vocabulary about core and radial objects and what they do (their function).
- The practitioner could take photos of all the objects and make a book of these, calling it 'Hayley's interesting objects'.

- Sometimes it might appear that children are stuck in their play, because they stay doing something for a long time; it might even appear to be obsessive.

Tuning in to children

The following case studies look at three different children. When the practitioner tunes in to each one, we can see that they all have completely different needs. Responding to each child individually is part of creating a rich learning environment indoors and outdoors.

AC 3.4 Make recommendations for the next stage of children's learning and development in relation to planned play opportunities

Using assessment to inform future planning

In order to plan for what is often called the child's 'learning journey', early years practitioners need to develop an understanding of:

- what children know
- the skills they have developed
- the attitudes they have towards learning, and
- the interests they have.

Sharing information

In addition to building this knowledge, practitioners need to share information gained from observation and assessment to:

- inform their future planning
- group children for particular activities and interests
- ensure that the curriculum meets the needs of all children
- promote continuity and progression.

Information should be shared between the setting and the home, so that a holistic picture of the child's needs, preferences and skills emerges. Parents have important information about their child's competence at home which will help practitioners to plan for their next stage of learning.

Reflective practice

Research shows that children develop and learn through their play and the first-hand experiences they are offered by adults who are interested in what they do, and who support and extend their learning. Children benefit from the relationships and companionship they find with other children. However, none of this can happen if the conditions are not favourable: the role of the adult is crucial in creating, maintaining and planning the general environment.

1 How can I take more account of children's home, social and cultural experiences when planning for play?
2 What types of play opportunities am I providing for the children inside and outside?
3 What themes, aims and learning goals am I supporting through the planned play opportunities?
4 How do I find out the level of engagement that children show in adult-led activities?

Assessment practice

1 Draw up a template for the plans you will be creating to provide play opportunities. Use this format to help you with all your planning.
2 Create a plan for play opportunities for (a) physical play; (b) creative play; (c) imaginative play; and (d) sensory play.
3 Describe how you would differentiate planned activities to meet individual needs.
4 Describe the features of an environment which support children's play, learning and development.
5 Lead a planned play opportunity in your own setting and support children's participation in this.
6 Why is it important to provide a balance of adult-led and child-initiated activities?

7 What can you do to encourage parents/carers to take an active role in children's play?
8 Evaluate how a planned play opportunity meets the play, learning and developmental needs of children.
9 How do the planned play opportunities in your setting relate to the current frameworks for learning?
10 What is meant by 'tuning in to children'?
11 Analyse your own role in relation to planned play opportunities.
12 What information would you gather to enable you to make recommendations for the next stage of children's learning?

Useful resources

Organisation

5x5x5creativity – this is an independent, arts-based action research organisation and has been influenced by the work in Reggio Emilia in Italy: www.5x5x5creativity.org.uk

Books and journals

Brooker, E. (2002), *Starting School: Young Children Learning Cultures*. Maidenhead: Open University Press.

Bruce, T. (1996), *Helping Young Children to Play*. London: Hodder & Stoughton.

Bruce, T. (2004), *Developing Learning in Early Childhood*. London: Paul Chapman Publishing.

Bruce, T. (2009), 'Learning through Play: Froebelian Principles and their Practice Today', *Early Childhood Practice: The Journal for Multi-professional Partnerships* 10(2): 58–73.

Bruce, T. (ed.) (2010), *Early Childhood: A Guide for Students* (2nd edn). London: Sage.

Kalliala, M. (2006), *Play Culture in a Changing World*. Oxford: Oxford University Press.

Langer, E. (1997), *The Power of Mindful Learning*. Harlow: Addison-Wesley.

Matthews, J. (2003), *Drawing and Painting: Children and Visual Representation* (2nd edn). London: Paul Chapman Publishing Ltd.

Ouvry, M. (2004), *Sounds like Playing: Music in the Early Years Curriculum*. London: BAECE/Early Education.

Sylva, K., Melhuish, E., Sammons, P., Siraj-Blatchford, I. and Taggart, B. (2004), *The Effective Provision of Pre-School Education (EPPE) Project: Final Report*. London: DfES/Institute of Education, University of London.

Unit 3.3 Apply theoretical perspectives and philosophical approaches to play

This unit provides the learner with underpinning knowledge of theories and philosophical approaches to how children play. It also provides the learner with the skills required to apply learning to their own practice.

Learning outcomes

By the end of this unit you will:

1 Understand theoretical perspectives which support play.
2 Understand philosophical approaches which influence play provision.
3 Be able to apply theoretical knowledge in own practice.
4 Be able to apply philosophical approaches in own practice.
5 Be able to review how theoretical perspectives and philosophical approaches to play contribute to own practice.

LO1 Understand theoretical perspectives which support play

AC 1.1 Identify theories which influence play

Throughout history, there have always been people who have been prepared to stand up and fight for what young children need. They are the pioneers who help everyone working with young children, past and present, to move forward. Theories about play are influenced by thinkers from the past and thinkers from around the world. A theory is something that helps us to explain and answer 'Why?' It helps us to look at the role of play in a child's development. The different theories of play emphasise different aspects. They all help us to learn more about children's play.

Jan Amos Comenius (1592–1670)

This Moravian educator and bishop anticipated some of the ideas of Friedrich Froebel (see below) by a century. He believed that children learn through the senses and through real, first-hand experiences. He thought that teachers should try to make learning interesting and enjoyable, and that learning by doing and helping children to play was part of this. He thought play was important because what children learnt through their play they would use later in life. In his book, *The Great Didactic*, published in Amsterdam in 1649 (the year Charles I was executed in England), Comenius emphasised movement and exercise; he believed that giving children interesting, real and play experiences was the key to education, and that children should understand the reasons for rules.

Friedrich Froebel (1782–1852)

Before theories about play were established, Froebel pioneered the view that play acts as a way of bringing together and organising learning. (It is sometimes called an **integrating mechanism**.) Play helps children to use what they know, to apply their knowledge and understanding as they think, have ideas and feelings, relate to people and be confident in their physical bodies. He thought that play helps children to show their deepest possible levels of learning. Play helps children to understand themselves, others and the universe. Froebel's influence is discussed in greater depth on p 285.

Karl Groos (1861–1946)

Groos wrote a book called *The Play of Animals* in 1898. He believed that play is a way for children to run off excess energy, but, more importantly, that play is preparation for later life, as it gives children opportunities to practise skills they will need later.

Johan Huizinga (1872–1945)

The Dutch cultural historian saw play within an evolutionary framework. This was because he said that animals inhabited the earth before humans did, and animals play, so this means that play is older than human culture. In 1938, Huizinga wrote a book called *Homo Ludens*, which translates as *Man the Player*. In it, he argues that play gives children freedom, and experiences that are more than their ordinary, real lives, beyond their local space and time. He said that play gives children a sense of order. No financial profit is gained from play.

Anna Freud (1895–1982)

Anna was the daughter of Sigmund Freud, who pioneered the idea of psychoanalysis. She was a teacher and a trained therapist. Anna Freud thought it was important to observe children at play, and to see how they use play to move in and out of reality, experimenting in this way with their feelings. Play is a self-healing process, and supports children in sorting out their feelings and learning to manage them. Anna Freud did not think that many children would need specialist therapeutic help, although some would. The most important thing is that children have a childhood in which they are loved, with clear boundaries and opportunities for natural play.

Lev Vygotsky (1896–1934)

Vygotsky thought that play creates a 'zone of potential development', in which children are able to function at their highest level of learning. He suggested that it is as if children become a 'head taller than they really are'. He valued imaginative play, so did not focus so much on play before the toddler age when that emerges. In his view, play creates a way of freeing children from the constraints of everyday life. Vygotsky believed that social relationships are at the heart of a child's learning, so his theory is called a social constructivist theory. (Also see Unit 3.2 for information on Goldschmeid and explanation of heuristic play.)

Donald Winnicott (1896–1971)

Winnicott developed his understanding of play through pioneering the idea of the transitional object. This can be a substitute for someone important to the child emotionally when that person is not present. Alternatively, it can help a child to enjoy the presence of someone they love who *is* present.

Transitional objects work in two ways: they make a healthy and natural link with those people the child loves – for example, teddy stands for the father who goes to work but returns; but teddy also has

an imaginative life, taking meals with the child, sleeping together and having adventures together.

Jean Piaget (1896–1980)

Piaget believed that play was just for pleasure, and while it allowed children to practise things they had previously learnt, it did not necessarily result in the learning of new things. In other words, play reflects what the child has already learnt but does not necessarily teach the child anything new. For Piaget, play is about keeping balanced. He thought this had two aspects:

- **accommodation** – adapting to a situation
- **assimilation** – confirming what you already know through your experiences.

Play is mainly to do with assimilation, using what is known, familiar and understood. It is about applying what has already been learnt. Play provides a relaxed atmosphere in which learning can easily occur. However, play is not the same as learning; cognitive development requires both assimilation and adaptation, while play is assimilation without accommodation.

Piaget thought there were two aspects to play, in a developmental sequence: sensory and movement play, and then imagination, pretend and symbolic play. In middle childhood, play increasingly turns into games with rules. For more information on Piaget's theories, see Unit 3.10.

Erik Erikson (1902–94)

Erikson was a student of Anna Freud. He thought that children are partners in their futures. In his view, children deal with difficult experiences by creating an ideal situation, which they then master and control. This helps them into their future lives.

Jerome Bruner (1915–)

Bruner suggests that children need a long childhood because there is so much for them to learn in preparation for their lives as adults. They learn about the technical aspects of life and about their culture. Bruner believed that:

- play is a tool for children to develop intellectually
- creating an imaginative play situation is seen as an opportunity to develop **abstract thinking skills**

- play in early childhood is the main way in which children experiment freely and learn to do this, and through which they are initiated into the culture
- children play with objects provided and chosen by adults, and by 'doing' (Bruner calls this **enactive learning**). They learn the rules of games from people who teach them as they play together, and they become familiar with the rules of the culture through their play.

Mildred Parten (1916–2009)

Mildred Parten was a sociologist who observed children in the first half of the twentieth century and discovered that children of different ages actually played together differently.

Parten's **stage theory of play** describes the ways children interact with each other:

- **Solitary independent play**: children play alone with objects without interacting with others even when they are near.
- **Parallel play**: children playing side by side with similar toys – next to each other, but not with each other.
- **Associative play**: children play with each other, but there is no particular goal or organisation to their play.
- **Cooperative play**: children cooperate with others to create play situations, with each child in the group playing an assigned role.

Parents and early years practitioners see mostly parallel and associative play with toddlers, although cooperative play emerges for most children by the end of this period.

Tina Bruce: the twelve features of play

Quite often practitioners will observe children at play, and will have a sense that this is a rich play scenario. But this does not help the adult to say why. The twelve features of play (see below) are often used to help practitioners share the importance of their children's play with parents and with other practitioners. Free-flow play arises out of the twelve features of play. Play will have low status unless practitioners can help parents and colleagues to see how richly it helps children to develop and learn.

If seven or more of the twelve features are present, then it is probably a rich play scenario. If only a few of the features are present, it does not necessarily mean that the child is not doing something worthwhile, but it may not be play. When you have read the next section, then observe a child at play and identify the features of play that are present. Is this rich play?

The twelve features of play are as follows:

1 Children use real, **first-hand experiences** in their play (such as going to the shops, preparing food).
2 Children have a sense of control when they play, and they begin to make up **rules** (the dog must be fed and his plate must be here, on the floor, because I say so). Children feel powerful when they play.
3 Children find, use and **make play props** when they play. This is creative, as they use things in flexible and new ways. It is imaginative as they rearrange their experiences to suit the play.
4 Children **choose to play**. No one can make a child play.
5 When children play, they sometimes **rehearse the future**, for example in their role play, when they pretend to be adults.
6 Children might **pretend** when they play – that they are the goodies chasing the baddies, for example. They organise their thinking, transforming it as they do so.
7 Children might choose to **play alone**, needing some personal space and time to reflect and try out an idea they have, for example with their small world garage.
8 They might **play with other children**, in parallel, associatively or cooperatively.
9 When children play they have a **personal play agenda**. They might want to put pretend jam on all the pretend cakes, or bath the dog. They will find a way to carry this out. Adults are welcome to play with children, providing everyone respects each other's personal play agenda.
10 Children involved in rich play become deeply **involved**, and are difficult to distract. Children wallow in their play.

11 Children **show us their latest learning when they play**. They might have just mastered riding a bicycle, and so in their play they keep riding their bike to post a letter, to go to the shops, to take their child to school … as long as they are on their bike!

12 **Play brings together the learning** children do. It organises the learning, so that it becomes connected and an integrated whole.

Janet Moyles' play spiral

This approach to play argues that children need play materials first (she gives the example of a plastic construction kit) so that children can explore freely. Then the adult demonstrates how to make a box with the materials, and discusses this with the children, who also make boxes. Children are then left free to use the kit without the adult and will, in Moyles' observations, use the adult's teaching in their free play. The adult is either directly teaching and showing, or leaving children without adult presence, to use materials in their own way.

Bob Hughes: a taxonomy of play types

Bob Hughes, a leading play theorist and practitioner in the UK, suggests that there are at least 16 different play types, displayed by children as they play. These play types help to provide playworkers and other practitioners with a common language for describing play:

1 **Communication play**: play using words, nuances or gestures – for example, mime/charades, jokes, play acting, mickey-taking, singing, whispering, pointing, debate, street slang, poetry, text messages, talking on mobiles, emails or internet, skipping games, group and ball games.

2 **Creative play**: play which allows a new response, the transformation of information, awareness of new connections, with an element of surprise. It allows children to design, explore, try out new

Figures 3.3.1 and 3.3.2 Note the storage of the equipment. The transparent boxes allow children to see what is in them. The flooring is flat enough for building with wooden blocks. The children are allowed to fetch cars, planes etc. to use with the blocks, because the two areas are next to each other. Perhaps these children are interested in up and under: the vehicle is under the bridge they have built. The plane is held up in the air. The boys are using their knowledge and experience of aeroplanes. They are very involved in their play (wallowing in it). They are playing cooperatively. They have chosen to play, and they have selected play props. They are pretending, and have created a play scenario, using their ideas (their play agenda).

ideas and use their imagination. It involves the enjoyment of creation with a range of materials and tools, texture and form, for its own sake, with freedom to mix and make whatever you wish without the necessity for an end result.

3 **Deep play**: play which allows the child to encounter risky or even potentially life-threatening experiences, to develop survival skills and conquer fear. For example, lighting fires with matches, making weapons and conquering fear such as heights, snakes, and creepy crawlies. Some find strength they never knew they had to climb obstacles, lift large objects, etc.; for example, leaping onto an aerial runway, riding a bike on a parapet, balancing on a high beam, roller skating, assault course, high jump.

4 **Dramatic play**: play which dramatises events in which the child is not a direct participator; for example, presentation of a television show, an event on the street, a religious or festive event, even a funeral.

5 **Exploratory play**: play to access factual information consisting of manipulative behaviours such as handling, throwing, banging or mouthing objects; for example, engaging with an object or area and, either by manipulation or movement, assessing its properties, possibilities and content – such as stacking bricks.

6 **Fantasy play**: this is the make-believe world of children. This type of play is where the child's imagination gets to run wild. Fantasy play rearranges the world in a way that is unlikely to occur. For example, playing at being a pilot flying around the world; pretending to be various characters/people; to be wherever they want to be; to drive a car, to become be six feet nothing tall or as tiny as they want to be … the list is endless, as is a child's imagination.

7 **Imaginative play**: play where the conventional rules, which govern the physical world, do not apply. For example, imagining you are …, or pretending to be a tree or ship, or patting a dog, which is not there.

8 **Locomotor play**: movement in any or every direction for its own sake – for example, chase, tag, hide-and-seek, tree climbing.

9 **Mastery play**: control of the physical and affective ingredients of the environments; for example, digging holes, changing the course of streams, constructing shelters, and building fires.

10 **Object play**: play which uses infinite and interesting sequences of hand–eye manipulations and movements; for example, examination and novel use of any object, such as cloth, paintbrush or cup.

11 **Recapitulative play**: play that allows the child to explore ancestry, history, rituals, stories, rhymes, fire and darkness. This enables children to access play of earlier human evolutionary stages.

12 **Role play**: play exploring ways of being, although not normally of an intense personal, social, domestic or interpersonal nature; for example, brushing with a broom, dialling with a telephone, driving a car.

13 **Rough-and-tumble play**: close-encounter play, which is less to do with fighting and more to do with touching, tickling and gauging relative strength – discovering physical flexibility and the exhilaration of display. This type of play allows a child to participate in physical contact that does not involve or result in someone being hurt. This type of play can use up lots of energy.

14 **Social play**: play during which the rules and criteria for social engagement and interaction can be revealed, explored and amended; for example, any social or interactive situation which contains an expectation on all parties that they will abide by the rules or protocols, i.e. games, conversations, making something together.

15 **Socio-dramatic play**: the enactment of real and potential experiences of an intense personal, social, domestic or interpersonal nature; for example, playing at house, going to the shops, being mothers and fathers, organising a meal or even having a row.

16 **Symbolic play**: play that allows control, gradual exploration and increased understanding without the risk of being out of one's depth. It could be playing with a piece of wood and using it as a sword, using string as a fishing line, making signs and marks as a code or making signs or noises as a language.

(Hughes, 2002)

Recent studies in neuroscience

The repetitive nature of play helps shape and builds networks in children's brains which they will use for other things. Children learn through play that involves them doing things themselves:

- using and expanding the knowledge they have through trying
- working out problems
- imagining and pretending
- talking and negotiating with others
- reasoning and explaining.

Recent research shows that children do not develop as if they are climbing up a ladder. Instead, brain studies show that their play develops like a network. In relation to stage theories, for example, sometimes children will play alone (solitary play). Sometimes they will play with others (parallel, associatively or cooperatively). These aspects of play are discussed in Unit 3.1.

Discussion point

Now that you have read about the different pioneers and theories of play, choose the two theories that you most agree with. In a small group, discuss the different theories and say what attracts you to the two theories you have chosen. Can you find a key message about which all these pioneers and theorists agree?

AC 1.2 Summarise how theories impact on own understanding of play

Activity

Look again at Tina Bruce's twelve features of play detailed on p 280. For each of the features, write a brief summary of how you have observed this in relation to children's play in your settings.

How have the theories you have read about in this unit impacted on your understanding of play?

Research activity

Find out more about:

- Janet Moyles' play spiral
- Bob Hughes' play types.

AC 1.3 Analyse how theoretical perspectives on play inform practice

Ideas about play from around the world

In Western Europe and the USA, children are often given toys to play with. Sometimes these are very expensive to buy. In other countries, specially designed toys may not be part of the way of life, and children will play mainly with natural materials, such as stones, twigs, sand, water and mud, and make their own pretend play.

In some cultures, adults think it is not a good idea to play with children. They let children play together and older children play with younger children (for example, Maori children in New Zealand). Other cultures believe that adults (usually mothers) ought to play with their children and teach them through their play.

How children become involved in their play and activities

Some theories emphasise the importance of childhood play because it encourages children to practise things they need to do later on in life. It helps them with the physical coordination of their bodies, objects and people.

Learning through practice play

There are two sides to practice play.

1 The biological side of practice play: studies of young animals playing show that, for example, lion cubs playing together quite naturally begin catching and chewing. This helps them to learn what they need to know later in order to hunt for their food and survive.
2 The social/cultural aspect of practice play: even newborn babies are very aware of other people. Children imitate people who are important role models for them.

The importance of play in supporting all aspects of development

Theories about the way that play progresses as children grow older help adults to plan appropriate play materials and play opportunities for different children according to their stage of development.

This is called knowing about **progression** in the development of play.

Play, feelings and self-esteem

There is a popular idea that learning through play means always having fun. Certainly, children will have plenty of fun as they learn through play. However, children also learn about sad and angry feelings. They are challenged to learn about difficult things such as:

● death
● being separated from people they love
● being hurt.

Some theories emphasise the importance of children's feelings. These are 'psychoanalytic' ideas about why children play. The play scenarios children create deal with their feelings of happiness, sadness, anger, and so on, in an emotionally healthy way. Although this helps any child, therapists particularly emphasise sad and angry feelings through play for the children they work with. Research shows that emotional health is helped through play, and leads to children developing positive self-esteem and resilience.

Play helps socially acceptable behaviour

Other theories show that children learn to think of others through their play. They learn to behave in ways that are socially acceptable as they play. This helps them to understand how other people feel and to develop morally (to value and respect others, and to care about other people). This is called **theory of mind**.

Play helps thinking and ideas (concepts) to develop

There are three important theories about how play helps children to have ideas and learn to think. They are all useful for adults working with young children. Two of these theories emphasise social/cultural learning.

Both Vygotsky's and Bruner's theories show that other people are important in developing a child's play.

1 Vygotsky found that children do their best thinking when they play with others. This is because play helps them to feel in **control** of their ideas, and to make sense of things that have happened. Play helps children to **think ahead**.

2 Bruner believes that play helps children to learn how adults do things in their culture. Adults observe children as they play and break things down into easily manageable steps for them. This is called **scaffolding the learning**.

3 Piaget's theory emphasised both biology and social/cultural learning, and is the most famous theory. Piaget emphasised that children are active learners. They learn through their senses (seeing, touching, hearing, smelling, tasting) and through their own movement.

● Sometimes children will play alone.
● Sometimes they will play with others (children or adults).
● Children are like scientists, exploring their world and working at different levels about the world.
● Children go through stages of play. Although each of the stages builds on the one before, they also overlap. Modern research shows some children do things earlier, and some later, than others.

Play and the development of conversation skills

Children experiment with language during play and use words to express their thoughts and ideas, to solve problems and to communicate their wishes.

Play and the development of physical coordination

Children vary, and develop at different rates. This depends partly on their biological stage. It also depends on where they grow up and what play opportunities and materials they are given. A child who has played with wooden blocks since toddler times might well be building towers that are castles by the age of four years. A child who has not had these experiences is unlikely to do this.

This shows that what children learn is influenced by how adults help their development. This is why *observing children* as they play is important, especially if they have disabilities.

LO2 Understand philosophical approaches which influence play provision

AC 2.1 Identify philosophical approaches which influence play provision

The following theorists all believed in integrated early years provision – that is, combining the two functions of care and education in one integrated service. This has a long and respected heritage, and the greatest influence in the UK from the nineteenth century has been that of Friedrich Froebel. Other theorists and philosophical perspectives include Susan Isaacs, Maria Montessori, Margaret McMillan, Rudolf Steiner, Reggio Emilia, Forest schools and Te Whariki.

Friedrich Froebel (1782–1852)

Friedrich Froebel was a forester and mathematician, and was the first person to write about the importance of play in development and learning. He started a community school where parents were welcome at any time. His staff were trained to observe and value children's play. Below is a summary of his beliefs and findings:

- It is important to talk with parents and learn with them how to help children learn through their play.
- He designed a set of wooden blocks (gifts), which are still used in early years settings today. He also designed many other kinds of play equipment (occupations) and movement games (action songs and finger-play rhymes and dancing) through which children learn by doing.
- Relationships with other children are as important as relationships with adults, and he had a strong belief in the value of imaginative and symbolic play.
- Froebel encouraged pretend play and play with other children.

- Both indoor and outdoor play are important.
- He helped children to make dens in the garden and to play with natural materials such as sand, water and wood.
- Teachers should be sensitive and approachable, and have qualities that the children can respect and imitate.
- He called his schools 'kindergartens' (for children aged two to eight). This word means 'children's garden' in German. Even today there are kindergartens all over the world. Froebel has had a profound influence on early childhood education and care.

Research activity

Investigating Froebel's work

1 Research a set of wooden hollow blocks and wooden unit blocks (examples of these are made by Community Playthings). Can you find any mathematical relationships between the different blocks? Plan how you could help children to learn about shape, using wooden blocks. Implement your plan, and evaluate your observations with children of three to seven years of age.
2 Try to find 12 examples of finger rhymes. These are songs or rhymes using the fingers for actions. Make a book of them for children to enjoy. Make sure you include a multicultural range of action songs, and also think about children with disabilities. Share the book with a child of between two and seven years of age. Evaluate your observations.
3 Research what children did in kindergartens in the twentieth century – for example, each child had his or her own little garden.
4 Imagine that you are Friedrich Froebel today. What do you think he might like or dislike about your early years setting?

In practice activity

Plan how you will organise a garden activity. What equipment will you need? Where will you do this? How will you clear up?

- Plant some flowers or vegetables with children, and watch them grow.
- Observe a child of between two and seven years of age, and evaluate your garden activity in relation to that particular child's cognitive and language development.

Susan Isaacs (1885–1948)

Susan Isaacs, like Margaret McMillan (see below), was influenced by Froebel. She was also influenced by the theories of Melanie Klein, the psychoanalyst. Isaacs made detailed observations of children in her Malting House School in Cambridge during the 1930s. A summary of Isaacs' ideas:

- Isaacs valued play because she believed that it gave children freedom to think, feel and relate to others.
- She looked at children's fears, their aggression and their anger. She believed that, through their play, children can move in and out of reality. This enables them to balance their ideas, feelings and relationships.
- She said of classrooms where young children have to sit at tables and write that they cannot learn in such places because they need to move just as they need to eat and sleep.
- Isaacs valued parents as the most important educators in a child's life. She spoke to them on the radio, and she wrote for parents in magazines. In her book, *The Nursery Years*, she wrote:

If the child has ample opportunity for free play and bodily exercise, if this love of making and doing with his hands is met, if his interest in the world around him is encouraged by sympathy and understanding, if he is left free to make believe or think as his impulses take him, then his advances in skill and interest are but the welcome signs of mental health and vigour.

- Isaacs encouraged people to look at the inner feelings of children. She encouraged children to express their feelings. She thought it would be very damaging to bottle up feelings inside.
- She supported both Froebel's and McMillan's view that nurseries are an extension of the home and not a substitute for it, and she believed that children should remain in nursery-type education until they are seven years of age.
- She kept careful records of children, both for the period they spent in her nursery and for the period after they had left. She found that many of them regressed when they left her nursery and went on to formal infant schools. Modern researchers have found the same.

Margaret McMillan (1860–1931)

Margaret McMillan (and her sister, Rachel) fought for the education of young children to emphasise physical care and development. They campaigned and were successful in introducing free school meals under the Provision of School Meals Act 1906, and they introduced regular medical inspections for school children by opening the first clinic especially devoted to school children in 1908. A summary of her beliefs:

- Children cannot learn if they are undernourished, poorly clothed, sick or ill with poor teeth, poor eyesight, ear infections, rickets, etc. (Recent reports emphasise that poor health and poverty are challenges still facing those who work with families in the UK today.)
- Children learn by exploring and achieve their whole potential through play; she placed an emphasis on craft and water activities, singing and model-making.
- Outdoor play and being taught in the fresh air are important; gardening was a regular activity.
- The importance of hygiene and cleanliness: parents should be educated about keeping their children clean and hygienic.
- The role of the 'home' in supporting a child's learning capability is very important.
- She stressed the importance of having trained teachers, and opened a special training school for the teachers in her schools. Children were taught in small groups, and McMillan expected teachers to be imaginative and inventive.
- A very close partnership with parents is essential: she encouraged parents to develop alongside their children, with adult classes in hobbies and languages made available to them.

The British nursery school, as envisaged by McMillan, has been admired and emulated across the world. McMillan Nursery schools have gardens, and are communities that welcome both parents and children.

Maria Montessori (1880–1952)

Maria Montessori was an Italian doctor who worked
in the poorest areas of Rome in the 1900s. She
did not believe that pretend play was important.
She thought children wanted to do real things, for
example, not *play* at being cooks but to actually
do some cooking. However, she did like Froebel's
play equipment, and she designed more (didactic
materials) to help them learn, for example, about
shapes, weight, colour, size and numbers. A
summary of her beliefs:

- All children have absorbent minds, and the
  way in which children learn is different from
  the way in which an adult learns. Children
  absorb information from the environment.
  Initially this learning is unconscious, but after
  the age of three the child absorbs information
  consciously. The ability to absorb language and
  to learn motor skills is initially without formal
  instruction, but later children use language to
  question.
- Children pass through sensitive periods during
  which they are particularly receptive to developing
  specific skills. A child will develop a particular
  interest in one specific skill or action, which they
  will repeat time and time again.
- Toys are not found in Montessori classrooms.
  Rather, they contain specially made learning
  equipment, which children use in specific ways.
  This equipment, known as 'didactic material',
  is designed to support children's expanding
  consciousness and to provide experiences for
  their current sensitivities; for example, response to
  colour, sound, touch, etc.
- Children should be guided by a trained adult
  to use the equipment until they can use it
  confidently on their own and independently.
- A Montessori teacher plays a very different role
  from that of a teacher in mainstream school

provision. The teacher, who is known as the
directress, is seen to guide or direct the children,
putting them in touch with their environment so
that they can learn for themselves.

Montessori called her schools Children's Houses,
and these are still to be found all over the world.

Rudolf Steiner (1861–1925)

Rudolf Steiner encouraged play through natural
materials, such as clay, beeswax, silk scarves for
dressing up and irregularly shaped wooden blocks.
The design of the child's environment is very
important; for example, the scale of the space should
not overwhelm a small child and so where possible
the ceilings are low, there are no 'hard' corners and
rooms are decorated in soft tones of pink to create a
gentle, secure feeling. A summary of his beliefs:

- Singing and dancing are important, and stories
  give children ideas for their play.
- Education is an artistic process. There must be a
  balance between artistic, creative and practical
  experiences on the one hand, and academic
  activities on the other.

Steiner schools do not provide **pre-structured
play environments** – for example, post offices,
launderettes or castles or ready-made toys. The
children arrive each morning into an open space,
where they may use the screens, the blocks, the
tables and the lengths of cloth to create their own
environments. Similarly, there are few objects that
represent the world outside the kindergarten: there
are no toy telephones or plastic play people.

Steiner believed that children pass through three
specific phases:

1 The **period of will** (birth to seven years) in which
  the active aspect predominates. Within this period
  there are three stages:
  - birth to three years – the main features are walking,
    speech and the ability to think in words

- three to five years – the development of the imagination and memory is important
- five years onwards – the stimulation for play tends to come less from external objects but more from ideas generated within the children.

2 The **period of the heart** (seven to 14 years): the feeling phase. The child is now ready for formal learning, although the role of the imagination is still very important.

3 The **period of the head** (14 years onwards): the cognitive phase. The adolescent stage is considered to be the period of thinking. At this stage children develop a healthy idealism, and may be very sensitive about their feelings.

Steiner's schools are now the largest independent school system in the world, with many of the schools situated in North America and Australia.

Research activity

Find out more about the Steiner schools in the UK. Visit the website: www.steinerwaldorf.org.uk

The Reggio Emilia approach

The Reggio Emilia approach to 'pre-school' education was started by the schools of the city of Reggio Emilia in Italy after the Second World War. There is much about Reggio Emilia's approach to childcare and education that distinguishes it from other efforts both inside and outside Italy, and attracts worldwide attention. All children are catered for – those with disabilities are considered to have 'special rights' rather than 'special needs'.

The key features of the Reggio Emilia approach are:

- **Community support and parental involvement**: the parents' role mirrors that of the community's, at both the school and classroom level. Parents are expected to take part in discussions about school policy, child development concerns, and curriculum planning and evaluation.

- **Administrative policies and organisational features**:
  - Every centre is staffed with two teachers per classroom (12 children in infant classes, 18 in toddler classes, and 24 in pre-primary classes).
  - Teachers are viewed as enthusiastic learners and researchers and not as imparters of knowledge. Each group of children has two teachers who remain with them throughout their time at school.
  - The role of the *atelierista* – a practising artist who supports the development of children's learning, creativity and imagination – is central to the Reggio approach. The *atelierista* works with classroom teachers in curriculum development and documentation, and several auxiliary staff.
  - There is no principal, nor is there a hierarchical relationship among the teachers.

- **The role of the environment**: the pre-schools are generally filled with indoor plants and vines, and awash with natural light. Classrooms open to a central piazza, kitchens are open to view, and access to the surrounding community is assured through wall-size windows, courtyards and doors to the outside in each classroom. Entrances capture the attention of both children and adults through the use of mirrors (on the walls, floors, and ceilings), photographs, and children's work accompanied by transcriptions of their discussions. These same features characterise classroom interiors, where displays of project work are interspersed with arrays of found objects and classroom materials, with clearly designated spaces for large- and small-group activities.

- **Long-term projects as vehicles for learning**: Teachers often work on projects with small groups of children, while the rest of the class engages in a wide variety of self-selected activities typical of pre-school classrooms. The topic of investigation may derive directly from teacher observations of children's spontaneous play and exploration. Projects begin with teachers observing and questioning children about the topic of interest. Based on children's responses, teachers introduce materials, questions and opportunities that provoke children to further explore the topic.

- **The hundred languages of children**: as children proceed in an investigation, generating and testing their hypotheses, they are encouraged to depict their understanding through one of many symbolic languages, including drawing, sculpture, dramatic play and writing. They work together towards the resolution of problems that arise. Teachers facilitate and then observe debates regarding the extent to which a child's drawing or other form of representation lives up to the expressed intent. Revision of drawings (and ideas) is encouraged, and teachers allow children to repeat activities and modify each other's work in the collective aim of better understanding the topic. Teachers foster children's involvement in the processes of exploration and evaluation, acknowledging the importance of their evolving products as vehicles for exchange.

In practice activity

Investigating different approaches

1 Research the different ways in which Froebel, Montessori and Steiner would:
   - introduce children to a set of wooden blocks, and
   - help children to use the blocks.
2 Implement each approach with a group of children in three separate sessions.
3 Evaluate your observations, noting the way in which your role as an early years practitioner changed according to which approach you used.
4 Note the differences in the way in which the children responded, especially in relation to creativity, language and play. Which approaches encouraged the child to be a symbol-user? Evaluate your observations.

Forest schools

The philosophy of Forest schools, which started in Denmark in 1950, is to encourage and inspire individuals of any age through positive outdoor experiences. Forest schools have demonstrated success with children of all ages who visit the same local woodlands on a regular basis, and through play have the opportunity to learn about the natural environment, how to handle risks and most importantly to use their own initiative to solve problems and cooperate with others. Forest school programmes run throughout the year for about 36 weeks, going to the woods in all weathers (except for high winds).

Forest schools aim to develop:

- a greater understanding of their own natural and man-made environments
- a wide range of physical skills
- social communication skills
- independence
- a positive mental attitude, self-esteem and confidence.

Te Whariki: New Zealand

Maori people and the Pakeha (white people) worked together to make the Te Whariki early childhood curriculum framework. This is based on four principles:

- empowerment (Whakamana)
- holistic development (Kotahitanga)
- family and community (Whanau Tangata)
- relationships (Nga Hononga).

It has five strands, each with its own goals:

1 **Well-being** (Mana Atua). *Goals*: to promote health; nurture emotional well-being; keep from harm.
2 **Belonging** (Mana Whenua). *Goals*: connecting links with the family and wider world are affirmed and extended; children know they have a place; they feel comfortable with the routines, customs and regular events; they know the limits and boundaries of acceptable behaviour.
3 **Contribution** (Mana Tangat). *Goals*: there are equitable opportunities for learning, irrespective of gender, ability, age, ethnicity or background; children are affirmed as individuals; they are encouraged to learn with and alongside others.
4 **Communication** (Mana Reo). *Goals*: children develop verbal and non-verbal communication skills for a range of purposes; they experience the stories and symbols of their own and other cultures; they discover and develop different ways to be creative and expressive.
5 **Exploration** (Mana Aoturoa). *Goals*: children's play is valued as meaningful learning, and the importance of spontaneous play is recognised; they gain confidence in and control of their bodies; they learn strategies for active exploration, thinking and reasoning; they develop working theories for making sense of the natural, social, physical and material worlds.

- How does the staffing of Reggio Emilia Schools differ from that of schools in the UK?
- What are the similarities between the principles of the Te Whariki curriculum and those of the EYFS?

AC 2.2 Summarise how philosophical approaches impact on own understanding of play provision

Activity

Consider each approach in turn and summarise how it impacts on your own understanding of play provision. In particular, think about the philosophy underpinning:

- Forest schools
- Steiner schools
- Montessori schools
- Reggio Emilia approach
- the Te Whariki early childhood curriculum.

AC 2.3 Analyse how philosophical approaches to play inform practice

Activity

In your own setting, choose different areas of play activity, and analyse ways in which different philosophical approaches inform practice.

LO3 Be able to apply theoretical knowledge in own practice

AC 3.1 Create a plan using theoretical perspectives on play to support the developmental stage and needs and interests of children aged: 0–5 years

Planning play to support the needs of babies from birth to 1 year 11 months

For very young babies – not yet sitting – think about the following ideas on which you could base your plan:

- exploring textures and sounds – using an activity mat and a range of materials and rattles and bells (Bruce, Bruner, Parten)
- providing a range of objects for babies to explore with their hands and mouths (Bruce, Parten).

Once a baby is able to sit unaided, you could choose to base your plan on:

- finger puppets and rhyming songs (Froebel, Bruce, Moyles, Hughes)
- heuristic play: using a treasure basket with carefully selected objects to promote holistic development (Goldschmied). See Unit 3.1 for more information on heuristic play.

For toddlers, you could choose to base your plan on:

- sand and water play (Piaget, Bruce, Parten)
- playing with balls – rolling, kicking and throwing, etc. (Hughes, Moyles)
- playing with things that screw and unscrew (Piaget, Hughes)
- puppet play and action rhymes (Froebel, Hughes, Bruce).

Planning play to support the needs of children from 2 to 2 years 11 months

Some ideas to plan for include:

- sand and water play (Piaget, Bruce, Parten)
- musical games (Bruce, Hughes, Bruner)
- matching and sorting games (Piaget)
- role play or pretend play (Bruce, Hughes)
- toys to ride and climb on (Piaget, Hughes, Bruner).

Planning play to support the needs of children from 3 to 5 years

Some ideas to plan for include:

- sand and water play (Piaget, Bruce, Parten)
- active pretend play with other children (Bruce, Parten, Moyles)
- creative play (Hughes, Bruce, Moyles)
- playing with dough (Hughes, Bruce)
- imaginative play (Bruce, Parten, Froebel)
- acting out puppet shows (Froebel, Hughes, Bruce)
- jigsaw puzzles and making models (Piaget, Bruner).

Creating a plan

For each plan you create, state the following:

1 The reason for your choice – the rationale.
2 How your activity will support the developmental stage of the child or children involved.
3 Which theoretical perspective you are using.
4 A detailed, timed plan – to include equipment and resources needed.
5 Any adaptations to the plan which could be made, if necessary. For example, you may need to provide non-slip mats during a drawing or messy play activity for a child with a physical disability.

• •

AC 3.2 Use theoretical perspectives on play which support the developmental stage and needs and interests of children aged: 0–1 year, 11 months; 2–2 years 11 months; and 3–5 years

Activity •

Implementing the plan

Having created your plan, arrange to implement it – and if possible, make an observation of the children during the activity.

• •

LO4 Be able to apply philosophical approaches in own practice

AC 4.1 Create a plan using philosophical approaches to play which support developmental stage, needs and interests of children aged: 0–5 years

Planning play to support the needs of children from birth to 1 year 11 months

For very young babies – not yet sitting – think about the following ideas on which you could base your plan:

- exploring textures and sounds – using an activity mat and a range of materials and rattles and bells (Steiner, Montessori, Reggio Emilia)

- providing a range of objects for babies to explore with their hands and mouths (Isaacs, Froebel).

Once a baby is able to sit unaided, you could choose to base your plan on:

- finger puppets and rhyming songs (Froebel, Isaacs, McMillan)
- heuristic play: using a treasure basket with carefully selected objects to promote holistic development (Goldschmied).

For toddlers, you could choose to base your plan on:

- sand and water play (Isaacs, McMillan)
- playing with balls – rolling, kicking and throwing, etc. (Isaacs, Forest schools)
- playing with things that screw and unscrew (Vygotsky, Bruner)
- puppet play and action rhymes (Steiner and Isaacs).

Planning play to support the needs of children from 2 to 2 years 11 months

Some ideas to plan for include:

- wooden block play (Froebel, Steiner, Montessori)
- sand and water play (Isaacs, McMillan)
- musical games (Steiner, McMillan)
- matching and sorting games (Piaget)
- role play or pretend play (Isaacs, McMillan)
- musical games – dancing and jumping to music (Isaacs).

Planning play to support the needs of children from 3 to 5 years

Some ideas to plan for include:

- wooden block play (Froebel, Steiner, Montessori)
- open-ended outdoor play (McMillan, Steiner, Froebel, Forest schools)
- making dens outdoors (Forest schools)
- cooking activity (Steiner, Montessori)
- active pretend play with other children (Steiner, Montessori, Reggio Emilia)
- creative play: painting, drawing, drama (Reggio Emilia)
- playing with dough (McMillan, Steiner)
- imaginative play: pretend play, small world play, dressing-up activities, play with puppets, dolls and teddies (Froebel)
- acting out puppet shows (Froebel, Steiner)

- jigsaw puzzles and making models (Piaget, Bruner)
- create a classroom terrarium in a clear fish tank; fill the tank with layers of gravel, sand, and soil and plant with mosses and ferns (Froebel's 'gifts').

AC 4.2 Use philosophical approaches to play to support the developmental stage and needs and interests of children aged: 0–1 year 11 months; 2–2 years 11 months; and 3–5 years

Activity

Implementing the plan

Having created your plan, arrange to implement it – and if possible, make an observation of the children during the activity.

LO5 Review how theoretical perspectives and philosophical approaches to play contribute to own practice

AC 5.1 Evaluate how theoretical perspectives and philosophical approaches to play support own practice

After each planned play activity, review how different approaches from theorists have contributed to your own practice.

Reflect on your own practice and evaluate how certain theoretical perspectives and philosophical approaches to play have supported your own practice.

AC 5.2 Share evaluation of how theoretical perspectives and philosophical approaches to play provision supports practice

Activity

Prepare a presentation

Choose one theoretical perspective and one philosophical approach, and prepare a presentation for the rest of the class. This could be a short talk, a PowerPoint presentation or a group discussion, and should include:

- a brief description of the main principles of theory and approach you have chosen
- the activity or play scenario
- how the chosen approach has supported practice
- a brief summary of what you have learnt.

Useful resources

Hughes, B. (2002), *A Playworker's Taxonomy of Play Types* (2nd edn). London: PlayLink.

Assessment practice

1 Identify theories which influence play.
2 How have theories impacted on your own understanding of play?
3 Analyse how theoretical perspectives on play inform practice.
4 Identify philosophical approaches which influence play provision.
5 How have philosophical approaches impacted on your own understanding of play provision?
6 Using theoretical perspectives on play, plan activities for children from birth to five years which support their developmental stage, needs and interests.
7 Using theoretical perspectives on play, implement your planned activities for children from birth to

five years which support their developmental stage, needs and interests.
8 Using philosophical approaches to play, plan activities for children from birth to five years which support their developmental stage, needs and interests.
9 Using philosophical approaches to play, implement activities for children from birth to five years which support their developmental stage, needs and interests.
10 Evaluate how theoretical perspectives and philosophical approaches to play support your own practice.
11 Share evaluation of how theoretical perspectives and philosophical approaches to play provision supports practice.

Unit 3.4 Contribute to enabling play environments

This unit provides the learner with the knowledge, understanding and skills required to contribute to enabling play environments.

Learning outcomes

By the end of this unit you will:

1 Understand the play environment.
2 Understand how the early years practitioner supports children's behaviour and socialisation within play environments.
3 Be able to support children's behaviour and socialisation within play environments.
4 Understand how the characteristics of an enabling indoor play environment meet the age, stage and needs of children.
5 Understand how the characteristics of an enabling outdoor play environment meet the age, stage and needs of children.
6 Be able to provide enabling play environments.
7 Be able to critically evaluate enabling play environments.
8 Be able to plan and lead opportunities which support children's understanding of the world.
9 Be able to plan and lead opportunities which encourage children's engagement in expressive arts and design.

AC 1.2 Identify types of environment

There is a wide variety of play environments in the UK: see Figure 3.4.1. See Unit 1.1 for more detailed information on different early years settings.

In addition, most areas also have private and local authority adventure playgrounds and soft play centres.

Research activity

Find out about the types of play environment provided in your local area. Which settings provide integrated education and care, using the EYFS or other national framework for learning?

LO1 Understand the play environment

AC 1.1 Explain what is meant by 'environment'

In an inclusive early years setting that embraces diversity, the layout and presentation of material provision offer a range of experiences and activities across the birth to five years framework. Increasingly, from the time they can walk, children are integrating with children in the Foundation years for parts of the day, which gives a more natural and family-group feeling. Children with special educational needs and disabilities are also included in settings. All this means that the traditions of wide provision are of central importance in providing an enabling play environment.

AC 1.3 Explain how environments support play

Creating environments which encourage and support play

Play does not just happen. It is true that babies and young children are biologically disposed to play, but they will not develop their play unless they meet people and experience situations that encourage the development of play. What adults provide has a direct impact on play. If adults encourage play and create an enabling environment that cultivates play, the quality of children's play will be deeper.

Continuous provision

There should always be a core of open-ended provision that is continuously offered – this means

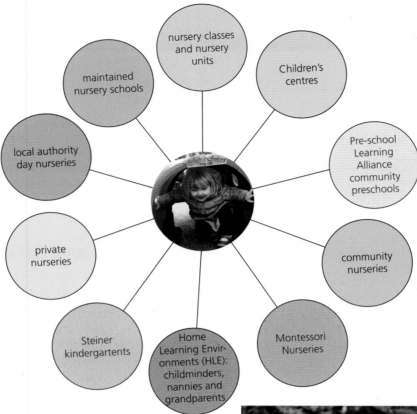

Figure 3.4.1 Different play environments in the UK

it is constantly available. Other experiences can be added in or changed, and may not be offered all day, every day in the same way.

The following are considered to be open-ended continuous provision:

- malleable natural materials (clay, mud, dough)
- home corner for domestic play
- workshop area, with found and recycled material for model-making and mark-making, and including masking tape and scissors that cut (for left- and right-handed children)
- small world play (dolls' house, farm, prehistoric animals, roads, trains)
- sand (wet and dry) and water.

Space and places to play indoors: room design

Freedom of movement is central to early childhood. Susan Isaacs, a pioneer in integrated early years provision, thought that children cannot learn if they are made to sit still.

Figure 3.4.2 The children are involved in parallel (companionship) play: both are digging in the sand and filling holes with water, watching it seep into the sand

Space and places to play outdoors: gardens, parks, forests, urban forests

Play does not happen to adult order. Challenging play helps children to play at their highest levels. Play outdoors gives children opportunities to consolidate and practise skills.

Settings now work hard to make their outdoor area an important part of the play environment. Children need to interact with nature, so plants, trees, flowers and vegetables need to be part of the play environment, and also encourage bird and insect life. Ideally, children are taken to forests, or to parks with copses of trees, so that they learn how to be in woodland and in open green spaces. To play in this situation strengthens the play and encourages creativity. Den-making is something children all over the world engage in. Dens, mud pies, hoops, beanbags and balls in zones all have a contribution to make to outdoor play.

Open-ended natural materials to play with

These encourage children to think, feel, imagine, socialise and concentrate deeply. This type of material encourages children to think about natural resources in the world (where does clay come from?). Children will tend to use a range of fine motor skills with these materials, such as working at the woodwork bench or making a clay coil pot. Examples of open-ended materials are:

- found materials, such as those used in junk modelling
- transforming raw materials, like clay and dough
- self-service areas
- dressing-up clothes and cookery items in the home area
- wooden blocks.

Carefully chosen and limited use of commercial toys and equipment

It is important to note that toys are often expensive and of doubtful quality in terms of educational experience. Pre-structured toys can only be used in one prescribed way, whereas open-ended material can be used as a prop for all kinds of play scenarios.

A set of wooden unit blocks has more potential for creative and imaginative play than one set of a plastic construction kit. It is best to keep adding to

Figure 3.4.3 It is quite a skill to avoid pouring the water over his feet – the child demonstrates this in his play. He also shows us that he is interested in pouring water on the concrete wall of the sandpit, as well as the sand inside the pit. He is noticing that the results are different: water seeps into sand; it splashes off concrete. He might enjoy discussing this later, if photos were taken and he shared them with his key person. Often children do not want to interrupt their play, but they do appreciate reflecting afterwards, and photos are an excellent way of doing this in a relaxed way

It is hard for children to develop their play if the day is timetabled into rigid slots, with routines that break up the day. If children are allowed to move about freely between the indoor and outdoor areas, research suggests that their play is calmer and of deeper quality.

There is also the advantage that giving children greater choice of where and how they play gives adults more time and opportunity to support children's play and choices, rather than organising and directing adult-led 'activities' for most of the day.

the wooden blocks, and to choose one construction kit that is as open-ended as possible, so that many different things can be constructed with it, and then to keep adding to that.

Activity

- How is play supported in your setting?
- Is there continuous provision of open-ended materials?
- Is the design of indoor and outdoor space both functional and attractive?

AC 1.4 Analyse the impact of philosophical approaches on current frameworks in relation to play environments

In Unit 3.3, we looked at the philosophical approaches which have influenced current early years frameworks in the UK. These include Froebel's approach, the Reggio Emilia approach, Forest schools, Steiner schools, and the studies undertaken by Margaret McMillan and Susan Isaacs.

EYFS 2012

The EYFS states that a truly enabling environment provides the stimulation and the positive relationships that support children to feel safe enough to explore. It also stipulates that the learning environment should provide opportunities for both **indoor** and **outdoor** play which will give young children the chance to:

- select and use activities and resources with help as per own request
- take turns and share resources with appropriate support as required
- talk to other children when playing together, including initiating conversations
- play cooperatively in a group, for example, demonstrating friendly behaviour
- form positive relationships with peers and familiar adults
- move confidently in a range of ways, for example, safely negotiating space when playing racing and chasing games, adjusting speed or changing direction to avoid obstacles
- handle tools effectively for the purpose, including mark-making.

Activity

Using the information in Unit 3.3, analyse the impact of the various philosophical approaches on the EYFS.

AC 1.5 Explain how to work collaboratively to provide enabling play environments in early years settings

Effective teamwork is essential when planning to provide enabling play environments.

The role of the practitioner is central

The role of the early years practitioner in supporting children's development and learning through developmentally appropriate materials provision, equipment and resources is central. The environment (people and provision) needs to support all children.

Clutter confuses children

There should be nothing in a learning environment, indoors or outdoors, that has not been carefully thought through and well organised. Children need to know what they are allowed to do, and what they are not allowed to do, and the environment needs to signal to children how it should be used and kept. When children feel insecure, they test boundaries.

The space indoors and outdoors should be flexible

Both indoor and outdoor spaces should be flexible, so that it can be set up and transformed for different uses in a variety of ways. Attention should be given to light, because the way that it shines into a building changes the atmosphere. If the sun is shining onto a child's face during story time, it will be difficult for the child to become engaged.

The temperature is important

Being too hot or too cold makes it difficult to learn. Outdoors, children need suitable clothing for all weathers (and so do the adults!), and indoors, the rooms should have good air circulation to encourage concentration and reduce the spread of infection.

LO2 Understand how the EYP supports children's behaviour and socialisation within play environments

AC 2.1 Describe the role of the EYP in supporting children's socialisation within play environments

Socialisation involves how children relate socially (and emotionally) to other people. Children need to learn how to deal appropriately with a whole range of emotions, including anger and frustration, within a supportive environment.

An essential aspect of socialisation involves supporting young children to behave in socially acceptable ways without damaging their self-esteem: that is, rejecting the children's unacceptable behaviour, not the children themselves. Socialisation begins from birth, as babies interact with the people around them and respond to their environment.

Encouraging positive social interactions

Having at least one secure personal relationship with a parent or carer enables children to form other relationships. Consistent, loving care from a parent or carer who is sensitive to the child's particular needs enables the child to feel secure and to develop self-worth. Children observe the behaviour of parents, carers and other significant adults (such as early years practitioners, play workers, teachers and teaching assistants), and their observations affect children's own behaviour, including how they relate to others. A child's ability to relate to others may also be affected by:

- special needs, for example communication and/or social interaction difficulties
- family circumstances such as separation or divorce
- death, abandonment or other permanent separation from parent or main carer.

All children need affection, security, acceptance, encouragement, patience and a stimulating environment. Children deprived of these in the first five to six years of life may find it difficult to relate to other people throughout childhood (and even adulthood). However, children are amazingly resilient, and subsequent sustained relationships

with caring adults in a supportive environment can help children to overcome early parental separation, rejection or neglect.

Adults who provide inconsistent or inappropriate care may unwittingly encourage inappropriate behaviour in children, which can lead to adults spending less time interacting with the child, resulting in the child having ineffective communication skills as well as difficulties in establishing and maintaining positive relationships with other people. Appropriate social interactions with adults (and other children) in various settings will lead to children being able to demonstrate positive ways of relating to others and using appropriate social skills.

Activity

- Which early social interactions can you remember (for example, at playgroup, nursery, school, clubs; hobbies, on holiday, early friendships)?
- How do you think these early social interactions influenced your attitudes and actions? For example, did they have positive or negative influences?

AC 2.2 Explain how modelling positive behaviours impacts on children's behaviour

Behaviour refers to the way we act, speak and treat other people and our environment. Children who develop well socially and emotionally at an early age are more likely to make friends, to settle well into school and to understand how to behave appropriately in different situations. They have strong self-esteem and a sense of self-worth, but also have a feeling of empathy for others. They understand what the boundaries are, and why they are necessary. A child with poor social and emotional development may be at risk of poor relationships with peers and unwanted behaviour.

Modelling positive behaviour

Children learn a lot of their behaviour from those around them. This is the principle of the social learning theory discussed in Unit 3.13.

Early years practitioners must be good role models – by modelling positive behaviour; this includes showing respect, being polite, showing consideration for others and waiting with patience.

Modelling positive behaviour is a useful way of helping children to resolve conflicts. For example, when talking to a pair of children who have been fighting, an adult might say, 'I wonder how Jason could have said he wanted the train, instead of grabbing it?' or 'Serena, I wonder how you could stop Jason grabbing the train, without hitting him?' It is important to encourage a culture where children can say how they are feeling. Sometimes it may feel like children, or a particular child, keep coming to you for help, and this may become wearing. But it is important that on every occasion you listen with sympathy and try to help the child. Adults can encourage children to be *assertive*. For example, they can help children to use phrases like 'I want a turn,' 'Can I go next?' and 'Can I have a turn when you're finished?' Encourage children to respond to things they do not like, by saying 'No' or 'I do not like that.'

Activity ·

Think about the behaviours modelled by you and your colleagues in the setting. How could you improve your behaviour when confronted with an aggressive child?

· ·

AC 2.3 Analyse strategies to support children to manage their own behaviour in relation to others

Helping children to recognise their emotions

Child development theory emphasises how children use **social referencing** to make sense of situations. In other words, children look back to see adults' expressions and pay close attention to their tone of voice and what they say. In practice, this can be used to help children understand situations and their emotions – for example, a smile and approval for a child as he or she plays positively with others reinforces the child's inner sense of enjoyment. Where children are in conflict, adults might intervene sharply to say 'No,' or to reprimand with terms like 'naughty' and 'nasty'. These responses can lead children to associate those situations with anger and criticism, and

a cycle of difficult behaviour can arise. An alternative approach is to try to help the children to understand what has happened and what they might be feeling. This means approaching an incident of inappropriate behaviour rather like a problem to be solved together.

Different approaches to supporting positive behaviour
Containment

Containment is a psychodynamic theory developed by Wilfred Bion. Containment occurs when you receive and understand someone else's emotional communication, like joy, fear, guilt or anxiety.

For example, a baby may communicate feelings of great fear and distress by crying and seeming inconsolable. Usually, the baby's mother can receive and then make sense of these feelings, for example

Case study

Learning to share

An experienced early years practitioner sees a child snatch a toy train from another child, who starts to cry. She goes over to the children calmly and says, 'I can see you really wanted that train, Harry. But Iqbal really wants it too.' After a moment, she asks Harry, 'Can you see that Iqbal is sad?' Harry nods, so she asks, 'What could we do to make him feel better?' Harry is not sure and does not answer. So she asks Iqbal, who points at the train. After a minute or so, Harry hands the train to Iqbal. The practitioner says, 'I wonder what you could do next time when you really want something like the train.' Harry does not reply, so she suggests, 'Maybe you could say, "Can I have a turn next?" Or perhaps you could look for another train?' Then she checks to see if Iqbal is all right, and suggests, 'Next time, if someone grabs something from you, you could say, "No, it is mine," or "Stop it. I do not like that." Shall we try saying that together?'

Consider the following questions:

1 How has the practitioner helped the children to acknowledge their feelings?
2 How has the practitioner given the children ideas to manage their behaviour in the group?
3 This approach would take a lot longer than just telling Harry off and making him give the train back to Iqbal. Do you think that the extra time and attention are worthwhile?
4 What might be the longer-term benefits of dealing with the incident in this way?

In practice

Factors influencing behaviour

If the behaviour of a particular child in your setting is difficult, consider the following factors:

- Does the child have a strong relationship with a key person?
- Are there plenty of stimulating things to do which match the child's interests?
- Are routines and demands appropriate for the child's development and age?
- Might the child feel tired or hungry?
- Have there been any recent changes in the child's family life that may have unsettled him or her?

You could share your thoughts with other members of staff in your setting, and discuss how you might improve the situation for the child.

It is important that you do everything you can to establish a good relationship with the child's parents. If a child has similar difficulties at home, and behaviour remains difficult over time in the early years setting or school, you may decide that this is a special educational need (SEN), and seek help and support from the special educational needs coordinator (SENCO).

by soothing the baby, understanding that the baby is feeling cold and hungry, and then feeding the baby. It is the mother, not the baby, who thinks through the fact that the baby is cold and hungry, and the feelings are said to have been 'contained'. When this positive experience is repeated many times, the baby begins to recognise and manage feelings like hunger without always becoming so distressed. In time, as a young child, he or she will be able to say 'I'm hungry' rather than getting into a distressed crying state. On the other hand, if a baby's needs are often neglected, then he or she may become a young child who gets highly upset by every little thing that goes wrong.

Case study

Containment

Jaydeen is three years old. It is five o'clock in the afternoon on a hot day. Her key person, Tara, sees out of the corner of her eye that Jaydeen is struggling to put the marble run together. After a few minutes, Jaydeen flings a piece to the floor in frustration and shouts so loudly that the child playing next to her starts to cry. Tara comes over and sits close to Jaydeen, comforting the child who is crying. Then she says to Jaydeen, 'I think you are probably fed up because you are hot and tired. Shall we all sit together and have a cuddle and a story?' Jaydeen puts her thumb into her mouth and snuggles up to Tara.

Consider these questions:

1 How does Tara provide a containing function for Jaydeen's emotions?
2 How might this change things for Jaydeen?

Key terms

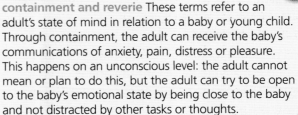

containment and reverie These terms refer to an adult's state of mind in relation to a baby or young child. Through containment, the adult can receive the baby's communications of anxiety, pain, distress or pleasure. This happens on an unconscious level: the adult cannot mean or plan to do this, but the adult can try to be open to the baby's emotional state by being close to the baby and not distracted by other tasks or thoughts.

Through reverie, the adult can process the baby's communications and hand them back to the baby, either sharing the pleasure in a loving and intimate interaction, or handing back distressing thoughts in a way that the baby can manage. This model was developed by the psychoanalyst Wilfred Bion.

social referencing When children check how adults respond to a situation as part of their own emotional response. An example would be a baby who sees something on the grass in a park and looks back at her mother before deciding whether to crawl confidently forward to grab it, or to stay away and watch warily.

Progress check

The importance of feelings

- Understand how children's feelings might influence their behaviour.
- Use some strategies to help children become more aware of how they are feeling.
- Work within the team to create an atmosphere that shows understanding towards children's feelings, but also puts some limits on how they can express those feelings.

Guidelines for helping children to recognise their feelings and to develop self-discipline

- By 'tuning in' to children and responding positively and warmly to them, you can help them to become aware of how they are feeling.
- Work with the team to set and maintain clear and agreed boundaries, so that children know what sort of behaviour is acceptable.
- Spend blocks of time with an individual child who is experiencing difficulties with behaviour, to build a close relationship with him or her.
- Help children to negotiate solutions to conflicts and disputes rather than just telling them off, so that in time they can solve problems themselves.

Behaviour modification: positive reinforcement

This theory can be applied to the management of children's behaviour. Behaviour is understood as a response to positive reinforcements – for example, if a child has a tantrum and is given sweets to help him or her to calm down, the sweets become a positive reinforcement, so the child may start to throw tantrums in order to get sweets. Following the approach of learning theory, if the parents stop giving the sweets, the learnt behaviour will no longer be reinforced and will wither away. This approach is often called **behaviour modification**, and it is used a great deal in early years settings and schools. It is underpinned by the following theories:

- Most behaviour – good or bad – is learnt.
- If behaviour is reinforced when it occurs, it will increase.
- If behaviour is ignored or punished when it occurs, it will decrease.
- Behaviour can therefore be changed, if consequences are always applied *immediately*. Rewards will increase the desired behaviour, and negative consequences (such as time out, ignoring) will decrease the undesirable behaviour.
- The timing of the reinforcements is crucial, especially for young children: it has to be immediate, otherwise the reward or punishment may not be associated with the behaviour.

Advantages of this approach

This approach to managing behaviour can work well in certain circumstances. Parents and carers often use it successfully to manage difficult issues such as going to bed or toileting, using star charts linked to rewards ('if you go to bed on time, you get a star; if you get five stars, you will get a reward, like a small toy'). In an early years setting it may be the only effective strategy if a child's behaviour is very difficult to manage; for example, aggressive behaviour could lead consistently to spending time out (sitting out and not being able to play for a short period of time, like one minute), while cooperative behaviour (such as managing to play alongside another child for two minutes) could be consistently rewarded with praise, and special time on a favoured activity.

Drawbacks of this approach

Children might not be able to generalise. A child might be punished consistently for drawing on books at home until this behaviour dies away, but then goes to his or her grandparents' house and draws on the walls. The child has stopped the *specific* behaviour, but does not understand the *general* requirement to be careful and avoid doing damage. Another drawback is that children might start doing things for rewards, which will affect their curiosity and general motivation.

Another drawback or limitation to this approach is that it takes no account of the child's inner world. A child's behaviour may be difficult because of previous experiences, such as experiencing the trauma of losing a parent in early childhood. Behaviour modification would only seek to control the child's behaviour, rather than seeking to help the child to grieve and find ways of expressing his or her feelings of sadness and anger.

Therapeutic help

If a child's behaviour is very difficult, other professionals may be called on to offer therapeutic help to the child. Some of these professionals are art, music or play therapists and child psychotherapists. In contrast to the behavioural modification approach outlined above, a **therapeutic approach** will generally involve an attempt to find the underlying causes of the child's difficult behaviour. Through play, art, music

Guidelines for dealing with inappropriate behaviour

- **Try to remain calm**: it is easier to control a difficult child or situation if you are in control of yourself. Listen to both sides of the story when there is conflict, and apologise if you have made a mistake.
- **Ignore attention-seeking behaviour**: children who desperately want adults to notice them will call out, interrupt, ask questions and frequently push in front of other children to show something they have made or done. It is important to ignore such behaviour as much as possible and to reward them by giving them attention *only* when they have waited appropriately, so that they are encouraged to do so again.
- **Use a distraction or diversion**: if two children are arguing over a toy, you could distract them by offering an alternative activity: 'Shall we go and play with the blocks instead?' Or you could use a volunteer task as a distraction, such as helping with handing out resources.
- **Blame the behaviour, not the child**: when you need to talk to children about their behaviour, it is important for them to feel that it is not personal – that you do not dislike the child, only his or her

behaviour. For example, you might say, 'Bailey, throwing toys is dangerous behaviour; I want you to stop right now!'
- **Give the child a choice**: explain that the child can choose how to behave. For example, you might say: 'Bailey, you now have a choice. You can stop throwing the toys and play nicely with them, or I'm afraid I will have to take them away.' Allow the child a few minutes to decide what to do. If he or she refuses to comply, follow through with the sanction by removing the toys.
- **Firmly state the rule in your setting if a child uses unacceptable language**: this includes swearing and name-calling that often result from children repeating what they have heard. Sometimes they are unaware that it is unacceptable in one setting but not another. In these cases they need to be told firmly not to say those words 'here' – you cannot legislate for language they may use at home or criticise their families. Some children will deliberately use unacceptable language to shock or seek attention. In these cases you should state the rule calmly and firmly.

or talking in a free way, the child can be helped to express his or her feelings. The therapist can help by giving the child a safe space for expression, and by interpreting the child's communications in a way that makes it more possible for the child to live with feelings of anger, loss or unhappiness. As the child is increasingly able to express and find ways of living with difficult emotions, he or she becomes more able to develop and grow throughout childhood, instead of being 'stuck'.

Research activity

To find out more about therapeutic help, read *Dibs: In Search of Self* by the American play therapist, Virginia Axline.

Find out more about how therapeutic ideas can be used in early years settings and schools, by reading *Wally's Stories* by Vivian Gussin Paley. See p 320 for full references.

De-escalate and diversion

Young children find it difficult to control their emotions, and are not easily able to understand

that what they are doing is unacceptable. Early years practitioners can help to prevent inappropriate behaviour from escalating by providing a distraction or diversion.

Boundary setting and negotiation

It is important that adults provide **boundaries**: they clearly tell children when their behaviour is not acceptable. Some young children bump into others, grab for equipment first, give others an aggressive look or generally intimidate other children. Other children say things to make others feel left out or foolish – 'You're not coming to my party' or 'Don't play with stupid Eleanor.' Behaviour like this can quickly escalate to more serious forms of bullying like open aggression, which is either **physical** (hitting, pushing) or **verbal** (name-calling). It is important that adults look out for this sort of behaviour and encourage other children to say confidently how it affects them.

Be consistent: it is normal for children to push at the boundaries set by adults. It is often tempting to 'overlook' inappropriate behaviour when we are feeling stressed or overworked, but children will better understand how you want them to behave if you always respond in a consistent manner.

Supporting children to reflect on and manage their own behaviour

In order to help children to learn positive behaviour in a group, one particularly important area to consider is how children can learn to manage the conflicts that will inevitably arise. If children are taught to depend on adults to sort out every dispute, their development will be held back.

Anti-bullying strategies

The EYFS requires that 'children's behaviour must be managed effectively and in a manner appropriate for their stage of development and particular individual needs'. Every early years setting needs to develop a policy around the support of children's behaviour and the prevention of bullying. In any group, there are likely to be instances of bullying, including early years settings and schools.

Supporting children to become assertive and to resolve conflicts can help to minimise bullying. But remember that, in the end, it is the adults' responsibility to uphold acceptable behaviour. Some children may not be able to stop others from being aggressive and domineering, however much they try to be assertive. When inappropriate or bullying behaviour occurs, take firm action when necessary. You may have to say to a child, 'Pushing like that is not allowed. Do you remember yesterday when Jason said he felt sad when you pushed him? So I am going to have to take you away from the trains for two minutes.' You can help the child by saying clearly which part of their behaviour is not acceptable, while not being negative towards the child personally. This is why you would *not* say, 'You are being naughty.' It is important that you follow this up by settling the child back into the play – 'We can go back to the trains, but I need you to remember that there is no pushing' – and then spend time in that area, helping the children to play together.

Key term

challenging behaviour This term has been used to refer to the unwanted or unacceptable behaviours that may be shown by children or adults. Such behaviours include *aggression* (hitting, kicking, biting), *destruction* (ripping clothes, breaking windows, throwing objects), *self-injury* (head banging, self-biting, skin picking), *tantrums* and many other behaviours. Normally, challenging behaviour puts the safety of the individual or others in some jeopardy, or has a significant impact on their quality of life.

Activity

Analyse strategies to support children in managing their own behaviour. How many of the strategies described have you seen being used in your setting?

AC 2.4 Explain how the EYP provides for group learning and socialisation

Group learning

Inevitably, group learning will be adult-led, rather than child-initiated. Children come together for stories, music, singing, dancing or physical education. For very young children, group times can be difficult. Sitting with a friend often helps children to settle into a group more easily as it provides the comfort of the familiar person.

When providing group learning activities the early years practitioner should:

- Select materials which are relevant to children's needs, interests, and preferences – and which promote social interaction.
- Give children ideas for using the materials or suggest ways to engage in an activity (for example, 'One of you might be the cook and someone else might be the server').
- Take children's characteristics into consideration when grouping children. For example, by pairing socially competent children with shy or less socially skilled children.
- Consider the number of children in each group to maximise social interaction.
- Give children with limited social skills several opportunities to interact with others.

- Use strategies such as modelling, prompting and role playing.
- Give children positive feedback when they engage in positive social interactions.

Socialisation

Socialisation occurs through the observation, identification, imitation and assimilation of the behaviour of other people. Children model their attitudes and actions on the behaviour of others. You need to be aware of the significant impact you make on children's social (and emotional) development, and ensure that you provide a positive role model.

Encouraging children to take turns is an essential element of helping them to interact appropriately with other children. From about the age of three, young children begin to cooperate with other children in play activities. By about five, they should be quite adept at playing cooperatively with other children. Gradually children should be able to participate in more complex cooperative play, including games with rules as their understanding of abstract ideas increases.

We live in a highly competitive society; we all want to be the best, fastest, strongest or cleverest. The media (television, magazines and newspapers) focus our attention on being the best. Most sports and games have only one winner, which means that all the other participants are losers. Winning makes the individual feel good, confident and successful; losing makes the individual feel bad, inadequate and unsuccessful. Competitive games can prepare children for the competitiveness of real life. However, competition can also contribute to:

- negative self-image and low self-esteem
- aggressive behaviour
- lack of compassion for others
- overwhelming desire to win at any cost.

Competitive sports and games can be beneficial to children's social development as long as they emphasise:

- cooperation and working as a team
- mutual respect
- agreeing on rules and following them
- participation and the pleasure of taking part are more important than winning
- everyone doing their personal best.

As well as being competitive, people can also be sociable and cooperative; we like to be part of a group or groups. Cooperative activities encourage children to:

- be self-confident
- have high self-esteem
- relate positively to others
- work together and help others
- make joint decisions
- participate fully (no one is left out or eliminated)
- have a sense of belonging.

Go to Unit 3.12 where you can learn more about the expectations/stages of PSED.

In practice activity

Observe a group of children during a play activity or a game. Focus on one child's social and emotional development.

In your assessment comment on: the child's level of social interaction; the child's ability to make choices or decisions; the child's use of language to express needs and/or feelings; the child's behaviour during the activity; the role of the adult in promoting the child's social and emotional development; suggestions for further activities to encourage or extend the child's social and emotional development including appropriate resources.

Activity

Plan a group activity which promotes group learning and socialisation.

LO3 Support children's behaviour and socialisation within play environments

AC 3.1 Model positive behaviour

Children model their attitudes and actions on the behaviour of others. They imitate the actions and speech of those they are closest to them, for example acting at being 'mum', 'dad', 'key person' or 'teacher'; copying the actions and mannerisms of adults around the home, childcare setting or school. All adults working with children need to be aware of the significant impact they make on children's development, including their behaviour, by providing positive role models. Observing the communication and interactions of parents and other significant adults (such as early years practitioners) affects children's own behaviour, how children deal with their own feelings and how children relate to others. This is why it is so important for adults to provide positive role models for children's behaviour. Group or family times provide a good opportunity to model positive interactions between siblings and family members.

You need to act as a positive role model for children. You can do this by:

- keeping calm when dealing with inappropriate behaviour
- listening to both sides of the story when there is conflict and apologising if you have made a mistake
- noticing good behaviour and praising it
- being consistent when dealing with inappropriate behaviour
- showing respect to children and other adults: by the way you listen, your facial expression, your body language and by what you say
- making sure that you do not make any negative comments in front of the children.

AC 3.2 Plan an environment which supports children's socialisation and group learning

See Unit 3.1 for a discussion of the EYP's role in socialisation.

In practice activity

- Plan, implement and evaluate a play activity which encourages or extends a child's social and emotional development. Use the assessment from previous observation of the child's social and emotional development as the basis for your planning.
- Encourage the child to use a variety of social skills and emotional abilities. For example: appropriate behaviour; independence (such as using self-help skills or making choices); effective communication skills; sharing resources; expressing needs and/or feelings; understanding the needs and feelings of others.
- Consider how you could meet the needs of children with behavioural difficulties with this activity.

AC 3.3 Use strategies when supporting children to manage their own behaviour

Read through the section AC 2.3 about the different strategies for helping children to manage their own behaviour and use them appropriately when working with children.

LO4 Understand how characteristics of an enabling indoor play environment meet children's age, stage and needs

AC 4.1 Explain the characteristics of an enabling indoor play environment

Given that children from birth to six years learn through the senses, the layout needs to support and extend this kind of learning. The layout from Reggio Emilia and Pistoia in Northern Italy has reminded practitioners in the UK of the importance of:

- an attractive and welcoming entrance area, where children and families are greeted, can find and share information, and feel part of a community
- natural light
- the feeling of space without clutter
- making spaces beautiful using natural materials.

The environment also needs to support and actively encourage and extend the symbolic life of the child, making one thing stand for another (for example, pretending a cardboard tube is a telescope). Understanding cause-and-effect relationships is also very important, and the learning environment needs to promote this (for example, kicking the ball hard makes it go a long distance, while tapping it with your toes makes it roll only a little way).

Planning a safe and predictable environment

Children need a safe and predictable environment. It is important for staff to work as a team so that different messages are not given by different people

– for example, if one adult allows children to sit on tables and another does not, children will push the boundaries because they are confused. When children feel safe, they explore and enjoy stimulating provision that has been planned for them.

Providing risk and challenge in the environment

Children are biologically driven to make risk assessments, but only if they are constantly encouraged to use these processes – for example, toddlers can be encouraged to come down the stairs (under supervision) sliding on their tummies, feet first. They will pause and check where they are every few steps, making their own risk assessment. Children who are not supported to make their own risk assessments, by an adult sensitive and helpful to their needs, are more likely to have accidents. For more information on risk and challenge, see Unit 1.2.

AC 4.2 Describe how an enabling indoor play environment meets the age, stage and needs of children

How an enabling indoor play environment meets the needs of babies
The importance of people – learning before sitting

It can be very boring to be a baby. This is because babies depend on adults to bring interesting experiences to them, as they cannot move about enough to reach for things when sitting, or crawl or walk to get them.

Bored, unhappy babies cannot learn much, and the important period of babyhood, when so much learning is possible, will then be lost. Studies of child development suggest that the first years of life are of great importance for development and learning, and also that this is the time when the child's willingness and ability for future learning are set.

Imagine what it would be like if you spent long periods on your back with only a ceiling to look at, or you were in a pram in the garden with a plastic cover hiding your view of the sky and trees, or you could hear voices, but could not see who was talking because they were standing behind you.

Material provision, equipment and resources for babies

Children from birth to three years enjoy and benefit from the companionship and stimulation of being with older children, but they also become exhausted if they do not have a safe base/haven/nest to return to, where they can be quiet and calm.

Babies need to be cuddled, held on your knee so that they can see things, talked to and sung to, and bounced in time with music. They need things to look at, swipe at, grab and hold, chew, suck and mouth, smell, shake and listen to. Babies need objects and people.

Quiet times

Sometimes babies need to be quiet, but they still need to feel that people are near. Of course, it is important that the sun is not in their eyes, and that they are comfortable in temperature and with a clean nappy.

Babies need times to:

- look at a mobile
- listen to gentle music playing
- hear the birds singing as they lie in a pram under a tree, looking through the branches at the patterns of the leaves against the sky
- sit propped up in a specially designed chair and watch what is going on
- watch other children
- follow voices they know because they spend time with them and love them
- receive warmth and affection.

Floor time

Anyone who observes babies finds that they are exploring the environment using their senses and movement. They need plenty of opportunities to be on the floor so that they can do this. When lying on their backs, they can watch mobiles or leaves and branches swaying and fluttering in the trees above their pram, and swipe at objects above them with their arms, or kick at them with their legs. But they also need to feel their arms, legs and tummies against the ground. Experts in physical movement development (like JABADAO, the National Centre for Movement, Learning and Health in Leeds) are finding that children often do not spend

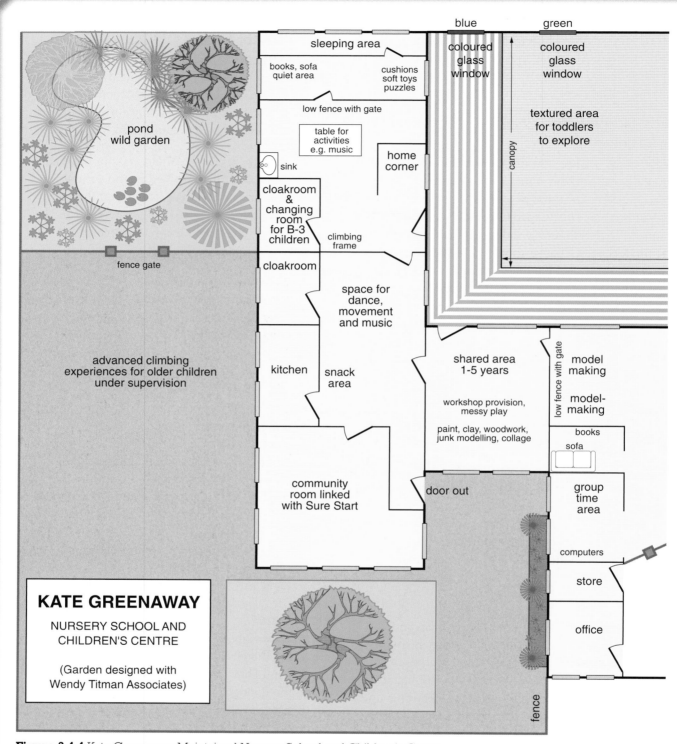

Figure 3.4.4 Kate Greenaway Maintained Nursery School and Children's Centre

enough time on the floor. They need to be given opportunities to crawl as well as to sit and lie down. It is exciting when children take their first steps, but they still need plenty of time down on the floor. This means that there should be plenty of spaces to do

this when working with very young children in the first year of their life.

Tummy time: Babies need time to be on the floor, on their tummies, with interesting natural objects

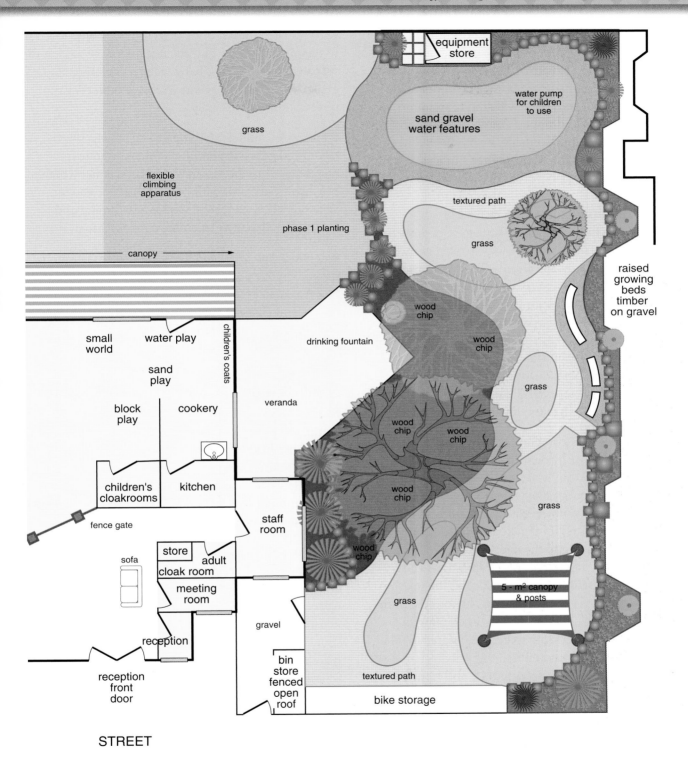

equipment store

water pump for children to use

sand gravel water features

grass

textured path

flexible climbing apparatus

phase 1 planting

grass

raised growing beds timber on gravel

canopy

small world

water play

sand play

block play

cookery

children's coats

drinking fountain

wood chip

wood chip

wood chip

grass

veranda

children's cloakrooms

kitchen

wood chip

wood chip

grass

fence gate

wood chip

staff room

grass

sofa

store

adult cloak room

meeting room

wood chip

5 - m² canopy & posts

grass

reception

gravel

reception front door

bin store fenced open roof

textured path

bike storage

STREET

(not plastic all the time) placed in front of them, which they need to reach for. Adults can be very encouraging and help babies to have things in reach, and at the point where the baby is trying to crawl, keep frustration at bay by making sure there is enough success to keep them trying. It is very difficult for a baby when they are trying to crawl forwards to get something they want, and they find they are moving backwards. Having something to push against can be just the right help at the right time!

Are there objects a baby can put in his or her mouth, touch and handle, smell, carry about, look at and make sounds with? They will learn more if everything is not made of plastic. The floors will need to be clean, as a baby will stop to examine every piece of fluff, dropped crumb or spillage. When the baby crawls outside, he or she will need surfaces such as grass, and rougher surfaces. But remember, babies put everything in their mouths.

Sitting babies – treasure baskets

Elinor Goldschmied pioneered treasure baskets for sitting babies. These are now widely used in most settings. It is very important that they are presented to babies in the correct way or the baby will not get the full benefit of the learning the treasure basket offers. Make sure the basket is the correct shape, height and size. It is distressing for the baby if it tips as they lean on it, or if they are unable to reach the objects on the other side. It is uncomfortable to sit at a basket that is too high (like an adult sitting at a table when the chair is too low for the table height).

The baby needs the companionship of an adult who sits near them (usually on a chair that is near to the ground in height), but who does not join in – simply there as an anchor, smiling when shown objects, but saying nothing. When adults are concentrating (perhaps writing and thinking hard), it would interrupt the flow of thought and the deep focusing to have someone make suggestions or ask questions and try to make conversation with them. Ideally, the treasure basket experience will take place away from the hurly-burly of the main area, perhaps screened off with a clothes horses draped with material, to signal to other, older, more mobile children that this is a quiet area, set aside for sitting babies to concentrate and learn.

The objects should not be made of plastic, but of natural materials or metals that can be washed and kept clean. This is because plastic does not offer much to the range of senses through which babies learn. As objects become shabby they should be removed, and there should be new objects to keep the interest of the baby who has regular use of the basket. As your observations of a baby build, you will be able to select objects with that baby's interests in mind. The baby who loves to bang and bash objects will choose different ones from the baby who loves to dangle and shake objects. It is deeply satisfying to try to work out what a baby will particularly enjoy exploring, especially when you have built on your observations successfully.

Babies need sufficient objects to be able to select from, so the basket should be full enough to encourage this. Examples would be: a small wooden brush, a small cardboard box, a loofah, a wooden spoon, a small metal egg whisk, a bath plug and chain, a small bag of lavender, a large feather.

Of course, you will need to make a risk assessment based on your observations of what a baby needs. Never put an object in the treasure basket that makes you anxious about its safety for a baby, and remember that some babies have allergies. Remember also that some babies are less adventurous than others and will need more support and encouragement to enjoy the treasure basket.

Providing opportunities for rest and sleep

Getting the right rest is crucial for the learning of babies and young children. Not all babies will need to sleep at the same time, and it is very worrying to find practice where all babies are expected to have their nappies changed at the same time and to sleep at the same time. These are very individual things.

It is important for babies to feel that they are near someone when they sleep. Some babies sleep best on a mat on the floor of a quiet area that is gated, with a cover to keep them warm; others sleep better in a darkened room, in a cot kept for them. This area should not be too full of stimulation. It is important to relax and let go when falling asleep. Neutral colouring is best, and the room should not be cluttered.

It is also important to keep to the sleep-time rituals and patterns that are familiar to the baby at home. Some babies need to have a cuddle, being lowered into their cot as they fall asleep. Others might never go to sleep on a lap, but need to be in a cot, in a quiet room with their teddy, in order to fall asleep.

Sleep is important for learning. It helps the memory to embed rich learning experiences with people, objects, events and places.

Guidelines for material provision, equipment and resources for babies

Expensive equipment is not necessary to create a rich environment in which babies can develop and learn. Babies are helped to develop and learn when they are:

- introduced to treasure baskets
- offered home-made or commercial toys – for example, baby mirrors, which help their sense of identity (who it that? is that me?); rattles to hold and shake, with and without sounds; wobbly toys and pop-up toys; bath toys that sink and float; a soft toy, such as a teddy bear
- provided with opportunities to crawl on comfortable surfaces – a mixture of carpets and other surfaces to explore, including grass

- have suitable places to sleep – some babies sleep best in a cot, others in a basket on a floor away from draughts, some tightly tucked in, others with loose bedclothes covering them; babies should *never* be left to sleep unsupervised when in group care
- eat in a family group – this is best for babies, as they are part of the conversation, and they are talked to and given attention in a way that is impossible with a group of babies
- share a book with their key person, which can calm them (they love to look at patterns, grids and circles – see Figure 3.4.5); books will be chewed and sucked, as babies learn through all their senses.

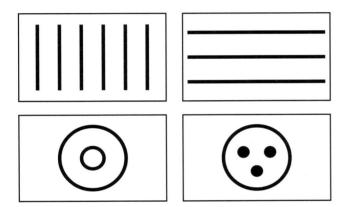

Figure 3.4.5 Babies love to look at patterns, grids and circles

How an enabling indoor play environment meets the needs of toddlers

The importance of people

Toddlers need adults who create a warm, affectionate atmosphere, support well-being, encourage children to try things, observe and tune in to their learning, and make individual plans to help them learn. Children need to feel valued, appreciated and respected.

When children feel their efforts are appreciated and valued, they develop a positive self-image and a good sense of well-being. This, more than anything else, helps them to learn. The key person in the setting is of great importance in this.

By this age, children are beginning to get a sense of the rhythms of time and passing time through the

day as they become familiar with the early years setting. They are helped in knowing the shape of the day if there is a predictable environment. This does not mean rigid routines, but it does mean having a consistent shape to the day, or to outings, so that children can begin to participate fully in preparations, having experiences and a sense of closure as they join in clearing things up each day. This means that staff need to work together as a team to create consistent boundaries and ways of doing things, so that children feel safe and secure and able to develop their intellectual lives. Then they can be explorers and problem-solvers, and they can make and use symbols, with reasoning and enquiring minds.

Heuristic play

This is a good time to offer crawling babies and toddlers heuristic play experiences, which are described in Unit 3.1, p 262.

Children need to be comfortable. Rather than a cold, draughty floor, they need a warm, inviting floor space, without lots of clutter to capture their attention. The space needs to be prepared in advance so that children come upon the carefully spaced piles of objects when they enter the area. All the objects are collected from everyday use, rather than toys.

One pile might include spheres, circular objects and cylinders, such as a cotton reel, a bobble from a hat, a bracelet. Another might be of metal objects, such as tins with smoothed edges, or a metal tea caddy. The adult sits quietly and provides a calm and concentrating atmosphere that supports the child's explorations without intervening, except to say something like,'Yes, you have a lovely tin'– but only if the child brings it to them. Otherwise, a warm smile is sufficient and the child then returns to his or her explorations.

The session varies in length, but careful observation will signal to the adult when to draw things to a close. Often children stay concentrating for half an hour. A further ten minutes or so should be taken to clear up with the children, who are encouraged to put the collections into the right type of bag. This is then hung on the wall, with the children watching. As long as children's efforts are valued, they enjoy helping. They do not respond well when nagged or criticised for putting an object in the wrong bag. They need encouragement and positive, sensitive support.

Double provision

Through double provision (providing more than one activity at a time), the different needs and interests of children from birth to five years can be attended to with quality. There might be a workshop area, with carefully selected and presented found materials, such as boxes, tubes, dried flowers, moss, twigs, wool, string, masking tape, glue, scissors and card. Here, older children could become involved in making models and constructions, and adults can help them to carry out their ideas without losing track of them on the way or becoming frustrated. Children can be helped as they try to join things, and make decisions about whether a string knot would be better than masking tape or glue.

Nearby, on the floor, there might be a beautiful basket full of balls of wool and string, which younger and less experienced children can enjoy unravelling and finding out how these behave. Other children might like to return to this earlier way of using string too. Remember that careful supervision is essential to prevent accidents.

It is a good idea to try to offer everything at different levels of difficulty, so that there is something for

everyone to find absorbing. Absorbed children behave better, on the whole.

Attractive presentation and tidy-up time indoors and outdoors

If an area is dirty, shabby or in a muddle, it is less attractive to children. Often a well-used area becomes cluttered and untidy halfway through a morning or afternoon, and the children leave it. It is important that adults do not neglect these abandoned areas. Children can be encouraged to help tidy it, but adults can role model this mid-session if children are very involved in other areas. At the end of the session, everyone needs to tidy up though, unless there are good reasons for a child not to, such as being upset or unsettled. Children should never be nagged or made to feel bad, but they should be encouraged and given specific but appropriate tasks as members of the learning community. Even a toddler enjoys putting rubbish in the bin. It is a question of finding something suitable for each particular child. The important thing is not to overdo the requests for help in tidying, and to remember that it is discriminatory to expect only a few children to do all the tidying.

Movement area

Important play provision for toddlers and children up to at least five years is on the floor! Making a movement corner is as important as making a book corner for brain development, learning and well-being. The floor needs to be clean and carpets should not be scratchy. Penny Greenland at JABADAO (the National Centre for Movement, Learning and Health) emphasises the importance of movement in early childhood.

Having an interested person, sensitively supporting and mirroring, is also important. Mirroring is another vital pattern for late learning, as research by Colwyn Trevarthen at Edinburgh University shows. Adults who make good play companions are a valuable resource as part of the play provision. The rough-and-tumble play traditional in mammals, including human children, just before sleeping, is often engaged in with adults in the family.

Figure 3.4.6 Boys engaged in imaginative play

Guidelines: indoor material provision, equipment and resources for toddlers

Children who are beginning to be confident walkers need:

- stable furniture to pull themselves up on and cruise between
- heuristic play
- a designated space for vigorous movement, with cushions on which to leap and roll about
- wooden and natural material objects to feel, mouth and hold
- simple towers to make and knock down
- finger-painting
- non-toxic crayons and felt-tip pens and paper
- wet and dry silver sand (not builder's sand)
- play dough – find some good recipes for play dough (some involve cooking, which makes the dough last longer); check the dough is safe to put in the mouth and even to eat, as some children might do this

- opportunities for water play, carefully supervised, at bath time, in paddling pools or with bowls of water – remember, children can drown in very shallow water, so always supervise these activities
- a tea set, toy cars and other play props to encourage pretend symbolic play with a willing adult
- objects to transport in trucks, bags, and so on
- boxes for children to put things into and take things out of
- blankets to cover teddies, dolls, and so on (enveloping)
- picture books and books with simple texts, and stories and rhymes, such as *Spot the Dog*
- simple dressing-up clothes – mainly hats, shoes and belts for toddlers
- action songs and finger rhymes.

Discussion point

The importance of people in the lives of toddlers
Having read the sections in this chapter about the importance of people, what do you think are the key messages? Discuss this in a small group, and make a set of commitments to work on in your practice. Write them down and review them in a month's time. Evaluate your progress.

Playing with an adult: interdependent relationships

The key person sat on the floor, facing Rebecca (two years old), and sang 'Row, row, row the boat' with her. She sang the song and did the actions twice through and then stopped. Rebecca touched her on the thigh and the key person responded, 'Again? You want to sing again?' The singing and moving were repeated, and Rebecca smiled with pleasure. In this play:

- Rebecca is helped to be imaginative
- her idea to repeat the song is taken up
- she is encouraged to use her initiative and not be passive
- she is learning the basis of drama, music and dance.

In practice activity

Audit – or make an assessment of – the provision in your setting/placement. If there are gaps in the provision, think about what would you introduce first, and why.

How an enabling indoor play environment meets the needs of children from three to five years

The importance of people

Communication, skilful body movements, play and the use of cultural symbols and creative and imaginative making of symbols are all important aspects of a child's development during this period. Adults have a huge role in supporting children as these overarching aspects emerge and strengthen.

Just as babies and toddlers need plenty of time to be in the garden/outdoors, so too do children from three to five years. They also enjoy toddler experiences, alongside increasingly complex experiences. They are able to take increasing responsibility for their own risk assessment (at the woodwork bench, when cooking and gardening), but they need adult support or they will not manage to do so. Children benefit from discussions about safety, and taking care of themselves, others and equipment. They also need adults who give them help in caring for others, thinking of others, looking after the material provision and equipment, and making decisions and choices which help their development and learning. Children do not respond well to being judged and chided by adults. They do respond well to being helped to take responsible decisions.

Figure 3.4.7 Dinosaurs could be the key for this child to learn many different things

Case study

Supporting learning through nurturing a child's interest

See Figure 3.4.7: this little boy is showing through the gesture of holding up the dinosaur that he wants us to look at it. It is his favourite; his eyes coordinate when he looks at it. It is important for children to hold objects and look at them as they play, as this will help later tracking of print on the page of a book. It will also help him if the adult names the dinosaur. Often we use the general word (dinosaur) instead of giving children the word for the type (in this case, Tyrannosaurus rex). He is ready to be given this vocabulary and delights in using the correct description of his dinosaur. Language helps children to sort and classify things in the world: he will be able to establish that the class of dinosaurs contains different types. He will learn the difference between a Tyrannosaurus rex and a brontosaurus, but only if he is in a language-rich, enabling environment. There need to be books of dinosaurs, people who help him look them up, show them to him and name them for him.

Guidelines: indoor material provision, equipment and resources for children from three to five years

Children from three to five years need access to the following every day:

- wet sand and dry sand (these are two entirely different learning experiences), with equipment nearby in boxes labelled with words and pictures for children to select
- clean water in a water tray or baby bath, with buckets, guttering, waterwheels, and so on, to make waterfalls, and boxes of equipment labelled with pictures and words
- found and recycled materials in a workshop area, with glue, scissors, masking tape, and so on
- book-making area, next to the workshop
- small world – dolls' house, train set, garage, cars, farms, zoos, dinosaurs
- paint/graphics materials in a mark-making area, with a variety of paper and different kinds of pencils, pens and chalks (this might be next to the workshop area)
- malleable clay or dough
- wooden set of free-standing blocks (not plastic, and not bits and pieces from different sets) – unit blocks, hollow blocks and mini hollow blocks (for example, from Community Playthings)
- construction kit (one or two carefully selected types, such as Duplo or Brio)
- book area, which is warm, light and cosy
- domestic play area
- dressing-up clothes (mainly hats and shoes)
- daily cookery with baking materials and equipment
- ICT, digital camera, computer – it is preferable to use computer programs that encourage children to use their imaginations, rather than responding to computer-led tasks
- nature table, with magnifiers, growing and living things, such as mustard and cress, hyacinths, wormery, fish tank
- woodwork bench, with glue to join things and tape to bind things together, saws, hammers and a vice
- a range of dolls and soft toys
- music and sounds area, with home-made and commercially produced instruments
- movement area (perhaps next to the music area)
- story props, poetry and song cards
- sewing table
- cooker/food preparation.

Guidelines for displays and interest tables

- Adults should not draw or write on children's work without their permission. After all, adults do not allow children to draw or write on their records without permission.
- Any writing or notes about a painting should be mounted separately underneath the child's painting or drawing. The label should be discussed with the child, who should agree to the wording.
- Any lettering should be done carefully on ruled lines so that it looks attractive. Your writing must project a good role model for children.
- Writing should not be at 'jaunty angles' on a display, as children are developing their understanding of which direction the print goes when reading.
- In English, writing goes from left to right; in Urdu it goes from right to left; in Chinese it goes up and down.

Open continuous provision indoors should be provided every day

Everything in the list for continuous, open-ended provision that is suitable for toddlers (see p 000) should also be provided for children aged three to five years. Children need to be able to experience materials at different levels of complexity, since at times they are operating at their highest levels of possibility, and at other times they need a quieter,

less exhausting day. None of us – adults or children – is at our best all day and every day.

It is always useful to move around the environment on your knees in order to see it from a child's-eye view (or crawl to gain a toddler or mobile baby's view). Lying on your back helps to understand a baby's view from a cot. In other words, what would a child see as they move about the environment?

Guidelines for making a display

- Use a piece of material that takes the eye to important parts of the display.
- Display the essential objects of the experience (for example, autumn leaves, conkers and tree bark).
- Include a non-fiction book on the subject (about autumn or seasonal rhythms).
- Include a book of literature, such as a poem or a story about autumn.
- Include photos/audiotape of sights/sounds of the garden in autumn and the children raking up leaves, to help children to link into the experience and reflect.
- Wall displays (such as photographs) for crawling babies should be at their eye height, along the floor, against the wall. Wall displays for older children should also be at their eye height, and not above. Remember not to clutter the walls. Leave some walls blank, and perhaps only put a display on one wall. Having too much on the walls is too exciting and colourful, and children become calmer when the walls are calmer, in natural shades.
- The Reggio Emilia approach reminds us that practitioners need to consider the following in setting up displays, which are seen as part of what they describe as the 'microclimate'. Consider:
  - how different parts of the display relate to each other in the way they are presented
  - how light shines and is part of the display
  - the way in which colours and materials create different experiences
  - that the display can smell as well as be touched
  - that sounds are an aspect to be built in to the display.

Figure 3.4.8 A display about numeracy

Displays and interest tables indoors

Issues of gender, culture and disability need to be thought through when it comes to setting up displays. Positive images and multicultural artefacts need to be discussed and planned by staff as a team. Seasonal and cultural festivals and educational visits across the year help children through special and one-off opportunities for exploration.

Displays should respect children's work – do not cut up children's paintings to make an adult's collage. The paintings children do should be mounted and displayed as they are.

LO5 Understand how the characteristics of an enabling outdoor play environment meet children's age, stage and needs

AC 5.1 Explain the characteristics of an enabling outdoor play environment

The outdoor environment has an important role to play in providing for the developmental needs of all children. In a well planned, enabling outdoor setting, with supportive adults, children's curiosity can be nurtured and their physical skills developed. Also, behaviour that may seem inappropriate or too boisterous indoors becomes perfectly natural when playing outside.

The garden and outdoor areas offer children major learning opportunities. They help children to learn about nature and gardening. Children can try out their physical skills and become competent, adventurous and confident in their physical bodies. Parents enjoy joining their children in the outdoor area, for picnics and other enjoyable experiences that make them feel part of the community.

Children need challenging places to climb and swing, and to be taught how to stay safe and be responsible. Children are biologically driven to make risk assessments, but only if this is encouraged. They need places to run, jump, skip and wheel.

Different ways of doing similar things – indoors and outdoors

The outdoor learning environment should echo and mirror the indoor area, but both will offer different experiences. Indoors, children will use felt-tip pens and pencils, while outdoors they might chalk on the ground and make marks on a larger scale. Indoors, they might use paint and brushes on paper, but outdoors they may have buckets of water and large brushes, and paint on walls and the ground.

Hoses for warmer weather and a water pump give children opportunities for learning in many ways, from not splashing others to the science of pumping and spraying. Gardening equipment is needed for the planting areas. Buckets, spades, sieves, and so on, are needed in the sand area. They will make dens, play in tents and may wear dressing-up clothes indoors or outdoors.

It is very important that great care is taken of equipment in both environments, so that jigsaw pieces do not end up on a flowerbed, for example. Sets (puzzles, crockery from the home corner, sets of zoo animals, wooden blocks) should not be moved from the area where they belong. If children have made a den and want to have a pretend meal in it, then a picnic box can be taken into the garden, full of bits and bobs. This allows children to learn to care for equipment.

Children should be able to learn outside for most of the day if they choose to do so. They need appropriate clothes (as do adults), so that everyone can be outside in all weathers. The idea that learning can only take place indoors is extraordinary when we stop to think about it.

There should be different surfaces – playground surfaces, grass, an earth patch to dig in, a large, drained sandpit, planted areas with trees and wild areas for butterflies. Settings that do not value the importance of the outdoor learning environment are only offering children half a curriculum.

AC 5.2 Describe how an enabling outdoor play environment meets age, stage and needs of children

How an enabling outdoor play environment meets the needs of babies

Many settings find that babies and toddlers sleep better outside in cool, fresh air in flatbed cots or prams. They tend to fall asleep more easily and move more gently into wakefulness with clouds or a leafy branch overhead and the sounds of nature and children playing outdoors.

Babies should also be given the opportunity to experience play outdoors:

- Non-mobile babies need to be placed in positions that give them plenty to look at, reach for, swipe at and grasp. Adults should carry them to interesting places or sit with them to share interest about the environment.
- Crawling babies need a variety of surfaces to provide different tactile experiences – for example, they will learn that grass is warm, soft and firm but may be wet, whereas paving is hard, cool and smooth. They will also learn how to adapt their newfound movement skills to each different surface.

How an enabling outdoor play environment meets the needs of toddlers

Toddlers who are mastering locomotion and coordination also need several kinds of surfaces in order to practise their skills. Once they are more confident walkers, they need less predictable surfaces to practice their skills.

Figure 3.4.9 Raking leaves

Guidelines: outdoor material provision, equipment and resources for working with toddlers

Children who are beginning to be confident walkers need:

- a range of surfaces to walk on, and to try to run
- a large, bouncy ball to kick and throw, bats, hoops, and beanbags
- flowers (these are for picking as far as a toddler is concerned); encourage children to pick daisies and dandelions rather than flowers from the flowerbed; they enjoy putting flowers in a vase of water to place on the meal table
- climbing opportunities, always carefully supervised: a small climbing frame or steps

- wheeled trucks to push and pull, pull-along toys, pushchairs for dolls and teddies and other soft toys
- plants and a growing area, and watering cans
- a well-drained sandpit
- a covered pond and fishing nets to use when supervised with an adult
- puddles to stamp in wearing wellies
- picnics
- mud pies and a digging area.

How an enabling outdoor play environment meets the needs of children aged three to five years

In her book, *Playing Outdoors: Spaces and Places, Risk and Challenge* (2007), Helen Tovey lists the following as important if children are to have a challenging and creative outdoor area. Children need:

- designated spaces (but children should be allowed to rearrange them and use them in a different way)

- connected spaces, which encourage children to join in (sand and water areas)
- elevated spaces (mounds, trees, ramps, steps, climbing frames)
- wild spaces, so that children do not only experience neat and trim tarmac areas
- spaces for exploring and investigating
- spaces for mystery and enchantment (dens)
- natural spaces (digging patches and opportunities to grow flowers and vegetables)
- space for the imagination (providing children with open-ended props, logs and so on)
- spaces for movement and stillness (climbing, dragging, swinging on bars, jumping, balancing and so on, as well as sitting in secluded, tucked-away places in peace and calm)
- social spaces (outdoor seats for chatting together)
- fluid places (flexible resources that can be moved about when needed).

It is important that resources are organised with a minimum of setting out equipment and arranging it – for example, making a den with a tea set in it. The children will want to change things about if they are thinking and using the environment well.

Bikes, scooters and carts

Bikes need to be three-wheeled and two-wheeled, with some needing two or three children cooperating in order to make them work. Two-wheeler bikes with no pedals are excellent for children, as they can tilt and balance without having to perform a complex combination of actions. Scooters and carts to push and pull are also important, as are prams and pushchairs for dolls and teddies.

Research activity

Investigate the different approaches to Forest schools in the UK and in countries such as Germany, Denmark, Norway and Sweden. (You will find useful websites listed in the Useful resources section on p 314.)

LO6 Provide enabling play environments

AC 6.1 Plan an enabling play environment: indoors; outdoors

Activity

Plan an enabling indoor play environment

Focus on just one area in the setting and make a plan which includes the relevant equipment and resources as described in LO5. For example, you could plan a role-play area or a water-play area.

Plan an enabling outdoor play environment

Focus on just one area in the setting and make a plan which includes the relevant equipment and resources as described in LO5. For example, you could plan a simple obstacle course or a small gardening project.

AC 6.2 Create an enabling play environment: indoors; outdoors

Activity

Implement your plans.

LO7 Critically evaluate enabling play environments

AC 7.1 Critically evaluate enabling play environments in own setting

Activity

Observe children in your own setting and critically evaluate the environment. Focus on:

- how the children played
- their enjoyment
- whether you think anything could be improved – and how it could be done

LO8 Plan and lead opportunities which support children's understanding of the world

In the Revised Early Years Foundation Stage, Understanding of the World is about how children get to know about other people, the place where they live and about all aspects of the environment. It is broken down into three aspects:

- people and communities
- the world
- technology.

People and communities

As children learn about the world around them, they find out about the past through talking to parents, grandparents and friends. They develop an interest in their own story as well as the stories in their family: this is the beginning of developing an understanding of the past, and helps them to learn about how other people are different from them, yet share some of the same characteristics and ideas.

The world

Understanding of the world develops as children take notice of everything around them, including places and all the things within them, such as trees in the natural environment and roads and traffic in the built environment. Finding out about places begins initially when a child learns about their own home and the things nearby, then later as children notice things on journeys to and from home – such as the sequence of the traffic lights or names on street signs. This awareness is extended by visiting places and finding out about different elements of environments in books, on television and through using other technology. This aspect also focuses on learning about cause and effect and is developed through having conversations with adults and other children about the things they observe.

Technology

Technology has become commonplace for many families, and children often see and use it quite

naturally when they activate a toy such as an ambulance or police car to make a siren sound. Recognising the role of technology at home or in a setting is important because this helps children to identify the different types of technology and what they are useful for.

AC 8.1 Plan opportunities which support children's understanding of the world

Finding out about the world around them is what babies and young children do very effectively when they investigate by touching, holding or pressing things and by climbing on and jumping off things. Older children love to explore and investigate how and why things work, and to test out their ideas of what will happen if they do a particular thing like pouring more and more water into a container, for example.

For ideas on planning opportunities which support children's understanding of the world, see Unit 3.2.

AC 8.2 Lead opportunities which support children's understanding of the world

Activity ·

Implement and evaluate the planned activities from AC 9.1.

· ·

LO9 Plan and lead opportunities which encourage children's engagement in expressive arts and design

In the Revised Early Years Foundation Stage, Expressive Arts and Design (EAD) is broken down into two aspects:

- exploring and using media and materials
- being imaginative.

Figure 3.4.10 Exploring natural objects

Exploring and using media and materials

This is about how children experiment with media and materials, finding out about their properties and modifying and manipulating them. It includes exploring sounds, patterns, movement and different tools and techniques.

Being imaginative

This is about children's explorations into the world of pretence, building on their experiences of the real world and transforming them into something new – whether through role play, music, pretend play, block play or small world play or a range of other areas.

AC 9.1 Plan opportunities which encourage children's engagement in expressive arts and design

Helping children to be creative is as much about encouraging attitudes of curiosity and questioning as about skills or techniques. Children

notice everything and closely observe the most ordinary things that adults often take for granted. Building on children's interests can lead to them creating amazing inventions or making marks on paper that represent for them an experience or something they have seen. Encouraging children to choose and use materials and resources in an open-ended way helps them to make choices and to have confidence in their own ideas. Retaining childhood confidence in their ideas and skills can easily be lost if others 'take over' and try to suggest what the child is making, thinking or doing. Just expressing an interest in the process a child has gone through is often enough, or asking open questions such as 'Can you tell me about it – that looks interesting,' may be all that is required to help a child hold on to their remarkable creativity. For ideas on planning opportunities which encourage children's expressive arts and design, see the section on creative and imaginative play in Unit 3.2.

AC 9.2 Lead opportunities which encourage children's engagement in expressive arts and design

Implement and evaluate the planned activities from AC 9.1.

Assessment practice

1 Explain what is meant by environment and identify types of environment.
2 Explain how environments support play.
3 Analyse the impact of philosophical approaches on current frameworks in relation to play environments.
4 Explain how to work collaboratively to provide enabling play environments in early years settings.
5 Describe the role of the early years practitioner in supporting children's socialisation within play environments.
6 Explain how modelling positive behaviours impacts on children's behaviour.
7 Analyse strategies to support children to manage their own behaviour in relation to others.
8 Explain how the early years practitioner provides for group learning and socialisation.
9 Explain how to model positive behaviour.
10 Plan an environment which supports children's socialisation and group learning.

11 Use strategies when supporting children to manage their own behaviour.
12 Explain the characteristics of an enabling indoor play environment and how such an environment meets the age, stage and needs of children.
13 Explain the characteristics of an enabling outdoor play environment.
14 Describe how an enabling outdoor play environment meets the age, stage and needs of children.
15 Plan and create an enabling play environment indoors and outdoors.
16 Critically evaluate enabling play environments in own setting.
17 Know and explain how you can plan and lead opportunities which support children's understanding of the world.
18 Plan and lead opportunities which encourage children's expressive art and design.

Useful resources

Organisations

Anna Freud Centre

The centre was established in 1947 by Anna Freud to support the emotional well-being of children through direct work with children and their families, research and the development of practice, and training mental health practitioners: www.annafreud.org

High/Scope

High/Scope is an American approach to early education and care, with several decades of research into its effectiveness. The website includes books, DVDs and news of training events and conferences in the UK: www.high-scope.org.uk

Kate Greenaway Nursery School and Children's Centre

This website includes news and policies for a centre based in central London: www.kategreenaway.ik.org

Kidscape

This charity was established specifically to prevent bullying and child sexual abuse. The website includes resources for parents, children and professionals, and

details of campaigns and training events: www.kidscape.org.uk

The National Strategies (Early Years)

The government's programme for developing practice in the early years, including statutory requirements, advice on best practice, and research findings: www.education.gov.uk and search for early years.

Books

Axline, V. (1971), *Dibs, In Search of Self: Personality Development in Play Therapy*. London: Penguin.

Dowling, M. (2010), *Young Children's Personal, Social and Emotional Development* (3rd edn). London: Sage Publications.

Paley, V.G. (1981), *Wally's Stories*. Cambridge, Mass.: Harvard University Press.

Sylva, K. and Lunt, I. (1982), *Child Development: A First Course*. Oxford: Blackwell.

Tovey, H. (2007), *Playing Outdoors: Spaces and Places, Risk and Challenge*. Maidenhead: Open University Press.

Unit 3.5 Develop emergent literacy skills of children

This unit provides the learner with the knowledge, understanding and skills to develop children's emergent literacy by providing a language-rich environment.

Learning outcomes

By the end of this unit you will:

1 Understand the language and communication needs of children.
2 Understand the characteristics of a language-rich environment.
3 Be able to support children's language and communication needs.
4 Understand strategies which support emergent literacy.
5 Be able to plan activities to support emergent literacy.
6 Be able to lead activities which support emergent literacy.
7 Be able to review how planned activities support emergent literacy.
8 Be able to work with parents/carers in a way which encourages them to take an active role in their child's play, learning and development.

LO1 Understand the language and communication needs of children

AC 1.1 Identify stages of language and communication development from birth to 7 years

From birth to one year

Babies are born with a need and a desire to communicate with others before they can express themselves through speaking. Learning how to communicate – to listen and to speak – begins with **non-verbal communication**. This includes:

- **body language**: for example, facial expression, eye contact, pointing, touching and reaching for objects

- **listening** to others talking to them
- **making sounds** to attract attention. The baby may stop crying when he or she hears, sees or feels her main carer
- **copying** the sounds made by others.

These skills develop as babies and young children express their needs and feelings, interact with others and establish their own identities and personalities.

The first year of a baby's life is sometimes called 'prelinguistic'. This is a rather misleading term. It is more positive and helpful to think of a baby as someone who communicates without words, and who is developing everything needed for conversations in spoken/signed language. This is sometimes called the period of emerging language.

From one to four years

From the second year of the baby's life until about the age of four years, there is a period of language explosion. Every aspect of language seems to move forward rapidly at this time. It is the best time to learn other languages, or to become bilingual or multilingual.

From four to eight years

From four to eight years of age, children are consolidating their communication and language learning. They build on what they know about communication with themselves, with other people, developing better articulation, and using more conventional grammar patterns. They think about whom they are talking to, with greater sensitivity and awareness. They are also more attentive to the context in which they are talking, and the situation. They can put their ideas and feelings into words more easily than when they were toddlers.

To learn more about the detail of the sequence of communication and development, look at the charts of normative development in Table 3.5.1.

In practice activity

Observing language development

Observe one of the following in either the home setting or the early years setting:

- baby aged six to twelve months
- child aged one to three years
- child aged three to five years
- child aged five to seven years.

Note sounds: vowels (ah, eh, ee, aye, oh, yu) and consonants such as p, g, b. Then look at the charts of normative development on language development below and analyse your observations.

Does the baby/child use single words or holophrases (single-word utterances that express several thoughts, ideas or feelings)? Does the child speak in sentences? Evaluate the language development of the child.

The stages of communication and language development

The first month

- Babies need to share language experiences and cooperate with others from birth onwards. From the start babies need other people.
- The baby responds to sounds, especially familiar voices.
- The baby quietens when picked up.
- The baby makes eye contact.
- The baby cries to indicate need, e.g. hunger, dirty nappy, etc.
- The baby may move his or her eyes towards the direction of sound.

From one to four months

From four to eight weeks:

- The baby recognises the carer and familiar objects.
- The baby makes non-crying noises such as cooing and gurgling.
- The baby's cries become more expressive.

From eight to twelve weeks:

- The baby is still distressed by sudden loud noises.
- The baby often sucks or licks lips when he or she hears sound of food preparation.
- The baby shows excitement at sound of approaching footsteps or voices.

During the first three months:

- The baby listens to people's voices. When adults close to the baby talk in motherese or fatherese (a high-pitched tone referring to what is around and going on) the baby dances, listens, replies in babble and coo.
- The baby cries with anger to show they are tired, hungry, and to say they need to be changed.
- The baby is comforted by the voices of those who are close to them and will turn especially to the voices of close family members.

From four to six months

- The baby becomes more aware of others so he or she communicates more and more.
- As the baby listens, he or she imitates sounds he or she can hear, and reacts to the tone of someone's voice. For example, the baby might become upset by an angry tone, or cheered by a happy tone.
- The baby begins to use vowels, consonants and syllable sounds, e.g. 'ah', 'ee aw'.
- The baby begins to laugh and squeal with pleasure.

From six to nine months

- Babble becomes tuneful, like the lilt of the language the baby can hear (except in hearing-impaired babies).
- Babies begin to understand words like 'up' and 'down', raising their arms to be lifted up, using appropriate gestures.
- The baby repeats sounds.

Table 3.5.1 The stages of language and communication development

The stages of communication and language development

From nine to twelve months

- The baby can follow simple instructions, e.g. kiss teddy.
- Word approximations appear, e.g. 'hee haw' to indicate a donkey, or more typically 'mumma', 'dadda' and 'bye-bye' in English-speaking contexts.
- The tuneful babble develops into 'jargon' and the baby makes his or her voice go up and down just as people do when they talk to each other. 'Really? Do you? No!' The babble is very expressive.
- The baby knows that words stand for people, objects, what they do and what happens.

From one year to two years

- The child begins to talk with words or sign language.
- By **18 months**: The child enjoys trying to sing as well as to listen to songs and rhymes. Action songs (e.g. 'Pat-a-cake') are much loved.
- Books with pictures are of great interest. The child points at and often names parts of their body, objects, people and pictures in books.
- The child echoes the last part of what others say (echolalia).
- The child begins waving his or her arms up and down which might mean 'Start again,' or 'I like it,' or 'more'.
- Gestures develop alongside words. Gesture is used in some cultures more than in others.

From two years

- Children are rapidly becoming competent speakers of the languages they experience.
- The child overextends the use of a word, e.g. all animals are called 'doggie'.
- The child talks about an absent object when reminded of it; e.g. seeing an empty plate, they say 'biscuit'.
- The child uses phrases (telegraphese), 'doggie-gone' and the child calls him- or herself by name.
- The child spends a great deal of energy naming things and what they do – e.g. 'chair', and as they go up a step they might say 'up'.
- The child can follow a simple instruction or request, e.g. 'Could you bring me the spoon?'
- The child increasingly wants to share songs, dance, conversations, finger rhymes.

From three years

- The child begins to use plurals, pronouns, adjectives, possessives, time words, tenses and sentences.
- The child might say 'two times' instead of 'twice'. The child might say 'I goed there' instead of 'I went there.' The child loves to chat and ask questions (what, where and who).
- The child enjoys much more complicated stories and asks for his or her favourite ones over and over again.
- It is not unusual for the child to stutter because he or she is trying so hard to tell adults things. The child's thinking goes faster than the pace at which the child can say what he or she wants to. The child can quickly become frustrated.

From four years

- During this time the child asks why, when and how questions as he or she becomes more and more fascinated with the reasons for things and how things work (cause and effect).
- Past, present and future tenses are used more often.
- The child can be taught to say his or her name, address and age.
- As the child becomes more accurate in the way he or she pronounces words, and begins to use grammar, the child delights in nonsense words that he or she makes up, and jokes using words.

From five to eight years

- The child tries to understand the meaning of words and uses adverbs and prepositions. The child talks confidently, and with more and more fluency.
- The child begins to be able to define objects by their function, e.g. 'What is a ball?' 'You bounce it.'
- The child begins to understand book language, and that stories have characters and a plot (the narrative).
- The child begins to realise that different situations require different ways of talking.

Table 3.5.1 The stages of language and communication development   (*Continued*)

· ·

1 How do babies communicate without using words?
2 At what stage can babies follow simple instructions and develop a tuneful babble?
3 At what stage do children typically 'name' objects and actions and overextend words?
4 When do children start asking questions, mostly asking: 'why?'
5 At what stage do children begin to understand book language?

· ·

AC 1.2 Describe factors which affect language and communication needs

Factors which impact on a child's ability to communicate effectively include:

- **any hearing impairments** – permanent or temporary
- **physical impairments** such as cleft palate and hare lip
- **speech dysfluency**: many children have some degree of dysfluency when they are learning to talk, repeating words and sounds, and stopping and starting again. This is especially common when a child is excited or agitated. Children may have episodes of dysfluency during the years of rapid language development between two and five years of age, and at other times speak quite normally
- other **medical conditions** which affect other aspects of development and, as a consequence, a child's confidence or self-esteem
- disorders which affect learning such as **autism**
- **an additional language** – children's home language must be valued; see below on bilingualism
- **lack of language input** (conversations) with an interested adult or positive role model
- **emotional factors** which can result in shyness, low self-esteem and a lack of confidence.

Key term

speech dysfluency The use of hesitators (sounds such as 'erm', 'ur'), pauses and repetitions which reflect the difficulty of mental planning at speed. Stammering (or stuttering) is a form of speech dysfluency.

AC 1.3 Explain how working with others supports children's emergent literacy from birth to seven years

Effective teamwork with your colleagues and with other professionals involves careful planning and organisation. Early years practitioners are expected to follow the guidelines in their own setting for ways in which to support children's language and literacy. This includes methods of promoting reading skills. Some settings use core texts that they have selected themselves, while others may use a reading scheme. There also needs to be a consistent approach to the promotion of writing skills.

Children need secure and loving relationships with their parents and/or a key person so that they become strong and autonomous readers and writers, conversationalists and listeners. They do not flourish when adults sit in judgement over them and use their power to control everything they do through adult-set and adult-led tasks, which are tightly structured and focused. But they blossom when they feel adults are alongside them, sensitive to their feelings and thoughts, and helping them to put these into words/signs.

When adults spend time engaging with children one-to-one or in small groups sharing non-fiction and fiction books, this:

- builds the feeling that reading is fascinating
- gives information about experiences
- deepens knowledge and understanding (for example, a book about pond dipping after an outing).

A wide range of fiction that includes stories, poems, rhymes, songs and music may introduce children to diversity and cultural differences, and help them to understand others through empathy with different characters and situations. See also p 346 (LO8) for information about working with parents.

· ·

Describe how you have contributed to maintaining a positive environment that supports children's speech, language and communication. Include information on: the physical environment; staff roles and responsibilities; training needs and opportunities; views of the child; appropriate involvement of parents or carers.

· ·

LO2 Understand the characteristics of a language-rich environment

AC 2.1 Explain what is meant by 'a language-rich environment'

A language-rich environment

It became apparent in the 1960s–70s that some children were not developing language as readily as others. At the time it was thought that children from working-class homes were disadvantaged because they used what the researcher Basil Bernstein called a restricted language code (using limited vocabulary and less complex forms of grammar). This was thought to hold them back at school. He thought that children from middle-class homes developed an elaborated language code, and that this was why they achieved better at school.

As a result, in both the USA and the UK programmes of compensatory education were developed with the aim of enriching the language and learning environments of young children, so that they would succeed in education.

But during the 1980s–90s it became clear that there is more to a language-rich environment than it seems. Gordon Wells found that it was important for practitioners working with young children to understand the background and culture of the children and families they were working with. Then they would be able to understand the richness of the child's own language and culture.

Recent research shows that children growing up in Japan who are described as lower class do badly in school compared with children described as upper class. But if the family moved to the USA, they were simply thought of as Japanese. It did not matter what class they had been described as back in Japan. In the USA there is a perception that Japanese children study well at school, and this positive attitude towards them seemed to influence things so that they did well in school, regardless of their perceived class in Japan. In other words, positive attitudes towards the children whom practitioners work with are essential if children are to develop good language skills.

The importance of context and a language-rich environment

The brain develops important interconnecting networks, which include movement, communication, play, symbol use, problem-solving and understanding why things happen (cause and effect). These become more complex as the networks for learning in the brain develop. Before five years of age, the language system is not yet mature. Reading and writing develop most easily and enjoyably once language is well developed.

Many experts believe that removing the meaningful context and teaching letter–sound relationships in isolation and separately, although methodical to the adult readers devising the system, actually make reading and writing more difficult for many children. This is particularly so for children who have disabilities such as visual or hearing impairments, or for children with English as an additional language.

AC 2.2 Analyse a language-rich environment in relation to current frameworks for children

National and local frameworks and policies

The EYFS 2012

The learning and development requirements of the EYFS define what early years providers must do to promote the learning and development of all children in their care, ensuring they are 'school ready'. The EYFS statutory framework asserts that:

- Literacy development involves encouraging children to link sounds and letters and to begin to read and write. Children must be given access to a wide range of reading materials (books, poems and other written materials) to ignite their interest.
- Educational programmes for developing young children's communication, language and literacy skills must encompass the following key issues:
  - **Communication and language development** is one of the prime areas and involves giving children opportunities to speak and listen in a range of situations and to develop their confidence and skills in expressing themselves.

- **Literacy development** that involves encouraging children to read and write, both through listening to others read, and being encouraged to begin to read and write themselves.

All early years practitioners must consider the individual needs, interests and stage of development of each child in their care, and must use this information to plan a challenging and enjoyable experience for each child in all of the areas of learning and development.

Communication, language and literacy (as for **all** the areas of learning and development) must be delivered through planned, purposeful play, adult-led activity and child-initiated activity. There should be a fluid interchange between activities initiated by children, and activities led or guided by adults. This will move increasingly towards adult-led learning as children start to prepare for reception class.

Go to page 332 for information on synthetic phonics and sustained shared thinking.

Six aspects of communication for EYFS

1 **Language for communication** is about how children become communicators. Learning to listen and speak emerges out of non-verbal communication, which includes facial expression, eye contact and hand gesture.
   Aims: children listen with enjoyment, and respond to stories, songs and other music, rhymes and poems and make up their own stories, songs, rhymes and poems. They speak clearly and audibly with confidence and control, and show awareness of the listener; for example, the use of conventions such as greetings, 'please' and 'thank you'.

2 **Language for thinking** is about how children learn to use language to clarify their thinking and ideas or to refer to events they have observed.
   Aims: children use talk to organise, sequence and clarify thinking, ideas, feelings and events. They use language to imagine and recreate roles and experiences.

3 **Linking sounds and letters** is about how children develop the ability to distinguish between sounds and become familiar with rhyme, rhythm and alliteration.
   Aims: children link sounds to letters, naming and sounding the letters of the alphabet. They use their **phonic** knowledge to write simple regular words and make phonetically plausible attempts at more complex words.

4 **Reading** is about children understanding and enjoying stories, books and rhymes.
   Aims: children explore and experiment with sounds, words and texts. They read a range of familiar and common words and simple sentences independently, and know that print carries meaning and, in English, is read from left to right and top to bottom.

5 **Writing** is about how children build an understanding of the relationship between the spoken and written word, and how through making marks, drawing and personal writing, children ascribe meaning to text and attempt to write for various purposes.
   Aims: children attempt writing for different purposes, using features of different forms such as lists, stories and instructions. They write their own names and other things such as labels and captions, and begin to form simple sentences, sometimes using punctuation.

6 **Handwriting** is about the ways in which children's random marks, lines and drawings develop and form the basis of recognisable letters.
   Aims: children use a pencil and hold it effectively to form recognisable letters, most of which are correctly formed.

> **Key term**
>
> **alliteration** When two or more words in a poem begin with the same letter or sound; for example, **R**abbits **R**unning over **R**oses.

Local frameworks

There are a number of projects and networks which work with a range of professionals to provide support for the development of children's communication, language and literacy skills.

Bookstart

Bookstart is the national early intervention and cultural access programme for every child. It gives away free book packs to every child in the four UK home nations. In their baby's first year parents receive a free *Bookstart Baby Pack* from their health visitor or other health professional. The pack has been chosen to include everything parents need to get started sharing stories, rhymes and songs with their baby: canvas shoulder bag for carrying books, two board books and a guidance leaflet 'Babies Love Books' on sharing books.

My Bookstart Treasure Chest is a pack for pre-school children aged three to four years which is usually gifted by the child's nursery, playgroup or other early years setting. It includes two books chosen especially for pre-schoolers, a list of handy book recommendations, tips for reading to pre-schoolers and more. For more information visit: http://www.bookstart.org.uk

Booktime

Booktime is the free books programme that follows on from Bookstart. A book pack is given to every reception-aged child during the autumn term. Packs include a book, selected by an expert panel, and guidance for parents and carers on shared reading. Additional interactive resources are also available to libraries, and many use them to support special events and activities that promote libraries and reading to families. For more information visit: www.booktime.org.uk

Talk To Your Baby

Talking to young children helps them become good communicators, which is essential if they are to do well at school and lead happy, fulfilled and successful lives. *Talk To Your Baby Community of Research and Practice* is an online network open to everyone who shares an interest in the development of young children's speech, language and communication. It brings together researchers and academics who are particularly interested in the development of theory, investigation and enquiry, with practitioners who are working with children and families to promote high-quality practice at home, in early years settings, and across local communities. For more information visit: http://www.literacytrust.org.uk/talk_to_your_baby

Every Child a Talker

Every Child a Talker (ECAT) was a national project to develop the language and communication of children from birth to five years of age. The project was set up after concern about the high levels of 'language impoverishment' in the UK, and how this affects children's progress in school and chances in life. For more information visit: http://www.talkformeaning.co.uk/everychild.php

The Young Readers Programme

This is the national programme that the National Literacy Trust uses to motivate disadvantaged children and young people to read for pleasure. The programme helps children and young people to acquire the skills they need to develop as readers, from knowing how to choose a book that engages them, to where they can find books once the project is over. All schools and Children's Centres are now able to participate in Young Readers Programme by purchasing a resource pack. For more information visit: http://www.literacytrust.org.uk/nyrp

London Literacy Champions

London Literacy Champions improves children's literacy by training local volunteers to support parents in disadvantaged areas. This Team London project is funded by the Mayor of London and the Reuben Foundation, and is delivered by the National Literacy Trust in partnership with 12 local authorities. For more information visit: http://www.literacytrust.org.uk/london_literacy_champions

Schools Network

The National Literacy Trust Schools Network supports schools to raise literacy attainment across the whole school, specifically by improving pupils' attitudes and behaviour towards literacy. For more information visit: http://www.literacytrust.org.uk/schools_network

Communities and local areas

The National Literacy Trust work focuses on families, helps local areas to target support to those with the greatest need, and helps communities to improve literacy levels and life chances. For more information visit: http://www.literacytrust.org.uk/communities

Activity ·

Analyse how the current frameworks in your own area support a language-rich environment.

· ·

LO3 Support children's language and communication needs

AC 3.1 Develop a language-rich environment for children

Policies and procedures which support the development of communication, language and literacy skills

You must know and understand the setting's policy and procedures for developing children's communication, language and literacy, including how this relates to the relevant national framework and curriculum guidelines for teaching English. The setting should have a clear and agreed policy on how they will deliver the EYFS's requirements for communication, language and literacy to meet the needs of individual children, their circumstances and the local community. The setting's policy and procedures for communication, language and literacy should include:

- **Policy statement**: a short statement about the setting's values and approaches to the development of children's communication, language and literacy skills.
- **Aims**: the setting's aims for managing, organising and developing children's communication and language skills; the setting's view on partnerships with parents.
- **Curriculum content**: the EYFS; curriculum planning and organisation including long-, medium- and short-term planning strategies and formats.
- **Roles and responsibilities of staff**: all staff members should have clear documents that outline their roles and responsibilities.
- **Teaching and learning**: planning and organisation; teaching styles and methods; matching children's learning needs and learning styles; the setting's policies and approaches for reading, writing, handwriting and spelling.

- **Equal opportunities**: equality of access to the curriculum; inclusion; supporting children with English as an additional language; promoting positive images; appropriate resources.
- **Special educational needs**: inclusion; differentiation; identification of children with special language and/or literacy needs; support programmes; special resources; involvement of outside agencies.
- **Resources**: books; reading schemes; spelling and handwriting schemes; writing tools; ICT; teaching resources including 'big' books and whiteboards; displays; book corner and/or library.
- **Assessment**: ongoing assessment; EYFS Profile; end of key stage target-setting; end of year group target-setting; marking policy; rewards; recording progress; reviewing targets with children and parents; reporting to parents.
- **Parent partnerships**: reading at home; reports and reviews; information to support parents; family literacy projects; parent helpers in school.
- **Professional development**: staff training; sharing good practice within the setting; learning from and with other practitioners outside the school (networks).
- **Monitor and review**: monitoring teaching, standards and resources for developing children's communication, language and literacy skills; roles and responsibilities; recording; review dates. See also Unit 3.11 for your role in developing a language-rich environment.

Activity ·

Find out about your role in developing a language-rich environment in line with the policies and procedures of your setting.

· ·

AC 3.2 Interact with children to meet individual language and communication needs

Children come into early years settings with a variety of language skills, having had different linguistic and cultural experiences. These experiences will influence their development in the language skills of speaking, listening and communicating.

Obtaining information about individual children's progress and planning appropriate activities

Assessment plays an important part in helping parents and early years practitioners to understand children's needs and plan activities to meet them. The EYFS requirement is that providers must assess children's progress on an ongoing basis, and complete assessments at two specific points:

- When a child is aged between 24 and 36 months, early years practitioners must review progress in the prime areas, and supply parents or carers with a short written summary of their child's development.
- A report on progress is required is the final term of the year in which the child reaches age five, and no later than 30 June in that term. At this point, the EYFS Profile must be completed for each child.

Assessment

Ongoing assessment (known sometimes as **formative assessment**) is an integral part of the learning and development process. It involves early years practitioners observing children on an ongoing basis, understanding their level of achievement, interests and learning styles, shaping learning experiences for each child and reflecting on their observations. Assessment should happen as part of practitioners' ongoing interaction with children, informed by feedback from parents, and other adults who interact with the child. Assessment must not entail prolonged breaks from interaction with children, nor does it require excessive paperwork. Key achievements and any concerns should be recorded periodically. Early years practitioners must give parents and carers regular updates on children's progress and achievements as part of their ongoing dialogue with families (DfE, 2011).

The Early Years Foundation Stage Profile

Assessment at the end of the Foundation Stage is called the EYFS Profile and provides parents, practitioners and teachers with a well-rounded picture of a child's knowledge, understanding and abilities, their progress against expected levels, and their readiness for school. The Profile should help teachers to plan activities for children starting Key Stage 1. Providers must make arrangements for each child to be assessed throughout the final year. The Profile report must reflect ongoing observation and should also take into account all relevant records held by the setting, and of any discussions with parents and/or carers.

Each child's level of development must be assessed (and recorded) against the 17 early learning goals. Early years practitioners must indicate whether children are not yet reaching, meeting or exceeding expected levels ('emerging', 'expected' or 'exceeding').

The **early learning goals** for communication, language and literacy are:

- **Listening and attention** – children listen attentively in a range of situations. They listen to stories, accurately anticipating key events and respond to what they hear with relevant comments, questions or actions. They can give their attention to what is being said to them and respond appropriately, while remaining involved in an activity.
- **Understanding** – children can follow instructions involving several ideas or actions. They answer 'how' and 'why' questions about their experiences and in response to stories or events.
- **Speaking** – children express themselves effectively, showing awareness of listeners' needs. They use past, present and future forms accurately when talking about events that have happened or are to happen in the future. They develop their own narratives and explanations by connecting ideas or events.
- **Reading** – children read and understand simple sentences in stories and information books, using phonic knowledge to decode regular words and read them aloud accurately. They demonstrate understanding when talking with others about what they have read, or what has been read to them.
- **Writing** – children write their own labels, captions, messages and simple stories which can be read by themselves and others. They use their phonic knowledge to spell words in ways which match their spoken sounds. They make use of letter patterns and sequences found in many words.

Aspect	Emerging	Expected (ELGs)	Exceeding
Listening and Attention	Children listen to others one-to-one or in small groups when the conversation interests them. When listening to familiar stories and rhymes children can join in at relevant points with repeated refrains and phrases and can anticipate key events. They can focus their attention by shifting between an activity and listening.	Children listen attentively in a range of situations. They listen to stories, accurately anticipating key events and respond to what they hear with relevant comments, questions or actions. They can give their attention to what is being said to them and respond appropriately, while remaining involved in an activity.	Children listen to instructions and follow them accurately, asking for clarification if necessary. They listen attentively with sustained concentration to follow a story without pictures or props. They can listen in a larger group, for example at assembly.
Understanding	Children respond to instructions when, for example, they are asked to get an item or put it away. They can understand the meaning of words such as 'on', 'under'. They can identify familiar objects by the way in which they are used.	Children can follow instructions involving several ideas or actions. They answer 'how' and 'why' questions about their experiences and in response to stories or events.	After listening to stories children can express views about the events or characters in the story and answer questions about why things happened. They can carry out instructions which contain several parts in a sequence.
Speaking	Children can connect ideas using talk, actions or objects and can retell a simple past event in correct order. They question why things happen and give simple explanations.	Children express themselves effectively showing awareness of listeners' needs. They use past, present and future forms accurately when talking about events that have happened or are to happen in the future. They develop their own narratives and explanations by connecting ideas or events.	Children show some awareness of the listener by making changes to language and non-verbal features. They recount experiences and imagine possibilities, often connecting ideas. They use a range of vocabulary in imaginative ways to add information, express ideas or to explain or justify actions or events.
Reading	Children know that print carries meaning. They show interest in books and can suggest how a story might end. They can segment the sounds in simple words and blend them together, and join in with rhyming and rhythmic activities.	Children read and understand simple sentences in stories and information books, using phonic knowledge to decode regular words and read them aloud accurately. They demonstrate understanding when talking with others about what they have read, or what has been read to them.	Children can read phonically regular words of more than one syllable as well as many irregular but high-frequency words. They use phonic, semantic and syntactic knowledge to understand unfamiliar vocabulary. They can describe the main events in the simple stories they have read.
Writing	Children give meaning to marks they make as they draw, write and paint. They can segment words orally, and use some clearly identifiable letters to communicate meaning, representing some sounds correctly and in sequence.	Children write their own labels, captions, messages and simple stories which can be read by themselves and others. They use their phonic knowledge to spell words in ways which match their spoken sounds, and make use of high-frequency spellings.	Children can spell phonically regular words of more than one syllable as well as many irregular but high-frequency words. They use key features of narrative in their own writing.

Table 3.5.2 Early Learning Goals (ELGs) for communication, language and literacy

Providers must supplement the Profile assessment with a *short commentary* on each child's skills and abilities in relation to the three key characteristics of effective learning which are:

- **Playing and exploring**: children investigate and experience things, and 'have a go'.
- **Active learning**: children keep on trying if they encounter difficulties, and enjoy achievements.
- **Creating and thinking critically**: children have and develop their own ideas, make links between ideas, and develop strategies for doing things.

This commentary will give Year 1 teachers helpful background and context when considering every child's stage of development and learning needs.

The Profile must be completed for all children, including those with special educational needs and disabilities. Children will have differing levels of skills and abilities across the Profile and it is important that there is a full assessment of all areas of their development to inform plans for future activities.

Supporting children with special educational needs

If a child's progress in developing communication, language and literacy skills gives cause for concern, early years practitioners must discuss this with the child's parents and continue to provide focused support in that area, reducing the risk that the child will struggle when starting Key Stage 1. Early years practitioners should consider whether a child may have a disability or special educational need, which requires specialist support, and should link with and/or help families to access relevant services as appropriate.

Supporting children whose home language is not English

For children whose home language is not English, early years practitioners must provide opportunities to develop and use the child's home language in play and learning, supporting their language development at home. Providers must also ensure that children have sufficient opportunities to learn and reach a good standard in English language during the EYFS, ensuring children are ready to begin Key Stage 1. When conducting assessments in communication, language and literacy, practitioners must assess children's skills in English. However if a child is not reaching the expected level in English, practitioners should discuss with parents the child's skills in the home language before reaching a conclusion on whether there is a language delay. In this way, the practitioner's role is vital in creating a language-rich environment, especially in trying to ensure that any impact on the overall expectations and aspirations of children is positive.

Activity •

Consider the individual language and communication needs of a child new to your setting and describe how you would interact with him or her to meet those needs.

• •

LO4 Understand strategies which support emergent literacy

Emergent literacy recognises the importance of early language experiences in supporting literacy development among children. Such experiences include talk, reading stories, mark-making and play; for example, when a child uses a book to 'read' a story to a doll even though he or she cannot actually read and the story does not match with what is in the book. The child has learnt how a book can be used to tell a story, and this provides an important foundation for later literacy.

Key term

emergent literacy A term that is used to explain a child's knowledge of reading and writing skills before he or she learns how to read and write words.

AC 4.1 Explain strategies to support the development of emergent literacy in relation to current frameworks

The EYFS in England provides a framework for emergent literacy. *Practical Guidance* for the EYFS states:

- **From 22 to 36 months**: the emphasis is on language and communication, facial expression and gesture, and special time to share. 'Find opportunities to tell and read stories to children, using puppets, soft toys or real objects as props.'
- **From 30 to 50 months**: the EYFS highlights storytelling: As children begin to understand how to use books, early years practitioners might observe 'children's familiarity with the way books work ... turning the pages and telling the story using the pictures and using phrases such as "Once upon a time"'. The next step for a child could be to 'suggest how the story might end'.
- **From 40 to 60 months+**: later, the same child might show their increasing knowledge of how a story is put together, demonstrating 'understanding of the elements of stories, for example, Mehmet refers to the "beginning" and "end" of a story. He says: "I don't like that ending. I think he should have run away and been happy ever after"'.

These examples from across the developmental stages in the EYFS show how progress in reading is not just about learning letter sounds or recognising words. In the *Practice Guidance*, 'Linking Sounds and Letters' and 'Reading' are separate sections, emphasising that equal value is given to children becoming familiar with books and how stories work.

Practical strategies

Early years settings are able to use a number of practical strategies to support the development of emergent literacy. These include the following:

Setting up a writing area

Encourage children to use emergent forms of writing, such as scribble writing, by providing:

- a writing area stocked with pens, pencils, markers, paper, sticky notes and envelopes
- shared writing demonstrations in which the practitioner writes down text dictated by children
- practical writing opportunities which are related to class activities – for example, sign-up sheets for popular activities, library book slips, postbox with postcards
- play-related writing materials (e.g. pencils and notepads for making shopping lists and receipts).

Promoting an awareness of print

1. Read 'big' books and other enlarged texts with children, and point to the print as it is read. While reading the text, draw children's attention to basic concepts of print such as:
   - the distinction between pictures and print
   - left-to-right, top-to-bottom sequence; and
   - book concepts (cover, title, page).
2. Read favourite stories repeatedly, and encourage children to 'read' along on the parts of the story they remember.
3. Introduce useful print linked to play areas and activities:
   - label play areas including both text and a photo or picture
   - label storage areas for toys and equipment using text and a picture of the item.
4. Write text beside children's artwork or photos of activities, recording exactly what the children said about them.
5. Include books related to play areas such as recipe books and shopping catalogues in the role-play area.

Supporting name recognition

Label areas with the child's name where their personal belongings – such as coats, hats and books – are kept.

Ask the children to sign in on arrival and assist them to find their name on the sign-in sheet.

Activity •

Check the provision for emergent literacy in your setting. Are there plenty of examples of text relevant to children's everyday experiences?

• •

AC 4.2 Explain systematic synthetic phonics in the teaching of reading

Systematic synthetic phonics

English is an irregular language, which makes it particularly hard to learn to read and write in English. Some argue that we should get children off to an early start for just this reason. Most early childhood experts take the view that the human brain needs to be sufficiently mature to tackle the fine detail of discriminating the sounds and look of English print. Even in countries where the language is very regular, such as Finland and Sweden, this is the approach. However, the brain does function easily and without stress in relation to learning about communication (both non-verbal and spoken/signed language) and music, gesture and movement. This means that singing and dancing, and talking with and listening to children all have a huge contribution to make in helping children towards reading and writing at six or seven years of age. This age is generally regarded, throughout the world, as the best time to learn to read and write, because the structures dealing with this level of symbolic functioning are present.

These rhyming strings of words nearly sound the same: 'pot', 'dot', 'got'; 'mess', 'cress', 'dress'; 'mum', 'chum', 'drum'. The last chunk rhymes, but the first chunk is different in each case. This is an aspect of **analytic phonics**. Many early childhood reading and writing experts consider that learning about rhyming through poems, songs, action rhymes, poetry cards and books is a more powerful way of helping young children to read in English than teaching isolated sounds, using flashcards (**synthetic phonics**) as the main strategy. A fierce debate about this seems to arise roughly every 10 years. Most experts argue that the more strategies we have to offer children as they learn to read, the more we can find the ones that suit each child best. One size does not fit all children.

There is great opposition by early childhood experts to the suggestion that young children should be directly taught synthetic phonics through daily drill in large groups. However, daily group time (remember, large groups are four to eight children), with song, dance and rhyme, and encouragement, helps children become:

- phonologically aware
- able to discriminate sounds with increasing ease
- able to link these with the print in the rhymes using poetry cards.

Key terms

analytic phonics Children are taught whole words and later analyse their constituent parts, such as c-at or str-eet.

synthetic phonics Children are taught the sounds of letters and letter combinations first, then combine those to form words: c-a-t or s-t-r-ee-t.

Sounds and how words look

Children need to learn to segment (break down) sounds and print. They also need to learn to blend (join) sounds and print. The smallest sounds are **phonemes** and the smallest print is a **grapheme**. Children need to make grapho–phonic relationships.

They need to begin to see that what they have segmented can be blended back into a word. The ideal age to do this, experts in most countries say, is between six and seven years of age.

Songs like 'Humpty Dumpty' are simple examples of this:

Humpty Dumpty sat on a wall,

Humpty Dumpty had a great fall …

Children quickly begin to see that the last chunk is the same (-all), while the beginnings are different ('w' and 'f').

AC 4.3 Describe how the EYP provides opportunities for sustained shared thinking to support children's emergent literacy

What is sustained shared thinking?

Sustained shared thinking is the means by which early years practitioners nurture and develop children's critical thinking skills. It involves seeking out opportunities to build upon the children's interests and challenging them to indulge in a deeper thought process.

Sustained shared thinking occurs when two or more individuals 'work together' in an intellectual way to solve a problem, clarify a concept, evaluate an activity, extend a narrative etc. Both parties must contribute to the thinking and it must develop and extend the understanding.

(Siraj-Blatchford et al., 2004)

Sustained shared thinking is a key approach in helping children to become lifelong learners with transferable skills. Children who have the ability to enquire, consider, reflect, reason, predict, evaluate and suggest creative solutions will be better equipped to succeed in a world where a job is no longer for life.

Recent theories supporting thinking skills

In the last few years, theories about thinking skills have led to different methods for actively teaching thinking skills when working with young children in Key Stage 1 of the National Curriculum or above. These include the following theories:

Researching Effective Pedagogy in the Early Years (REPEY)

One of the key findings of this report concerns the development of thinking skills:

- Good outcomes for children were found to be linked to adult–child interactions that included 'sustained shared thinking' and open-ended questioning to extend children's thinking.
- Adult 'modelling' is often combined with sustained periods of shared thinking.
- Freely chosen play activities often provided the best opportunities for adults to extend children's thinking.

Instrumental Enrichment (Reuven Feuerstein)

The basic principle of the Feuerstein Method of Instrumental Enrichment is that every human being – regardless of age, disability or socio-economic background – has the ability to improve their learning potential and therefore their level of functioning. The method is a comprehensive approach encompassing philosophy and systematic tools that can be implemented in a variety of clinical and educational techniques. The result is that individuals not only learn new information, but how to learn; how to question, how to analyse and how to think in a logical, critical way.

Philosophy for Children – Thinking through stories (Matthew Lipman)

Lipman talks about children as born philosophers because of the natural curiosity they have for the world. He believes that education taught facts, people in authority taught opinions, but no one was teaching children to think. His approach was to provide children with stories which promote thinking: these stories promote questioning and discussion and are used in many countries of the world to support the development of reasoning skills.

Thinking Hats (Edward de Bono)

De Bono's method uses colour-coded 'hats' for children to wear physically and mentally. There are six hats: white for information gathering, red for feelings, black for negative feelings, yellow for positive points, green for creativity, blue for organisation and planning. Children work in a small group on a problem, and are encouraged to use one 'hat' at a time to understand the different ways they can tackle the problem. When they are familiar with the method they can apply it to working alone as well as in group work. This method is generally used with children aged five and over as it is vital that they are able to understand their own and other's feelings while problem-solving. The idea behind his method is that by learning to understand how emotions affect their thought process, children can develop their creative and logical thinking.

Thinking through Primary Teaching (Steve Higgins)

Higgins believes that developing children's thinking and understanding of their own learning is a key factor in effective primary teaching. By encouraging children to think about their learning, teachers can help them to grow into effective learners. Higgins monitored and evaluated several methods for teaching thinking skills and devised subject-specific skills for teachers to integrate into their lessons.

Providing opportunities for sustained shared thinking

Working with babies

Babies communicate through facial expressions, gestures and body movements as well as through sounds.

- Make eye contact and use exaggerated facial movements to convey your message and watch for the response you get.

- Encourage babies to interact with one another through the use of some shared resources, and talk aloud in a running commentary on what you and the babies are doing, thereby letting them know that they are important members of the social group.
- Give them time to respond and time to think through their ideas, rather than asking questions or commenting.
- Discuss with parents the importance of them talking to their babies at home, and of being receptive to their babies' responses.
- For families whose home language is not English, it is helpful to ask the parents to teach you a few key words in their own language, which you can then use when talking to their baby in the setting.

Working with toddlers

Talk with toddlers about the routines during the day. This helps them to understand that they are active participants in the daily life of the setting.

- Encourage them to become independent by giving them opportunities to make choices and to take an increasing responsibility for how they spend their time.
- Value their early attempts at using language and listen carefully to what they are saying.
- At the same time, value the non-verbal language which children use to express their thoughts and needs. When disputes arise – often over sharing toys – use these as opportunities to help children develop negotiation and conflict resolution skills. The more opportunities they have to practise these skills, the more confident they will become in extending their own learning as part of a team.

Working with three- to five-year-olds

A good way to support individual children's learning is to listen to children and follow their interests.

- Provide time at the start of the day for a group discussion: Give children the opportunity to discuss together what is on offer for them to do. Listen carefully to the children's responses. By keeping questions open-ended and following up on their suggestions there will be new ideas and avenues to explore.
- By becoming engaged in sustained shared thinking alongside the children, adults can provide the ideal role model for active learning. Provide a

comfortable atmosphere where children feel confident in expressing their thoughts and ideas, without fear of ridicule or contradiction.

- Provide time during the day for children to reflect on their ideas and actions and talk about what they have done. By sharing reflections in this way, children will refine and develop their thinking, as well as seeing that their play and learning are valued and respected.

Activity

How does your setting provide opportunities for sustained shared thinking? List the activities which positively promote these opportunities.

LO5 Plan activities to support emergent literacy

AC 5.1 Plan for children's participation in activities which support and extend emergent literacy

When planning, implementing and evaluating activities to support the early years framework for learning, your overall aims should be to:

- support *all* the children you work with
- ensure each child has full access to the relevant curriculum
- encourage participation by all children
- meet children's individual learning and development needs
- build on children's existing knowledge and skills
- help all children achieve their full potential.

Before starting to plan activities to support emergent literacy, you need to find out about each individual child's needs and preferences. The stages outlined in this unit are merely a guide to the *sequence* of development. Remember that each child is unique, and will develop in his or her own way.

The stages of development of reading skills
Babies and toddlers (birth to age two to three years)
General stages:

- looking at patterns, fluttering leaves on trees, or in books for newborns

- sharing a focus, as you follow the baby/toddler's gaze at a picture or object
- talking about what you see together: position chairs so that adult and child face each other to encourage talking about what you see together
- finger rhymes
- action songs.

Sharing books:

- describing pictures, especially photographs of familiar people and objects
- pausing to let the child respond
- encouraging the child to turn the page (thick card or cloth pages are helpful)
- encouraging the child to make sounds in the story, or complete repetitious phrases
- enjoying the rhythms of the phrases and rhymes
- emphasising key words as they are said.

Two to three years, and five to six years
In general:

- singing finger rhymes and action songs becomes easier, and children begin to anticipate the movements and actions while singing or chanting the words
- they engage with the sounds of the rhyming
- they engage with the rhythms
- they engage with alliteration (repetition of initial sounds)
- they play spontaneously with sounds
- they are interested in sounds around them, such as police sirens, ambulances, animals and birdsong, or the rhythmic sounds of machinery; in London, children are often heard chanting on the underground trains, 'Mind the gap'
- they make nonsense rhymes, or repeat sounds in a string
- they enjoy games with sounds, led by adults
- children like to dictate shopping lists or messages on a card for someone they love. They often want to read these back, and do so with pride and a sense of achievement.

From five to six years, to eight years

- Children learn how texts work, and how to build words and break them up, so that they develop word recognition and understanding. They do so

without understanding what they read; at this stage children do not read for meaning (this is often called barking at print).

- By the end of this part of childhood, most (but by no means all) children are becoming fluent readers and confident writers.
- Almost all children can learn to read and most really want to learn. The majority of children learn to read between the ages of four-and-a-half and six years old. Research shows that pre-school children who are exposed to plenty of language (books and conversation) tend to do better at school.

The importance of books
Children need to find out that what people say, think, feel and do can be written down, or printed in a book, which may then be read by someone else. They need to work out where the text begins and where it ends, and have to learn which direction they have to read the text in (left to right in English). Bilingual children need to learn to switch direction if reading a language that is presented in a different way. If they speak Urdu and English equally well, they need to learn to read from left to right in English, and right to left in Urdu. A close partnership with parents is important in helping children to achieve this.

Enjoying looking at books
Children use 'reading-like' behaviour; this is a rehearsal for the fluent reading which comes later. They pretend to 'read' in their role play. They memorise texts of books that are favourites. Many settings now introduce core texts, chosen carefully

by the staff, and favourite texts that children consistently select from the book area.

Enjoying listening to stories

Though not all children will be read to at bedtime, they will benefit from spending some time every day sharing a book with an adult, while sitting on a sofa; this activity, which may take place either on a one-to-one basis or with two children and an adult, is one of the most important early reading experiences adults can give to children.

Figure 3.5.1 Sharing stories is important

Children love to talk about what is being read to them, as they listen. This is why it is important for adults to share books with children in very small groups, or one-to-one. Children relate the stories that are read to them to their own experiences of people and the world they live in. They bring their own ideas, thoughts and feelings to the book. This is what adults do when they read, but they do not do this out loud in the way that young children need to do. It is therefore important to be clear that in small groups, or one-to-one, children can literally share the text as an active 'reader' would do silently.

In larger groups (and with this age group it is usually wise not to have more than six to ten children in a large group) children can be introduced to the core texts chosen by staff, with the expectation that they listen to the whole story without interruption. This helps them to focus on the music, rhythms, rhymes, alliteration and sounds as the story unfolds. It also gives children the sense of a complete narrative/story with its characters.

Reflective practice

- What key communication skills (verbal and non-verbal) does a young child have?
- How could you more effectively support the development of these skills?

How to use constructive feedback to support children

Early years practitioners should find opportunities, wherever possible, to discuss the learning with the children, giving them feedback and identifying next steps. This should all form part of the 'assessment *for* learning' process, and should be done, when possible, without interrupting children's play.

Practitioners should always recognise young children's competence, and appreciate their efforts when they show their understanding of new words and phrases. Make sure that children understand what they are being praised for by responding immediately; saying, for example, 'Well done, Daniel, you told that story very well.' It is important to use encouraging words when a child is putting in a lot of effort, even if he has not managed to achieve his aim. Children need to receive positive feedback in order to develop confidence and good self-esteem. Then they will be more likely to try again and to persevere until they succeed.

Progress check

Giving positive feedback

- **Be specific**: make sure that the child knows what you are referring to when you say: 'Well done!' or 'I really liked that …'
- **Be positive and constructive**: comment on particular ideas the child expressed in writing. *First*, praise the child for what he or she has achieved and emphasise the good points. *Next*, focus on what you feel the child needs to learn. *Then*, suggest ways the child can improve – and end on a positive note.
- **Ask open-ended questions**: engage the child's interest by showing interest yourself: 'Why did he or she include the dog in the story …?' 'What sort of dog is your dog in the story?'
- **Be reassuring**: adapt the feedback to the developmental stage of the individual, taking account of the child's self-confidence. Always end on a positive note, reassuring the child that however difficult they may find it, it will soon seem much easier.

Reflective practice

Communicating with children

- Do you encourage repetition, rhythm and rhyme by reciting poems and rhymes and singing?
- Do you encourage playfulness and turn-taking with babies using games such as peek-a-boo?
- Do you use different voices, to tell stories and get young children to join in, sometimes using puppets, soft toys or real objects?

The barriers to learning how to read and write

Poor levels of attainment in reading and writing at primary school are associated strongly with later low achievement. There are various factors which create barriers for children when learning to read and write – both inside and outside their own homes. These include:

- **Social and cultural attitudes** to the importance of reading and writing in everyday life: this will affect children's interest and motivation to learn literacy skills.
- **Socio-economic status**: this may affect access to books and often influences how much time is available for reading and being read to.
- **Access to pre-school provision**: effective pre-school provision promotes children's language development through a rich variety of activities involving talking and listening, including reading stories, singing songs, so familiarising them with the value of written text.
- **Lack of familiarity with the sounds of language**: children who are learning a second language or who have a language delay will have difficulties in both reading and writing. Children from minority ethnic groups, particularly those whose first language is not English, and Traveller children may require additional support.
- **Access to public libraries**: this includes parental knowledge of what materials are available within them; and parental attitudes from their own success or failure at reading.

AC 5.2 Use strategies to plan activities which encourage: speaking and listening; reading; sustained shared thinking; writing; digital literacy

Activities to develop speaking and listening skills

These activities can be divided into five basic categories:

1 exploration
2 description
3 conversation
4 discussion
5 instruction.

Exploration

- Toys and other interesting objects to look at and play with such as household objects (remember safety).
- Sounds to listen to including voices, music, songs and rhymes.
- Noisemakers such as commercial and home-made musical instruments.
- Bath toys and books.
- Construction materials including wooden bricks, plastic bricks and 'junk' modelling.
- Natural materials such as water, sand, clay, dough and cooking ingredients.
- Creative materials such as paint, paper and glue.
- Outdoor activities and outings including gardening, visits to parks and museums, swimming.
- Animals including visits to farms and wildlife centres, looking after small pets.

Description

- News time, circle time.
- Recording events, outings, visits and visitors.
- Books and stories appropriate to age/level of development including cloth books, board books, activity books, pop-up books, picture books, audio books, textbooks, novels, encyclopaedia.

Conversation

- Talking about their day, experiences and interests in a variety of settings with other children and adults, such as playgroup, nursery, school, after-school clubs, youth clubs.

- Talking during imaginative play activities such as playing with pretend/role-play equipment; for example, dressing-up clothes, home corner, play shop, puppets; playing with dolls, teddies and other cuddly toys; playing with small-scale toys such as toy cars, garages and road systems, train set, dolls' houses.
- Talking about special events such as birthdays, new baby, religious festivals.
- Talking while doing activities – not necessarily related to the task!

Discussion

- Problem-solving during activities such as mathematics, science and technology.
- Follow-up discussion after an activity or event, such as watching DVD/television or live performance, listening to a story or recorded music.
- Cooperative group work.
- Games and puzzles.

Instruction

- Preparation before an activity.
- Explanation of what to do – verbal and/or written on a board.

- Instructions during an activity to keep the children on task.
- Extra support for individuals.
- Introducing or extending knowledge on a specific skill.
- Step-by-step instructions.
- Worksheets, workbooks and work cards.
- Delivering verbal and/or written messages, carrying out errands.

Activity

Using your own experience

Describe an example activity for *each* of the five categories, based on your own experiences of working with children.

Activities to develop early reading skills

In order to learn to read, children must recognise that a certain pattern of letters represents a particular sound. They need to build up a set of skills that will help them to make sense of words, signs and symbols.

Early reading skill	Activities to promote the skill
Shape recognition and matching: the ability to recognise shapes and to differentiate between them is important. Children learn to match shapes and patterns first and this helps them to match letters and, finally, words.	Snap Shape sorter Picture pairs Lotto Jigsaws Dominoes
Rhyming: research shows that children who can understand about rhyming words have a head start in learning to read and, even more, to spell.	Rhyming games such as 'I Spy with my little eye, something that rhymes with cat' (hat or mat). Leave off the end of rhymes for the child to complete, e.g. 'Humpty Dumpty sat on a wall, Humpty Dumpty had a great…?' Reading simple poetry.
Language skills: the more experience children have of language, the more easily they will learn to read. Children need to hear and join in conversations (with adults and children), and to listen to stories and poetry of all sorts.	Talking. Reading stories. Encouraging children to talk. Share their favourite stories again and again: repeating phrases helps to build children's language. ➔

Table 3.5.3 Activities to promote early reading skills

Early reading skill	Activities to promote the skill
Concepts of print: this means 'how we look at books' and includes following print the right way (from left to right), turning the pages, looking at pictures.	Children need to learn practical skills: ● how to hold a book (the right way up!) ● how to turn pages singly ● let the child see your finger following the print when reading.
Letter skills: children need to learn what sounds the letters can make.	Begin with letters with an interesting shape that makes them easy to recognise or a letter which is important to the child, such as their own initial. Use the letter sounds rather than letter names; e.g. 'a for ant', not 'ay for ape'. Try a letter hunt: looking for objects which begin with a particular letter.
Motor skills: since reading and writing are best taught together, pencil control is important.	Encourage creativity: drawing and painting with lots of different tools and materials to encourage pencil and brush control. Playing with small toys, especially construction sets, help to develop fine motor skills.
Looking at a variety of **printed materials**: newspapers, magazines, packaging, street and shop names, etc.	Point out words in the environment: e.g. 'Push', 'Pull', 'Open', 'Closed', etc. Visit the library to encourage familiarity with the idea of books for everyone.
Memory skills: words are made up of sequences of letters and sounds, and children need to remember this before they can read.	Memory games: such as 'I went to the shops and I bought a...' and pairs (Pelmanism) all help to improve children's memory skills and to increase their attention span. Sequencing: book page layout can be reinforced by, for example, laying out the child's clothes to be selected first from left then to the right: vest, pants, top, trousers, socks, shoes.

Table 3.5.3 Activities to promote early reading skills   (*Continued*)

The use of story and rhyme in supporting communication, language and listening
Storytelling

There is a difference between reading stories from a book and storytelling. A love of stories is common to all young children, and by telling stories, rather than reading them, a storyteller can really bring the story to life and make it a more interactive experience for the children. To enhance the experience of storytelling, you can use:

● visual aids or props – objects related to the story
● sound effects – children could be encouraged to make appropriate sounds
● pictures or photographs
● children's drawings and paintings.

When telling (or reading) a story to a group of children, it is important to arrange seating comfortably, and to ensure that all children can see and hear both you and the book or visual aids. Early years practitioners should also find opportunities to read or tell stories to individual children or very small groups. Having extra attention at story time allows children to point, to comment and to help with page turning.

Rhyme

Sharing rhymes with young children helps them listen to the patterns of language. Children first begin to notice that certain words have the same sounds at the end (rhyme). Later they notice that many words share a pattern in the way they are spelled. Understanding these links makes learning to read much easier.

Rhyming words helps children appreciate beginning and ending sounds – for example, 'cat', 'pat' and 'mat'. Rhyming activities suggested in the EYFS include:

● Share, recite and encourage joining in with rhymes, action songs and games. For example, as the children come to join the circle for group time, say the rhyme: 'I know a name which rhymes with hen, he's sitting in the group and his name is …' and encourage the children to provide the name (for example, Ben). For children whose names do not lend themselves to rhyme, say for example, 'I know a girl whose name I can sing, Jodie's coming next and she's in the ring.'

● Encourage repetition, rhythm and rhyme by using tone and intonation. Use rhymes from a variety of cultures, including those shared by parents from home. Increase children's repertoire of familiar and traditional rhymes.
● Encourage the children to use a microphone and recording equipment to record their own rhymes.

Methods of teaching reading

You can help children to read by enjoying a book or poetry card together, without any pressure. Children can see how a book is used, where to begin, how to turn a page and the direction of print, using pictures as clues, finding familiar words and guessing. Being able to guess and predict what the print says is important. Children are usually fascinated by guesses that go wrong, realising this as they learn to link what they read with meaning, and to work out the words using their increasing ability to segment and blend the graphemes and phonemes. It is important to say, 'What do you think he says next?' Show the child any patterns – for example, a phrase that is repeated – and talk about the letters, words and sentences as you go. Picture cues are very important when learning to read, so talk about these and the clues they give.

Alphabet books and friezes are important as they help children to segment words, and to focus on the initial grapheme and phoneme in a word, while offering a meaningful picture to help the child along. Regularly singing the alphabet is helpful too.

Pointing out children with the same letter at the beginning of their names helps, and there can be fascinating discussions about why George is pronounced with a 'j' sound, while Gary is with a 'g' sound. English speakers need to learn early to spot exceptions with detective joy!

Children often know favourite stories by heart; this gives children a sense of control and the ability to feel they can predict what the text says. It gives them a can-do feeling, which is crucial in learning. Decide as a team which books you will introduce as *core texts*, to help children become familiar with them. Note which books are favourites of particular children, and use these with the child in the same way. Above all, remember that learning to read should be fun, and it should hold meaning for the child.

In practice activity

Stages of reading

Observe children aged three to seven years. Identify which children are emergent, beginner and fluent readers. What are the factors that you use to decide this? What can you do to support children in their enjoyment of books?

Sustained shared thinking

In addition to the ideas suggested on pp 333–34 (AC 4.3), try to use open-ended questioning with young children and other words to promote children's confidence in self-expression. This will encourage sustained shared thinking. Examples include:

● 'I don't know, what do you think?'
● 'That's an interesting idea.'
● 'I like what you have done there.'
● 'Have you seen what J has done – why?'
● 'I wondered why you had … ?'
● 'I've never thought about that before.'
● 'You've really made me think.'
● 'What would happen if we did x or y?'

Informative displays set at the children's eye level are also an effective way to prompt discussion and conversation about a subject. Such displays might feature posters or photographs with extracts of information and questions about a project in the setting.

Writing

Writing has two aspects:

● what it says – the construction of meaning
● the look of it – the handwriting and letter shapes (transcription).

When children begin to write, they are constructing a code. Most languages have a written code. Writing develops when children begin to use

Figure 3.5.2 Early mark-making

symbols. Often they begin by putting letter-type shapes into their drawings. These gradually get pushed out to the edges of the drawing, to look more like words and sentences. Early years practitioners need to observe the shapes, sizes and numbers that children experiment with. Children need to be free to experiment, without criticism or pressure. Left-handed children must never be encouraged to write with the right hand. Young children find capital letters, which are more linear, easier to write than lower-case letters, which have more curves, so they tend to experiment with capitals first. It is when children begin to experiment with curves that they are indicating they have more pencil control, so can begin to form letters more easily.

Children need:

- to manipulate and try out different ways of 'writing', using their own personal code – tracing or copying letters undermines this because their own movement patterns and laying down of neural pathways are an important part of the process
- to explore what writing is

- adults who point out print in books and in the environment – for example, on notices and street signs.

It is important to talk with children about environmental print, and to pick out their favourite letters (often those in their name). A child's own name is important to them, and they often write the names of people they love, plus the words 'love from'.

Learning to write

Writing and spelling are more difficult to learn than speaking and reading. The child's first word written from memory is usually his or her own name. Most of the activities shown to promote early reading skills will also help children to learn to write. They also need to develop the following basic skills.

Children need to know how to:

- control the pen or pencil – this involves fine manipulative skills
- form letters including upper and lower case
- recognise letter direction, e.g. b, d and p, q
- write in a straight line and to space out words
- punctuate – understanding when writing needs a comma or full stop

- plan what they are going to write in advance
- sit still for some time with the correct posture for writing.

Children learn how to copy letters from as early as two years, and the skills of learning to write develop gradually as they become competent readers.

How writing develops

It is important to remember that children will progress through the different stages at different rates and ages, depending on their experiences and developmental abilities. All children begin their journey into writing by **making marks**. This early writing follows a sequence:

Stage one
The child:

- holds the pencil or crayon in the palm of the hand in a palmar – or fist-like – grasp
- makes early attempts at mark-making which feature lots of random marks, often made over other marks. This is often described by adults as scribbles
- cannot usually distinguish between her writing and her picture.

Stage two
The child:

- may hold the pencil or crayon in a pincer grip between the thumb and index finger
- makes a definite attempt to make individual marks
- attempts to close shapes making an inside and an outside. These shapes are often circular
- combines shapes and lines. These marks will often represent one word.

Stage three
The child:

- copies adults and makes marks going across the page. These are often zigzags and curvy lines
- has a clearer idea of the marks she wants to make
- may use either hand for writing.

Stage four
The child:

- forms symbols and some recognisable familiar letters that follow on next to each other
- is becoming aware of the left-to-right direction of print and can point to where the print begins

- is becoming aware that writing conveys meaning and may 'read' own writing.

Stage five
The child:

- writes a message using familiar letters
- writes some upper-and lower-case letters
- writes her name reliably.

Stage six
The child:

- writes most of the alphabet correctly using upper- and lower-case letters
- writes first one or two letters correctly then finishes with a jumbled string of letters
- begins to write capital letters and full stops at the beginning and end of work
- writes a longer sentence and can read it back
- attempts familiar forms of writing such as letters and lists.

Stage seven
The child:

- makes individual marks and uses some letters from her own name to communicate a message
- begins to understand that drawing and writing are different
- is becoming aware that print carries a message.

> **Key term**
>
> **mark-making** When children realise that marks can be used symbolically to carry meaning, in much the same way as the spoken word, they begin to use marks as tools to make their thinking visible.

How to promote mark-making and writing skills
Settings should provide:

- **Materials for mark-making**: these can include a range of pencils, felt tips, different sized paper, envelopes, little books and recycled cards. Also useful are other materials such as alphabet friezes, name cards and magnetic letters.
- **Meaningful contexts**: a 'writing-rich' environment where writing and mark-making

Figure 3.5.3 Boys writing on whiteboards

are encouraged for a wide variety of purposes or when adults take part in writing with children.

- **Examples of other people writing**: these can include activities such as staff completing records, parents and carers leaving messages and visits to the local environment to see adults writing in shops, banks or post offices.
- **Encouragement and praise**: all attempts at writing made by children should be positively encouraged. Early years practitioners help children to understand that their writing is important and valuable if they take time to discuss with children what marks mean.

> ### In practice activity
>
> **Observe** a child engaged in a writing activity. **Assess** the child's writing skills, by commenting on:
>
> - manipulative skills
> - concentration
> - creativity of the finished piece of writing.

Scribing

Sitting down with children at the mark-making table, at their level, and scribing their messages for them are all important aspects of working sensitively with children. Children do not offer adults their writing for it to be judged and found wanting. They give their effortful early attempts at writing with love, and trust that the adult will appreciate and value them. Then they begin to share with the adult those aspects they found difficult, and accept help that is proffered willingly.

Reasons for writing

Children are attracted to activities such as writing labels for the photograph album, as they engage with talking about what they were doing, or their friends and family. Writing messages such as 'closed' and 'open' for the shop helps children to see the reasons for writing.

Remember, you cannot plan the next steps for a child unless you first observe what interests the child and what engages them in learning. Observation helps practitioners to create a learning environment, indoors and outdoors, which supports the development of writing.

Digital literacy
The use of technology to support language and literacy

The use of information and communication technology in the EYFS is based on the needs of the children, the focus of the curriculum, and whether the technology will add to children's educational opportunities and experiences.

The use of computers

Fine and gross motor skills develop at varying rates, and learning to write can be tedious and difficult as children struggle to form letters. A word processor allows them to compose and revise text without being distracted by the fine motor aspects of letter formation. If computers are used with children in kindergarten, pre-school, or other early years settings, the computer should be one of many activity choices they can explore.

- **Three- to five-year-olds** generally spend about the same amount of time at a computer as they do on other activities such as playing with blocks or drawing. Most children of this age are limited to icons and pictures on the screen for understanding. They are also more interested and less frustrated when an adult is present; their computer use is usually facilitated by the teacher or practitioner.
- **Five- to eight-year-olds**: as they mature, children use computers more independently, and the teacher's role moves from guidance towards monitoring and active support. Software programs for this age group should be limited in number

and appropriate for children's skill level and the intended use. More opportunities for independent use become available with increasing language and literacy skills. For example, simple word processors become important educational tools as children experiment with written language.

Recording equipment

Recording equipment such as MP3 players can support early literacy experiences by integrating all aspects of literacy: speaking, listening, reading and writing. They allow children to listen to recorded stories or songs, or to follow along in a book as they hear it being read on tape. Children can record family stories, their own made-up stories, poems, and songs, or themselves reading aloud. When adults write down children's stories from children's dictated words or from the recording equipment, children see how the spoken word can turn into the written word. They can also help children develop their own storytelling ability and an understanding of how sound translates to print.

Cameras

Cameras (film, video or digital) can record children's activities while they are working, as well as performances and special events. Children can tell a story in pictures and write or dictate captions. Photos can be used to share the learning with other children and with parents. Photos can also introduce teachers and staff members to new students and families during home visits.

LO6 Lead activities that support emergent literacy

AC 6.1 Lead an activity to support emergent literacy

As outlined in Unit 3.2, leading an activity involves managing the activity from the planning stage to evaluation. Using your plans, arrange to implement the activity and evaluate it.

Activity ·

Plan, lead and evaluate an activity using the strategies outlined in this unit.

· ·

AC 6.2 Identify benefits to children's holistic learning and development when supporting emergent literacy

Child development should always be viewed in the round, or holistically. This is because each area of development is linked with and affects every other area of development. Unit 3.10 looks at the benefits to children's holistic learning and development when communication skills are promoted. Read through the section on pp 427–9 to find out how all aspects of communication benefit children's learning holistically. These are the same for emergent literacy skills. Children will benefit by gaining independence skills as well as in self-esteem and confidence.

LO7 Review how planned activities support emergent literacy

AC 7.1 Evaluate how planned activities support emergent literacy in relation to current frameworks

How to monitor progress and keep appropriate records

The EYFS outlines:

- the ways in which early years practitioners and teachers monitor children's progress
- when and how to keep records
- when and how to refer a child for specialist help (for example, the local speech and language team).

It is important that schools use the EYFS to build on with children in Year 1 as well as those in reception classes. The EYFS helps Nursery, Reception and Key Stage 1 (Years 1 and 2) teachers to see how the six area of the EYFS link to literacy in Key Stage 1. This is not about getting children ready for the next class. It is about building on what children know and can do, supporting them in this, and using what they know to help them into the less familiar. Then they continue their learning journey with high well-being, eager to learn more.

The EYFS Profile helps early years practitioners and teachers to plan activities for children starting Key Stage 1. Evaluate your planned activities in relation to the Early Learning Goals for communication, language and literacy.

AC 7.2 Analyse own role in relation to planned activities

Reflective practice

Your role will vary from one activity to the next. It is important to be reflective about your role in providing activities. In particular, analyse your role by answering the following questions:

- Have I ensured that children are not rushed but are supported in ways that are right for each child's stage of development?
- Do I take into account the children's previous experiences, current interests and developmental needs?
- Have I encouraged the use of language and provided access to a rich vocabulary?
- Do I manage children's time so that they have the opportunity to become deeply involved in their activities?
- Have I identified learning opportunities that arise spontaneously through play?

However well planned, it is important to be flexible. As the EYFS says (EYFS Practice Guidance 2.9),

It is important to remember that no plan written weeks before can include a group's interest in a spider's web on a frosty morning or a particular child's interest in transporting small objects in a favourite blue bucket. Yet it is these interests which may lead to some powerful learning. Plans should therefore be flexible enough to adapt to circumstances.

AC 7.3 Make recommendations for meeting children's individual literacy needs

Each setting will have its own policy and methods for assessing the progress of children's literacy skills. Your role is to aim to meet each child's individual literacy needs. This can be done by:

- identifying problems and monitoring progress

- providing activities targeted to individual needs
- providing a language-rich environment for learning to read and write
- evaluating the effects of your practice – what worked well and not so well?

How to provide and prepare resources to support learning and development

The British Association for Early Childhood Education (www.early-education.org.uk) produces a wide range of publications and resources to support early years practitioners and parents to support young children to learn effectively. The booklet on *Core experiences for the EYFS* from Kate Greenaway Nursery School and Children's Centre can also be ordered from this website.

Centre for Literacy in Primary Education has undertaken pioneering work in supporting and training practitioners to enjoy helping children to love stories and books. It offers excellent training for those working with children in Reception and Key Stage 1: www.clpe.co.uk

The National Literacy Trust (www.literacytrust.org.uk) provides information relating to early years provision and literacy, including news, research, events, policy, resources and further information about their work in this area.

LO8 Work with parents/carers to encourage them to take an active role in their child's play, learning and development

AC 8.1 Work with parents/carers to encourage them to take an active role in their child's play, learning and development

Parents play a vital role in all aspects of their children's development, but particularly in the development of communication skills. Being told stories promotes language and, by feeding the child's imagination, develops abstract thought. An international study by OECD (2011) found that children whose parents frequently read with them in their first year of school are still showing the benefit when they are 15.

Throughout this book, the importance of developing a partnership with parents is emphasised. There are several ways in which parents can be involved in their child's learning journey. These include:

- **information-sharing** – sharing information with parents about their child's learning and preferences, and encouraging parents to share information about their child's interests and needs
- **setting up a library in the setting** – this could double as an opportunity for parents to borrow books to share with their child at home and also for parents and early years practitioners to interact in a relaxed atmosphere
- **involving parents** in assessments of their child.

Activity

Are parents involved in coming into the setting to help with emergent literacy activities, such as reading or musical activities with the children?

Assessment practice

1 Describe the different stages of communication, language and literacy development for children aged from birth to seven years.
2 Describe the factors that can affect language and communication needs.
3 How can working with others support children's emergent literacy?
4 What is meant by a 'language-rich environment'?
5 Find out about the different frameworks and policies relating to your home country which guide provision for children's learning in communication, language and literacy from birth to seven years years.
6 Know how to provide a language-rich environment for children.
7 How can you interact with children to meet individual language and communication needs?
8 Explain strategies to support the development of emergent literacy in relation to current frameworks.
9 Explain how you can use synthetic phonics in the teaching of reading.
10 What is sustained shared thinking? How can you provide opportunities for this to support children's emergent literacy?
11 Describe three activities that support children's learning to promote:
   - speaking skills
   - listening skills
   - reading skills.
12 Lead activities to support and extend emergent literacy, and identify benefits to children's holistic learning and development when supporting emergent literacy.
13 Evaluate how planned activities support emergent literacy in relation to current frameworks in your area.
14 Analyse your own role in relation to planned activities.
15 Make some recommendations for meeting children's individual literacy needs.
16 How can you work with parents/carers in a way which encourages them to take an active role in their child's play, learning and development?
17 Identify three barriers to learning how to read and write.

Useful resources

Books and journals

Conteh, J. (ed.) (2006), *Promoting Learning for Bilingual Pupils 3–11: Opening Doors to Success*. London: Sage.

Nyland, B., Ferris, J. and Dunn, L. (2008), 'Mindful hands, gestures as language: Listening to children', *Early Years* 28(1): 73–80.

Palmer, S. and Bayley, R. (2004), *Foundations of Literacy: A Balanced Approach to Language, Listening and Literacy Skills in the Early Years*. Edinburgh: Network Educational Press.

Siraj-Blatchford, I. Sylva, K., Melhuish, E.C., Sammons, P. and Taggart, B. (2004),*The Effective Provision of Pre-School Education (EPPE)*. London: DfES / Institute of Education, University of London.

Trevarthen, C. (2004), *Learning about Ourselves from Children: Why a Growing Human Brain needs Interesting Companions*. Perception-in-Action Laboratories, University of Edinburgh.

Whitehead, M. (2010), *Language and Literacy in the Early Years 0–7* (4th edn). London: Sage.

Unit 3.6 Develop emergent mathematical skills of children

This unit provides the learner with the knowledge, understanding and skills to develop children's emergent mathematical development.

Learning outcomes

By the end of this unit you will:

1 Understand how concepts of mathematics relate to children's everyday lives.
2 Understand the curriculum requirements that inform mathematical learning for children from birth to seven years.
3 Understand how to create an environment which supports children's emergent mathematical development.
4 Understand the role of the early years practitioner in relation to supporting children's emergent mathematical development.
5 Understand how opportunities support children's emergent mathematical development.
6 Be able to implement activities to support children's emergent mathematical development.
7 Be able to review how planned activities support children's emergent mathematical development.
8 Be able to work with parents/carers in a way which encourages them to take an active role in their child's play, learning and development.

LO1 Understand how concepts of mathematics relate to children's everyday lives

AC 1.1 Describe how mathematics is evident in children's everyday lives

Mathematics is an important part of the way in which children (and adults) make sense of the world. Many early years practitioners may not like mathematics or perhaps may feel they are not good at it. These negative feelings often stem from their memories of how they experienced maths teaching in school. In the UK in the past, there has been a tendency in mathematics to teach as if it were simply something to be imparted by adults to passive child recipients. Although many adults claim

to be 'no good at maths', we are all primed from birth to seek out patterns and to solve problems – both of which are key elements of mathematical understanding.

The bills we pay, the coins we use, the shopping comparisons we make, the measurements we take all require calculations and thinking about mathematics. We also use maths to get to work on time, to work out when to cross the road or when preparing a meal. Maths is important in skills such as laying floor or roof tiles, and in dressmaking and other handicrafts. Most people need to be able to read a bus or train timetable, graphs from the internet and tables from various magazines. Some will also need to be able to read and interpret spreadsheets.

Mathematics is important in the everyday life of children. It is present in children's play, in their interactions with their physical and natural world. Children use mathematics in their block play and construction games, and in deciding whether things are fair.

Every day, children may experience the following mathematical concepts:

- Numbers:
  - counting, estimating, adding and subtracting
  - hours and minutes on a clock display
  - finding a certain house number down the street (counting by twos)
  - operating a microwave oven – counting backwards
  - counting the number of seconds before hunting for a friend in a game of hide and seek
  - finding numbers on a remote control to locate their favourite television programme.
- Shape, space and measures:
  - stacking containers in the cupboard
  - weighing, estimating and making comparisons
  - cooking in the kitchen
  - weighing out ingredients.

AC 1.2 Analyse factors which affect children's learning of mathematical concepts

Factors which affect children's learning of mathematical concepts include:

● **Lack of parental support**: it is estimated that 15–20 per cent of adults in the UK do not have basic functional numeracy skills, so many parents and carers may lack confidence to support their child's learning.
● **Economic factors and social deprivation**: these can also contribute to learning difficulties in all subjects.
● **Attitude towards mathematics**: a practitioner's attitude towards mathematics combined with a lack of confidence in their own mathematical abilities is an important factor in the way the subject is taught.
● **Dyscalculia:** dyscalculia is like dyslexia for numbers. But unlike dyslexia, very little is known about its prevalence, causes or treatment. Current thinking suggests that it is a congenital condition, caused by the abnormal functioning of a specific area of the brain.

Key term 🔑

dyscalculia The DfE defines dyscalculia as: 'a condition that affects the ability to acquire arithmetical skills. Dyscalculic learners may have difficulty understanding simple number concepts, lack an intuitive grasp of numbers, and have problems learning number facts and procedures. Even if they produce a correct answer or use a correct method, they may do so mechanically and without confidence.'

LO2 Understand the curriculum requirements that inform mathematical learning for children from birth to 7 years

AC 2.1 Describe the process of mathematical development in relation to current frameworks

England: EYFS (2012)

In the EYFS (2012), mathematics is divided into two aspects:

● numbers
● shape, space and measures.

Early learning goals

Each aspect sets out some early learning goals that a child is expected to reach by the end of Reception year, at the age of five:

1 **Numbers**: children count reliably with numbers from one to twenty, place them in order and say which number is one more or one less than a given number. Using quantities and objects, they add and subtract two single-digit numbers and count on or back to find the answer. They solve problems, including doubling, halving and sharing.
2 **Shape, space and measures**: children use everyday language to talk about size, weight, capacity, position, distance, time and money to compare quantities and objects and to solve problems. They recognise, create and describe patterns. They explore characteristics of everyday objects and shapes, and use mathematical language to describe them.

Before revision of the EYFS in 2012, the specific area involving mathematics was termed Problem-solving, Reasoning and Numeracy. Problem-solving is considered part of the whole curriculum, not just mathematics. Children learn about topological space (on/off, over/under, in/out, surrounding, across, near/far) before they learn about Euclidian space (circles, squares and so on).

Research activity

Find out more about the curriculum framework and methods of assessment for learning mathematics in the EYFS.

The process of mathematical development

From the time they are born, babies are particularly stimulated through sensory experiences. Shapes are important: babies react instinctively to the arrangement of shapes which make up the human face, and will seek out the pattern over and over again. Babies' and children's mathematical development occurs as they seek patterns, make connections and recognise relationships through finding out about and working with numbers and counting, with sorting and matching and with shape, space and measures. Children use their knowledge and skills in these areas to solve problems, generate new questions and make connections across other areas of learning and development.

Number

Number has several different aspects:

- matching – this looks like this (two identical cups in the home corner)
- sorting – this looks different from this (the cup and the saucer)
- one-to-one correspondence – one biscuit for you, one biscuit for me
- cardinal numbers – the two cups remain two cups, however they are arranged (this means that the child understands the number, such as two)
- ordinal numbers – this is first, second, third (for example, the sequence in cooking: first, I wash my hands; second, I put on my apron …).

Children learn about number in the following ways:

- reciting – number songs
- nominal understanding – they pick out numbers on house doors, buses, in shops, on shoe sizes, etc.
- **subitising** – remembering number patterns to recognise how many: for example, four dots, one on each corner of a square, or on a domino (chimpanzees can do this with numbers up to seven)
- counting backwards – 5, 4, 3, 2, 1, lift-off!

There are three counting principles:

1 **The one-to-one correspondence principle**: a number word is needed for every object that is counted. Children match the counting words they are saying to the items they are counting.
2 **The stable-order principle:** this refers to the child's understanding that the order of counting words is always the same – 1, 2, 3 (not 1, 3, 2).
3 **The cardinal number principle**: when children count, they have grasped the cardinal number principle if they understand the three-ness of three. Three objects are the same number whether they are spread out or are together.

Key term

subitising Instantly recognising the number of objects in a small group, without counting (from the Latin 'subito', meaning 'immediately'): for example, when you can see that there are five coins without counting.

Guidelines for developing an awareness of numbers

- Do not do exercises or tasks with young children that are isolated from their experience.
- Remember that children learn mathematics through cooking, tidy-up time, playing in the home area, painting and being in the garden. Mathematics is everywhere.
- Numbers are found on rulers, calibrated cooking jugs, the doors of houses, and so on.
- Counting is only one part of exploring numbers. It is one thing for children to be curious about numbers on calibrated jugs, weights and measures, but they need to be free to experiment and explore. This is very different from formally teaching them numbers through adult-led tasks, unrelated to real life.

Understanding time

Time has two aspects:

- **Personal time**: it feels like a long time before a car journey ends – it might be an hour, but it feels like a day.
- **Universal time,** including:
  - succession: Monday, Tuesday, Wednesday…
  - duration: day, night, an hour, a minute …

Shape and size

Children need adults to describe things that are 'bigger than' and 'smaller than' in order to learn that these things are relative, not absolute sizes. Something is 'big' only in relation to something else. Always use relative terms with children.

Introduce words like 'cylinder' and 'sphere' before 'oblong' and 'circle'. Use everyday things, like tins of food or a football, to explain what a cylinder and a sphere look like.

Length

Use words such as 'longer than' or 'shorter than'. Children need to have rulers and tapes in their environment so that they become aware that things can be measured. Which is the tallest plant? Who has the longest foot? Gradually, they develop an understanding of the exactness of absolute measurements.

Volume and capacity

'This glass is full.' 'This bucket is nearly empty.' Listen to yourself speak and you will be surprised at how often you use mathematical language in everyday situations.

Area

You can introduce the concept of area using an example of a blanket that covers the bed mattress. Another example would be a pancake covered with lemon and sugar – the lemon and sugar cover the area of the pancake. Children often explore area in their block play.

Weight

Introduce the concept of weight using relative ideas: 'This tin of soup is heavier than that apple.' Rather than using a weighing machine, use a balance scale, so that children see this. Remember that young children need to experience weight physically. They love to carry heavy things. They love to lift each other up, and often carry bags around.

Case study

Exploring weight

Kit (aged three years) picked up a large piece of ice while out for a walk in the winter. He enjoyed throwing it and watching it skim across an icy stream. He kept saying, 'This is heavy.' His parents helped him to make comparisons: 'Is it heavier than this stone?' 'Is it heavier than this twig?' The natural outdoor environment was an ideal place for Kit to learn about weight.

Computers

The most appropriate computer programs invite children to be interactive. Children benefit from using a word processor and printer, as well as using digital cameras. They enjoy picking out letters and punctuation marks, and through this kind of play they learn about important aspects of reading, writing and numbers, which will be used in a more elaborate way as they get older.

AC 2.2 Explain how working with others supports children's emergent mathematical development

Effective teamwork with your colleagues and with other professionals involves careful planning and organisation. Early years practitioners are expected to follow the guidelines in their own setting for ways in which to support children's emergent mathematical development. This includes methods of promoting the understanding of number counting skills and of mathematical concepts. See also LO8 for information on working with parents.

LO3 Understand how to create an environment which supports children's emergent mathematical development

AC 3.1 Describe how to create an environment which supports children's emergent mathematical development in relation to current frameworks for children from birth to 7 years

Mathematical understanding includes the development of:

- **abstract thought** – through the use of imagination and symbolic representation
- **mathematical abilities** such as estimating, predicting or hypothesising – or, in other words, guessing
- **the language of mathematics** – it is now widely agreed that becoming a mathematician is like learning another language.

An environment that supports children's mathematical learning needs to be carefully planned and resourced. Children need both **indoor** and **outdoor environments** that provide the following:

- **opportunities for mathematical problem-solving** – an environment which encourages children to 'have a go' and to be creative when trying to solve problems
- an area for mathematical **graphics** – or mark-making
- **stories, books and rhymes** which reflect mathematical ideas, represent concepts and foster imagination
- **spaces** to go up, over, into, on and through; things to climb on to, up, down and under
- a **clock** and a timetable for the day that is visible to all children

- **the use of routine activities** to promote mathematical language and problem-solving
- **real-life mathematical ideas** represented in role-play resourcing; for example, petrol stations, shops, supermarkets and natural environments such as beaches and woods
- **plans for mathematical learning** which reflect and take into account children's current interests.

It is also important to provide a range of resources which ensure that children with additional needs can access them. For example, provide tactile number cards, and number lines with large print for children with impaired vision.

Graphics area (mark-making)

The graphics area – so important for the development of children's literacy – should also include resources for mathematical graphics. For example, include:

- real money
- number lines
- clocks
- stamps
- tape measures and rulers
- raffle tickets
- calculators.

Using everyday routines to support children's mathematical development

There are many opportunities for mathematical learning during the daily routines in a setting.

- Self-registration: children can make a mark or add their names to a list.
- Water play: involve children in setting up the water tray/table and learning about mathematical concepts (see below for more ideas).
- Sandpit or tray: talk to children, as they play with water or sand, to encourage them to think about when something is full, empty or holds more. Which containers shall we use today? Should we put more sand in? How much more? How can we fill it?
- Snack and lunch time: counting out and cutting pieces of fruit; counting items of cutlery and glasses; discussing which shape of cloth would be best to use – round, square or hexagonal. How many children having lunch today? How many chairs will we need?

- Tidy-up time: is there room for all the hats in the basket? Have we enough space to put all the trikes in the shed? How can we empty the sand tray?

Using the language of mathematics

Using mathematical language comes naturally when playing with children. Throughout the day one uses words such as 'first', 'next', 'this one is bigger, smaller', etc. The use of open-ended questions also gives young children opportunities to think and to work out the solutions to problems by themselves.

Number lines and tracks

Number lines provide a mental strategy for addition and subtraction. Children make a natural progression from counting to basic addition – but there is an important milestone on the way. This occurs when they realise they do not have to count all the way from one each time. For example, children start out by counting on fingers from one to three, then they count four more to get seven. This method is a natural progression, but involves some unnecessary counting. When children realise this, they start at three and then count on to seven. Number lines are a useful way to accelerate this development. Numbers that can be easily moved on a string are excellent for using flexibly where children can discuss, for example, the numbers they want to hang on the line. The advantages of using number lines include the following:

- Adults can easily refer to the number lines to support any number conversation or group activity.
- Often children will look at their age number or door number to initiate a conversation.
- Number lines of different lengths are useful to show children that numbers go beyond 10, and that the children can also see the number sequence and how numerals are written.

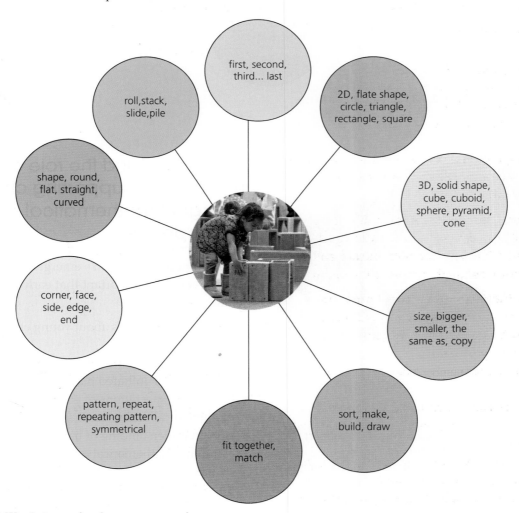

Figure 3.6.1 Words to use for shape, space and measures

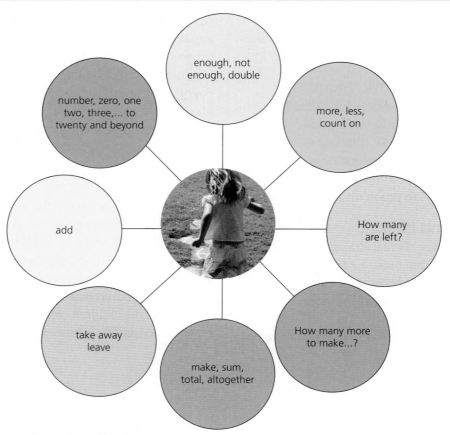

Figure 3.6.2 Number words to use

Figure 3.6.3 A hanging number line

Activity •

- Can children easily access resources which support their mathematical development?
- Is every area of mathematics covered – that is, number, weight, time, measurement for length, space, and money?

• •

LO4 Understand the role of the EYP in relation to supporting children's emergent mathematical development

When supporting children's emergent mathematical development, it is important that early years practitioners:

- share positive beliefs about young children learning mathematics
- are aware of the mathematics that arises through children's self-initiated play
- have high expectations of young children's mathematical understanding
- gain an understanding of babies' and young children's mathematical development from reflecting on observations and through discussions with their team

use the knowledge gained from this understanding to 'tune into' the mathematics that children explore within their play.

AC 4.1 Describe reasons for scaffolding children's mathematical development

According to theorist Lev Vygotsky, for the curriculum to be developmentally appropriate, the teacher or practitioner must plan activities that incorporate not only what children are capable of doing on their own but also what they can learn with the help of others. He called this the **zone of proximal** (or potential) **development**. Jerome Bruner further developed these ideas and has described the sort of help given by others as **scaffolding**. See also Unit 3.10, p 303.

There are three ways in which scaffolding can be used to support learning. The adult can take on three different roles during learning. The adult may:

- **model concepts to children** – for example, singing or saying lots of number rhymes – up to five, up to ten and up to twenty; saying the number names up to three when about to pick up a baby from the changing table.
- **work together with a child** on something, with the child doing what they can and the adult doing the rest. For example, when you know a child can count up to five, you let them do this part, and then you do the next sequence of numbers (e.g. up to ten). When you know that a child is confident in the counting routine, you say 'one', 'two' and then wait to allow the child to say 'three'.
- **encourage the child to do or demonstrate the concept on their own**. (The adult will only do this if they feel confident that the child already knows the concept or can do the task without support.) For example, when you feel confident that a child knows the number sequence, you encourage them to lead the group in the rhyme or song and will ask them

to predict what numbers come after ten or twenty. When you feel confident that a toddler knows the number order to three, invite them to recite it.

Thinking, making meanings and understanding are significant aspects of mathematics. By valuing children's ideas and supporting their mathematical explorations, adults help to 'scaffold' children's thinking. They also help children to go beyond what they already understand and can do.

AC 4.2 Analyse reasons for valuing individual interests when supporting children's emergent mathematical development

Children will become more deeply involved when you provide something that is new and unusual for them to explore, especially when it is linked to their interests. It is important to support children's interests over time, reminding them of previous approaches and encouraging them to make connections between their experiences. Children should be encouraged to explore and talk about what they are learning.

The EYFS says that individual children's interests should inform planning for children's learning and development. In practice, this means that practitioners will:

- value children's ideas and their ways of doing things
- start with what children are naturally drawn to and interested in; this inspires children to learn and be actively involved in their learning
- encourage children to express their thoughts and feelings and respond by showing these are valued
- offer children opportunities to make choices, develop individual interests and enable them to be involved in decisions that affect them.

Activity

Why do you think it is important to value children's interests when supporting their mathematical development?

AC 4.3 Describe how the EYP provides opportunities for sustained shared thinking to support children's emergent mathematical development

Sustained shared thinking is a key approach in helping children to become lifelong learners with transferable skills. Children who have the ability to enquire, consider, reflect, reason, predict, evaluate and suggest creative solutions will be better equipped to succeed in a world where a job is no longer for life.

Engaging in discussion with children means that the practitioner is genuinely interested in learning from the children about their ideas. Using open-ended questions encourages children to talk about their thinking. This will allow ideas to be developed and shared between adult and child, and meanings to be negotiated and understood.

Case study

Thinking out loud

Using sustained shared thinking, a practitioner may model the problem-solving process by verbalising her own inner speech – often called 'thinking out loud'. This is an excellent way of involving the children in the problem-solving process while valuing their contributions and letting them understand the process.

A practitioner is doing a cooking activity with a group of children.

'Our recipe says that we need one cup of flour. I haven't got a measuring cup that big. I have a half-cup. What could I do with that? How many half cups would I need to make a whole cup?'

Several children give answers.

'I think two sounds right. When Jack had the play dough earlier today, he gave Megan one half. Then Jack had two pieces: one for himself and one for his friend. So I think two half cups is the answer.'

Activity

Describe ways in which you have used sustained shared thinking to support children's emergent mathematical development.

LO5 Understand how opportunities support children's emergent mathematical development

AC 5.1 Explain strategies to support emergent mathematical development in relation to current frameworks for children from birth to 7 years

A wide range of activities supports the teaching and learning of mathematics including:

- observation of number and pattern in the environment and daily routines
- board games
- large and small construction
- stories, songs, rhymes and finger games
- sand and water play
- two- and three-dimensional work with a range of materials
- imaginative play
- cooking and shopping
- outdoor play and 'playground' games.

AC 5.2 Describe opportunities which support children's understanding

Number

Children develop their awareness of number through play, exploration and everyday routine activities. To become proficient at counting, children need opportunities to:

- learn the vocabulary of number: comparison words, such as more, less, the same, etc.
- recite numbers in the right order – counting candles on a birthday cake or singing a number song

Guidelines for developing emergent mathematical skills of children

Mathematical understanding is best developed through stories, songs, games and imaginative play.

Early years practitioners should provide opportunities for:

- indoor and outdoor play, some of which will focus on mathematical development, and some of which will evoke the mathematical learning in other activities
- observing numbers and patterns both in the environment and in daily routines
- practical activities that are related to real-life situations, for example: 'How many cups do we need for everyone at this table to have one?'

- modelling mathematical vocabulary during the daily routines and throughout play activities
- children to have sufficient time and support to use 'new' words and mathematical concepts and language during child-initiated activities in their own play
- supporting those children who have additional communication needs in developing and understanding specific mathematical language
- regular observations, assessment and planning for the next stage in children's learning.

- count out a given quantity of objects – such as toy animals
- count items in a set
- count things that cannot be seen – such as someone tapping on a drum or playing notes on a recorder
- count physical movements, like the number of hops or steps.

When selecting number songs and rhymes, try to include those that children are familiar with from home. Also make sure that they include:

- counting back *and* counting forward
- 'no' or 'none' ('Five little ducks went swimming one day')
- counting in pairs ('2 ,4, 6, 8, Mary at the cottage gate')
- counting to five, ten and beyond.

Shape, size and pattern

Children explore the properties of shapes at home and in the setting. They play with natural objects that differ in size and shape, and they learn the vocabulary of shape: for example, this path is straight and this one is curvy. Children need an environment in which pattern is evident and discussed – in resources, routines, music and the way in which festivals and changing seasons are celebrated. Patterns help children learn to make predictions, to understand what comes next, to make logical connections, and to use reasoning skills.

Children need opportunities to:

- Investigate the properties of shapes, including 2D shapes – lines, circles, triangles and squares, and 3D shapes –cubes, cylinders, cones and pyramids; rather than just learning the names of shapes, children need to learn about what shapes can and cannot do; which shapes fit together and which shapes do not.
- Explore and build with 2D and 3D materials: include large objects, such as blocks, cardboard boxes and crates, and smaller ones, such as sets of small bricks, construction kits and shaped blocks.
- Investigate patterns, which are simply things – numbers, shapes, images – that repeat in a logical way. Examples of activities to investigate pattern include:
  - sorting patterns in wall paper or fabric samples
  - exploring raindrops in puddles – concentric circles
  - threading activities
  - tessellating games
  - playing with dominoes
  - icing and decorating cakes/biscuits to a counted plan.

Weight, volume and capacity

While children are comparing the length, weight, volume or capacity of objects, they are also beginning to gain an understanding of **conservation** of measures. They understand that the properties of an object – its weight, volume and so on – do not change arbitrarily, even though the appearance of an object might change.

Children need opportunities to:

- Use the relevant vocabulary: *volume* – big, little, small, thick, wide, thin; *capacity* – full, half-full, empty, holds, container; *weight* – weigh, balance, heavy/light, heavier/lighter, heaviest/lightest.
- Learn how to weigh large and small items; provide a range of scales, such as bucket-balances, kitchen scales, stand-on scales and any other weighing machines that will give the children an opportunity to weigh large and small items.
- Talk about lengths, distances and weight without measuring them. You could encourage a conversation about what a long way it is to the park, or how heavy a box is to carry.
- Compare two things directly, one against the other: find which dinosaur is the larger, or the longer; and which bowl holds more by filling one with mini pasta shapes and tipping it in to the other bowl.
- Introduce measuring tools, such as centimetre tapes, rulers, jugs with measures and litre containers. Using real measuring equipment gives children the opportunity to practise being measurers.

Space and time

Time is a difficult concept to grasp. For very young children, time only exists in the moment. By about the age of three, a child begins to understand that time is a continuum and that things took place before now and will take place after now. After this age, time gradually becomes associated with days of the week and times of the day.

To build up an understanding of space and time, children need opportunities to:

- Discuss familiar routines: practitioners can remind them of what happens before or after these routines, for example, washing your hands before lunch.
- Recreate everyday events in their lives: you could set up the home area as a bedroom and include all the resources that children will need to get ready for bed: a bed, a toothbrush, a teddy bear, slippers,

a hot water bottle, pyjamas or nightie, slippers and a storybook.

- Practise measuring time: provide sand-timers to show how time passes and play games such as 'Let's see if we can get dressed before all the sand gets to the bottom'.
- Play with adult ideas of time and learn how adults measure time: provide clocks, calendars, stopwatches, digital watches and sand-timers in role-play areas. Timers with buzzers can be used in a variety of games.
- Learn about their own growth over time: young children are fascinated to see how they looked as babies and how they have changed. Talking about themselves, their families and other significant people will involve references to past, present and future.
- Observe seasonal changes: go for walks to collect natural treasures like conkers, acorns and sycamore wings.
- Read books and stories to develop understanding of celebrations and events, time, sequence and chronology.

See suggestions for books exploring the concept of time in Useful resources, p 362.

Matching and sorting

When children explore their environment, they notice how things are alike, and how they are different. Sorting involves separating objects into groups according to their similarities. Children begin to sort them by characteristics that have meaning to them, such as colour, size, shape, texture and sound. Children then begin matching objects that have the same characteristics. It is easier for children to begin matching pictures after they have had experience matching concrete objects. As children begin to master their matching skills, they will try more complex mathematical activities.

In order to support understanding of matching and sorting, children need opportunities to:

- Help with household tasks, such as putting away the shopping or sorting the laundry.
- Pair or match objects in everyday situations, such as laying the table for tea – making sure that each person has 'one' of each item of cutlery, etc.

- Play card games such as Snap, Happy Families, Pelmanism and Old Maid. For very young children, play Snap using two separate piles of cards, and show them how to turn the cards over.

Data representation

Involving children in collecting and presenting data for graphs, charts or pictograms helps them to understand the information. This also helps them to begin to make comparisons between quantities – an important mathematical skill.

To support their understanding of data representation, children need opportunities to:

- Be involved in collecting and presenting data in such a way that helps them to more fully understand the skills and processes involved, as well as what the information means when presented graphically.
- Record their interests and preferences in a visual way; for example, children could vote for their favourite fruit by placing their name or photo in a box with a fruit picture on it. Then, when the votes are counted out in front of all the children, each child can see that their preference is represented.
- Contribute to pictograms and 3D bar charts. For example, a chart to show children's favourite colours could be represented by towers of different coloured bricks. Each child places a brick with their name sticker on of their favourite colour on the tower.

Problem-solving

In order to develop problem-solving skills, children need opportunities to:

- Use the vocabulary of problem-solving: *Words*: pattern, puzzle, listen, join in, say, think, imagine, remember, explain, describe, different way, another way. *Useful open-ended questions*: what could we try next? How do you think you'll work it out?
- Learn in an environment where exploration and 'having a go' are seen as more important than getting the right answer.
- Encounter both planned 'set-up' problems and everyday problems which occur as part of normal activities and involve some kind of mathematics.

For example, placing the right number of bulbs in a flower pot, or putting each cup back on a hook
- Discuss the problem with others in order to share ideas about strategy.

LO6 Implement activities to support children's emergent mathematical development

AC 6.1 Plan an activity to support children's emergent mathematical development

When planning, implementing and evaluating activities to support the early years framework for learning, your overall aims should be to:

- support *all* the children you work with
- ensure each child has full access to the relevant curriculum
- encourage participation by all children
- meet children's individual learning and development needs
- build on children's existing knowledge and skills
- help all children achieve their full potential.

Before starting to plan activities to support children's emergent mathematical development, you need to find out about each individual child's needs and preferences. The stages outlined below are merely a guide to the *sequence* of development. Remember that each child is unique, and will develop in his or her own way.

Stages in developing mathematical skills

Remember that children develop at their own rates, and in their own ways. As with all normative stages of development, these age bands are merely a guide.

Between 18 months and two years, three months, children:

- are learning to classify by organising and arranging toys with increasing intent
- categorise objects according to their properties.

Between two and three years, children:

- begin to make comparisons between quantities
- know that a group of things changes in quantity when something is added or taken away.

Between two-and-a-half and four years, children:

- compare two groups of objects, saying when they have the same number
- show an interest in number problems
- separate a group of three or four objects in different ways, beginning to recognise that the total is still the same.

Between three-and-a-half and five years-plus, children:

- find the total number of items in two groups by counting all of them
- use own methods to work through a problem
- say the number that is one more than a given number
- select two groups of objects to make a given total of objects
- count repeated groups of the same size
- share objects into equal groups and count how many in each group
- begin to use the vocabulary involved in adding and subtracting, when discussing activities
- use language such as 'more' or 'less' to compare two numbers.
- find one more or one less than a number from one to ten
- begin to relate addition to combining two groups of objects and subtraction to 'taking away'.

Example of an activity to support children's mathematical development: water play

Water play provides many opportunities to develop mathematical language and an understanding of mathematical concepts. For example, inviting the children to help set up the water tray and to think about questions such as:

- How much water shall we use?
- How deep shall we make it?
- How can we find out how many centimetres deep the water is today?
- Which containers shall we use today – the short tubes or the long ones?
- How many jugs of water will we need to make it that deep?

The following list contains a sample of mathematical concepts that can be built through water play:

empty/full	many/few	before/after
thick/thin	more/less	same/different
heavy/light	shallow/deep	greater/less than
sets	classification	rational counting
liquid measure	ordinal counting	linear measure

AC 6.2 Lead an activity to support children's emergent mathematical development

As outlined in Unit 3.2, leading an activity involves managing the activity from the planning stage to evaluation. Using your plans, arrange to implement the activity and evaluate it.

Activity

Plan, lead and evaluate an activity using the strategies outlined in this unit.

LO7 Review how planned activities support children's emergent mathematical development.

AC 7.1 Evaluate how planned activities support children's emergent mathematical development in relation to current frameworks

Activity

Evaluate your planned activities in relation to the Early Learning Goals for mathematics or Experiences and Outcomes for mathematics.

AC 7.2 Analyse own role in relation to planned activities which support children's emergent mathematical development

Activity

Analyse your own role in relation to one planned activity. Write a reflective account of your role.

AC 7.3 Make recommendations for meeting children's emergent mathematical needs

Each setting will have its own policy and methods for assessing the progress of children's mathematical development. Your role is to aim to meet each child's individual mathematical needs. This can be done by:

- identifying problems and monitoring progress
- providing activities targeted to individual needs
- providing an environment rich in mathematical print and mathematical resources in every area
- evaluating the effects of your practice – what worked well and not so well?

How to provide and prepare resources to support learning and development

The British Association for Early Childhood Education (www.early-education.org.uk) produces a wide range of publications and resources to support early childhood practitioners and parents to support young children to learn effectively. The booklet on *Core experiences for the EYFS* from Kate Greenaway Nursery School and Children's Centre can also be ordered from this website.

LO8 Work with parents/carers to encourage them to take an active role in their child's play, learning and development

AC 8.1 Work with parents/carers to encourage them to take an active role in their child's play, learning and development

Parents play an important role in supporting children's number and mathematical development through the activities in which they engage their children. Parents can build mathematics-related opportunities into their child's play. They can also capitalise on situations in which mathematics is a natural part of everyday tasks, such as grocery shopping or cooking. Young children have many opportunities to learn about mathematics in their home environment. They:

- learn about money as they go shopping with parents
- become aware of numbers as they count the stairs to bed
- learn about the concept of time as they become familiar with the routine of their day – wash, dress, breakfast, etc.
- learn about number, shape, sorting and sharing:
  - setting places at the table – a cup for me, a cup for you
  - helping to sort the washing, matching socks, big shirt/small shirt
  - putting similar items together, for example, when tidying up or matching lids to saucepans.

During daily activities, parents can:

- observe their children carefully, seeing what they do and encouraging and extending their use of number symbols and language
- encourage counting – for example, they can count small food items or the number of cups at the table
- ask children to tell them about their problem-solving – for example, using open-ended questions such as: 'What did you mean by that?' or 'Why did you do it that way?'
- engage in activities that involve playing with blocks, building things and board games.

Throughout this book, the importance of developing a partnership with parents is emphasised. There are several ways in which parents can be involved in their child's learning journey. These include:

- **information-sharing** – sharing information with parents about their child's learning and preferences, and encouraging parents to share information about their child's interests and needs
- **setting up a maths workshop** – this could double as an opportunity for parents to find out how mathematical concepts are introduced, and also for parents and practitioners to interact in a relaxed atmosphere
- **involving parents** in assessments of their child.

Activity

Are parents involved in coming into the setting to help with activities for emergent mathematical skills – such as cooking activities – with the children?

Case study

Mathematics and cooking

Jamal's father said that after a cooking activity he understood the link between doing division sums in mathematics and sharing. He had not wanted to share the biscuits he had made when he cooked. He had been shocked by his own feelings, and it made him understand how Jamal might feel when told that the biscuits must be shared. He had not previously seen this as doing a division sum in mathematics. He thought it was a very good way to learn mathematics.

Assessment practice

1 Describe how mathematics is evident in children's everyday lives.
2 Analyse factors which affect children's learning of mathematical concepts.
3 Describe the process of mathematical development in relation to current frameworks.
4 Explain how working with others supports children's emergent mathematical development.
5 Describe how to create an environment which supports children's emergent mathematical development in relation to current frameworks for children from birth to seven years.
6 Describe reasons for scaffolding children's mathematical development.
7 Analyse reasons for valuing individual interests when supporting children's emergent mathematical development.
8 Describe how the early years practitioner provides opportunities for sustained shared thinking to support children's emergent mathematical development.
9 Explain strategies to support the development of emergent mathematical development in relation to current frameworks for children from birth to seven years.
10 Describe opportunities which support children's understanding of number; shape, size and pattern; weight, volume and capacity; space and time; matching and sorting; data representation; and problem-solving.
11 Plan and lead an activity to support children's emergent mathematical development.
12 Evaluate how planned activities support children's emergent mathematical development in relation to current frameworks.
13 Make recommendations for meeting children's emergent mathematical needs.
14 How can you work in a way that encourages parents/carers to take an active role in their child's play, learning and development in relation to this unit?

Useful resources

Organisation

NRICH

The NRICH Project aims to enrich the mathematical experiences of all learners. To support this aim, members of the NRICH team work in a wide range of capacities, including providing professional development for teachers wishing to embed rich mathematical tasks into everyday classroom practice: www.nrich.maths.org

Books and journals

Boaler, J. (2009), The Elephant in the Classroom: Helping Children Learn and Love Mathematics. London: Souvenir Press.

Early Education (2012), *Development Matters in the Early Years Foundation Stage (non-statutory guidance)*. London: BAECE (www.early-education.org.uk).

Pound, L. (2008), Thinking and Learning about Mathematics in the Early Years. Nursery World/Routledge.

Books supporting children's emergent numeracy

Waddell, M and Dale, P (2001), *Once There Were Giants*. London: Walker Books. As a baby girl grows up and becomes an adult, the 'giants' in her family seem to grow smaller.

Hutchins, P. (1991), *Happy Birthday, Sam*. London: HarperCollins.

Ormerod, J. (2002, 2005), *Sunshine and Moonlight*. London: Frances Lincoln. These companion titles and classic, wordless picture books look at the daily routines of a young girl in the morning and at night.

Carle, E. (2002), *The Very Hungry Caterpillar*. London: Picture Puffin.

Unit 3.7 Understand the needs of the child in preparing for school

This unit provides the learner with the knowledge and understanding required to support children during transition to school.

Learning outcomes

By the end of this unit you will:

1 Understand 'school readiness' in relation to the role of the early years practitioner.
2 Understand 'school readiness' in relation to the current framework.
3 Understand how working in partnership with others contributes to children's school readiness.

LO1 Understand 'school readiness' in relation to the role of the EYP

In most of Europe, children start school much later than they do in the UK. In fact, no child is regarded as being 'ready for school' – in other words, ready for formal teaching and learning – until they are at least six years of age. The UK Government has introduced formal curricula at ever-earlier points in school and, in its latest publication of curriculum frameworks and related guidance, has prescribed that children should be 'made ready' for school by the age of five. School readiness is a complicated issue when one considers the following issues:

● Children born in the UK in the summer are entering school a whole year before those who are born after 31 August. With single-form entry to schools, children may only just be four years old as they enter school, which is compounded significantly if you are a summer-born boy, were born prematurely, have special educational needs or are learning a second language.
● Children who join Key Stage 1 in the first year of statutory schooling may be as little as a month older than children in the final year of the EYFS who are in Reception year. And yet they will often be moving from a child-focused setting which facilitates play, choice and autonomy in learning,

to a classroom based on a subject-led curriculum, determined and led by the class teacher.

What is 'school readiness'?

At the launch of the revised EYFS in 2012, the Minister of State for Children and Families at the time stated:

What really matters is making sure a child is able to start school ready to learn, able to make friends and play, ready to ask for what they need and say what they think. These are critical foundations for really getting the best out of school. It's vital we have the right framework to support high quality early years education. Our changes, including the progress check at age two, will support early years professionals and families to give children the best possible start in life.

The revised EYFS Statutory Framework (2012) includes many references to children being 'school ready'; for example:

The EYFS sets the standards that all early years providers must meet to ensure that children learn and develop well and are kept healthy and safe. It promotes teaching and learning to ensure children's 'school readiness' and gives the broad range of knowledge and skills that provide the right foundation for good future progress through school and life.

AC 1.1 Describe characteristics of 'school readiness'

Research shows that children who enter school *ready to learn* appear to achieve more academically. Academic success has been linked to improved social, economic and health outcomes. The concept of school readiness can be used to include the:

1 readiness of the individual child
2 school's readiness for children, and
3 the ability of the family and community to support optimal early child development.

The **AcE Programme (Accounting Early for Life Long Learning)** sets out what a child needs early for lifelong learning and termed this as making the child '*life* *ready'* rather than *'school ready'*. The Programme describes four underpinning – or 'prime'– capacities for a young child as they move into school and later childhood life:

1 Language development and communication skills, including:
   - language exploration
   - language agency (or use)
   - language range
   - language processing.

2 Attitudes and dispositions, including:
   - independence
   - creativity
   - self-motivation
   - resilience.

3 Social competence and self-esteem, including:
   - effective relationships
   - empathy
   - responsibility
   - assertiveness
   - self-worth.

4 Emotional well-being, including:
   - emotional literacy
   - empowerment
   - connectedness
   - positive self-esteem.

AcE also stresses that progress and the pattern of development of individual children will depend on:

- their particular strengths and interests
- their experiences and culture in the home
- their time and experiences in a range of settings, and
- their age.

These four capacities in the young child make him or her an effective learner; it is particularly important that the skills are established in the child's formative years, as it becomes increasingly more difficult to learn later on in life. Children should exit the EYFS equipped with these capacities – or abilities – to be a lifelong learner.

Discussion point

The characteristics of school readiness
Read the following statements about school readiness:

Firstly, school readiness; If there is one theme which predominates in the conversations I have had with primary school teachers in the last year or so it is the difficulty they have in dealing with children who arrive in reception class totally unprepared to learn. Teachers report to me that a growing number of children cannot form letters or even hold a pencil. Many cannot sit and listen. Many can scarcely communicate orally, let alone frame a question. Many cannot use a knife and fork. Many cannot even go to the lavatory properly. Some express their frustration through displays of inarticulate rage.

(Michael Gove, Secretary of State for Education, 2011)

There is a mischievous mistruth in the belief that doing certain things early helps children get ready for the next stage. The best way to help a child to get ready to be 5 is to let her be 3 when she is 3 and let him be 4 when he is 4, and to hold high expectations of what children in their first 48 months of life might achieve.

(Cathy Nutbrown, 1996, p.54)

In research conducted by the Professional Association for Childcare and Early Years (PACEY), 97% of the childcare professionals surveyed agreed that the term 'school ready' should be defined as being children who: (a) are curious about the world, (b) have a desire to learn, (c) can cope emotionally with being separated from their parents, and (d) are relatively independent with their personal care. Only a third of childcare professionals believe that a definition of 'school ready' should include a child having a good basic understanding of reading, writing and arithmetic.

In a group, discuss each statement.

- Try to arrive at a description of the characteristics of school readiness with which the majority agrees.
- Do you agree with the idea that children should start school as early as possible (as in the UK), or do you think the Scandinavian countries are right in leaving formal schooling until much later?

AC 1.2 Describe factors affecting children's readiness for school

It is important to be aware of children's developmental needs when considering their readiness for school. These needs are fully discussed in Unit 3.8.

During the early years, the following factors have particular significance:

- the nature of early relationships with parents and other carers
- the extent of intellectual stimulation
- access to adequate nutrition and health care, and
- other resources, such as a safe home and neighbourhood environment.

Research from the EPPE project (Siraj-Blatchford et al., 2004) confirms that parental involvement in activities such as reading to children, visits to the library, drawing and painting together, singing songs and rhymes together, playing with letters and numbers and so on will influence children's social and behavioural achievements over the pre-school period. Such activities are significant in accounting for differences in their social and behavioural development at the start of primary school.

Factors affecting children's readiness for school

Children's school readiness is affected by the following factors:

Emotional development

This includes:

- being able to separate from parent/carer, to say goodbye and to join other children
- the ability to deal with new situations and to cope with changes in routine
- being able to manage their emotions appropriately – for example, not crying when confronted with minor problems.

Independence

This covers a wide area, and includes:

- being reliably clean and dry, i.e. toilet trained
- telling an adult when they need to go to the toilet
- being able to wash and dry hands without help

- being able to manage clothing – that is, taking off and putting on coat, jumper and shoes
- being able to eat independently, pour a drink, etc.
- being able to state name, address and age.

Social development

This includes:

- being able to take turns in play
- engaging readily with other children in play
- agreeing to share toys and materials with other children.

Behaviour

This includes:

- being able to contain frustration and temper
- understanding boundaries and set rules
- mostly doing as they are told
- refraining from distracting and interfering with other children.

Communication skills

These include:

- speaking clearly – so that they are understandable to others
- understanding simple commands
- being able to listen: this is developmental, and the listening skills and abilities of a four-year-old are not the same as an older child or adult
- being able to take part in a conversation and begin to understand that other people may have different ideas
- enjoying a wide variety of books, songs, poems and rhymes.

AC 1.3 Explain how the EYP supports children to prepare for school

Preparing children for transition to school is not about teaching them to read and write (although some four-year-olds *will* be able to read short books and to write some words or even sentences). The most important factors in easing the transition is about making sure children are confident, and able to deal with the social, practical and behavioural demands of the classroom and the playground. It involves preparing children socially and emotionally as well as intellectually and educationally.

Guidelines: supporting children to prepare for school

- **Listen to children**: try to find out how the child feels about a move – what they might be excited about or feel anxious about.
- **Encourage children to talk**: about what they already know and how they think they will adjust to the change.
- **Recognise the needs** of an individual child and his or her family in relation to attachment needs and separation anxiety. Some will be more vulnerable than others at this time.
- **Reassure children that you are there for them**: show them that you will always respond to their needs – for example, for a comfort object or a particular routine to provide stability when they are handling separation.
- **Show respect** for a child's way of making it work for themselves, by listening to the child and to their parents or carers about how they want to handle the

separation from each other, and adapting your plan to include this information.
- **Plan carefully for transition**, making sure you collect and make use of all the information from parents and from previous settings.
- **Offer support**: additional time and support may be needed for those who are younger or less mature or less confident, who are less able, or who have special educational needs or English as an additional language.
- **Organise some fun sessions at the setting** about getting ready for 'big' school; for example, a school role-play corner with uniforms from local schools.
- **Visit the primary 'feeder' schools** in the summer term to get a clear idea of the school day and challenges for young children.

Early years practitioners need to work with an awareness of, and sensitivity to, each individual child as they are supported for the transition to school.

Case study

Supporting Noah in preparation for school

Noah is four years two months old and has attended the same private nursery full-time since he was nine months old. Noah will be starting primary school in two months' time.

- Using the information from other units about the stages and sequence of development and the categories in AC 1.2 above, make a simple checklist to assess Noah's holistic needs in relation to school readiness.
- Identify the assessment strategies applied during Noah's time in the EYFS.
- Explain your role in relation to preparing Noah for school.
- Describe partnership working that will support Noah as he prepares for school.

LO2 Understand 'school readiness' in relation to the current framework

A strong start in learning and development helps prepare children for the school environment, so they are ready and able to manage transition into reception class and the move to year 1. Children who are not ready for school may experience difficulties

that disrupt their learning, and that of others. Early years providers must guide the development of children's capabilities with a view to ensuring the children in their care complete the EYFS ready to benefit fully from school.

(EYFS, 2012)

AC 2.1 Describe areas of learning and development within the current framework which relate to school readiness

Most people agree that what is important is not the age at which children start school, but whether their experiences once they are in school are appropriate to their age and stage of development. Many people have interpreted the use of the term 'ready for school' to indicate the Government's expectation that children should be prepared for the established primary school system and its fixed Year 1 curriculum. In England, the EYFS applies to young children in early years settings and in Reception class (the first year at infant school).

Foundation Stage units

Increasing numbers of schools and local authorities are setting up Foundation Stage units/settings where nursery and Reception provision might be:

- closely linked
- combined for parts of the day
- completely integrated.

The increased familiarity with staff and the learning environment that this allows means that transition is not such a problem for children and their families. This is particularly true in units where there is complete integration of children from three to five years old. As children spend a minimum of two years with the same staff, in the same learning environment, there is no break to their progress through the Foundation Stage, and practitioners are able to build strong relationships with the children and their families, possibly gaining greater insight into their needs.

Early years education in the rest of Europe

Statistics provided by the European Commission show that over half of the 33 European countries they investigated have age six as the official school starting age, and in three Scandinavian countries and five Eastern European countries the starting age is seven.

Areas of learning and development

Many early years practitioners believe that the important issue is not *where* young children's educational needs are met, but whether the types of curriculum they are offered are of high quality, appropriate for their developmental needs and offered through appropriate teaching methods. Some would argue that it is more appropriate to ensure that the school is ready for the children, rather than the children being ready for the school.

During the first year in Reception at Primary School in England, children are still in the EYFS. When they move to Year 1, they enter Key Stage 1 of the National Curriculum.

Key Stage 1 of the National Curriculum

Key stage 1 applies to children aged between five and seven (Year Groups 1 and 2). The compulsory subjects consist of: English, Mathematics, Science, Information and Communication Technology, Design and Technology, History, Geography, Art and Design, Music, Physical Education.

In addition there is a non-statutory framework for Personal, Social and Health Education (PSHE) and Citizenship. Primary schools must also provide Religious Education and Sex Education, although parents may withdraw their children from these lessons if they wish to do so.

AC 2.2 Identify assessment strategies in relation to the current framework

See pp 329–30 for more detailed information on the EYFS Profile.

The current framework requires that the EYFS Profile is carried out in the final term of the year in which the child reaches age five, and no later than 30 June in that term. The primary purpose of the EYFS Profile is to provide a reliable, valid and accurate assessment of individual children at the end of the EYFS.

The primary uses of EYFS Profile data are as follows:

- to inform parents about their child's development against the ELGs (Early Learning Goals) and the characteristics of their learning
- to support a smooth transition to Key Stage 1 by informing the professional dialogue between EYFS and Key Stage 1 teachers
- to help Year 1 teachers plan an effective, responsive and appropriate curriculum that will meet the needs of all children.

In addition, the Department for Education considers that a secondary purpose of the assessment is to provide an accurate national data set relating to levels of child development at the end of the EYFS, which can be used to monitor changes in levels of children's development and their readiness for the next phase of their education both nationally and locally (school readiness). Children with additional needs are assessed by means of the Common Assessment Framework (CAF). This is discussed in Unit 3.13.

Research activity

Find out more about how the EYFS Profile is compiled. Visit www.education.gov and follow links to EYFS and EYFS Profile.

AC 2.3 Evaluate the current framework's assessment process in supporting children's preparation for school

When evaluating the effectiveness of the assessment processes in your own setting, practitioners should consider:

- child development, both the biological and cultural aspects, and its impact on how learning may best be supported
- planning which ensures a relevant, motivating, flexible and interesting curriculum
- provision of an environment which truly enables successful learning by all children in their care
- the need for detailed understanding of the framework for assessment in order to gather accurate, reliable and meaningful information
- the importance of high-quality adult interaction which is sensitive and adaptive to the needs of individual children and capable of promoting learning; and
- organisational aspects of provision, resources, curriculum and people.

LO3 Understand how working in partnership with others contributes to children's school readiness

In England it has been recognised that the move children make from the EYFS to Key stage 1 (KS1) can be too abrupt and cause problems. One way of minimising the problem is to ensure that everyone concerned with the children and their families is involved in the transition process. This will include the children themselves, teachers in Reception, teachers in Year 1, support staff in the school and the children's parents and carers.

AC 3.1 Identify others involved in helping children prepare for school

The starting point when planning for any transition is to know the children and their families well. This enables teachers to plan an effective programme for transition. Smooth, planned transitions from the EYFS to KS1 cannot be achieved without

wholehearted support from the whole school, and it needs to be seen as a shared responsibility between EYFS staff and their KS1 colleagues in Year 1.

Children in Reception

Following these guidelines can ease transition to KS1:

- Reception children are told who their teacher is as early as possible. They feel more secure if they can name and talk about their new teacher.
- They visit Year 1 to work and play alongside 'buddies' – carefully selected children assigned to look out for children making the transition to Year 1.
- They draw a picture of themselves on their visit to Year 1, so that the Year 1 teacher can use these to make a display to welcome children at the beginning of the September term.
- They prepare their coat-peg label/tray on their visit to Year 1, ready for the start of the new term.
- They visit Year 1 in small groups to 'interview' the Year 1 teacher and ask the questions they want to ask (prepared for with the Reception teacher).

After transition

- Children visit Reception class in small numbers to share projects or experiences.
- They have lunch at same time as Reception so as not to face the noisy whole-school dinner hall.
- They are initially accompanied to the lunch hall by a familiar adult (not a dinner lady who has other children to supervise).
- They feed back on 'things to look forward to' in Year 1, ready for the next cohort of children.

Parents and carers

Parents and carers also need to have their voices heard, because they will have a different view of transition – possibly from the experiences of older children in the family – and should be able to share these experiences with the school.

- Consult parents about their feelings about transition, before and after the event.
- Hold a meeting for parents of children moving to Year 1, to explain the KS1 approaches to learning.
- Hold meeting for parents of new Year 1 children after the start of the new term, to explain further the approaches in Year 1 and see if there are any concerns or queries.

- Hold workshops for parents new to KS1 to explain how children's learning needs are met across the curriculum.

Reception and Year 1 staff

One visit to the new class is not enough. Children need time to get to know new teachers and new classrooms – and teachers need time to get to know their new children.

- Attend any necessary courses about developmentally appropriate practice that builds on the EYFS.
- Visit each other's classes to become familiar with expectations of children and learning experiences of children when they move on.
- Swap classes and teach for a morning, afternoon, day or on a regular basis (thus no supply cover is required).
- Undertake joint observations of selected children and share possible 'next steps' of learning.
- Meet to pass on information from children's records or profiles, including any knowledge gained from home visits.
- Meet to plan for the long- and medium-term stage curriculum coverage.
- Move with the children each year on a rolling programme, so the Reception teacher becomes the Year 1 teacher and the Year 1 teacher takes Reception (this can also apply to support staff).

Case study

In one primary school, the Year 1 teachers swapped classes every Friday with their Foundation Stage colleagues. In this way the Year 1 teachers came to understand the ways in which children were learning in the EYFS and what made them confident and motivated to learn. They were then able to plan a programme for the early weeks of children's Year 1 experience which mirrored the children's experiences in the Foundation Stage.

Head teachers and senior management teams

Head teachers and senior management teams need to recognise how important it is for children – and staff – to have time to prepare for transition properly and to ensure that adequate financial resources

are set aside to support the process. All senior staff need to understand how children learn in KS1 so that when they monitor the quality of teaching and learning, they have appropriate expectations for planning, practice and evidence of learning.

Activity

Identify others involved in helping children prepare for school. Find out how the transition from EYFS to Year 1 is carried out in your setting.

AC 3.2 Describe the information required to enable the school to meet the individual needs of the child during transition

Within every class, there is a wide range of children with an equally diverse range of learning needs and abilities. Some five-year-old learners in the Reception class are ready to learn elements of the Year 1 curriculum. Some children in Year 2 struggle to learn the objectives that are meant for children in Year 1. Children need to be treated as unique individual learners – rather than as a homogeneous group who all happen to be 'in Year 1'.

Schools need to receive the following information from early years settings:

- names and contact details of children moving into Reception
- any additional needs of the children and their families – for example, English as an additional language
- transfer forms
- special educational needs information; if a child has special educational needs, contact the school SENCO as early as possible after confirmation of a place.

They also need each individual child's EYFS Profile or equivalent assessment documentation.

The EYFS Profile

All early years providers must complete an EYFS profile for each child in the final term of the year in which they turn five years old. For most children this is the Reception year in primary school. The main purpose is to provide an accurate assessment of individual children at the end of the EYFS. The profile describes each child's attainment against 17 early learning goals (ELGs) together with a short narrative about their learning characteristics. For information on the 17 ELGs which make up the EYFS Profile, see p 380 in Unit 3.8.

The revised EYFS 2012 goes a step further than the old EYFS 2008 in stating that transition from Reception into Year 1 must also be in place:

- Teachers must be given a copy of the Profile report together with a short commentary on each child's skills and abilities in relation to the three key characteristics of effective learning. These should inform a dialogue between Reception and Year 1 teachers about each child's stage of development and learning needs, and assist with the planning of activities in Year 1.
- There is a duty placed on schools regarding information-sharing in the statutory guidance:
- If a child moves to a new school during the academic year, the original school must send their assessment of the child's level of development against the early learning goals to the relevant school within 15 days of receiving a request.

AC 3.3 Explain the role of the EYP in encouraging parents/carers to take an active role in their child's play, learning and development in preparation for school readiness

Provide information for parents

Early years settings can be a valuable bridge between the setting and the new school:

- **Contact the main feeder primary schools** to find out about induction sessions and dates, additional school events (such as a summer fair) and actual school start dates for children in September. Also ask the schools to send you copies of their new starter booklet or welcome pack.
- **Distribute this information to all parents**, making sure that their child's key person provides any additional support needed to parents with poor literacy skills or with English as an additional language.

- **Provide some workshops** for parents about children's development and learning needs in relation to school readiness. Some Children's Centres run such workshops during the summer months.

Supporting parents in preparing children for school

There are various practical tips to suggest to parents when preparing for their child's transition. The most important factor to consider is to promote their child's skills of independence and self-care:

- **Promote a sense of independence in your child**: this will enable them to cope with practical tasks, such as managing their shoes and socks, PE clothes and hygiene needs, as well as giving them greater resilience to cope with change and the self-esteem and confidence to ask for help when required.
- **Think ahead to snack and lunch times**: make sure that children can open all their lunchtime cartons and bottles by themselves, otherwise they may have a long, hungry wait until an adult is free.
- **Help children to identify their own belongings easily**: name all their belongings and customise their PE bag and rucksack so that they can find it quickly.
- **Ensure that their uniform is free of complicated fastenings** to make it easy for the child to get it on and off independently; try adding a key ring pull to the zips on the child's coat and rucksack to enable little fingers to pull them up easily.
- **Drinks**: invest in a rucksack with drink holders on the side so that drinks do not spill inside the bags at the end of the day and wet all the child's letters, work or reading books.
- **Comfort object**: consider giving them a transitional toy, such as a teddy, to take to school on the first few days.

Activity

How would you encourage parents to take an active role in preparing their child for school? Does your setting have a system which encourages parents to play an active role in their children's learning?

Figure 3.7.1 This boy can manage to put his jacket on

Assessment practice

1 Describe characteristics of 'school readiness'.
2 Describe factors affecting children's readiness for school.
3 Explain how the early years practitioner supports children to prepare for school.
4 Describe areas of learning and development within the current framework which relate to school readiness.
5 Identify assessment strategies in relation to the current framework.
6 Evaluate the current framework's assessment process in supporting children's preparation for school.
7 Identify others involved in helping children prepare for school.
8 Describe the information required to enable the school to meet the individual needs of the child during transition.
9 Explain the role of the early years practitioner in encouraging parents/carers to take an active role in their child's play, learning and development in preparation for school readiness.

Useful resources

Books and journals

Fisher, J. (2010), *Moving On to Key Stage 1 – Improving Transition from the Early Years Foundation Stage*. Maidenhead: Open University Press.

Likierman, H. and Muter, V. (2006), *Prepare Your Child for School*. London:Vermilion.

Nutbrown, C. (ed.) (1996), *Respectful Educators – Capable Learners: Children's Rights and Early Education*. London: Sage.

Siraj-Blatchford, I. Sylva, K., Melhuish, E.C., Sammons, P. and Taggart, B. (2004),*The Effective Provision of Pre-School Education (EPPE)*. London: DfES / Institute of Education, University of London.

Whitebread, D. and Bingham, S. (2012), *School Readiness; a critical review of perspectives and evidence*. Occasional Paper No:2, published by The Association for the Professional Development of Early Years Educators (TACTYC).

Unit 3.8 Understand how to plan to meet the needs of the developing child

This unit provides the learner with the knowledge and understanding to plan to meet the needs of the developing child.

LO1 Understand approaches to planning when working with children from birth to seven years

AC 1.1 Explain why the EYP plans to meet individual needs of children

The revised EYFS says:

Practitioners must consider the individual needs, interests, and stage of development of each child in their care, and must use this information to plan a challenging and enjoyable experience for each child in all of the areas of learning and development.

Early years practitioners working directly with young children have an important role. Children remember and look back with pleasure and affection to those who supported and extended their learning in their earliest years. It is important to note that there is a shift from making curriculum plans (which are too rigid to meet the needs or develop the interests of individual children) to curriculum planning, which is flexible and ever-changing. The principles on which the curriculum frameworks are based inform the planning alongside observations of individual children. This means that the emphasis is on *planning within an effective curriculum framework*, rather than making a plan using a rigid and prescribed curriculum syllabus.

Your role in planning to meet individual needs of children

As appropriate to your particular role, you will need to plan, implement and evaluate curriculum plans according to the requirements of your setting. When planning, implementing and evaluating curriculum plans, your overall aims should be to:

- support all the children you work with
- ensure each child has full access to the relevant curriculum
- encourage participation by all children
- meet children's individual learning and development needs
- build on children's existing knowledge and skills
- help all children achieve their full potential.

Your planning should be flexible enough to allow for children's individual interests and unplanned, spontaneous opportunities for promoting children's development and learning. For example, an unexpected snowfall can provide a wonderful opportunity to talk about snow and for children to share their delight and fascination with this type of weather. A child might bring in their collection of postcards, prompting an unplanned discussion about the collections of other children; this could be developed into a 'mini-topic' on collections if the children are really interested. It is important that children have this freedom of choice to help represent their experiences, feelings and ideas.

Activity

Why is planning central to your work with children? How can you ensure that your plans are not too rigid and that they allow opportunities to respond to unplanned, spontaneous events?

Planning for individual children

1 **Observe the child** at different times, in different places, indoors and outdoors, at mealtimes, home time, with different people. What does the child choose to do? What interests the child?

2 **Support the learning**. Are there plenty of opportunities to repeat the experiences which the child has chosen? Is there open and continuous material provision, rather than closed and prescribed activities? Do children have plenty of choice about how they spend their time? What kind of help do the children need? Do adults recognise when help is needed, and do they join children as companions and sensitively engage them in conversations? Do adults know not to interfere when the children are deeply involved?

3 **Extend the learning**. Learning can be extended in two ways:

   ● **Broadening and deepening the learning** – it is important not to think automatically that children constantly need new experiences. They might need

to play with the same dinosaurs for several weeks. If they do, this is an opportunity to help them learn the names of different dinosaurs, what they ate and the habitat they lived in. Dinosaur scenarios could be built with sand and water and plants in seed trays, so that children create their own small worlds about dinosaurs. This is often the best way to extend learning.

   ● **Onwards and upwards** – it is important not to rush children into new learning when what they really need is to consolidate what they know. A child might have enjoyed cooking roti or bread rolls. Making a carrot cake is a similar experience, but it involves adding eggs and the mixture is stirred and beaten rather than pummelled. These differences could be talked about, but children will need to make the roti and the carrot cakes so that the conversation will be possible. A book of recipes with pictures is helpful – you could make these and laminate them.

AC 1.2 Describe approaches to planning to meet individual needs of children in the short term and the long term

Approaches to planning

Rigid plans hold back learning: they do not meet the learning needs or develop the interests of individual children, and lead to an activity-based curriculum which does not help the group or individual children to develop and learn. Planning begins with the observation of the child as a unique, valued and respected individual, with their own interests and needs. We could say this is all about getting to know the child, but further general planning is also necessary, because there is only so much that children can learn on their own. They need an environment that has been carefully thought through, plus the right help from adults in using that environment. This aspect of planning ensures that the learning environment indoors and outdoors is balanced in what it offers, so that it helps all children in general, but also caters for individual children.

In this way, the curriculum:

● differentiates for individual children
● is inclusive and embraces diversity
● offers experiences and activities which are appropriate for most children of the age range (the group), because it considers the social and cultural context and the biological aspects of children developing in a community of learning.

You could use the following sources in your planning:

● the children's interests and preferences
● observations and assessments
● the children's parents and carers
● your colleagues in the setting
● other professionals such as Portage workers or health visitors.

Long-term planning

Long-term planning focuses on the following:

● What is known about the general development and learning needs of most children between birth and five years of age.

- General provision arising from this first point, in considering what is planned indoors and outdoors.
- A general sense of direction, making everyone aware of the principles, values and philosophy that support the curriculum. Using the information provided here, create a plan which includes a balance.
- A particular emphasis for a period of time (perhaps for several months); for example, the way in which children and adults communicate; how to get the most from the outdoor environment; how to support children settling in to the setting; creativity; play. It is important to note, long-term planning is not just important for children aged 0–3 but also for other age groups and in other situations.

Continuous provision

As part of long-term planning, early years practitioners need to be fully aware of how the daily routines and the organisation of the inside and outside environments offer children opportunities for development and learning across all the prime and specific areas of learning and development. See Unit 3.4 for more information.

This can be called 'continuous provision' and accounts for a significant part of the planning process. Continuous provision includes:

- daily and weekly routines
- activities or experiences that children enjoy on a regular basis.

Routines

Routines should also be carefully planned:

- the start of the session including registration/ 'handover' time for babies from parents/carers to their key person
- snack and meal times
- hand washing and toilet/nappy-changing routines
- tidy-up time
- story, singing and circle times
- the end of the session/'handover' from key person to parent/carer.

Medium-term planning

This is the way in which the principles and general framework set by the long-term planning are applied. The medium-term plan will need to be

adjusted constantly because it will be influenced by the observations made of individual children.

For children from birth to three years, it needs to include reviews of care routines, key person relationships and the way in which the day is organised to offer play and experiences, including materials and physical resources.

If short-term planning (see below) is effective, many settings find that medium-term planning becomes unnecessary. If the daily plans are good, they often extend over several weeks and become medium-term plans, which are adjusted slightly each day. This is especially so if the curriculum offers continuous open-ended materials, equipment and resources, indoors and outdoors.

Short-term planning

This is based on observation sheets of individual children's interests and needs. (If a medium-term plan is used, the observations will inform how to adjust and change the plan so that it is responsive to the individual child's interests and needs.)

One type of plan widely used is called PLOD (Possible Lines Of Direction). This was first developed with staff at Redford House Workplace Nursery at Froebel College in Roehampton, and later developed with staff at Pen Green Children's Centre. These can be used for one child (as in Figure 3.8.1), or for several children with similar interests.

Individual learning plans

In many settings observations are recorded in the Individual Learning Plan, sometimes called the Individual Learning Journey. This plan usually shows the different activities, organised into the EYFS areas of learning, and charts the child's development and learning by recording when an activity was introduced. It may also record the child's continued interest in and repetition of the activity and the child's level of competence noting the skills or abilities demonstrated in each area of learning. Many early years settings now focus on particular children on particular days. This means that every child is observed regularly, and the curriculum is planned in a differentiated way to cater for the interests and needs of individual children.

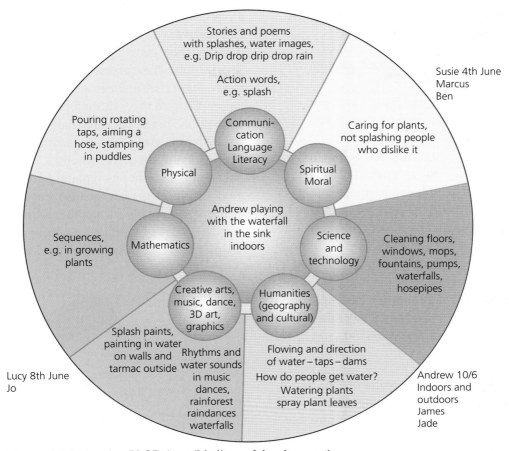

Stories and poems
with splashes, water images,
e.g. Drip drop drip drop rain

Action words,
e.g. splash

Susie 4th June
Marcus
Ben

Pouring rotating
taps, aiming a
hose, stamping
in puddles

Communi-
cation
Language
Literacy

Caring for plants,
not splashing people
who dislike it

Physical

Spiritual
Moral

Andrew playing
with the waterfall
in the sink
indoors

Science
and
technology

Cleaning floors,
windows, mops,
fountains, pumps,
waterfalls,
hosepipes

Sequences,
e.g. in growing
plants

Mathematics

Creative arts,
music, dance,
3D art,
graphics

Humanities
(geography
and cultural)

Splash paints,
painting in water
on walls and
tarmac outside

Rhythms and
water sounds
in music
dances,
rainforest
raindances
waterfalls

Flowing and direction
of water – taps – dams
How do people get water?
Watering plants
spray plant leaves

Lucy 8th June
Jo

Andrew 10/6
Indoors and
outdoors
James
Jade

Figure 3.8.1 Planning PLOD (possible lines of development)

Individual Education Plans

Every child with special educational needs should have an Individual Education Plan (IEP). These are discussed in Unit 3.14 on p 493.

Every child with special educational needs should have an Individual Education Plan (IEP). These are discussed in Unit 3.14 on p 493.

Activity ·

Describe approaches to planning to meet individual needs of children, in the short term and the long term. What do you think are the advantages in such planning?

· ·

Case study

Observation and planning

In one setting, observations of the target child (Andrew) over a week showed that a 'waterfall' consisting of three beakers of graded sizes was greatly used. Andrew lined them up next to the tap so that the water fell exactly as he wanted it to. He had a bowl of corks under the waterfall; he aimed the water at them one by one, to make them bob about.

When the tap was turned on, a waterfall was created, which led to much glee and discussion. The long-term plan identified science as a major area for attention.

The practitioner reported this observation of Andrew to a group of staff. They decided to put the waterfall out again. In addition, they provided a bigger version in the outside area, using buckets and old water trays.

They planned who will be in which areas, and aimed for Andrew to learn that water:

- flows
- splashes
- cascades in the outdoor waterfall more than the indoor waterfall
- flows downwards if it can
- makes a trajectory (a moving line)
- has the force to move things that are in its way.

To extend Andrew's interest, the staff planned a visit to the local shopping mall where there is a fountain. They also linked the short-term plans made for Andrew with the medium-term plan (see Figure 3.8.1) and the long-term plan, which had a focus on knowledge and understanding of the world (science).

AC 1.3 Explain planning in relation to current frameworks

EYFS: The Observation, Assessment and Planning Cycle

The EYFS (2012), the core statutory framework for children from birth to the end of their Reception year, should inform all planning. There are no set rules about what planning should look like in the revised EYFS, nor about what types of planning should be in place. The only requirement is that planning should be fit for the purposes described in the revised document, and should meet the requirements set out by individual schools, settings or groups of settings. Underpinning all planning should be evaluative questions about its usefulness and whether it makes a difference to teaching and learning in the setting, regardless of whether a child is five months old or five years old.

The child at the centre

The EYFS puts the child at the centre of the observation, assessment and planning process. The surrounding layers build up the bigger picture that will influence or be influenced by the observation, assessment and planning process.

Starting in the centre, observation, assessment and planning will meet the immediate needs and interests of children in the moment, in short (daily/weekly) and medium (two to six weeks) terms. This will inform longer-term plans and shape how continuous provision is organised, the organisation of the day, approaches to learning and development, etc.

The outer layers include summaries of children's learning and development, self-evaluation and the EYFS statutory requirements, as well as leadership, management and governance structures. These require certain standards and processes to be in place and will have a direct effect on practice. But they will also be shaped by the children, families and practitioners at the centre.

The KEEP (Key Elements of Effective Practice) planning cycle

Figure 3.8.2 shows how observation and assessment inform the planning process. The cycle is a continuous one, and settings adapt their provision to suit the needs of the children and families they are working with at any one time. It is through close observation, monitoring and assessment that staff can ensure that they introduce appropriate changes in their practice to meet the specific needs of individual children, as well as the whole group. This is particularly relevant to identifying children's schemas, which can be taken into account when planning. It ensures that practitioners plan the next steps that take account of a child's development, interests and needs. It marks significant points in a child's learning journey and helps assessment for learning as a continual process.

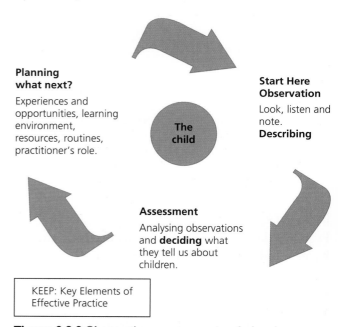

Planning what next?
Experiences and opportunities, learning environment, resources, routines, practitioner's role.

The child

Start Here Observation
Look, listen and note. **Describing**

Assessment
Analysing observations and **deciding** what they tell us about children.

KEEP: Key Elements of Effective Practice

Figure 3.8.2 Observation, assessment and planning are a continuous cycle of activity in the early years

Activity

Assessing children's development across the EYFS

- Use a single, long observation to tell you about a child's all-round holistic development in the seven areas set out in the EYFS.
- Work as a team to find out whether there are some areas of development and learning that you do not observe often, and think about how you will address this problem.
- Spend time talking to parents, children and colleagues about your observations, so that you gain other perspectives.

Case study

Tyrone

Tyrone is six months' old, and it is his third day during his settling-in period at nursery. His mother carries him into the nursery and they are both greeted by their key person, Debbie. Tyrone's mother sits down next to Debbie and then places Tyrone on her lap. Debbie starts to sing a song that Tyrone had enjoyed the day before in nursery and he smiles briefly. Tyrone explores the treasure basket that is in front of them briefly, putting a few different objects in his mouth, but he is not really involved in the treasure basket and keeps looking at his mother.

Tyrone's mother says goodbye to him and agrees with Debbie that she will leave him for ten minutes. She says that Tyrone may be hungry, and that she has left some baby rice in his bag. Tyrone starts to cry as his mother is leaving and he reaches towards her, so Debbie has to hold him on her lap. She starts singing again, and this soothes Tyrone a little bit, but he is not happy. A few minutes later he starts to explore another item in the treasure basket, but his main focus is on the door. Debbie continues to sing and Tyrone moves a little in rhythm with the song. Then he starts to cry again. Debbie soothes him and, wondering if he is hungry, gets out some baby rice. Tyrone angrily rejects the baby rice and pushes the spoon away. When his mother comes back a few minutes later, Tyrone is still crying. She cuddles him, and when she offers him some rice he eats it hungrily.

(**Grenier and Elfer, 2009**)

Research activity

This activity will help you to practice using observation and assessment to:

- evaluate the quality of a nursery setting, and consider how well it meets the EYFS commitments
- consider a child's starting points in nursery
- consider what you might plan to do next, in order to support the child's development and well-being.

Before you start, have a copy of the EYFS at hand or go to this website: www.nationalstrategies.standards.dcsf. gov.uk/earlyyears. First, carefully read the case study above on Tyrone. Under the EYFS *Positive Relationships* heading, the *Key Person* section states that:

- A key person helps the baby or child to become familiar with the setting and to feel confident and safe within it.
- A key person develops a genuine bond with children and offers a settled, close relationship.
- When children feel happy and secure in this way, they are confident to explore and to try out new things.
- Even when children are older and can hold special people in mind for longer, there is still a need for them to have a key person to depend on in the setting, such as their teacher or a teaching assistant.

1 How well do you think that this setting is working towards meeting the EYFS commitment to positive relationships?
2 What next steps would you take, if you were Debbie, to continue to meet this commitment?

We can also use observations to assess children's development, learning and well-being. These assessments help us to think about how we might work with parents and our colleagues to provide further support for children in order to meet their needs, and build on children's development and learning.

Look at the 'Personal, Social and Emotional Development' section in *Development Matters*, which is part of the EYFS. Carefully read the 'Birth to 11 months' sections.

3 What evidence can you find to show that Tyrone's development is securely in this band? For example, do you think the observation shows that he can 'Gain physical, psychological and emotional comfort from "snuggling in"'?
4 Now read the 'Look, listen and note' column. What might you be looking out for next, as you observe Tyrone? For example, one suggestion is to look for 'How young babies respond to attention, such as making eye contact or vocalising'. Do you think this would be a good focus for future observations of Tyrone?
5 Read the 'Effective practice' column. Does this give you some good ideas of what you might do next, if you were Tyrone's key person? For example, the guidance suggests that you should 'talk to a young baby when you cannot give them your direct attention, so that they are aware of your interest and your presence nearby'. Do you think that this would help Tyrone?
6 Finally, read the 'Planning and resourcing' column. What might you plan to do next, in discussion with Tyrone's family and your colleagues? For example, the guidance suggests that you should 'Have special toys for babies to hold while you are preparing their food, or gathering materials for a nappy change'. Is this something you might plan to do? →

7 Now turn to other sections of *Development Matters*. What does this observation tell you about different areas of Tyrone's development, such as communication or physical development?

This shows how just a few good-quality observations can inform you about a child's starting points. Good-quality observations help you to evaluate your practice and think of next steps for the child. Perhaps most importantly, observations like this help you to get to know a child, and give a focus for discussions with the child's parents.

LO2 Understand how to plan to meet the needs of children

AC 2.1 Describe information the EYP requires to plan to meet the needs of children

Information required for planning

Every child needs their practitioners to know:

- what I can do
- how I learn
- what I enjoy
- who I am
- who my special people are.

Some practitioners collect a great deal of information about children, through observations, photographs and collecting drawings. But the value of their work is limited if they just collect information and do not put it to any use. Equally, other practitioners plan activities for children without any thought to what they have observed the children doing. They simply pluck ideas from the air – 'Let's do play dough with glitter on Wednesday; we have not done that for a while.' This makes it unlikely that the children will be able to build on their learning over time.

Planning to meet the needs of children

When children feel their efforts are appreciated and celebrated, they learn more effectively. If adults only praise and recognise results (**products of learning**), children are more likely to lose heart and become less motivated to learn.

Planning should therefore focus on process and the efforts which children make (**processes of learning**) as much as the product. An example would be finger-painting rather than handprints, so that children can freely make their own patterns in the paint. At the end, the paint is cleared away, with no pressure on children to produce a product. However, staff might photograph the processes involved in finger-painting and display these on the wall, to remind children of what they did. Children love to share process books later with interested adults, other children and their parents or carers.

Figure 3.8.3 Children who are just discovering paint also need to experiment with it – painting does not have to have an end product

AC 2.2 Explain the reasons for identifying children's needs, interests and stage of development prior to planning

Effective planning for children's early learning is based on every child's individual needs, abilities and interests; this is why accurate observations and assessments are so important. These needs have to be integrated into the curriculum requirements for your particular setting and the age groups of the children you work with, for example the learning and development requirements of the EYFS.

From observations of children, we can build up a picture of their needs and their interests. The focus should always be on the attitudes and dispositions that we want to promote through planned play activities. There has to be flexibility in all planning. Many settings choose a topic to plan activities around, for example, a well known and popular story, such as *The Gruffalo's Child* by Julia Donaldson. However, children will learn best when they are able to pursue their own particular interests, so planning should be able to be modified and adapted to take account of individual interests. This does not mean that a well-planned set of themed activities needs to be abandoned; just that allowance should be made to take advantage of a spontaneous expression of interest in something that has just occurred.

AC 2.3 Explain the role of observation in planning

Observation is an essential tool in planning to meet children's needs. Observation is important as it enables early years practitioners to:

- evaluate individual needs and to share their evaluation with others
- tune in to what interests an individual child, and to see how to support and extend their interests
- ensure that their planning and practice are informed by the knowledge gained from observations
- build a fuller picture of each child that informs assessment.

The evaluation of individual needs through observation

Every early years setting must work closely with other professionals and agencies to ensure that each child has the best possible opportunities in their learning. These professionals and agencies are discussed more fully in Unit 2.5.

Observing children as individuals

In order to plan a quality curriculum framework, the first step is to observe children as individuals. Observation helps adults tune in to what interests a child, and to see how to support and extend their interest. When children are interested in the experiences and activities they are offered, they learn more effectively, and adults can add to this and provide children with what they need.

Observation informs planning and practice

Giving children what they need means linking the child's interests with what is needed in the official curriculum framework documents of the country. The role of the early years practitioner is to observe, support and extend the child's learning.

Throughout, this book stresses the importance of observation and how it informs the way practitioners can become involved in:

- creating learning environments indoors and outdoors, based on what they have observed that children are interested in

- supporting the individual and group interests of children
- extending the interests of individual children, when appropriate
- meeting the needs of children as unique individuals
- sharing and exchanging through rich dialogue and observations with parents/carers.

The revised English EYFS (from birth to five years of age) covers the year leading into Key Stage 1 with the Foundation Profile. This helps practitioners to assess the development, learning and well-being of children across the year, using observations which make formative assessments to plot progress. It is a holistic approach, covering the areas of learning set out in the EYFS theme called 'Learning and Development'.

The early learning goals are not expectations, but aspirations. For example, more than half the children in England achieve the goals for personal, social and emotional development, but only about one-third reach the goals for communication, language and literacy because, against advice of early childhood experts, the goals were set too high. Children in other countries are not expected to reach this level as they turn five years of age, and yet they do better in the long term, despite being taught to read and write later (typically at six to seven years of age). Looking at the progress of children across the six areas of learning has proved important. For example, it has been shown that children who achieve well on the goals for physical development are achieving better in pencil control in the literacy goals. There are important discussion points here:

- Early is not best.
- Narrow approaches constrain rather than help development and learning.
- Learning with quality takes time to embed.
- Children learn through a variety of richly deserved experiences, and so it is often difficult to track down their exact learning journey. Indirect teaching is powerful.
- Adult-led teaching needs to be very sensitive and be based on observation, tuning in to the child at the right time in the right way. Table 3.8.1 shows the Early Learning Goals against which each child's level of development must be assessed and recorded.

Aspect	Expected level of development (ELGs)
Personal, social and emotional development	
Self-confidence and self-awareness	Children are confident to try out new activities and can say why they like some more than others. They are confident to speak in a familiar group and will talk about their ideas, and choose the resources they need for activities they have decided on. They can say when they do or do not need help.
Managing feelings and behaviour	Children can talk about how they and others show feelings and know that not all behaviours are acceptable. They can talk about their own and others' behaviour and its consequences. They can work as part of a group or class and understand and follow the rules. They can adjust their behaviour to different situations and take changes in routine in their stride.
Making relationships	Children can play cooperatively, taking turns when playing. They can take account of one another's ideas about how to organise their activity. They can show sensitivity to the needs and feelings of others and form positive relationships with adults and other children.
Physical development	
Moving and handling	Children show good control and coordination in large and small movements. They move confidently in a range of ways, safely negotiating space. They handle equipment and tools effectively, including pencils for writing.
Health and self-care	Children know the importance for good health of physical exercise and a healthy diet and can talk about ways to keep healthy and safe. They can manage their own basic hygiene and personal needs successfully, including dressing and going to the toilet independently. →

Table 3.8.1 Early Learning Goals (ELGs)

Aspect	Expected level of development (ELGs)
Communication and language	
Listening and attention	Children listen attentively in a range of situations. They listen to stories, accurately anticipating key events and respond to what they hear with relevant comments, questions or actions. They can give their attention to what is being said to them and respond appropriately, while remaining involved in an activity.
Understanding	Children can follow instructions involving several ideas or actions. They answer 'how' and 'why' questions about their experiences and in response to stories or events.
Speaking	Children express themselves effectively, showing awareness of listeners' needs. They use past, present and future forms accurately when talking about events that have happened or are to happen in the future. They develop their own narratives and explanations by connecting ideas or events.
Literacy	
Reading	Children read and understand simple sentences in stories and information books, using phonic knowledge to decode regular words and read them aloud accurately. They demonstrate understanding when talking with others about what they have read, or what has been read to them.
Writing	Children write their own labels, captions, messages and simple stories which can be read by themselves and others. They use their phonic knowledge to spell words in ways which match their spoken sounds, and make use of high frequency spellings.
Mathematics	
Numbers	Children use numbers up to ten in order to do simple addition and subtraction to solve practical problems. They can find a total by counting on, and can calculate how many are left from a larger number by counting back.
Shape, space, and measures	Children use everyday language to describe and compare size, weight, capacity, time, position and distance. They know and talk about patterns and the properties of flat and solid shapes.
Understanding the world	
People and communities	Children talk about past and present events in their own lives and the lives of family members. They know that other children do not always enjoy the same things and are sensitive to this. They know about similarities and differences between themselves and others, and among families, communities and traditions.
The world	Children know about similarities and differences in relation to places, objects, materials and living things. They can talk about the features of their own immediate environment and how environments might vary from one another. They can make observations of animals and plants and explain why some things occur, and talk about changes, including in simple experiments.
Technology	Children recognise that a range of technology is used in places such as homes and schools. They select and use technology for particular purposes.
Expressive arts and design	
Exploring and using media and materials	Children sing songs, make music and dance and experiment with ways of changing them. They use and explore a variety of materials, experimenting with colour, design, texture, shape and form.
Being imaginative	Children use what they have learned about media and materials in purposeful and original ways. They represent their own ideas, thoughts and feelings through art and design, music, dance, role play and stories.

(DfE, 2011; adapted from Appendix 4)

Table 3.8.1 Early Learning Goals (ELGs) (*Continued*)

Observation informs assessment

See also Unit 3.14 for information on assessment and observation.

Baseline assessment: when we first meet a child we need to get to know them and their family/carers. We use our first observations as a way of doing this, along with what parents/carers know and understand.

Formative assessment: as our observations build, we are able to gain a fuller picture of the child, and we literally form assessments as we accompany the child on their learning journey.

Summative assessment: at regular points (depending on whether a child has special needs) or when the child is leaving the setting and moving on, we take stock and pause to reflect on an aspect of development and learning, or on the whole child's learning. See Unit 3.14, p 514 for guidelines on developing your skills in observation and assessment.

AC 2.4 Devise a plan to meet the needs of an individual child

Devising a plan

This assessment task is to show that you can devise a plan to meet the developmental needs of an individual child. The following guidelines will help you to develop a plan.

- Having used different observational techniques, make an assessment of a child's developmental needs. Remember to practise confidentiality and anti-bias practice.
- Encourage the child to take responsibility for his or her own development plan. Even young children can help in planning activities by suggesting things they enjoy doing.
- Involve parents or carers in the assessment of their children.
- Devise a structure for the plan (your setting may use a regular format for plans). Include the following details:
  - the date and the child's name
  - the aim and purpose
  - the period of time involved – or timescale

- the activities suggested to meet the child's needs, including a list of resources
- the targets or goals to use in order to measure the success of the plan
- the name of the person/s responsible for implementing the plan
- the date for review of the plan.

Implementing the plan

Many plans are drawn up in consultation with colleagues – either individual plans or those focused more broadly on a whole group or class of children. Early years practitioners should ensure that they prepare for the implementation: for example, by organising a time slot, providing equipment and resources, arranging for others to help if necessary, and so on.

Evaluating and revising the plan

The plan should be evaluated by considering whether the targets or aims were fully met or only partially met. You should also evaluate it in terms of how enjoyable it was for the child. Having evaluated the plan, you then need to consider if it could be improved; it is important to let children have a role in reviewing the plan and in suggesting possible changes.

> **Key term**
>
> **evaluate** Describe and summarise in relation to advantages and disadvantages.

Activity •

Describe how you plan provision to promote children's learning and development in your setting. Include examples of any planning sheets you use.

• •

AC 2.5 Explain why the EYP involves others in planning for the next steps of children's development

Home-setting diaries

These are a useful way of including parents and carers in the Observation/Assessment/Planning cycle.

- They can be completed daily or weekly and include significant events throughout the day for the child concerned.
- They should be easily accessed by parents and enable both practitioners and parents to gain an insight into both the setting and the child's home life, and how parents and practitioners can work together to support the child further.
- Some settings use a combined diary and reading record for the Reception-aged children. This ensures information can be passed between home and setting in a more multipurpose way.
- Other settings may only use home-setting diaries on a more short-term basis, for example for a child who has found it difficult to settle.

Learning journeys

Learning journeys (sometimes referred to as learning journals) are used in early years settings. The term refers to a collection of different documents collected by early years practitioners which:

- Provide a picture of a child's development under the areas of learning identified in the EYFS.
- Consist of photos, art-work, mark-making, etc.
- Should be combined with observations made by practitioners including notes of relevant conversations or comments made by the child.
- Practitioners should match any observations to the EYFS curriculum guidance.
- The aim of a Learning Journey is to build a unique picture of what each child knows, feels and is able to do – as well as his or her particular interests and learning style. This picture can then be used to identify learning priorities and plan appropriate learning experiences.

AC 2.6 Explain the role of the EYP in encouraging parents/carers to take an active role in their child's play, learning and development

Parents not only benefit from being involved in their child's care and education, they also have a right to feel included. One way of ensuring this is to consistently share important information with parents on a daily basis, where possible.

In practice

Involving parents and carers

Early years practitioners could do the following:

- Use informal (verbal) exchanges of information as parents or carers drop off and collect their children.
- Use more formal exchanges of information – such as baby care sheets, parent-held records, documented observations of the child during the day, home-setting diaries and children's profiles.
- Provide displays of children's work.
- Have digital photographs of the day's events on display where parents can choose whether or not to look at them.
- Provide video footage, where parents agree, for parents to take home with them of their child that day.
- Provide opportunities for parents to spend time in the setting and opportunities for support and discussion with parents within the home.
- The learning journey should involve contributions from a variety of adults who have contact with the child, including the child's family.

Progress check

Recording and reporting are a means of:

- promoting partnership with parents
- sharing information with children, colleagues and other professionals, and
- shaping the next steps in learning.

Records begin when a child is preparing to start the early years setting. Parents and children complete statements such as 'I can …' and 'I enjoy …', with pictures or photographs and statements. This helps to involve children in recognising their capabilities and also values the learning which they have already achieved.

AC 2.7 Describe reasons for tracking children's progress

Careful observations enable you and your colleagues to make objective assessments concerning children and their individual care needs, behaviour patterns, levels of development, skills/abilities, and their learning needs and achievements. Assessment of this information can help highlight and celebrate a child's strengths as well as identifying any gaps in their learning. This can then form the basis for the ongoing planning of appropriate care routines, play opportunities and learning activities and they may also be a useful starting point for future learning goals.

Assessing and recording

You should draw on everyday observations and your knowledge of individual children to inform your assessments. After you have provided play and learning activities, you will need to assess and record the child's progress. Some assessment and recording may occur during the activities, providing continuous assessment of each child's performance (for example, child observations and checklists). Some assessment and recording may occur shortly afterwards (for example, record sheets and formal assessments.) It is important to assess and record children's progress so that you can:

- discover if the activity has been successful (have the aims and learning outcomes been met?)
- consider how the activity might be modified/ adapted to meet the needs of the child or children
- inform a senior practitioner, teacher, SENCO or other professionals whether or not a particular activity has been successful.

Methods of recording children's learning and development

Effective recording of children's learning and development should:

- be clear and concise
- be dated and signed or initialled by the practitioner
- be positive in tone and describe children's individual achievements and progress
- reflect the whole child's learning and development

- highlight significant moments within each area of learning
- involve and inform the EYFS team in the setting and also the child's parents and carers
- show clear next steps and the results of the follow up
- be flexible and take a variety of forms including sticky notes, annotated photographs, short observations, learning stories, longer observations, group observations, evidence from home, annotated pictures and collages and quotes
- be manageable and part of each adult's role and daily routine.

Many settings create learning journeys, learning stories, learning diaries and other forms of documentation relating to a child's time in a setting. The purpose of these varies depending on the setting.

Assessment in the 2012 EYFS

Assessment in the 2012 EYFS plays an important part in helping parents and practitioners to understand children's needs and plan activities to meet them, supporting children's progress. It is particularly important that parents are left in no doubt about their child's progress and development, and that learning and development needs are identified early and addressed in partnership with parents and other relevant practitioners. Early years providers must assess young children's progress on an ongoing basis, and also complete assessments at two specific points which are described in the assessment profile.

Assessment practice

1 Why is it important to plan to meet the individual needs of children? Give three reasons.
2 What is meant by long-term planning? And short-term planning?
3 What is the role of planning in relation to current frameworks?
4 What information does the early years practitioner need in order to plan to meet the needs of children? How is such information gathered in your setting?
5 Why is it important to identify children's needs, interests and stage of development before you begin planning?

6 Describe four benefits of observation to planning.
7 Devise a plan to meet the needs of an individual child.
8 Why is it important to involve others when planning for the next stage of children's development?
9 How can the early years practitioner encourage parents and carers to take an active role in their child's play, learning and development?
10 Why is it important to track children's progress, and how is this achieved in your setting?

Useful resources

Websites

Early Years Foundation Stage

The government's website, including all the statutory requirements for the EYFS, as well as guidance: www.education.gov.uk and search for 'Early Years Foundation Stage'.

Early Years Foundation Stage Profile videos

Expertly selected video footage of children learning in the EYFS, together with notes and guidance: www.qcda.gov.uk/assessment/352.aspx

Books and articles

Bartholomew, L. and Bruce, T. (1993), *Getting to Know You: A Guide to Record-keeping in Early Childhood Education and Care*. London: Hodder & Stoughton.

Berk, L.E. (2006), *Child Development* (7th edn). Boston, MA: Pearson International Edition.

Bertram, T. and Pascal, C. (1997), *Effective Early Learning: Case Studies in Improvement*. London: Hodder & Stoughton.

Bruce, T. (2005), *Early Childhood Education and Care* (3rd edn). London: Hodder Arnold.

Dahlberg, G., Moss, P. and Pence, A. (2007), *Beyond Quality in Early Childhood Education and Care: Languages of Evaluation*. London: Routledge.

Elfer, P. and Grenier, J. (2010) 'Personal, social and emotional development' in Bruce, T. (ed.) *Early Childhood: A Guide for Students*. London: Sage.

Unit 3.9 Facilitate the cognitive development of children

This unit provides the learner with the knowledge, understanding and skills to facilitate the cognitive development of children from birth to seven years.

Learning outcomes

By the end of this unit you will:

1 Understand about cognitive development in children.
2 Understand theory underpinning cognitive development.
3 Be able to facilitate the development of cognition in children.
4 Be able to implement a learning experience which supports the development of sustained shared thinking in children.
5 Be able to critically evaluate the provision for supporting cognitive development in own setting.

LO1 Understand about cognitive development in children

AC 1.1 Describe sensory development in the first year of life

Everything a baby tastes, hears, sees, feels and smells, and all of a baby's own movements, will influence the way the brain makes its connections, so the more varied and appropriate the play experiences we offer, the better these neural pathways are formed. It is important to give babies interesting sensory experiences, as well as the love and care that are essential. Babies will cry less when they are engaged with their senses and are perceptually aware. This kind of awareness leads to early **concepts** (an important aspect of intellectual development), which researchers are beginning to discover are formed earlier than was previously thought. Our feelings, thoughts and physical movements all work together as we learn.

Sensory development refers to the maturing of the five familiar senses: hearing, smell, taste, touch and vision. It also involves the way a baby's nervous system receives input from these senses and then forms an appropriate motor or behavioural response. This is known as sensory processing or **sensory integration**.

Babies are born with most of these senses almost fully developed. In their first year, babies explore their world through their senses:

Hearing

The middle ear of a newborn is full of fluid and this impairs hearing to a slight extent. The sense of hearing is still immature; that is why newborn babies respond best to high-pitched, exaggerated sounds and voices.

- Newborn babies are unable to hear certain very quiet sounds.
- By about three months, babies will show that they can hear a sound by turning their head toward the direction of the sound.
- By four to eight months, babies can hear the full range of sound frequencies.

Smell

- A newborn baby's sense of smell is so well developed that he or she can already tell the difference between the smell of her mother's milk and that of another mother. Researchers conducted experiments where two breast pads (one from the baby's mother, the other from another lactating mother) were placed at the sides of the babies' heads. The babies consistently turned towards the breast pad of their own mothers.
- By about the age of five years, children can identify some foods by smell.

Taste

A newborn baby can differentiate between sweet, salty, sour and bitter tastes. Babies show a preference for sweet taste, such as breast milk, and for salty tastes later on.

By 12 to 18 months, babies usually attain a full sensitivity to taste.

Touch

Touch is a term used to describe all the physical sensations that can be felt through the skin. There are separate nerve receptors in the skin to register heat, cold, pressure, pain and touch.

- Newborn babies can distinguish between hot and cold temperatures, and can feel pain. Their hands and mouths are particularly sensitive to touch.
- Between one and nine months of age, babies can distinguish differences in textures with their hands and mouths.
- By the age of three years, children can distinguish size and shape differences by touch.

Vision

Newborn babies prefer to look at faces over other shapes and objects, and at round shapes with light and dark borders – for example, an adult's eyes.

- Newborn babies can focus on objects about eight to fifteen inches away. This is the ideal distance to be able to focus on the face of the adult who is feeding a baby.
- Newborn babies have limited colour vision.
- By one month, babies can see objects about three feet away.

- Between four and seven months of age, full colour perception is achieved.
- Between three and seven months, babies develop depth perception – the ability to perceive the relative distance of objects in one's visual field.
- During the second year, babies possess the same visual acuity as an adult.

Activity ·

Describe sensory development in the first year of life. Include a brief description of development in the following areas: hearing, touch, smell, taste and vision.

· ·

AC 1.2 Identify stages of cognitive development in children from birth to 7 years

Cognitive (or intellectual) development is development of the mind – the part of the brain that is used for recognising, reasoning, knowing and understanding. It involves:

- what a person knows and the ability to reason, understand and problem-solve
- memory, concentration, attention and perception
- imagination and creativity.

Learning through play

See Unit 3.1 for more information on learning through play.

The stages of cognitive development
The first month
Babies explore through their senses and through their own activity and movement.

Touch

- From the beginning, babies feel pain.
- The baby's face, abdomen, hands and the soles of his or her feet are also very sensitive to touch.
- The baby perceives the movements that he or she makes, and the way that other people move them about through his or her senses.
- For example, the baby gives a 'startle' response if they are moved suddenly. This is called the 'moro' or startle reflex.

Sound

- Even a newborn baby will turn to a sound. The baby might become still and listen to a low sound, or quicken his or her movements when he or she hears a high sound.
- The baby often stops crying and listens to a human voice by two weeks of age.

Table 3.9.1 An overview of the stages of cognitive development

The stages of cognitive development

Taste

The baby likes sweet tastes, e.g. breast milk.

Smell

The baby turns to the smell of the breast.

Sight

- The baby can focus on objects 20 cm (a few inches) away.
- The baby is sensitive to light.
- The baby likes to look at human faces – eye contact.
- The baby can track the movements of people and objects.
- The baby will scan the edges of objects.
- The baby will imitate facial expressions (e.g. he or she will put out their tongue if you do). If you know any new-born or very young babies, try it and see!

From one to four months

- The baby recognises differing speech sounds.
- By three months the baby can even imitate low- or high-pitched sounds.
- By four months the baby links objects they know with the sound, e.g. mother's voice and her face.
- The baby knows the smell of his or her mother from that of other mothers.

From four to six months

- By four months the baby reaches for objects, which suggests they recognise and judge the distance in relation to the size of the object.
- The baby prefers complicated things to look at from five to six months and enjoys bright colours.
- The baby knows that he or she has one mother. The baby is disturbed if he or she is shown several images of his or her mother at the same time. The baby realises that people are permanent before they realise that objects are.
- The baby can coordinate more, e.g. see a rattle, grasp the rattle, put the rattle in his or her mouth (they coordinate tracking, reaching, grasping and sucking).
- The baby can develop favourite tastes in food and recognise differences by five months.

From six to nine months

- The baby understands signs, e.g. the bib means that food is coming.
- From eight to nine months the baby shows that he or she knows objects exist when they have gone out of sight, even under test conditions. This is called the concept of object constancy, or the object permanence test (Piaget). The baby is also fascinated by the way objects move.

From nine to twelve months

- The baby is beginning to develop images. Memory develops and the baby can remember the past.
- The baby can anticipate the future. This gives the baby some understanding of routine daily sequences, e.g. after a feed, changing and a sleep with teddy.
- The baby imitates actions, sounds, gestures and moods after an event is finished, e.g. imitate a temper tantrum he or she saw a friend have the previous day, wave bye-bye remembering Grandma has gone to the shops.

From one year to two years

- The child understands the names of objects and can follow simple instructions.
- The child learns about things through trial and error.
- The child uses toys or objects to represent things in real life (e.g. using a doll as a baby, or a large cardboard box as a car or a garage).
- The child begins to scribble on paper.
- The child often 'talks' to him- or herself while playing.

→

Table 3.9.1 An overview of the stages of cognitive development (*Continued*)

The stages of cognitive development

From two years

- The child has improved memory skills, which help his or her understanding of concepts (e.g. the child can often name and match two or three colours – usually yellow and red).
- The child can hold a crayon and move it up and down.
- The child understands cause and effect (e.g. if something is dropped, he or she understands it might break).
- The child talks about an absent object when reminded of it (e.g. he or she may say 'biscuit' when seeing an empty plate or bowl).

From three years

The child develops symbolic behaviour. This means that:

- The child talks.
- The child pretend plays – often talking to him- or herself while playing.
- The child takes part in simple non-competitive games.
- The child represents events in drawings, models, etc.
- Personal images dominate, rather than conventions used in the culture, e.g. writing is 'pretend' writing.
- The child becomes fascinated by cause and effect; the child is continually trying to explain what goes on in the world.
- The child can identify common colours, such as red, yellow, blue and green – although may sometimes confuse blue with green.

From four years

- At about age four, the child usually knows how to count – up to 20.
- The child also understands ideas such as 'more' and 'fewer', and 'big' and 'small'.
- The child will recognise his or her own name when it is written down and can usually write it.
- The child can think back and can think forward much more easily than before.
- The child can also think about things from somebody else's point of view, but only fleetingly.
- The child often enjoys music and playing sturdy instruments, and joins in groups singing and dancing.

From five to eight years

- Communication through body language, facial gestures and language is well established, and opens the way into literacy (talking, listening, writing and reading).
- The child includes more detail in their drawings – e.g. a house may have not only windows and a roof, but also curtains and a chimney.
- The child will recognise his or her own name when it is written down and can usually write it him- or herself.
- Thinking becomes increasingly coordinated as the child is able to hold in mind more than one point of view at a time. Concepts – of matter, length, measurement, distance, area, time, volume, capacity and weight – develop steadily.
- The child enjoys chanting and counting (beginning to understand number). The child can use his or her voice in different ways to play different characters in pretend play. The child develops play narratives (stories), which he or she returns to over time. The child helps younger children into the play.
- The child is beginning to establish differences between what is real and unreal/fantasy. This is not yet always stable, so the child can easily be frightened by supernatural characters.

Table 3.9.1 An overview of the stages of cognitive development (*Continued*)

Activity

- Identify the main stages of cognitive development in children from birth to seven years.
- When do babies develop what Piaget called the concept of object permanence?
- When does a child typically begin to understand cause and effect?
- What is meant by symbolic behaviour – and at what age does a child typically develop symbolic behaviour?
- When do children begin to establish differences between what is real and what is unreal – or fantasy?

AC 1.3 Summarise current scientific research relating to neurological and brain development in early years

Current research into the development and learning of babies and young children focuses mainly on neuroscience. In the past, some scientists thought that the brain's development was determined genetically, and that brain growth followed a biologically predetermined path. Now neuroscientists believe that most of the brain's cells are formed before birth, but most of the connections among cells are made during infancy and early childhood. They refer to the 'plasticity' of the brain and believe that:

- early experiences are vital to healthy brain development
- the outside world shapes the development of a baby's brain through experiences that a child's senses – vision, hearing, smell, touch and taste – take in.

It is estimated that at birth, a baby's brain contains thousands of millions of neurons, or nerve cells, and that almost all the neurons that the brain will ever have are present. Babies start to learn in the womb, particularly in the last three months. When they are born, babies are able to recognise familiar sounds and they have already developed some taste preferences. The brain continues to grow for a few years after birth, and by the age of two years, the brain is about 80 per cent of the adult size.

The neurons are connected together to form even more billions of different neural pathways. Whenever we have a new experience, a new neural pathway in the brain is used. Each new experience changes our behaviour – this is called learning. If the experience is repeated, or the stimulus is very strong, more nerve impulses are sent along the new pathway. This reinforces the learning process and explains why repetition helps us to learn new things. Repetition strengthens the connections between neurons and makes it easier for impulses to travel along the pathway. This process is commonly known as hard wiring, and 90 per cent of the hard-wired connections will be complete by the age of three. It is very important to our understanding of brain development in early childhood, and explains and illustrates the long-lasting impact of early experiences.

Key term

neuroscience Studies of the brain which provide evidence to help early years specialists working with young children.

Sensory deprivation

A congenitally blind baby (a baby who is born blind) will develop a more sophisticated sense of touch than a sighted baby, although they both start life with the same touch potential. As the sense of touch develops, so the area of the brain normally assigned to touch increases in size for the blind baby, and the area of the brain normally assigned to sight decreases.

Similarly, in a congenitally deaf baby, the part of the brain that normally receives auditory stimuli is taken over by the visual and movement input from sign language.

Activity

Why is knowledge about neuroscience important in early years studies? Summarise the current scientific research relating to brain development in early years.

AC 1.4 Explain how current scientific research relating to neurological and brain development in early years influences practice in early years settings

The following findings from studies in neuroscience have had an impact on early years practice.

- Brain development occurs as a result of a complex interweaving of one's genetic potential and experiences.
- Early experiences have an effect on the 'design' of the brain, and influence the nature and extent of adult capabilities.
- Early interactions impact on the way the brain is 'wired' as well as creating the context for development and learning.
- Brain development is non-linear: at certain times there are 'sensitive' periods at which conditions for particular kinds of learning are optimal.

- In the early years children's brains are much more active than are adults' brains; high levels of activity have reduced considerably by adolescence.

Early years practitioners already appreciate the importance of providing a learning environment rich in opportunities for children to learn through the full range of their senses. The identification of sensitive periods – or windows of opportunity – in brain development is also important to early years practice. These are not clearly defined as fixed periods; rather, they exist more as subtle differences in the brain's ability to be shaped by the environment. Sensitive periods for learning mainly involve visual, movement control, language and memory functions that are learnt naturally in an enabling environment. It is thought that if a child misses an opportunity, his or her brain may not develop its circuitry – or hard wiring – to its full potential for a specific function.

Activity ·

How do you think research into brain development has impacted on early years practice? Find out about the criticisms of neuroscience when applied to early years practice. One critic is the scientist, John Bruer; see Useful resources for information.

· ·

LO2 Understand theory underpinning cognitive development

Theories of child development – a holistic approach

A theory of child development is someone's idea about how a child might develop. Theories help people to predict, for example, that before children talk, they usually babble. Theories about how children develop are products of research, so are influenced by the culture in which they are thought out. Research by human beings provides all the evidence for and against various theories of child development. It is very important to remember this, because humans are not objective – they agree and disagree. You must realise that there is no such thing as 'the truth' about child development. We always need to stop and ask: Who is doing the research? Who is formulating the theory?

Two examples illustrate this point.

- The child psychologist **Lev Vygotsky** grew up in the Soviet Union, where Marxist and communist ideas dominated. He came from a large family. Is it coincidence that his theory emphasises social relationships and the community?
- The psychologist **Jean Piaget** grew up in Europe. He was an only child. Is it coincidence that his theory emphasises the child as an individual and as an active learner, trying to experiment and solve problems?

AC 2.1 Describe theoretical perspectives in relation to cognitive development

Aspects of cognitive development

Concentrating and attending, being engaged and involved

Children concentrate best when they:

- find something interesting and enjoyable
- have a choice of experiences
- are with an adult who is interested in what they are doing
- are with an adult who will help them, but without doing things for them.

Activity ·

Look at the photographs in this chapter and link each of them with the bullet points about when children concentrate best.

· ·

Figure 3.9.1 The adult lends a helping hand when needed to the child who is learning to use a spoon

Figure 3.9.2 The boy is fascinated by the egg. This is not the moment for a conversation; it is the time to fully experience what is happening

Figure 3.9.3 Cooking for someone's pleasure involves advance planning

Figure 3.9.4 Boys cooking

Theory of mind – me and you

Being able to appreciate another person's way of thinking from their point of view is an incredible thing to be able to do. The neuroscientist

Sarah-Jayne Blakemore outlines the sequence of development:

- Until they walk, talk and pretend, babies concentrate on what they see, want and feel.
- Once they pretend, they begin to have some understanding of what is real and unreal.
- Gradually, they begin to talk about their beliefs (that the biscuits are in the kitchen cupboard).
- By the end of the first five years, typically they are beginning to know that people can have different beliefs from theirs, and that theirs can be changed too.

There are two approaches to studying theory of mind: one is to set up laboratory experiments to test it and the other is to observe children within their own families.

The Sally–Anne false belief task – the laboratory test approach

The Sally–Anne experiment involves placing a doll on a table and telling the child that this is Sally. Sally has a basket. Then a doll called Anne is introduced and she is placed next to Sally. Anne has a box.

Sally has a marble, which she places in her basket. She goes for a walk. Anne takes the marble out of the basket while Sally has gone. Anne puts the marble in her box. Sally comes back. She wants to play with the marble. The child is asked, 'Where will Sally look for the marble?'

The child may or may not realise that Sally will not know that Anne has moved the marble to her box while she is away. The answer the child gives will show whether the child understands what it is like to see things from either Sally's or Anne's point of view in terms of their 'knowledge' of the situation. If the child says that Sally will look in Anne's box for the marble, it shows they do not understand that Anne has moved it there, but that Sally would not know this as she had left the room when this was done. They are not yet looking at this from Sally's point of view.

In practice activity

Carry out the Sally–Anne false belief task with a child aged three years and a child aged four years. What does this tell you about each child's thinking? Make sure the children do not observe each other doing the task.

Observing children in natural situations

Observing children in their homes, Judy Dunn found that even toddlers showed a practical grasp of how to annoy or comfort other children. From the time they walk, talk and pretend, they begin to understand other people's feelings, but only within the circle of people who love them and whom they love.

This confirms the pioneering work of Jean Piaget in the 1930s, that children are – and Piaget admitted this was an unfortunate description – intellectually egocentric (selfish) until the age of about four or five years. Margaret Donaldson, using laboratory techniques in the late 1970s, and Judy Dunn, observing in natural situations in the 1980s, have demonstrated that children perform at a more advanced level:

- in surroundings that they know and in which they feel comfortable
- when they are with people who love them and whom they love
- when a situation makes what Donaldson called 'human sense' to them.

Case study

Theory of mind

Mandie, who is three years old, gives her mother the celery stick because she know she likes this. She gives Granny a cucumber stick for the same reason. She takes a carrot stick from the plate because she likes those the best. If she were with people she did not know, she would not have the knowledge to demonstrate her understanding of others.

Instead of talking as Piaget did, about children gradually shedding intellectual egocentricity, we now talk about developing theory of mind (ToM), which is more positive.

In practice activity

Observe a child over the course of a day to see where he or she is in his or her journey towards understanding how other children and adults feel and think. Observe the child in the familiar setting, and when he or she is with adults who know and care for the child. Link your observations to what you have read in this unit.

Problem-solving and making hypotheses and theories

Children are natural problem-solvers from the moment they are born. It used to be thought that, at first, children tried to solve problems through trial and error, and that only later could they develop a theory or hypothesis. More recently, however, researchers have found that even newborn babies can make a hypothesis. Making a hypothesis means having a theory that can be tested to see if it is right. It is amazing to think that babies can do this, rather than the cruder trial-and-error approach to solving problems.

Case study

Baby makes a hypothesis

This experiment, conducted in the 1970s, would be considered unethical today (because honey is now known to be dangerous to some babies under one year of age), but it does show how a baby makes a hypothesis. A newborn baby turned towards the sound of a buzzer and was given a honeyed dummy to suck on. The baby also turned to the sound of a bell, but was not given a honeyed dummy. Soon the baby turned only for the buzzer. Once the baby had tested the hypothesis – that the buzzer signified honey and the bell did not – the hypothesis was confirmed. Soon the baby was bored with confirming the hypothesis again and again, so the baby did not turn to either buzzer or bell.

Key term

hypothesis A hypothesis makes a prediction that something will happen and tests it out in a scientific way to see if it is true or not.

Making a false hypothesis is an important part of childhood

Children can be very obstinate about a theory they have! Experts think that finding out that a hypothesis is wrong is a very important part of learning to solve problems. In order to learn about problem-solving, children need to test out their incorrect hypotheses as well as correct ones. The reasoning they employ is invaluable for intellectual development.

Case study

Learning by hypothesis

Segun (four years) saw some paint that glowed in the dark. His mother told him (wrongly) that it was called fluorescent paint. He asked his mother for some. Having painted the stone owl from the garden, Segun put it in his bed, so that it would glow in the dark. It did not glow in the dark! He then painted all sorts of stones from the garden. He put them in his bed each night. They did not glow in the dark either! Next he painted sticks from the garden and put them on his bed each night. They did not glow in the dark!

Segun's uncle visited him and told him that what he needed was iridescent paint. Segun, however, carried on with his idea of making objects glow in the dark using fluorescent paint. Then he saw a pot that glowed in the dark. He asked the owner what sort of paint they had used. The answer was, 'Iridescent'. He decided to try the new paint, and his owl glowed in the dark; so did his sticks and stones.

Segun had worked out, thorough exploration, that the hypothesis that fluorescent paint glows in the dark was incorrect. He will now know this for the rest of his life. He also knows from experience that iridescent paint does make things glow in the dark. This is real learning that no one can take away from him. It shows he is making predictions through his hypothesis, reasoning and problem-solving.

Memory

Memory is about the way in which experiences are stored, retained and recalled in the brain. There are different kinds of memory: short-term memory and long-term memory.

Short-term memory

When you make a phone call, you need to remember the number for long enough to dial. Remembering ten or so digits is quite hard to do. It becomes easier for the brain if the numbers are 'chunked', ideally into a maximum of three numbers per chunk, some chunks with two numbers.

Imitation and memory are linked: if you poke out your tongue at a newborn baby, they will imitate you.

Short-term memory relies hugely on hearing (acoustic) and also on seeing (visual). This is why it is difficult to remember words that sound similar (bog, dog, log, fog). The difference between 'dog' and 'cat' is easier for the brain to hear.

Short-term memories do not last long in the brain; they are limited. Neuroscientists now know that our feelings, sensory perceptions and memories are all bound together in a seamless whole. This means that the feelings children have are of central importance in the way memory develops.

Long-term memory

We remember things that engage our interest and hold meaning for us. One famous example comes from Jean Piaget's daughter Jacqueline when she was a toddler. She saw a friend (aged 18 months) have a temper tantrum. She was very impressed by this dramatic event, and the following day she tried it out on herself, imitating the tantrum.

Whereas short-term memory relies on sound and sight, long-term memory depends on meaning (semantics). Unless something makes sense, it cannot find its way into the long-term memory.

Between the ages of two and three years, children are able to remember more. The advantage of developing a longer-term memory is that children can organise their thinking a bit more. They remember what they have done before in similar situations with people, and they can use this memory to think about what to do in a new situation. This is called 'inhibition to the unfamiliar'. It means children begin to 'think before they do'.

Early concepts

Concepts take time to form because they rely on being able to organise information. Children develop concepts of time, space, love, beauty and number (to name just a few), which continue to develop over the years. Some aspects of concept formation are biological, and some are social and cultural. Our brains quite literally change according to whom we meet and the experiences we have. This can be summed up by the phrase 'nurture shapes nature'.

An emerging concept of faces

Hannah cried when her Uncle Dan, who was bald, came to the house. This happened every time she saw her Uncle Dan for a month or so. She had to adjust to her new knowledge that some people do not have hair on the top of their heads.

Babies get to know the faces of people in their family and of their carers. They begin to develop an early concept of what faces look like. By the age of about six to nine months, typically, they find faces that seem different rather frightening because they do not fit with what they know. At first, Uncle Dan was very upset, but he was reassured when this was explained.

Schemas – part of concept formation

A schema is a pattern of behaviour that is repeatable. It helps children to take in experiences. Schemas become generalised and tried out in a variety of situations. They become coordinated with each other and grow increasingly complex as children develop and learn. Knowing about schemas helps parents and practitioners to relate to children more easily and to enjoy their company more. It helps adults to understand some of the annoying things children do too, and to work positively with children. Schemas, which are part of brain development, help children to learn. See Table 3.9.2.

There is a developmental sequence in schemas:

- At first, babies develop action schemas, using their actions, senses and movement. These develop out of the reflexes that they are born with, and include, for example, sucking and gazing. These remain throughout life.
- Then the sensory motor action schemas begin to develop into two deeper levels:
  - symbolic (making one thing stand for another)
  - cause and effect (understanding that if I do this, then that will happen).

Transmission models of learning

In the seventeenth century, the British philosopher John Locke thought that children were like lumps of clay, which adults could mould into the shape they wanted. At the beginning of the twentieth century, the American psychologist John B. Watson and the Russian psychologist Ivan Pavlov were developing

Figure 3.9.5 Trajectory schema – at a cause-and-effect level. This means the child is continuing to experience and try things out and learn through her senses and movement, but is also beginning to experiment with trajectories. It is as if she is asking herself, 'What if I do this? This happened last time, but will it happen again? Does this action always bring this result?'

similar theories about how people learn. In the past, these theories have had a strong influence on thinking about development.

Classical conditioning

Ivan Pavlov (1849–1936) experimented with conditioned responses in dogs. He liked to be described as a physiologist, rather than as a psychologist, because he believed that psychological states (such as conditioning) are identical to physiological states and processes in the brain. He thought this approach was useful and scientific. In his experiments, there was a neutral conditioned stimulus (CS), which was a church bell ringing. This was paired with food, which was an unconditioned

Name of schema	Description
Transporting	A child may move objects or collections of objects from one place to another, perhaps using a bag, pram or truck.
Positioning	A child may be interested in placing objects in particular positions, for example on top of, around the edge of, or behind something. Paintings and drawings also often show evidence of this.
Orientation	This schema is shown by interest in a different viewpoint, as when a child hangs upside down or turns objects upside down.
Dab	A graphic schema used in paintings, randomly or systematically, to form patterns or to represent, for example, eyes, flowers or buttons.
Dynamic vertical (and horizontal)	A child may show evidence of particular interest by actions such as climbing, stepping-up and down, or lying flat. These schemas may also be seen in constructions, collages or graphically. After schemas of horizontality and vertically have been explored separately, the two are often used in conjunction to form crosses or grids. These are very often systematically explored on paper and interest is shown in everyday objects such as a cake-cooling tray, grills or nets.
The family of trajectories	(a) **Vertical** (up) and **Horizontal** (down) A fascination with things moving or flying through the air – balls, aeroplanes, rockets, catapults, frisbees – and indeed, anything that can be thrown. When expressed through the child's own body movements, this often becomes large arm and leg movements, kicking, or punching, for example. (b) **Diagonality** Usually explored later than the previous schemas, this one emerges via the construction of ramps, slides and sloping walls. Drawings begin to contain diagonal lines forming roofs, hands, triangles, zig-zags.
Containment	Putting things inside and outside containers, baskets, buckets, bags, carts, boxes, etc.
Enclosure	A child may build enclosures with blocks, Lego or large crates, perhaps naming them as boats, ponds, beds. The enclosure is sometimes left empty, sometimes carefully filled in. An enclosing line often surrounds paintings and drawings while a child is exploring this schema. The child might draw circles, squares and triangles, heads, bodies, eyes, wheels, flowers, etc.
Enveloping	This is often an extension of enclosure. Objects, space or the child him- or herself are completely covered. The child may wrap things in paper, enclose them in pots or boxes with covers or lids, wrap him- or herself in a blanket or creep under a rug. Paintings are sometimes covered over with a wash of colour or scrap collages glued over with layers of paper or fabric.
Circles and lines radiating from the circle	(a) **Semi-circularity** Semi-circles are used graphically as features, parts of bodies and other objects. Smiles, eyebrows, ears, rainbows and umbrellas are a few of the representational uses for this schema, as well as parts of letters of the alphabet. (b) **Core** and **Radials** Again common in paintings, drawings and models. Spiders, suns, fingers, eyelashes, hair and hedgehogs often appear as a series of radials.
Rotation	A child may become absorbed by things which turn – taps, wheels, cogs and keys. The child may roll cylinders along, or roll themselves. The child may rotate their arms, or construct objects with rotating parts in wood or scrap materials. →

Table 3.9.2 Schema focus sheet

Name of schema	Description
Connection	Scrap materials may be glued, sewn and fastened into lines; pieces of wood are nailed into long connecting constructions. Strings, rope or wool are used to tie objects together, often in complex ways. Drawings and paintings sometimes show a series of linked parts. The opposite of this schema may be seen in separation, where interest is shown in disconnecting assembled or attached parts.
Ordering	A child may produce paintings and drawings with ordered lines or dabs; collages or constructions with items of scrap carefully glued in sequence. They may place blocks, vehicles or animals in lines and begin to show interest in 'largest' and 'smallest'.

It is important to remember that the sensory-motor stage of the schema is at an earlier level, and that the cause and effect, together with the symbolic levels, both emerge out of this.

Table 3.9.2 Schema focus sheet   (*Continued*)

stimulus (UCS). The dogs were fed when the church bells rang. This produced an unconditioned response (UCR), which was saliva flowing in the dog's mouth when the food appeared. Gradually, the sound of any bell would produce a conditioned response (CR) in the dogs, which would produce saliva, ready for the food that usually accompanied the ringing of the bell.

Classical conditioning is the way in which responses come under the control of a new stimulus. In this case, food normally produces salivation. Classical conditioning changes the stimulus, so that the sound of a bell produces salivation. Pavlov would have fed the dogs whether or not they salivated at the sound of the bell.

Figure 3.9.7 Pavlov's dog: an illustrated summary of the experiment

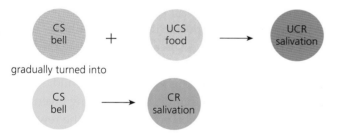

Figure 3.9.6 A summary of Pavlov's experiment

Case study

An example of learning through classical conditioning

Year 2 children (aged six and seven years) in a primary school were working in groups. One group was painting, one was writing, one was involved in a maths game and one was cooking. The school bell rang. Immediately, the children stopped what they were doing and started to tidy up quickly and go out to play. The children were conditioned to expect playtime when the bell sounded, so they tidied up in readiness. They would have tidied up even if they had not subsequently been allowed to go out to play.

Bell (CS) + Playtime (UCS) = Tidy up (UCR)

Bell (CS) = Tidy up (CR)

Operant conditioning

B. F. Skinner (1904–90) was a behavioural psychologist who worked in the USA. He did not believe it was useful to theorise about mental states that could not be observed. He thought this was unscientific.

Whereas Pavlov fed his dogs when the bell rang whether they salivated or not, Skinner only fed his rats or pigeons if they behaved as he required. For example, Skinner gave rats a reward of food if they pressed a lever. This was positive reinforcement: the desired behaviour was rewarded.

Conversely, undesired behaviour could be negatively reinforced. For example, the rats might receive an electric shock each time they went near one area of a maze. They would then begin to avoid that area. The undesired behaviour was extinguished and the desired behaviour was encouraged.

Chris Rice is a lecturer in early childhood courses at Clydebank College in Scotland, and explains how positive and negative reinforcement can work for children:

Positive and negative reinforcement

Positive reinforcement is concerned with a child behaving in a certain way, leading to a pleasing outcome; then the behaviour will be repeated. For example, a baby points to a toy monkey and looks at the adult. The adult hands the baby the toy, making appropriate monkey noises, which they both find funny. The baby then repeats the behaviour with other objects, in order to be similarly amused (positive reinforcement).

Negative reinforcement is concerned with a child behaving in a particular way in order to avoid something unpleasant, to stop pain or to prevent discomfort. For example, the baby cries because he or she has a wet nappy and feels uncomfortable. The adult responds by changing the nappy and the baby feels better. The next time the baby feels discomfort he or she will repeat the behaviour – that is, repeat the crying – in order to stop the unpleasant feeling.

A **reinforcer** causes the behaviour to be repeated; it may be some form of reward for showing a desired behaviour or something that is linked to the avoidance of unpleasantness or pain.

In the positive reinforcement example, the monkey noises are the reinforcer – the entertaining reward for asking for the toy.

In the negative reinforcement example, getting a nappy change is the reinforcer – the reward for crying. In both these situations, the baby is learning that a certain behaviour will elicit a certain response from other people.

As long as these responses occur, the baby will repeat the behaviour. If the adult ignores the behaviour instead of rewarding it, it will stop eventually (this is called **extinction**). See table 3.9.3.

Links to practice (AC 2.2)

Another example of negative reinforcement would be that while playing at the water tray, a toddler might try to take a jug from another child. Neither child will let go and both will look to the nearest adult, with cries of distress to get attention. If in the past this has led to a satisfactory conclusion – the adult finding a bottle that one child accepts as a substitute – the children will repeat the behaviour in the future.

Bribery and behaviour-shaping

Bribery is quite different from behaviour-shaping or behaviour modification. We might want a child to put away the floor puzzle that he or she has been working on that is spread all over the floor. If we tell the child that he or she can have a sweet if he or she tidies it up, this is bribery. The child, understandably, feels that he or she is being given a choice, and weighs the behaviour against the reward. Is it worth it? The child may decide it is not – and he or she will be baffled if the adult is displeased with his or her choice. (Older children may see this as an opportunity to negotiate, asking for two sweets!) With bribery, the child learns that the point of the behaviour is to please the adult and gain the reward – in this case, a sweet – not to ensure that all the pieces of the puzzle are stored safely for another time.

Link to practice (AC 2.2)

In behaviour-shaping or modification, there is no 'if' and no mention of reward. The reinforcer comes only after the behaviour has appeared, usually in a way that is linked to the behaviour. 'Well done,' the adult might say, 'you have tidied that up quickly.' When using behaviour shaping, the only time that there is any mention of future outcome is in terms of what will be happening next – for example, 'When everyone is sitting quietly, then we can start the story.'

Just as positive reinforcement must not be confused with bribery, negative reinforcement must not be confused with punishment. Ignoring undesirable behaviour (leading to extinction), together with clear and consistent reinforcement of desired behaviour, is more effective than punishment.

Problems with behaviourist techniques

It is important that adults are very clear about their purpose if they use these techniques.

● What behaviour is to be extinguished?
● What behaviour does the adult want to increase?

The adult must make sure that what they intend is what actually happens, and that the child does not pick up an entirely different message. For example, a child may learn that if he says sorry within an adult's hearing and quickly enough after hitting another child, he may avoid punishment, irrespective of whether or not he has any feelings of remorse.

Often, adults ignore children when they are behaving appropriately, only giving them attention when they are disruptive. However, children need to realise the advantages (enjoyment and satisfaction) of cooperating with others in different situations, so that enjoyment and satisfaction become the reinforcers. Other kinds of reward are then not necessary.

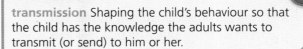

Key term

transmission Shaping the child's behaviour so that the child has the knowledge the adults wants to transmit (or send) to him or her.

Subject	Behaviour	Reinforcer	Outcome
child	has tantrum in supermarket	GETS sweets	Positive Reinforcement – Behaviour Will Be Repeated
salesperson	meets sales target	GETS bonus	
teenager	pushes over old woman in street	GETS money from handbag	
dog	sits up and begs	GETS food	
baby	points to toy	GETS toy handed to them	
holidaymaker	puts on suntan oil	AVOIDS sunburn	Negative Reinforcement – Behaviour Will Be Repeated
tutor with headache	takes aspirin	STOPS headache	
driver	slows down before speed camera	AVOIDS speeding ticket	
student	hands medical certificate in	AVOIDS losing bursary	
baby with wet nappy	cries	STOPS discomfort (adult changes nappy)	
neighbour	complains about loud music next door	STOPS noise	

Table 3.9.3 Operant conditioning

With permission from Chris Rice, Clydebank College

Leave it to nature: a *laissez-faire* model

In the eighteenth century, the French philosopher Jean-Jacques Rousseau thought that children learnt naturally, and that they were biologically programmed to learn particular things at a particular time. He thought that just as a flower unfolds through the bud, so a child's learning unfolds – for example, babbling leads into language, and then on into reading and writing; and kicking the arms and legs leads to crawling and walking.

In this approach, adults help children to learn by making sure that the environment supports the child's learning as it unfolds. For example, children learn the language that they hear spoken as they grow up. If children hear Chinese, they learn to speak Chinese. If they hear English, they learn to speak English. If children hear more than one language, they are able to learn more than one language and become bilingual or multilingual. This model of learning suggests that children are naturally programmed to learn languages.

This view of learning suggests that children naturally do what they need to in order to develop and learn. It sees children as active in their own learning. Children may be helped by other people or may learn on their own. Because adults do not need to act, according to this theory, it is sometimes referred to as a *laissez-faire* (letting things take their own course) view of how children learn. See table 3.9.4.

Arnold Gesell

In the 1930s, Arnold Gesell mapped out some norms of development (normative measurement was discussed earlier in this unit – see pp 387–9). These were used to chart milestones in the child's development as it unfolded. Gesell believed that normal development progressed according to a set sequence. His milestones could be used to check that the pattern of development was 'normal'. Gesell's developmental scales looked at motor, adaptive, language and personal – social areas. If children reached particular milestones, such as walking, within the 'normal' age range, then their development was said to be making 'normal' progress. This approach is depressing if used with children with special educational needs, as they are constantly labelled 'not normal'.

Case study

An example of learning through a 'leave it to nature' approach

Because most children of around three to four years of age begin to enjoy drawing and painting, the rooms in a nursery school were set up to support this. Great care was taken in the way that a variety of colours were put out in pots, with a choice of thick and thin paintbrushes. Children could choose paper of different sizes. A drying rack was close to the area and children could choose to paint at a table or on an easel.

Adults would be on hand to help if needed, but would be careful not to talk to children while they were painting, in case they cut across the children's thinking. Adults would not 'make' children paint, because not all children would be ready to do so. Readiness is important in this approach to learning.

The social constructivist/interactionist approach

In the eighteenth century, the German philosopher Immanuel Kant believed that a child's learning was an interaction between the developing child and the environment. He said that children constructed their own understanding and knowledge about things. The approach is called a social constructivist view of how children learn. This model:

- is the approach currently most favoured by early years practitioners
- has the best support from research into child development in the western world
- draws on both the transmission model and the *laissez-faire* model of a child's learning, rearranging elements of both into something that is helpful to those working with children.

Piaget, Vygotsky and Bruner all used a social constructivist/interactionist approach; their work is discussed below.

Jean Piaget (1896–1980)

The important elements of Piaget's theory of how children learn are that:

- children go through **stages** and **sequences** in their learning
- children are active learners

Advantages	Disadvantages
• Adults can learn about how to offer the right physical resources, activities and equipment for each stage of development.	• Adults may hold back too much because they are nervous of damaging the child's natural development: for example, by not talking to a child while she is drawing or by holding back from playing with children.
• Children can actively make choices, select, be responsible, explore, try things out and make errors without incurring reproach or a feeling of failure.	• Adults only support children in their learning, rather than extending the learning children do.
• Adults value observing children and act in the light of their observations. This might mean adding more materials, and having conversations with children to help them learn more.	• Children might be understimulated because adults are waiting for signs of readiness in the child. The signs might never come! Adults wait too long before intervening.
• Adults are able to follow the child's lead and be sensitive to the child.	• Children might not be shown how to do things in case it is not the right moment developmentally to teach them, which leaves them without skills.
	• Children with special educational needs or from different cultures might be labelled 'abnormal' or 'unready'. In fact, they might reach a milestone earlier or later, but still within the normal sequence. They might develop unevenly but in ways which make 'normal' life possible. Milestones in one culture might be different in another culture.

Table 3.9.4 Advantages and disadvantages of the 'leave it to nature' view of development and learning

- children use **first-hand experiences** and prior experiences in order to learn
- children **imitate** and transform what they learn into **symbolic behaviour**.

Piaget did not explicitly emphasise the importance of the social and emotional aspects of learning, and he did not dwell on social relationships as much as the other social constructivists. This means that he took social and emotional development for granted and did not write about it in detail. Instead, his writing emphasises intellectual or cognitive development and learning. Piaget's theory is called constructivist (rather than social constructivist) for this reason.

Lev Vygotsky (1896–1934)

Vygotsky stressed the importance for development of someone who knows more than the child and who can help the child to learn something that would be too difficult for the child to do on his or her own. He described:

- the **zone of proximal development (ZPD)**, sometimes called the zone of potential

development – this means that the child can do with help *now* what it will be possible for him or her to do alone with no help *later in life*
- the **importance of play** for children under seven years, allowing them to do things beyond what they can manage in actual life (such as pretend to drive a car) – it is another way through which children reach their zone of potential development
- the **zone of actual development** – this is what the child can manage without help from anyone.

Vygotsky believed that social relationships are at the heart of a child's learning, so his theory is called a social constructivist theory.

Jerome Bruner (1915–)

The essence of Bruner's theory is that children learn through:

- **doing** (the **enactive** mode of learning)
- **imaging** things that they have done (the **iconic** mode of learning)

- making what they know into **symbolic codes** – for example, talking, writing or drawing (the **symbolic** mode of learning).

Scaffolding: helping children to learn

Bruner believed in the importance of scaffolding in helping children to learn. Adults can help develop children's thinking by being like a piece of scaffolding on a building. At first, the building has a great deal of scaffolding (i.e. adult support of the child's learning), but gradually, as the children extend their competence and control of the situation, the scaffolding is progressively removed until it is no longer needed.

Scaffolding can be described as anything a teacher can provide in a learning environment that might help a student learn. This means that children can learn any subject at any age. They simply need to be given the right kind of help. This includes anything that allows the student to grow in independence as a learner – such as:

- clues or hints
- reminders
- encouragement
- breaking a problem down into smaller steps
- providing an example.

For example, when a baby drops a biscuit over the side of the high chair, the baby can learn about gravity if the adult 'scaffolds' the experience by saying something like: 'It dropped straight down to the floor, didn't it? Let's both drop a biscuit and see if they get to the floor together.' Bruner's theory is also called a social constructivist theory, as social relationships are central to 'scaffolding'.

Key terms

enactive learning This is about learning by doing, through first-hand experiences.

iconic thinking When an image stands for a person, experience or object, perhaps through a photograph.

Discussion point

Scaffolding an activity

Calum and his father were out shopping. Calum stopped walking and was obviously struggling to do up the zip on his jacket, but was becoming increasingly frustrated. His father stood behind him and – using his own hands to guide Calum's – helped him to insert the end of the zip into the metal fitting. When Calum had managed to slot it in, he was easily able to pull the zip up by himself and was delighted.

In class, think about the following scenarios and discuss how you could scaffold the child's learning:

- learning to ride a two-wheeled bike
- learning how to tie shoelaces.

Case study

An example of a social constructivist/ interactionist view of development and learning

Using a team approach to record-keeping in an early years setting, staff had built up observations of children. They noted that Damian (five years old) kept punching; he punched other children, furniture and other objects. It seemed to be his main way of exploring.

The staff decided to introduce activities that allowed punching.

- They put huge lumps of clay on the table.
- They made bread and encouraged energetic kneading.
- They sang songs like 'Clap your hands and stamp your feet' and 'Hands, knees and bumps-a-daisy'.
- They encouraged vigorous hand-printing and finger-painting.

- They helped children to choreograph dance fights when acting out a story.
- Damian told the group about 'baddies' from another planet.
- He helped to beat the carpet with a beater as part of spring-cleaning.
- He spent a long time at the woodwork bench, hammering nails into his model. He soon stopped hitting other children, and began to talk about what he was doing in the activities with adults and other children.

Observation enabled adults to support Damian's learning in educationally worthwhile ways. Adults were also able to extend his learning, so that hitting people stopped and became learning to hit in a rich variety of ways that did not hurt anyone.

Advantages	Disadvantages
• This approach is very rewarding and satisfying because adults and children can enjoy working together, struggling at times, concentrating hard, stretching their thinking and ideas, celebrating their learning, and sharing the learning together.	• It is very hard work compared with the other two approaches to learning that we have looked at in this chapter. This is because there is much more for adults to know about, more to think about, more to organise and do.
• Trusting each other to help when necessary creates a positive relationship between children, parents and staff. It means taking pride in the way that indoor and outdoor areas of the room are set up, organised, maintained and cared for.	• It is much more difficult for those who are not trained to understand how to work in this way.
• It means teamwork by the adults, which is the way to bring out everyone's strengths in a multiprofessional group of teachers and early years workers.	
• It means sharing with parents and children all the learning that is going on.	
• It means adults need to go on learning about children's development. When adults continue to develop as people professionals, learning alongside children, they have more to offer the children.	

Table 3.9.5 Advantages and disadvantages of the social constructivist/interactionist view of learning

The nature–nurture debate

The nature–nurture debate is concerned with the extent to which development and learning are primarily to do with the child's natural maturing processes, and the extent to which development and learning progress as a result of experience.

The debate has been very fierce, and it is not over yet. Modern psychologists such as Sir Michael Rutter believe that the child's learning is probably about 60 per cent nature and 40 per cent nurture.

Neuroscientists such as Colin Blakemore stress the importance of relationships (nurture), and how these actually cause the brain to change and be altered physically.

We can think about the developmental theories in terms of nature and nurture:

- The transmission approach stresses experience and nurture.
- The 'leave it to nature' approach stresses maturation and nature.

Case study

The Brooklands experiment

A group of children with severe learning difficulties were taken from the wards of the Fountain Hospital in London in 1960. They were placed in a stimulating environment of people and first-hand interesting experiences. Their intelligence was found to develop rapidly. This research project, led by Jack Tizard of the University of London, was called the Brooklands experiment. Research like this led, in 1971, to children with special needs living in hospitals or attending day care centres, receiving education as well as care, by law. Until then, it was considered impossible to educate children with IQs below 50.

- The social constructivist approach to learning stresses both nature and nurture. A modern way of describing this is to say that both the biological and sociocultural paths of development are important for learning.

Intelligence – fixed or elastic?

The idea that children are born with a fixed amount of intelligence, which can be measured and does not change throughout their lives, was not seriously challenged until the 1960s.

Before the 1960s, children were frequently tested to find their IQ (intelligence quotient), using scales such as the Stanford–Binet or Merrill–Palmer tests. Because these tests were developed by white, male psychologists with middle-class ways of looking at life, they favoured white, middle-class, male children, who therefore scored higher than other groups of children. This began to worry some researchers, who found that IQ tests:

- favour children from the culture from which the tests emerged, which means the tests are not as objective as they were first thought to be
- measure particular types of intelligence, such as memory span and ability with numbers and language, so that intelligence is only looked at in a narrow way, which does not help us to consider outstanding ability in dancing, music or sensitivity to others, for example
- lead to children being labelled 'bright', 'average' or 'low ability'
- cause practitioners to have predetermined expectations of children (for example, 'Well, she's only got an IQ of 80')
- are sometimes useful if used as part of a range of tests (especially for children with special educational needs), but they are not useful used in isolation from other forms of assessment
- do not show the motivation (will) a child has to learn; two children might have the same IQ, but the one with the greater will to learn is likely to do better.

During the 1960s, Piaget's work made researchers think again about what intelligence/cognition is. His theory (which has been confirmed by later work in neuroscience) suggested that intelligence is not fixed and unchangeable, but elastic. This means it can stretch, grow and increase. We now know that intellectual/cognitive development is helped if children:

- engage with adults and other children who are interesting to be with and who are interested in them
- experience a stimulating environment that encourages thinking and ideas, emotional intelligence and social interaction.

Educating children: compensating for deficits or building on nature?

Following either of these two approaches leads to entirely different ways of working with babies and young children.

An approach based on the idea of compensating for deficiencies prevailed in the late 1960s in the USA (Headstart programmes) and in the early 1970s in the UK (Halsey studies). This was because researchers were beginning to realise that intelligence is elastic. Children who were growing up in non-stimulating environments were placed in education programmes that compensated for the poverty and social disadvantage of their lives. However, this approach did not place enough emphasis on:

- the language and cultural background of the children
- the importance of the child's parents and family life.

By contrast, the Froebel Nursery Research Project, directed by Chris Athey from 1972 to 1977, worked in close partnership with parents.

Activity

Remembering our learning

Think back to your own schooldays. Were any of the lessons based on a transmission model of learning? Evaluate your learning experience.

Guidelines: using the different approaches to development and learning

1 Table 3.9.4 shows that in a 'leave it to nature' approach to learning, children make a very high contribution to the learning they do, but adults hold back and take a very small part.
2 This is very different from the transmission model. In this approach, the adult has a very high input into the child's learning, taking control over the child's learning. The child's contribution is quite low.
3 The 'by-the-book' approach to learning is not valuable and has not been covered in this unit. Here,

both the adults and the children have a very low level of participation. It is not really an approach to learning; it is just a way of keeping children occupied. Worksheets, colouring in, tracing, templates, filling in gaps and joining the dots all fall under this heading.
4 In the social constructivist (sometimes called interactionist) approach to learning, both the adult and the children put an enormous amount of energy into active learning.

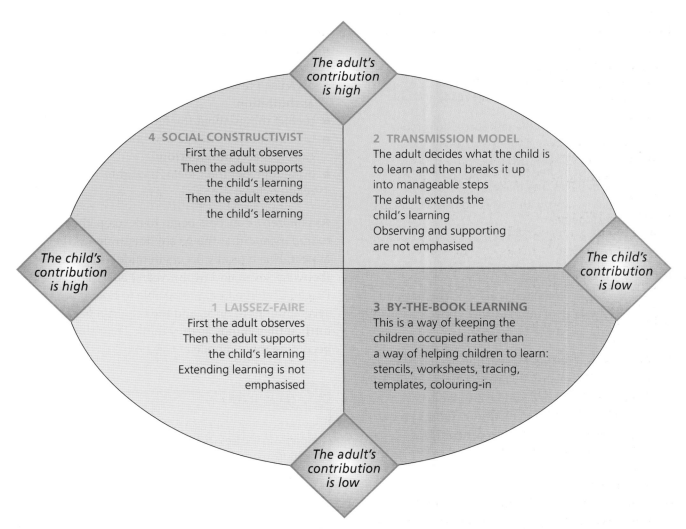

Figure 3.9.8 The four approaches to development and learning

Activity ·

Models of learning

Make a chart with these three headings:

● Transmission model of learning
● *Laissez-faire* or 'leave it to nature' model of learning
● Social constructivist or interactionist model of learning.

Which of the following sentences go under which heading?

1 Adults should mould children's learning. After all, adults know more than children.
2 Children know what they need in order to learn.
3 Do you want to have a story first, or tidy up first?
4 We need to tidy up; we'll have the story after.
5 Children are full of ideas if they are encouraged to have them.
6 Do it because I say so.
7 That child has been off-task all morning.
8 Children are born with everything they need in order to learn.
9 Children enjoy conversations with adults.
10 Children must be free to try things out.
11 Children will learn when they are ready and not before.
12 That child performed the task successfully today.
13 Nature knows best.
14 Adults know best.
15 Children must be free to try things out and to learn from the mistakes they make.

Compare your answers with a working partner. Discuss your answers together.

· ·

Piaget's theory of concepts

Although Piaget pioneered work on schemas and concepts, a great deal more is now known, allowing our knowledge of these to develop.

Young children become increasingly able to think forwards and backwards in time in quick succession, because every event is a bit like a separate photograph. They need to focus (or centre) on one thing at a time. Piaget calls this **centration**.

As children begin to link their previous experiences more easily, the experiences they have become more like a moving film than a sequence of still photographs. Piaget calls this period of development 'pre-operational'. However, most early years workers do not like the idea that children are 'pre' anything, because it concentrates too much on what children

cannot do, giving a negative image of the young child. It is much more useful to think in terms of developing operations, which provides a more positive emphasis.

As a child's early concepts emerge and develop, they begin to:

● link past, present and future around a particular idea
● develop memory, which helps them to know more
● organise their thinking
● understand sequences, with a beginning, middle and end
● understand transformations
● seriate, so that they understand the differences between things (different shapes, sizes, colours, objects and animals)
● classify, so that they see the similarities between things (cats and dogs are animals)
● organise previous experience – Piaget calls this **assimilation**
● predict things about the future
● take in new knowledge and understand it – Piaget calls this **accommodation**
● bring together their ideas, thoughts, feelings and relationships.

As children's concepts begin to develop, they begin to understand that things are not always as they appear. This typically occurs in middle childhood (between seven and twelve years) according to Piaget. Children begin to be able to hold in mind several things at once, and they can run back and forth in their minds as they think. Their thinking is becoming more mobile at this point.

Key terms

centration The child cannot hold in mind several ideas at once, so focuses (centrates) on one aspect. The child might focus on the height of a mug, for example.

assimilation This is the process by which new information and experience is taken into (assimilated) the existing structures (schemas or concepts) in the brain.

accommodation Sometimes it is not possible to simply take in experiences, and then alterations can be made which adapt/alter (accommodate) the brain.

There are several ways of examining Piaget's theory. One is to look at the way he explores:

- **biological sequences** of development (the way children grow, develop and mature)
- **social** knowledge (other people and the way children relate to them)
- the **equilibrium** of learning (accommodating to new ideas and assimilating experiences into what is already known); because we are always learning, we are always balancing (as we do on a two-wheel bicycle)
- the importance of **experience** in development and learning – Piaget pioneered the idea that experience is important in the development of intelligence and cognition (thinking).

Usually, Piaget's work is looked at through the biological sequences of development rather than through the other aspects of his theory.

The following section outlines the stages of development that occur in a child according to Piaget. The exact ages vary, and are different in different cultures and for children with complex needs and disabilities, but the sequences are still thought to be useful.

Piaget's stages of cognitive development
Sensory-motor stage (birth to about 18 months)
There are six stages:

1 Ready-made behaviours (reflexes) that the baby is born with are adapted and used – for example, the baby actively tries to reach for the nipple (teat) with his or her hands as soon as it touches the baby's lips.
2 Hands become coordinated with sucking; sounds are looked for; objects are seen and reached for; hand-watching is important.
3 Babies begin to show intention. They try to prolong or repeat something that interests them.
4 Babies begin to experiment with making things happen. They begin to work out that although they do the same thing (for example, throw) each time, the object they throw might behave in a different way – a ball will bounce, a biscuit will crumble, milk will spill.

5 Around the end of the first year, babies deliberately modify their actions in order to produce the result they want. They like trying out new things, and they follow through and search for a ball if it rolls under the sofa, expecting to find that it has rolled out the other side.
6 They can think about the past and the future. They might imitate the action of eating a lollipop the day after they had one as a treat.

Developing operations (about 18 months to seven years)
Children are involved in:

- imitation (and increasingly imitating things after the event)
- pretending (imagining things from the past or in the future)
- forming images inside their heads.

The first part of this phase is often called the period of symbolic behaviour. This is linked to play, imagination and creativity. We see the child becoming more and more able to think about and reflect on things he or she actively experiences. The second part of this phase is known as intuitive. The child develops a sense of right and wrong.

In practice activity

Conservation of number

Show a child two rows of identical buttons. Check that the child agrees that the rows have the same number of buttons. Spread out one row to make it longer. Ask the child which row has the most buttons. Children under seven years usually do not conserve number in a formal task situation like this. This means they are likely to think that the spread-out row has more buttons. Children cannot yet hold in mind more than one thing at a time.

Concrete operations (about seven to 12 years)
Although children are beginning to be able to think in more abstract ways, they still need plenty of real and first-hand experiences in order to understand things. There is a Chinese proverb that says, 'I do and I understand.' During these years of middle childhood, children become increasingly able to:

- hold in mind several things at once
- deepen the way they use symbols as they draw, make models, dance, make music, write, read, make stories and use mathematical numbers and mark-making
- conserve ideas (be able to see beyond the superficial appearance of how things look) about shape, number, quantity, volume, and so on – for example, to work out that although five sweets look like more when they are spread out than when they are bunched up, there are still five sweets
- understand the rules of games, such as football or snakes and ladders.

Formal operations (about 12 years to adulthood)

In the stage of concrete thinking, children need real and present situations so that they can have their deepest thoughts – for example, they can understand a great deal about what is fair and unfair if one child is given a present and the other is not. But formal operations allow older children and adults to think in abstract ways.

- Supposing only your class survived a global disaster. How would you create rules and laws to live fairly together?
- What do we mean by peace and justice? These are abstract ideas.

Some adults never reach this stage, and for most of the time adults continue to rely on concrete, real situations when they think. It is hard to think in the abstract, without a real situation to help the thinking along, so we do not manage it all the time.

Figure 3.9.9 How do you fill a bottle with water? A funnel solves the problem

In practice activity

Permanence of the object

Piaget used a test called 'the permanence of the object'. He would cover an object, and the baby had to sit and watch this. By nine months of age, the baby would reach for the object by uncovering it and picking it up; younger babies did not do this. It is now thought that babies have to realise that two objects (the object and the cover) can be in one place in order to complete the test.

Later researchers gave babies of five months of age an object which might be put in either their right hand or their left hand. When the light went out they found that the babies reached for the object as soon as it was dark. The object could not be seen, but the babies still reached out and almost always they reached out in the right direction. The babies seemed to know that the object was still there, even though they could not see it in the dark. They also know that they only have one mother, and so become disturbed if they are shown multiple images of her as early as five months old.

Using the information provided, carry out Piaget's permanence of the object test. You will need to find the equipment required, and a sitting/crawling baby who is relaxed and wanting to play with you.

1 What are your findings?
2 What does this tell you about the baby's thinking and ideas?

Social and cultural relationships

These are now thought to be just as central to a child's development as the other kinds of experience that Piaget emphasised more, such as the way that children build up an understanding of objects. Recent research is helping us to remember that it is important to have a balanced approach which emphasises:

- the importance of people and positive relationships for thinking and learning
- first-hand experiences that are physical, cultural and social
- learning and thinking in indoor and outdoor situations
- the importance of children having experiences that are of interest and that hold meaning for them
- that children are active learners, but are not isolated learners – they need other children and adults to help them learn and think.

Children perform less well in test situations

When children are put into laboratory test situations, they find it harder to do their best thinking. They find it difficult to understand exactly what the experimenter is asking them. When they are in a situation that makes 'human sense' to them – at home or in their early years setting with their mother or key person – they are in a familiar situation and they can think well.

Cultural sensitivities

Recent researchers are beginning to look more at the importance of context. One of Piaget's conservation tests, to see if a child has a concept of looking at a view from different visual perspectives, involves asking a child to look at model mountains. The child is asked to say what a doll will see when placed at different points around the model. A child growing up in the Norfolk Broads where the land is flat will not experience the mountains of Switzerland in the way that the children whom Piaget studied did. The Swiss children saw views from different angles as they moved round the mountains, in a way that children living in Norfolk would not, so children living in flat countryside might appear to be less able according to the conservation test. In this example,

the conservation test is culturally biased in favour of the Swiss children. Biases like this are called 'cultural sensitivities'.

Transforming – you are never the same again

Piaget's stages of development are now seen as too linear. Instead, researchers look at the way networks of behaviour develop in sequences. Piaget's basic idea is that one stage transforms as it changes into the next persists, but we now know that it is a very complex series of biological transformations, and we are trying to understand and learn about the detail.

Activity

It may help to describe the theories relating to cognitive development if you describe them using Figure 3.9.8 on p 405: i.e. social constructive theories – Piaget, Vygotsky, Bruner; transmission model theories – Pavlov and Skinner; *laissez-faire theories* – Rousseau and Gesell. (The fourth approach – by-the-book learning – has no useful underpinning theory!)

AC 2.2 Analyse how theoretical perspectives in relation to cognitive development impact on current practice

Some of the links to practice with theoretical perspectives on cognitive development have been identified and placed immediately next to the theories being described in AC.1 – and are labelled 'AC 2.2 Link to practice'.

The use of schemas to support effective learning

Schemas are a very useful learning tool, which can help practitioners to better describe the complexities and the connections in children's play. They are important to early years practice because they:

- make children's thinking and ideas visible
- can support children's abstract thinking.
- help practitioners to describe, in more detail, the ways in which children are approaching their learning
- enable practitioners to support parents' understanding of their children's learning

- help inform planning: schemas emphasise children's individual interests, preferences, knowledge and abilities.

In practice activity

Schemas

Observe a child throughout one day – either a baby, a toddler or a child up to five years old – using narrative observations and, if possible, photography. Then analyse your observations to see if you have any examples of consistent use of a schema or schema cluster (rotation is often strong when enclosure is present; the two schemas form a cluster). Use Table 3.9.2 (p 396) to help you identify schemas.

1 Note the child's favourite experiences in the setting. Can you see if there are links with the child's schemas?
2 Ask the parent(s) what the child is interested in at home and share your observations with them. Are there any connections between what the child enjoys and finds interesting in the setting and at home?
3 What can you do to support and extend the child's schemas? For example, if the child is particularly interested in rotation, you might add whisks and spinners to the water tray.

Chris Athey: learning through schemas

Chris Athey developed Piaget's idea of schemas when working on The Froebel Nursery Research Project, which she directed in 1972–7, working in close partnership with parents. Schema theory derived from Athey's work has a strong place in early years practice in the UK, and indeed some other countries too, most notably New Zealand. It is used successfully in many early years settings. Features of Athey's pioneering work include the following:

- The home language of the children was respected and valued.
- Children were offered interesting, real experiences through a quality curriculum. This curriculum included:
  - gardening
  - cooking
  - play indoors and outdoors
  - a home area
  - woodwork
  - clay
  - painting and drawing
  - modelling with found materials.

The objective of the Project was to support children from less socially advantaged homes, and was very successful. The IQs of the children rose, especially the younger children who joined the Froebel project as babies. This approach builds on what children naturally and biologically do, as well as placing great emphasis on the social and cultural aspects of learning in a caring educational community. Children learn to talk and communicate, and to develop their thoughts and ideas more easily when they spend their time with adults who care about what they think and are interested in.

LO3 Facilitate the development of cognition in children

AC 3.1 Describe the role of the EYP when facilitating the development of cognition in children

Activities for babies and young children in early years settings are carefully planned to promote their holistic development. Your role is to plan and implement activities to facilitate the development of cognition – or learning – at all stages of children's development.

Promoting active learning

Active learning is learning that engages and challenges children's thinking using real-life and imaginary situations. It takes full advantage of the opportunities for learning presented by:

- spontaneous play
- planned, purposeful play
- investigating and exploring
- events and life experiences
- focused learning and teaching.

These opportunities for learning are supported when necessary through sensitive intervention to support or extend learning. All areas of the curriculum can be enriched and developed through play.

Children need opportunities to follow their own interests and ideas through free play. Children's learning is most effective when it arises from **first-hand experiences** (whether spontaneous or structured), and when they are given time to play without interruptions and to a satisfactory conclusion.

Key term

first-hand experience One that is lived through personally rather than experienced by someone else and seen or heard about.

Unit 3.2 describes how active learning can be promoted through well-planned play.

The skills children need to learn effectively

The frameworks for learning for children in the UK are designed to promote these skills and to assess each child's skills throughout their early years and schooling.

Guidelines: facilitating the development of cognition in children from birth to five years

- Observe children's thinking and the ideas they develop; carefully note your observations and share them with parents and colleagues.
- Remember the sequences of development in thinking, so that you can help the child in ways that tap into this.
- Use your observations to make sure that you do not underestimate or overestimate a child's thinking.
- Offer a wide range of experiences (not narrow activities and tasks that allow little choice on the part of the child).
- Be prepared to be flexible. Take your lead from the children when judging when a project is 'finished' – perhaps allowing projects to run over sessions, even days if necessary, as this will build motivation and perseverance.

- See children as active learners.
- Try not to expect children to do things that are boring for them.
- Do not expect children to perform tasks that are too difficult for them and therefore discourage them.
- Encourage children to have ideas and to be creative and imaginative.
- Encourage children to try new things.
- Give children sensitive help in carrying out their ideas.
- Help the child while respecting and showing sensitivity to their ideas, helping only when needed.
- Adapt experiences to suit children with special educational needs, complex needs and disabilities.

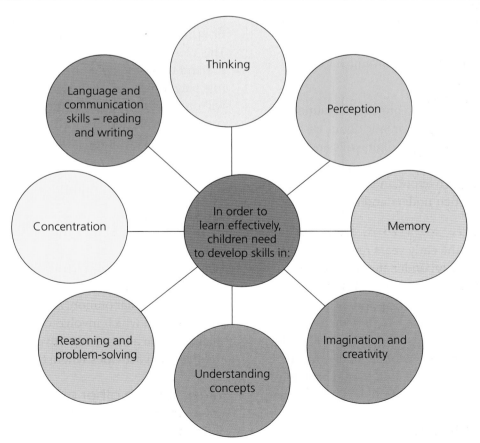

Figure 3.9.10 Skills for effective learning

AC 3.2 Analyse the use of technology in supporting the development of cognition in children

Learning about information and communications technology (ICT) starts from birth because technology is now a fundamental part of every young child's environment. Children are surrounded by ICT, in the same way as they are surrounded by language, print and numbers. In the home, technology encompasses remote controls for television, DVDs and sound systems, toys which have buttons, dials and buzzers, mobile phones, washing machines, microwave ovens and other machines that require programming – and of course, computers.

Outside the home, children are also surrounded by technology: they see automatic doors, cash machines, barcode scanners, digital tills and security cameras. Technology is something children are going to grow up with, learn about and master, and use as a tool to increase their understanding in all areas of learning.

Many activities in the early years revolve around children developing an understanding of their environment. Settings encourage children to explore, observe, solve problems, predict, discuss and consider. ICT resources can provide tools for using these skills as well as being examined in their own right, with computers not being the only ICT resources. ICT equipment added to role play reflects the real world, builds on children's experiences and allows them opportunities to understand how, why, when and where different forms of technology are used in everyday life.

The Early Learning Goals in the EYFS (2012) state:

Technology: Children recognise that a range of technology is used in places such as homes and schools. They select and use technology for particular purposes.

According to a report by DATEC (Developmentally Appropriate Technology in Early Childhood), seven general principles have been identified for determining the effectiveness of ICT use in the early years. These principles aim to help practitioners provide the best possible experiences. They are:

1 Ensure an educational purpose.
2 Encourage collaboration.
3 Integrate with other aspects of curriculum.
4 Ensure the child is in control.
5 Choose applications that are transparent.
6 Avoid applications containing violence or stereotyping.
7 Be aware of health and safety issues.

Parental involvement is also important in this area.

Ensure an educational purpose

This could be something as simple as providing a pretend mobile telephone to encourage imaginative role play, which children from a very early age will do quite naturally. Children need a variety of computer applications which encourage a range of development, including creativity, self-expression and language. Ideally, apps should be used only after a thorough discussion with staff and parents about the educational benefits and limitations of the particular application.

Encourage collaboration

Children can access programs individually, but the best applications provide a valuable means of encouraging collaboration. Activities requiring 'joint attention' and which involve 'children learning to share' provide a better cognitive challenge for young children than activities where they work alone.

Integrate with other aspects of curriculum

ICT applications should be integrated as far as possible with other play and project work, and all should work together to help make the curriculum relevant to children. Many settings use computer programs which manage information as part of their project work so that, for instance, children might collect information on a topic about the body (hair colour or height, perhaps) and make simple graphs on the computer using these data. Computers should only be used as a means to fulfil a function which cannot be achieved better through other means. Questions to ask relating to this are: what does this program enable the children to do that they couldn't do otherwise? Is it helping towards particular skills and understanding?

Ensure the child is in control
Generally, the child should control the application; the application should not control the child's interaction through programmed learning or any other behaviourist device. Such an approach is contrary to current ideas of what constitutes good educational practice. Many early years practitioners feel that programmed learning operates against the principles of developing children's awareness and positive outlook towards literacy and numeracy.

Choose applications that are transparent
As far as possible, ICT applications should be 'transparent'; their functions should be clearly defined and intuitive. In practice, this means that the application can complete each clearly defined task in a single operation. A good example of this is the 'drag and drop' facility on the computer, which allows the user to pick an item up with a click, drag

it to somewhere else and then drop it in that place with another click. It is a perfect simulation of what happens in real life when something is moved.

Avoid applications containing violence or stereotyping
Computers can empower all young children to be more independent, but research shows that issues of equality are very important. A number of studies have shown that:

- girls often use computers less often than boys
- the presence of computers in a setting does not always ensure access
- teachers, while concerned about equality issues, often hold attitudes which hinder access, for example use of the computer may be granted as a reward, or its use may be restricted to drill-and-practice tasks for less able children
- children from low-income families often have less access and/or lower-quality access to computers in the home.

When selecting applications for use in early years settings it is important to ensure that they do not include stereotypical or patronising images or actions related to social class, ethnicity and gender.

Be aware of health and safety issues
Serious concerns have been voiced about the consequences of encouraging extended use of desktop computers by young children. It is therefore advisable that a typical use of any desktop computer

Guidelines: introducing ICT to children in an early years setting

- Encourage children to observe and talk about the uses of ICT in their environment. On local walks, for example, talk with children about traffic lights, telephones, street lights or the barcode scanners which identify prices in shops.
- Encourage play with improvised pretend or real technological objects to support their imaginative role play.
- Join in the play as a co-player or observing children at play in order to identify more clearly how they are making sense of ICT in their worlds and their learning needs.
- Involve parents in their children's use of ICT:
  - use digital, still and video pictures on a television or computer in the reception area – recording outings,

  the day's activities, curriculum presentations, and any special events
  - use digital pictures in the records
  - ask parents to trial new software
  - use closed circuit televisions to enable parents to watch children at play and learning
  - loan recording equipment to take home
  - make CDs of children singing
  - develop a website.

See also the list of suggested ICT resources at the end of this unit.

application by a child should be comparatively short, usually no more than ten to twenty minutes for three-year-olds, extending to no more than forty minutes by the age of eight. However, if a child or group of children is totally engaged in an activity and the completion of this requires a longer period at the computer this should be allowed, but it is not recommended that children do this regularly.

AC 3.3 Create an environment which facilitates cognitive development of children in own setting

As children learn through well-planned play, revisit Units 3.2 and 3.4 to enable you to create an environment which facilitates cognitive development in your own setting.

LO4 Implement a learning experience which supports the development of sustained shared thinking in children

AC 4.1 Plan a learning experience which supports the development of sustained shared thinking in children aged: 0–1 year 11 months; 2–2 years 11 months; 3–5 years

The EPPSE longitudinal study identifies sustained shared thinking as a key strategy in supporting and extending children's learning and thinking. It is defined as

an episode in which two or more individuals 'work together' in an intellectual way to solve a problem, clarify a concept, evaluate activities, extend a narrative, etc. Both parties must contribute to the thinking and it must develop and extend.

For more information on sustained shared thinking, see Unit 3.5, p 333.

When children explore and share their ideas with others they try to solve problems and develop their thinking together – constructing their own learning. Sustained shared thinking involves the adult being aware of children's interests and their understanding and the adult and children working together to develop an idea or skill.

Sustained shared thinking occurs most often when the child or children have initiated and led an activity, and the practitioner has responded to this by using the children's interests to shape the planning and the curriculum. This includes the planning of focused activities and guided teaching, for example, through storytelling, using a phonics session to extend the 'pirate language' the children have already created, or finding a film on the internet of outer space to show the children what stars look like on closer inspection.

Iram Siraj-Blatchford identifies the following range of strategies to support sustained shared thinking:

- **Tuning in**: listening carefully to what is being said, observing body language and what the child is doing.
- **Showing interest**: giving their whole attention to the child, maintaining eye contact, smiling, nodding.
- **Respecting children's own decisions and choices by inviting children to elaborate**: saying things like 'I really want to know more about this,' and listening and engaging in the response.
- **Recapping**: 'So you think that…'
- **Offering the adult's own experience**: 'I like to listen to music when I cook supper at home.'
- **Clarifying ideas**: 'Right, Darren, so you think that this stone will melt if I boil it in water?'
- **Suggesting**: 'You might like to try doing it this way.'
- **Reminding**: 'Don't forget that you said this stone will melt if I boil it.'
- **Using encouragement to further thinking**: 'You have really thought hard about where to put this door in the palace – where will you put the windows?'
- **Offering an alternative viewpoint**: 'Maybe Goldilocks wasn't naughty when she ate the porridge?'
- **Speculating**: 'Do you think the three bears would have liked Goldilocks to come to live with them as their friend?'

- **Reciprocating**: 'Thank goodness you were wearing wellie boots when you jumped in those puddles. Look at my feet, they're soaking wet!'
- **Asking open questions**: 'How did you...?' 'Why does this...?' 'What happens next?' 'What do you think?' 'I wonder what would happen if...?'
- **Modelling thinking**: 'I have to think hard about what I do this evening. I need to take my dog to the vet because he has a sore foot, take my library books back to the library and buy some food for dinner tonight. But I just won't have time to do all of these things.'

Reflective practice

- Can you join in with children's play in the home area, or the role-play area you have created with the children (the hospital room or the monster's house) and take a part, following the children's lead, and participate *alongside* the play?
- Can you keep an open mind about the children's play and listen to their ideas before adding your own?
- Do you encourage children to ask questions rather than asking questions yourself?

Activity

Using the ideas in Unit 3.2 and suggestions from your colleagues, plan a learning activity to support the development of sustained shared thinking for *each* of the following age groups: children aged: birth to one year, 11 months; two to two years 11 months; three to five years.

AC 4.2 Lead a learning experience which supports the development of sustained shared thinking in children aged: 0–1 year 11 months; 2–2 years 11 months; 3–5 years

Activity

Using the ideas in Unit 3.2. and suggestions from your colleagues, lead a learning activity to support the development of sustained shared thinking for *each* of the following age groups: children aged

- birth to one year 11 months
- two to two years 11 months
- three to five years.

LO5 AC 5.1 Critically evaluate the provision for supporting cognitive development in own setting

Evaluating the provision for supporting cognitive development of children in your own setting

When evaluating the effectiveness of our provision and practice, we need to be able to identify and record ways of continually improving our practice.

Assessing the effectiveness of planned provision

The main way of evaluating our practice is by observing children's participation and assessing whether their needs have been met. The following points should be considered:

Observing and assessing children

Select one child (or a group of children) and carry out a structured observation over a number of sessions or a few weeks. Your aims are to find out how their cognitive development has been supported – in particular their progression in thinking and problem-solving.

Obtaining feedback

From the child or children: you can obtain direct feedback from the child or children by listening to them and noting their comments or by asking them questions. It is usually easy to see whether children have enjoyed a certain activity, as they will often be clamouring to do it again.

From colleagues and parents: parents know their own child best and they are often able to provide valuable insight into the effectiveness of activities. Colleagues are often well placed to give feedback as they may be able to observe children during an activity. Feedback can also be obtained by filming the children during the activity and observing the children's reactions and comments.

Identifying and recording areas for improvement

Having obtained feedback, you now need to identify areas for future development. This can be recorded as an action plan. You should draw up a plan that identifies:

- areas for improvement
- reason for action
- detail of action to be taken
- equipment and resources needed
- date for implementation.

Assessment practice

1 Describe sensory development in the first year of life.
2 What are the stages of cognitive development in children from birth to seven years?
3 What is the current scientific research relating to neurological and brain development in the early years and how does this influence practice in early years settings?
4 Describe the main theoretical perspectives in relation to cognitive development and analyse how they impact on current practice.

5 What is the role of the EYP when facilitating the development of cognition in children?
6 How can technology support children's cognitive development?
7 What makes a good environment that facilitates children's cognitive development?
8 Plan and lead a learning experience that supports the development of sustained shared thinking in your setting.
9 Critically evaluate the provision for supporting cognitive development in your own setting.

Useful resources

Books and journals

Bruer, J.T. (1999), *The Myth of the First Three Years: A new understanding of early brain development and lifelong learning*. New York: Free Press.

Siraj-Blatchford, I. (2009), 'Conceptualising Progression in the Pedagogy of Play and Sustained Shared Thinking in Early Childhood Education: A Vygotskian Perspective', *Education and Child Psychology* 26 (2).

Websites

BBC CBeebies: http://www.bbc.co.uk/cbeebies/

BBC Games: http://www.bbc.co.uk/cbbc/games/index.shtml

Berit's Best Sites: http://www.beritsbest.com/

Enchanted Learning Online: http://www.enchantedlearning.com/categories/preschool.shtml

Kids @ National Geographic: http://www.nationalgeographic.com/kids/

Kids Domain: www.kidsdomain.com

Kid's Wave: http://www.safesurf.com/safesurfing/

Microsoft Kids Website: http://www.kids.msn.com/

Peter Rabbit: http://www.peterrabbit.com/

PBS Kids: http://pbskids.org/

Thomas the Tank Engine: http://www.hitentertainment.com/thomasandfriends/uk/

Unit 3.10 Develop the speech, language and communication of children

This unit provides the learner with the knowledge, understanding and skills to develop the speech, language and communication of children.

Learning outcomes

By the end of this unit you will:

1 Understand theory and current frameworks which underpin children's speech, language and communication development.
2 Understand how the early years practitioner supports the development of speech, language and communication of children.
3 Be able to create a language-rich environment to develop the speech, language and communication of children in own setting.
4 Be able to lead activities which support the development of speech, language and communication of children.
5 Be able to critically evaluate provision for developing speech, language and communication for children in own setting.

LO1 Understand theory and current frameworks underpinning children's speech, language and communication development

AC 1.1 Define the terms: speech, language and communication

Communication is the exchange of messages or meanings. It uses all the senses, although we often focus on language and speech because they convey the most complex meanings. **Language** is a structured system that conveys meaning. We usually use spoken language, but can also communicate using writing or sign language. Language is more formal than communication, following a set of rules that allows the user to express new ideas and to convey complex meanings. Different languages use different sounds and follow different rules from

one another. **Speech** is made up of the sounds that are used to communicate words and sentences in spoken language. Children acquire the ability to use speech as they gain control over the muscles of the mouth and face.

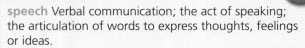

Key terms

speech Verbal communication; the act of speaking; the articulation of words to express thoughts, feelings or ideas.

language A recognised system of gestures, signs and symbols used to communicate.

communication The transmission of thoughts, feelings or information via body language, signals, speech or writing.

What is communication with and without words?

Communication is probably one of the most important ways in which we develop and learn throughout life. Babies, children and adults communicate all the time. However, approximately 80 per cent of communication is without words. Even when we use the spoken word (verbal communication), we continue to communicate non-verbally.

Figure 3.10.1 These babies are communicating with each other in non-verbal ways. The object is used as an invitation to open up communication between them

We communicate in order to understand ourselves and develop a strong, confident sense of our identity, and to understand and relate to other people, their feelings, ideas and thoughts. See Figure 3.10.2, which demonstrates that communication does not always require words. The adult holds the child in a way that makes the child feel secure. They share an experience: the adult smiles, looking at the child, which gives an atmosphere of warm affection, without overwhelming. The child is sitting in a relaxed way, with one foot under the other, and feels confident about looking at what is happening around them. They are not feeling rushed or under pressure.

Figure 3.10.2 There are several kinds of communication here that do not involve words

Gestures, pointing, props, signals and links

Personal communication can include:

- gestures
- pointing
- props – the handbag represents mother when she goes for coffee, and the child knows she is coming back because her handbag is there
- signals that give evidence – the footprint in the sand tells us someone was there
- links – the child has a teddy bear while the parent or carer is away that links the child to them; the communication is personal between this child and this parent or carer.

Naming

Once children are beginning to gesture and point, they often begin to name things. The naming is at first very personal to the child – for example, a baby of 14 months calls a horse 'hee haw', but also uses this word to describe dogs, cats and any four-legged animal.

Activity

Find out more about the definitions for speech, language, communication, and speech, language and communication needs. Explain in your own words what each of these terms means: speech; language; communication.

In practice activity

Communicating

Sit with a child, either between one and three years, or between three and five years. Note the communications you have between you that do not depend on words. Make a list of examples.

Not all human beings communicate through a spoken language, for one reason or another, but the vast majority of people in the world do. What is more, they often speak two or three languages fluently from an early age.

Key terms

receptive language Learning to listen and understand language: the child listens, watches people talking, and begins to understand what is being said.

expressive language Learning to speak and to use language. This involves using the face expressively, making gestures and speaking (or signing).

AC 1.2 Describe theoretical perspectives in relation to speech, language and communication development

There are four main theories about how language is acquired:

- imitation
- nativist
- interactionist
- input.

Imitation theory

For a long time, it was thought that language was acquired – or 'picked up' – by a simple process of imitation and reinforcement. This learning theory is particularly associated with the behaviourist, Skinner, and has the following features:

- Adults – particularly parents – react to random, babbling sounds made by babies and toddlers. They conclude that the baby is asking for something, e.g. 'bi-bi' or 'bis-bis' means biscuit. They respond by providing the biscuit and by giving the correct name for it. As the toddler is eating the biscuit, he or she repeats the sound 'bi-bi', and the association between the sound and the child's experience of eating the biscuit is reinforced by the adult saying: 'Yes, that's right, you've got a biscuit.'
- Children may also acquire language through imitating and echoing sounds made by adults in particular situations; for example, the adult says: 'Harry's gone to school' and the child echoes: 'school' or more probably 'kool'. A child has learnt that by saying 'I want … (my teddy, a biscuit, Mummy),' they will get what they want. They learn to preface all requests with the words 'I want' by a process of reward and reinforcement.
- Sounds and words that are not part of the language that the child will eventually speak are not reinforced and therefore are extinguished. This is called operant conditioning. See Unit 3.9 for information on operant conditioning.

Criticisms of imitation theory

The theory of imitation does not explain the rules of grammar that are applied in children's speech.

For example, children often make simple errors when using plurals, which they cannot have heard adults use: 'boaties', 'shoppies' and 'mouses' for boats, shops and mice. Similarly, when a child says 'taked' or 'digged' he or she is actually showing an understanding of the rule of making regular past tenses (i.e. by adding the regular suffix '-ed'). The theory that language is acquired through imitation and reinforcement is not supported by research into the ways in which parents communicate with small children. Parents rarely correct their children's grammar – and when they do, studies by Katherine Nelson (1988) show that these children have smaller vocabularies than those children who were corrected less. The idea that parents 'shape' their children's learning in this way is flawed.

Nativist theory

This theory was proposed by Noam Chomsky, an American psycholinguist writing in the 1960s. Chomsky argued that much of a child's speech was composed of original constructions and therefore could not have been copied from an adult. He believed that children must be born with an **innate** capacity for language development.

The main features of the nativist (or innateness) theory are:

- Human beings are born with a biological (innate) capacity for language – it is part of their genetic inheritance. Chomsky termed this the Language Acquisition Device (LAD). The LAD is programmed to recognise the universal rules that underlie the particular language that a child hears. Using the machine analogy, the LAD may be described as computing hardware.
- All children possess innate mental structures that allow them to recognise and to use the complex grammatical rules of a language.
- All languages share universal key rules – nouns and verbs and ways of posing questions, issuing commands and expressing negatives.
- Children could not possibly learn all they know through imitation, as many behaviourists argue.
- Experience cannot modify the way the LAD works – as it is innate – i.e. something we are born with.
- The critical period hypothesis: the nativist view describes an apparent critical period for language

acquisition. If the left hemisphere of the brain (which is responsible for the specialisation of language functions) is damaged, the extent of potential recovery from that damage is determined by age, and is at its highest point prior to puberty.

Chomsky proposed that language development should be described as 'language growth' because the 'language organ' simply grows like any other organ. He later abandoned the term LAD – using instead the term Universal Grammar – but the importance of innate mental structures in cognitive development remains the core of nativist theory.

Criticisms of nativist theory

If all children are born with an innate capacity for language, it does not account for the years taken to develop language skills. It also does not explain the mistakes made by children and the use of over- and under-extensions. The theory also fails to explain the wide variation in language ability between individual children. Furthermore, an adult is able to learn a second language to proficiency, which means that the critical period hypothesis is also called into question.

Interactionist theory

This theory argues that language acquisition must be viewed within the context of a child's cognitive development. Piaget associated language acquisition with the emergence of representational thought, which he saw as clearly shown in a variety of ways, including in the search for hidden objects and pretend play. The main features of interactionist theory are:

- Children's language development is closely linked to their cognitive achievements; skills

learnt provide essential resources for language acquisition.
- Children do not use hypothetical statements until they have formed concepts, rather than having simply acquired grammar.
- The cultural view of language acquisition (proposed by Bruner and others) emphasises that the social environment is organised to incorporate the child as a member of an already existing language-using group. Bruner uses the term 'format' to refer to a socially patterned activity in which adults and children interact – an example is the game 'peek-a-boo'.

Piaget saw language as depending entirely on thought, simply mirroring what was in the child's mind. Bruner saw language as a tool that amplifies and enhances thought.

Vygotsky also offered an interactionist explanation for language acquisition. He thought that language emerged from social interactions and relationships. In that sense, language begins outside the child. But as the child takes part in the cultural life of the family, it becomes the way in which children begin to reflect on and elaborate their experiences. Language development takes children on a personal journey in their individual thoughts, but it also gives them social experiences that are important in their culture and society.

Vygotsky believed that language and thought were interrelated in profound ways. He thought that the talking aloud and to themselves that we see young children do gradually becomes internalised. It becomes inner speech, which is silent. In this way, children begin to gain control over their thoughts, so that they can plan, organise, remember and solve problems.

He suggested that this silent inner speech and spoken social speech are connected to the way concepts and the understanding of shared ideas develop together. In other words, there are two strands of development in learning to talk which have a deep influence on the way a child develops their ability to think:

- inner speech (silent and inside yourself)
- social communication using speech.

Criticisms of interactionist theory

Piaget's approach to the development of language fails to explain the ability of very young children to use and understand complex grammatical structures. Language would not develop ahead of a child's basic thought processes. For example, before the child can use expressions of comparison – e.g. 'this cake is bigger than that one', they need first to have developed the ability to make relative judgements of size. In her book, *Children's Minds*, Margaret Donaldson suggests that Piaget may have underestimated children's language and thinking abilities by not giving enough consideration to the contexts he provided for children when conducting his research. There is currently more acceptance of the interactionist views of Bruner and Vygotsky, which stress the importance of social interaction in language development.

Input theory

This theory stresses the importance of the language used by adults – particularly mothers. This language used to be called motherese, but is now more commonly known as Child Directed Speech (CDS). Many adults speak to young children differently from the way they speak to adults. CDS has the following features:

- It is spoken in a higher-pitched voice.
- Sentences are shorter and key words are emphasised.
- Speech is slower and the sentences use simple grammar.
- It is highly repetitive; the same sentences, or variations, may be used over and over again, e.g. 'Where is the teddy? Can you see the teddy? There's the teddy!' The adult often repeats the child's sentences, sometimes correcting the grammar in the repetition. A child using telegraphic speech – for example, 'Daddy car' may obtain the response: 'Yes, Daddy's gone to work in his car.'
- The vocabulary is limited to words that the child will understand, and tends to refer to 'concrete' objects that are immediately present.
- Diminutive or duplicating words are common, e.g. 'doggie' or 'choo-choo'. English makes particular use of a 'y/ie' ending, and similar forms are found in other languages, e.g. the Japanese 'ko'.
- There is a high frequency of question forms, and many sentences end on a higher intonation, e.g. 'Yes?' and 'All right?'

Although CDS or something resembling CDS exists in most cultures and contexts, it is not found in every society. Research has shown that even newborn babies can discriminate between CDS and adult-directed speech, and that they prefer to listen to CDS. This may be due to the lilting, musical quality of the speech patterns. The input theory relies on the fact that children who hear a lot of language develop vocabulary more rapidly in the early years than do those children who are talked to less.

Criticisms of input theory

Research into the language development of children from different cultures has shown that in cultures where the parents do not speak CDS, the children still manage to learn the language. Although the amount of input from adults in terms modification of speech (as in CDS) – and greater involvement in storytelling and symbolic play – *does* affect the rate at which language is learnt, it does not appear to be necessary to language learning.

Stan Kuczaj: a combined perspective

Each of the four theories outlined above offers some insight on the acquisition of language, but Stan Kuczaj provides a different perspective. He makes the distinction between **input** and **intake**. Although adult input is important to some extent, it is the child's use of the input that is crucial. Kuczaj argues that language development is affected by three factors:

1. **Innate organising predispositions**: this is the basic brain structure that forms the basis for neural connections (nervous pathways). Very young infants are 'pre-programmed' to pay attention to the beginning and ending of strings of sounds, and particularly to stressed sounds.

2. **Input**: the set of language experiences actually encountered by the child. Many of the studies on the use of CDS concentrate on the frequency of use of CDS-type constructions in adult speech. Kuczaj suggests that once a minimally sufficient amount of exposure to a particular construction has occurred, additional exposure is

not necessarily helpful to the child's acquisition of it. Some forms of input are more helpful to the child than are others, for example repetitions and expansions.

3 **Intake**: what the child does with the input is crucial to language acquisition. The child may be selective in *what* he or she uses from the adult input and *when* it is used. The intention behind the particular construction of speech used is equally important. For example, a child is more likely to *attend* to CDS that is meant to praise or to encourage rather than to chide or scold.

This combined perspective seems to account for the striking similarities seen among children in their early use of language. All children share the same set of 'pre-programmed' rules, and most children are exposed to very similar input from the people around them.

Activity

Theories of language development

Note three key messages from each theory that you find helpful in your work. How will you use these in your practice?

AC 1.3 Analyse how theoretical perspectives relating to speech, language and communication development inform current frameworks

The early learning goals for communication and language are organised in a set of three new aspects, aimed at clarifying the building blocks of communication and language. Instead of noting mainly how children use language to talk, the revised aspects place increased attention on the underlying skills a child develops before they can begin to talk. These aspects are drawn from those that have proved very useful to practitioners in understanding and supporting children's communication and language development through Every Child a Talker.

Communication and language are a prime area of the EYFS, and the early learning goals for

children at the end of the EYFS are Listening and attention; Understanding; and Speaking. The ELGs for Communication, Language and literacy are described in Unit 3.5.

Listening and attention

This refers to the way babies and children 'tune in to' sounds around them, becoming aware of similarities and differences between sounds and learning to distinguish the sounds that make up spoken language. This aspect includes the early stages of phonological awareness through playing with words, sounds and rhymes that will lead eventually to making links to letters as part of literacy.

Listening and attention also include the development of *purposeful* attention. This means being able to pay attention to more than one thing at a time; it is not the same as becoming deeply engrossed and paying close attention to an activity, which can be seen at each stage of development. Having purposeful control over attention does develop over time, from a baby who immediately turns round when distracted, through to a toddler being able to pay attention to only one thing at a time, to a child who is able to change the focus of attention at will.

Piaget sees language as a social part of development, something that needs other people, so that ideas can be shared and developed. For children who find it hard to listen to what is being said and are not yet able to shift their attention at will, practitioners can help them become ready to listen by saying their name first to help them to turn their attention to the speaker.

Understanding

Children need to understand words and what words mean when they are put together into phrases and sentences before they can use these themselves. They learn from the models of language that they have heard.

Children can be helped to understand language when we tell them a range of words for objects and experiences that they are directly engaged with – in other words, teaching in context. We also help children understand what is said to them by using lively voices, gestures and pictures. Listening to stories helps children to understand more complex language, since the types of sentences used in texts are different from the way we tend to talk in conversation. Stan Kuczaj's work on input and intake emphasises the importance of individual experiences to language development.

Speaking

Speaking refers to children using language to express themselves, but it does not just refer to speaking aloud. This aspect also includes children who do not make speech sounds to express themselves but use language in other ways – for example, through Makaton or signing.

Children need lots of practice in expressing themselves in order to develop both skills and confidence in using language. Bruner stresses the importance of a warm affectionate atmosphere in supporting language development. The adult role as a good listener is vital in providing the right environment for conversation. Children are most likely to develop more complex language when they talk about what they are most interested in, so it is important to follow their lead in one-to-one conversations about their own activities, ideas and play. Vygotsky's theory of the zone of proximal development fits in with the idea of the adult extending children's talk by modelling just one step beyond what the child is currently saying.

LO2 Understand how the EYP supports children's development of speech, language and communication

AC 2.1 Describe the role of the EYP when supporting the development of speech, language and communication

Early years practitioners need to be able to demonstrate methods of providing support for speech, language and communication development, taking into account the age, specific needs, abilities and interests, and home language (where this is

different from that of the setting) of the children in your setting. These methods may include:

- adapting your own language
- scaffolding the child's language
- giving children the time and opportunity to communicate
- facilitating communication between children and each other
- learning through play
- working with parents and carers.

Adapting your own language

It is important to communicate with children in a manner that is clear and concise and appropriate to their age, needs and abilities. This involves:

- using words and phrases that children will understand
- actively listening to children
- responding positively to children's views and feelings
- clarifying and confirming points to reinforce children's knowledge and understanding.

When communicating with children:

- ask and answer questions to prompt appropriate responses from them and to check their understanding
- encourage them to ask questions and contribute their own ideas
- adapt communication methods to suit their individual language needs if they have special needs such as a hearing impairment or they are bilingual.

Scaffolding the child's language

As well as enabling children to use language, early years practitioners can also help young children to understand the rules of language. Once children start to combine words to make sentences, they progress through various stages as the structure and organisation of language becomes gradually more systematic. This systematic structuring of language is called 'grammar'. For example:

- **Stage 1**: very young children use simple two- or three-word phrases or sentences. Grammatical indicators are not present at this stage: no plurals, e.g. 'Many car'; no possessive 's', e.g. 'Tom teddy';

no tense markers such as 'ed' or 'ing', e.g. 'It rain'; no auxiliary verbs such as 'is' or 'do', e.g. 'No like cake'. Young children only use nouns, verbs, adjectives and adverbs such as 'now' or 'soon'.

- **Stage 2**: young children begin to use grammatical indicators that were previously missing. Note the irregular use of past tense forms, e.g. 'camed' (came) and 'goed' (went), and plurals, e.g. 'sheeps' (sheep). Gradually, children begin to use grammar in increasingly adult forms.

Children do not learn grammar through imitation alone; they need opportunities to discover the rules of language for themselves by experimenting and being creative with words in a variety of situations.

Early years practitioners can help children with grammar by repeating back the correct form of language when the child makes a grammatical error. Some examples are:

- Possessive pronouns: the child says, 'This Tom hat and that Teena hat', so the adult replies, 'Yes, that is your hat and this is my hat.'
- Possessive 's': the child says, 'Here Marley boots and teacher boots', so the adult replies, 'Yes, these are Marley's boots and those are Ms Kamen's boots.'
- Plurals: the child says, 'We saw sheeps', so the adult replies, 'Yes, we saw some sheep at the farm.'
- Tense markers: the child says, 'The cat goed out', so the adult replies, 'Yes, the cat went outside,' or the child says, 'Mummy come!', so the adult replies, 'Yes, your mummy is coming into the nursery now.'
- Auxiliary verbs: the child says, 'We done play dough', so the adult replies, 'Yes, we did make play dough this morning,' or the child says, 'We is walking to the park', so the adult replies, 'Yes, we are walking to the park.'
- Negatives: the child says, 'I not eat 'nana', so the adult replies, 'I see you haven't eaten your banana.'
- Questions: the child asks, 'More?', so the adult asks, 'Would you like some more milk?'

You should give positive feedback, praise and encouragement to all children by commenting positively on their efforts to communicate in different ways. Remember to be positive towards each child's attempts at language and communication by considering children's individual interest and abilities, valuing children's home or community language(s), and being aware of children's special language needs. (See relevant sections below.)

Giving children the time and opportunity to communicate

Early years practitioners need to provide appropriate opportunities for language and to ask the right type of questions to stimulate communication. You can do this by providing a wide range of materials and by encouraging young children to talk about their interests, what they are doing and what is happening around them. You need to provide appropriate activities and experiences to enable young children to develop their speech, language and communication skills in meaningful situations; for example, providing opportunities for children's self-expression and self-evaluation through discussion, news time, circle time, painting, drawing, writing, music making, drama and dance.

Facilitating communication between children

The early years practitioner needs to act as a facilitator by providing opportunities for communication between children. For example:

- talking about their day, experiences and interests with other children and adults
- talking about special events such as birthdays, a new baby, religious festivals
- talking during imaginative play activities: playing with pretend/role-play equipment such as dressing-up clothes, home-play area, play shop, puppets; playing with dolls, teddies and other cuddly toys; playing with small-scale toys such as toy cars, garages and road systems, train set, dolls' houses
- playing games and puzzles
- problem-solving during activities such as mathematics, science and technology
- follow-up discussion after an activity or event, such as watching a DVD/television or a live performance, or listening to a story or recorded music

- cooperative group work
- talking while doing activities – not necessarily related to the task!

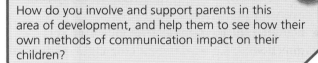

Reflective practice

- How aware are you of your own styles of *non-verbal* communication?
- How effectively do you read others' body language as a way of improving communication?
- How do you explain to the children your strategies for negotiation, problem-solving and resolving conflicts?

Learning through play

Early years practitioners need to provide opportunities for play which are appropriate to the children's ages/levels of development, especially activities and materials which encourage language and communication, such as:

- toys and other interesting objects to look at and play with, such as household objects (remember safety)
- sounds to listen to, including voices, music, songs and rhymes, and noise-makers such as commercial and home-made musical instruments
- construction materials including wooden bricks, plastic bricks and 'junk' modelling
- natural materials, such as water, sand, clay, dough and cooking ingredients
- creative materials, such as paint, paper and glue
- imaginative play materials (see above)
- outdoor activities and outings including playgrounds, gardening, visits to parks and museums, swimming.

Working with parents and carers

Early years practitioners also need to work with parents and carers to encourage their support and participation in activities which help to develop children's speech, language and communication both at home and in the setting. For example, encourage parents and carers to:

- share books and stories (appropriate to the age/level of development of their children) at home, including cloth books, board books, activity books, pop-up books, picture books, audio books, simple textbooks and encyclopaedias

- visit their local library, including special story sessions for the under-fives
- share books and stories with children in the setting, for example bilingual story time
- participate in activities within the setting, for example cooking, sewing and gardening activities
- participate in special events in the setting, such as festivals
- participate in special events outside the setting, such as visits to parks, museums, farms and wildlife centres.

Reflective practice

How do you involve and support parents in this area of development, and help them to see how their own methods of communication impact on their children?

In practice activity

Observation of a language activity

Observe a small group of children involved in a language activity.

In your assessment, comment on each child's language and communication skills:

- use of verbal language (e.g. vocabulary, sentence structure, babbling, imitating sounds)
- use of non-verbal communication (e.g. body language, gestures, facial expressions, signing)
- level of participation in the group situation (e.g. frequency of language, need for prompts from other children/adults)
- level of social interaction (e.g. ability to take turns in speaking and listening, following instructions for the activity or rules of a game).

Suggest practical ideas to assist the children's language and communication skills in future activities.

How to work with children with English as a second language
Advantages of bilingualism

Children need to feel a sense of belonging in an early years setting. It has been known for children to be labelled as having 'no' language, when in fact they simply speak a different language from English.

It is important that children feel their bilingualism is valued and that they see it as the advantage that it is. In most parts of the world, it is common to speak three or four languages fluently. Bilingualism is a positive advantage for all sorts of reasons:

- Learning a language means learning about a culture.
- Knowing about different cultures through living the language means that children who are bilingual experience cultural diversity in rich and important ways. For example, in Guajarati, 'thank you' is only used for special situations as an expression of deep gratitude; in English, people thank each other often, and it is just a form of everyday politeness.
- Bilingual speakers come at an idea from several directions, because different languages emphasise different things. This makes their thinking flexible and analytic. Recent studies in neuroscience provide evidence to support this.
- Children can think in different ways about the same thing when they speak different languages. For example, the Inuit language has several words for 'snow', which makes it possible to think about snow in greater detail than is possible in English.
- Children who are bilingual grow up understanding different ways of thinking. This helps them to respect and value differences between people.
- Children find it easier to understand that names for objects can be changed.
- Children who are bilingual are often more sensitive to the emotional aspects of intonation. They can interpret situations more easily.

Promoting bilingualism
Allow for a period of silence
Before children speak a language, they need to listen to it and tune in. They will make intonational sounds as they try out the sounds of the language. Look at a baby to see this process. It takes about two or three years before the baby turns into a talking toddler. In order to learn to speak a language, it is also important to see the shapes the mouth makes. The mouth looks different when the sound 'oo' is made compared with the sound 'ee'.

Comprehensible input
The researcher Stephen Krashen suggests that children need to make sense of what is being said. If an adult picks up a cup, points at the jug of orange juice and asks, 'Would you like a drink of orange juice?' the meaning is clear. If the adult just says the words, without the actions or objects being visible, the meaning is not at all clear. The adult could be saying anything.

Transitional bilingualism
In some early years settings the child's home language has been valued only as a bridge into learning English. This is transitional (sometimes called **subtractive**) bilingualism. It is assumed that the child will no longer need to speak their home language once English begins to take over. For example, a child who speaks Punjabi at home might be expected to speak English at school and gradually to speak English rather than Punjabi at home.

In fact, children will need to continue their home language to help them transfer later on to reading and writing in English. If the child's home language is not valued alongside English, the opportunities for bilingualism and the advantages that bilingualism brings will be wasted. The home language is important for children to express their feelings and for thinking.

Additive and successful bilingualism
The home language (L1) is the language of thinking and feelings. English as an additional language (L2) is only useful if the home language is strong. Then children think and manage feelings with deeper skill and understanding. This is called **additive bilingualism**.

The EYFS gives specific advice with regard to bilingualism. Practitioners:

- should be aware of the needs of children learning English as an additional language from a variety of cultures and ask parents to share their favourites from their home languages
- should give children opportunities both to speak and to listen, ensuring that the needs of children learning English as an additional language are met, so that they can participate fully

- should value non-verbal communications and those offered in their home language for those children learning English as an additional language.

Key term

balanced bilingualism This is when a child speaks more than one language, each with equal fluency. In fact, the child's home language is usually more fluent than English. Very few children are completely balanced across two languages. For most, one language is more developed than the other.

Reflective practice

- How far are you able to include phrases from a child's home language when talking with them?
- How do you provide opportunities for children to use their first language, and to hear and experience a variety of other languages?

Activity

Supporting children with special language needs
Describe how you have provided (or could provide) support for children with special language needs in your setting. Include examples for children with additional communication and/or interaction needs.

Activity

- Give examples of how your setting promotes language development.
- How do (or could) you provide support for the communication skills of bilingual children?

AC 2.2 Describe benefits to children's holistic learning and development when supporting speech, language and communication development

Child development should always be viewed holistically. This is because each area of development is linked with and affects every other area of development.

- **Personal, social and emotional development** is interwoven with communication development, as both are crucial in the formation of relationships. Children experience difficulties when they are not able to put their feelings into words or to express them in any way. This has a damaging impact on their sense of self and identity, and on their self-confidence. If children are full of anger, anxiety, frustration or fear, they need to express this. Talking about feelings is just as important as talking about ideas. Children who cannot explain or put into words/signs how they feel often have temper tantrums or show other kinds of challenging behaviour. Unless children develop the language of emotion, they will not be able to express their feelings in ways that others find acceptable. This will cause difficulties with relationships and will have a damaging influence on their social development.
- **Physical development** is part of communicating, whether with body language or using the muscles of the mouth. Children become more aware of their motor skills when they have the vocabulary of movement, such as pull, push, spin, roll, fast and slow. They also use their developing communication skills as part of growing independence in their choice of food and in self-care skills – such as dressing, washing, etc.
- **Cognitive development**: language and thinking are often considered to be particularly closely linked. Can we think without words? Some researchers have suggested that we cannot have concepts without having language (spoken or signed languages such as BSL). Certainly, language is important for abstract thinking. It would be difficult to have an idea of what is fair or honest without any language. But some ideas can be expressed without words or sign language, and feelings and relationships often do not need language at an abstract level. Effective communication is not just about conversations with young children. It also involves children being able to understand and use the **language of learning**. That is, the language needed to understand concepts, to participate in problem-solving and to develop ideas and opinions.

- **Behaviour development**: we use language to set limits and firm boundaries for children's behaviour. To do this, adults need to effectively communicate and exchange information with children according to their age, needs and abilities. Language plays an important part in encouraging children to behave in acceptable ways as it enables them to:
  - understand verbal explanations of what is and is not acceptable behaviour
  - understand verbal explanations of why certain behaviour is not acceptable
  - express their own needs and feelings more clearly
  - avoid conflicts when handled by sensitive adults
  - reach compromises more easily
  - have a positive outlet for feelings through discussion and imaginative play.

How language benefits children's holistic development

Language helps children (and adults) to:

- talk to ourselves: children and adults often talk out loud to themselves; as we develop our language skills, what we say out loud becomes 'internal speech', so that we are increasingly able to think of the words rather than saying them out loud
- move from the here and now into thoughts about the past or the future, and back again
- use and make different symbols, from spoken/signed language to the languages of dance, music, mathematical symbols, drawings, sculptures and models
- develop ideas, some of which become concepts, and put them into words
- express creative and imaginative thoughts and ideas
- express and communicate personal ideas
- think in abstract ways
- plan
- express feelings, think about emotional responses and manage them, becoming increasingly self-disciplined.

The positive effects of adult support for children's speech, language and communication development

Positive effects may include improvements in: speech, language and communication skills; social interaction; behaviour; emotional development/self-confidence.

Praise and encouragement are essential components when supporting young children's speech, language and communication development. Young children need immediate and positive affirmations or rewards to show that their language and learning are progressing in accordance with the adult's (and child's) expectations. Adults should emphasise the **positive** aspects of young children's attempts at developing their speech, language and communication skills. Children gain confidence and increased positive self-esteem when they receive praise/rewards for their efforts and achievements, including encouragement to try new activities and experiences.

There are four main methods used to praise and encourage children:

1 **Verbal**, for example: 'praise' assemblies; positive comments about the child's behaviour or activities, such as 'Well done, Tom! This is a lovely story! Tell me what happened next.'
2 **Non-verbal**, for example: body language, leaning forward or turning towards a child to show interest in what the child is communicating; facial expressions: smiling; sign language – 'good boy/girl!'
3 **Symbolic**, for example: 'smiley faces' for carefully done work or positive behaviour; stickers for being a good listener or for reading well; stars or merit points for attempting and/or completing tasks.
4 **Written**, for example: merit certificates; written comments in head teacher's book; newsletter recording achievements; comments written (or stamped) on child's work such as 'Well done!' or 'Good work!'

Children's social and emotional development is closely linked with their language development, as communication involves social interaction with at least one other person. Confidence, self-esteem and self-image affect the way we all interact with other people, so this will necessarily affect the development of communication skills.See sections on self-esteem and self-image in Unit 3.13.

Activity

Praise and encouragement

What methods do you use to provide positive praise and encouragement for the efforts and achievements of children in your setting? Think about occasions when you have used praise and encouragement and noticed the positive effects on the child's language and communication skills.

AC 2.3 Analyse how the use of technology supports the development of speech, language and communication

Design and technology are essentially a creative activity including many of the craft and practical skill-based activities currently undertaken in early years settings. Technology is about doing: making something for a purpose. It involves putting ideas into practice and having an awareness of the possibilities and limitations of different materials. Children need to experience at first hand the consequences of the decisions they have made, rather than being shown by an adult how to get it 'right'. Digital literacy and ICT are discussed in Unit 3.5.

Good design and technology need children to be:

- actively involved in their learning
- given opportunities to exercise their creativity
- encouraged to work both independently and collaboratively as part of a small group
- supported in their choice of materials and equipment
- shown how to use the materials with judgement
- supported to select and use appropriate equipment with guidance.

Well-planned, purposeful activity and appropriate intervention by practitioners will engage children in the learning process and help them make progress in their learning. The use of technology in the early years includes the resources shown in Figure 3.10.3.

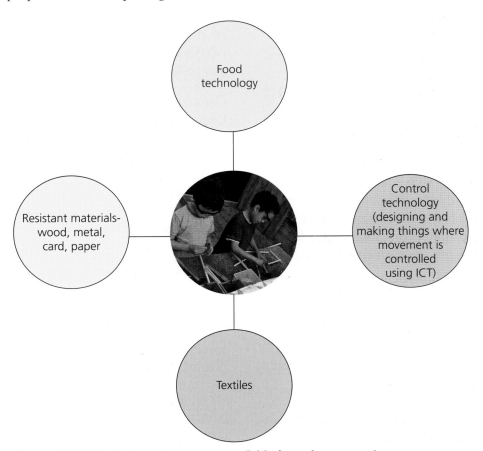

Figure 3.10.3 Technological resources available for early years settings

The use of technology supports the development of speech, language and communication in the following ways:

- Discussing ideas about designs and plans with others develops language for thinking and for communication.
- Talking about what they have made offers children opportunities to talk about their choices and to evaluate their own work and that of others.
- The fine motor or manipulative skills required to construct things contribute to handwriting skills.
- Reading and writing are given a purpose in the context of making greetings cards, notices for a shop or menus for a cafe.

In practice activity

Observe a group of children using technology – perhaps using paper and card – to make something they have planned. Observe the conversations they have – both with other children and with practitioners. Analyse how the use of technology supports their communication and language development.

LO3 Create a language-rich environment to develop children's speech, language and communication in own setting

Children learn speech and language through listening, watching, exploring, copying, initiating, responding, playing and interacting with others. During children's early years, most of the important interaction is going to be between the child and their parents, carers and maybe siblings. Parents and practitioners should provide a language-rich environment. This should be:

- **a nurturing environment**: giving children love and affection and building their self-confidence
- **a learning environment**: creating a place where language and learning can take place together
- **a language-rich environment**: using every opportunity to use language, to interact, to share a common focus, to talk and to take turns.

One of the biggest things to be aware of when using language around young children is the level and complexity of the language you use. A young child will generally understand more words than he uses in speech.

AC 3.1 Create a language-rich environment which develops children's speech, language and communication in own setting

It is important that children spend time with people who speak fluently, so that they hear the patterns of the language they are trying to learn. A language-rich environment which encourages children to talk is crucial. Hearing other people speak fluently means experiencing **comprehensible input**: if the adult says, 'Oh dear, you've bumped your knee. Shall I rub it better?' and points at the child's knee and makes a rubbing mime, then the child has enough clues to understand what is being said. This is very important for young children, children with language delay and children who are learning English as an additional language (EAL).

Children learn by doing, so language is best learnt when children are active in their learning. The practitioners might say to a three-year-old child, 'You've got to the top of the slide, haven't you? Are you going to come down now?'

Creating a language-rich environment

From the moment a baby is born, communicating begins. Babies have a different kind of cry for different situations: they cry for food, to say they are tired or with distress or pain. Babies listen to people's voices; they like the human voice more than other sounds. Babies 'call out' for company, as they become lonely if they spend too much time alone.

When we talk to babies, we speak in a high-pitched tone, in short phrases, placing emphasis on the key words and using a great deal of repetition. As we saw earlier, this is called CDS, 'motherese' or 'fatherese'. However, in some cultures adults do not speak to babies in this way. Instead, the babies watch their mothers working and talking with other adults.

When we converse with babies, we look at the baby and the baby looks at us. Eye contact is part of communication. Visually impaired babies respond by becoming still and listening intently, whereas sighted babies 'dance' in response to speech. Adults will pause and be still when they have said something to the baby, and the baby will usually 'reply' in babble, moving as he or she does so. We move when we talk to babies (body language). Researchers describe this dance-like movement interaction as part of these early conversations, which are called **proto-conversations**. They have all the ingredients of a conversation, but without the words or signs.

Communication between babies, children and adults involves:

- facial expressions – smile, frown, raised eyebrows, eye contact
- gesture and body language – hugs, beckoning, clapping hands, shrugs, jumping with surprise, being stiff and ill at ease, feet and arms moving in response to someone talking to you
- moving together (in synchrony) in a proto-conversation – this can be either mirroring each other or imitating the other's movements and sounds
- movements of the hands and face – especially important for communication and language development
- pauses – these are very important; often we do not give babies and young children enough time to make their response
- rhythms, tone and melody of a language (musical aspects) – these are important in developing communication and spoken language
- intonation – the voice may be used to express fear, anger, pleasure, wanting to play, cooing, relaxing, and so on
- babies finishing a phrase in a musical way, according to research – adding a note that seems to complete the phrase when they respond to people talking to them; this seems to be cross-cultural
- spoken language and sign languages (such as BSL) – these are agreed codes that develop according to the cultures in which they arise
- verbal or sign language – a child might say 'oggie' for dogs and all animals, so that only close family understand what the baby is saying; this is a personal language, not yet a shared language beyond a close circle of people
- Makaton – a communication system that uses agreed and shared signs but is not a full language

- objects of reference – these build a personal communication system with an individual child, and are only shared between the child, the family and practitioners working with the child and the family.

Encouraging conversations and group discussions

Conversations need to:

- be two-way
- involve sharing feelings and ideas
- involve thinking of each other
- be a real exchange of feelings and ideas between children and other children, and between children and adults
- include turn-taking as the conversation flows
- involve thinking about what will be of interest to each other, as well as things that are of interest to oneself.

One-to-one conversations with young children

Young children are beginning to establish a strong sense of self, realising that they are a separate person; this is why their favourite words are often 'no' and 'mine'.

Researchers have noticed that although toddlers often turn their backs on their mother (or other adults they are familiar with and have a close relationship with, such as their key person) and say 'No!' to a suggestion, they do in fact take up and imitate the idea offered to them. Adults need to be aware of this, and to realise that when a toddler says 'No!' they really mean they want to do something for themselves, and to make the decision for themselves, rather than feeling controlled. It is all part of developing a strong sense of self.

Remember:

- Children need to be spoken to as individuals.
- They need to spend time with adults who are patient with them and who listen to them. It is hard for young children to put their feelings and thoughts into words, and it takes time, so adults need to be aware of this. It is very tempting to prompt children and say things for them. Instead,

try nodding or saying, 'Hmm'. This gives children time to say what they want to.

- Do not correct what children say. Instead, elaborate on what they have said, giving them the correct pattern. For example, Shanaz, at two years, says, 'I falled down'. The adult replies, 'Yes, you did, didn't you? You fell down. Never mind, I will help you up.'
- It is important that all children experience unrushed, one-to-one conversations with adults and with other children – for example, when sharing a drink together at the snack table, chatting while using the clay or sharing a book together.
- Value and respect the child's language and culture.
- Have genuine conversations with children, using gestures, eye contact and props.
- Encourage children to listen to and enjoy stories, including those of their own culture.
- Introduce 'book language', such as 'Once upon a time …'.

Small group discussions

Children need help when taking part in group discussions. Groups should be no more than four to eight children, and wherever possible should be with the key person whom the children know well. Having to wait for a turn frustrates young children, as does having to wait until everyone is sitting quietly. It is best to start a song or a dance with plenty of actions, so that everyone can join in from the beginning of the group time. Children are then much more likely to be willing to sit quietly for a story.

In a small group, children can take part in the discussion more easily. Group times should be no longer than ten to fifteen minutes in length.

Children who do not speak

It is important that children who do not speak when they attend a group setting (elective mute or children who stammer) are not put under pressure to speak. But it is also important to create an environment that encourages children to communicate and talk/sign. This can be achieved by:

- observing to see how the child spends the day in the setting – share your observations with your line manager and the team

- checking that a silent child can see and hear – this is very important
- bearing in mind that a child under emotional stress may become withdrawn and will need sensitive encouragement to talk/sign
- inviting a child to talk about something during small group time, or perhaps in a one-to-one story, but respecting their decision if they turn down the invitation to speak, so that they do not feel bad about it
- using stories and rhymes with props and pictures to make them easy to understand
- making sure that the child has understood what you have said – it may be necessary to try different ways of explaining something
- remembering that other children can often explain something to another child in a way that helps them to understand.

Reflective practice

- What strategies do you use to extend conversations with children as sustained shared thinking – not just questions and answers?
- How do you make the most of children's playful interest in words, repetitive sounds, nonsense rhymes, humour and jokes?

In practice activity

Nathan (aged six years) is a quiet and shy child who needs lots of encouragement to participate in group discussions. He enjoys books and ICT activities. Suggest ways in which you can encourage his communication skills.

For more information on creating a language-rich environment, see Unit 3.5, p 328.

The physical environment

The early years setting should be equipped with a basic set of resources and books appropriate to the ages and developmental needs of the children. You should organise resources so that they are equally accessible to all children in the setting, and enable choice and independence. You should encourage children to be actively involved in decisions about their environment, such as the selection of play and learning resources. Children should be taught how to use all resources correctly and safely, with care and respect and with regard for health and safety, and waste. Remember that resources should reflect the cultural and linguistic diversity of our society. General resources may include:

- Visual aids: wall displays including children's work, maps, posters, pictures and posters; interest tables with interesting objects related to topic work; 3D displays of children's work including construction models; videos; computer graphics; books.
- Indoor and outdoor play equipment appropriate for the children's ages and levels of development and suitable for children of all abilities, including children with special needs.
- Groups of tables for group work including literacy and numeracy activities.
- Groups of tables for 'messy' practical activities (e.g. arts and crafts, design technology) including storage for art/design materials and equipment such as paint, paint pots, drying rack; sink for washing paint pots and brushes; basin for washing hands.
- Computers and printers with selection of appropriate software.
- CD players with headphones with a selection of CDs.
- Book/story corner with appropriate range of fiction and non-fiction books, including some dual-language books.
- Quiet area where children can go for privacy, rest or sleep depending on their individual needs, including cushions, mats or cots appropriate to the ages of the children.
- Whiteboard, overhead projector and teaching base in settings supporting children's literacy and numeracy skills, with marker pens, transparencies, textbooks, teaching manuals and other resources needed by staff on a regular basis.
- Writing and drawing materials including a variety of writing tools (crayons, pencils, pens, pastels, chalks) and different shapes, sizes and types of paper (plain, coloured, graph).
- Specialist resources for specific curriculum areas stored in the appropriate curriculum resource cupboard/area.

- Children's work trays to store individual workbooks, folders for topic work, reading books, reading logs, personal named pencils, crayon tins.
- Area with individual coat pegs for children's coats and PE bags.

The importance of labelling

Very young children respond to labels even before they can read them; they will ask adults what labels say. Using pictures or objects as well as written words helps children to make sense of labels and to develop their own literacy skills.

Labelling introduces young children to one of the important purposes of written language: providing information or directions. Labels encourage children's independence in reading and writing. A special place for children to keep their belongings (whether on a hook, in a drawer, tray or basket) clearly labelled with each child's name, is an essential part of the effective language-rich environment. With very young children, a picture on the left-hand side of the label helps them to remember to work from left to right in reading and writing activities.

> ### Reflective practice
>
>
> - How does the environment stimulate and support children to communicate through meaningful activities and experiences?
> - Is the learning environment rich in symbols and signs, words, dance and art which take account of and extend children's cultural experiences?

LO4 Lead activities which support the development of speech, language and communication of children

Young children need to be encouraged to **learn through play** and to focus on an activity rather than on practising a specific language skill. They need to:

- enjoy themselves
- pretend
- to feel comfortable when communicating with others

AC 4.1 Plan an activity which supports children's development of speech, language and communication of children aged: 0–1 year 11 months; 2–2 years 11 months; 3–5 years

The following activities all encourage children to listen and talk to others.

Role play

Children use a rich variety of language to communicate during role play. They enjoy being someone else and acting out a situation, for example: at the shop, at the post office, or driving a car. Children naturally use role play in their own language situations; e.g. 'I'll be Mummy and you be Daddy.'

Reading aloud

Reading aloud to children is a natural way to encourage two-way communication. Talking and listening to young children develops their literacy skills and the social skills of sharing and taking turns. Reading books aloud has many benefits:

- It is an important source of new vocabulary – words for characters and objects.
- It introduces children to the exciting world of stories and helps them learn how to express their own thoughts and emotions.
- It provides topics for discussion, with many opportunities for learning the *context* of language.
- It provides parents and practitioners with a structure to help them talk aloud to children and listen to their responses.
- It combines the benefits of talking, listening and storytelling within a single activity and helps to build the foundation for language development.

Choose stories with repetition like 'The Three Little Pigs', or *The Very Hungry Caterpillar*.

Puppets and props

Children often use puppets or dolls to express themselves verbally, and props like masks or dressing-up clothes help them to act out roles in their own pretend play. Playing with hand puppets offer great opportunities to develop listening and talking skills. Children usually find it easy to talk to their own and other people's puppets, and this gives them confidence to express their ideas and feelings.

Games and puzzles

Children quickly learn to use the language necessary to take part in simple games, such as I Spy, Spot the difference, etc. As they get older, children enjoy board games such as Ludo and Junior Scrabble.

Songs and rhymes

These help children to learn new words in an enjoyable way. Songs and rhymes are also a good way to help children's talking and listening skills. When singing rhymes and songs:

- **Make them fun**: change the sound of your voice, make up some actions or add the children's names. Or make up alternative endings and encourage the children to supply the last word of the nursery rhyme.
- **Encourage them to join in**: when child joins in, show that you have noticed by giving lots of encouragement.
- **Link language with physical movement**: use action songs and rhymes, such as 'The wheels on the bus' or 'We're going on a bear hunt', etc.
- **Talk about similarities** in rhyming words, and draw attention to the similarities in sounds at the beginning of words, emphasising initial sounds

Speaking and listening activities in group settings

These range from individual conversations between adult and child to whole-class or group 'news' times. In addition there are many games and activities that provide ideal opportunities for children to use and practise their speaking and listening skills. For very young children, sharing rhymes (traditional nursery, finger and action), songs and books with an adult are both valuable and enjoyable.

As language and listening skills develop, older children will be able to play games which involve **active listening** such as:

- **'What (or who) am I?'** This involves the adult (or a child – perhaps with help) giving clues until the animal/person/object is identified. 'I have sharp

Guidelines: your role in promoting children's communication skills

- Know how to 'tune in to' the different messages babies and young children are attempting to convey.
- Model the correct use of key words, rather than correcting what children say.
- Talk about things that interest young children – both indoors and outdoors.
- Support children in using a variety of communication strategies including gestures and signing, where appropriate.
- Take time to listen to children and respond with interest to what they say.
- Help children to expand on what they say, introducing and reinforcing their vocabulary.

teeth. I have a long tail. I have a striped coat. I eat meat.' *Answer:* 'I'm a tiger or a tabby cat.'

- **Taped sounds**: these can be environmental (a kettle boiling, a doorbell, someone eating crisps) or related to a particular topic – farm animals, pet animals, and machines – or of familiar people's voices.
- **Taped voices**: Reception or Year 1 children tape their own voices giving clues about themselves but without saying who they are. 'I have brown eyes. I have two brothers. I have a Lion King lunchbox. I have short, dark hair. Who am I?' This activity is best done with a small group so they are not guessing from among the whole class! They find it difficult not to say their own names but love hearing themselves and their friends. The enjoyment factor makes it valuable and ensures concentrated listening once the excitement has died down.
- **Feely box**: use varied objects for children to feel (without being able to see) and encourage them to describe the shape, size, texture, surface, etc. This can be topic-related, e.g. fruit or solid shapes, and is a very good activity for extending children's vocabulary.
- **'Snowball'** games that involve active listening and memory – 'I went to market and I bought …'. There are many versions of this. It can be used for *number* – one cabbage, two bananas, three flannels, etc.; or to reinforce the *alphabet* – an apple, a budgie, a crane, etc.; or it could be *topic*-related – food items, transport items, clothing, etc.
- **Chinese whispers**: this is appropriate for older children who are more able to wait patiently for their turn.
- **Circle activities** in which children and the practitioner/s sit in a circle and the person who

is speaking holds a 'special' object. Rules are that only the person holding the object is allowed to speak – the object is passed around in turn or to whoever wants to say something – adult supervision needed! Alternatively a large ball can be rolled across the circle and the person rolling the ball makes her contribution (this can be on a theme – favourite foods/colours/games, etc.) and the person who receives the ball makes the next contribution.

These **group activities** encourage children to:

- take turns
- use language to express their thoughts, feelings and ideas, and
- gain confidence as communicators.

The circle activities are particularly good for encouraging shy or withdrawn children who may not otherwise get a word in – literally!

How to engage children's interest and attention

Children who have had a lack of social interaction or poor role modelling in the early years of their lives may present with listening and attention difficulties. It is important to build their confidence early on by providing activities that are relatively easy to start with – offering quick success and rewards. They can then be adapted and developed as the children's listening and attention skills improve. Suitable activities to engage children's interest and attention are:

- matching games, such as Lotto
- 'spot the difference' games that require the child to observe closely and to respond when a difference is noticed

- board games that require the child to take turns and to know what to do when it is her turn
- musical games where the child has to complete the song.

Every Child a Talker

As we saw in Unit 3.5, Every Child a Talker (ECAT) is a developmentally appropriate approach that emphasises the importance of a supportive and stimulating environment in which children are encouraged to develop communication and language. It supports the work of the EYFS in England, in home learning environments (childminders) and in group settings of all kinds. It helps practitioners to:

- identify what helps communication and language to develop
- audit their language provision and plan appropriately
- work with children with EAL
- make the most of everyday activities and experiences that promote communication and language
- make a good partnership with parents.

In practice activity

Observe a small group of three or four children with an adult. Note examples of turn-taking and any of the things you would expect to find in a conversation that have been identified in this chapter. Was there a difference in the number of times individual children spoke in the group? In what way? Evaluate the pros and cons of small groups and large groups.

Activity

Using the information in this section, plan an activity which supports the development of speech, language and communication of children aged:

- birth to one year 11 months
- two years to two years 11 months
- three to five years.

AC 4.2 Implement an activity which supports the development of speech, language and communication of children aged: 0–1 year 11 months; 2–2 years 11 months; 3–5 years

In practice activity

- Plan, implement and evaluate a language activity for a small group of children, such as news time, circle time, discussion, story time or phonics session.
- You could use your suggestions from the observation on p 425 (AC 2.1) as the starting point for planning this activity.
- The activity should encourage the children's active participation, including attentive listening and communicating with others during the activity, as well as supervising and maintaining the children's interest throughout the activity.

Activity

Implement the *three* activities you have planned for AC 4.1.

AC 4.3 Reflect on own role in relation to the provision for supporting speech, language and communication development in own setting

Quality early years provision for young children can only be delivered through caring, personal relationships between young children and early years practitioners. In group settings such as a crèche or day nursery, a **key person system** is essential to provide links between individual practitioners and individual children.

Training needs and opportunities

To provide effective support for a child's speech, language and communication, practitioners may need to access additional training opportunities. Early help is very important, and effective early assistance with communication difficulties can prevent more complex problems later on. Early intervention is important because:

- Language and communication skills are essential to the learning process.
- Language has a vital role in the understanding of concepts.

- The main foundations of language are constructed between the ages of 18 months and four-and-a-half years, during which time the majority of children fully integrate language as part of the thinking and learning process.
- It is easier to assist with language development and communication skills during this critical three-year period than to sort out problems once children have reached school age.
- Effective communication skills are essential to positive social interaction and emotional well-being.

There are a number of agencies which offer advice, support and/or training for children's speech, language and communication development; for example: health visitors, speech and language therapists, educational psychologists, Portage workers, advisory teachers,; charities such as Afasic, National Autism Society, RNIB and RNID.

Research activity

Find out about training relating to supporting children's speech, language and communication which is available in your setting and/or the local community.

Views of the child

You should provide a caring and responsive environment by:

- providing flexible routines to support children's well-being
- explaining any foreseeable changes to the child's environment clearly and honestly
- providing reassurance, explanations and comfort for any unforeseen changes
- being flexible and responsive to children's changing needs and circumstances.

You should allow children to take responsibility for themselves and others by providing opportunities which encourage them to become more independent according to their age, needs and abilities. This includes taking the child's views into account and providing opportunities for children to make choices or be involved in decision-making, for example choosing play activities and/or resources.

Appropriate involvement of parents/carers

Positive working relationships with parents/carers are essential to provide continuity of care for young children. Partnership between parents and practitioners depends on regular and open communication where contributions from both parties are acknowledged and valued. Friendly communication on a regular basis ensures continuity and consistency in providing shared routines and timing any necessary changes. Parents and practitioners can keep up to date with what a young child has learnt or is nearly ready to do through regular conversation when they can exchange information and share delight about the young child's discoveries and interests (Lindon, 2002).

Take the time each day to chat briefly with the parents when you hand the child back into their care. Keep it short so that the child can interact with the parents as soon as possible. Sort out how you will share more detailed information about the child with the parents, for example, keeping a diary or daily log of the child's day including food/drink intake, hours slept, play and early learning activities done, any developmental progress made. You could also make a brief note of any specific plans for the next day, for example, reminders about outings such as going swimming or to the library. The parents can also use the diary/daily log to share information with you, for example, if the child did not sleep well the night before, and reminders about immunisations, dental check-ups or returning library books.

Reflective practice

Think about the ways in which you plan group activities to provide opportunities for children to:

- exchange and extend their own ideas
- express their feelings
- explore the language of negotiation and reconciliation
- express themselves through song, dance and poetry.

Activity

Describe how you have contributed to maintaining a positive environment that supports children's speech, language and communication. Include information on the physical environment, your own role and responsibilities, training needs and opportunities, views of the child and the appropriate involvement of parents or carers.

LO5 AC 5.1 Critically evaluate provision for developing speech, language and communication for children in own setting

You need to evaluate the effectiveness of speech, language and communication support for children in your setting as this will enable you to:

- understand the wide range of speech, language and communication development demonstrated by young children
- know and understand the sequence of children's development
- use this knowledge to link theory and practice in your own setting
- assess children's language and development and communication skills
- plan activities appropriate to children's individual language needs.

Observing children's speech, language and communication

Adults working with young children need to be able to look and to listen attentively to how children communicate. By observing carefully, you can discover the range and variety of language used by the children in your setting and improve your own skills in providing appropriate opportunities for encouraging and extending children's speech, language and communication development.

Regular observations are also helpful in identifying any potential problems children may have with their speech, language and communication skills. The observing adult can identify the ways in which each child communicates, how the child interacts with others, the child's social skills, and any difficulties the child has in communicating.

A continuous record of a child's language difficulties (for example, in a diary format) can help the adult to identify specific problems. Working with parents, colleagues and specialist advisers (if necessary), the early years practitioner can then plan a suitable programme to enable the child to overcome these difficulties. Observations can provide a check that children's language is progressing in the expected ways.

You can observe children's language in a variety of situations. Remember, we all use language in some form in *everything* we do. For example, you could observe the following situations:

- a child talking with another child or an adult
- an adult talking with a small group of children
- a small group of children engaged in a role play activity
- a child playing alone
- small or large group discussions such as news time or circle time
- an adult reading or telling a story to a child or group of children
- a child or group of children participating in a creative activity such as painting or drawing
- a child or children playing outside
- a child involved in a literacy activity such as writing news, a story or a poem.

Research activity

Find out about the policies in your setting with regard to child observations, language assessments, record-keeping and confidentiality. Remember to keep this information in mind when doing your own observations of children within the setting.

Evaluating children's speech, language and communication

Once you have recorded your observation of the child's language and communication skills, you need to assess this information in relation to:

- the aims of the observation
- what you observed about this child's language and communication skills in *this* situation
- how this compares to the expected language development for a child of this age
- any factors which may have affected the child's language ability such as the immediate environment, significant events, illness, the child's cultural or linguistic background, and any special needs
- how the adult supported the child's speech, language and communication.

Your college tutor or assessor should give you guidelines on how to present your observations.

In practice activity

Observe a young child communicating with another child or adult. Focus on the child's speech, language and communication skills. In your assessment, comment on:

- any vocabulary used by the child
- the complexity of the child-centred structure
- any non-verbal communication used, such as body language, gestures, facial expressions
- the child's level of social interaction; for example: Did the child appear confident when speaking? Did the child have a friendly and relaxed manner? Did the child need coaxing to communicate?
- the role of the adult in supporting the child's speech, language and communication.

Planning to support a child's speech, language and communication

Following your observation and assessment of a child's speech, language and communication, your recommendations can provide the basis for planning appropriate activities and experiences to encourage or extend the child's abilities in these areas.

Effective planning is based on children's individual needs, abilities and interests, hence the need for accurate child observations and assessments. These needs have to be integrated into the curriculum requirements of your particular setting; for example, themes and activities may be related to the EYFS.

When you have decided on the appropriate activities and experiences (in consultation with colleagues and/or parents as relevant to your setting), you can then implement them. Remember to evaluate the plan afterwards. Further observations and assessments will be necessary to maintain up-to-date information on each child's developmental needs.

Activity

Use the observations you have made to critically evaluate the provision for developing children's speech, language and communication in your own setting. Suggest recommendations for improvement to the provision.

Useful resources

Books and articles

Lindon, J. (2002), *Child Care and Early Education: Good Practice to Support Young Children and Their Families*. London: Thomson Learning.

Statutory Framework for the Early Years Foundation Stage (March 2012). DfE.

Whitehead, M. (1997), *The Development of Language and Literacy*. London: Hodder and Stoughton.

Assessment practice

1 What is meant by the terms speech, language and communication?
2 Describe the main theories which underpin children's speech, language and communication development.
3 How do the theoretical perspectives relate to the current frameworks in your home country?
4 What is your role in supporting the development of children's speech, language and communication?
5 What are the benefits to children's holistic learning and development of supporting their speech, language and communication development?
6 How does the use of technology support the development of children's speech, language and communication?
7 How could you create a language-rich environment? What would you describe as the main characteristics of such an environment?

8 Plan three activities to support the development of children's speech, language and communication.
9 Implement three activities to support the development of children's speech, language and communication.
10 Evaluate three activities to support the development of children's speech, language and communication.
11 Reflect on your own role in relation to provision for developing children's speech, language and communication.
12 Critically evaluate provision for developing children's speech, language and communication.

Unit 3.11 Promote the physical development of children

This unit provides the learner with the knowledge, understanding and skills to promote the physical development of children from birth to seven years.

Learning outcomes

By the end of this unit you will:

1 Understand physical development of children.
2 Understand theory and current frameworks in relation to children's physical development.
3 Be able to promote physical development.
4 Be able to implement opportunities which promote the physical development of children.
5 Be able to critically evaluate the provision for promoting the physical development of children in own setting.

LO1 Understand physical development of children

AC 1.1 Identify stages of physical development of children from birth to 7 years

The difference between growth and physical development

Growth

Growth refers to an increase in physical size, and can be measured by **height** (length), **weight** and **head circumference**. Growth is determined by:

● hereditary factors
● hormones
● nutrition
● emotional influences.

Physical development

Physical development involves the increasing skill and functioning of the body, including the development of:

● motor skills (or skills of movement)
● skills of coordination (for example, hand–eye coordination)
● balance.

Common patterns in physical growth and development
Height

The most important factors controlling a child's growth in height are the genes and chromosomes inherited from the parents. From birth to adolescence there are two distinct phases of growth:

● **From birth to two years**: this is a period of very rapid growth. The baby gains 25 to 30 cm in length and triples his or her body weight in the first year.
● **From two years to adolescence**: this is a slower but steady period of growth. The child gains 5 to 8 cm in height and about 3 kg in body weight per year until adolescence.

Body proportions

As a child grows, the various parts of his or her body change in shape and proportion, as well as increasing in size. The different body parts also grow at different rates – for example, the feet and hands of a teenager reach their final adult size before the body does. At birth, a baby's head accounts for about one-quarter of the total length of this or her body, whereas at seven years old, the head will be about one-eighth of the total length. This difference in body proportions explains why newborn babies appear to have such large eyes, and also why adolescents often appear to be clumsy or awkward in their physical movements.

Measuring growth

Centile charts are used to compare the growth pattern of an individual child with the normal range of growth patterns that are typical of a large number of children of the same sex. The charts are used to plot height (or, in young babies, length), weight and head circumference. (See Unit 1.6.)

Physical development

Physical development is the most visible of all the abilities shown in childhood and includes the less observable development of all the **senses**:

hearing, vision, touch, taste and smell. Development follows a sequence:

- **From simple to complex** – for example, a child will walk before he or she can skip or hop.
- **From head to toe** – for example, head control is acquired before coordination of the spinal muscles. Head control is important from birth in order for the baby to feed.
- **From inner to outer** – for example, a child can coordinate his or her arms to reach for an object before he or she has learnt the fine manipulative skills necessary to pick it up.
- **From general to specific** – for example, a young baby shows pleasure by a massive general response (eyes widen, legs and arms move vigorously). An older child shows pleasure by smiling or using appropriate words and gestures.

Primitive reflexes: movements of the newborn baby

Newborn babies display a number of reflex actions. A reflex action is one made automatically, without needing a conscious message from the brain – such as swallowing, sneezing or blinking. The presence of some of the newborn's primitive reflexes is essential to survival. The most important of these reflexes is breathing, closely followed by the 'rooting' and 'sucking' reflexes that help them to search out the breast and to feed successfully. The reflexes are replaced by *voluntary* responses as the brain takes control of behaviour; for example, the grasp reflex has to fade before the baby learns to hold – and let go of – objects which are placed in her hand. Doctors check for some of these reflexes during the baby's first examination.

If the reflexes persist beyond an expected time it may indicate a delay in development.

The swallowing and sucking reflexes

When something is put in the mouth, the baby at once sucks and swallows; some babies make their fingers sore by sucking them while still in the womb! The swallowing reflex is permanent but the sucking reflex disappears after about four months.

The rooting reflex

If one side of the baby's cheek or mouth is gently touched, the baby's head turns towards the touch and the mouth purses as if in search of the nipple, usually looking for food. This is very useful when learning to breastfeed a baby as it helps the baby to 'latch on' well to the breast in the first weeks of life. This reflex should have disappeared by three to four months of age.

The grasp reflex

This is demonstrated by placing your finger or an object into the baby's open palm, which will cause a reflex or automatic grasp or grip. If you try to pull away, the grasp will get even stronger. This reflex should have disappeared by around three months of age.

The stepping or walking reflex

When held upright and tilting slightly forward, with feet placed on a firm surface, the baby will make forward-stepping movements. This reflex is present at birth, disappears at around two to three months and then reappears when the child is ready to learn to walk later on.

The startle reflex

This is the baby's generalised alarm reflex, which provides protection against danger before the brain is developed enough to determine what is and is not dangerous. When an adult fails to support or hold the baby's neck and head or if the baby becomes startled by a sudden loud noise, bright light or sudden touch, the arms of the baby will thrust outward and then curl in as to embrace themselves. This reflex should disappear between two to four months of age.

The asymmetric tonic neck reflex (ATNR)

This reflex involves a coordinated movement of the baby's neck, arm and leg in conjunction with the head. If the baby's head is turned to one side, she will straighten the arm and leg on that side and bend the arm and leg on the opposite side. The ATNR reflex begins about 18 weeks after conception and should be fully developed at birth. Later this reflex plays an important role in hand–eye coordination and object and distance perception.

The falling reflex

This is often called the Moro reflex. Any sudden movement which affects the neck gives the baby the feeling that she may be dropped; she will fling out her arms and open her hands before bringing them back over the chest as if to catch hold of something. This reflex will disappear by four to six months.

Key terms

neonatal Relating to the first few weeks of a baby's life.

neonate A newborn infant, especially one less than four weeks old.

voluntary Intentional or controlled by individual will.

involuntary Controlled by the autonomic nervous system, without conscious control.

reflex An involuntary action or response, such as a sneeze, blink, or hiccup.

Proprioception

The word 'proprioception' comes from the Latin proprius - meaning 'one's own'. Proprioception

Key terms

proprioception The ability to recognise and use the physical sensations from the body that give feedback on balance and the position of our limbs.

tracking The smooth movements made by the eyes in following the track of a moving object (sometimes called 'smooth pursuit').

– or proprioceptive learning – means knowing the position of our bodies and where our bodies begin and end, without us having to look at them. When babies kick their legs repeatedly and wave their arms around, they are starting to develop the sense of proprioception, as information is constantly sent to the brain from the muscles and joints to the brain, both when our muscles and joints are moving and when they are still.

Sensory development is discussed in Unit 3.10.

An overview of the stages of physical development

The first month

Gross motor skills	Fine motor skills
• The baby lies **supine** (on his or her back).	• The baby turns his or her head towards the light and stares at bright or shiny objects.
• When placed on his or her front (the **prone** position), the baby lies with head turned to one side, and by one month can lift the head.	• The baby is fascinated by human faces and gazes attentively at carer's face when fed or held.
• If pulled to sitting position, the head will lag, the back curves over and the head falls forward.	• The baby's hands are usually tightly closed.
	• The baby reacts to loud sounds but by one month may be soothed by particular music.

From one to four months

Gross motor skills	Fine motor skills
From four to eight weeks:	
• The baby can now turn from side to back.	• The baby turns her head towards the light and stares at bright or shiny objects.
• The baby can lift the head briefly from the prone position.	• The baby will show interest and excitement by facial expression and will gaze attentively at carer's face while being fed. →

Table 3.11.1 An overview of the stages of physical development

An overview of the stages of physical development

● Arm and leg movements are jerky and uncontrolled.	● The baby will use his or her hand to grasp the carer's finger.

From one to four months

● There is head lag if the baby is pulled to sitting position.	

From eight to twelve weeks:

● When lying supine, the baby's head is in a central position.	● The baby moves his or her head to follow adult movements.
● The baby can now lift head and chest off bed in prone position, supported on forearms.	● The baby watches his or her hands and plays with his or her fingers.
● There is almost no head lag in sitting position.	● The baby holds a rattle for a brief time before dropping it.
● The legs can kick vigorously, both separately and together.	
● The baby can wave his or her arms and bring his or her hands together over the body.	

From four to six months

Gross motor skills	Fine motor skills
● The baby is beginning to use a **palmar grasp** and can transfer objects from hand to hand.	● The baby now has good head control and is beginning to sit with support.
● The baby is very interested in all activity.	● The baby rolls over from back to side and is beginning to reach for objects.
● Everything is taken to the mouth.	● When supine, the baby plays with his or her own feet.
● The baby moves his or her head around to follow people and objects.	● The baby holds his or her head up when pulled to sitting position.

From six to nine months

Gross motor skills	Fine motor skills
● The baby can roll from front to back.	● The baby is very alert to people and objects.
● The baby may attempt to crawl but will often end up sliding backwards.	● The baby is beginning to use a **pincer grasp** with thumb and index finger.
● The baby may grasp feet and place them in his or her mouth.	● The baby transfers toys from one hand to the other and looks for fallen objects.
● The baby can sit without support for longer periods of time.	● Everything is explored by putting it in his or her mouth.
● The baby may 'cruise' around furniture and may even stand or walk alone.	

From nine to twelve months

Gross motor skills	Fine motor skills
● The baby will now be mobile – may be crawling, bear-walking, bottom-shuffling or even walking.	● The baby's pincer grasp is now well developed and he or she can pick things up and pull them towards him or her.
● The baby can sit up on his or her own and lean forward to pick up things.	● The baby can poke with one finger and will point to desired objects. ➜

Table 3.11.1 An overview of the stages of physical development   (*Continued*)

An overview of the stages of physical development

From nine to twelve months

• The baby may crawl upstairs and onto low items of furniture.	• The baby can clasp hands and imitate adults' actions.
• The baby may bounce in rhythm to music.	• The baby can throw toys deliberately.
	• The baby can manage spoons and finger foods well.

From one year to two years

Gross motor skills	Fine motor skills
At 15 months:	
• The baby probably walks alone, with feet wide apart and arms raised to maintain balance. He or she is likely to fall over and often sit down suddenly.	• The baby can build with a few bricks and arrange toys on the floor.
• The baby can probably manage stairs and steps, but will need supervision.	• The baby holds a crayon in palmar grasp and turns several pages of a book at once.
• The baby can get to standing without help from furniture or people, and kneels without support.	• The baby can point to desired objects. • The baby shows a preference for one hand, but uses either.
At 18 months:	
• The child walks confidently and is able to stop without falling.	• The child can thread large beads.
• The child can kneel, squat, climb and carry things around with him or her.	• The child uses pincer grasp to pick up small objects.
• The child can climb onto an adult chair forwards and then turn round to sit.	• The child can build a tower of several cubes.
• The child can come downstairs, usually by creeping backwards on his or her tummy.	• The child can scribble to and fro on paper.

From two years

Gross motor skills	Fine motor skills
• The child is very mobile and can run safely.	• The child can draw circles, lines and dots, using preferred hand.
• The child can climb up onto furniture.	• The child can pick up tiny objects using a **fine pincer grasp**.
• The child can walk up and down stairs, usually two feet to a step.	• The child can build a tower of six or more blocks (bricks) with longer concentration span.
• The child tries to kick a ball with some success but cannot catch yet.	• The child enjoys picture books and turns pages singly.

From three years

Gross motor skills	Fine motor skills
• The child can jump from a low step.	• The child can build tall towers of bricks or blocks.
• The child can walk backwards and sideways.	• The child can control a pencil using thumb and first two fingers – **a dynamic tripod grasp**.

→

Table 3.11.1 An overview of the stages of physical development   (*Continued*)

An overview of the stages of physical development	
• The child can stand and walk on tiptoe and stand on one foot.	• The child enjoys painting with a large brush.
• The child has good spatial awareness.	• The child can use scissors to cut paper.
• The child rides a tricycle, using pedals.	• The child can copy shapes, such as a circle.
• The child can climb stairs with one foot on each step – and downwards with two feet per step.	
From four years	
Gross motor skills	**Fine motor skills**
• A sense of balance is developing – the child may be able to walk along a line.	• The child can build a tower of bricks and other constructions too.
• The child can catch, kick, throw and bounce a ball.	• The child can draw a recognisable person on request, showing head, legs and trunk.
• The child can bend at the waist to pick up objects from the floor.	• The child can thread small beads on a lace.
• The child enjoys climbing trees and frames.	
• The child can run up and down stairs, one foot per step.	
From five to eight years	
Gross motor skills	**Fine motor skills**
From five years:	
• The child can use a variety of play equipment – slides, swings, climbing frames.	• The child may be able to thread a large-eyed needle and sew large stitches.
• The child can play ball games.	• The child can draw a person with head, trunk, legs, nose, mouth and eyes.
• The child can hop and run lightly on toes and can move rhythmically to music.	• The child has good control over pencils and paintbrushes. He or she copies shapes, such as a square.
• The sense of balance is well developed.	
• The child can skip.	
From six to seven years:	
• The child has increased agility, muscle coordination and balance.	• The child can build a tall, straight tower with blocks and other constructions too.
• The child develops competence in riding a two-wheeled bicycle.	• The child can draw a person with detail, e.g. clothes and eyebrows.
• The child hops easily, with good balance.	• The child can write letters of alphabet at school, with similar writing grip to an adult.
• The child can jump off apparatus.	• The child can catch a ball thrown from one metre with one hand.

Table 3.11.1 An overview of the stages of physical development   (*Continued*)

Figure 3.11.1 The majority of babies start walking around the age of one year to 15 months, but this varies greatly

Figure 3.11.2 Threading large beads promotes hand–eye coordination, spatial awareness and the development of fine motor skills

Activity ·

Identify the stages of physical development from birth to seven years old. What are the major features or milestones in a child's development? Why is it important to have a knowledge of how children develop physically?

· ·

AC 1.2 Describe the development of children's physical skills

The development of motor skills

The sequence of physical development involves gross motor skills first – these involve control of large muscles in the body. This is followed by development of fine manipulative skills, which depend on small muscle coordination – these are sometimes called skills of **movement**. Children need experience of large-muscle movements in order to develop the small-muscle movements which come later. For example, they need lots of opportunities to strengthen their large arm muscles in physical play, before the smaller arm muscles are ready for writing and drawing.

Gross motor skills use the large muscles in the body – the arms and legs – and include walking, running and climbing.

Fine motor skills use the smaller muscles and include:

● **gross manipulative skills**, which involve single-limb movements, usually the arm – for example, throwing, catching and sweeping arm movements
● **fine manipulative skills**, which involve precise use of the hands and fingers for drawing, using a knife and fork, writing, and doing up shoelaces and buttons.

The ability to grasp

Grasping is the ability to hold onto objects and use them for specific purposes.

- **Reflex grasp**: very young babies have a reflexive grasp; their hands automatically close tightly when pressure or stimulation is applied to their palms.
- **Palmar grasp**: using the whole hand to grasp an object. From about four to six months a baby will start to 'rake' an object towards him or herself, and will start passing objects from one hand to the other, using the whole hand.
- **Inferior pincer grasp**: using the thumb and fingers to grasp an object. At around eight or nine months, a baby will be able to pick up small objects such as raisins by resting a forearm on a table and using the sides of thumb and the index finger.
- **Superior pincer grasp**: using the thumb and tip of the first finger to grasp an object. At around 12 months, a baby will be able to pick up and release a tiny object such as a piece of cereal by using the tip of the index finger and thumb while holding wrist off the surface.
- **Static tripod grasp**: the pencil is held between the thumb, index finger and middle finger (i.e. three fingers are touching the writing tool). Commonly seen between the ages of three and four years.
- **Dynamic tripod grasp**: the pencil is placed between the thumb and index finger. The side of the middle finger gently supports the pencil, with the third and little fingers lightly curled under. This is considered the most efficient grasp for handwriting and drawing, as intricate and detailed marks can be made.

Locomotion and balance

Locomotion is the ability to move around on one's own. It is central to the pattern of development changes that occur at the end of the baby's first year, and it begins with crawling or bottom shuffling.

Balance is the first of all the senses to develop. It is crucial to posture, movement and proprioception.

The eight-month-old child who rolls backwards and forwards across the floor, with no particular goal in sight, is preparing her balance for sitting, standing and walking.

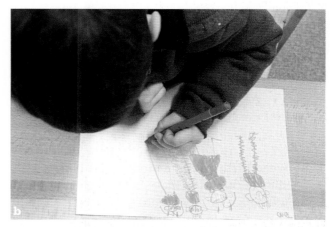

Figures 3.11.3 (a) palmar grasp (b) pincer grasp (c) dynamic tripod grasp

There are several aspects of physical skills development, which are outlined in Table 3.11.2 below.

The skills of locomotion

Babies go through the '**pre-walking**' stage between birth and 11 months:

Gross motor skills (locomotion or movement)	Fine motor skills (manipulation)	Balance and stabilisation
walking	throwing	bending
running	catching	stretching
skipping	picking up	twisting
jumping	kicking	turning
hopping	rolling	balancing
chasing	volleying	squatting
dodging	striking	transferring
climbing	squeezing	landing
crawling	kneading	hanging

Table 3.11.2 A summary of activities related to physical skills development

1 **Between birth and five months**, the baby is learning to turn from their side to their back and from their back to their side.
2 **Between four and 10 months**, the baby is developing the ability to roll from their back to their stomach.
3 **Around 11 months**, the baby should reach the pre-walking progression of being on his/her hand and knees.
4 Between the ages of five and 12 months the walking stage occurs. This stage begins with:
   ● stepping movements, followed by the ability to walk while holding onto furniture, followed by
   ● walking with help until he or she can walk alone. This ability should be gained by around 17 months of age, and coincides with the development of the ability to walk well.
5 **Up to the age of 24 months**: the final stages that the baby should go through in order to achieve locomotive abilities are:
   ● developing the ability to walk sideways and backwards
   ● walking up and down stairs with some help, which should develop until around 23 months of age, and finally the ability to walk with one foot on a walking board, which occurs up to around 24 months of age.

Walking develops further and becomes more efficient after the age of two. Children then become able to vary their walking by including a tiptoe action and a walking backwards action, and by being able to walk in different circumstances (e.g. uphill or downhill or on uneven surfaces) and at different paces.

As walking becomes an increasingly automatic function, children learn to multi-task and can carry out other actions while walking – for example, transporting objects when walking from one place to another.

Running

Another key development that occurs in the early years is that of the ability to run. Children begin to run at around 18 months, and by the age of two years, most children can run.

Between the ages of four and six years, children begin to be able to run with ease and begin to play running games.

Key term

locomotion Movement or the ability to move from one place to another.

Jumping and hopping

In the development of **jumping**, the age of achievement varies, but all children follow the same stages:

● At 18 months, the ability to step down occurs, which is then followed by the ability for two-foot take-off.
● At around two years: a key milestone for young children is the two-foot jump from the ground, which develops from around two years of age.

In the development of **hopping**:

● by around three-and-a-half years, children can hop once
● by around five years, they can hop about 10 times.

Hopping can lead to the development of other locomotor activities such as skipping and galloping. Skipping begins to develop at around three-and-a-half years (with the ability to skip on one foot) to five years (with the ability to skip on alternating feet). Researchers have found that there are gender differences in this ability; for example, 55 per cent of boys are able to enact five continuous skips at five-and-a-half years compared to 91 per cent of girls.

Figure 3.11.4 Jumping requires a good sense of balance

A sense of balance

Balancing is not always seen as a developmental skill, but rather as a means of developing skills such as running, hopping, skipping and climbing. However, at around two years of age, a child can momentarily stand on one foot and can walk along a line on the ground. By three years of age, children can generally stand on one foot for around five seconds and can walk around a circular line on the ground. Finally, by age five, most children can stand alone on one foot for around ten seconds.

Eye–hand coordination

The ability to reach and grasp objects in a coordinated way requires months of practice and close attention:

- In the first months after birth, hand–eye coordination takes effort.
- By around nine months of age, a baby can usually manage to guide his or her movements with a single glance to check for accuracy – for example, when feeding themselves with a spoon.

Foot–eye coordination

The ability to execute actions with the feet, guided by the eyes, is necessary for many movement activities: for example, climbing stairs, and kicking or dribbling a ball.

There are several aspects of movement skills, which are outlined in Table 3.11.3.

Travel Travelling movements where the child moves from one point to another	Object control Objects being sent, received or travelled with	Balance and coordination
walking	throwing	bending
running	catching	stretching
skipping	picking up	twisting
jumping	kicking	turning
hopping	rolling	balancing
chasing	volleying	squatting
dodging	striking	transferring
climbing	squeezing	landing
crawling	kneading	hanging

Table 3.11.3 Movement skills

A learning experience

Chloe walks towards a ball. She wants to pick it up. She leans over to touch the ball, but instead her foot hits it and the ball slides across the floor. She walks towards it again, and this time she tries to kick the ball on purpose. She misses the ball; her foot goes past the left side of the ball. Chloe tries again and again. She kicks it and begins to run after the ball, tries to stop in front of it and falls forward. She stands up and kicks it to a new location and she laughs.

- How old do you think Chloe is?
- What has Chloe learnt during this activity? Try to list at least six things and then compare them with the list at the end of this chapter (p 458).

• •

AC 1.3 Describe the role of the EYP when promoting physical development in children from birth to 7 years

In Unit 1.2, the provision of opportunities for physical *exercise* in the setting is examined. In order to promote holistic physical development, practitioners need to support children's physical development in the following ways. This includes provision for:

- continuous open-ended, indoor and outdoor opportunities for physical play and for sensory stimulation
- access to a rich outdoor environment, with a variety of natural obstacles, surfaces and structures
- spaces for sensory play opportunities which are freely available to the children at all times. Provide a range of malleable play materials such as dough, clay and gloop, wet and dry sand, and water, to encourage manipulation and so support fine motor control
- opportunities for tummy-time play for babies
- time and space for activities which encourage children to use their whole bodies, including rough-and-tumble or active play, crawling, climbing, sliding, rolling, running, hopping and jumping
- more time using the floor for play activities (and less time sitting)

- activities which include lifting, carrying and tasks such as sweeping and digging
- space for creative activities, both indoors and out, where children can be messy and have opportunities to use the floor rather than sitting at tables
- periods of rest and relaxation and opportunities for affectionate touch and physical comforting
- opportunities for children to be able to make their own risk assessments relating to their activities, for themselves, rather than removing all risk for them
- promoting health awareness in young children – particularly in relation to healthy eating and self-care. See also Unit 1.2 for information on providing risk and challenge in physical play.

Figure 3.11.6 This boy enjoys playing on the climbing apparatus

The importance of floor play and tummy time for babies

Floor play

Floor games which involve the pushing and kicking of legs help to promote motor skills for babies who are not yet walking. Once walking, toddlers can be provided with indoor and outdoor play surfaces of varying textures and slopes.

Tummy time

There are many physical benefits to building opportunities for tummy time. Placing babies on their tummies enables them to:

- develop their neck muscles so that they can hold up their head
- develop their back muscles – which are needed for rolling and for sitting
- use their hands to bear their own weight; this also helps to develop the full palm stretch, which is important for *literacy skills* as it promotes strength of grasp and fine motor skills
- learn to shift their weight – a crucial skill for later crawling and walking
- focus their eyes at close range and 'track' objects in their line of vision
- develop movement across the mid-line of the body. These cross-lateral connections are thought to be important for higher-level thinking and memory skills.

Health and self-care

A requirement of the EYFS (2012) relating to the prime area of physical development is that:

Children know the importance for good health of physical exercise and a healthy diet, and talk about ways to keep healthy and safe. They manage their own basic hygiene and personal needs successfully, including dressing and going to the toilet independently.

Promoting health awareness

Practitioners can promote health awareness by talking with children about physical exercise, its effect on their bodies and the positive contribution it can make to their health. Similarly, the setting can provide different methods of displaying information about healthy foods, so that children become aware of the choices they can make to eat healthily.

Supporting children to manage their own basic hygiene and personal needs

See Unit 1.3 for more information on supporting children to manage their own personal needs.

Guidelines for promoting health awareness

Physical exercise

- Encourage children to be active and energetic by organising lively games, since physical activity is important in maintaining good health and in guarding against children becoming overweight or obese in later life.
- Talk with children about why you encourage them to rest when they are tired or why they need to wear wellingtons when it is muddy outdoors.
- Encourage children to notice the changes in their bodies after exercise, such as their heart beating faster or feeling tired and hot.
- Encourage children to tell an adult when hungry or tired or when they want to rest or play.

Healthy eating

- Be aware of eating habits at home and of the different ways people eat their food, e.g. that eating with clean fingers is as valued as using cutlery.

- Display a colourful daily menu showing healthy meals and snacks, and discuss choices with the children, reminding them, for example, that they tried something previously and might like to try it again or encouraging them to try something new.
- Help children to enjoy their food and to appreciate healthier choices by combining favourites with new tastes and textures.
- Involve young children in preparing food.
- Give children the chance to talk about what they like to eat, while reinforcing messages about healthier choices.
- Create time to discuss options so that young children have choices between healthy options, such as whether they will drink water or milk.

Children like to feel independent, but sometimes they need an adult's encouragement to feel that they are capable and that adults believe that they can do it. Teaching independence with self-care skills such as hand washing, brushing teeth, and dressing and undressing is an important step in development that can be achieved when children are supported in a positive and encouraging way.

Hand washing

Hand washing is an important skill that children need to learn. It can be made into a fun activity, and children soon learn that it is a routine task that must always be done after going to the toilet, before meals and after playing outdoors.

Dressing and undressing

Children need plenty of time and support to learn how to dress and undress themselves. You can help by breaking the process down into steps and encouraging them when they have mastered the first step by offering descriptive praise.

Toileting

It is important to encourage self-care skills when children are using the toilet independently. They should be encouraged to pull their own pants down and shown how to wipe their bottoms – for example, showing girls how to wipe from the front to the back. You also need children to learn that going to the toilet is a private activity; you should withdraw by partially closing the door while remaining nearby in case help is needed.

Brushing teeth

It is essential to establish a tooth-brushing routine. Children should brush after meals, after snacks, and before bedtime, so that it becomes a lifelong habit. Offering children a choice during routines increases the likelihood that they will do the activity and gives them a sense of control. So for example, when brushing teeth, you could say, 'Do you want to use the minty toothpaste or the strawberry toothpaste?'

Engaging with children during care routines to support their learning and development

See Unit 1.3 for advice and guidance on engaging with children during care routines.

Activity

Describe your role when promoting physical development in children from birth to seven years. Include the promotion of motor skills and promoting health awareness and self-care – which make up the prime area of physical development in the EYFS.

Guidelines for promoting self-reliance skills throughout childhood

Babies:

- Encourage babies to cooperate when getting them dressed and undressed – for example, by pushing their arms through sleeves and pulling off their socks.
- Provide finger foods from about eight months and tolerate mess when babies are feeding themselves.
- Set out a variety of toys to encourage them to make choices.

Children aged between two and four years:

- Encourage children to help tidy away toys.
- Allow children to have a free choice in their play.
- Encourage children in self-care skills – washing hands, brushing hair and getting dressed; be patient and provide them with adequate time.
- Talk with children about the importance of hand washing.

- Build choice into routines such as meal and snack times.
- Encourage children to enjoy simple cooking activities.

Children aged between five and eight years:

- Provide activities which promote problem-solving skills, such as investigating volume and capacity in sand or water play.
- Allow children to take responsibility for set tasks – such as wiping the tables, caring for plants, etc.
- Encourage them to learn specific skills – such as using scissors and threading large needles.
- Allow children the opportunity to make choices and encourage them to assess risks when supervised.

AC 1.4 Describe the benefits to children's holistic learning and development when promoting physical development

How promoting physical development benefits children's holistic learning

Physical development is linked to other areas of development, such as personal, emotional and social development, and cognitive and language development. Each affects and is affected by the other areas. For example:

Emotional development

- **Developing independence and confidence**: once babies have mastered crawling, they are free to explore the world on their own – they become more independent and confident when away from their familiar adults. When a child falls over but gets back on the climbing frame, they are becoming resilient.
- **Expressing emotions**: children become aware that they can use their bodies to express themselves by moving in different ways as they respond to their moods and feelings, to music or to imaginative ideas.
- **Personal care routines**: learning how to brush one's teeth, wash one's hands and to dress oneself – doing up buttons and zips, etc. help to promote children's self-esteem and confidence – and also develop fine motor skills.

Cognitive development

- **The ability to reach and grasp objects** (usually achieved at around six months) develops babies' understanding of the nature of objects. This often results in a surprise – for example, when they try to pick up a soap bubble or a shaft of sunlight. Babies are interested in edges (of a book or a floor, for example). Where does one object end and the next object begin?
- **Exploring what their bodies can do** and becoming aware of their increasing abilities, agility and skill. Children's awareness of the space around them and what their bodies are capable of can be extended by climbing and balancing on large-scale apparatus, such as a climbing frame, wooden logs and a balancing bar, and by using small tricycles, bicycles and carts.
- **Solving problems and having ideas of their own**: children solve problems as they make models, paint and draw. They think ahead, estimate sizes, use shapes and make choices.
- **Developing an understanding of why things happen:** e.g. 'If I jump from the second step I need to push off harder and to bend my knees when I land, otherwise I will fall.'

Social development

- **Cooperating with others in physical play and games**: children become aware of physical play both as individuals and as a social activity: in playing alone or alongside others, in playing throwing and catching with a partner, in using a seesaw or push cart, or in joining a game with a larger group.
- **Helping with household tasks**: washing up, pouring drinks, carrying bags are all cooperative tasks which also develop fine motor skills.

Communication and language development

- **Self-expression through movement** and dance is an effective form of communication.
- **Learning to listen carefully** to the words associated with movement helps to develop language skills
- **Adults and children talk together as they use materials**: e.g. 'Does it fit? Do you have enough? It's too big, will you pass me the scissors, please.'

LO2 Understand theory and current frameworks in relation to children's physical development

AC 2.1 Describe theoretical perspectives in relation to physical development

Motor skills and learning

One of the most important cognitive skills to develop in the first two years of life is learning about cause and effect. Young babies have difficulty with determining cause and effect, but as they develop, they are increasingly able to understand the cause-and-effect relationship – and then can intentionally make the desired result of an action occur. Research shows that motor play contributes to this kind of causal thinking. For example, one study found that the longer seven-month-old babies played with a toy that produced an interesting result, the better they were able to cause that result to occur again in later play. In the study, babies were provided with a toy that made a noise when they pushed a button. When presented with the toy again after a period of time, the infants immediately and repeatedly pushed the button, suggesting that they had learnt how to perform an action to cause the sound.

'Back to sleep' and 'Prone to play'

Recent research has shown that *positioning* babies properly for play will improve their motor skills. The 'back to sleep' campaign, begun in 1992 to protect babies from sudden infant death syndrome, has led to an unfortunate trend: some parents are placing their babies on their backs during waking periods as well. In addition, the increased use of car seats and bouncy chairs also means that many babies are left with fewer opportunities for playing on their tummies. The research shows that babies who are placed on their tummies to play have improved motor skills compared with those who spend a lot of their waking hours on their backs. Current advice uses the phrases: 'back to sleep' and 'prone to play' to remind parents and practitioners of the importance of tummy time for babies.

The ecological systems theory: Urie Bronfenbrenner (1917–2005)

Bronfenbrenner developed the ecological systems theory to explain how everything in a child and the child's environment influences how a child grows and develops. He labelled different aspects or levels of the environment that affect children's development:

- **the microsystem**: the microsystem is the small, immediate environment the child lives in. This will include any relationships or organisations that the child interacts with, such as their immediate family or carers and their early years setting or school. How these groups interact with the child will have an effect on how the child grows and develops; the more nurturing these relationships and places are, the better the child will be able to grow. In turn, each child's unique genetic and biologically influenced personality traits, what are known as temperament, result in influencing how others treat them.

- **the mesosystem**: this system describes how the different parts of a child's microsystem work together for the sake of the child. For example, if a child's parents or carers take an active role in a child's setting or schools, such as involving themselves in activities and attending parent meetings, this will help to ensure the child's holistic development. Conversely, if there is disagreement about the ways of bringing up a child between two sets of parents or carers – such as might occur in a stepfamily – the child will receive conflicting messages and this will hinder the child's overall growth and development.

- **the exosystem**: this system includes the other people and places that the child may not interact with often himself but that still have a large affect on him, such as parents' workplaces, extended family members, the neighbourhood, etc. For example, if a child's parent loses his or her job, that may have negative affects on the child because the parents are unable to pay rent or to buy groceries; however, if the child's parent is promoted at work, this may have a positive affect on the child because the parents will be better able to meet his physical needs.

- **the macrosystem**: this includes the largest and most remote set of people and things in relation to a child, but which still have a great influence over him or her. The macrosystem includes things such as the relative freedoms permitted by the national government, cultural values, the economy, wars, etc. These things can also affect a child either positively or negatively.

Sally Goddard Blythe

Sally Goddard Blythe is a consultant in neuro-developmental education and writer of many books, including *The Well-balanced Child*. She states:

without balance we could not stand, walk nor run. We couldn't see images in sharp detail as we move, or navigate without visual landmarks, or perhaps even think clearly.

She describes the importance of balance for a child in the following ways:

- **Balance is the first of the sensory systems to mature** and is an essential player in how the brain interprets information from the other senses. How a child sees, hears and feels the world around him is intimately connected to the functioning of balance.
- **Balance provides the platform for the development of coordination**, stable eye movements and visual perception – or how a child 'sees' the world. These abilities are crucial to all aspects of learning, from being able to control the body at sports to being able to sit still, track a moving object at speed such as catching a ball, or more slowly to control the eye movements needed to follow along a line of print when reading.
- **Balance is 'the art of not moving'**: the ability to remain totally still is the most advanced of all levels of movement. It is really hard for a young child to be still, because they have not done enough moving yet. It can take seven years for the vestibular pathways to be fully developed. A child who continues to have difficulty being still as they get older needs *more* opportunities for movement, rather than fewer.
- **Balance is also important for emotional stability** in order to feel secure, perceive the outside world as it is and to be in control of oneself. Disturbances of balance result in physical and psychological feelings of anxiety with no obvious external cause. Just as the balance mechanism itself is hidden from view, so the origins of anxiety, avoidance and depression can also have a hidden cause.

Forest schools

See Unit 3.3 for information on Forest schools.

In an attempt to raise standards of physical development, Forest schools were introduced to Britain in 1995. The Forest school initiative was developed in Scandinavia in 1950s and the idea is to use a woodland setting as an 'outdoor classroom' as a way of helping young people learn about the natural world. A qualified Forest school leader devises a programme of learning that is based on the children's interests and which allows them to build on skills from week to week, at their own pace. The programmes are designed to give children a varied experience of the woodland through experimental and hands-on tasks and activities. Forest schools provide a safe woodland environment for the children to explore, embedded in routine that is established early within the programme. Forest schools also place an emphasis on children assessing levels of risk and challenge for themselves.

AC 2.2 Analyse how theoretical perspectives in relation to physical development inform current frameworks

The EYFS states:

The physical development of babies and young children must be encouraged through the provision of opportunities for them to be active and interactive and to improve their skills of coordination, control, manipulation and movement. They must be supported using all of their senses to learn about the world around them and to make connections between new information and what they already know. They must be supported in developing an understanding of the importance of physical activity and making healthy choices in relation to food.

(EYFS, p 90)

Physical development: Early Learning Goals

Moving and handling: children show good control and coordination in large and small movements. They move confidently in a range of ways, safely negotiating space. They handle equipment and tools effectively including pencils for writing.

Health and self-care: children know the importance for good health of physical exercise and a healthy diet and talk about ways to keep healthy and safe. They manage their own basic hygiene and personal needs successfully, including dressing and going to the toilet independently.

LO3 Be able to promote physical development

Outdoor physical play opportunities should, ideally, be provided every day. Children need physical play to:

- learn how to control their bodies
- develop their gross and fine motor skills
- improve their hand–eye coordination and body balance
- help them to use energy and prevent obesity.

AC 3.1 Describe own role when promoting physical development in own setting

Your role is to:

- Recognise the **skills** that children have developed.
- Provide plenty of **opportunities** for children to practise their skills.

- Make sure that children have the freedom to explore their environment **in safety**.
- Be there for children; offer them **reassurance**, encouragement and praise.
- Provide access to a **range of facilities and equipment**; this need not be expensive – a visit to the local park, a pre-school group (playgroup or one o'clock club) or an adventure playground will provide facilities not available in a small flat.
- Promote **outdoor play** whenever possible; even in cold or windy weather, children will enjoy running around outside as long as they are warmly wrapped up. (If you are supervising, make sure that you are warmly wrapped up too.)

AC 3.2 Create an environment which promotes physical development in own setting

Guidelines for promoting physical development

- Think about how and where you position yourself to support physical play and exercise. You may choose to be an observer or a participant in physical play. This will vary according to the age and stage of development of the children playing.
- Always supervise physical activities but resist the role of being overprotective and getting in the way of potentially exciting explorations.
- Think of ways to redirect and encourage alternative ways of playing if children become too boisterous. For example, you could lead the children in role play – by suggesting they take on different roles in the play.

- Use your knowledge of individual children to know when to allow children to work out how to deal with difficult manoeuvres or to recover their balance after a fall.
- Some children become overexcited or particularly stressed by lots of physical play. Try to scaffold their play and to provide oases of calm.
- Be a good role model – by demonstrating safe ways to fall and to explore their environment by talking through emotions and ideas as they are playing.

Reflective practice

- How do the planning and layout of the environment in your setting facilitate physical development through the characteristics of effective learning?
- Is there room to run, jump, stretch and climb both indoors and out? If not, how can you achieve this, making sure, for example, that 15 minutes of walking

to the park is balanced by 15 minutes of physical activity that leaves both practitioners and children out of breath?

- Are opportunities for physical activity balanced by opportunities for rest and quiet, and provision of regular healthy snacks and drinks?

LO4 Implement opportunities which promote the physical development of children

AC 4.1 Plan an opportunity which promotes the physical development of children aged: 0–1 year 11 months; 2–2 years 11 months; 3–5 years

Activity . . . .

Using the guidelines in this Unit, plan an opportunity which promotes the physical development of children in each of the following age groups: 0–1 year 11 months; 2–2 years 11 months; 3–5 years

. . . .

AC 4.2 Provide an opportunity which promotes physical development for children aged: 0–1 year 11 months; 2–2 years 11 months; 3–5 years

Activity . . . .

Using the guidelines in this unit, implement your plans in AC 4.1.

. . . .

AC 4.3 Reflect on own role in relation to the provision for promoting physical development in own setting

Activity . . . .

Reflecting on your own practice

Reflect on your daily practice and think about how well you provide appropriate physical play experiences for the children you work with. For example:

- How do you consider the balance between child-initiated activity and adult-led activity?
- Do you join in with physical activity?
- How do you enable children and their parents to express opinions and be listened to?
- How confident are you in planning for children's individual needs and in observing and assessing their progress?
- How do you ensure that there is sufficient challenge in the activities you provide?
- How can you improve your practice?

. . . .

LO5 AC 5.1 Critically evaluate the provision for promoting the physical development of children in own setting

See Unit 3.11, p 440 for advice on how to critically evaluate the provision for promoting the physical development of children in your setting.

Assessment practice

1 Identify the stages of physical development of children from birth to seven years.
2 Explain the difference between growth and physical development.
3 Describe the development of children's physical skills.
4 Describe the role of the early years practitioner when promoting physical development in children from birth to seven years.
5 Describe the benefits to children's holistic learning and development when promoting physical development.
6 Describe theoretical perspectives in relation to physical development.
7 Analyse how theoretical perspectives in relation to physical development inform current frameworks.
8 Describe your own role when promoting physical development in your own setting.
9 Create an environment which promotes physical development in own setting.
10 Plan and provide an opportunity which promotes the physical development of children aged: birth to one year 11 months; two years to two years 11 months; three to five years.
11 Reflect on your own role in relation to the provision for promoting physical development in your own setting.
12 Critically evaluate the provision for promoting the physical development of children in your own setting.

Useful resources

Books

Blythe, S.G. (2006), *The Well-Balanced Child: Movement and Early Learning*. Stroud: Hawthorn Press.

Greenland, P. (2000), *Hopping Home Backwards*. Leeds: Jabadao, www.jabadao.org.

A learning experience: Answers to activity on p 450

1 Chloe has just had her second birthday.
2 These are some of the things you may have listed; you may have found more. Chloe has learned:
   - That you need to watch your feet as well as your hands

- If you hit something with your foot it moves
- You have to aim at the ball, not just swing your leg
- Not to give up even when it is difficult
- Not to run too fast when you go after a ball
- To slow down before trying to stop
- To start stopping at a certain distance ahead, depending on the speed at which you are moving
- How to assess speed, distance and force
- The connections between cause and effect
- To keep trying because you can succeed
- That learning is fun.

Unit 3.12 Promote the personal, social and emotional development of children

This unit provides the learner with the knowledge, understanding and skills to promote the personal, social and emotional development of children from birth to seven years.

Learning outcomes

By the end of this unit you will:

1 Understand personal, social and emotional development of children.
2 Understand theory and current frameworks underpinning personal, social and emotional development of children.
3 Be able to promote the personal, social and emotional development of children.
4 Be able to implement an opportunity which promotes the personal, social and emotional development of children.
5 Be able to critically evaluate the provision for the personal, social and emotional development of children in own setting.

LO1 Understand personal, social and emotional development of children

The educational programme for personal, social and emotional development (PSED) is a prime area in the revised EYFS and states that PSED involves helping children to:

- develop a positive sense of themselves and others
- form positive relationships and develop respect for others
- develop social skills and learn how to manage their feelings
- understand appropriate behaviour in groups; and
- have confidence in their own abilities.

Personal, social and emotional development is made up of the following aspects:

- **Dispositions and attitudes**: how children develop interest in – and become excited and motivated about – their learning.

- **Self-confidence and self-esteem**: how children have a sense of their own value and develop an understanding of the need for sensitivity to significant events in their own and other people's lives.
- **Forming relationships**: this refers to the importance of children forming good relationships with others and working alongside others sociably.
- **Behaviour and self-control**: how children develop a growing understanding of what is right and wrong and why, along with understanding the impact of their words and actions on themselves and others.
- **Self-care and independence**: how children gain a sense of self-respect and concern for their own personal hygiene and care, and how they develop independence.
- **Sense of community**: how children understand and respect their own needs, views, cultures and beliefs, and those of other people.

Emotional development involves the:

- growth of feelings about, and awareness of, **oneself**
- development of feelings towards **other people**
- development of **self-esteem** and a **self-concept**.

Key terms

self-esteem The way you feel about yourself (good or bad) leads to high or low self-esteem.

self-concept How you see yourself, and how you think others see you; sometimes called **self-image**.

Personal development: personality and temperament

Everyone has a different **personality**. Research is increasingly suggesting that a child's temperament in early childhood is the foundation of his or her adult personality. It used to be thought that personality

Figure 3.12.1 The thoughtful and sensitive presence of a familiar adult gives these children a feeling of security

was fixed at birth (just as it used to be thought that intelligence was fixed at birth and unchangeable thereafter). As in other areas of development, it seems that a child's temperament is partly biological, but is also influenced by other factors:

- life experience and culture
- physical challenges, including special needs and disabilities
- the people whom children meet.

Temperament is the style of behaviour that is natural to the child. So, the child's temperament influences the personality that emerges later on, during late childhood and early adolescence.

Laura E. Berk (2012) summarises Mary Rothbart's important theory that babies and young children have differing levels of **reactivity**. Reactivity describes their:

- levels of activity
- capacity to pay attention for a time

- fearful distress, especially when faced by new situations
- irritable distress, especially finding it difficult to get comfortable, 'fussing'
- positive emotional response and state: how often they appear to be happy and experiencing pleasure.

It is very important that adults working with young children do not favour smiling children at the expense of those children who seem more 'difficult', or seem inactive and 'slow to warm up'. It is also critical that they do not form negative opinions of children with more difficult temperaments. Working professionally with children means being determined to uphold principles of equality of opportunity and inclusivity (see Unit 2.4).

Babies and young children can also take some control themselves and be resilient. This is called **effortful control** – for example, managing their frustration by turning their attention to something else, rather than becoming increasingly angry or just giving up on difficult things.

As children grow, their temperament can change with their development. The 'easy' baby who is content to lie back may be very fearful about exploring and crawling, while the 'fussy', wriggly baby who never seems to settle may love the physical sensations of movement and enjoy getting around.

Key terms

effortful control Children's capacity to override their immediate wants, desires and responses with a more socially acceptable and effective response. Children who can see that there are cakes on the table, but wait for the adult to say it is all right to have one, are showing high levels of effortful control.

reactivity This refers to the intensity and speed of the child's emotional responses, the child's ability to focus attention and the child's movement.

Social development

Social development in the EYFS social and emotional aspects of development is described as 'how children come to understand themselves in relation to others, how friends are made and recognition of rules and expectations are formed'. All of these underpin the aspect 'Making relationships', which focuses on children's ability to form positive relationships, and to develop respect for and hold a positive sense of themselves and others.

Relating to others

From the start, it seems as if babies are born to relate to other people: they are interested in others and want to gain people's attention and respond to them. It is important to encourage sociability by providing opportunities for babies and young children to meet other children and adults. As early as six months of age, babies can enjoy each other's company. For example, when they sit together, they touch each other's faces; they look at each other and smile at each other.; they enjoy peek-a-boo games with adults and older children. This is an

early example of **cooperative social behaviour**. It involves turn-taking and is the foundation of having a conversation with someone else. Babies delight in having a shared idea, and they really laugh with pleasure.

- Toddlers' behaviour also shows how very young children cooperate socially. One child might pick up a toy and another will copy. They laugh together. There is plenty of eye contact. One drops the toy intentionally, and the other copies. They laugh with glee. They have a shared idea that they can enjoy together.

- By the age of two or three years, the widening social circle becomes important. Children need varying amounts of help and support as they have new social experiences. This might include joining an early childhood group of some kind.

Figure 3.12.2 Young children in nursery showing cooperative social behaviour

AC 1.1 Describe stages of personal, social and emotional development of children from birth to 7 years

The table below shows the normative 'milestones' or stages in a child's personal, social and emotional development from birth to seven years. These show what *most* children can do at a particular age. It is important to understand that while the *sequence* – or order – of development is fairly general to all children, the *rate* – or speed – of development can vary a great deal. When children do things earlier than the milestones suggest is normal, it does not necessarily mean that they will be outstanding or gifted in any way. Parents sometimes think that because their child speaks early, is potty-trained early or walks early, he or she is gifted in some way.

Stages of personal, social and emotional development
The first month
<ul><li>A baby's first smile in definite response to carer is usually around five to six weeks.</li><li>The baby often imitates certain facial expressions.</li><li>The baby uses total body movements to express pleasure at bath time or when being fed.</li><li>The baby enjoys feeding and cuddling.</li><li>In the first month, babies are learning where they begin and end, e.g. his or her hand is part of them but mother's hand is not.</li></ul>
From one to four months
From four to eight weeks:<ul><li>The baby will smile in response to an adult.</li><li>The baby enjoys sucking.</li><li>The baby turns to regard nearby speaker's face.</li><li>The baby turns to preferred person's voice.</li><li>The baby recognises face and hands of preferred adult.</li><li>The baby may stop crying when he or she hears, sees or feels her carer.</li></ul>From eight to twelve weeks:<ul><li>The baby shows enjoyment at caring routines such as bath time.</li><li>The baby responds with obvious pleasure to loving attention and cuddles.</li><li>The baby fixes his or her eyes unblinkingly on carer's face when feeding.</li><li>The baby stays awake for longer periods of time.</li></ul>
From four to six months
<ul><li>The baby shows trust and security.</li><li>The baby has recognisable sleep patterns.</li></ul>
From six to nine months
<ul><li>The baby can manage to feed herself using his or her fingers.</li><li>The baby is now more wary of strangers, sometimes showing stranger fear.</li><li>The baby might offer toys to others.</li><li>The baby might show distress when his or her mother leaves.</li><li>The baby typically begins to crawl and this means he or she can do more for him- or herself, reach for objects and get to places and people.</li><li>The baby is now more aware of other people's feelings. For example, he or she may cry if their brother cries.</li></ul>

Table 3.12.1 An overview of the stages of personal, social and emotional development

Stages of personal, social and emotional development

From nine to 12 months

- The baby enjoys songs and action rhymes.
- The baby still likes to be near to a familiar adult.
- The baby can drink from a cup with help.
- The baby will play alone for long periods.
- The baby has and shows definite likes and dislikes at mealtimes and bedtimes.
- The baby thoroughly enjoys peek-a-boo games.
- The baby likes to look at him- or herself in a mirror (plastic safety mirror).
- The baby imitates other people – e.g. clapping hands, waving bye-bye – but there is often a time lapse, so that he or she waves after the person has gone.
- The baby cooperates when being dressed.

From one year to two years

- The child begins to have a longer memory.
- The child develops a sense of identity (I am me).
- The child expresses his or her needs in words and gestures.
- The child enjoys being able to walk, and is eager to try to get dressed – 'Me do it!'
- The child is aware when others are fearful or anxious for him or her as he or she climbs on and off chairs, and so on.

From two years

- The child is impulsive and curious about their environment.
- Pretend play develops rapidly when adults encourage it.
- The child begins to be able to say how he or she is feeling, but often feels frustrated when unable to express him- or herself.
- The child can dress him- or herself and go to the toilet independently, but needs sensitive support in order to feel success rather than frustration.
- By two-and-half years the child plays more with other children, but may not share his or her toys with them.

From three years

Pretend play helps the child to decentre and develop theory of mind (the child begins to be able to understand how someone else might feel and/or think).

- The child is beginning to develop a gender role as they become aware of being male or female.
- The child makes friends and is interested in having friends.
- The child learns to negotiate, give and take through experimenting with feeling powerful, having a sense of control, and through quarrels with other children.
- The child is easily afraid, e.g. of the dark, as he or she becomes capable of pretending. The child imagines all sorts of things.

From four years

- The child likes to be independent and is strongly self-willed.
- The child shows a sense of humour.
- The child can undress and dress him – or herself – except for laces and back buttons.
- The child can wash and dry his or her hands and brush their teeth.

From five to eight years

- The child has developed a stable self-concept.
- The child can hide their feelings once they can begin to control them.
- The child can think of the feelings of others.
- The child can take responsibility, e.g. in helping younger children.

Table 3.12.1 An overview of the stages of personal, social and emotional development   (*Continued*)

Describe the stages of personal, social and emotional development in children from birth to seven years.

- During the first few weeks, how does a baby express pleasure?
- At what age does a child become aware of gender – of being male or female?
- At what age does a baby begin to offer toys to others?
- When is a child able to hide their feelings and also think of the feelings of others?
- When does a baby start to cooperate when being dressed?
- When does a child begin to develop a sense of identity?

· ·

LO2 Understand theory and current frameworks underpinning children's personal, social and emotional development

AC 2.1 and **AC 2.2** Describe theoretical perspectives in relation to personal, social and emotional development and Analyse how theoretical perspectives in relation to personal, social and emotional development inform current frameworks

Attachment theory: Bowlby, Ainsworth and Winnicott

John Bowlby (1907–90) drew on ideas from animal studies, psychology and psychoanalysis to develop a body of work known as **attachment** theory (1969).

Babies and the people who care for them usually form close bonds. As the baby is fed, held and enjoyed, these emotional, loving relationships develop and deepen. Babies who find that adults respond quickly to their cries become trusting of life and are securely attached in stable, warm relationships. They know that they will be fed, changed when soiled, comforted when teething, and so on. Babies and parents who, for one reason or another, do not make close emotional bonds, experience general difficulty in forming stable, warm and loving relationships.

Bowlby looked at:

- how babies become attached to the mother figure (**attachment**)
- what happens when babies are separated from the mother figure (**separation**)
- what happens when babies experience **loss and grief** after being separated from the people to whom they feel close.

Mary Ainsworth (1913–99) who worked with Bowlby, found that if adults responded quickly to a baby's cries, the child was less demanding by three years of age than those babies who had generally been left to cry. The individual temperament of a baby becomes obvious very early on and has an effect on the carers. For instance, some babies become hysterical very quickly when hungry, while others have a calmer nature. Bonding is partly about adults and babies adjusting to and understanding each other; learning how to read each other's signals.

Bowlby thought that early attachment was very important – that the relationship between the mother figure and the baby was the most important. This was because in the 1950s mothers tended to be at home with their babies. He did not believe that the most important attachment figure must be the natural mother, but he did say that babies need one central person, or a mother figure. It is now understood that babies can have deep relationships with several people – mother, father, brothers, sisters, carers and grandparents. Indeed, babies develop in an emotionally and socially healthy way only if they bond with several different people. In many parts of the world and in many cultures, this is usual. Babies might enjoy playing with one person and having meals with another. It is the quality of the time which the child spends with people that determines whether or not the child becomes attached to them.

Attachment can be difficult at first, especially in cases where it is hard for the adult and child to communicate; for example:

- the birth has caused mother and baby to be separated, and the mother is depressed. For more information on post-natal depression refer to Unit 1.6.

- the child is visually impaired and eye contact is absent
- the child is hearing-impaired and does not turn to the parent's voice; eye contact is also harder to establish here because the child does not turn to the parent's face when he or she speaks
- the child has severe learning difficulties and needs many experiences of a person before bonding can become stable.

AC 2.2 Links to practice

Bowlby's work on attachment was important because it led to the following changes in practice:

- The introduction of the key person system in early years settings.
- Parents can often stay in hospital with their children; there may be a bed for a parent next to the child's bed.
- Social workers are extremely careful about separating children and parents when families experience difficulties.
- Most early years settings have policies on how to settle children so as to make it a positive experience.
- Children are fostered in family homes rather than placed in large institutions.

Separation anxiety

By five or six months, many babies are so closely attached to the people they know and love that they show separation anxiety when they are taken away from these attachment figures. Researchers have found that toddlers will happily explore toys and play with them if an attachment figure (usually their parent) is present. If the parent goes out of the room, however, young children quickly become anxious, and stop exploring and playing. They need the reassurance of someone they know to be able to explore, play and learn. Children who have had many separations from those with whom they have tried to bond find it very difficult to understand social situations and relationships.

Key term

attachment An enduring emotional bond that an infant forms with a specific person. Usually the first attachment is to the mother, formed between the ages of six and nine months.

Donald Winnicott (1896–1971) emphasised the importance of play for the emotional and social development of the child, but stated that all developmental stages in a child's play are related to the child's capacity to learn. Winnicott's work focused on transitional or comfort objects and is discussed in Unit 1.4.

Psychodynamic theories: Freud and Erikson

Sigmund Freud (1856–1939) is the founder of psychoanalytic theory. Freud linked thinking, feeling, and sexual and social relationships with early physical behaviour, such as breastfeeding, toilet training and separation from parents. He believed the following:

- Our unconscious feelings direct the way we behave; we are not aware of these feelings, and this means that we often do not know why we behave as we do in a particular situation.
- Our earliest childhood experiences deeply influence what we believe and how we feel as adults.
- People go through psychosexual stages of development which he called oral, anal, phallic, latency and genital stages.
- He could help the people he psychoanalysed to understand their behaviour and feelings, and even to change.

Freud thought that people have:

- an **id**, which makes 'want' demands
- an **ego,** which tries to resolve conflicts between the id and the superego
- a **superego,** which conveys the demands made by parents or society about how to behave.

Erik Erikson (1902–94) took Sigmund Freud's work as the rock on which he based his own personality theory. He was also a pupil of Anna Freud, Sigmund's daughter. Erikson concentrated on the superego and on the influence of society on a child's development. He showed how, when we meet a personal crisis or have to deal with a crisis in the world (for example, living through a war), we are naturally equipped to face the difficulties and to deal with them. Erikson thought that there were eight developmental phases during a person's life (five during childhood and three during adulthood). He said that during each phase we have to face and sort out the particular kinds of problem that occur during that phase.

In the days before equal opportunities, Erikson called his developmental stages the Eight Phases of Man. It is important to bear in mind that theories evolving from Freud's ideas are based on white, middle-class patients in Western Europe. The theories need to be used carefully for that reason. However, they still seem to be useful in many of Erikson's eight developmental phases.

1 **Babyhood**: we have to sort out whether we feel a basic sense of trust or mistrust in life. This phase is about being a hopeful person or not.
2 **The toddler and nursery years**: we develop either a basic sense of being able to do things ourselves (autonomy), or a basic sense of doubt in ourselves, leading to shame. This phase is about our self-identity.
3 **The infant school years**: we either take the initiative and go for it or we feel guilty and hold back in case we upset people. This phase is about leading an active life with a sense of purpose, or not.
4 **The junior years**: we either begin to be determined to master things or we do not try hard in case we cannot manage something. This phase is about becoming skilled.
5 **Adolescence**: we either begin to be at one with ourselves or we feel uncertain and unsure. We learn to have faith in ourselves, or not.
6 **Young adults**: we begin to have a sense of taking part in our society and of taking responsibility in it as a shared venture, or we think only of ourselves and become isolated.
7 **Middle age**: we begin to be caring of the next generation and the future of our society, or we reject the challenge.
8 **Old age:** we return to our roots and overcome feelings of despair, disgust about new lifestyles or fear of death, or not. This is Erikson's phase of wisdom.

Social learning theory: Bandura

Social learning theory emphasises that young children learn about social behaviour by:

- watching other people
- imitating other people.

Albert Bandura (1925–) found that children tend to imitate people in their lives who they believe hold status, especially if those people are warm or powerful personalities. This research study did not replicate a natural situation for the children, but it does suggest that adults can be very influential on a child's behaviour. This should lead us to think about our own behaviour and the effect we have on children:

- If children are smacked by adults, they are likely to hit other children.
- If children are shouted at by adults, they are likely to shout at others.
- If children are given explanations, they will try to explain things too.
- If children are comforted when they fall, they will learn to do the same to others.
- People who work with young children are very important status figures in the child's social learning.

The Bobo doll study

The Bobo doll is an inflatable doll, five feet tall with a weighted base. No matter how hard the doll is hit, it always springs back. Bandura showed three groups of children a film in which an adult was hitting a Bobo doll and shouting at it. The film had a different ending for each of the three groups:

- First ending: the adult was given a reward for hitting the doll.
- Second ending: the adult was punished for hitting the doll.
- Third ending: nothing was done to the adult for hitting the doll.

Then the children were given a Bobo doll like the one in the film. The children who saw the adult rewarded for hitting the doll tended to do the same.

AC 2.2 Link to practice: role play as social learning

Children copy directly what adults do, but they also pretend to be adults (that is, they role play being adults) when they begin to play imaginatively. The child's home – or the home area in an early years setting – is an important area for this, and so is the outdoor area, which can become all sorts of places (shops, markets, streets and building sites, for example). The problem with this approach is that it does not see role play as children experimenting with different ways of doing things: it suggests that children merely copy what they see. We now know that role play is a more complex activity than the social learning theory would suggest.

Activity ·

Think about what the theories teach us about this aspect of child development. Analyse how each theory informs current frameworks in your home country.

· ·

AC 2.3 Describe the role of the EYP when promoting the personal, social and emotional development of children

In relation to personal, social and emotional development, the EYFS states that practitioners can help parents and children by the factors shown in Figure 3.12.3.

Progress check

Putting theories into practice

- Know how children's temperaments might affect their well-being in nursery.
- Work as a team to use words like 'thinking', 'imagining' or 'wondering' to match children's developing theory of mind.

- Spend blocks of time with a child who seems fearful to explore and play, showing your interest in what the child is doing.

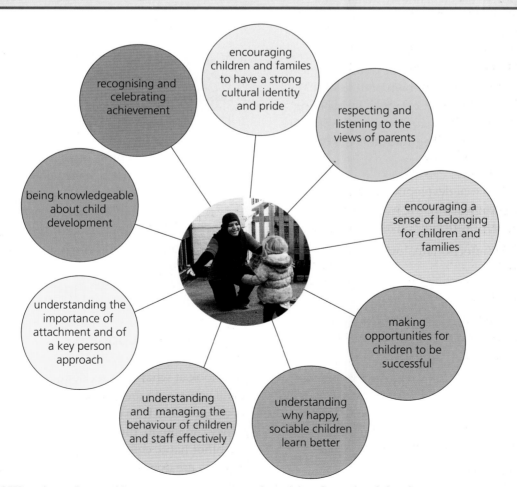

Figure 3.12.3 Ways for early practitioners to promote personal, social and emotional development

Attachment

Children become securely attached and begin to trust when someone:

- smiles back at them
- comforts them when they are upset
- feeds them when they are hungry.

Research shows that babies who receive quick and affectionate responses to their expressed needs typically learn to cry much less and sleep more at night. At the same time, when babies are calmed by being comforted or fed, the brain's stress-response systems are turned off. Babies' brains begin to create the network of cells that help them learn to self-regulate – or to soothe themselves.

Remember: You cannot spoil a young baby by responding to his or her needs.

Emotional security

When unhappy, babies will often frown or switch their focus from the carer to objects in the room. This is their way of expressing their feelings. As babies gain more experience with their carers' soothing responses to their signals of unhappiness, babies begin to develop their own pattern of soothing self-regulation, for example, by babbling to themselves before going to sleep or on wakening. A key component of **self-regulation** is the baby's emotional security.

To promote emotional development, you should make sure you know about the ways babies and children develop holistically. You also need to:

- be interested, affectionate, loving, and responsive
- hold, touch, rock, sing, and smile at babies and children
- build an understanding of the needs and temperaments of each child
- continually observe each baby or toddler to discover which skills he is ready to explore and eventually master
- have an overall plan for each day – one which includes materials and activities that are appropriate for the development stage of each child
- always work to enhance sensitivity and respect.

Getting on with other children

A young child, seeing a friend distressed, may make a gesture spontaneously – such as giving them a treasured teddy bear – to ease the pain and provide comfort. This means that young children can be, in their own way, very *giving*. They are also very *forgiving*. Being able to give means that a young child has managed to think of someone else's needs and control his or her own behaviour accordingly. It takes enormous effort for young children to do this. It is an ability that will come and go depending on the situation, the people involved and how tired the child is. Children who become skilled in this way are often popular leaders, and other children want to be with them.

Children tend to behave according to the way they experience life. If they are ridiculed or smacked, they are likely to laugh at and hit others, especially children younger or smaller than themselves. This is because children use social referencing to guide their behaviour and responses to others. Some children need a great deal of support to play well and get on with other children. Children who know how to join in get on better with other children. They have good **access strategies**:

1 First, a child will tend to circle around the edge of an activity, perhaps on a tricycle, trying to work out what is happening, or will watch what is happening from the safe viewpoint of being at the sand tray or water tray.
2 Then they will imitate what the other children are doing – for example, pouring sand in and out of pots and laughing as each pot is upturned. We call this using a **side-by-side** strategy. Doing the same helps the child to join in with other children.

How you can support a child to join in

You might say to the child, 'Do you want to join in? Let's look at what they are doing, shall we? Don't ask if you can do the same as them, just do the same as them.' This advice is given because if children ask if they can join in, they are usually rejected. If, on the other hand, children simply do what the other children are doing, they are very likely to be accepted into the group. This is an important access strategy that adults can help children to develop. It is also a useful strategy for adults to use if they are joining a group of children. Adults can also support young children by modelling phrases such as, 'Can I have a go next?' or 'Can I have that when you're finished?' which can help children to find a way between being left out and never getting a turn, or being impulsive and grabbing things to force their way in.

In practice activity

Spend some time observing a child who is finding it difficult to play with others. Set up an activity based on what you have observed the child is interested in, and see if you can help the child to play with another child with similar interests.

Progress check

Supporting play

- Know about some of the ways that play helps children's emotional and social development.
- Work within your team to help children find appropriate ways to join in with play when they feel left out.
- Spend time with a child who is finding it difficult to share and play alongside others, acting as a positive model by suggesting phrases like, 'I would like a turn when you have finished.'

Case study

Active communication

William (aged 10 months) plays with the xylophone that his key person, Leanne, has given him. He then lies down and begins whining. Leanne sits him up and plays the xylophone as she talks to him softly. 'Now, it's your turn, William!' she says enthusiastically. William stops whining and plays with the xylophone again as Leanne strokes his hair and says, 'William is making a lovely sound.'

Leanne is quick to respond to William's 'cue' that he is unhappy as she helps him to control his feelings. Once he is calm and begins playing with the xylophone again, Leanne reassures him further by talking to him softly as she strokes his hair. In her daily interactions, Leanne often 'contains' a baby; that is, she helps the baby to remain involved in an activity.

Helping children to manage their feelings in their social relationships

Learning to be assertive

Children might bully others because they feel bad about themselves, or because others have bullied them. They can pick on weaker children or children who are different – for example, they tease or make racial, gender or disability insults. Teaching all children to value the way others are different, rather than to mock or be nervous, and to be assertive in their response to name-calling or hitting, can help to prevent bullying.

Supporting children to develop assertiveness

Do not use labelling words like 'bully' or 'disruptive'. These can give a child a bad name that the child will then live up to – and often children do not really understand what these words mean anyway. Instead, talk to children in ways they understand, about what they can see or feel; for example, 'When you shout like that, it makes Adam sad. Can you see he is crying now? What would be a better way to get your turn on the bike?'

Swearing can create similar problems to name-calling. Often it is simply the case that swearing is an everyday part of the child's language experience. However, it is quite a different thing when children swear in order to shock. Any child who swears needs help in:

- learning which words they cannot use in the early years setting
- finding new words to replace the swear words (they still have to be able to express their thoughts and feelings)
- building up their vocabulary so that they have wider choice of words.

Progress check

Helping children to be assertive

- Know about some strategies to use when children show angry feelings and act these feelings out by being aggressive.
- Work within your team to help children to become appropriately assertive.
- Acknowledge children's emotions of all kinds – happy, sad and angry.

Supporting children to manage strong feelings

Children live life to the full. This means that they have powerful feelings. They need adult help to learn to deal with the strength of their feelings. Feelings are hard to manage – even adults do not always succeed in dealing with how they feel. These strong feelings can quickly overwhelm children. This can lead to:

- sobbing and sadness
- temper tantrums that are full of anger and rage
- jealousy that makes a child want to hit out
- joy that makes a child literally jump and leap with a wildness that is unnerving to many adults.

Children's body language

Children need to express their feelings, and not just through words. They do so through:

- **physical actions** – like stamping with rage, screaming with terror, hitting out, jumping with joy or seeking a cuddle
- **facial expressions** – a pout tells the adult the child is not happy, compared with eyes that are shining with joy
- **the position of the body** – playing alone with the dolls' house or hovering on the edge of a cooking session might indicate that the child wants to join in but does not know how; playing boats right in the centre of a group of children tells an adult something quite different
- **body movements** – children who keep twisting their fingers together are not at ease, compared with children who sit in a relaxed way.

Figure 3.12.4 Facial expressions can say a lot about how you are feeling; children enjoy being with adults who reflect their body language and emotions

Putting feelings into words

It helps children to manage their feelings if they can put them into words. The child who can say, 'Stop hitting me! That hurts! I don't like it!' has found an appropriate way to deal with an unpleasant situation.

- The cries that a baby makes are early attempts to 'tell' others how he or she feels. By trying to 'tune in' to the baby and understand the cause of his or her distress, you help the baby's developing confidence by showing that he or she is understood by other people.
- It takes time, experience and adult support for young children to learn how to express their feelings in words and to negotiate in dialogue with others. It can help to give them examples of sharp-sounding words, such as 'Stop it!' so that they can take control of situations. Children learn the language of feelings through real situations that hold great meaning and that engage their whole attention.
- Stories that relate to an area of difficulty for the child can help them to develop more understanding. Some children find it hard to say goodbye to their parents at the start of nursery. Hearing a story such as *Owl Babies* by Martin Waddell might be a way to start talking about those feelings of loss, and the relief the babies feel when their mother returns.

Helping children under emotional stress

When children do not experience warm, loving relationships, they react differently according to their personality. They may:

- become aggressive
- be very quiet, watchful and tense
- begin bedwetting or soiling themselves
- find it difficult to eat
- regress in development – they may want a bottle again or a comforter; they might want to be held and cuddled or carried about; they might want help with eating and dressing.

When children are under emotional stress, their behaviour can change quite quickly. It is important, therefore, that early years practitioners are alert to the changes listed above and that they respond sensitively and with understanding. If you suspect a problem of this kind, it is important to talk with your line manager about your observations and consider how best to discuss it with the child's family. The discussion will probably open up to the staff team. You will all look at the child's progress and agree what steps should be taken, depending on whether the situation is a temporary one for the child or one that is more likely to be long-term. Where children continue to experience difficulties of these kinds for more than a few weeks, and where there is no obvious cause – for example, a new baby or a sick parent – it may be important to involve another professional, such as a clinical child psychologist.

Case study

Supporting a child who is distressed

Jack, aged 11 months, became very distressed when his mother had to leave for work, sobbing and trying to hold on to her. His key person, Lisa, held him gently, rubbing his back as his mother did when he was upset. As she held him, she spoke to him quietly, acknowledging his feelings – that he was upset and that he wanted his mother to stay. As he became calmer, Jack started to look around at the other babies, and Lisa talked about what they were doing. As he seemed particularly interested in Lettie playing with a basket of Duplo® bricks, she sat with Jack next to Lettie and supported him as he started to explore them, gradually becoming absorbed in playing.

Guidelines: helping children to understand their feelings and manage their emotions positively

1. Children need to begin to understand, express and manage their feelings.
2. Children need to develop positive relationships with people.
3. Children feel things deeply and need a great deal of help in coming to terms with their emotions. Feelings are hard to deal with. Anyone – child or adult – can be overwhelmed by their emotions for a time, and need someone sympathetic to stay with them and look after them.
4. Children need help to learn how to make up when they have hurt someone else. Insisting children say 'sorry' can lead to a half-hearted apology, while putting the problem back to the child and saying, 'How can we make Iqbal feel a bit better now?' can be more productive.

Children who express themselves or relate to others in particular or challenging ways

The shy or withdrawn child

Although it is important for every child to have his or her own personal space and be allowed opportunities to do things alone, some children have difficulty socialising with other children or with adults. There are a number of things that you can do to support a child to overcome his or her shyness.

- **Making introductions**: when an adult is new to the child, you can introduce them. 'Michael, this is Jane. Jane wants to do a painting. Can you help her to get started? Can you tell her how to find the colours she wants?'
- **Being welcoming**: if a child is shy with adults, it can be helpful to join the child with a warm smile, but to say nothing. You might find that a welcoming gesture, such as handing the child a lump of clay if they join the clay table, reassures them.
- **Observing children**: keeping good observations of children's social relationships is important. If a child who is normally outgoing and has the full range of social behaviour suddenly becomes quiet, withdrawn and solitary, this should be discussed

with the team and parents should be included in the discussion. Multi-professional help from outside may be required if the problem cannot be solved within the team.

The over-demanding child

Having too much individual adult attention can lead to children being labelled as 'spoilt' or 'over-demanding'. This negative image of the child is not helpful. Some children – for example, children with no brothers or sisters – are the main focus of their family and are given one-to-one attention by adults most of the time. They have not experienced waiting for things or taking turns. Is it the child's fault if he or she seems demanding of adult attention, insecure or ill at ease with other children? This child needs sensitive help to become involved in parallel, associative and cooperative social behaviour with other children.

Some children gain attention by being dominant and demanding. These are the so-called 'bossy' children. But this is another negative and unhelpful image. Such children need help in turn-taking and learning to give and take. They are usually afraid of losing control of situations – for example, in the play and home areas, they may control the other children by saying what the storyline is going to be and by making the other children do as they say. These children need an adult to help them to see that the 'story' will be better if other children's ideas are allowed in. It takes a bit of courage for the child to dare to let the play 'free-flow', because no one knows quite how the story will turn out. For more on free-flow play, see Unit 3.3.

Sibling jealousy

When a new baby is born, it can be hard for a child who is used to having a lot of attention. Sibling jealousy often results in very demanding behaviour, which may last for some time, until the family adjusts to its new social relationships. Recent research shows that the older child needs to feel that he or she is being treated in exactly the same way as the new baby – for example, getting some special attention at times.

Key term

behavioural, emotional and social difficulties (BESD) Signs that a child may have BESD include withdrawn or isolated behaviour, highly disruptive or disturbing behaviour, hyperactivity and significant difficulties with social interactions. It is difficult to assess whether a young child has BESD, and an educational psychologist or clinical child psychologist should always be involved.

Children and 'status possessions'

From two years of age children may become eager to own objects. Owning possessions helps them to gain attention and enables them to control things. Children who have not experienced secure social relationships are often especially anxious to possess fashionable objects that carry high status – for example, a special toy or particular clothes and shoes. Advertisers pressurise children into wanting goods branded with their favourite characters: there are now hundreds of Thomas the Tank Engine products, for example, including clothes, bedding, games and rucksacks.

Adults can help children in a number of ways. It is probably best to avoid any kind of branded goods in an early years setting: it is inevitable that a Bob the Builder hammer will create a huge amount of conflict. Branded goods are also restrictive: you can only be Batman in a Batman suit, while with a length of dark fabric you can be Batman, or a monster, or a baby wrapped up for sleep. Playing with equipment and materials like this can help children to see that branded objects are not vital for having friends and being part of the group. Children need to learn that friends like you because of who you are, not because you have a certain brand of trainers.

Angry children

Hitting, kicking, spitting, biting, swearing and disrupting other children's activities are behaviours that children use to demand attention. When children behave like this, they can soon become labelled as naughty or impossible to manage, and it is only a short step to these children starting to live up to their label, and staff starting to speak and act towards them in an anxious or hostile way. For more information on the impact of labelling, see Unit 2.4. So it is important to break this cycle, to try to hold on to the positive aspects of the child's behaviour and appeal to these.

The following strategies may help:

- **Try to imagine what it might be like to be a child in the setting**. Does it sometimes feel like there is a great mass of children, all demanding attention and seeking the same equipment? You can help by taking time with individual children, listening to them and observing them, encountering them as special individuals and not just one many in the group.
- **Try to become aware of your own feelings**. Angry children provoke angry responses from adults. Can you work on your responses and become calmer and clearer, and reduce confrontations? Saying, 'I can wait a minute, but then I really do need you to come and sit down' will often work much better than demanding 'Sit down now!'
- **Look for patterns in children's behaviour**. If a child is often angry at a particular time of the day, during a particular activity or in response to particular children, try to plan the day to minimise these times.

Dealing with temper tantrums

Temper tantrums can be:

- **noisy** – the child might hurl themselves about, perhaps hurting themselves, usually in rather a public way
- **quiet** – the child holds their breath and might even turn blue.

It is almost always best to deal with temper tantrums in a quiet and matter-of-fact way, however much you sense your own feelings boiling up. Try to give as little attention as possible to the tantrum, and encourage other children away. It can be helpful to stay near the child, offering quiet reassurance, but it is usually best not to talk: the child is in no state for discussion. At the end, you might say something like, 'Now you are calmer, we can talk about this and see what we can do about it,' and help the child return to playing with others.

Activity •

Describe your role when promoting the personal, social and emotional development of children. How important do you think the key person approach is in promoting emotional and social development?

LO3 Promote children's personal, social and emotional development

AC 3.1 Create an environment which promotes children's personal, social and emotional development in own setting

Every early years setting has its own ethos and ambience. To promote young children's personal, social and emotional development, the environment should be inclusive and welcoming. The people working in the setting are the most important elements in creating such an environment:

- **A key person system**: this should always be planned around the needs of the children. A key person should let 'their' children know if they are going to be absent at the start or end of the day, and name the person who will fulfil their role. This promotes the child's sense of belonging and provides emotional security.
- **Quiet, cosy corners**: spaces where babies and young children can feel both physically safe and free to explore at their own pace.
- **Islands of intimacy**: the 'islands of intimacy' were first described by Elinor Goldschmied, well known for her work on heuristic play. These spaces enable babies and children to be together at significant points of the day as well as for spontaneous chats and cuddles with an adult. In some settings, the 'island' is a special rug only used during the session – 'island time' is an opportunity for children and their key person to get to know each other better, and for the children to receive directed, meaningful praise about what they are doing.
- **Promoting social confidence and self-help skills**: encouraging children to come together at times during the daily routine, such as snack or meal times. Children are encouraged to take it

in turns to pour the water out for each other or to pass the glasses round. Pro-social behaviour is modelled for the children by their key person.

- **Promoting a sense of belonging**: a sleep room that provides each baby and young child with their own cot/sleep nest and their own bedding. Comfort objects should be readily available and labelled with the child's photograph. Babies could have their favourite story read to them before sleeping.
- **A relaxed environment**: the nappy changing area should not be too clinical and should provide a cheerful, relaxed atmosphere where the child and key person can enjoy each other's company in an unhurried routine.

Reflective practice

Consider these questions for your own setting:

- What level of emotional well-being are children displaying?
- Are there any factors in the child's life that need to be considered?
- How do practitioners respond to and praise children?
- Are each child's efforts valued?
- Do practitioners use sustained shared thinking with the child?

LO4 Implement an opportunity which promotes the personal, social and emotional development of children

AC 4.1 Plan an opportunity which promotes the personal, social and emotional development of children aged 0–1 year 11 months; 2–2 years 11 months; 3–5 years

Activity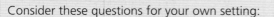

Using the ideas in Unit 3.2 and suggestions from your colleagues, plan an opportunity which promotes the personal, social and emotional development for *each* of the following age groups: children aged: birth to one year 11 months; two years to two years 11 months; three to five years.

AC 4.2 Provide an opportunity which promotes the personal, social and emotional development of children

Activity

Using your plans for AC 4.1, provide an opportunity which promotes the personal, social and emotional development for *each* of the following age groups: children aged: birth to one year 11 months; two years to two years 11 months; three to five years.

AC 4.3 Describe the benefits to children's holistic learning and development when promoting personal, social and emotional development

Child development should always be viewed holistically. This is because each area of development is linked with and affects every other area of development. It is important to remember that it is not possible to isolate emotional and social development from any other areas of development.

- A baby who feels secure and has strong attachments will be able to explore a wider environment, promoting their physical development. They will want to reach out, move about and practise physical skills, such as crawling.
- As children develop a relationship with their key person and with others, their communication and language development will benefit.

The process of **social referencing** is an example of how areas of development overlap: the child who feels prevented from playing with a new toy or approaching another child in the park by his carer's look of anxiety and fear is not only affected emotionally (perhaps becoming anxious and shy), but also cognitively by missing out on new play experiences.

Similarly, if carers do not try to think about what a child means when he or she cries or gets angry, the child in turn might be unable to think about how other people feel. Empathy is the ability to understand and share the feelings of another, and should not be confused with sympathy. Some people find it easy to appreciate how someone else is feeling by imagining themselves in that person's position. Peter Fonagy, a psychoanalyst and clinical psychologist, uses the term **mentalisation** to describe the ability, through imagination, to interpret what other people do and say. Mentalisation is needed to develop friendships, which depend on being able to imagine how another person is feeling; and it is also needed in order to take part in role play, enjoy books and a whole host of other experiences. For example, Julia Donaldson's book, *The Gruffalo*, depends on the reader or listener being able to imagine that the animals are afraid of a mysterious big monster in the forest.

In practice activity

1 Observe a two-year-old child for an hour.
2 How many examples of social referencing do you see?
3 How do adult responses (facial expressions, tone of voice, words spoken) help the child to feel confident exploring?
4 How do they help the child to take care and be aware of danger?

Key terms

mentalisation The ability to understand another person's mental state through observing their behaviour – for example, a child saying, 'I think Sophie wants to be my friend; she is trying to hold my hand.'

social referencing This is when a baby or young child checks an adult's emotional response before deciding on their own. If the adult looks pleased as a child moves to pick up a toy, the child is likely to smile too. If the adult looks fearful, the child is likely to shy away.

AC 4.4 Reflect on own role in relation to the provision for promoting children's personal, social and emotional development in own setting

One of the roles of a key person is to provide a **healthy dependence** from which independence can grow. Peter Elfer et al. support this viewpoint, describing the relationship between a key person and child as an invisible piece of elastic. It stretches to give the child independence but springs back to the key person when the child is need of reassurance or comfort.

Activity

Think about your role in supporting children's personal, social and emotional, using the following questions:

- Do I value my relationship with children and support them in developing independence?
- Do I take enough time to ensure that I have heard what a child is trying to tell me, rather than assuming I have understood and imposing my thoughts on them?
- Do I acknowledge a child's feelings as real and encourage children to express their feelings – giving them the vocabulary to say how they feel?
- Do I allow children to make choices and decisions and to take risks within safe boundaries and a secure relationship?
- Do I share mealtimes with children, so supporting the empowerment of babies and young children, their independence, and their social skills?

LO5 AC 5.1 Critically evaluate the provision for children's personal, social and emotional development in own setting

Using the information in Unit 3.2, critically evaluate the provision for promoting personal, social and emotional development in your own setting.

Assessment practice

1 Describe the stages of personal, social and emotional development of children from birth to 7 years.
2 Describe theoretical perspectives in relation to personal, social and emotional development.
3 Analyse how theoretical perspectives in relation to personal, social and emotional development inform current frameworks.
4 Describe the role of the early years practitioner when promoting the personal, social and emotional development of children.
5 Create an environment which promotes the personal, social and emotional development of children in own setting.
6 Plan an opportunity which promotes the personal, social and emotional development of children aged from birth to one year 11 months; two years to two years 11 months; three to five years.
7 Provide an opportunity which promotes the personal, social and emotional development of children aged from birth to one year 11 months; two years to two years 11 months; three to five years.
8 Describe the benefits to children's holistic learning and development when promoting personal, social and emotional development.
9 Reflect on own role in relation to the provision for promoting the personal, social and emotional development of children in own setting.
10 Critically evaluate the provision for the personal, social and emotional development of children in your own setting.

Useful resources

Books and articles

Elfer, P., Goldschmied, E. and Selleck, D. (2003), *Key Persons in the Nursery: Building Relationships for Quality Provision*. London: David Fulton.

Berk, L. (2012), *Child Development*. Oxford: Pearson.

Bowlby, J. (1969), *Attachment and Loss. Vol. I: Attachment*. London: Hogarth Press.

Dowling, M. (2010), *Young Children's Personal, Social and Emotional Development* (3rd edn). London: Sage Publications.

Elfer, P., Grenier, J., Manning-Morton, J., Dearnley, K. and Wilson, D. (2008), 'Appendix 1: The key person in reception classes and small nursery settings', *Social and Emotional Aspects of Development: Guidance for Practitioners Working in the Early Years Foundation Stage*. Nottingham: DCSF Publications, available at http://nationalstrategies.standards.dcsf.gov.uk/node/132720.

Freud, A., in collaboration with D. Burlingham (1973), *The Writings of Anna Freud. Vol. III: Infants Without Families [and] Reports on the Hampstead Nurseries, 1939–1945*. New York: International Universities Press.

Paley, V.G. (1981), *Wally's Stories*. Cambridge, Mass.: Harvard University Press.

Waddell, M. (1995), *Owl Babies*. London: Walker Books.

Winnicott, D.W. (1964), *The Child, the Family and the Outside World*. London: Penguin Books.

Unit 3.13 Support children with additional needs

This unit provides the learner with the knowledge, understanding and skills required to support children with additional needs.

Learning outcomes

By the end of this unit you will:

1 Understand biological, environmental and developmental factors which may result in children needing additional support.
2 Understand how personal experiences, values and beliefs impact on the role of the early years practitioner.
3 Understand the principles of inclusive practice.
4 Understand the role of early intervention in partnership working.
5 Be able to support the additional needs of children.
6 Be able to critically evaluate the provision for children with additional needs in own setting.

LO1 Understand biological, environmental and developmental factors which may result in children needing additional support

AC 1.1 Define the terms 'biological' and 'environmental'

Biological

In this context, biological means that a child may need additional support because of:

- genetic causes – when a faulty gene leads to a disabling condition, or
- developmental causes – something goes wrong when the foetus is growing in the womb.

Environmental

In this context, environmental means that a child may need additional support because of positive and negative influences on development, derivable from external factors. These external factors include:

- illness
- accidents
- life experiences.

Genetic factors

The growth and development of the embryo and foetus are controlled by genes. Abnormal genes can cause abnormal growth and development (see Table 3.13.1).

Dominant gene defects

A parent with a dominant gene defect has a 50 per cent chance of passing the defect on to each of their children. Examples of dominant gene defects are:

- tuberous sclerosis (a disorder affecting the skin and nervous system)
- achondroplasia (once called dwarfism)
- Huntington's chorea (a disorder of the central nervous system).

Recessive gene defects

These defects are only inherited if two recessive genes meet. Therefore, if both parents carry a single recessive gene defect, each of their children has a one in four (25 per cent) chance of being affected. Examples of defects transmitted this way are:

- cystic fibrosis (a genetic condition in which the lungs and digestive system become clogged with thick sticky mucus)
- sickle cell anaemia (an inherited blood condition)
- phenylketonuria (a defective enzyme disorder)
- thalassaemia (a blood disorder)
- Tay-Sachs disease (a disorder of the nervous system)
- Friedreich's ataxia (a disorder of the spinal cord).

Chromosomal defects

These vary considerably in the severity of their effect on the individual. About one in every 200 babies born alive has a chromosomal abnormality – which means that the structure or number of chromosomes varies from normal. Among foetuses that have been spontaneously aborted, about half have such an abnormality. Examples of defects transmitted this way are:

- **Down's syndrome**: Trisomy 21 is the term used for the chromosomal abnormality that results

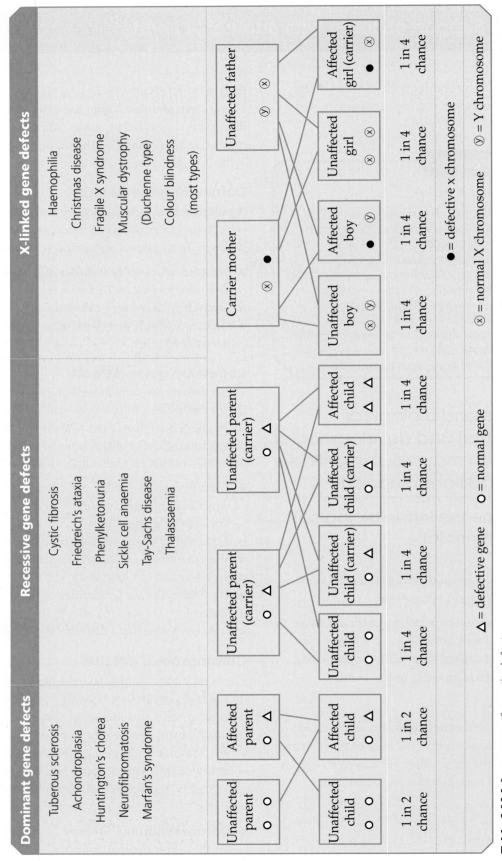

Table 3.13.1 A summary of genetic defects

in Down's syndrome. The extra chromosome is number 21, and affected individuals have three, instead of two, number 21 chromosomes. This results in short stature, as well as learning difficulties and an increased susceptibility to infection.

- **Klinefelter's syndrome**: 47XXY is the term used for the chromosomal abnormality that results in Klinefelter's syndrome. The affected male has one or more extra X chromosomes (normally the pattern is XY). This results in boys who are very tall, with hypogonadism. Hypogonadism is when the sex glands produce few or no hormones. In men, these glands (gonads) are the testes; in women, they are the ovaries.
- **Turner's syndrome**: 45XO is the term used for the chromosomal abnormality which results in Turner's syndrome. Most affected females have only 45 chromosomes instead of 46; they have a missing or defective X chromosome. This results in girls with non-functioning ovaries, a webbed neck and a broad chest; they may also have cardiac malfunctions.
- **Cri du chat syndrome**: this is a very rare condition in which a portion of one particular chromosome is missing in each of the affected individual's cells.

Genetic counselling is available for anyone with a child or other member of the family with a chromosomal abnormality, and chromosome analysis is offered in early pregnancy.

Developmental factors

The first three months (the first trimester) of a pregnancy are when the foetus is particularly vulnerable. The lifestyle of the pregnant woman affects the health of the baby in her womb. Important factors are:

- a healthy diet
- the avoidance of alcohol and other drugs
- not smoking
- regular and appropriate exercise.

Rubella

Rubella ('German measles') is especially harmful to the developing foetus as it can cause deafness, blindness and learning disability. All girls in the UK are now immunised against rubella before they reach child-bearing age, and this measure has drastically reduced the incidence of rubella-damaged babies.

Thalidomide

A drug called Thalidomide was widely prescribed in the early 1960s, to alleviate morning sickness in pregnant women. Unfortunately, it was found to cause limb deformities in many of the babies born to women who had used the drug, and it was withdrawn in 1961.

Toxoplasmosis

Toxoplasmosis is an infection caused by the protozoan toxoplasma gondii. It may be contracted when pregnant women eat undercooked meat (usually pork) from infected animals, or by poor hygiene after handling cats or their faeces. In about one-third of cases, toxoplasmosis is transmitted to the child and may cause blindness, hydro-cephalus or learning difficulty. Infection in late pregnancy usually has no ill effects.

Irradiation

If a woman has X-rays in early pregnancy or receives radiotherapy for the treatment of cancer, the embryo may suffer abnormalities. Radiation damage may also result from atomic radiation or radioactive fall-out (following a nuclear explosion or a leak from a nuclear reactor). There is also an increased risk of the child developing leukaemia in later life after exposure to radiation.

Activity ·

What are the main factors resulting in children needing additional support? Define biological and environmental factors.

· ·

AC 1.2 Analyse the impact of biological factors on children's development

Cerebral palsy

This is the general term for disorders of movement and posture resulting from damage to a child's developing brain in the later months of pregnancy, during birth, in the neonatal period or in early childhood. The injury does not damage the child's muscles or the nerves that connect them to the spinal cord – only the brain's ability to control the muscles. (Palsy literally means 'paralysis'.)

Cerebral palsy affects two to three children in every 1,000. In the UK, about 1,500 babies either are born with or develop the condition each year. It can affect boys and girls, and people from all races and social backgrounds.

Types of cerebral palsy

Cerebral palsy jumbles messages between the brain and muscles. There are three main types of cerebral palsy which correspond to the different parts of the brain affected:

- **Spastic cerebral palsy**: affected children find that some muscles become very stiff and weak, especially under effort, which can affect their control of movement. This is the most common type of cerebral palsy and it affects different areas of the body.
- **Athetoid cerebral palsy**: affected children have some loss of control of their posture, and tend to make involuntary movements. Their speech can be hard to understand, and hearing problems are also common.
- **Ataxic cerebral palsy**: affected children usually have problems with balance. They may also have shaky hand movements and irregular speech.

Often, children will have a mixture of the different types of cerebral palsy. In some children, the condition is barely noticeable, whereas others will be more severely affected. No two children will be affected in quite the same way.

Causes of cerebral palsy

Cerebral palsy is most commonly the result of a failure of part of the brain to develop, either before birth or in early childhood. Occasionally, it is due to an inherited disorder. It is sometimes possible to identify the cause of cerebral palsy, but not always.

The impact of cerebral palsy on children's development

Cerebral palsy may not be recognised until the child is several months' old. A child with cerebral palsy may have some or most of the following features, in varying degrees of severity:

- slow, awkward or jerky movements
- stiffness of the arms and legs when being picked up
- delayed sitting or walking
- feeding difficulties
- muscle spasms
- floppiness
- unwanted (involuntary) movements.

Some children with cerebral palsy do have learning difficulties, but this is by no means always the case. Some have higher than average intelligence, and some have average intelligence. Some children have difficulty in learning to do certain tasks (for example, reading, drawing or arithmetic). Because a particular part of the brain is affected, it is termed a 'specific learning difficulty' and should not be confused with the child's general intelligence.

Care of children with cerebral palsy

There is no cure for cerebral palsy. It is a non-progressive condition; this means that it does not become more severe as the child gets older, but some difficulties may become more noticeable.

Therapy can help children with cerebral palsy. Physiotherapists, occupational therapists and speech therapists often work very closely together to devise a treatment programme that will meet the needs of both the child and the family. As the nature of cerebral palsy varies immensely, the therapy is adapted to the needs of the individual child.

Research activity

Find out more about cerebral palsy at www.scope.org.uk or search online for SCOPE.

Blindness and partial sight (visual impairment)

The picture of total darkness conjured up by the word 'blindness' is inaccurate: only about 18 per cent of blind people in the UK are affected to this degree; the other 82 per cent all have some remaining sight. In the UK, there are just over one million blind and partially-sighted people, of whom 40 per cent are blind and 60 per cent are partially sighted (or have a visual impairment).

Causes of visual impairment

The main causes of visual impairment in children are:

- abnormalities of the eyes from birth, such as cataracts (cloudiness of the lens)
- nystagmus (involuntary jerkiness of the eyes)
- optic atrophy (damage to the optic nerve)
- retinopathy of prematurity (abnormal development of retinas in premature babies)
- hereditary factors such as retinoblastoma, a tumour of the retina which is often inherited.

Childhood glaucoma and diabetic retinopathy are quite rare in children, but are common causes of visual impairment in adults.

Treatment of visual impairment

Some conditions that cause visual impairment are treatable, particularly if detected at an early stage; for example:

- glaucoma can be halted by medical or surgical means
- a cataract may be removed by removal of the lens
- laser therapy is also now being used to correct various visual defects.

The impact of visual impairment on children's development

Impaired vision from birth or in early childhood can have a profound impact on a baby's or child's development. It has the potential to restrict participation in social, physical and educational opportunities.

Development of all the senses

Encourage exploration of materials by touch, smell and taste, allowing for plenty of time. Listening is especially important for a child with a visual impairment as a way of finding out what is going on. Babies and toddlers may seem still and uninterested, when in reality they are listening out for every sound. Remember to communicate the warmth that you would convey with a smile, with a warm tone of voice, and when the child smiles, show your warmth through words or touch.

Language development

A lot of language development ordinarily depends on being able to see. Children see objects and hear the names of objects in daily life. You can help a visually impaired baby or child by naming items every time the child uses or explores them. This might include clothes, bottles, cups, cutlery and toys. But remember that all children need uninterrupted time to play and explore – do not overwhelm the child with words. Finger and other action rhymes are a fun way to associate movements and body parts with words. Story tapes with interesting sound effects can be a good way into stories.

Exploratory play

Touching and feeling objects can be scary. Encourage and soothe the child. You can introduce messy play with tiny dabs of substances, first on fingertips, and slowly building up until you judge the child is ready to dip a finger into the wet sand or shaving foam.

Physical play

Encourage movement: it is important to create good open spaces for babies to crawl and toddle in. Older children need opportunities to move freely inside and outside.

Visual development

Encourage looking: nearly all babies and young children with a visual impairment have *some* sight. Shiny and sparkly objects and light toys can be used to stimulate the child's vision. Hold things close to the child in good light and give plenty of time. Children's eyes will not be damaged by sitting close up to computers and televisions.

Developing independence

Starting to eat solid foods is an important part of a child's development, but it is frustrating too – and all the more so for a child with a visual impairment. It is good to allow plenty of time for the child to 'feel' food and not to worry too much about mess. A bowl or plate resting on a non-slip mat is helpful, as it is difficult to manage when things keep moving around. You will need to judge the balance between allowing for experimentation and exploration, and the need for the child to eat something without becoming too frustrated.

Support within the setting

In early years settings, good natural lighting, without too much glaring artificial light, makes for the best possible environment. Well-ordered and uncluttered storage systems, and plenty of space in areas for play will help the child with a visual impairment to get used to where things are and operate more independently. These approaches will also help all children to find the setting or school an ordered and relaxing environment.

The Royal National Institute of Blind People (RNIB) has produced an excellent booklet, *Focus on Foundation*, which offers practical advice on the inclusion in early years settings of children who are blind and partially sighted.

Education for children with visual impairment

More than 55 per cent of visually impaired children in education attend mainstream schools along with sighted children. Most will have a Statement of Special Education Needs (see p 492) which details the support and special equipment they need.

Case study

Mothers' response to blind babies

Research by Selma Fraiberg from 1974 to 1977 showed that blind babies begin to smile at about the same age as sighted babies (roughly four weeks), but that they smile less often. The blind infant's smile is also less intense and more fleeting than the sighted baby's smile. In addition, blind babies do not enter into a mutual gaze, which is an important factor in the formation of a deep attachment or bond between parents and their baby. Fraiberg's research found that most mothers of blind babies gradually withdrew from their infants. They needed help in learning to 'read' their baby's other signals, such as body movements and gestures. This help led to an improved interaction between mothers and their babies.

Activity

Promoting an awareness of visual impairment

Tutors or learners (or both) may wish to send away for copies of the booklet produced by the RNIB (see Useful resources, p 503) to enable them to carry out the first of the following activities.

Arranged into groups, your task is to plan and mount a display on 'Children with visual impairment'. Using the booklets as a guide, each small group should plan and mount a display on one of the following topics:

- developing the senses
- establishing routines

- movement games
- play and toys.

When the displays are up, the groups should evaluate each other's displays, using a set of criteria agreed beforehand: is the information presented in an easy-to-understand format? Does the material used illustrate the points effectively?

Try to contact a local group of parents of visually impaired children, and invite them to view the display. Health visitors or social services departments may be able to make the first contact for you here.

Deafness and partial hearing (hearing impairment)

Deafness is often called 'the hidden disability' as it may not be outwardly apparent that a person is deaf. As with total blindness, total deafness is rare and is usually congenital (present from birth). Partial deafness is generally the result of an ear disease, injury or degeneration associated with the ageing process.

There are two types of hearing loss:

- **conductive**: when there is faulty transmission of sound from the outer ear to the inner ear
- **sensori-neural**: when sounds that do reach the inner ear fail to be transmitted to the brain (often referred to as 'nerve' deafness).

Causes of conductive hearing loss

The most common causes of this kind of deafness in children are:

- **otitis media**: infection of the middle ear
- **glue ear**: a build-up of sticky fluid in the middle ear, usually affecting children under eight years.

Causes of sensori-neural hearing loss

Common causes of sensori-neural hearing loss are:

- **heredity**: there may be an inherited fault in a chromosome
- **birth injury**: this may cause nerve or brain damage
- **severe jaundice**: in the newborn baby with severe jaundice, there may be damage to the inner ear
- **rubella**: there may be damage to the developing foetus if the mother is infected with the rubella (German measles) virus during pregnancy

- **Ménière's disease**: this is a rare disorder in which deafness, vertigo and tinnitus result from an accumulation of fluid within the labyrinth in the inner ear
- **damage to the cochlea or labyrinth (or both)**: this can result from an injury, viral infection or prolonged exposure to loud noise.

Diagnosis of hearing impairment

Hearing tests are performed as part of a routine assessment of child development. The early detection of any hearing defect is vital in order that the best possible help can be offered at the time when development is at its fastest. Go to Unit 1.6 for more information on hearing impairments.

Treatment of hearing impairment

For conductive hearing loss, treatment is usually a hearing aid while they are waiting to be admitted to hospital for corrective surgery.

For sensori-neural hearing loss, treatment is also a hearing aid, but also special training, for example in language acquisition, speech therapy or perceptual motor training. A bilingual approach using British Sign Language (BSL) and verbal speech is often recommended.

Hearing aids

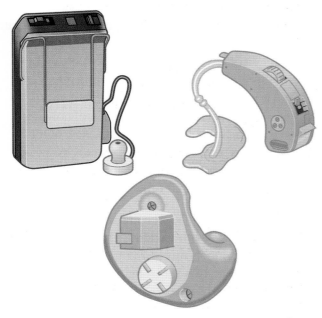

Figure 3.13.1 Different types of hearing aid

There are three types of hearing aid (see Figure 3.13.1):

1 **A body-worn hearing aid**: this is often strapped to the child's waist, with a wire connecting it to the earpiece. This type of aid is used for profound hearing loss as it enables greater amplification of sound than in the smaller devices.
2 **A post-aural hearing aid**: this fits comfortably behind the ear, and can be used even with small babies.
3 **An in-the-ear hearing aid**: this is generally reserved for use with older children.

The aim of all hearing aids is to amplify sounds. In children whose hearing is not helped by such aids, a cochlear implant may be considered instead.

The impact of hearing impairment on children's development

- **Communication**: if possible, children should learn to express themselves through a recognisable speech pattern (language acquisition). **Isolation** may result from the deaf child's inability to hear the familiar voices and household noises that a hearing child takes for granted.
- **A lack of auditory stimulation**: this may lead to delayed development.
- **A potential for injury**: this is related to a failure to detect warning sounds, such as traffic or warning shouts.
- **Anxiety and coping difficulties**: this is related to reduced social interaction and loneliness.
- **Parental anxiety**: this is related to having a child with impaired hearing.

> ### Discussion point
>
> #### A hearing problem
> Carla, a baby of 15 months, has just been diagnosed with a severe hearing impairment. When she has her nappy changed, Mary, the baby room supervisor, notices that Laura, one of the early years practitioners, changes her nappy in silence, although she always smiles, chats and plays with the other babies during nappy-changing routines. When Mary asked her why she does not do the same with Carla, Laura replied that she did not see the point because Carla cannot hear anything.
>
> 1 Why is Mary concerned about Laura's childcare practice?
> 2 Discuss ways in which practitioners could promote Carla's development and meet her holistic needs.

Guidelines for working with children with a hearing impairment

- A baby with a hearing impairment may not show the 'startle' reaction or reflex to a loud noise which is evident shortly after birth.
- A baby of about four months will visibly relax and smile at the sound of his or her mother's voice, even before he or she can see her. If the baby does not show this response, there may be some hearing loss.
- If babbling starts and then stops after a few weeks, this is often an indication of hearing loss.
- A child with hearing loss will be much more observant and visually aware than a hearing child – be aware that the child may respond to the ringing of doorbells and telephones by reading the body language of those around them and reacting appropriately.
- Toys that make a lot of noise are still popular, because children can feel the vibration, even if they cannot hear the sound. Dancing to music is also popular for the same reason.
- A child with a profound hearing loss may still react quite normally, even turning round in response to someone's approach, since they may be using their other senses to compensate for the loss of hearing – for example, they may notice a smell of perfume, or see the reflection of the person in a window or other reflective surface.

Autism/autistic spectrum disorder

Autism is a disability that disrupts the development of social interaction and communication. Children are affected in many different ways by autism, which is why we use the term 'autistic spectrum'. The most seriously affected children have profound learning disabilities and delayed language, and will need intensive support and care. At the other end of the spectrum, children with Asperger's syndrome may manage the intellectual demands of schooling very well, although they will still find aspects of social interaction and communication difficult.

Causes of autism

Research suggests that there is no single cause, but that there may be a physical problem affecting those parts of the brain that integrate language and information from the senses. The condition is *not* caused by emotional problems in families or emotional deprivation. The onset of autism is almost always before the age of three years. It affects four times as many boys as girls.

The impact of autistic spectrum disorder on children's development

The degree to which children with an autistic spectrum disorder are affected varies, but all those affected have what is known as the 'triad of impairments' or the 'three impairments'. The Early Support guide to autistic spectrum disorders describes these as follows:

- **Social interaction** – difficulty understanding social 'rules', behaviour and relationships; for example, appearing indifferent to other people or not understanding how to take turns.
- **Social communication** – difficulty with verbal and non-verbal communication; for example, not fully understanding the meaning of common gestures, facial expressions or tone of voice.
- **Rigidity of thinking and difficulties with social imagination** – difficulty in the development of interpersonal play and imagination; for example, having a limited range of imaginative activities, possibly copied and pursued rigidly and repetitively.

Working with a child who has an autistic spectrum disorder

There is a great deal of controversy about the different interventions that may help a child with an autistic spectrum disorder (ASD), ranging from behavioural interventions to dietary and medical programmes. It is not advisable to attempt to implement any approach without careful consideration of how well it would suit a particular child, and a review of the independent research evidence for its effectiveness. The best starting point for information is the National Autistic Society (www.nas.org.uk).

However, there is wide agreement that early years settings and schools can be difficult places for children with an ASD. A lot of early learning is based on language and play, two areas of great difficulty for a child with an ASD. The noise and amount of visual stimulation from displays and boxes of equipment can quickly become overwhelming. In this context, a

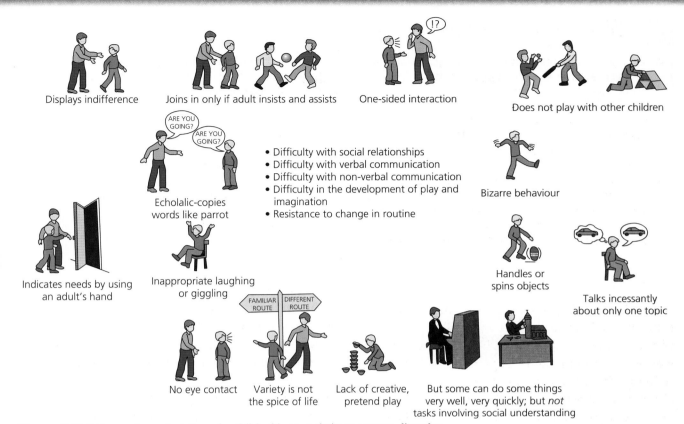

Figure 3.13.2 Some characteristics of a child with an autistic spectrum disorder

child with an ASD might gain some feeling of security by rigidly following the same sequences of activity, or repeating the same action over again. While it is important not to deprive a child under stress of actions that provide some comfort, constant repetition is not the basis for successful development and learning, and the child will need skilled and sensitive support to interact with others and to extend his or her interests.

Guidelines: how you can help a child with an autistic spectrum disorder

- **Visual learning is stronger than language-based learning or learning through exploratory play** – putting things into symbols really helps children with an ASD. A visual timetable, showing the main sequence of events and routines in the day, can help the child to understand what is going to happen next. Symbols that the child can pick up or point to, in order to make choices and express preferences, will aid early communication.
- **Reduce visual stimulation** – keep displays and labels orderly: pictures all over the windows and labels at jaunty angles can be visually overwhelming. Have some places with blank walls, which can be calming.
- **Keep everything as clear and consistent as you can** – while for most children a sudden announcement of a trip or a special activity is fun, for many children with an ASD such changes in routine are very scary. As far as possible, keep routines consistent and alert

the child when something is about to happen by using symbols or the visual timetable. When something new is coming up, try to prepare the child as much as you can. You might have a symbol that means 'a change', or be able to use a photograph to signal what is going to happen. Use as few words and as few symbols as possible: communicate clearly and briefly.
- **Show how things work** – a child with an ASD can be helped when adults show, step by step, how to put Lego® bricks together, or model pretending to eat in the home corner. Allow plenty of time and encourage the child to copy.
- **Introduce new things slowly** – sensory play can be very difficult. Start with just a very brief attempt, and introduce materials in small amounts in areas of low distraction. To encourage sand play, for example, start in a quiet zone, without any children, and encourage the child to touch a small amount of sand on a table top or on the floor.

AC 1.3 Analyse the impact of environmental factors on children's development

There are a number of environmental factors – apart from the conditions described above – which can affect a child's ability to learn, including the following:

- **emotional**: the effects of trauma, such as bereavement or abuse
- **the wider environment**: the effects of poverty, lack of stimulation, poor provision for play
- **cultural**: different cultural expectations and experience
- **social**: lack of a stable relationship with adults, poor role models.

Each of these factors may prevent or delay a child's development; for example, lack of stimulation will prevent the child from experiencing early learning activities, which help in the development of concepts.

Loss and separation

There are many ways in which children and young people can experience loss and separation. Refugee children arriving in the UK, for example, face huge disruption to their lives and are usually separated from their wider family members and their familiar cultural context. Children of parents who are separated or divorced also face temporary upheaval. Bereavement is one extreme form of loss, especially if the child's parent dies. How children respond to the death of an important person in their life depends on a number of factors:

- their age and stage of development and consequently their understanding of death
- the nature of their relationship with the person who has died
- the circumstances of the death
- the reaction of other family members to the death

- the overall effect on the family unit
- their culture and family's spiritual beliefs
- their self-esteem and feelings of self-worth.

Children's reactions can vary from deep despair to denial or active protest. Whatever their reaction, it is important that they are allowed to express their feelings without being stopped or urged to 'be brave'. Children suffering bereavement through violent death (for example, murder or suicide) are more likely to need specialist professional help, both at the time of the death and also in the years to come, as they mature and reflect on the death and why it happened.

Normal signs of grief in young children include:

- bedwetting
- loss of appetite
- tummy upsets
- restlessness
- disturbed sleep
- nightmares
- crying: a tendency to tears at the least little thing, over a number of weeks
- attention-seeking behaviour
- increased anxiety and clinginess
- difficulty in concentrating.

These only become a cause for concern when they persist over a prolonged period of time.

Normal signs of grief in older children include:

- changes in personality – some may experience a depressed mood
- mood swings
- rudeness
- learning difficulties
- lack of concentration
- refusal to go to school
- sleep and appetite disturbances
- poor schoolwork – although other children will throw themselves into their schoolwork and end up by overworking.

These changes may not occur immediately after the bereavement, but could show themselves months or even years after the event. Children return to grief at different stages of their development. Teachers and early years practitioners need to be aware of the date when the death occurred and be sensitive by not avoiding the reality of the special days which may be difficult for the child. These include the anniversary of the death, Father's Day or Mother's Day, Christmas and birthdays.

The Child Bereavement Trust (a charity) has a training programme for primary, secondary and special schools. The courses are designed to provide managers, teachers and support staff with information and resources to enable them to better understand how to support pupils experiencing a loss. Guidance is given on introducing the subject into the classroom.

The emotional and social impact of illness on children's ability to learn

Any child with an illness or disability may have a problem in developing a positive self-concept. Children need to feel confident and successful in order to learn effectively. Children's **self-esteem** may be adversely affected because they:

- **feel different from others**: they may notice that they are different from their peers; their siblings may resent them, seeing them as the brother or sister child who is spoilt or never punished
- **are overprotected**: parents who try to cocoon their child can find that this is counterproductive. Children need to be equipped for life and can only learn by making mistakes
- **lack freedom of choice**: parents may take freedom of choice away from the child (for example in trying new activities), thereby disempowering them
- **miss out on social opportunities**: friendships may be affected as parents often dictate where and with whom the child plays. In this way, they are depriving them of an opportunity for valuable social learning
- **may be bullied**: differences are often seen as weaknesses by other children, who might tease or reject the child.

Deprivation and abuse

As we have seen in Unit 2.2, there are many forms of child abuse and neglect. All such deprivation will affect the child's ability to learn and form relationships with adults and other children.

Physically abused children may be:

- watchful, cautious or wary of adults
- unable to play and be spontaneous
- bullying other children or being bullied themselves
- unable to concentrate, underachieving at school and avoiding activities that involve removal of clothes (such as sports).

Emotionally abused or neglected children may:

- be slow to learn to walk and talk
- find it hard to develop close relationships
- get on badly with other children of the same age
- be unable to play imaginatively
- think badly of themselves and have low self-esteem
- be easily distracted and underachieve at school.

Medical conditions

Some medical conditions can affect children's learning. The child's condition may cause him to become quickly tired, or may lead to frequent absences for treatment. Examples of this include childhood leukaemia or chronic lung disease. Other medical conditions, like asthma or diabetes, may be adequately managed by taking medication and do not need to cause significant interference in the child's development and learning.

AC 1.4 and AC 1.5 Analyse impact of the stage of development on children's learning and Describe factors which affect children's development in the short term and the long term

The stage of development reached by an individual will have an effect on their holistic development. Look again at the normative sequence and stages of development in Units 3.9, 3.10, 3.11 and 3.12, and analyse the impact this might have on children's learning. Additional support needs may be of short duration, perhaps a few weeks or months, or could be long term over a number of years. The factors which may give rise to additional support needs are wide and varied because they relate to the circumstances of individual children, and an individual may have additional support needs arising from more than one of the factors listed below.

Short-term needs

A child may need additional support in the short term – that is, has a temporary additional need – because he or she:

- is being bullied or is bullying
- has sustained an injury or illness requiring hospitalisation
- is temporarily hearing impaired – for example, has 'glue ear' or recurrent ear infections
- is highly able – or gifted – and may not be challenged sufficiently
- has specific reading or writing problems and may not be receiving the appropriate support
- is bereaved
- has a home life disrupted by poverty, homelessness, domestic abuse, parental alcohol or drug misuse, or parental mental or physical health problems
- is looked after by a local authority.

The same factor may have different impacts on individual learning. For example, one child may find that difficulties at home have an adverse impact upon his or her learning. Another child in apparently similar circumstances may experience a minimal impact on his or her learning.

Long-term needs

A child may need additional support in the long term because he or she has:

- a disability caused by a genetic/chromosomal defect, e.g. Down's syndrome
- a physical disability: difficulty with movement – e.g. cerebral palsy
- a visual or hearing impairment
- a specific language impairment
- autistic spectrum disorder
- learning or attention difficulties, such as attention deficit hyperactivity disorder (ADHD)
- a chronic or a debilitating illness.

LO2 Understand how personal experiences, values and beliefs impact on the role of the EYP

AC 2.1 Analyse how personal experiences, values and beliefs impact on the professional practice of the EYP

Your own personal experiences, values and beliefs impact on your work with young children and their parents.

Your attitudes, values and behaviour should demonstrate your commitment to diversity, inclusion and participation. You need to be able to think clearly and fairly about issues related to diversity, inclusion and participation. This will enable you to care for young children with due attention to their *individual needs* as well as promoting their development and early learning in ways which open up opportunities for their future. It is important to be aware of the effect that your use of language can have on others:

- The words you use to express yourself affect the development of your own attitudes, values and behaviour.
- The language you use shapes the way you think and may lead you to distorted or limited opinions. Language reflects and influences how you think about yourself and others.
- Language can reinforce the development of stereotyped and prejudiced ideas, or it can help you to think more constructively and treat others respectfully. See also Unit 2.4 (AC 4.3). Evaluate the impact of own attitudes, values and behaviour when supporting equality, diversity and inclusive practice.

LO3 Understand the principles of inclusive practice

The principles of inclusive practice

Inclusive practice is a term used within education to describe the process of ensuring equality of learning opportunities for all children and young people, whatever their disabilities or disadvantages. This means that all children have the right to have their needs met in the best way for them. They are seen as being part of the community, even if they need particular help to live a full life within the community. So, while integration is about bringing people who are different together, inclusion is about providing the support that is needed to enable different people to be together in a community. Despite the moves towards inclusion, there are arguments for keeping a minority of children in special schools.

Inclusion is about the child's right to:

- attend the local mainstream setting
- be valued as an individual
- be provided with all the support needed to thrive in a mainstream setting.

Inclusive provision should be seen as an extension of the early years setting's equal opportunities policy and practice. It requires a commitment from the entire staff, parents and children, to include the full diversity of children in the local community. This may require planned restructuring of the whole childcare environment to ensure equality of access.

Discussion point

Excluded from an outing

The nursery manager at a private nursery explains to a child's parents that their son, Thomas, will not be able to join the rest of his group on a visit to a local children's theatre production of 'The Gruffalo's Child'. Thomas has Down's syndrome and learning difficulties. The nursery staff had met to discuss the problem and had concluded that there was no point in Thomas going as he would not appreciate the show and would probably disrupt the other children. Thomas' mother is very unhappy with their decision and has accused the nursery of discriminating against Thomas on account of his disability.

Discuss the following questions in a group:

- Do you think the nursery staff were justified in their decision?
- What could the nursery staff have done in order to enable Thomas to join the others?
- Do you believe the nursery has discriminated against Thomas?

Key term

inclusion 'a process of identifying, understanding and breaking down barriers to participation and belonging' (Early Childhood Forum).

AC 3.1 Identify the requirements of current legislation in relation to inclusive practice

With reference to inclusive practice, the EYFS (2012) framework makes it clear that all providers have a responsibility:

to ensure that diversity of individuals and communities is valued and respected and that no child or family is discriminated against. Settings need to provide individualised opportunities based on each child's needs, particularly those related to ethnicity, language and disability.

Current legislation in relation to inclusive practice is discussed in Unit 2.4.

AC 3.2 Explain the medical and social models of disability

The difference between the social model and medical model of disability

The **medical model of disability** sees people with disabilities as having the problem. Disabled people have to adapt to fit into the world as it is. If this is not possible, then they are excluded in specialised institutions or isolated in their homes. The medical model of disability emphasises the person's impairment and provides support for stereotypical views of disability that evoke pity, fear and patronising attitudes towards disabled people. The medical model creates a cycle of dependency and exclusion. In addition, the design of the physical environment (e.g. play, leisure, school and work facilities) presents disabled people with many barriers, making it very difficult or sometimes impossible for their needs to be met, and limiting their day-to-day activities.

The **social model of disability** views the barriers that prevent disabled people from participating in any situation as what disables them. The social model suggests that disabled people are individually and collectively disadvantaged by a complex form of institutional discrimination as fundamental to our society as sexism and racism. Disabled people are often made to feel that it is their fault that they are different. The only difference is that they have an impairment that limits their physical, mental or sensory functions. Restructuring physical environments and accepting people with disabilities for who they are without fear, ignorance and prejudice benefit everyone.

Medical model thinking	Social model thinking
Child or young person is faulty	Child or young person is valued
Diagnosis	Strengths and needs defined by self and others
Labelling	Identify barriers and develop solutions
Impairment becomes focus of attention	Outcome-based programme design
Assessment, monitoring, programmes of therapy imposed	Resources are made available to ordinary services
Segregation and alternative services	Training for parents and professionals
Ordinary needs are put on hold	Relationships nurtured
Re-entry if normal enough *or* permanent exclusion	Diversity welcomed: child is included
Society remains unchanged	Society evolves

Table 3.13.2 The differences between the medical and social models of disability (from Disability Equality in Education website)

The human rights model

The human rights model of disability can be seen as the most recent development of the social model. It states that:

- All human beings are equal and have rights that should be respected without distinction of any kind.

- People with disabilities are citizens and, as such, have the same rights as those without impairments.
- All actions to support people with disabilities should be 'rights based'; for example, the demand for equal access to services and opportunities as a human right.

The human rights model is similar to the social model, as it places responsibility for addressing the problems of disability on society rather than on the person with disabilities.

AC 3.3 Evaluate inclusive practice in relation to current frameworks for children from birth to 7 years

For inclusive practice to be successful, the child, parents and family must be at the centre of the processes, practices and decision-making. Early years settings should be creating their services around the needs of those they serve. For example, by:

- involving parents and carers in policy and procedure decisions
- finding out from parents and other users of the setting what their needs are, and developing services around these
- personalising learning through building on individual children's interests, skills and strengths.

As an early years practitioner, you should know how to judge whether the setting is inclusive and supportive of diversity. You should be able to demonstrate that you support inclusion and diversity through your words, actions and behaviours in the setting. You must know and understand the importance of promoting the setting to children who may experience barriers to participation, e.g. children with disabilities or those from other minority groups. Inclusion is about the child's right to:

- attend the local mainstream setting
- be valued as an individual
- be provided with all the support needed to thrive in a mainstream setting.

Inclusive provision should be seen as an extension of the setting's equal opportunities policy and practice. It requires a commitment from the entire staff, parents and children to include the full diversity of children in the local community. This may require planned restructuring of the whole childcare environment to ensure equality of access.

Kidsactive defines inclusive provision as:

provision that is open and accessible to all, and takes positive steps in removing disabling barriers, so that disabled and non-disabled people can participate.

(Douch, 2006)

The following inclusion indicators may help you to identify whether inclusion is being put into practice in your setting.

Inclusion indicators

1 Visitors can see:
   - nobody makes a fuss about the presence of disabled children
   - activities are designed around the interests and enthusiasms of all children who attend and with regard to any dislikes or impairments they may have
   - each person, adult or child, is welcomed on arrival
   - all children, including disabled children, have choices and are able to exercise those choices.

2 The leader/manager:
   - has sought out families, schools and services for disabled children and built links to promote the involvement of disabled children
   - runs regular staff meetings designed to enable staff to reflect on their practice together and develop good future practice
   - can identify action taken and progress made towards inclusion, and also the things he or she still needs and plans to do to make the setting more inclusive.

3 The staff:
   - have received disability equality training and/or attitudinal training and continue to undertake other training relating to inclusion
   - feel that they are consulted and informed by the leader/manager.

4 Disabled and non-disabled children:
   - report being involved in making rules/policies or 'having a say in what goes on'
   - say they are generally happy with the setting.

5 Parents of disabled and non-disabled children:
   - feel welcome and valued
   - say they are consulted about how best to meet their children's needs.

6 Policies and paperwork indicate that:
   - a commitment to inclusion is explicit in public and internal documentation
   - staff that have particular support roles with individual disabled children are full members of the team and have job descriptions which stress the inclusion of the child, rather than just one-to-one support.

(Douch, 2006)

LO4 Understand the role of early intervention in partnership working

AC 4.1 Identify children's additional needs in relation to expected stages of development

Your role includes enabling children with additional needs to gain access to age- and developmentally appropriate learning, play or leisure opportunities. Time, commitment and good communication skills are essential to engaging with disabled children. You need to spend time with both the child and family to gain their trust and build their relationship within the setting. You can demonstrate your engagement with disabled children in the following ways:

- Liaising with the child/family to understand the child's particular requirements for accessing the setting, e.g. home visits, talking with the child/family about their needs.
- Work with colleagues and the child/family to identify how best to meet those requirements from the beginning, e.g. establishing links with key person, induction programme.
- Ensure the setting recognises and develops its existing good practice as the basis for welcoming any child, e.g. all staff have disability awareness and/or inclusion training.

- Show the child and family how the setting is able to meet the needs of children, e.g. disabled access, specialist equipment, individual programmes.
- Identify any additional resources required to meet the child's needs, and work with the family to obtain these resources, e.g. medical interventions, recruitment of additional staff, loan or purchase of equipment, sign language or inclusion training.

When trying to identify children's additional needs, you will be expected to have an understanding of the normative stages of development. You will not be expected to offer a diagnosis or a prediction! The main reason for being able to identify the additional needs of children is to be able to provide the resources – both in terms of staff and equipment – to meet those needs.

AC 4.2 Describe the reasons for early intervention when meeting children's additional needs

The range of additional needs is enormous, from severe to relatively minor, from temporary or short-lived to permanent. Young children with a disability will often arrive in an early years setting or school with difficulties that have not yet been understood or assessed. Sometimes parents have not noticed the difficulties, but it is more usual that there is a general anxiety or sense that all is not well with the child.

Where factors that impact on a child's ability to learn and to develop are just starting to become apparent, partnership working involving all the adults in a child's life becomes very important. The earlier a need for additional support is identified, the more likely it is that early intervention can prevent certain aspects of a child's development or behaviour developing into a persistent difficulty.

Parents and carers find that getting a diagnosis for their child is important. Being given a name for their child's condition or special need enables them to discuss their child's development needs with health, social services and education professionals. Getting information about what they and their children are entitled to, as early as possible, is very important. This applies to the benefits they are entitled to as well as the services.

Early years practitioners need to actively seek out information about a possible underlying disability. When you have worked with many children in a particular age group, your experience will help you to notice those children who appear to have specific difficulties which lie outside the range of ordinary child development. By working closely with the parents and other specialist professionals, you may be able to help identify that a child has a disability. The early support that can follow early identification can make a real difference to a child's well-being, quality of life, and later achievement and enjoyment in school.

AC 4.3 Explain strategies for early intervention

The assessment process

In the UK about 17 per cent of all schoolchildren have a special educational need. Most (around 60 per cent) are taught in **mainstream** schools, where they receive additional help from a range of services. Children with special educational needs but *without* a statement will have their needs met through Early Years Action or Early Years Action Plus. (When children reach school age these are called School Action and School Action Plus.)

The framework in England that enables assessment to be carried out of the development and progress of all young children is the EYFS. As we have seen in earlier chapters, the EYFS focuses on seven areas of learning and development:

- personal, social and emotional development
- physical development
- communication and language
- literacy
- mathematics
- understanding the world
- expressive arts and design.

Practitioners help to assess each child's development using the EYFS Profile.

The Statement of Special Educational Needs

The Statement of Special Educational Needs is a legal document produced by LEAs following multi-professional assessment and contributions from parents or carers. It specifies the precise nature of the child's assessed difficulties and educational needs, and the special or additional provision that should be made in order to meet that pupil's needs. Statements must then be reviewed at least annually.

An assessment must take account of the following five factors:

1 **Physical factors**: the child's particular illness or condition.
2 **Psychological and emotional factors**: the child's intellectual ability and levels of anxiety or depression will lead to different needs and priorities (for example, severe anxiety may adversely affect all daily activities, and its alleviation will therefore assume top priority).
3 **Socio-cultural factors**: whether or not the child is part of a family, the family's background and the relationships within the family will all influence needs. Similarly, the individual's wider community and the social class to which they belong are also influential.
4 **Environmental factors**: a child living in a cold, damp house with an outside toilet will have different needs from someone who is more comfortably housed.
5 **Political and economic factors**: poverty or belonging to a disadvantaged group leads to reduced choice in day-to-day living.

The Early Support programme: for babies and young children under five

Early Support is an integral part of the delivery of the EYFS for babies and young children under five with disabilities or emerging special educational needs. It helps staff in early years settings to identify impairments early and to work in partnership with families and other services to provide the best possible care and support for young disabled children. An important part of the Early Support programme is the **Family File**, which the family holds. The Family File:

- is used by the professionals and the family together, to plan appropriate support to be provided for the child
- informs the family about the different professionals they may meet and what their role is

- explains how the different health, education and social services can provide support
- allows parents and carers to share information about their child with the professionals they meet, without having to say the same things to every new person
- provides information about sources of financial support and childcare.

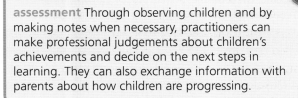

Key term

assessment Through observing children and by making notes when necessary, practitioners can make professional judgements about children's achievements and decide on the next steps in learning. They can also exchange information with parents about how children are progressing.

Common Assessment Framework (CAF)

The Common Assessment Framework was introduced in 2005 as an assessment tool that can be used by the children's workforce to assess the additional needs of children and young people at the first signs of difficulties. See Unit 2.5 for more details on the CAF.

Individual Education Plans

Every child with special educational needs should have an Individual Education Plan (IEP) (see Table 3.13.3 on page 495). The IEP's purpose is to detail the ways in which an individual child will be helped; for example:

- what special help is being given
- who will provide the help
- how often the child will receive the help
- targets for the child
- how and when the child's progress will be checked
- what help parents can give their child at home.

The child's teacher is responsible for the planning and should discuss the IEP with the parents or carers and with their child, whenever possible. IEPs are usually linked to the main areas of language, literacy, mathematics and behaviour and social skills. Sometimes the school or early years setting will not write an IEP but will record how they are meeting the child's needs in a different way, perhaps as part of the whole-class lesson plans. They will record the child's progress in the same way as they do for all the other children.

In addition, practitioners should:

- assess how accessible the setting is for children who use wheelchairs or walking frames, or who are learning English as an additional language, and take appropriate action to include a wider range of children
- work together with professionals from other agencies, such as local and community health services, to provide the best learning opportunities for individual children.

Discussion point

IEPs set out targets which can be described as SMART (Specific, Measurable, Achievable, Relevant, Time-limited). Here is an example of a SMART IEP target:

Here is an example of a target which is *not* SMART: 'For all staff to help James to improve his language.'

Target	Who will support	When and for how long?	Review
For James to use 4 Makaton signs while playing: hello, me, yes, no.	Vicky to model every day. All staff to use these signs with James. Teach all children the signs at group time.	Vicky to plan a 5-minute play session every morning. All staff throughout the session. James's parents to organise 5 minutes playing time every day at home with just James, using the signs.	6 weeks: evidence that James can use the signs in 5-minute sessions with Vicky. Evidence he uses the signs freely with other children.

In a small group, or with another learner, look at the following targets. Which targets do you think are SMART, and why?

- To help James to play in the sand.
- To help James to lift both feet off the ground with a daily 10-minute trampoline session.
- To encourage James's familiarity with other children by pointing to a photo card of each child in turn at group time and saying their names.

- To encourage James to play for one minute with messy materials, by providing a daily five-minute session using wet sand, play dough or paint.
- Stop James from pushing and hitting other children by teaching him the Makaton for 'no' and 'me'.

In practice activity

Outline your setting's procedures for ensuring that IEPs for children are in place and regularly reviewed. Provide examples of the relevant forms: IEP review sheets for child's comments, parents' comments and staff comments. Remember confidentiality.

AC 4.4 Evaluate the principles of working in partnership with others to meet children's additional needs

The principles of working in partnership with other agencies and professionals

In addition to liaising with parents, you will also need to liaise with other professionals regarding disabled children and those with specific requirements, as well as providing effective support for colleagues in the setting (see below). You may be involved in coordinating a network of relationships between staff at the setting and other professionals from external agencies, such as:

- **Local education authority**, e.g. educational psychologist, special needs support teachers, special needs advisers, specialist teachers, Portage workers, education welfare officers.
- **Health services**, e.g. paediatricians, health visitors, physiotherapists, occupational therapists, speech and language therapists, play therapists, school nurses, clinical psychologists.
- **Social services department**, e.g. social workers specialist social workers: sensory disabilities, physical disabilities, mental health or children and families.

Individual Education Plan: Autumn Term 2014		
Name: Lucas	Year Group: 1	Pastoral Teacher: Maggie Conran
Targets to be achieved by: Feb 2015	Method/resources	Outcome (tick best descriptor) Date:
Independence: for L to collect milk from the fridge and come back without needing an adult to shadow him.	Give L this job frequently. Begin with shadowing him and gradually reduce the support as he improves.	Achieved Ongoing Partially Not achieved
Communication: for L to use his communication book to request an activity he enjoys in the classroom, in addition to using it at snack times.	Provide L with photos of favoured activities in class. Introduce them to him and how to exchange them to receive the activity. Encourage L to get his book out of his drawer if he wants a specific activity.	Achieved Ongoing Partially Not achieved
Maths and CLL: to sort coloured objects into pots of the same colours (up to 3 colours).	Structured session with L in his chair (helps him focus). Model what is required and then encourage him to do the same. Plenty of repetition.	Achieved Ongoing Partially Not achieved
CLL: To select his own name from a choice of 2 in a variety of places, such as on a name card and on the whiteboard screen.	Frequent use of name card and name on other games etc., and contrast with longer/different names for him to choose from.	Achieved Ongoing Partially Not achieved
Physical: to stand up from the floor from a half kneel to standing, using support of a person or object.	Encourage L to stand in this way as often as possible. Model it and also encourage him to get to his knees before asking him to get up.	Achieved Ongoing Partially Not achieved
Parent's contribution: to help Lucas become more independent at home, e.g. fetching and pouring own drinks, and using his communication book to express his preferences.		
Parent's signature		Date
Teacher's signature		Date

Table 3.13.3 A sample IEP

- **Charities and voluntary organisations**, e.g. AFASIC, British Dyslexia Association, Council for Disabled Children, National Autistic Society, RNIB, RNID, SCOPE.

In practice activity

Describe how you work with other agencies to help families access specialist support.

Include information on how you exchange information with families and other agencies, such as keeping records of contacts and information in line with agreed policies and procedures, e.g. confidentiality and data protection procedures.

The roles and responsibilities of partners that are typically involved with disabled children and those with specific requirements

Statutory services include health, education and social services. A number of different services or agencies may work together to support children and their families. Support services provided by different statutory agencies should be carefully coordinated to meet the needs of children and families more effectively. Some areas already provide a single multi-agency service for young children and families which bring together health, education and social services, e.g. Children's Centres.

The **Right from the Start Template** is a working document designed to help professionals develop the policies, procedures and practice required to ensure that more families with disabled children receive a better service. The principles and good practice framework included in the Right from the Start Template are applicable to professionals working with all children in need, not just children with disabilities – see www.rightfromthestart.org.uk

The role of the key person or lead professional

The key person is a named professional who assists families in accessing information and support from specialist services. Sometimes the key person is known as the lead professional. In Team Around the Child approaches (see Figure 3.13.3), a professional with regular contact with the family takes on the role of key person or lead professional, as well as their existing responsibilities for supporting the family.

The core responsibilities of the lead professional are:

- Make sure the family have all the information they need and, where necessary, help families to understand and use the information received.
- Ensure that everyone (e.g. other agencies) has up-to-date information about the child and family.
- Coordinate assessment support and intervention.
- Ensure that a joint plan is formulated which keeps the family at the centre of decision-making and involves all the professionals and agencies in contact with the child.
- Facilitate the regular review and updating of support plans.
- Maintain regular contact with the family and, where appropriate, provide emotional support.

(DfES, 2001)

The Framework for the Assessment of Children in Need and their Families provides a systemic framework to help professionals identify children and young people in need and assess the best approach to help children in need and their families (see above).

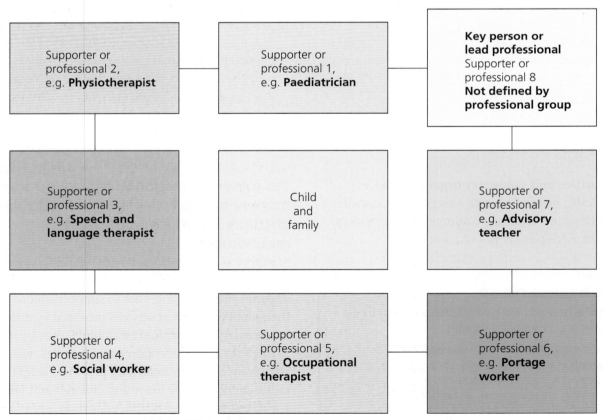

Figure 3.13.3 Team Around the Child approaches

Compile an information booklet which includes the following:

- Links with other professionals from external agencies established by your setting.
- A diagram which illustrates how you and your colleagues work with other professionals to provide effective support for disabled children and young people in your setting.
- Your role and responsibilities in liaising with other professionals to support disabled children and their parents.
- Where to obtain information about the roles of other professionals in the local area.

LO5 Support the additional needs of children

AC 5.1 Identify the individual needs of children in own setting

You need to know and understand the details about particular disabilities as they affect the children in your setting and your ability to provide a high-quality service. Children with disabilities and those with specific requirements in your setting may include children with:

- hearing impairment
- visual impairment
- physical disabilities
- behavioural difficulties
- emotional difficulties
- communication difficulties
- learning difficulties.

Some children may require additional support in the setting due to specific requirements such as additional sensory and/or physical needs, as a result of hearing, visual and/or physical impairment. As children with sensory or physical impairments may be dependent on others for some of their needs, it is essential to provide opportunities for them to be as independent as possible. Give them every chance to join in, to express opinions and to interact with their peer group. Remember to focus on each child as a unique person with individual strengths rather than focusing on the child's particular disabilities, e.g. what they can do rather than what they cannot.

Techniques for supporting the learning of children with additional needs

Many children with additional needs will have personal priority needs which are central to their learning and quality of life. Some children may need the provision of a specific therapy or may require paramedical care. Others need to have existing equipment or activities modified or adapted to suit their particular needs. This might involve:

- adapting standard equipment, for example by having a tray on the table so that objects stay on the table, so that a child with a visual impairment does not 'lose' objects that fall off
- providing the opportunity to learn sign languages, for example Makaton or PECS
- helping children to maintain good posture, appropriate muscle tone and ease of movement, and promoting skills in independent mobility
- helping children to manage eating and drinking; there is a wide range of specialist aids for eating and drinking, such as angled spoons and suction plates
- promoting relaxation and support to help children manage stress and anxiety; some settings use a sensory room, but a quiet, comfortable area will benefit all children
- providing palliative treatments for painful or degenerative conditions to ensure children's health and well-being
- promoting children's autonomy and independence through the use of specialist aids and equipment, for example non-slip table mats and specially designed cutlery for eating
- developing children's self-esteem (e.g. by encouraging and praising effort as well as achievement)
- allowing children's behaviour and alternative ways of communicating to be acknowledged and understood
- providing appropriate therapies, for example speech and language, occupational or physiotherapy. Support from health services is generally set out as non-educational provision in a child's statement, but speech and language therapy may be regarded as either educational or non-educational provision

- planning the use of music, art, drama or movement therapy: these therapies may play a complementary role in the curriculum for individual children and will need to be planned as part of the whole curriculum
- using specialist environments, for example ball pools, warm-water pools or light and sound stimulation rooms
- providing ramps for wheelchair users
- providing thick pencils and brushes for children with poor fine motor skills
- positioning children so that they learn effectively, for example by making sure the light falls on the adult's face, so that a child wearing a hearing aid is able to lip-read and a child with a visual impairment can use any residual eyesight to see facial expressions.

The use of a sensory curriculum for profound needs
The multisensory curriculum
All teachers differentiate the curriculum (that is, they provide different learning experiences) in order to meet the range of learning needs in their class. Children who are multisensory-impaired are likely

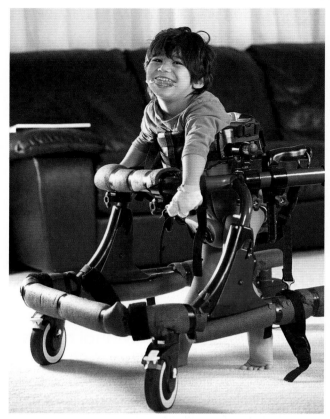

Figure 3.13.4 Using a walking frame or rollator

Case study

Providing for Holly's needs
When Holly, a partially sighted baby, joined the nursery, her key person, Simon, discussed her needs with her parents and contacted the RNIB for information about ways of supporting her development. Simon decided to plan a set of activities that could be used by Holly – and by sighted babies too – based on his research, which found that for profoundly blind and partially sighted babies it is important to:

1 Offer as wide a range of **tactile experiences** as possible right from the beginning. Simon started collecting tactile objects, such as:
  - a foil survival blanket to scrunch and reflect
  - a flat silky cushion containing polystyrene beads
  - pan scourer, lemon reamer, pasta strainer, dish-washing brush.
2 **Encourage movement**: helping babies to become aware of whole body movements and to learn to tolerate different positions, such as being placed on their stomach. Simon:

- provided some brightly lit and sound-producing toys to provide the motivation to roll and reach
- rearranged the nursery furniture to provide a logical sequence to support the baby when moving – and to help 'mental mapping' of her environment.
3 Encourage exploration of sound, rhythm and timing. Simon provided:
  - tactile nursery rhyme prompt cards: He made these using A4 cards and stuck on different fabrics to link touch to a particular song. For example, a piece of fur fabric stuck on card to make a link with 'Round and Round the Garden like a Teddy Bear', or a single shiny silver star stuck onto dark blue card to make a link with 'Twinkle, twinkle little star'
  - a handbell, rolling chime ball, musical xylophone and a drum.
4 Simon used some of the tactile objects in a treasure basket that could be enjoyed by all the babies in the setting.

to need the curriculum differentiated *individually*, because each child's combination of hearing impairment, visual impairment, other disabilities and learning characteristics will be different.

Some settings have a multisensory room which provides opportunities for children with a wide range of special needs. This room features a variety of lights, smells, sounds and touch sensations which help to stimulate each sense. Staff need to be trained in the use of a sensory room so that it works optimally for each child.

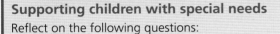

Reflective practice

Supporting children with special needs

Reflect on the following questions:

- How well does your setting provide for the special needs of children?
- Is there effective communication between the child's parents or carers and the setting?
- Do the play experiences and activities avoid stereotyping and ensure that each child has an equal opportunity to take part in activities?

AC 5.2 Plan activities in partnership with others to meet children's additional needs

When working with children, you should maintain a balance between flexibility and consistency in your approach to time allocation to ensure that the needs of individual children are met. An **individual support plan** will ensure that this time allocation takes into account:

- the individual child's learning, play or leisure needs in terms of staffing, resources and equipment, e.g. mobility and communication aids
- the management of medical issues and personal care routines, e.g. epilepsy or difficulties with eating and drinking
- approaches to minimising the impact of sensory and physical impairments, e.g. the use of specialised lighting or appropriate positioning of equipment

- individual counselling and the management of difficult emotions and behaviour, e.g. helping the child recognise what triggers outbursts and how to respond
- the use of therapeutic treatments, e.g. speech and language therapy, physiotherapy, hydrotherapy, etc.

An effective individual support plan:

- builds on the child's understanding of their own support needs, as well as the views and contributions of parents, carers, families and others
- uses the expertise and involvement of a range of professionals from different agencies that may include therapists, nursing staff, social workers and representatives from the voluntary sector
- can make a significant contribution to an effective and inclusive environment for a disabled child or young person, by ensuring that parts of therapeutic programmes are successfully integrated in the activities of the setting

Your contribution to the planning of an individual support plan will depend on your exact role and responsibilities within the setting. You may be involved in developing a plan with an individual child to support learning, play or leisure needs. You may be involved in a variety of planning sessions and meetings, or simply be required to implement the plans of others such as teachers and/or specialists. An individual support plan may be either short term (e.g. a week, a month or half term) or long term (e.g. a term, several months or a whole year) and can cover a range of developmental and learning needs, including social, physical, intellectual communication or emotional. A plan for several months or the whole year will, of course, require more work than a plan for a week or two.

An individual support plan should be based on detailed observations and assessments of the child's learning and development. These assessments will include information from parents and appropriate professionals, as well as the observations and assessments made by you and your colleagues.

Observe a child with additional needs over a period of time (e.g. a week, a month or half a term) which is appropriate to your role in the setting. Using your observations, assess the child's development and make suggestions for the child's future learning needs.

As part of your role in the planning process, you may be involved in making suggestions for the specific content of an individual support plan. You will work in conjunction with colleagues, the special educational needs coordinator (SENCO) and possibly a specialist such as an educational psychologist, speech and language therapist, physiotherapist or occupational therapist.

The individual support plan should include:

- the child's age and level of development
- the specific area of impairment or special need
- the intended length of the plan
- where and when the plan is to be implemented, e.g. at home, in the setting or both
- details of the activities to be provided to support learning, play or leisure needs
- who will provide the activities and any necessary support
- the resources required, including any specialist equipment.

AC 5.3 Work in partnership with others to provide activities to meet children's additional needs

As appropriate to your own role and responsibilities, you will implement the individual support plan, including providing activities to support the child's learning, play or leisure needs. It is essential that you understand your own role (and that of colleagues) in the planning and implementation of the programme. In addition to following the general information on promoting learning and development (see Unit 3.2), you also need to consider implementing activities in ways that maximise benefit to the child. For example:

- Implement at a time when the child is receptive.
- Avoid unnecessary distractions for the child.
- Keep disruptions to the usual routines of the setting to a minimum.
- Use appropriate resources, including any specialised learning materials and/or equipment.

In practice activity

Developing a support plan for a child with additional needs

Develop a possible individual support plan for a child with additional needs, based on your observations and assessments from the previous activity (AC 5.2).

You could do an **outline plan** to include the following:

- spidergram of activities and/or skills to be developed using headings appropriate to your setting and the child's learning, play or leisure needs, e.g. the EYFS
- list of the planning and preparation for the activities, including resources and organisation
- inclusion of the child's activities into the usual routines of the setting, including any necessary modifications
- your role in supporting the child during the activities
- any health and safety issues
- timetable of the first week's activities from the plan
- detailed description of the implementation of at least one activity from the plan (remember to review and evaluate this activity afterwards)
- review and evaluate the whole plan.

If you have never done an outline plan before, ask your tutor for guidance or advice on a format which might be more appropriate to your role within the setting.

Activity

Provide examples of how you have supported children with additional needs to enable them to participate in the full range of activities and experiences in your setting, e.g. encouraging the child to participate in activities, or modifying activities to meet the child's individual learning, play or leisure needs.

AC 5.4 Work with parents/carers to encourage them to take an active role in their child's play, learning and development

Working in partnerships with families is particularly important when a child has additional support needs. Each parent or carer should be made to feel welcome and valued as an expert on his or her child, playing a vital role in helping practitioners to enable their child to participate and learn.

Parents usually know more about their children and their children's specific requirements, so it is important to listen to what parents have to say. The role of the early years practitioner is the following:

- Actively encourage positive relationships between parents (or designated carers) and the setting.
- Only give information to parents consistent with your role and responsibilities within the setting; for example, do not give recommendations concerning the child's future learning needs directly to parents, if this is the responsibility of another professional.
- Ensure that any information shared with parents is agreed with the relevant colleagues such as the child's key person.
- Ensure that any information about a child shared with their parents is relevant, accurate and up to date. Always follow the confidentiality requirements of the setting.

When liaising with parents about the additional needs of their children, you should consider the family's home background and the expressed wishes of the parents. You must also follow the setting's policies and procedures with regard to specific requirements, e.g. inclusion strategies, policies, procedures and practices. You may need to give parents positive reassurance about their children's care, learning and development. Any concerns or worries expressed by a child's parents should be passed immediately to the appropriate person in the setting. If a parent makes a request to see a colleague or other professional, then you should follow the relevant setting policy and procedures.

Parents and carers often find that the most helpful sources of information and advice come from others with shared experiences. There are many organisations which exist to provide support and answer questions; for example, Contact a Family, The Down's Syndrome Association, Mencap and The Royal Society for the Blind. There are many more – most with their own website and helpline.

Communicating with parents and carers
The principles of effective communication are discussed in Unit 2.5. One of the main purposes of communicating with parents and carers is to provide and to share information about the child and about the setting – both about the early years setting and the home. Practitioners need to build up a partnership with parents and carers, and to do this they need to promote a feeling of trust.

Providing flexible support for the family
Parents and carers want support which is flexible enough to respond to their particular family's needs, and which is both available in an emergency and can also be planned in advance. Children want support which enables them to do the kinds of things their peers do: this can vary from going swimming with their siblings to spending time away from home with their friends. The most popular services are generally those developed by parents or carers themselves, or by local disability organisations.

Coordinating the support
A single point of contact for the family (such as a key person, link worker or care coordinator), with a holistic view of the child and family, can help the family to find out about what services are available and the roles of different agencies, and to get professionals to understand their needs. Families with a single point of contact report better relationships with services, fewer unmet needs, better morale, fewer feelings of isolation and burden, more information about services, greater satisfaction, and more parental involvement than families without this service. Care coordination should ensure that the family's needs for information, advice and help are identified and addressed.

Types of support and information include:

- communication aids such as learning to use sign language, Makaton, speech board
- social and emotional support such as coming to terms with the impact of disability on own family
- financial support such as claiming benefits
- information about services and availability such as housing adaptations
- information about children's and families' rights
- information for parents about their child's condition and how they can support their child's development
- information for children and their family about their condition and treatment, about how to

live with the condition and how to overcome disabling barriers

- support that enables families to do activities together, as a whole family
- short-term breaks and domiciliary services
- accessible and appropriate play and leisure services.

Parent partnership services

The Parent Partnership Scheme (PPS) is a statutory service that offers the following support:

- information, advice and support for parents or carers of children with SEN
- putting parents or carers in touch with other local organisations
- making sure that the views of the parent or carer are heard and understood, and that these views inform local policy and practice.

Some parent partnerships are based in the voluntary sector, although the majority of them remain based in their LEA or Children's Trust. All parent partnerships, wherever they are based, work separately and independently from the LEA, which means that they are able to provide impartial advice and support to parents and carers.

For more information, visit the NPPN (National Parent Partnership Network) website at: www. parentpartnership.org.uk.

Activity

Find out about the services available to provide support and information for families with disabled children in your local area. Examples may include domiciliary services, special nursery provision, play and leisure services, Portage, and Home-Start.

AC 5.5 Reflect on own practice in meeting children's additional needs

You should be able to reflect on your own practice as part of your everyday learning. In this way, every experience – whether positive or negative – will contribute to your development and personal growth.

Reflective practice

In relation to meeting children's additional needs, reflect upon the following questions:

- Have you regularly observed individual children to help you to identify their holistic needs?
- Have you found out more about a child's particular additional need?
- Have you established a good relationship with the child's parents?
- Do you understand your own role within the setting in planning for children's additional needs?
- Are you able to plan activities to meet the play and learning needs of a child with additional needs?
- Do you regularly review and evaluate your plans and activities?
- Have you identified what you have achieved and what you still need to work on?

LO6 AC 6.1 Critically evaluate the provision for children with additional needs in own setting

You should be able to critically evaluate the provision for children with additional needs in your own setting by considering the following **characteristics of quality inclusion** – and evaluating how your setting provides for children's additional needs:

- Through their attitudes and behaviour, children, practitioners and parents demonstrate how unremarkable it is that disabled children are part of a wide cross-section of the local community using the setting.
- Children's interests, interactions or enthusiasms lead their play, and activities take into account individual likes, dislikes as well as access or support requirements.
- Everyone is welcomed on arrival and wished well on departure in a way that suits them.
- Each child is respected and valued as an individual with equal rights and choices, and is given equality of opportunity to exercise those rights and choices.
- Each child is supported when he or she chooses to play with others, to play alongside others, to play alone or not to take part in the activity.
- Risks are assessed and managed to enable each child to experience and enjoy risky play, while

managing their preferences and their own and others' safety.

- Children and adults each initiate communication with one another in a variety of ways.
- Each child has opportunities to actively participate in formal and informal consultation, using their chosen communication methods, so that they can express their views and opinions on the play sessions and the setting as a whole.

- All children report that practitioners seek their views, and listen and act on their requests.
- Each child indicates they are happy in the play/ childcare environment, and have opportunities to experience a range of emotions.
- Each child is encouraged to show their parent(s) what they have been doing, in their own way.

(PIP, 2008)

Assessment practice

1 List four biological factors and three environmental factors which may result in children needing additional support.

2 Describe the impact on children's development of **one** of the biological factors and **one** of the environmental factors you listed above.

3 Analyse the impact of the stage of development on children's learning.

4 Describe factors that affect children's development in the short and long term.

5 How do your personal experiences and value system impact on your professional practice?

6 What is meant by inclusive practice? What do you think you need to do to create an environment which promotes the personal, social and emotional development of children in your own setting?

7 What is meant by the medical and social models of disability? Which model is used now and why?

8 Evaluate inclusive practice in relation to current frameworks for children.

9 How can you identify children's additional needs in relation to expected stages of development?

10 Why is early intervention important in meeting children's additional needs, and what strategies are in place to facilitate early intervention?

11 Evaluate the principles of working in partnership with others to meet children's additional needs.

12 Show that you have been able to reflect on your own practice and also to critically evaluate the provision for children with additional needs in your setting.

13 Write a brief summary of the ways in which you have been able to plan (with others) to meet children's additional needs.

14 Describe the principles of working in partnership with other professionals and agencies to meet children's additional needs.

15 How can practitioners encourage parents and carers to take an active role in their child's play, learning and development?

16 Critically evaluate the provision for children with additional needs in your own setting.

Useful resources

Organisations

The Alliance for Inclusive Education

The Alliance for Inclusive Education is a national campaigning organisation led by disabled people: www.allfie.org.uk

Early Support

Early Support provides materials for families and professionals, including a service audit tool, a family pack, information for parents and developmental journals on the deaf, Down's Syndrome and visual impairments: www.earlysupport.org.uk

KIDS

KIDS works for disabled children, young people and their families: www.kids.org.uk

British Dyslexia Association (BDA)

The BDA is a national charity working for a 'dyslexia-friendly society' that enables dyslexic people of all ages to reach their full potential: www.bdadyslexia.org.uk

National Autistic Society (NAS)

The NAS aims to champion the rights and interests of all people with autism, and to provide individuals with autism and their families with help, support and services: www.nas.org.uk

Royal National Institute of Blind People (RNIB)

The Royal National Institute of Blind People (RNIB) has produced an excellent booklet, **Focus on Foundation**, which offers practical advice on the inclusion in early years settings of children who are blind and partially sighted: www.rnib.org.uk

Royal National Institute for Deaf People (RNID)

The RNID is the largest charity in the UK offering a range of services for people who are deaf or have a hearing impairment, and providing information and support on all aspects of deafness, hearing loss and tinnitus: www.rnid.org.uk

Scope

Scope is a charity that supports disabled people and their families. Its vision is a world where disabled people have the same opportunities as everyone else. Scope specialises in working with people who have cerebral palsy: www.scope.org.uk

Books and journals

Alcott, M. (2002), *An Introduction to Children with Special Needs*. London: Hodder & Stoughton.

Contact a Family (2004), *Caring for Disabled Children: A Guide for Students and Professionals*. Available from: www.cafamily.org.uk/students.pdf

DfES (2001), *The Special Educational Needs Code of Practice 2001*. Available free at: www.teachernet.gov.uk/_doc/3724/SENCodeOfPractice.pdf

Dickins, M. and Denziloe, J. (2004), *All Together: How to Create Inclusive Services for Children and Their Families*. National Children's Bureau.

Douch, P. (2006), *It Doesn't Just Happen – Inclusive Management for Inclusive Play*. London: Kids.

Horwath, J. (2001), *The Child's World: Assessing Children in Need*. London: Jessica Kingsley Publishers.

Lindon, J. (2005), *Understanding Child Development: Linking Theory and Practice*. London: Hodder Arnold.

Mortimer, H. (2001), *Special Needs and Early Years Provision*. London: Continuum International Publishing Group.

Wall, K. (2006), *Special Needs and Early Years: A Practitioner's Guide*. London: Paul Chapman Publications.

Wilson, R. (2003), *Special Educational Needs in the Early Years*. Abingdon: Routledge Falmer.

Unit 3.14 Use observation, assessment and planning to promote the development of children

This unit provides the learner with the knowledge, understanding and skills to use observation, assessment and planning to promote the development of children from birth to seven years.

Learning outcomes

By the end of this unit you will:

1 Understand the role of observation when working with children.
2 Understand observation methods.
3 Understand professional practice in relation to the observation of children.
4 Be able to carry out observations in own setting in line with current frameworks.
5 Be able to work with parents/carers in a way that encourages them to take an active role in their child's play, learning and development.

LO1 Understand the role of observation when working with children

AC 1.1 Explain how observations are used: to plan for individual children's needs; for early intervention; to review the environment; during transition, and when working in partnership

Becoming skilled in observation and assessment is one of the most important parts of your training and developing practice.

By **observation**, we mean closely watching, listening to and generally attending to what a child is doing, and recording your findings as accurately as you can. While you are observing, you should try to avoid drawing any conclusions, and to stay as focused on the child as possible.

By **assessment**, we mean making judgements about what your observation says about the child's development, learning, health and well-being.

How observations are used to plan for individual children's needs

Effective planning for children's early learning is based on every child's individual needs, abilities and interests; this is why accurate observations and assessments are so important. These needs have to be integrated into the curriculum requirements for your particular setting and the age groups of the children you work with, for example the learning and development requirements of the EYFS.

All early years practitioners must consider children's individual needs, interests and levels of development, and must use this information to plan a challenging and enjoyable experience for each child in all seven areas of learning and development. For example, you might notice that a child is making lots of progress in their communication, but you have no observations of their exploratory play and early scientific learning. You will need to plan to look out for the child's play and learning in that area. You might need to think of ways of encouraging the child to participate in those sorts of experiences by focussing on their interests.

How observations are used for early intervention

Throughout the early years, if a child's progress in any of the prime areas of learning gives cause for concern, practitioners must discuss this with the child's parents and continue to provide focused support in that area, reducing the risk that the child will struggle when starting Key Stage 1. Practitioners should consider using observations and assessments to determine if a child has an underlying developmental delay or if there is a concern that a child may have a special educational need or disability which is affecting their development. Early identification should reduce the risk that the child will continue to struggle in certain areas. The importance of early intervention is discussed in Unit 13.

How observations are used to review the environment

When observing children in the early years setting, focused observations can help you to analyse such issues as the use of different play areas. Event sampling and time sampling will enable practitioners to assess the quality of the setting in providing for children's learning in all the EYFS areas. Sometimes settings might identify that there are significant patterns in their observations and assessments:

- If there are many observations of boys in the block play area, but none of girls, you will need to think of how you will encourage girls to take part in construction play.
- If boys spend little time in the book area, you might need to change the types of books on display, or try adding home-made books about children's play and interests.
- If the bilingual children in the early years setting make less progress than those who speak English as a first language, you will need to focus on whether your setting is providing enough appropriate support.

How observations are used during transition

When a young child is experiencing a transition – such as starting a new nursery or getting used to having a new sibling in the family, observations can help practitioners to build up a picture of the child's needs during transition. The practitioner could, for example, visit the child's home before he or she starts at the nursery to observe their behaviour and to find out about any worries that the parents or carers might have. This will make it easier to plan for the separation and so ease the transition.

How observations are used when working in partnership

Even the most experienced early years practitioners may find that, although they have observed a child and made efforts to adapt their provision, they need help from outside the setting. This is particularly true if there is a specific medical condition or developmental delay. In these cases, the people who best know the child – almost always the parents or main carer – will provide the most

valuable suggestions, alongside the advice and guidance of other expert or specialist professionals. The development of an individual 'care plan' or special educational programme will take account of evidence gathered from different sources – for example, from parents, early years practitioners, health visitors, doctors, social services, speech and language therapists, and so on. These provisions can only meet the child's needs when there is cooperation between all the services involved, and those who are competent to do so make accurate assessments. This is called **partnership working**.

Progress check

It is important to become skilled in observing and assessing children so that you can:

- get to know the children
- have purposeful discussions with parents, carers and colleagues
- think about what to plan next
- identify children's strengths and also their areas of difficulty
- monitor children's progress and offer help if a child does not seem to be accessing a particular area of the curriculum or does not seem to be making good progress
- reflect on the quality of your work as a practitioner and the overall quality of your setting.

LO2 Understand observation methods

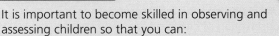

AC 2.1 Evaluate observation methods in relation to current frameworks

It is generally accepted as good practice to observe children in a familiar environment, playing and interacting with family and friends. In early years settings, the EYFS promotes **observation-based assessment**. Observations are assessed using the 'Development matters' scales or the EYFS Profile (at the end of the Reception year); see p 000 below. There are other scales to help assess particular areas of development – for example, in the Every Child a Talker (ECAT) programme.

As you become more skilled at making observations of children, there are many further approaches that will complement your work and give you a broader picture. Some of these are explored below.

Leuven Involvement Scale

The Leuven Involvement Scale is a method for assessing the quality of children's learning, using associated scales in children's well-being and practitioner sensitivity. Taken all together, these can give you valuable information about how effective your setting is. But because children are only observed for very short lengths of time (two minutes), the scales will tell you more about the overall quality of the setting than about the learning and development of particular children. The scale is used by settings involved in the popular **Effective Early Learning programme** (Bertram and Pascal, 1997).

Activity ·

Evaluate observation methods in relation to current frameworks. Look at the framework for learning for children from birth to seven years in your home country.

· ·

Figure 3.14.1 The look of concentration on this girl's face as she waters her plants, and the careful way she is holding and tipping the watering can, show that she is deeply involved

Level	Description
Level 1: Extremely low	The child hardly shows any activity: no concentration, daydreams, has an absent/passive attitude, displays no signs of exploration or interests, doesn't partake in goal-orientated activity and doesn't seem to be taking anything in.
Level 2: Low	The child shows some degree of activity but it is often interrupted: limited concentration, often looking away during activities and dreaming, is easily distracted, and action only leads to limited results.
Level 3: Moderate	The child is busy the whole time, but without real concentration: attention is superficial, doesn't become absorbed in activities and these activities are short lived, limited motivation, does not feel challenged and the child does not use his/her capabilities or imagination to the full extent.
Level 4: High	There are clear signs of involvement, but these are not always present to their full extent: engaged in activities without interruption, displays real concentration although sometimes the attention can be more superficial, the child feels challenged and motivated, the activities engage the child's capabilities and imagination to a certain extent.
Level 5: Extremely high	During the observation the child is continuously engaged and completely absorbed in the activity: concentrates without interruption, is highly motivated and perseveres, is alert and shows precision and intense mental activity, is not easily distracted, even by strong stimuli, addresses his/her full capabilities/imagination and enjoys being engrossed.

Table 3.14.1 The Leuven Involvement Scale

AC 2.2 Evaluate observation methods: Event Sample; Time Sample; Sociogram; Narrative/Free Description; Target Child; Checklist; Child Tracker/Movement Record

The range of observation methods

Perhaps the most common is the **narrative** or **descriptive observation**. This type attempts to record everything that happens, as it happens, with plenty of detail. Methods that fit into the 'narrative' framework are:

- descriptive/running record
- target child action
- diary description
- anecdotal record
- tape and transcript (may be considered to fit into this category so long as the section focused upon

and used for evaluation purposes is continuous and not a series of edited extracts)

- video recording (as for tape and transcript).

Target Child Observation

The Target Child Observation (Painter, Roy and Sylva, 1980) is a technique based on narrative observation, which also includes a coding system to help you interpret your findings. The Target Child Observation involves observing individual children for ten or twenty minutes, allowing you to gain in-depth information about each child. You will need time for the observation and then allow at least the same amount of time again for the coding and analysis of your results. The Target Child Observation approach was used in the Oxford Preschool Research project in the 1970s and the EPPE (Effective Provision of Preschool Education) project, which has been in progress since 1997.

RP = role play, SOL = solitary, SG = small group, LG = large group, TC = target child, C = child, A = adult, BC = book corner, SW = small world, W = waiting			
Child initials: JG Gender: M Age: 3 yrs 10 mths Date/Time: 1/10/05 2.15 p.m.			
ACTIVITY RECORD	**LANGUAGE RECORD**	**TASK**	**SOCIAL**
1 min TC on carpeted area, playing with farm animals and buildings.	TC→C My cow wants to come in your field. C→TC No. You'll have to wait till my tractor has finished.	SW	SG
2 min TC sitting at edge of carpet, looking at wall display.		W	SOL
3 min Now in dressing-up area, putting on a floppy hat and laughing.	C→TC You look funny in that. TC→C Let me see. Where's the mirror?	RP	SG
4 min Sitting in a small chair at a table, holding a knife and fork in his hands.	TC→C Where's my tea? I want my tea. Not fish fingers again!	RP	SG
5 min Standing at 'cooker' and stirring something in a pan.	A→TC What are you cooking? TC→A I'm a good cooker. It's basgetti.	RP	SG
6 min Taking off hat and tidying equipment.		RP	SOL
7 min Sitting in story corner, looking at book.		BC	LG

Figure 3.14.2 Example of a target child observation

Time sample

Time sampling involves making a series of short observations (usually up to two minutes each) at regular intervals over a fairly long period. The interval between observations and the overall duration is your decision, depending on exactly what you are observing and why. For example, you may choose to record at 20-minute intervals over the course of a whole day, or every 15 minutes during a half-day session.

It can be a useful way of finding out how children use particular toys or resources, to monitor how a new child has settled in or to observe the behaviour of an individual child. When observing an individual child's behaviour, time sampling can raise awareness of positive aspects which may be overlooked in the normal run of a busy day. Staff can then make a point of noticing and appreciating the incidents of positive behaviour, and encourage these as part of a strategy to reduce unwanted aspects.

It is difficult to keep stepping away at regular intervals from whatever else you are doing, in order to make the record. Negotiation with colleagues is essential so that children's safety is not put at risk.

You can choose your own headings for the chart format to match the detail you need to include. Usual headings are 'Time', 'Setting or location', 'Language' and 'Social group', but you may want to include 'Actions' and 'Other'.

Child observed = HR   Teacher = T   Other children = A, B, C, D, E.
LG = large group, SG = small group, P = pair of children
Aim: To find out how well a child, newly arrived from another school, has settled in, looking particularly at interaction with other children.

Time	Setting	Language	Social group	Other
9.00	Registration – sitting on carpeted area.	None	LG	At back of class group, fiddling with shoelaces and looking around the room.
9.20	At a table, playing a language game.	HR: 'It's *not* my turn.'	SG	One parent helper and 3 other children.
9.40	On floor of cloakroom.	HR: 'You splashed me first and my jumper's all wet, look.'	P	Had been to toilet and is washing hands.
10.00	In maths area, carrying out a sorting activity using coloured cubes.	T: 'Can you find some more cubes the same colour, HR?' HR: 'There's only 2 more red ones.'	SG	Concentrating and smiling as he completes the task.
10.20	Playground – HR is standing by a wall, crying.	Sobbing sounds – won't make eye contact with or speak to T on duty.	SOL	Small group of children look on.
10.40	Music activity – playing a tambour to beat the rhythm of his name.	Says his name in 2-syllable beats.	LG	Showing enjoyment by smiling – T prises him.
11.00	Tidying away instruments with another child.	A→HR: 'We have instruments every week. It's good, isn't it?' HR → A: 'Yeh. i liked it.'	P	
11.20	Playing with construction equipment with A and B.	B→HR + A: 'I've got loads of Lego at home.' HR→B + A: 'So have I. I like the technical stuff best.' B→HR: 'What's that like?'	SG	Children working together to build a garage for toy cars.
11.40	HR fetching reading book to read to T.	Humming to himself.	SOL	
12.00	Lining up with other children to go for lunch		LG	Nudging A, who is standing in front of him. A turns round and grins.

Figure 3.14.3 Example of a time sample in a Year 1 class

Event sample

This involves the observation of specific actions, incidents or behaviour. The event to be observed is usually decided in advance, and a chart format is most often used to record events as they happen.

Diary description

This is usually kept to monitor the learning and development of an individual child (but can also be used for a group) and provides a day-to-day account of significant events. It may include anecdotal records (see below) and other forms of observation. A diary is time-consuming to keep, and you need to be sure that the information gathered is helpful and remains objective, rather than being mundane, repetitive and subjective. This type of observation can help to record the progress of every child in a group over time.

Anecdotal record

This is a brief description of an incident written soon after it has occurred. This is a widely used method of observation and is useful because it is recorded only a short time after the incident. The adult records a significant piece of learning, perhaps the first steps a baby takes unaided, or an important development in relationships with other children. Anecdotal observations can be made in a different coloured pen, to show that they are not 'on-the-spot', but recalled events.

Flow diagram (or movement chart)

This method allows you to present information about an individual child or a group of children, activities, safety in a work setting or use of equipment. It can be very simple, with very basic information (see Figure 3.14.4), or more detailed to highlight more than one aspect (see Figure 3.14.5). If you want to track one child from one area or activity to another during the course of a morning session, it might help to have a prepared plan of the room on which to map her or his movement.

From this type of observation you can see:

- which activities the child visited
- the order in which he or she visited them
- how long he or she spent at each one
- which activities he or she visited on more than one occasion
- which activities he or she did not visit at all.

The more detailed version provides the following additional information:

- which activities had adult-led tasks
- which ones had an adult permanently supervising or helping
- which other children were at an activity when the observed child arrived.

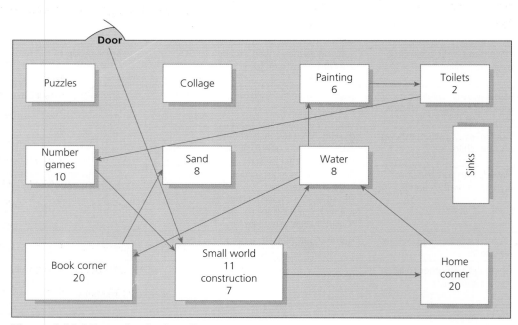

Figure 3.14.4 Example of a flow diagram

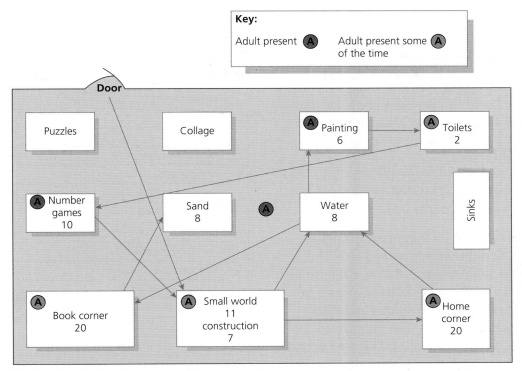

Figure 3.14.5 Flow diagram – with extra detail

From this level of detail you may gain further insight into the child's movements. Repeated observations may enable you to find out if the child never visits the sand, always heads for an activity with an adult present or always follows another child.

Sociogram

This is a diagrammatic method used to show an individual child's social relationships within a group, or to find out about friendship patterns between several children within a group (see Figure 3.14.6). Identifying girls and boys separately can sometimes make it immediately clear whether girls play with girls, and boys with boys, or if they play in mixed gender groups. You should record the ages of the children involved. You may find that an older child habitually plays with a group of much younger

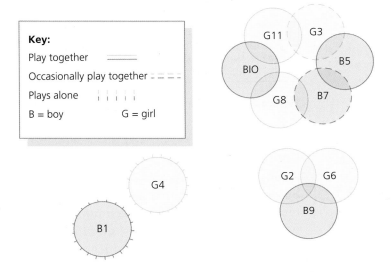

Figure 3.14.6 Sociogram

children. You will be able to identify any child who always plays alone or who always seeks the company of an adult. There are many factors that will affect the play relationships – friendship of parents, proximity of homes, presence of siblings and, not least, pattern of attendance. These factors need to be taken into account when drawing your conclusions.

Growth charts

These can be used to plot the height and/or weight of an individual child over a period of time. An example of a growth chart is shown in Unit 3.12.

Make sure you use one for the correct gender as there are variations between boys and girls. The chart cannot be submitted in isolation, but must be accompanied by your analysis of the information which makes reference to percentiles and shows your understanding. You must use the chart to interpret 'your' child's information. This type of chart is good to include in a longitudinal study. Even if you are studying a child aged two years or over, it is quite likely that the parents will have a record of length/ height and weight at birth and at some intervening intervals that you can plot.

Checklists

This form of recording has its limitations, including the following:

- giving no detail or supporting evidence
- being narrow in focus
- making practitioners feel that they have more information than they really do
- being time-consuming to create.

However, if these limitations are appreciated and the checklist is well thought out, it can be a very straightforward method of recording your observation. It should only be used in addition to other methods. It can be used to help:

- monitor developmental progress of an individual child or several children
- assess children on a regular basis over a period of time
- staff to plan for children's changing needs
- consideration of one area of development
- assess a child's behaviour.

	CHILD 1 yrs m	CHILD 2 yrs m	CHILD 3 yrs m
1. WALKING			
Looks ahead			
Walks upright			
Avoids objects			
Small steps			
Strides			
Walks heel to toe			
Arms by side			
Arms swinging			
Other observation			
2. BALANCE			
Stands on one foot			
Balances for 3–4 seconds			
Balances for longer			
Leans to one side			
Arms stretched out			
Arms by side			
Arms folded			
Can walk on narrow line			
Other observation			
3. RUNNING			
Runs on tiptoe			
Runs flat-footed			
Swings arms			
Arms by side			
Arms folded			
Able to change speed			
Changes direction			
Runs round corners			
Other observation			

You can add to this chart for other gross motor skills, such as skipping, hopping, climbing, swinging etc., by identifying the important components of the action.

Figure 3.14.7 Example of a gross motor skills checklist

Longitudinal study

A longitudinal study consists of a series of observations of different aspects of development, recorded using a variety of techniques over a period of time – a few weeks, months, a year or more. It provides opportunities to look at the 'whole' child by observing and assessing

Possible use: for monitoring reading skills Title of book used: *The Birthday Cake* Date: Skill	Child 1	Comment	Child 2	Comment
1. **Holds book right way up**	✓	Held book correctly in both hands	✓	Took book from me and turned it right way
2. **Knows which is the front of a book**	✓	Looked at front cover before opening book	✓	Pointed to character on cover picture
3. **Follows text/pictures left to right**	✓	Followed pictures as story was read	✓	Head movements showed was doing this
4. **Knows text 'works' top to bottom**	✓	As above	✓	As above
5. **Can point to known characters in illustrations**	✓	Pointed to Chip and Floppy	✓	Named characters as they appeared in illustrations
6. **Can talk about illustrations**	✓	Did so when prompted	✓	Pointed to things in pictures which he found funny
7. **Can recap the story partway through**	✗	Needed prompting and had to turn back through pages	✓	Good recall of what had happened
8. **Can suggest what might happen next**	✗	Could offer no ideas	✓	Good suggestions with reasons
9. **Identifies some individual letters**	✓	Named and pointed to 'c', 'd' and 'a'	✓	Named and pointed to 'c', 'd', 'a', 'g', 'h', 'l', 'b', 'n', 'w', 't', 's', 'r', 'y', 'p'
10. **Can identify a capital (upper-case) letter**	✓	Named and pointed to 'c' – own initial letter	✓	Named and pointed to 'C', 'F', 'B', 'H', 'T', 'R'
11. **Can identify a full stop**	✗		✗	

Figure 3.14.8 Example of an expanded checklist showing reading development

progress in all areas of development. As a student you are most likely to carry out such a study on a child whom you know well or whose family you know well. In this case, you may be given permission to include photographs and/or video footage. The initial part of the study will involve gathering background and factual information, followed by observations carried out at agreed intervals (not necessarily regular). You may get the chance to observe special events, such as outings, birthdays, clinic visits, as well as the child's time spent in a setting.

When you have recorded all your observations you can collate the information. You might choose to present them in strict chronological order or in groups of observations of different developmental areas. This will depend on the focus of your study and the individual observations.

In work settings, a longitudinal study can be useful in planning long-term strategies for a child with special needs.

Video, photography and audio recording of children

Early years practitioners are increasingly using video, photography and audio recording of children. There are many advantages that have come with new technology, especially as digital cameras and MP3 recorders are cheap and easy to use. If you want to study a child's language development and discuss it with parents, then an audio or video recording might be a very good way of doing this. Likewise, nothing records a child's construction or model as well as a carefully taken photograph.

In practice

Using cameras, camcorders and MP3 recorders

- Before you make an audio or video recording of a child, or take photographs, check the policy of the setting.
- Think about how you will store data safely and with parental consent. It is not advisable to download photos or video onto your personal computer, for example. Best practice would be to keep everything on a computer in the setting, with password protection or encryption.
- Think about how you will position yourself. You will need to be quite close to the children to pick up their voices clearly, for example.
- Analysing video and audio recordings is extremely time-consuming. You may get the best results if you record for just a minute or two at the right

moment – when a child is really engaged in his play or in full conversational flow. Accurately transcribing even a few minutes of children's conversation can take half an hour or more.
- Think about how you will display and share information:
- Digital slide shows of well-taken photos can be a powerful and accessible way of showing a child's learning story, for example, or how a range of children play and learn in a particular area.
- Many settings put together profile books of individual children. These usually consist of photos with written observations and assessments. You will need to take care that a profile book is not merely a scrapbook of photos, without any commentary on the child's learning and development.

Progress check

Using a range of tools for observation and assessment

- Experiment with different ways to observe a child's development.
- Talk as a team about any checklists that you use, and consider whether these are useful.
- Share different types of observations and assessments with parents in order to develop a dialogue about children's progress and areas of difficulty.

Research activity

You can learn more about observation techniques in detail, with sections of film to develop your skills, by viewing the Observation Technique DVDs produced by Siren Films (see Useful resources section).

Observation in practical contexts

Assessment should occur as part of early years practitioners' ongoing interaction with young children. Ongoing assessment should also be informed by feedback from the child's parents and other adults who interact with the child. Assessment must not entail prolonged breaks from interaction with children, and should not require excessive paperwork. Key achievements and any concerns should be recorded periodically. Practitioners must give parents and carers regular updates on their children's progress and achievements as part of their ongoing partnerships with families (DfE, 2011).

Guidelines for developing your skills in observation and assessment

The following points will help you to develop your skills, both as you start out on your work with children and as you develop into an experienced practitioner.

- **Plan ahead**: think about when the majority of the children are likely to be settled enough in what they are doing so that you can start your observation.
- **Think about exactly what you need information about**: if you are observing a baby's feeding routine and the baby's responses, you will need to know exactly how much milk the baby has, how

the baby likes to be held, what interaction soothes the baby and makes the experience enjoyable, and what happens at the end of the feed. Equally, if you have pages of observations of a child's early writing and lots of examples, you will need to plan to gather information about an area you know less about.

- **Choose your approach with care**: if you are building up a profile of a child, you might plan to observe him or her systematically over a number of days, choosing different times and places. You can gather information about the start of the day, different types of play inside and out, mealtimes, settling to sleep or resting, and so on. If your focus is assessment for learning, you need to find times when the child is involved in something worthwhile, so you will have plenty of material to think about. An observation of a child drifting from one table to the next and looking bored will tell you little about the child's development and learning – it might be better to help the child there and then.

- **Respond quickly, on the spur of the moment**: life with young children is unpredictable, which is what makes it so interesting. You may be busy with a hundred different things, but notice out of the corner of your eye that William has gone to the easel and is doing a painting for the first time. You might be cooking with three children and need to concentrate totally on helping them with the recipe, but be noticing lots of things about what they can do. These are times to write a quick note on a sticky note when you get a moment, or at the end of the session, to add to

children's records. Just state very briefly what you saw that was important and always include the date.

- **Try to observe as accurately as possible**: focus on what you see and hear, and try to get everything down with as much detail as possible.
- **Take photos or collect examples where possible**: subject to the policies of your setting, a series of photos of a child painting will really bring an observation to life. Photocopy a child's early attempts at writing his or her name, as well as observing how he or she went about this.
- **Share your thoughts with others**: ask the child to talk to you about what you observed, share the observation with a colleague and talk to the child's parents. You will find that you will deepen your understanding this way.

The Welsh Government has produced a brief and helpful guide to observation in the Foundation Phase that will give you more ideas. You can find the guide by searching online for 'Foundation Phase Observing Children'.

Figure 3.14.9 This boy is concentrating very intently as he sits on his teacher's lap, shaving a piece of wood; observing this carefully can tell you about his confidence and concentration, his physical development and his understanding of the properties of materials

LO3 Understand professional practice in relation to the observation of children

AC 3.1 Define the terms 'objectivity' and 'subjectivity'

Objectivity
Objectivity is being open-minded and suspending judgement. When observing children, it is important for practitioners to be objective – that is, to ensure that personal opinions, experiences and/or prejudices do not affect their judgement.

Subjectivity
Subjectivity is judgement based on individual personal impressions, feelings and opinions rather than external facts.

Observations should be a factual record of what has taken place:

- Remember to write down only what you see or hear.
- Describe what the child is doing, how they are doing it, when they are doing it and with whom.
- Do not write down your opinion about why they are doing it.

Objective versus subjective observations

A subjective anecdotal record

Asha is playing with Maisie. They are not playing well together because Maisie keeps pestering Asha. They only play together for a short time before Asha goes to play alone. She does not like to play with Maisie.

An objective anecdotal record

Asha and Maisie are building a house with wooden blocks. Maisie knocks over the house. Asha puts it up again. Maisie knocks it over a second time. Asha says, 'I'm not playing any more.' Asha goes and sits on a cushion in the book corner, picks up a doll, and rocks it.

1 What are the main problems in being subjective when recording observations?
2 How can you ensure that you are objective when recording observations?

Your evaluation of the objective record will be done later. Value judgements should never be included in any recorded observation of children.

AC 3.2 Evaluate the reasons for objectivity when recording observations

The importance of objectivity

One of the most important skills to develop when observing children is the skill of objectivity. The more preconceived ideas we have about people, the less able we are to see them objectively. When you are observing and assessing children, you will need to be able to work towards putting into practice the anti-discriminatory, anti-bias approaches outlined in Unit 2.4. This is not always easy to do. We all have our own personal prejudices which can result in us being subjective and making value judgements.

Child development charts, including the 'Development matters' section in the EYFS, can be criticised for trying to 'normalise' each child. In other words, instead of seeing development as varied and influenced by different cultures and backgrounds, charts can present an 'ideal child'. This is a problem if any child who develops differently is seen as abnormal and problematic.

For example, Laura E. Berk (2006, p 333) summarises a large number of American research studies which suggest that the communication styles of some ethnic minority families are very different from the styles which are expected and valued in schools. Observations indicated that wealthier, white families were likely to ask questions such as: 'How many beads have you got?' and 'What colour is that car?' Children who are used to answering questions like this do well in schools where such exchanges are common.

On the other hand, in many of the ethnic minority families observed, only 'real' questions were asked – where the parent genuinely does not know the answer. Often, questions asked by parents called for individual responses, not 'right' answers – for example, 'So, what do you think of that car then?'

Any observation and assessment system that focuses on children giving correct answers to questions would be likely to favour those from wealthier, white backgrounds. Children who could not answer lots of direct questions about the colour and numbers of things might be seen as deficient. But a more flexible observation and assessment system would be able to recognise the particular strengths of children with a range of conversational styles.

Observations that try to record accurately what children do and say will be more objective and less biased. One child's discussion of his views about a car can be valued just as much as another's correct description of the car's colour and features.

It is not possible to avoid cultural bias, or any other kind of bias, when observing children. You can minimise subjectivity and bias, however, by:

- focusing on what children actually do and say
- raising your awareness of cultural diversity
- learning from parents about how they play and talk with their children at home, and what they value
- involving children – ask them to tell you what their thoughts are about what you have noticed and heard.

It is important not to confuse objectivity with holding back from making judgements. If you never make judgements about children's development, you will never notice which children are experiencing difficulties and therefore who needs to be offered extra help. Although you will be trying to uphold equal opportunities, the result will be that children with special needs and other difficulties will miss out on the extra help they need.

When you are observing and assessing children, you need to make robust judgements about:

- the child's approach to play and learning – for example, involvement, enjoyment and toleration of frustration
- the child's rate of progress – can you see development over time?
- whether the child is making sound progress or needs extra help.

The important thing is that you try to base your judgements on the information you have recorded, not merely on your opinions and impressions. You should also be open to the views of others – parents, carers and your colleagues, for example. Be prepared to explain why you have formed your opinion, but be open to changing your mind. Each practitioner will, however, have their own opinions and perspectives, and therefore it is good practice to use all practitioners within a setting to carry out observations over a period of time. This will help ensure that the information acquired will be balanced and provide a fuller picture of the child, children or area being observed.

> ### Discussion point
>
> On an outing to a live music event, a class of 28 children was seated in the front rows. They all thoroughly enjoyed the jazz-style pieces and many of them were standing up and swaying or moving in time with the music. Chantelle was the only mixed-race child present, being part Afro-Caribbean and part white English. After the concert, when the children had all gone home, an adult helper (who had watched the children with pleasure) said to you, 'I suppose it's because she's black that Chantelle has such a good sense of rhythm.'
>
> This adult has based her comment on a stereotypical view of black children. How would you reply to her comment? After you have thought about what you might say, discuss your ideas with another learner or in a group. Can you think of three or more ways in which stereotyping might get in the way of making an accurate observation of Chantelle and the other children?

> ### Key term
>
> **anti-bias practice** Anti-bias practice means going beyond equal opportunities and actively opposing forms of discrimination and prejudices in your work – for example, letting all children take part in woodwork upholds equal opportunities. Inviting a woman joiner into the nursery and displaying pictures and books about women doing woodwork, and talking these issues through with children, is an anti-bias approach.

AC 3.3 Evaluate the requirement for confidentiality during the observation process

The importance of appropriate sharing of confidential information

Many difficult issues arise when professionals record and share information about children. These include the following.

Consent

Information on a child should only be collected and stored with the consent of the child's parents, who should have free access to this information on request. Information should only be shared between professionals with the express consent of parents, which should be gained formally with a signature. The only exceptions are the very small number of cases where the child might otherwise be at risk of immediate and significant harm if you shared a piece of information with the parent. See Unit 2.2 for specific guidance on safeguarding.

Confidentiality

It is important that information is securely stored so that it cannot be freely accessed by anyone. Practitioners, including students, should not discuss or otherwise share this information – for example, when chatting in the staffroom or with friends at the weekend. If information is kept on computers or sent by email, steps must be taken to ensure that it could not fall into the hands of other people (for example, the use of encryption software).

However, where good, cooperative working is achieved between professionals, with clear consent, there are numerous benefits for parents:

- **Openness**: a Common Assessment Framework (CAF) is shared, so parents can see what the different views of the professionals are, and can put across their own viewpoint too. See Units 2.5 and 3.13 for more information about how to use the CAF.
- **Not having to repeat the same information over and over again**: if information is shared, a parent will not have to tell each professional in turn about something distressing, like their baby's difficult birth. They need only tell their story once.
- **Not being bombarded with different advice**: if there is a CAF in place for a child, there will be a single agreed set of advice and action plan. Otherwise, a parent might find that everyone has a different opinion about how to help his or her child, and might feel overwhelmed or confused. When professionals and parents cooperate well and share information in this way, children benefit.
- **They do not have to be constantly assessed by different people**: if a paediatrician has information about a child's development and learning in nursery, she or he will not need to undertake a long assessment at the clinic, but can focus instead on areas of particular importance.
- **Consistent programmes can be put together to help the child**: if a child has received speech and language therapy in a clinic, with the target of putting two words together, then consistent help with this at home and in nursery will provide significantly more benefit.

It is important to focus on children holistically, and think about their all-round development. The child

who has a speech and language delay might be a strong and graceful mover. If we fail to think of *the whole child*, we can end up seeing children with problems that need fixing, rather than as individuals with strengths and special qualities as well as needs.

Figure 3.14.10 A photo can tell you a great deal about a child's development and learning, like the concentration and skill shown by this two-year-old child

parent that you will find out and answer the question in due course. Offer parents regular opportunities to look at your observations.
- Ask for a signature to show formal consent.
- **Maintain anonymity** (for example, refer to children only by their initials, not their full names) and **confidentiality** – do not discuss what you find out about children with friends or family.

- **Plan when, where and how often you will observe the child**: make sure that everyone on the staff team is aware of this. You do not want to create a situation where staff are expecting you to supervise an area and play with children, but you are expecting to be able to hold back and spend time observing.
- **Share your observations with staff in the setting**: this will be a way in which you can help them with their record-keeping, assessment and planning.

Here is an example of a letter to a parent, asking for consent.

Dear parent of [*child's name*]

My name is [*your name*] and I am on placement in [*name of setting*] for [*dates of your placement*].

One of the things I will be learning about is how children play, develop, learn and socialise with each other. To help me do this, I will be observing some individual children over time and I would like to ask for your consent to observe your child.

I would like to make it clear that:
- you are free to give or withhold your consent
- you can withdraw your consent at any time, without having to give a reason – just let me know
- you can ask to see my observations and notes at any time.

I will keep my observations and notes in a safe place where they cannot be read by other people. I will only share them with my tutors and with staff here at the nursery.

I will offer times to meet with you to share what I have observed. It will be very helpful if you are able to tell me about your child too, as you will know so much more than me.

Please sign below if you agree to allow me to observe your child.

Name:

Signature:

Date:

The rights of children

It is very important to remember that everything that happens in the nursery must, as far as possible, be in the children's interests. Children cannot give informed consent in the way that adults can. But you can follow the same principles with the children:

If you think your observation might be causing distress or discomfort, you should stop. Look out for times where the child:
- keeps looking at you and seems inhibited from playing
- seems uncomfortable
- shrinks or looks away when you get close enough to observe
- indicates through body language or words that she does not want you to observe her.

If a child asks you what you are doing or shows interest:
- explain that you are watching his or her play and that you are very interested in what he or she is doing
- show the child your notebook or paper, and explain that you are writing things down
- wait patiently for the child to go back to his or her play or activity, without trying to shoo the child away; you will usually find that children get used to observations and stop noticing you.

If a child might be about to have an accident, or if you think a child is about to be hurt or bullied, you will need to stop your observation and intervene (or ask a member of staff to help).

It is also good practice to share your observations with children, taking account of their age and stage of development. With very young children, you may want to look at photos together and consider the child's responses (such as smiles, frowns, lack of interest). Many children from the age of three years upwards will be able to talk to you for a time.

In practice activity

Share your observations with children

- Show a child some photos you have taken and talk about them together. Try to find out the child's point of view. What does the child think he or she was playing or learning to do?
- Tell a child about what you have observed and what you think, and ask for his or her comments. For example, 'I've noticed you spending lots of time with the blocks. What do you like about playing with them?'
- Ask a child what they would like to do next or make suggestions. For example, 'I know you like playing with the trains a lot. Shall we go to the station one day and see some real trains?'

Article 12 of the United Nations Convention on the Rights of the Child says that children have a right to express an opinion. Their opinion should be taken into account if any matter or procedure affects them.

Key term

informed consent Informed consent means that you check carefully that someone has understood your request. If you said to a parent in passing, 'Do you mind if I do an observation of your child today?' you have not obtained informed consent. You need to arrange a time to meet, explain what you are planning to do, make time to answer any questions and obtain the parent's signature.

Progress check

- Know the policies of the setting on confidentiality and consent, and the legal requirements.
- Make sure you ask parents and carers for informed consent.
- Explore ways of seeking consent from children of different ages.
- Some settings have a specific Observations Policy. If your setting has one, make sure you follow the policy.

Guidelines: how to maintain confidentiality in your observations

Ensure that you have permission for making an observation – from your supervisor and the parent/main carer (this is confirmed by an authorising signature).

- Use codes rather than names to refer to the individuals involved – you should never use a child's first name. An initial or some other form of identification (e.g. Child 1) is sufficient. (You may use 'T' or 'A' for 'teacher' or 'adult'.)
- Understand and abide by policies and procedures in the setting.
- Remember that photographic and taped evidence can reveal identity, and should only be used with appropriate authority.
- Take extra care when sharing observations with fellow students – they may have friends or family involved in a setting and could easily identify individuals.
- Never discuss children or staff from your work setting in a public place (e.g. when sitting on a bus or in a cafe).
- Never identify individuals when talking at home about your daily experiences (e.g. they could be neighbours' children).

LO4 Be able to carry out observations in own setting in line with current frameworks

How to record observations of children
There is some information that should be included in any observation, but other aspects will depend on the purpose of the observation. If it is to consider the child's fine motor skills, then the detail will probably be different from one that is to find out about his/her social development – even if the same activity or situation is being observed. You should also record some *introductory* information (see below).

When you carry out a written observation it is usually because you want to find out something about an individual child or a group of children. This provides an **aim**, which should be identified at the start of your work. For example:

'**Aim**: To see what gross motor skills Child R uses in a PE lesson and consider how confident he is on the apparatus.'

A clear aim explains what you want to find out and the activity or context that you have decided will best show you. This is better than saying you will 'watch Child R in a PE lesson'. The aim you identify should affect what information you write in your introduction and in the actual observation.

As well as an aim, your observation should also have the following:

- date carried out
- start and finish times
- who gave permission
- where it took place (setting)
- number of children present
- number of adults present
- age of child/ages of children
- names or identification of children (remember confidentiality)
- method used (brief reason for choice)
- signature of supervisor or tutor.

How observations should be recorded

Your tutors will have their own preferences for how they want you to present your work but, generally, each observation should include the following sections: **Introduction**; **Actual observation**; **Evaluation**; **Bibliography**.

Introduction

In this section you must state where the observation is taking place (e.g. at the sand tray in a reception class) and give some information about what is happening (e.g. the children had just returned to the classroom from assembly). If there is any relevant information about the child, you might include it here (e.g. Child R has been ill recently and has missed two weeks of school). Include information that is relevant to your aim – it may be important to know whether he is of average build if you are dealing with physical skills, but not particularly relevant if you are dealing with imaginative play.

Actual observation

There are many different methods of recording, and your tutors will help you decide which one is best –

perhaps a 'chart' format, a checklist, or a written record describing what you see as it happens. Remember only to write what you see and, if appropriate, hear. **Do not write your judgements, opinions, assessments, and so on**. Make sure you include information about other children or adults involved, if it is relevant.

When recording your observation remember to maintain **confidentiality** by only using a child's first name or initial, or some other form of identification (e.g. Child R). You may use 'T' or 'A' for 'teacher' or 'adult'.

Evaluation

An evaluation is an assessment of what you have observed. This section can be dealt with in two parts.

1   You need to look back at your recorded information and summarise what you have discovered. Example: 'Child R was looking around the classroom and fidgeting with his shoelaces during the story, and appeared bored and uninterested. However, he was able to answer questions when asked so he must have been listening for at least part of the time.' This is a review of what you saw.

2   You then need to consider what you have summarised, and compare your findings to the 'norm' or 'average' or 'expected' for a child of this age and at this stage of development. What have you, yourself, learnt about this particular child/ group of children, and how has this helped you to understand children's development more widely? Use relevant books to help you and make reference to them – or quote directly if you can find a statement or section that relates to what you are saying or the point you are making. Your tutor or assessor wants to know what you understand, not information he or she could read in a book, so use references carefully.

As observation of children can help carers to plan for individual needs, try to suggest what activity or caring strategy might be needed next. You may also, in this section, give your opinion as to reasons for the behaviour, and so on – take care not to jump to conclusions about the role of the child's background, and never make judgements about the child or the child's family.

Bibliography

The bibliography is a list of the books you have used when reading and researching for information relating to your observation.

Interpreting and evaluating observations

Your observations of children need to be interpreted and evaluated to assess development and meet individual needs.

Using developmental theory to interpret observations

Theories about the way in which children learn, think and behave can help when making observations of children. Applying your knowledge of a particular theory can help in a number of ways. For example, using theories can help you to:

- understand the reasons behind children's thinking and behaviour
- plan activities which are developmentally appropriate
- decide which aspects of development to observe
- assess a child's strengths or identify any gaps in learning
- adapt your practice to take account of different theoretical approaches.

Example: Linking Vygotsky's theory to practice

As we saw in Unit 3.9, Vygotsky stressed children's active role in human development and (unlike Piaget) believed that a child's development occurs as a result of the child's attempts to deal with everyday problems. He also thought that in dealing with these problems, the child always develops strategies collaboratively, that is, in interaction with others. A significant proportion of children's everyday activities take place in Vygotsky's zone of proximal development (ZPD). The case study shows the ZPD 'in action' as the practitioner provides the 'scaffolding' of the activity.

The evaluation of individual needs through observation

All early years practitioners must consider children's individual needs, interests and levels

Case study

Vygotsky's zone of proximal development (ZPD)

A group of children aged four loved to run down a steep grassy slope in the outdoor play area. Margo, an early years practitioner, noticed that they were always keenly watched by the younger children, who could also climb to the top confidently, but then hesitated when they looked down. When the younger children asked for help, she would hold their hands and take them slowly down the slope, gradually increasing the pace each time as they increased in confidence. Once the children were ready to 'go it alone', Margo stood at the bottom to catch them as they came down. Then they did it all by themselves.

of development, and must use this information to plan a challenging and enjoyable experience for each child in all seven areas of learning and development.

AC 4.1 Observe in line with current frameworks: an individual child; a group of children; indoor provision, and outdoor provision

Activity

Using the guidelines above, and possibly with extra guidance from your tutor, carry out observations on:

- an individual child
- a group of children
- indoor provision
- outdoor provision.

AC 4.2 Reflect on outcomes of observations carried out in own setting in relation to: an individual child; a group of children; indoor provision and outdoor provision

Part of being a reflective practitioner is being able to reflect on the outcomes of the observations you have carried out. You could choose the most relevant questions from the list below to help you to reflect on the observations carried out as part of AC 4.1.

Progress check

These areas of focus refer to individual children. For **group observations**, you may want to reflect on the outcome of a particular group activity, such as a cooking activity, or a creative project.

- **Health and physical development**: what kinds of large motor and small motor activities does the child prefer? How does the child manipulate scissors and crayons? Does the family have any concerns about the child's health?
- **Emotional and social development**: can the child generally be described as flexible and easy going? Slow to warm up or cautious or fearful?
- **Skills and abilities**: what does the child do well? What does the child find challenging? What skills is the child trying to achieve?
- **Interests and preferences**: what activities cause the child's eyes to light up? What does the child talk about? When given a choice, what does the child choose to do?
- **Culture and home life**: how does the child express cultural or family traditions during play? How is discipline handled and affection expressed at home?
- **Approach to learning**: how does the child approach a new activity? How would you describe the child's interaction with materials?
- **Communication skills**: how much verbal language does the child have? Does the child talk to other children? Other adults? What does the child talk about?
- **Use of body language**: how does the child move? Does the child use gestures? Is the child physically expressive?
- **Social interaction**: does the child interact with other children? How does the child initiate interactions? How does the child handle conflicts?
- **Cognitive skills**: does the child show interest in books and other print material? Does the child notice similarities and differences?
- **Group activities**: was the group activity suitable for each child? Did each child become involved? Did you fulfil your stated **aim**?
- **Indoor provision**: did you identify any areas of indoor provision that worked particularly well? Did you evaluate the resources used – in terms of staff and equipment? Were there any aspects of the provision that could be improved?
- **Outdoor provision**: did you identify any areas of indoor provision that worked particularly well? Did you consider the role of risk and challenge in outdoor play? Were there any aspects of the provision that could be improved?

AC 4.3 Work with others to plan next steps in relation to the needs and interests of: an individual child; a group of children

Early years practitioners need to share information gained from observation and assessment to:

- inform their future planning
- group children for particular activities and interests
- ensure that the curriculum meets the needs of all children
- promote continuity and progression.

Information should be shared between the setting and the home, so that a holistic picture of the child's needs, preferences and skills emerges. Parents have important information about their child's competence at home which will help practitioners to plan for their next stage of learning.

Activity

For each of the observations carried out for AC 4.1, you should work with others to plan the next steps in relation to the children's needs and interests.

AC 4.4 Reflect on own role in meeting the needs and interests of children in own setting

Reflect on:

- the ways in which you communicate with children
- the variety of activities you provide for children – both indoors and outdoors
- the ways in which you use regular observations to find out about children's needs and interests.

Think about these aspects of your work in relation to supporting children's developmental needs. For example:

- Do you vary your method of communication to account for the individual child's needs and stage of development?
- Do you provide a wide range of activities which are designed to promote particular skills?
- Do you plan activities to promote development for individual children?
- Do you use observations to build up a picture of children's interests and needs?
- Do you involve parents in the observations you carry out with their children?

Activity ·

After considering these questions, can you think of ways in which you could improve your practice?

· ·

LO5 AC 5.1 Work with parents/carers in a way which encourages them to take an active role in their child's play, learning and development

See Unit 3.5, LO8 for advice and information on working with parents and carers in this way.

Assessment practice

1 Explain how observations are used to plan for individual children's needs.
2 How can observations help in early intervention?
3 What is the role of observations in reviewing the early years environment?
4 How can observations help during transition?
5 How would you use observations when working in partnership?
6 Describe the different observation techniques. For each method of observation, give an example of its possible application.
7 Why is it important to be objective when carrying out observations?

8 How do you practise confidentiality when carrying out observations?
9 Observe a group of children in line with current frameworks and reflect on the outcomes of these observations.
10 How can you work with others to plan the next steps in relation to the needs and interests of a group of children?
11 Reflect upon your own role in meeting the needs and interests of children in own setting.
12 How can you work with parents/carers in a way which encourages them to take an active role in their child's play, learning and development?

Useful resources

Books

Berk, L. E. (2006), *Child Development* (7th edn). Boston, MA: Pearson International Edition.

Bertram, T. and Pascal, C. (1997), *Effective Early Learning: Case Studies in Improvement*. London: Hodder & Stoughton.

Harding, J. and Meldon-Smith, L. (1996), *How to make Observations and Assessments*, London: Hodder Arnold.

Sylva, K., Roy, C. and Painter, M (1980), *Childwatching at Playgroup and Nursery School*. London: Sage Publications.

Unit 3.15 Use longitudinal studies to observe, assess and plan for children's needs

This unit provides the learner with the knowledge, understanding and skills to carry out observations in order to assess and plan for children's changing needs over time.

Learning outcomes

By the end of this unit you will:

1 Understand the purpose of undertaking longitudinal studies.
2 Be able to use observations to assess and plan for the developmental needs of children in line with current frameworks.
3 Be able to critically evaluate the outcomes of longitudinal studies.

LO1 Understand the purpose of undertaking longitudinal studies

A longitudinal study is an observational research method in which data is gathered for the same subjects repeatedly over a period of time – often as long as one year or more. In relation to child development and care, longitudinal studies can serve many different purposes and have the following characteristics:

- They are very useful for studying the developmental trends in children, or the effects of particular variables over time, for example, how violence on television affects children.
- As the participants form one group, the children will have similar experiences and cultural influences; for example, the programme *Child of our Time*, in which the BBC set out on a project to follow the lives of 25 children after their birth at the turn of the millennium. All the children are living in and going to school in the UK, being influenced by similar social and cultural variables (excluding social class and ethnicity).

When conducted on a grand scale, such studies tend to be very expensive and time-consuming.

Also participants may drop out of the study – and researchers may move on to other projects.

AC 1.1 Explain how longitudinal study is used as an assessment tool

This unit guides you through the process of completing two longitudinal studies. Each comprises a set of observations on an individual child; the observations carried out in the study provide us with valuable information about individual children:

- where they have reached in their development and learning
- their progress in the different areas of development
- aspects of their health and well-being
- personality, temperament, likes and dislikes
- response to different experiences
- behaviour in a range of contexts, for example in different social and physical environments.

This information gathered over a period of time will enable the practitioner to:

- find out more about different aspects of child development
- identify ways in which children learn
- reflect on what providers must do to promote development and learning and, thus, further develop good practice
- assess the development of the child or children
- plan for the next stage of development.

AC 1.2 Evaluate benefits of undertaking a longitudinal study

As you may imagine, a longitudinal study is not something which can be achieved through a single observation. It consists of a series of observations of different aspects of development, recorded using a variety of techniques over a period of time – a few weeks, months, a year or more. It provides opportunities to look at the 'whole' child by observing and assessing progress in all areas of development. As a student, you are most likely to carry out such a study on a child whom you know well or whose family you know well. In this case you may be given permission to include photographs and/or video footage.

The initial part of the study will involve gathering background and factual information, followed by observations carried out at agreed intervals (not necessarily regular). You may get the chance to observe special events, such as outings, birthdays, clinic visits, as well as the child's time spent in a setting. When you have recorded all your observations, you can collate the information. You might choose to present them in strict chronological order or in groups of observations of different developmental areas. This will depend on the focus of your study and the individual observations.

In settings, a longitudinal study can be particularly useful in planning long-term strategies for a child with additional needs.

The benefits of undertaking a longitudinal study for the child

Following the progress of an individual child over a period of time enables you to build up a picture of his or her:

- holistic development
- needs – and how these change over time
- interests and preferences.

The relationship that develops between you, the child and the wider family is an important one. You will be well placed to notice the different milestones in development and to use your understanding of child development to suggest play activities that will promote holistic development.

The benefits of undertaking a longitudinal study for early years practitioners

The main benefit to practitioners in undertaking a longitudinal study is the relationship that develops between you, the child and the family. As you get to know the child, you will find it easier to focus on specific aspects of development; to find out what particularly interests the child, and to further your knowledge of child development.

The benefits of undertaking a longitudinal study for others

Parents and carers should benefit from your study of their child. Because you are focusing solely on the individual child, you will have the time and understanding to record special and routine events, to evaluate play provision and to suggest ideas for future ways of promoting holistic development. You will also be well placed to notice if the child is not progressing as well in any area, and can offer ideas for intervention, where necessary.

LO2 Use observations to assess and plan for the developmental needs of children in line with current frameworks

Good observational skills develop over a period of time and through experience, but they are essential for all early years practitioners. It is worth learning and practising these skills now, as a learner, so you have a foundation for your future work with children. There is a wide range of methods to choose from and you will be given opportunities to try several, if not all. Deciding what to observe and which method will best suit your purposes is, in the initial stage, a question of following whatever guidance you are given. The more methods you try for yourself, the better able you will be to make your own selection and justify it.

AC 2.1 Carry out longitudinal studies using methods of observation to assess the changing developmental needs of children

For this AC you are required to complete **two longitudinal studies** of two children from two age ranges in a real work environment. Your tutor will give you extra guidance to help you make choices and to plan the studies.

The studies both require a focus on one child in one specific area of development.

Each longitudinal study will be made up of a total of **four** observations. Throughout the studies a minimum of **two different observation methods** must be used.

Practitioners will make their choices by selecting **two age ranges** from the following:

- birth to one year 11 months
- two years to two years 11 months
- three to five years.

On completion of each observation, a **summative evaluation** must be completed in order to plan the next steps for the child based on the assessment of the child's needs.

Each plan must be implemented with the child and used to inform the next observation as part of the observation and assessment cycle.

Once each longitudinal study has been completed, an **overall evaluation** must be completed in relation to:

- the child's developmental stage, interests and needs
- the learner's role
- choice of methods
- current frameworks
- theoretical perspectives
- partnership working.

Guidelines: carrying out longitudinal studies

Consider the following factors when planning to undertake the studies:

- reasons for choosing the child or age group
- aspects of development you intend to observe – including physical, intellectual, emotional, social, language and communication
- initial information about the child
- how you will observe them – the different observational techniques you intend to use
- any ethical considerations
- observation comparisons
- limitations which may affect your observations and/ or recordings.

NB You will also need to ensure that you maintain confidentiality and objectivity.

AC 2.2 Maintain records of observation, assessment and planning

Effective planning for children's early learning is based on every child's individual needs, abilities and interests; this is why accurate observations and assessments are so important. These needs have to be integrated into the curriculum requirements for your particular setting and the age groups of the children you work with, for example the learning and development requirements of the EYFS.

It is important that you maintain records of all your observation, assessment and planning activities. These should be stored in a secure place, and confidentiality must be upheld. For more information, see Unit 3.14.

AC 2.3 Evaluate observations in relation to: expected developmental stages; current frameworks, and theoretical perspectives

For information on evaluating observations, see Unit 3.14.

AC 2.4 Devise plans which meet the developmental needs and interests of children

For information on planning to meet developmental needs, see Unit 3.8.

AC 2.5 Implement plans which meet the developmental needs and interests of children

For information on implementing plans to meet developmental needs, see Unit 3.8.

LO3 AC 3.1 Critically evaluate the outcomes of longitudinal studies

When you have completed the two longitudinal studies, you need to be able to evaluate them critically. This involves:

- showing that you have interpreted your observations during your study, for the purpose of assessment and recording. You should include evidence of these interpretations with your studies.

- evaluating the observational techniques used – including the longitudinal study method.

Assessment practice

1 Explain how longitudinal study is used as an assessment tool.
2 Evaluate benefits of undertaking a longitudinal study for: the child, early years practitioners, others.
3 Carry out longitudinal studies using methods of observation to assess the changing developmental needs of children
4 How can you maintain records of observation, assessment and planning?

5 Evaluate your observations in relation to: expected developmental stages; current frameworks; theoretical perspectives.
6 Devise plans which meet the developmental needs and interests of children.
7 Implement plans which meet the developmental needs and interests of children.
8 Critically evaluate the outcomes of longitudinal studies.

Useful resources

Speak to your tutor for further guidance on useful resources.

In profile

I work in a nursery that has children from 3 months to 5 years so planning for their individual needs is paramount. We have a planning system in place across the nursery that bases all activities on individual needs and interests. Every resource that is set out for the children has a purpose behind it- we call this purposeful play activities. All resources are enhanced in various ways to make the learning behind the play varied and significant in their progress.

Children are observed through written, photographic and sound recordings which are done throughout the nursery on a daily basis. The observations are then taken to plan the next steps and activities that will be provided in the next few days. The planning sheets are displayed on the walls so that all practitioners can see them when they are setting up the room.

We enhance the play opportunities provided with other resources, including natural materials. For example, the toy animals would be put on a piece of material to enhance the texture/sensory aspect. Children would also have natural logs and wood to create hills and higher/lower play. By doing this, not only is the language enriched but opportunities are also provided to experience maths, communication and language (including extended vocabulary), knowledge of the world, role-play and social skills. We have found that by making these simple changes, the children are more engaged in activities, learn more from participating and also enjoy their time at nursery more because every day is different.

4.1 Engage in professional development

Unit 4.1 Engage in professional development

This unit provides the learner with the knowledge, understanding and skills required to engage in professional development.

Learning outcomes

By the end of this unit you will:

1 Understand professional development.
2 Understand theoretical perspectives in relation to reflection.
3 Be able to use reflective practice to contribute to own professional development.

LO1 Understand professional development

Professional development and reflective practice are both fundamental to those who work with children in a wide range of settings. Engaging in professional development has a positive influence on improving the status of early years practitioners, as well as enabling them to share examples of effective practice with others. Early years settings benefit from employing early years practitioners who are able to reflect on and improve their professional expertise.

AC 1.1 Explain 'professional development'

Professional development is important for anyone working within a profession. Each profession has a set of standards and rules which govern its practice. Professional development:

- concerns the acquisition of skills and knowledge both for personal development and for career advancement
- involves all types of learning opportunities, ranging from college degrees to formal coursework, conferences, study days, specialist courses and informal learning opportunities while in practice.

In relation to early years practice, professional development also includes mentoring and reflective practice. Continuing professional development (CPD) is fully explored in Unit 2.1.

Being a professional early years practitioner means having sufficient knowledge and understanding of children in relation to their learning and development. It also means being able and willing to challenge everyday practice and to adapt it where necessary, through regular analysis of how best to meet children's holistic needs.

The effect of your own experiences on your practice

Your professional development includes your own 'growth' as a person:

- Your experiences at work and at home can change your attitudes, priorities and ambitions.
- Changes in home circumstances influence decisions you make about your work, for example the hours you work, where you work and the level of responsibility you take on. If you are without family responsibilities, you may welcome the extra challenge of a training course to develop your career. However, if you have to strike a balance between career and home life, and additional time is not available for training, then this might seem a burden.
- Sometimes a personal interest will influence the course of your professional development. For example, you may become involved with the disabled child of friends, which sparks an interest in working with children with physical difficulties.

Self-awareness

An important part of your personal development is self-awareness. Self-awareness means:

- knowing who you are and what you enjoy doing
- being able to recognise your skills, strengths and weaknesses
- being able to recognise your effect on other people.

Key areas for self-awareness include our personality traits, personal values, habits and emotions.

Self-awareness helps you to exploit your strengths and cope with your weaknesses. The process of being self-aware can be uncomfortable when you realise that something you have done or said has had a negative impact on someone else. However, unless we face such self-awareness, we can never really develop and improve our practice. What is important here is that you have a network of colleagues that you can call upon for support and guidance should you require it.

Self-awareness is also crucial for developing effective interpersonal skills and building positive relationships with children and their families. Additionally, being self-aware allows you to identify your own learning needs and the ways in which those learning needs can be met – and then it is involved in your evaluation of whether those needs have been met.

Being non-judgemental

It is very important to be non-judgemental. It is easy to criticise others and to believe that you would approach things in a better way. However, parents and carers can only learn to trust you if they know that you are not judging their actions.

Activity

Read through the section on CPD in Unit 2.1. Then think about how an understanding of the importance of professional development could improve your working life. Make a list of the areas of practice you would like to develop, and find out how to access opportunities for further training and education.

AC 1.2 Describe methods for identifying professional development opportunities

It is important to keep abreast of all the changes in early years practice by reading the relevant magazines and journals, such as *Nursery World* and *Early Years Educator*, and by being willing to attend training courses when available. Nationally and locally, both public services and private companies will offer a variety of opportunities on diverse topics – for example, courses on:

- EYFS
- Learning and Development
- Leadership and Management
- SEND and Inclusion
- Safeguarding and Welfare Requirements
- Paediatric First Aid.

TACTYC, the Association for the Professional Development of Early Years Educators, is an early years organisation for anyone involved with the education and training of those who work with young children.

When you have completed the CACHE Early Years Educator course, you may wish to take further training and education. These opportunities include:

- a Foundation degree in Early Years
- Early Years Teacher Course
- Early Years Professional Status (EYPS), a graduate-level qualification combining both high-level practitioner skills and leading other practitioners in a variety of settings.

Activity

Identify professional development opportunities using the Internet and your local authority websites.

LO2 Understand theoretical perspectives in relation to reflection

AC 2.1 Summarise theoretical perspectives on reflection in relation to professional development

There are many different theoretical perspectives on reflective practice. Three of the best known and respected in the area of both education and health studies are those of Schön, Kolb and Gibbs.

Schön: the reflective practitioner

Donald Schön (author of *The Reflective Practitioner*) defined reflective practice as the practice by which professionals become aware of their implicit knowledge base and learn from their experience. He introduced the following three ideas:

- **Reflection in action**: reflect on behaviour as it happens, so as *to optimise* immediately following the action.
- **Reflection on action**: reflecting after the event, to review, analyse and evaluate the situation, so as to gain insight for improved practice in future.
- **Ladders of reflections**: action and reflection on action make a ladder. Every action is followed by reflection and every reflection is followed by action in a repetitive manner. In this ladder, the products of reflections also become the objects for further reflections.

Kolb's cyclical model of experiential learning

David Kolb views learning as an integrated process, with each stage being mutually supportive of and feeding into the next. It is possible to enter the cycle at any stage and follow it through its logical sequence.

- **Stage 1: Concrete experience** – the first stage of the process is to have a learning experience.
- **Stage 2: Observing and reflection** – at this stage learners are encouraged to reflect on what they learnt, how and why they learnt it and whether the experience could have been improved on (evaluation and self-reflection). This reflection can take many forms. It can be in conjunction with the teacher, peers or privately by the learner.
- **Stage 3: Forming abstract concepts** (generalising) – at this stage it is useful to use other experiences as a form or reference, and use other modes and models of thinking to inform your ideas. At the beginning of learning, this may be hard to do.
- **Stage 4: Testing the learning in new situations** – the final stage involves placing the learnt material into context within one's own life. If this does not happen, it is likely that the new knowledge gained will be forgotten quickly. It also involves thinking about how the learner will implement the knowledge and how they could make the next learning experience more

beneficial. The cyclical nature of the model implies there is no end: the cycle starts again when you reach the last point as you would start to implement what you have learnt in a new 'concrete experience' (Stage 1).

Gibbs' reflective cycle

Graham Gibbs' reflective cycle is a process involving six steps:

1 **Description** – what happened?
2 **Feelings** – what did you think and feel about it?
3 **Evaluation** – what were the positives and negatives?
4 **Analysis** – what sense can you make of it?
5 **Conclusion** – what else could you have done?
6 **Action Plan** – what will you do next time?

It is a 'cycle' because the action one takes in the final stage will feed back into the first stage, beginning the process again. The nature of a 'never-ending' cycle is one of the benefits of reflective practice, so that the learner does not stop learning or continuing to reflect on their practice.

Activity ·

Theories of reflection all emphasise the cyclic or repetitive nature of reflection. Why do you think this is? How would you summarise these perspectives?

· ·

LO3 Be able to use reflective practice to contribute to own professional development

What is a reflective practitioner?

A reflective practitioner is an individual who has developed the ability to gain self-knowledge – both of him- or herself and of his or her practice. Reflection allows the practitioner to learn about, evaluate, develop and take a position on his or her practice.

Reflective practice is associated with learning from experience; it is an important strategy for all who work in the caring field and is grounded in the individual's range of values, knowledge, theories and practice, which influence the judgements made about a particular situation.

Reflective practice requires a set of skills that the practitioner must use, such as:

- self-awareness
- the ability to view situations from multiple perspectives
- critical analysis and searching for alternative explanations
- the ability to use evidence in supporting or evaluating a decision or position.

Other skills include the ability to integrate new knowledge into existing knowledge, while making a judgement on the incident or situation. This is because evaluation is central to developing any new perspective.

The reflective cycle
See Figure 4.1.1

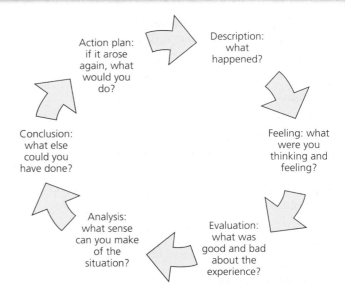

Figure 4.1.1 The reflective cycle (G. Gibbs (1988), *Learning by Doing*. Oxford: Further Education Unit)

Case study

Using the reflective cycle

Description of experience: what happened?
Claire and I were supervising about 12 children aged three years who were using the outdoor play equipment. One of the children, Sasha, climbed to the top of the little slide and pushed Ben very hard so that he fell and bruised his knees. I picked Ben up to examine his knees and to comfort him. Claire – who is my room supervisor – rushed towards Sasha and gave her an angry shove, saying, 'You naughty girl – now you know what it feels like!' I then told Claire that I was taking Ben indoors to deal with his injury. By the time I came back outside, Sasha was playing happily on the trikes; Ben was no longer crying and he went off to play indoors at the water tray.

Feelings: how did it make you feel?
I was quite shaken. I felt that Claire had reacted instinctively and lashed out without thinking first. She has quite a short fuse, but I have never seen her do anything like that before. I was annoyed that I did not say anything to Claire about it.

Evaluation: what was good and what was bad about the experience?
The good part about the experience was that ultimately neither child was seriously hurt. The bad part was that I had not felt able to talk to Claire about it and felt that the opportunity for telling her how I felt was now lost.

Analysis: what sense can you make of the situation?
I lacked assertiveness. I felt ashamed that I had witnessed bad practice and done nothing about it. I think Claire has been under a lot of stress recently as her mother is in hospital. I think I was hesitant to challenge her because she is senior to me and because normally I would trust her judgement.

Conclusion: what else could you have done?
I could have told Claire that I would like to discuss her behaviour towards Sasha, and could have arranged to see her after work.

Action plan: what would you do if it arose again?
I would try to remember what I have learnt about being assertive without being aggressive. I would definitely speak to Claire about how I felt and hope that it could be discussed rationally.

Problem-solving in the workplace as a reflective practitioner
A problem occurs when there is a difference between what 'should be' and what 'is' – between the ideal and the actual situation. Problem-solving is important in childcare contexts, both for the children's learning and for the adult's practice. Problem-solving is:

- a tool, which helps you to achieve a goal
- a skill, because once learnt, it stays with you for life, in the same way as being able to read and write
- a process, because it involves taking a number of steps.

Problem-solving is also the foundation of a young child's learning. Opportunities for problem-solving occur in the everyday context of a child's life; by observing the child closely, practitioners can use the child's social, cognitive, physical and emotional experiences to encourage problem-solving and to promote strategies which will be of lasting value.

One of the skills of being a reflective practitioner is to learn how to solve problems effectively.

A problem-solving cycle

There are different models of problem-solving cycles. Some are more suited to engineering problems where scientific investigation is important.

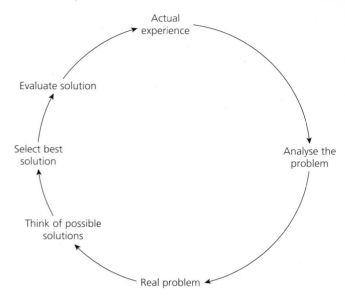

Figure 4.1.2 A problem-solving cycle

Case study

A worked example

1 **Actual experience**: this is something which is identified as a problem – there is a difference between what 'should be' and what 'is'. Bethany, aged three-and-a-half, attends a nursery on four days a week. She is a very lively girl and her key person, Emma, has noticed a problem during story time. Bethany wriggles and fidgets throughout the story; she gets up and walks around. She picks toys up and 'whizzes' them through the air. Bethany sometimes copies the other children when they are responding to the adult, but usually whines when fetched back to sit in the group.

2 **Analyse the problem**: gather information about the problem, through observation and data from other sources. Emma observes Bethany, using an event-sampling observational technique. She discusses the problem with Bethany's mother and also tables it to be discussed at the next team meeting. Bethany's mother tells Emma that Bethany is always lively at home and does not even sit still at mealtimes. She has a new baby brother at home who is now three months old.

3 **Real problem**: after analysing the information obtained, the cause of the problem is decided. Emma decides that the real problem is one of attention-seeking behaviour. Bethany did not have this problem until after the birth of her brother.

4 **Think of possible solutions**: brainstorm and analyse data; ensure that many possible ideas are explored and as much relevant data as possible is gathered. After discussion at the team meeting, Emma comes up with a range of possible solutions:
- Encourage Bethany to improve her listening skills by working one-to-one with her and reading.
- Encourage Bethany to choose a friend with whom to listen to a story read by an adult.
- Plan story times to include more opportunities for active movement.
- Set up a system of rewards – such as a star chart – which would apply to all the children at story time, rewarding wanted behaviour. Bethany's parents would be encouraged to continue this system at home.
- Encourage play with an infant doll – involving Bethany in feeding and caring for the doll.
- Choose books which promote discussion about young babies in the family.

5 **Select best solution**: make sure the solution is achievable within time and resource constraints. It is decided to encourage Bethany to play with a doll and to read books about the birth of a new baby in the family, with one-to-one attention. If this does not work, Emma will introduce a reward system, with the parents' cooperation.

→

6 **Evaluate solution**: how effective was the solution? If the problem was not solved, you may need to start the whole process again.

Bethany responds well to both strategies. She begins to carry the doll around at home and 'care' for it just like Mummy is caring for her brother. She also enjoys sitting quietly while an adult reads to her. Story time behaviour is greatly improved. Emma plans to work

with mothers who are expecting a baby to prepare the older sibling for the event, using books and dolls – both in the nursery and at home.

Observations, discussion and involving the parents were essential to solving the problem and also encouraged reflective practice.

Case study

Tensions in the nursery

Helen is the manager of a day nursery in an inner-city area. There are six full-time members of staff at the nursery, caring for 34 children. Two newly qualified nursery nurses have recently been employed, and Helen has noticed new tensions within the nursery. One of the new workers, Sarah, has asked for three weeks' annual leave at Christmas, so that she can visit her family in Australia. Darren, who has worked there for eight years, always takes two weeks off at that time, to visit Ireland. The other new staff member, Dianne, has suggested a more positive approach to equal opportunities, with more emphasis on multicultural provision, the observance of festivals and more variety in the daily menu, etc. One of the more experienced members of staff claims that the nursery already offers equal

opportunities and that any changes are both unnecessary and expensive; she also claims that parents are not in agreement with such plans.

In addition, another staff member, Pat, has had a great deal of time off work because her father has recently died; the rest of the staff feel that her absences have gone on for an unreasonable length of time, and they are tired of having to take on extra work.

Divide into groups and discuss the following questions:

1 How should Helen deal with these issues?
2 Do you think they are all equally important, or should any one issue be addressed before the others?

Feed back each group's answers into the whole group and summarise the strategies for solving the problems.

Activity

Problem-solving

Try a similar problem-solving exercise in your workplace, using the problem-solving cycle above. Use structured observations to help monitor the problem you have identified.

AC 3.1 Develop a curriculum vitae

It is always useful to compile a curriculum vitae (CV) and to keep it up to date. The purposes of a CV are to:

- provide a brief outline of your life history
- set out basic factual information in a concise manner
- help in filling out application forms.

Microsoft Word and Open Office both have templates for a CV or résumé. The main headings to include are:

- first name and family name
- personal details: date of birth, full postal address, and telephone number
- education and qualifications: include names of schools and colleges attended with dates and qualifications obtained
- employment history: if you have not worked before, include work, involvement in local organisations or babysitting experience, college work groups, and sport and leisure interests
- other experience: include any voluntary experience and Saturday and holiday jobs
- referees: give the names, positions and address of two people who are willing to provide references for you. Always ask their permission first.

CVs should be neatly typed and presented and free from any mistakes. Use your spellchecker, and also ask a friend to check it through for you. In general, if you are applying for a post in a school or local authority Children's Centre or day nursery, CVs will not be accepted. Read the guidance on job applications very carefully before you complete the forms to apply for a post.

Activity ·

Compile a CV, using the guidelines above.

· ·

AC 3.2 Analyse own professional development needs in relation to the role of the EYP

Reflect on your work activities

You should get used to reviewing and reflecting on your experiences as part of your everyday learning. In this way, every experience – whether positive or negative – will contribute to your development and personal growth. Ways to reflect include:

- setting yourself some goals or targets when you start studying, and using feedback from your tutor and placement supervisor to monitor your progress
- working out what you have achieved and what you still need to work on
- making a record of your thoughts and reflections, to help you to keep track of your ideas and see how far they have developed over a period of time
- recording your thoughts on any difficulties or challenges you are facing
- talking things through with another person, such as another learner or a trusted friend.

Progress check

Reflective practice

Using **reflective practice** will help you to review and evaluate your own practice. General and specific reflective questions will help to organise this evaluation – for example:

- Was your contribution to the planning meeting or activity appropriate?
- Did you achieve your targets? If not, was it because the targets were unrealistic?
- What other methods could be used?
- How can I improve my practice?
- Who can I ask for advice and support?
- How can I help a child to settle in again after his hospital stay?
- What is making a child behave inappropriately at mealtimes?

Key term

reflective practice A learner should consider their actions, experiences or learning and their implications in order to suggest significant developments for future action, learning or practice. These are recognised cycles of reflective practice. Reflective practice can also show that a learner performed exceptionally well.

Using feedback to analyse and improve your practice

Feedback is structured information that one person offers to another, about the impact of their actions or behaviour – in other words, how you are doing in your study or work role. It is vital to the success of most workplace tasks, and is an activity we engage in on a daily basis. Feedback should not be confused with **criticism**, which is often an unprepared reaction to people who are not behaving in the way you want them to. Criticism can make the recipient feel undervalued or angry – both unproductive emotions.

The information you hear when receiving feedback from others may be new – and even surprising. You may react with strong emotion. Positive feedback is an offer of information, not a diagnosis of your character or potential, so you should not react angrily or take it personally.

Receiving feedback can:

- help you become aware of your progress – the positive and the negative, what is working and what is not
- give you some ideas to help you plan your own development, in order to reach your full potential
- give you a 'reality check' – you can compare how you think you are, with what other people tell you.

Feedback from a number of different people helps you make a balanced decision about the information you are hearing. Apart from the feedback you receive through formal appraisals of your performance, you may receive other forms of feedback, such as:

- informal observations by colleagues
- **mentoring**: a mentor supports you by modelling good practice, and guiding you to look critically at your own practice, helping you to decide how it can be improved

- **questionnaires**: these are useful in obtaining feedback from parents and carers about the setting.

Barriers to the feedback process

Feedback is sometimes difficult to give or receive. The giver and receiver both need to be open to receiving feedback, and open to the possibility that the feedback being given may be based on incorrect assumptions. You may find it difficult to **give** feedback because you:

- believe that feedback is negative and unhelpful
- worry that the other person will not like you
- believe that the other person cannot handle the feedback
- have had previous experiences in which the receiver was hostile to feedback.

Receiving corrective feedback may be difficult because you:

- have the urge to rationalise, since the criticism can feel uncomfortable
- believe that your self-worth is diminished by suggestions for improvement
- have had previous experiences in which feedback was unhelpful or unjustified.

Guidelines: developing effective feedback skills

- **Ask questions**: state what you want feedback about. Be specific about what you want to know. Give the other person time to think about what they want to say.
- **Listen**: listen attentively. Do not interrupt or digress. Ask for clarification if you are not sure that you have understood what you have heard. Try not to be defensive or to reject the information. You need to listen, but not necessarily to agree. Take notes of what is said.
- **Check**: check what you have heard. Repeat back what the other person has said and ask for examples of what they mean. Give your reactions to the feedback or ask for time to think about it if necessary. Ask for suggestions on how to improve.
- **Reflect**: feedback is information for you to use – it is not a requirement to change. If you are unsure about the soundness of the feedback, check it out with other people. Work out the options open to you and decide what you want to do. It is up to you to evaluate how accurate and how useful the feedback is.

AC 3.3 Review own learning needs, professional interests and development opportunities

Accessing support to review your progress and achievements

Work with an appropriate person, such as your tutor or placement supervisor, to express your opinions and develop an individual plan that includes:

- **targets** that clearly show what you want to achieve in your learning, work or personal life, and how you will know if you have met these
- the **actions** you will take (action points) and dates for completing them (deadlines) to help you meet each target
- **how to get the support you need**, including who will review your progress, and where and when this will take place.

Your tutor or trainer will help you to discuss your progress; he or she will enable you to reflect on *what* you learnt, *how* you learnt, and *what* has been successful or unsuccessful. You should also aim to:

- **identify the targets** you have met, by checking your plan to see if you have done what you set out to do
- **identify your achievements** by finding out what you need to do to improve your performance (the quality of your work, and the way you work)
- **use ways of learning** suggested by your tutor or supervisor, making changes when needed to improve your performance.

Activity

Review your own learning needs, professional interests and development opportunities.

AC 3.4 Maintain subject knowledge across curriculum subjects which are of personal interest

Reviewing current research and using professional literature

Using professional literature will help you to inform your practice and in turn promote professional development. Reviewing literature is carrying out an analysis of what others have said or found out about the research area in question.

The first step is to decide which literature is most relevant to you. In other words, what are you hoping to find out? Through the literature, you should be able to confirm your concerns – discarding, modifying or adding to them as you read. As a result, you will identify a number of themes and sub-themes within your original topic which will provide the framework for your enquiry. You then need to focus on the themes you have identified.

1 **Be systematic**: keep a careful record of all you read, including exact bibliographic references. One useful method of keeping track of reading is to use a card index file (either a paper or digital version). Each time you find a book or an article which you think will be useful, note it down on a card, remembering to record a full note of the author, etc. You should include a few notes for each reference to remind you of the main issues raised by the author when you return to it. For example:

   ● **Quotes and references**: if you come across a statement which you might wish to quote, or one which you feel summarises the issues well and you might wish to refer to, make sure you write down a full reference, including the page number. This will help you to find it again and, if you use the quotation in writing up the study, you should cite the page number.

   ● **Reading in greater depth**: this allows you to identify competing perspectives within each sub-theme, to compare and contrast them and to identify strengths and weaknesses in the views given.

   The search may include books, journals, policy statements, professional journals and other publications, including electronic ones. While books are important, journals tend to be more up to date in their treatment of the issues which you might be researching. Many of the articles available online through the internet are highly topical.

2 **Be critical of what you read**: most writers have a particular viewpoint on an issue and you should consider the validity and reliability of statements made, the authority of the author and the professional relevance of the issues raised. Some journals are more authoritative than others.

3 **Read reviews** of books and reports in journals, and follow up those which seem promising.

4 Ask yourself questions about what you read:
   Presentation: is the style appropriate, clear, and readable?
   Authors: who are they and where are they from?
   Target audience: is it aimed at practitioners, academics, or researchers?
   Relevance: does it raise significant issues?
   Evidence: what is the evidence for arguments made? Is it appropriate? Do you have enough information to know if they drew appropriate conclusions?
   Plausibility: does it convince you?

If the focus of your enquiry is the effectiveness of a new policy within your area, for example, on learning and teaching in schools, it will be important to understand and analyse policy documents as well as any other relevant official publications. However, government policy documents will always take a rather one-sided view of the issues, so you need to balance this by reading about aspects of, for example, philosophy (child-centred education), psychology (how children learn) and sociology (poverty and discrimination).

5 Libraries can be very useful in showing you the way to find appropriate information on a particular topic.

Activity . . . .

Choose a subject area which particularly interests you. Find out how to access literature and other information to research the topic.

. . . .

AC 3.5 Work with others to agree own personal development plan

The importance of setting targets

Setting targets or goals as part of a personal development plan will help you to become more involved in your learning. Remember, your targets are personal; they may be quite different from those of other people in your class.

Learning targets can help you to:

- decide what is most important to you in your learning
- fit your studies in with your other commitments
- decide on how you will study
- become an active learner
- think about your personal and professional development.

Each member of a team needs to know exactly what is expected of them. These expectations are called targets or 'objectives'. Your learning targets should be **SMART**, which is an acronym for:

Specific	They must be easy to understand and say exactly what you want to happen.
Measurable	Success can be measured by checking back carefully against the instructions that have been given.
Achievable	The targets can be reached with reasonable effort in the time you are allowed.
Relevant	The targets must be appropriate, building on previous strengths and skills.
Time-related	The targets have clearly set deadlines and are reviewed frequently.

Activity ·

Using SMART targets

Look at the following scenarios and see how SMART targets can help individuals and teams to plan and to achieve their objectives.

1 *Scenario 1*: Paula has been asked if she would organise a display for the nursery room. The only instructions she has been given are:
'Paula, can you put up a nice, colourful display in the nursery room, please?'

2 *Scenario 2*: At a different nursery, Mark has also been asked to organise a display. On Wednesday, he was given these instructions:
'Next Monday we need to create an interactive display for the nursery room. It will be on the theme of Autumn. We've already collected some pine cones and autumn leaves, and we also have some good posters, but I'd like you to plan what else we

need and let me have a list of resources required by tomorrow lunchtime.'

Using targets for personal and professional development

Write down in two or three sentences what you hope to achieve through your course, and how you think it will help you in the future.

- What do you want to be able to do, think, feel, understand or know?
- How would this learning be recognised by others?
- What are the steps you need to take to reach the end result?

Now write your personal plan and learning targets based on these ideas, using the notes above as a guide.

· ·

AC 3.6 Use learning opportunities to support own professional development

Your early years setting should keep you informed about opportunities for progression, but it is your responsibility to:

- take advantage of opportunities to gain new knowledge and skills
- identify the new knowledge and skills which will be useful in your work
- use support to find out how to use the new skills and knowledge in your work
- use the new knowledge and skills to improve your practice
- use support to ask for feedback on improvements to your practice.

Activity ·

Describe how you have used learning opportunities to support your own professional development.

· ·

AC 3.7 Explain how reflective practice leads to improved ways of working

As an early years practitioner you need to know and understand the techniques of reflective practice:

- questioning what, why and how
- seeking alternatives
- keeping an open mind

- viewing from different perspectives
- thinking about consequences
- testing ideas through comparing and contrasting
- asking 'what if?'
- synthesising – or pulling together – ideas
- seeking, identifying and resolving problems.

Activity

Reflecting on your own practice

1 How do you monitor the processes, practices and outcomes from your work?
2 Give examples of how you evaluate your own professional practice including: self-evaluation; reflections on your interactions with others; sharing your reflections with others; using feedback from others to improve your own evaluation.
3 Describe how you have used reflection to solve problems and improve practice.

AC 3.8 Record progress in relation to personal development

Self-evaluation is important because it helps you to improve your own practice and to modify plans to meet the learning needs of the children.

Compile a record of your progress, and remember to add to it as your course progresses. In particular, make a record of:

- your own strengths and weaknesses
- areas you want to improve
- learning from observations and assessment of children
- activities with children that have gone well or badly – with evaluation
- learning opportunities you have accessed – e.g. courses, study sessions, in-service training, etc.
- reflections on your practice
- feedback you have received.

Assessment practice

1 What do you understand by the term professional development?
2 How would you go about identifying professional development opportunities?
3 Describe two theoretical perspectives on reflection in relation to professional development.
4 Develop a personal CV.
5 What do you perceive to be your own professional development needs?
6 Review your own learning needs and professional interests.
7 Maintain subject knowledge across curriculum subjects which are of personal interest.
8 How can you work with colleagues, trainers, tutors and managers to agree your own personal development plan?
9 Use learning opportunities to support your own professional development.
10 Explain how reflective practice has helped you to improve your practice.
11 Record your progress in relation to personal development.

Useful resources

Organisation

TACTYC Association for the Professional Development of Early Years Educators: An early years organisation for anyone involved with the education and training of those who work with young children: www.tactyc.org.uk

Books

Gibbs, G. (1988), *Learning by Doing: A Guide to Teaching and Learning Methods*. Oxford: Further Educational Unit, Oxford Polytechnic.

Kolb, D.A. (1984), *Experiential Learning Experience as a source of Learning and Development*. New Jersey: Prentice Hall.

Schön, D. (1983), *The Reflective Practitioner*. New York: Basic Books.

In profile

Professional development within the nursery in which I work is seen as an essential part of the staff training. As manager, I conduct weekly room observations, which are unannounced and look at the play environment, the interaction between staff and children, activities provided and the opportunities for sustained thinking among other things. These observations at first were daunting for the staff but as they became a natural part of the day, staff are now more relaxed. It has also helped them prepare for the Ofsted inspection as they are now used to being observed.

The observations will have action points which are discussed with the room leader or the relevant member of staff. After the observation, photographs are also taken as a record of room development. Staff also have a one-to-one with myself or my deputy every 8 weeks. This is an opportunity for staff to talk about their room development, planning, key children and any training/professional development needs and wishes. From these one-to-ones, the staff member is given action points to complete before the next meeting.

Staff also have yearly and half yearly appraisals, this is where 3 targets are set for the development of the nursery and their own professional development for the forthcoming year. They are reviewed after 6 months at the half yearly appraisal and support is put in place to help them achieve their goals.

Assessment – Information and tips

Any assessment of an award or qualification is designed to test your knowledge and understanding of the topics studied and how you apply that knowledge in practical situations. Assessments consider how you link what you have learnt (theory) to professional practice. Assessments can take many different forms, such as essays or multiple-choice question papers.

For this qualification there are three assessments, all of which have the requirement that you, the learner, produce written material, in some appropriate format. Each assessment will cover several units.

The assessments for this qualification are:
● a Short Answer Examination of six questions
● a Reflective Study
● an Extended Essay.

There is no set order for the completion of the assessments. The order is up to your centre and tutors. You do, however, have to achieve a pass grade in all three assessments in order to achieve the full qualification.

The units and themes covered by each assessment are set out in the table below:

Format	Content covered
Short Answer Examination	Theme 1: Units 1.1, 1.2, 1.3, 1.4, 1.5
	Theme 2: Units 2.1, 2.2, 2.3, 2.4
Reflective Study	Theme 3: Units 3.1, 3,3, 3.4, 3.8–3.15
	Theme 4: Units 1 and 2
Extended Essay	Theme 3: Units 3.5, 3.6, 3.7

The Assessment – Short Answer Examination

As you can see in the above table, this assessment covers several units. These units all relate to Theme 1 – Health and well-being, and Theme 2 – Legislation, frameworks and professional practice. This assessment consists of six questions, which are together on one question paper. The questions change for each paper, so it is very unlikely that they will be repeated. However, the topics being assessed remain the same.

The six questions test you in different ways and so need different approaches in order to answer appropriately. The examples given here aim to help you understand the format of the questions and give you some ideas of how to approach and develop your answers. The six questions are marked by CACHE external examiners, not your tutors, and are graded from D, the lowest grade, to A*, the highest grade. The more relevant detail and in-depth knowledge you can show, the greater opportunity for you to achieve higher grades. Every Short Answer Examination will be of equal difficulty so it will not matter when you take this test. Assessments that are marked by CACHE are called External Assessments.

The six questions of the Short Answer Examination are answered under examination conditions, and you have two hours to write your answers. You do not have to answer the questions in order, but you should attempt all of the questions on the paper.

Tip

Remember – if you do not write anything, you cannot be awarded any marks. If you cross something out it may not be considered, so it is probably best not to cross anything out until you are absolutely sure that you do not need it!

Your centre and tutors have guidance for the Short Answer Examination which has been issued by CACHE. This guidance has been produced to help you prepare for the examination, and you are strongly advised to read it.

How marks are awarded

Marks are awarded for each question if you can show that you can correctly recall factual information, and appropriately use and apply your knowledge using correct terminology. For example, use 'key person', not 'key worker'.

Higher grades can be achieved if you develop your knowledge and ideas with more detail, linking to practical examples, such as work placements, making relevant links to theory, current research, legislation and frameworks. The examiners will also be looking for evidence in your answers that you have looked at the subject, topic or idea from several different points of view, made judgements and drawn logical and relevant conclusions.

Before you can answer the questions successfully, it is important that you understand some key words or terms that could be used in a question; for example:

- **Evaluate** the impact of diet on the well-being of a child aged two years.
- **Discuss** the nutritional requirements of babies and young toddlers up to two years old and children between two and three years old.
- **Analyse** the impact of equalities legislation in maintaining an inclusive setting.
- **Explain** why it is important for practitioners to implement health and safety legislation in relation to children's well-being.

If you do not understand the difference between 'analyse' and 'explain', you may not be able to achieve a higher grade for your answer. This is because you may not have provided sufficient relevant and appropriate detail or information. You should avoid using jargon in your answers. However, you should use terminology and language that is appropriate to the childcare and early years sector; for example, Early Years Foundation Stage, next steps, early learning goals.

Terminology and other related language used must be correct and used appropriately; for example, The Children Act (2004) and not the Children's Act; children, not kids.

> ### Tip
>
> The language you use should be uncomplicated and straightforward. There is always the danger that if you use a complex word, that you think sounds impressive, it could be completely wrong or inappropriate. This would mean that marks cannot be awarded!

The table below gives a definition or explanation of some of the most frequently used words or key terms in the questions. These are also referred to as command words or command verbs.

Word or key term	Definition
analyse	Break down the subject into parts or ideas. Write about each part separately. Show how the parts or ideas are related and why they are important.
apply	Give details of how existing knowledge can be linked or used in different or new situations, contexts or circumstances.
assess	Measure, make a judgement or consider an idea.
clarify	Put an idea or topic into simple, clear words that someone who does not have knowledge of childcare and early years education would understand.
compare	Look at a topic, subject or idea and think about similarities and differences.
critically compare	Look at the similarities and differences of a topic, idea or subject in great detail so that you can make judgements.
consider	Think about something so that you can make a decision or judgement.
describe	Write in detail about an idea, topic or subject, using language that is straightforward and not jargon. →

develop	Take an idea, topic or subject and make it bigger, building on the main points.
differentiate	Identify or highlight the differences between two or more ideas, topics or subjects.
discuss	Write a detailed account which includes a range of views or opinions, using plain language and no jargon.
draw conclusions	Identify judgements, or outcomes that could lead to recommendations, consequences or deductions.
evaluate	Look at information from different views or opinions and make a reasoned conclusion or judgement.
critically evaluate	Consider strengths, weaknesses or positive and negative points of an idea, topic or subject and then make detailed judgements which lead to an overall conclusion.
explain how	Write clear and detailed information about the way in which something may happen or work.
explain why	Write clear and detailed information about the reasons something happens or is carried out.
extrapolate	Make clear the relevant and/or significant points, with reasons, using available information.
identify	List, recognise or single out several ideas or topics that are usually linked to a common subject.
judgement	An informed decision, opinion based on facts.
reflect	Think about or consider a subject, topic or idea so that conclusions or judgements can be made.

For more information on different words and phrases that may be used in examination questions, look at CACHE 'Finding the level', which can be downloaded from www.cache.org.uk.

All of the questions test your **knowledge** and **understanding** of topics studied in Themes 1 and 2. In order to answer this type of question, you have to recall factual information and write about it in detail. You must focus on the question and only include relevant information. With any question it is always good practice to read it very carefully, probably at least twice, and make absolutely certain that you are clear in your mind what you have to write about.

Tip

Some people like to write down a plan or list with all their ideas for a question. This can be done in any way that makes sense to you. As you write about each idea it can be crossed off your plan or list. A plan helps to keep your writing focused and stops you wandering off the point or repeating yourself.

A question that tests your knowledge and understanding could be:

 Explain the benefits of exercise to children's development and learning

One way to plan this type of question:

1 Look at what the question is asking you to do. What is the command word? In this case it is 'Explain'. Check that you understand what explain means.

2 What is it that you are being asked to explain? In this question it is the benefits of exercise to development and learning.

3 List the areas of development and learning.

4 How does exercise benefit children in each area *or* instead of points 3 and 4:

5 List as many benefits of exercise as you can remember.

6 Consider each benefit in relation to holistic development.

Tip

The more relevant details you can include, the greater your opportunity to be awarded a higher grade.

In this question you could also relate key points to personal workplace experiences and give practical examples of how you have observed the benefits of exercise for children. For example, you may have been involved in an outdoor play activity where children were running about and playing (Unit 1.2).

You might have discussed with children how they felt after running around outside, and talked with them about feeling breathless, hot, thirsty, excited, good, worn out and tired. Using language like this with young children will help to introduce new words to their vocabulary, which links to the communication and language area of learning and development.

You should include information about healthy lifestyles, diet and nutrition, physical development and exercise. Consider how often children have opportunities for exercise, both indoors and outside, and make judgements whether in your view this is sufficient or not, and what could be improved. When children take part in exercise, they are also going to become more aware of their own bodies, which is part of understanding the world. Children may also become aware of the feelings and needs of others as they exercise and engage in physical activities. This links to their personal, social and emotional development.

There are several theorists who advocate the benefits of outdoor play and exercise for children. These include Friedrich Froebel (1782–1852), Margaret McMillan (1860–1931) (both covered in this book) and more recently the Forest school movement. You might also like to conduct research into the work of Robert Owen (1771–1858). Including appropriate and relevant references and links to theory will help you to achieve higher grades.

Legislation in the form of the Statutory Requirements of the Early Years Foundation Stage has sections that include healthy lifestyles, so if you are aiming for a high grade, reference should be made to this document. (Unit 2.3)

How you **apply and use your knowledge and understanding**, rather than just recalling it, is the key to the Short Answer Examination. It makes sense to use your personal experience of working with children to help you answer the questions rather than making up situations. You will be able to write with more confidence if you are actually thinking about real-life situations, and so your answers should have more details and relevant information.

The questions could also ask you to make **judgements** or **evaluate** how well certain methods or actions have been. Again it is important to read the question very thoroughly and, if it fits your way of working, make a plan. Include your plan in your examination paper when handing it in for marking. If you run out of time but have identified a key issue on your plan, you could be given credit for it.

An example of a question that tests your application of knowledge could be:

 ### Explain why it is important for practitioners to implement health and safety legislation in relation to children's well-being

First of all, decide which are the key or significant words in the questions. In this case they are **'why it is important'**. 'Important' in the context of this question means central, significant, key, crucial, vital. The question is also focusing on the **'implementation of health and safety legislation'**. These words need to be your focus and so should run through all of your answer.

You must know which health and safety legislation is relevant; this is the recall of knowledge part.

Tip

When you write about any piece of legislation in an answer, make sure that you write the full title correctly.

You must understand what is meant by children's well-being; not just recalling knowledge of basic facts but being able to apply and reflect upon that knowledge. The question is asking you to explain **why**; in other words, write in a detailed and clear way the reasons that health and safety legislation is important. This is where you apply and use your knowledge, so use practical examples from your work placement.

You could write about how the policies and procedures in your workplace setting are carried out so that children's well-being is promoted. The Safeguarding and Welfare Requirements of the Early Years Foundation Stage 2012 (3.42 to 3.65) cover all aspects of health and safety and must inform policies and procedures. You could include, for example, why it is important that your workplace records accidents, incidents and emergencies, how sick children are managed or how medicines are stored and administered.

Theorists such as Margaret McMillan placed great significance on the importance of wholesome meals in relation to children's well-being; so it would help to achieve a higher grade if you made reference to relevant theories in your response to the question. This reinforces your knowledge to the external examiner, and shows that you can apply it. This is a question that includes aspects of Theme 1 – health and safety – and Theme 2 – legislation, frameworks and professional practice.

Some questions assess your ability to **analyse** a topic, subject or idea. In these questions you are given a topic, subject or idea and you need to break it down into smaller parts and write about each part in detail. If you find this concept difficult, in a light-hearted way try to think of the whole question as a cake and the analysis would be writing about each of the ingredients of the cake.

An example of a question that tests your ability to analyse is:

Analyse the role of the early years practitioner in meeting children's individual dietary requirements

A possible plan for this question:

1 Identify the command word: analyse.
2 Identify what it is you are analysing. This question is about professional practice (Unit 2.1), so you need to use your own experiences in the workplace to support your answer.

3 In your plan, think about all the possible ways that your role and professional practice have an effect a child's diet. This is not just about being aware of allergic reactions to certain foods and considering cultural differences. It includes respecting different lifestyle choices, such as vegan or vegetarian groups, or parents' preferences on how food is produced, such as organic or ethically produced.
4 What is a healthy and balanced diet?
5 You also need to think about how you make sure that children are offered a healthy and balanced diet that meets their individual requirements.
6 Think about partnership with parents and carers, plus effective communication methods. This is important because it is how you find about a child's individual dietary requirements. (Unit 2.5) This idea may also trigger your thoughts about how you communicate with parents/carers and children and how you take into consideration their likes and dislikes, preferences and requirements.
7 An understanding of the different stages of child development will help you answer this question more fully. Children's dietary requirements can change as they get older. For example, a very young baby will have different needs to those of an active toddler.

You may also want to include reasons why it is important to treat children as individuals in all aspects of their care and development, not just dietary needs. This could lead to a discussion in your answer about equality, diversity and inclusive practice. (Unit 2.4) Think about which theorists, contemporary thinkers or legislation have stressed the importance of meeting a child's individual needs. The Children Act 2004 places great emphasis on the unique child, so decide if something about this piece of legislation should be included in your answer, perhaps as part of your professional role and responsibilities. Do not forget the Statutory Requirements of the Early Years Foundation Stage (2012).

Think about which theorists, contemporary thinkers or legislation have stressed the importance of meeting a child's individual needs. Current researchers such as Gillian Pugh and Jay Belsky, to name only two, write extensively about individual needs and you may want to research them in more detail. Having a healthy diet and issues around obesity are high on the government's agenda. Making reference to this (for example, reducing a child's sugar intake) may be relevant.

> **Tip**
>
> You should always keep focused on the command word and the main point of the question which in this case was to *analyse* the role of the early years practitioner in meeting children's individual dietary requirements.

By now you have probably realised that the answer to a question that asks you to analyse an idea, topic or subject could be quite lengthy. Planning your answer is important, as mentioned earlier, but even more so in a question like this. It is so easy to wander off the point and lose focus.

You will not get a higher grade if you write lots of repetitive information, and the danger is that without a plan you will repeat yourself or lose focus. Planning your time is something that you will have to consider. Two hours may initially seem a very long time, but actually can whizz by. Running out of time and so not answering all six questions are poor planning and inefficient use of time; but it is your responsibility. You cannot be given marks or credit for unwritten answers. Bear in mind that a question that is about analysing a topic could take you longer to write than one that asks you to recall your knowledge.

Being able to **evaluate** or **assess** is an important skill, so there are questions that test this. Many people think that evaluating is a complex skill, but in reality it is something that we all do many times in our daily lives. For example, it is highly unlikely that you would buy a new article of clothing without looking at it first and making a judgement, or assessment. Even if you buy online you evaluate colour, shape and overall appearance, and read other people's reviews. You decide on the article's good points and bad points if any.

As you work with children on a daily basis, you are most likely evaluating and assessing all the time, sometimes without being really aware. You think

about strengths and good points, and possible weaknesses. For example, as children are playing you watch and listen to them, and from their reactions you decide if the children are learning, developing and extending their skills and enjoying their play. This is a form of evaluation because you are making judgements.

These judgements may not be written down and formally recorded, but nevertheless you have thought about the strengths and weaknesses of the play activity. As a result, you might suggest to another member of staff that the play activity is repeated again as the children gained a lot from it. This is a strength or positive feature. You could suggest that the activity is changed in some way, or different resources used, or more time allowed for the children to play. These are recommendations that address possible weaknesses. You are making these suggestions as a result of evaluating the play activity and considering its strengths and weaknesses.

An example of a question that tests your ability to evaluate and assess is:

 Evaluate the impact of implementing a policy for confidentiality in an early years setting

The command word in this question is 'evaluate'. Make sure you understand what this means. Evaluating is about assessing strengths and weaknesses and then making judgements as to whether the good, positive points (the strengths) outweigh the negative ones (the weaknesses). So in this question, think about the positive and negative aspects of having a confidentiality policy, but as always, remain focused – do not waffle.

In your plan, make sure you include the key features of the question:

1 Why do settings need a confidentiality policy? The prime reason for a confidentiality policy is to protect and safeguard children, so why is that a good thing?

2 How is it implemented or put in place? Some parents and carers may not fully understand a confidentiality policy. Parents could, for example, ask you for the names and contact details of their child's friends, so that they can invite them to a party. Parents may not appreciate why you cannot give out this information. This could jeopardise your relationship with a parent, and you could consider this a negative point.

3 A confidentiality policy covers how children's records and personal details are stored and who has access to them. Think about how settings you have worked in store such information. Decide whether these settings have good, secure systems or not, and include this judgement in your answer with clear reasons why you reached this conclusion.

4 Your evaluation should include the reasons why safeguarding children is a legal requirement. Make reference to the relevant pieces of legislation, making sure that you write the title of the appropriate act, for example, Data Protection Act 1998, not Data Act.

5 The question asks you to evaluate the impact of implementing the policy; so you should consider the effects for staff, children and parents/carers. The way a policy is written and the language used can be very important in the effectiveness of its implementation. A policy is more effective if all people who have to implement it are involved in some way in its creation, development and implementation, so this could be another aspect for you to evaluate.

6 The last part of the answer should pull together all the reasons and judgements that you have made. This is the conclusion and is a significant part of writing an evaluative answer. You do not need to repeat yourself, but at this point it is good practice to read through what you have written so that you can refocus on the strengths and weaknesses, positive and negative ideas.

Make an overall decision that makes reference to the question; for example, 'implementing a confidentiality policy in an early years setting is vitally important because …'.

By now you may have realised that a question that asks you to evaluate needs careful thought and planning. You also have to take into consideration that you have limited time so your plan should be precise and very focused. An example of a possible plan for the example question is given below.

Strengths	Weaknesses
Safeguarding children	Not understood properly by parents
Secure storage of records/details	Not accessible sometimes
Safeguarding staff	Not fully understood by staff
Teamwork to implement	No team, poor management

- My setting – actual examples of practice
- Legal requirement of Early Years Foundation Stage, Children Act 2004, Data Protection Act 1998
- Conclusion

This is not a perfect plan and it may not match your preferred learning style; but it is a start. Obviously as you write your answer you will develop each point, and do not forget to include relevant practical examples for your personal experiences.

A Reflective Study

As with the Short Answer Examination, the Reflective Study covers several units and your tutor should have information from CACHE to help and guide you. The assessment is a reflection on the main theme 3 Play, development and learning for school readiness. It uses examples from your Longitudinal Study of a child to support your answer.

A Longitudinal Study is one that relates to a child's learning and development, and takes place over a period of time, probably several months.

Throughout your course you will be working on your Longitudinal Study of a child and so it will be a large piece of work.

There is no set format or way for you to present your Longitudinal Study; however, there are guidelines from CACHE which your tutor should give you.

You have to complete two longitudinal studies of two different children in your work placement. The children should be from different age groups. For example, you could study a child between 0 and 1 year 11 months, and another between 2 years and 2 years 11 months, or between 3 and 5 years. You cannot study two children from the same age group.

You must choose one area of development for each longitudinal study. You can choose from:

- cognitive development
- physical development
- speech, language and communication
- personal, social and emotional development.

You cannot use the same area of development for each study.

For each child you must observe, assess and plan for their development and learning needs. This information provides the basis of the reflective study.

In addition your tutor will record that you have completed certain elements or key issues in your study. You should have studied several aspects of child development including the value of play, holistic development, observation and assessment, and aspects of professional practice. To a certain extent, your Longitudinal Study is descriptive but detailed; however, it must also be analytical and evaluative.

The Reflective Study is given the title:

The Early Years Practitioner promotes and supports children's play, learning and development

There is a word allowance of up to 5,000 words, but there is no minimum word limit. Work that is more than 10 per cent above the word limit, an extra 500 words, will not be marked. This synoptic assessment is marked by CACHE external examiners and is graded from D to A*. Descriptions of what is required for each grade have been given to your tutor by CACHE, so make sure that you have a copy.

Your Reflective Study can be completed in sections, but you must cover all the required elements. For example, you could write about observation and assessment first, then holistic development followed by theoretical approaches, and so on.

The order that you write your study will depend on your own stage of learning and progression through the course. However, you cannot present your Reflective Study for marking until it is complete. The CACHE guidance for each of the grade criteria could be used as a checklist to make sure that you give yourself the best opportunity to achieve a high grade.

> **Tip**
>
> Remember, whatever you write must be evaluative and analytical, not descriptive.

You need to combine ideas from different sources, such as textbooks, the internet and professional publications, a setting's policies and procedures, current research and regulatory frameworks. Remember that any references or source material that you use must be acknowledged in your work.

> **Tip**
>
> You must make sure that references in your work are clear. You do not need to write out the title of the book, date of publication and publisher in your work as you make the reference, but you must clearly indicate the source. This detailed information goes in the bibliography or reference list. You should put the name of the author, the date and the page number if relevant.

References from websites should be shown in full and include the date that you accessed the site. A detailed and accurate bibliography must be included at the end of the Reflective Study. It is good practice to make a note of any material that you use at the time you use it and then compile your bibliography or reference list. Your tutor should be able to suggest ways of recording your bibliography. However, an alphabetical list of authors followed by the date of publication (or when you accessed the website), and title of the book, magazine or article, is a well-used method for a bibliography.

You must also include at least two references in your Reflective Study which are traceable, to support your work. A reference is when you copy into your study the words of someone else and do not claim that they are your own. It is good practice to put references in a different font or colour in the text of your study so that they can be clearly seen by the examiner. If you pass off someone else's work as your own you can be accused of plagiarism, in other words fraud, deception and copying.

The Reflective Study is your opportunity to make judgements and draw conclusions about aspects of children's development and learning from your longitudinal studies. It can be described as a conclusion of your longitudinal studies, but must be, above all, reflective. It is also an opportunity for you to demonstrate to the examiner that you have good knowledge, are reflective and have good professional skills taking into consideration equality, diversity and inclusion.

A Reflective Study is one that is
- **detailed**
- **thoughtful**
- **logical**
- **philosophical**.

A **detailed** piece of work is thorough and wide-ranging and should cover topics, subjects and ideas in depth.

Presenting a piece of work that is described as **thoughtful** means that it is well-planned and shows that you have considered the key issues carefully.

A **logical** study is one that is well-organised, precise and accurate; it is focused, does not wander off the point or waffle, and is not repetitive.

If you are writing in a **philosophical** way, you are showing relevant and appropriate knowledge. This must be backed up with personal research and reading, considering the work of theorists, using references in the text and a bibliography or reference list of where you have found your information. A philosophical way of writing will also link theories and theoretical perspectives to practice and real-life scenarios.

If you are to produce a high-quality Reflective Study, you must plan your work carefully. No one can really do this for you. It should be a personal plan that works for you, fits in with your way of studying and learning, and also takes into consideration timescales. There is little point in planning to work on a Reflective Study every day for two weeks if you already know that for three days you are going to stay at a friend's house and will not have access to your computer. So, make sure that your plan is realistic and achievable.

Your reflective study must **analyse** key issues. For example, the child studied in your longitudinal studies will have taken part in many play activities and experiences; some may have been very successful, others not so. So, analyse the educational programme planned and offered to the children, and relate your analysis to theory. This analysis is a key issue. You are not being asked to make an evaluation of the Early Years Foundation Stage, but you could consider how the child's likes and dislikes, preferences, needs, interests and next steps for development were planned and provided for. This example naturally leads to an **evaluation** of the planned educational programme and opportunities to make reasoned judgements.

Another example of a key issue to analyse might be ways of observing the children. There are many different ways or formats of recording observations of children. Depending on the situation, context and activity, some formats are more appropriate than others. For example, a written note can give information about how a child approached an activity. Some settings use photographs (with written parental permission), which can support a written note or capture facial expressions of pleasure and joy.

Another observation format is a checklist, which can quickly assess physical skills, specific knowledge of numbers, colours or shapes, for example. However, a photograph cannot provide information on a child's knowledge of numbers, and a checklist could not provide information on a child's feelings. This would then lead you to write in an **evaluative** style and make judgements.

As you write your Reflective Study, you should consider different theories and perspectives of how children develop and learn, not forgetting current researchers. If you can relate these theories and opinions to things that you have actually written about in your Longitudinal Study, it will make better sense to you and be more relevant. For example, you may have written about a behavioural concern in a day care setting. This might, for example, lead you to look at the work and theory of Jay Belsky or the nature/nurture debate. Look at the work of contemporary thinkers and theorists, such as Urie Bronfenbrenner, Martin Hughes, Vivian Gussin Paley, as well as the better known theories of Jean Piaget, Lev Vygotsky, Jerome Bruner and B. F. Skinner.

Your Reflective Study must include reference to appropriate professional skills, including reflective practice. Researchers such as Graham Gibbs, David Kolb and Christopher Johns have studied reflective practice. You can find information on Kolb and Gibbs in Unit 4.1, and you may want to conduct research into the work of Johns. These may be helpful in any judgements that you make on the benefits of reflective practice in relation to the role of the practitioner in helping children to progress. This means that you must be clear about the roles and responsibilities of an early years practitioner. You should understand the Safeguarding and Welfare Requirements of the Early Years Foundation Stage as these underpin all professional practice. If you do not have access to a copy of the Statutory Requirements of the Early Years Foundation Stage, you can download one at https://www.education.gov.uk/publications/standard/AllPublications/Page1/DFE-00023-2012.

The grades for the reflective study are not stand-alone achievement 'hurdles'. In other words, it is not necessary to complete the D grade, and then write the C grade, then the B and so on. In doing this, there is the danger that you could repeat yourself; and remember, there is a word limit. The higher grades are a development of the earlier ones; for example, parts of the A and A* grades are a development of aspects of the C grade. Therefore it does make sense to include the A and A* parts when writing the C grade. In the same way, parts of the D grade are further developed in the B

grade. The links between the grades are shown in the guidance. In general, of course, the higher the grade, the more detail and evidence of knowledge and understanding are required. The links between each of the grades are shown in the guidance issued by CACHE.

While reflective practice is covered in greater detail in the A grade, it is the main focus of your Study. You should evaluate the benefits of reflective practice for your own professional practice and how this enables you to support children to progress in their learning and development. You should also develop your ideas in the D grade on play and enabling environments, evaluating all aspects including both positive and negative features. For example, the impact on children's learning and development could be very significant if children do not have access to regular outdoor play opportunities.

The highest grade is A*. To achieve this grade you should critically evaluate the current and different approaches to learning that you write about for Grade C. You could consider ways that children learn and the characteristics of effective teaching and learning. Your work should give a detailed, reasoned and balanced argument of the key issues and present an in-depth, logical conclusion. You should give recommendations for future practice and as before refer to your own Longitudinal Study and practical work experiences.

As mentioned earlier, the final part of your reflective study is the bibliography or reference list. This is not included in the word count so can be as detailed and extensive as you like. In the same way, any reference and quotations in the actual text of your study are also not included in the word count; another reason why it is good practice to put these in a different font or colour. A bibliography and at least two references are a requirement of the assessment and as such are vitally important.

The Extended Essay

This assessment is an Extended Essay of up to 5,000 words, with no minimum word count. It is marked by external examiners appointed by

CACHE. The essay is graded from D to A* like the other synoptic assessments. CACHE sets the title for the assessment in advance and the title will not remain the same, year on year. However, there is an overarching title of 'The Early Years Practitioner develops children's emergent literacy and emergent mathematical skills and contributes to children's school readiness'.

As with the Reflective Study, CACHE has issued guidance for your tutors and you. As suggested before, you could use this as a checklist to make sure that you cover all the key points for each grade. Although this assessment is called an extended essay, it must cover the criteria of each grade band and so it will not follow a traditional essay structure. As with the Reflective Study , the higher grades build on information from the lower grades; for example, aspects of the C and B grades are developed further in the A grade.

The extended essay can be completed in sections, as you work through your course. It should not be handed in for marking until you are completely satisfied that it is complete and you have not missed anything out. Your tutor will set deadline dates when you must hand in your work for both the Reflective Study and the Extended Essay.

Remember that your work is sent away to be examined and so if you are late handing in your Extended Essay it will not be accepted for marking until the next submission date set by CACHE. Therefore your results will be much later. The best way to make sure you have included all relevant material is, as mentioned before in this section, to have a personal study plan. As with the Reflective Study the plan will help to keep your work focused, and hopefully stop repetition and waffle.

Tip

Having a sensible, appropriate plan that is followed could mean the difference between a well-constructed piece of work that could achieve a high grade, and one that looks as is if has been written very quickly and misses out important material.

As with the Reflective Study, you will need to have references in your work to practical work experiences and evidence of personal research and reading. You should refer to theorists and consider different views on emergent literacy and mathematical skills, such as synthetic phonics. Think about how children can be prepared for school and ways of making transitions easier. Think about the different ways that children learn and the characteristics of effective teaching and learning.

As you write, remember to think about the length of the sentences. Generally speaking, long sentences have a tendency to wander off the point. They can be confusing for the reader or in this case, examiner. Long sentences often contain different ideas and can appear a random collection of thoughts joined by words such as 'and'. It is good practice to try to write short sentences that express one idea. This is usually known as the subject of a sentence.

Read the following sentence:

'When children are quite young they show emergent writing in many ways as they play in perhaps sand or during messy play using their fingers, hands and feet to make shapes and marks which may seem quite random but are the beginnings of handwriting.'

This is an example of a very long sentence that has several different ideas or subjects and is quite difficult to read with understanding. It would be better as:

'Young children can show emergent writing in many different ways. Messy play, for example, can provide opportunities to make marks with their hands, fingers or feet. These marks are the beginnings of handwriting.'

This is by no means perfect. However, three reasonably short sentences are better and easier to read than the first example.

There are three main ideas to consider in the Extended Essay. First of all is to think about the **role of the early years practitioner in developing children's emergent literacy**. The second idea concerns **your role in developing emergent mathematical skills** and finally **preparing children for school**. You can combine the first two ideas, but make sure that you give them both equal consideration.

Emergent literacy is a key part of communication and language. Your essay should show that you have good understanding of what literacy means for young children. You need to understand theories about how children learn to read and write. This could include theorists such as Hey (1870–1913), Frank Smith and Margaret Meek, who will be useful for you to research.

You might also want to think about different methods or approaches such as alphabetic, synthetic phonics, whole words and whole sentence that have been used to help children read. Informing your work should also be an understanding of the Rose review (2005). However, remember this essay is about the **role** of the early years practitioner in supporting children's learning and development, not a theoretical overview of literacy.

Mathematical skills include an understanding of numbers, shape, space and measures. It also includes how children solve problems and use mathematical language to describe objects and things. This should include a discussion on sustained shared thinking.

Think about the practical ways you have seen or been involved with in your workplace that have provided mathematical learning opportunities. In many ways, it can be quite difficult to separate out mathematical learning from other areas of learning and development as they are all interconnected. For example, using different containers to fill and pour water might have been planned as a mathematical activity, but it will also include aspects of personal, social and emotional development as children play together. It may also cover aspects of knowledge of the world as they explore the water.

As all areas are interconnected, it could be very easy to wander away from the main focus of the essay. This again highlights the need for a plan. You may want to include aspects of the theories and opinion of theorists and researchers such as Jean Piaget, Chris Athey, Jerome Bruner and Howard Gardner.

In order to effectively support children's emergent literacy and mathematical skills, you must have a good understanding of the importance of planning and assessment, so include this knowledge in your essay. You should consider different ways of meeting and supporting children's individual interests and needs. Each setting will have its own way of doing this, so this could make your Extended Essay very different from those of other learners. One common theme, however, is likely to be the scaffolding of children's learning and development. So, consider the importance of scaffolding, how you do it, or have seen others doing it. Analyse and evaluate scaffolding, including the possible consequences for not scaffolding learning and development.

School readiness is the subject of much debate and discussion. You need to be clear in your mind as to what is meant by 'school readiness'. What skills, attitudes and attributes would you expect to see in children who are 'school ready'? This does not necessarily mean at the age of five years, as we all know that children develop and learn at different rates and are unique.

One place to start your research could be by looking at the Effective Provision of Pre-School Education (EPPE) Project (1997–2003) and its findings on different forms of pre-school provision. You could also look at the ways in which early years practitioners promote the characteristics of effective teaching and learning in relation to school readiness.

Part of your role in preparing children for school will be to support their transitions. Successful transitions between the early years setting and school can be key to a child making progress in their learning, and so it is important that you understand how to plan and provide a supportive, inclusive environment.

Running through this Essay is the key feature of the role of the early years practitioner. When you focus on children's emerging literacy and mathematical skills, you should also reflect on your own learning. This should lead you to make recommendations for future practice. Use practical examples from your own personal experiences of working with children to support your ideas and recommendations. You must also support your ideas by personal research and reading. Do not forget to include references in the actual text of the Extended Essay, and list everything you use to complete this essay in the bibliography.

Tip

Remember, if you go over the word count, no matter how brilliant your work is, it will not be considered or marked. It is so important that you plan your use of words as well as the content of your essay. Stay focused, keep your work relevant and read it through after you think you have finished.

Enjoy your course of study; you are embarking on a very fulfilling career, and of course, good luck with all your assessments.

Appendix: Useful acronyms

ADD	Attention deficit disorder
ADHD	Attention deficit hyperactivity disorder
ASBO	Anti-social behaviour order
ASD	Autistic spectrum disorder
BASW	British Association of Social Workers
BEST	Behaviour and Education Support Team
BME	Black and Minority Ethnic
BTEC	Business and Technology Education Council
C&G	City and Guilds
CAB	Citizens Advice Bureau
CACHE	Council for Awards in Care, Health and Education
CAF	Common Assessment Framework
CAFCASS	Children and Family Court Advisory and Support Service
CAMHS	Child and Adolescent Mental Health Services
CCLD	Children's Care, Learning and Development
CCW	Care Council for Wales
CPD	Continuing professional development
CRE	Commission for Racial Equality
CWDC	Children's Workforce Development Council
CWN	Children's Workforce Network
CYP	Children and Young People
DCS	Director of Children's Services
DH	Department of Health
DTI	Department for Trade and Industry
EBSD	Emotional, behavioural and social difficulties
ECaT	Every Child a Talker
ELPP	Early Learning Partnership Project
EPPE	Effective Provision of Pre-School Education Project
EWO	Education Welfare Officer
EYFS	Early Years Foundation Stage
EYP	Early Years Professional
EYPS	Early Years Professional Status ➜

FPI	Family and Parenting Institute
FST	Family Support Team
FSW	Family Support Worker
FYJ	Forum for Youth Justice
GP	General Practitioner
IQF	Integrated Qualifications Framework
LLUK	Lifelong Learning UK
LP	Lead professional
LRN	Learning Resource Network
LSC	Learning and Skills Council
LWS	Local Workforce Strategy
MAT	Multi-agency team
NASWE	National Association of Social Workers in Education
NCB	National Children's Bureau
NCERCC	National Centre for Excellence in Residential Child Care
NCH	National Children's Home (The Children's Charity)
NCVCCO	National Council of Voluntary Child Care Organisations
NDNA	National Day Nurseries Association
NEET	Not in education, employment or training
NGfL	National Grid for Learning
NISCC	Northern Ireland Social Care Council
NOS	National Occupational Standards
NVQ	National Vocational Qualification
OCW	One Children's Workforce
	Ofsted Office for Standards in Education
PACEY	Professional Association for Childcare and Early Years
PHCT	Primary Health Care Team
PLA	Pre-school Learning Alliance
PRU	Pupil Referral Unit
QCA	Qualification and Curriculum Authority
QTS	Qualified Teacher Status
RNIB	Royal National Institute for the Blind
RNID	Royal National Institute for the Deaf
SEAL	Social and emotional aspects of learning →

SEN	Special educational needs
SENCO	Special Educational Needs Co-ordinator
SSDA	Sector Skills Development Agency
SSSC	Scottish Social Care Council
TAC	Team Around the Child
UCAS	University and Colleges Admission Service
VRQ	Vocationally Related Qualification

Glossary

accommodation Sometimes it is not possible to simply take in experiences, and then alterations can be made which adapt/alter (accommodate) the brain.

active listening Active listening is about focusing not only on what is being said, but the accompanying emotions and feelings that are being expressed in other ways. It provides a safe structure for a child to voice his or her concerns, and to receive feedback from the adult. Active listening includes the use of verbal and non-verbal skills.

adult-led activities Adult-led activities are those which adults initiate. The activities are not play, and children are likely not to see them as play, but they should be **playful** – with activities presented to children which are as open-ended as possible, with elements of imagination and active exploration that will increase the interest and motivation for children. As well as focused activities with groups of children, adult-led activities can include greeting times, story times, songs and even tidying up.

agency In this context, this term covers the range of organisations, services and professional groups who provide services to children and their families.

allegation A safeguarding allegation means the giving out of information that might commonly be kept secret, usually voluntarily or to be in compliance with legal regulations or workplace rules. (Allegation used to be known as disclosure). For example, a child tells an adult something that causes him or her to be concerned about the child's safety and wellbeing.

allergy Abnormal sensitivity reaction of the body to substances that are usually harmless.

alliteration When two or more words in a poem begin with the same letter or sound; for example, **R**abbits **R**unning over **R**oses.

alpha-fetoprotein A protein produced by the foetus's liver which can be detected in the mother's blood most accurately between the 16th and 18th weeks of pregnancy. High levels of AFP may be associated with spina bifida; low levels may be associated with Down's syndrome.

amniotic sac Often called 'membranes' or the 'bag of waters', the amniotic sac is the bag of amniotic fluid that surrounds and cushions the foetus.

analytic phonics Children are taught whole words and later analyse their constituent parts, such as c-at or str-eet.

anaphylaxis An immediate and severe allergic response; a shock reaction to a substance.

anaphylaxis A severe allergic reaction that affects the whole body. It can lead to **anaphylactic shock**.

anaphylactic shock A potentially fatal immune response when the body system literally shuts down. The most common causes are a severe allergic reaction to peanuts, insect stings and certain drugs.

anterior fontanelle A diamond-shaped, soft area at the front of the head, just above the brow. It is covered by a tough membrane; you can often see the baby's pulse beating there under the skin. The fontanelle closes between 12 and 18 months of age.

antibias practice Antibias practice means going beyond equal opportunities and actively opposing forms of discrimination and prejudices in your work – for example, letting all children take part in woodwork upholds equal opportunities. Inviting a woman joiner into the nursery and displaying pictures and books about women doing woodwork, and talking these issues through with children, is an antibias approach.

antibodies Antibodies are proteins made by the body's immune system.

anti-discrimination An approach which challenges unfair or unlawful treatment of individuals or groups based on a specific characteristic of that group (such as colour, age, disability, sexual orientation, etc.).

assessment Through observing children and by making notes when necessary, practitioners can make professional judgments about children's achievements and decide on the next steps in learning. They can also exchange information with parents about how children are progressing.

assimilation This is the process by which new information and experience is taken (assimilated) into the existing structures (schemas or concepts) in the brain.

attachment A warm, affectionate and supportive bond between child and carer that enables the child to develop secure relationships. Usually the first attachment is to the mother, formed between the ages of six and nine months.

balanced bilingualism This is when a child speaks more than one language, each with equal fluency. In fact, the child's home language is usually more fluent than English. Very few children are completely balanced across two languages. For most, one language is more developed than the other.

behavioural, emotional and social difficulties (BESD) Signs that a child may have BESD include withdrawn or isolated behaviour, highly disruptive or disturbing behaviour, hyperactivity and significant difficulties with social interactions. It is difficult to assess whether a young child has BESD, and an educational psychologist or clinical child psychologist should always be involved.

blastocyst The rapidly dividing fertilised egg when it enters the woman's uterus.

Caesarean section A Caesarean section (sometimes referred to as a C-section) is when the baby is delivered through an incision in the mother's abdomen and uterus. It is used when a woman cannot give birth vaginally or if the baby is in distress or danger.

centile charts Also known as percentile charts or growth charts, these are used to monitor a child's growth regularly and are contained in the child's PCHR.

centration The child cannot hold in mind several ideas at once, so focuses (centrates) on one aspect. The child might focus on the height of a mug, for example.

challenging behaviour This term has been used to refer to the unwanted or unacceptable behaviours that may be shown by children or adults. Such behaviours include aggression (hitting, kicking, biting), destruction (ripping clothes, breaking windows, throwing objects), self-injury (head banging, self-biting, skin picking), tantrums and many other behaviours. Normally, challenging behaviour puts the safety of the individual or others in some jeopardy, or has a significant impact on their quality of life.

child-initiated activity Child-initiated activity is wholly decided upon by the child, based on the child's own motivation, and remains under the child's control. It may involve play of many types, or it may be seen by the child as an activity with a serious purpose to explore a project or express an idea which the child may not see as pure play.

Children's Centre These centres bring together early education, childcare, health services, family support and help for parents wanting to return to work.

chromosomal abnormality An abnormality in the number or structure of chromosomes. Chromosomes are the structures that hold our genes.

colic Colic is persistent, unexplained crying in a healthy baby between two weeks and five months of age.

colostrum Colostrum is the first 'milk' that the breasts produce, as a precursor to breast milk. It is rich in fats, protein and antibodies, which protect the baby against infection and kick-start the immune system. Colostrum is low in fat, and high in carbohydrates, protein and antibodies to help keep the newborn baby healthy.

communication The transmission of thoughts, feelings or information via body language, signals, speech or writing.

containment and reverie These terms refer to an adult's state of mind in relation to a baby or young child. Through containment, the adult can receive the baby's communications of anxiety, pain, distress or pleasure. This happens on an unconscious level: the adult cannot mean or plan to do this, but the adult can try to be open to the baby's emotional state by being close to the baby and not distracted by other tasks or thoughts. Through reverie, the adult can process the baby's communications and hand them back to the baby, either sharing the pleasure in a loving and intimate interaction, or handing back distressing thoughts in a way that the baby can manage. This model was developed by the psychoanalyst Wilfred Bion.

cyanosis A bluish discoloration of the skin and mucous membranes resulting from inadequate oxygenation of the blood.

cystic fibrosis A condition which affects certain organs in the body, especially the lungs and pancreas, by clogging them with thick sticky mucus. New treatments mean people with cystic fibrosis can live relatively healthy lives.

differentiation Altering and adapting the way in which activities are presented to children to enable them to access them and to make progress.

disclosure See **allegation**.

discrimination Treating a person less favourably than others in the same or similar circumstances.

diversity The differences in values, attitudes, cultures, beliefs, skills, knowledge and life experience of each individual in any group of people.

Down's syndrome A genetic disorder resulting from the presence of an extra chromosome; children usually, but not always, have learning difficulties.

dyscalculia The DfE defines dyscalculia as 'a condition that affects the ability to acquire arithmetical skills. Dyscalculic learners may have difficulty understanding simple number concepts, lack an intuitive grasp of numbers, and have problems learning number facts and procedures. Even if they produce a correct answer or use a correct method, they may do so mechanically and without confidence'.

early intervention This approach seeks to offer extra help and support to a family before the child starts to lag behind in development or experience neglect or abuse. Early intervention is about working cooperatively with parents and carers, giving them a chance to make choices about which services they need.

effortful control Children's capacity to override their immediate wants, desires and responses with a more socially acceptable and effective response. Children who can see that there are cakes on the table, but wait for the adult to say it is alright to have one, are showing high levels of effortful control.

embryo The unborn child during the first eight weeks after conception.

emergent literacy A term that is used to explain a child's knowledge of reading and writing skills before he or she learns how to read and write words.

empathy The ability to understand and share the feelings of another.

endometrium The lining of the womb which grows and sheds during a normal menstrual cycle and which supports a foetus if a pregnancy occurs.

environment The provision that is made for children in which they can learn, play and relax. It encompasses both the physical environment (such as the layout, equipment and furniture) and the 'emotional' environment (the atmosphere or ambience that is created).

enactive learning This is about learning by doing, through first-hand experiences.

equality Ensuring that everyone has a chance to take part in society on an equal basis and to be treated appropriately, regardless of their gender, race, disability, age, sexual orientation, language, social origin, religious beliefs, marital status and other personal attributes.

evaluate Describe and summarise in relation to advantages and disadvantages.

extended school A school which provides a range of services and activities, often beyond the school day, to help meet the needs of its pupils, their families and the wider community.

expressive language Learning to speak and to use language. This involves using the face expressively, making gestures and speaking (or signing).

fertilisation The moment when sperm and egg meet, join and form a single cell. It usually takes place in the Fallopian tubes. The fertilised egg then travels into the uterus, where it implants in the lining before developing into an embryo and then a foetus.

first-hand experience One that is lived through personally rather than experienced by someone else, and seen or heard about.

foetus The unborn child from the end of the eighth week after conception until birth.

genes The individual instructions that tell our bodies how to develop and function. They govern our physical and medical characteristics, such as hair colour, blood type and susceptibility to disease.

half-brother or half-sister A sibling with one shared biological or adoptive parent.

hazard A source of potential harm or damage, or a situation with potential for harm or damage.

hypothermia A potentially fatal condition that occurs when body temperature falls below 35°C (95°F).

hypothesis A hypothesis makes a prediction that something will happen and tests it out in a scientific way to see if it is true or not.

iconic thinking When an image stands for a person, experience or object, perhaps through a photograph.

immunisation Immunisation protects children (and adults) against harmful infections before they come into contact with them in the community.

immunity A condition of being able to resist a particular infectious disease.

inclusion Ensuring that every child, young person, adult or learner is given equality of opportunity to access education and care, by meeting their specific needs. Defined by the Early Childhood Forum as 'a process of identifying, understanding and breaking down barriers to participation and belonging'.

inclusive practice Inclusion in education and care is one aspect of inclusion in society, and means taking necessary steps to ensure that every child, young person, adult or learner is given an equal chance of taking advantage of the opportunities offered to them.

information-sharing The term used to describe the situation whereby practitioners use their professional judgement and experience on a case-by-case basis to decide whether personal information should be shared with other practitioners in order to meet the needs of a child or young person.

informed consent When anyone, child or adult, is given sufficient information to be able to make a genuine decision to say 'yes' or 'no' to a request. This means that you need to check carefully that someone has understood your request. If you said to a parent in passing, 'Do you mind if I do an observation of your child today?' you have not obtained informed consent. You need to arrange a time to meet, explain what you are planning to do, make time to answer any questions and obtain the parent's signature.

inter-agency protection plan If a child's health or development has been significantly impaired as a result of physical, emotional or sexual abuse or neglect, an inter-agency protection plan may be drawn up. The plan will identify the steps that the family needs to take to safeguard the child, with the support of Children's Services and other agencies. The child's safety, health, development and well-being will be regularly monitored throughout the plan.

involuntary Controlled by the autonomic nervous system, without conscious control.

key person The EYFS glossary defines a key person as 'The named member of staff with whom a child has more contact than other adults. This adult shows a special interest in the child through close personal interaction day to day. The key person can help the young child to deal with separation anxiety.'

key person system A system within an early years setting in which care of each child is assigned to a particular adult, known as the key person. The role of the key person is to develop a special relationship with the child, in order to help the child to feel safe and secure in the setting. The key person will also liaise closely with each child's parents.

language A recognised system of gestures, signs and symbols used to communicate.

lanugo Downy, fine hair on a foetus. Lanugo can appear as early as 15 weeks of gestation, and typically begins to disappear sometime before birth.

lead professional The lead professional takes the lead to coordinate provision, and acts as a single point of contact for a child and his or her family when a TAC is required.

locomotion Movement or the ability to move from one place to another.

malnutrition A person's diet is lacking the necessary amounts of certain elements that are essential to growth, such as vitamins, salts and proteins.

mark-making When children realise that marks can be used symbolically to carry meaning, in much the same way as the spoken word, they begin to use marks as tools to make their thinking visible.

meningitis Infection or inflammation of the membranes (meninges) that cover the brain and spinal cord.

mentalisation The ability to understand another person's mental state through observing their behaviour – for example, a child saying, 'I think Sophie wants to be my friend; she is trying to hold my hand'.

neonatal Relating to the first few weeks of a baby's life.

neonate A newborn infant, especially one less than four weeks old.

neural tube defects This term includes anencephaly, encephalocoele and spina bifida. These conditions occur if the brain and/or spinal cord, together with its protecting skull and spinal column, fail to develop properly during the first month of embryonic life.

neuroscience Studies of the brain which provide evidence to help early years specialists working with young children.

nutrients The essential components of food which provide the individual with the necessary requirements for bodily functions.

orthoptist A professional who investigates, diagnoses and treats defects of vision and abnormalities of eye movement.

over-extension The opposite of under-extension. It occurs when a word is given a broader, more general meaning than it should have. An example is using the word 'daddy' not just for the child's father but for other men as well.

partnership working When all the services and professionals supporting children work together effectively to put the child at the centre, meet their needs (and those of their parents or carers) and improve their lives. Also called multi-agency working or integrated working.

perineum The skin between the vagina and the rectum.

physically active play Play that involves movements of all the major muscle groups, e.g. legs. It can range from activities with small intermittent movements, such as clapping hands, to large movements involving the whole body, such as climbing and running. It tends to be used to describe young children's physical activity.

policy A safeguarding policy is a statement that makes it clear to staff, parents and children what the organisation or group thinks about safeguarding, and what it will do to keep children safe.

possetting When a baby regularly vomits small amounts of her feeds but has no sign of illness. Usually caused by a weakness of the muscle at the opening of the stomach.

post-natal The first days and weeks after the birth of the baby (post = after, natal = birth).

posterior fontanelle A small, triangular-shaped soft area near the crown of the head; it is much smaller and less noticeable than the anterior fontanelle.

pre-eclampsia A condition that a mother may develop late in pregnancy, marked by sudden oedema, high blood pressure and protein in the urine. It can lead to eclampsia where the mother has convulsions; antenatal care staff monitor women carefully for the warning signs.

premature (or preterm) baby A baby who is born before 37 weeks of gestation.

proprioception The ability to recognise and use the physical sensations from the body that give feedback on balance and the position of our limbs.

puerperium The period of about six weeks which follows immediately after the birth of a child.

reactivity This refers to the intensity and speed of the child's emotional responses, the child's ability to focus attention and the child's movement.

receptive language Learning to listen and understand language: the child listens, watches people talking, and begins to understand what is being said.

reflective practice A learner should consider their actions, experiences or learning and their implications in order to suggest significant developments for future action, learning or practice. These are recognised cycles of reflective practice. Reflective practice can also show that a learner performed exceptionally well.

reflex An involuntary action or response, such as a sneeze, blink or hiccup.

retinopathy of prematurity An abnormal growth of blood vessels in the retina at the back of a premature baby's eye; when severe it can cause loss of vision.

reverie See **containment and reverie**.

Reye's syndrome A very rare condition that causes serious liver and brain damage. Many children who developed Reye's syndrome had previously taken the painkiller aspirin to treat their symptoms.

risk The possibility of suffering harm or loss; danger.

risk assessment The assessments that must be carried out in order to identify hazards and find out the safest way to carry out certain tasks and procedures.

Sense A national charity that supports and campaigns for children and adults who are deaf blind. Sense provides tailored support, advice and information as well as specialist services to all deaf blind people, their families, carers and the professionals who work with them. It also supports people who have a single sensory impairment with additional needs.

Scope A charity that works with disabled people of all ages and their families, across England and Wales.

self-concept How you see yourself, and how you think others see you; sometimes called self-image.

self-esteem The way you feel about yourself (good or bad) leads to high or low self-esteem.

sibling A brother or sister.

signs of illness Those that can be observed directly, for example, a change in skin colour, a rash or a swelling.

social referencing This is when a baby or young child checks an adult's emotional response before deciding on their own. An example would be a baby who sees something on the grass in a park and looks back at her mother before deciding whether to crawl confidently forward to grab it, or to stay away and watch warily.

speech Verbal communication; the act of speaking; the articulation of words to express thoughts, feelings or ideas.

speech dysfluency The use of hesitators (sounds such as 'erm', 'ur'), pauses and repetitions which reflect the difficulty of mental planning at speed. Stammering (or stuttering) is a form of speech dysfluency.

spina bifida This occurs when the spinal canal in the vertebral columns is not closed (although it may be covered with skin). Individuals with spina bifida can have a wide range of physical disabilities. In the more severe forms the spinal cord bulges out of the back, the legs and bladder may be paralysed, and obstruction to the fluid surrounding the brain causes hydrocephalus.

step-brother or step-sister A child who has brothers or sisters through the remarriage of a parent to somebody who has children.

step-family Step-families consist of married or co-habiting (living together) couples who, between them, have at least one child from a previous relationship who either visits or lives with them.

step-parent (step-mother or step-father) The individual who is not the biological parent of the child or children is referred to as the step-parent.

subitising Instantly recognising the number of objects in a small group, without counting (from the Latin 'subito', meaning 'immediately'): for example, when you can see that there are five coins without counting.

sustained shared thinking A process which involves the adult being aware of the child's interests and understanding, and the adult and child together developing an idea or skill.

symptoms of illness Those experienced by the child, for example, pain, discomfort or generally feeling unwell.

synthetic phonics Children are taught the sounds of letters and letter combinations first, then combine those to form words: c-a-t or s-t-r-ee-t.

tracking The smooth movements made by the eyes in following the track of a moving object (sometimes called 'smooth pursuit').

transition Any significant stage or experience in the life of a child that can affect his or her behaviour and/or development.

transitional object Often a soft toy or blanket to which a child becomes attached, a transitional object is used by a child to provide comfort and security while he or she is away from a secure base, such as parents or home.

transmission Shaping the child's behaviour so that the child has the knowledge the adults wants to transmit (or send) to him or her.

umbilical cord The cord connecting the foetus to the maternal placenta. It contains blood vessels that carry nutrients to the placenta and remove waste substances from the placenta.

under-extension A common semantic error made by children. It occurs when a word is given a narrower meaning than it has in adult language. An example is using the word 'cat' for the family pet but not applying it to other cats.

under nutrition This occurs when people do not get enough to eat.

vaccine A substance that stimulates the body's immune response in order to prevent or control an infection.

vernix A protective white greasy substance that often covers the skin of the newborn baby.

viable Able to maintain an independent existence – to live after birth.

voluntary Intentional or controlled by individual will.

Index

NREM sleep 53
nuchal fold translucency test 120
nuclear families 227
number lines 353, 354
number skills 350–1, 356–7, 381
Nursery Milk Scheme 3
nursery schools and classes 145, 146, 285, 286, 306–7
nurture-nature debate 403
nutrients 2
nutrition 2–24
   see also diet
   healthy eating 2–16
   and learning 286
   malnutrition and undernutrition 16–17
   special needs 18–24
nuts 6, 7, 16
OAE test 133
obesity 26
object permanence 408
object play 282
objective observation 516–17
   see also observation
objectivity 515
objects of reference 431
observation
   see also assessment
   for assessment 383–4, 415
   and confidentiality/consent 517–20, 521
   definition 505
   in developmental checks 136–8
   discussion with child 520
   evaluation 521–2
   function 505–6
   identifying needs 79, 83, 379, 505–6
   in illness 93, 101
   and information sharing 517, 518, 523
   in language development 322, 425, 438, 439
   methods 506–14, 525–8
   objectivity 515–17
   Observation, Assessment and Planning cycle 376
   for planning 31, 35, 265–6, 270, 376, 378–80, 383
   of play activities 303
   record-keeping 520–2, 527
   of schemas 410
Observation, Assessment and Planning cycle 376
OMEP 211
one hundred languages 189, 270

one-to-one conversations with adults 431–2
one-to-one correspondence principle 350
open days/evenings 234
open door policy 111
open posture 154
open questions 314, 415
operant conditioning 398–9
operational development stage 407
operations (medical), support for 106
operations (Paiget theory), concrete 407–8
Organisation Mondiale Education Pre-Scholaire (OMEP) 211
otitis media 88, 482
otoacoustic emissions (OAE) test 133
outdoor play
   environments 30–1, 35, 188, 190, 192, 196, 314–17
   Forest schools 289
   frameworks 26
   imaginative play 269, 311
   outings 181–4, 295
   wheeled toys 264, 317
outings 295
   safety procedures 181–4
outline plans 500
over-demanding children 17, 301, 472
over-extensions 420
over-protection
   disabled or sick children 487
   and risk management 193
paediatricians 131
pain, signs of 103
painting activities 267, 378
pallor 94
palmar grasp 443, 447
parallel play 253–4, 280, 294
parent and baby/toddler groups 233
parent consent forms, medicines 104
Parent Partnership Scheme 502
parent-administered medication form 145
parental involvement 233–4, 239–40
   additional needs support 500–2
   benefits 71–2, 229–34
   child abuse concerns 173
   child development 244, 328, 346–7, 361–2, 383, 425, 437
   communication 237–9, 437
   exercise needs 22, 28